FIRST AMENDMENT, FIRST PRINCIPLES

Verbal Acts and Freedom of Speech

REVISED EDITION

John F. Wirenius

HOLMES & MEIER
New York / London

Published in the United States of America 2004 by
Holmes & Meier Publishers, Inc.
160 Broadway • New York, NY 10038

Book design by Brigid McCarthy

Typesetting by Alpha Graphics

This book has been printed on acid-free paper.

Library of Congress Cataloging-in-Publication Data
Wirenius, John F.
    First Amendment, first principles : verbal acts and freedom of speech/John F.
Wirenius.—Rev. ed.
      p. cm.
    Includes bibliographical references and index.
      ISBN 0-8419-1434-6 (cloth : alk. paper) — ISBN 0-8419-1435-4 (pbk. : alk.
paper)
      1. Freedom of speech—United States.   I. Title.
    KF4772.W57 2003
    342.7308'53—dc22   2003062867

Manufactured in the United States of America

10 9 8 7 6 5 4 3 2 1

Contents

For Kellene, with love, and for Jan Kulas, *in memoriam*

Acknowledgments

As a rule, a new author does not complete a first book without stockpiling karmic debts, and I am no exception. I am grateful to the many scholars and legal experts who assisted me.

Vincent Blasi and Robert Amdur evaluated my first writing on freedom of speech, and their helpful comments drew to my attention certain analytical traps which I have kept in mind in this work. Also at Columbia, Charles L. Black, William F. Young, and Vivian O. Berger each encouraged me to continue my scholarly pursuits. Bill Young and Vivian Berger were particularly generous with their time and advice.

Nat Hentoff and Bruce E. H. Johnson provided insightful criticism and, while enthusiastic about the general thrust of the book, led me to devote expanded treatment to specific permutations of the general theme of the first edition. The Honorable Jed S. Rakoff, United States District Judge for the Southern District of New York, was both gracious and generous in his assessment of the first edition and strongly urged me to continue writing about free speech. Judge Rakoff's comments are especially encouraging in view of his outstanding scholarship and fidelity to the constitution.

After the publication of the first edition, Vince Blasi and Peter Strauss, my first instructor in Constitutional Law gave me invaluable advice for furthering my work for free expression. I am also grateful to Nadine Strossen for her helpful input.

Gerald Gunther, in an unexpected and disarming response to my review of his biography *Learned Hand: The Man and the Judge* (1994), discussed in an illuminating way the connection (or lack thereof) of Judge Hand to the Law and Economics Movement, of which Hand has become an avatar. Professor Gunther exemplified the scholarly community's generosity by the zest with which he encouraged my conclusions, even when they diverged from his own. Professor Tracy Higgins of Fordham University Law School likewise challenged my first evaluation of the work of Catharine A. MacKinnon and my original understanding of the evolution of free speech doctrine in her piece *Giving Women the Benefit of Equality: A Response to Wirenius,* 20 Ford. Urb. L.J. 77 (1992). In that her close critique of my assumptions about freedom of speech led me to examine the jurisprudence from its beginning, Professor Higgins can be said to have started me along the road to Brandenburg and beyond.

On that road, Michael T. Fois has played Bing Crosby to my Bob Hope (or vice-versa; we're not sure). Each of these chapters presented here has benefited from his criticisms, suggestions, and probing questions. Catherine Isobe (at the time a student at Fordham) provided research assistance for Chapter 3, and drew my attention to the 1996 symposium concerning Ronald Dworkin's *The Moral Reading of the Constitution.* The symposium participants, particularly Professor Dworkin, gave me much food for thought. Perhaps in view of the substantial disagreement expressed in this work with her First Amendment theory, I should note that I found Professor MacKinnon's presentation to be informative and, I confess, inspiring. Across the gulf of ideological disagreement, I salute a fine advocate.

Joseph Arvay, Q.C., who represented the Little Sisters bookshop in its challenge against censorial practices by Canadian Customs, was a gracious source of information about the practical impact of governmental balancing of the equality and liberty principles, and the pitfalls such balancing entails. The struggle of Little Sisters exemplifies more than any other single case the dangers of equality-based balancing to the very minority groups it is purportedly meant to favor. Patrick Califia most graciously provided me with his perspective on that case, and on the issues surrounding censorship of so-called pornography, and I thank him.

Finally, I have received unstinting support and encouragement from several sources which made the writing of this book possible: my family, especially my parents John D. and Claire F. Wirenius, and my incomparable sister and brother-in-law, Karen and Bill Brandon; friends such as Martha Rix, with whom I have discussed these issues for longer than either of us will admit, Harold Ferguson (same comment), and my first mentor in the law, Stanley A. Teitler. Alan M. Schlesinger of the City of New York Law Department has been an invaluable foil to my sometimes overly academic approach, bringing to my attention the practical impact of First Amendment theory. Kellene Wirenius, my wife, continues to typify my ideal audience. She even helped proofread both the first edition and the revised edition. To perform so daunting a task can only be explained by true love and I remain, delightedly, in her debt. I am unable to find words that adequately convey my appreciation of her love and support.

At the Office of the Corporation Counsel, I had the rare experience of litigating these issues in the real world, rather than confining my jousts to paper. Paul A. Crotty, former Corporation Counsel, knew of this book's pendency when hiring me, and neither he nor Michael D. Hess, his successor, requested to review it or otherwise see its contents in advance; indeed the office allowed me every scholarly freedom, and expressed only pleasure at the venture. James R. Sandner and the rest of my colleagues at New York State United Teachers have been uniformly interested and supportive. As before, I note that, of course, the views expressed here, and mistakes made, are mine and mine alone.

Earlier versions of three chapters and portions of a fourth have been published in law reviews: an earlier version of Chapter 2 was published under the same title in volume 43 Drake Law Review 1 (1994) and is included here by permission; an earlier version of Chapter 3 was published under the same title in volume 26 Capital University Law Review 331 (1996); Chapter 5 was published under the same title in volume 32 of the Seton Hall Law Review, and I thank its editors for their suggestions and editing assistance. Portions of Chapters 7 and 8 have cheerfully been cannibalized from *Giving the Devil the Benefit of Law: Pornographers, the First Amendment and the Feminist Attack on Free Expression*, 20 Fordham Urban Law Journal 27 (1992).

1

Introduction

FREEDOM OF SPEECH is always a contentious subject. It is easy to say with Voltaire that "I disapprove of what you say, but I will defend to the death your right to say it,"[1] when the speech at issue does not really offend us, but when it is our own sensibilities being trodden upon, or our own feelings of self-worth being verbally undermined—well, that is a different story.

The noble virtue of tolerance has never found many fans, except in the abstract. Tolerance—we all love it but have an exception (or two) to the rule, which usually comes down to what really hurts our feelings. And *that* is one of the reasons for the passion that fuels many disputes over free speech. Each segment of the population believes in the general rule of tolerance but knows of a really important exception to that rule, which the rest of society cannot fully appreciate. This phenomenon cannot be explained by racial, ethnic or class demographics alone. The lawsuit against television talk show host Oprah Winfrey demonstrated that an expression of concern about the safety of beef can spark litigation by angry cattle ranchers.[2]

One other reason: words hurt. I am rejecting the easy way out that many writers on free speech have adopted—the claim that we are dealing with "only words."[3] This claim, which allows us to both sanitize and trivialize the right of free speech, also requires us to put from our minds truths learned on the nursery school playground: Words can hurt.

---

1. S. G. Tallentyre, *The Friends of Voltaire* (1907) at 199.
2. *See New York Daily News*, 27 February 1998, at 1, *et seq.*
3. In an (entirely proper) effort to show derision for the attitude that speech should be free because it is in the last analysis harmless, Catharine A. MacKinnon entitled one of her essays arguing for the censorship of what she defines as pornography *Only Words* (1994).

Our society asks those on the receiving end of painful words to accept that there is no redress, no vindication. Just like on the playground, they have to take the insult, or the painful reminder of past events—or watch as cruel and distorted images of the gender/racial/ethnic/sexual group to which they belong are disseminated. There is no teacher or parent to protect and defend the verbally assailed. Indeed, we do not even offer much sympathy to those on the receiving end of verbal attacks. The presumption is, somehow, that the reciprocal right of free speech—the right to what has been called "counterspeech"[4]—is in itself a sufficient remedy, or that the offended party must be too fragile a plant for our rough-and-tumble society.

Yet somehow the right to answer back (what do you say to an Illinois Nazi? "So's your mother"?) is not an emotionally adequate response to the march of members of the Nazi Party on Skokie.[5] Nor, for many women, is it enough to calmly (or even heatedly) point out that violent sexual imagery reinforces sexual stereotypes and helps men so disposed to believe that rape is actually consensual because women are whores by nature.[6]

Which brings us to another reason why censorship is popular: Words cannot only inflict emotional or psychic pain in themselves, they can create or reinforce attitudes that may in turn lead to antisocial behavior, or at the very least undermine the already seriously bruised civility that citizens in a (hopefully) egalitarian society bring to social intercourse. All of which is a polite way of saying that people who hear "hate speech" (by which I mean speech that reflects bigotry, whether that bigotry is racial, ethnic-religious, or based on sexual orientation) often enough, and especially early enough, will come if not to believe it, then to carry it with them throughout their lives. The "good" white person may never use the "N word," for example, but that doesn't mean it isn't available, and that it doesn't run through his or her mind.

Feminists who claim that "porn is the theory, rape is the practice" point to instances in which rapists have lifted scenarios from pornographic publications or videos and enacted them upon their victims. Gays and lesbians are assaulted by youths or roughnecks—or even off-duty military personnel— who were taught, through words, to hate "queers." We're not just talking about hurt feelings or offended sensibilities here.

In short, in the overwhelming majority of cases we ask those who are hurt by words, both directly and through the climate that words help create, to

---

4. Vincent Blasi, *The Checking Value of the First Amendment*, 1977 American Bar Foundation Research Journal 521 (1977).
5. *See Collin v. Smith*, 578 F. 2d 1197, 1199 (7th Cir.), *cert. denied*, 439 U.S. 916 (1978). (Federal civil rights lawsuit involving First Amendment right of American Nazi Party to conduct march).
6. Andrea Dworkin, *Pornography* (1980).

live with their injuries, or to seek redress against only the physical assailant, sacrificing all hope of legal redress against the fomenter of the hate. As I argue in this book, I think that we *need* to make these sacrifices—for a host of reasons. That these sacrifices must be made, however, does not mean we have the right to ignore them, or to pretend that our rule of free speech is cost-free. Such argument by denial plays right into the hands of the censors.

This book will explore the path by which the American understanding of free speech has evolved, and where it may go next. In the course of tracing that path, both the dangers that have been successfully overcome (as well as those that haven't) and the dangers that might be lurking just around the corner will be looked at. In the process, two claims will be made.

The first is that the conventional history of free speech—that the United States Supreme Court essentially ignored the First Amendment until the Red Scare of 1919 was in full swing and then created a repressive, intolerant set of rules that allowed censorship to run rampant until the late 1960s—is wrong. In fact, the much-maligned 1919 series of cases marks the beginning of real protection of speech in American constitutional law, and in a sense are the midpoint, not the beginning, of the Supreme Court's evolution toward the expansive protection we give to speech in the American legal system today.

If we give such expansive protection to speakers, why are there so many bitter battles about free speech? In part, the fault belongs to the Supreme Court. Having taken the first steps toward protecting speech that fell short of "conduct" or "incitement" (concepts explored in Chapter 2), and as the consequences of such broad immunity became clear, a group of justices flinched, and came up with the idea (right out of George Orwell) that not all speech is *speech*, as that word is used in the First Amendment. These justices carved out exceptions to the First Amendment, finding justification in a throwaway line from a trivial case that was decided shortly after the U.S. declared war in 1941. A bare majority of the Court based its decisions on an inherently subjective question: Was the speech at issue of "high" or "low" value to society as a whole?

Increasingly since then, and especially in the last few years, as censorship has become the darling of *both* the left and the right, these censorable areas of "low-value" speech have continually expanded from "narrow exceptions" to become the principal method by which free speech issues are resolved. Some legal academics (and some judges) approve wholeheartedly of this approach, despite the utter absence of any such language in the text of the First Amendment or of any historical justification for it. (These issues are explored in Chapter 3).

The end result, and the second claim made by this book, is that although the function of the Supreme Court is to *interpret* and *enforce* the Constitution (and the laws passed under it, of course) and not to declare what it thinks is good social policy, the justices are upholding state and federal regulation of speech based solely on their own opinions of the merits of the speech. If this result seems a little beyond the scope of the job description—well, it is.

Those who are familiar with the debates that surround the issue of free speech are probably now saying, "So the alternative is First Amendment absolutism, right?" and getting ready to demonstrate how absolutism is unworkable as a practical matter, however attractive it may be in theory. Absolutism, the belief that restrictions on the right to speak are never valid unless the speech is an integral component of an illegal act (usually a violent act), is principally associated with Justices William O. Douglas and Hugo L. Black. And yes, the so-called absolutist view of Douglas and Black is far more nuanced and viable than the usual portrayal of these justices as, respectively, a judicial eccentric and a Baptist parson manqué who has substituted an old copy of the Constitution for Holy Writ would indicate. But this is not a book about First Amendment absolutism. Rather, the concept underlying their First Amendment jurisprudence, especially Douglas's, the century-old concept of the "verbal act," provides a possible rationalizing factor that has long been neglected in First Amendment academic writing, but one with a strong support in the decisions of judges.

Before we can even try to resolve our differences, a common language, a functional and nonsubjective language, is needed. In the next three chapters, I try to provide it, based on a new look at the First Amendment rule as applied to what everyone agrees *is* speech under the amendment. Rather than limit "speech" to the narrowest possible category of communication, I suggest that (because any exception means a disregard by the government of the language of the First Amendment) we should to the greatest possible extent treat all communication as speech. Whatever the rule we then decide upon, at least we will not be dodging the Constitution by saying that it does not apply.

After exploring the ways in which the justices have carved up the various kinds of speech and assigned each a different degree of protection from government regulation, and then trying to map out a less schizophrenic approach, the discussion turns to the pressing issues of free speech at the end of the century. The present approaches to these issues, including hate speech and regulation of new forms of communication (such as the Internet), will be explored. For example, the elimination by CompuServe of access—worldwide—to various electronic bulletin boards found by German provincial authorities to be "obscene" opens the door to the prospect that the "Information Superhighway" may be turned into a bike path rather than face trouble in any, even the most restrictive, locale. Although the elimination of cyberporn might not slow the advance of the mind (*that* will be discussed later), what happens when the Internet reaches more—sometimes dramatically more—restrictive nations? Will servers follow the pusillanimous example of CompuServe and regulate discussions of women's issues, modern literature, or even microbrewery beer in deference to the mores of such nations?

This last issue, like the questions associated with regulation of speech (or record albums, or videogames, etc.) in the interest of children, raises a complex and dangerous issue. The impact of regulation, or even consumer pressure (itself a First Amendment–protected right), could be profound, especially as coterie publishing and book, record, and video distribution are being dramatically reduced in favor of mass marketing. Soon—perhaps sooner than we would like to admit—mainstream culture may be the *only* culture. In regulating that culture, or even in creating it through community expressions of approval or disapproval, both government and private citizens have an obligation to avoid overly homogenizing it. Milk is a wonderfully nutritious food for children, but an unvarying diet of it soon becomes bland.

FREE TO CHOOSE?

So far, the questions of what the law regarding freedom of expression *should* be and what it *is* have been dealt with as almost synonymous—that is, as if the Supreme Court could expand and collapse the protections of the First Amendment at will. Many legal academics and political activists presume that this is, in fact, the case and pitch their arguments not on what the Constitution says, but on their ideas of what is good social policy. Such arguments have been made by those who consider themselves protectors of the First Amendment and by those who believe it has been elevated in our society to a shibboleth.[7]

---

7. For example, Vincent Blasi in *The Checking Value in First Amendment Theory*, 1977 Am. Bar. Found. Res. J. 521 (1977) and in *The Pathological Perspective and the First Amendment*, 85 Colum. L. Rev. 449 (1985) argues that the First Amendment's protections should be kept to a limited class of speech, but should be stringent, essentially calling for "a lean and mean" First Amendment. Similarly, G. Sidney Buchanan, *The Hate Speech Case: A Pyrrhic Victory for Freedom of Speech?*, 21 Hof. L. Rev. 285, 296–297 (1992) advocates that the Court be flexible in upholding or rejecting government regulation of speech on social policy grounds.

Those who believe that the values of the First Amendment should occasionally yield to other values often express themselves as if the Court has a free hand in delineating the scope of the First Amendment. *See* Steven H. Shiffrin, *Dissent, Injustice and the Meaning of America* (1999); Tracy Higgins, *Giving Women the Benefit of Equality: A Response to Wirenius*, 20 Ford. Urb. L.J. 77, 87 (1992); Frederick Schauer, *Codifying the First Amendment: New York v. Ferber*, 1982 Sup. Ct. Rev. 285, 315–317 (1983); Cass R. Sunstein, *Neutrality and Constitutional Law*, 92 Colum. L. Rev. 1 (1992); *see also* Sunstein, *Pornography and the First Amendment*, 1986 Duke L.J. 589 (1987). This point of view unites all the contributors to David S. Allen and Robert Jensen, *Freeing the First Amendment: Critical Perspectives on Freedom of Expression* (1995).

Eminent law professors such as Ronald Dworkin argue that the goal of constitutional interpretation should be to make of the Constitution the most morally sound blueprint for government possible.[8] Others believe that the language of the Constitution must give way to the "original intent" of the Framers.[9] This approach is studded with difficulties. Who were the "Framers"—the drafters? the delegates to the Constitutional Convention? the state ratifiers? How can we ascertain views that were often unrecorded?[10]

Dean Lee Bollinger's *The Tolerant Society* grounds the First Amendment's purpose—and thus its correct interpretation—in the molding of the character of the U.S. citizenry, in the inculcation of the civic virtue of tolerance, so necessary to prevent our patchwork democracy from unraveling.[11] Similarly, Justice Louis D. Brandeis grounded the amendment's purpose in the inculcation of courage, although (unlike Bollinger) Brandeis does not suggest that this end should in every case guarantee immunity to the speaker— as witnessed by the fact that Brandeis and Oliver Wendell Holmes *concurred* in the upholding of the conviction of Anita Whitney.[12]

Recently, some scholars (an increasing number) have suggested that the fundamental purpose of the Constitution is to create an egalitarian society, and that to the extent that the constitutional language, the original intent, or the nation's history get in the way of this single overarching good, the document does not deserve our fidelity.[13] Others argue for an instrumental fidelity to the Constitution—arguing that because the constitutional structure is flexible enough to permit judicial redesigning of the U.S. political structure, and thus to advance the achievement of equality, it should be

---

8. Ronald Dworkin, *Freedom's Law: The Moral Reading of the American Constitution* (1996); *see also* Ronald Dworkin, *The Arduous Virtue of Fidelity: Originalism, Scalia, Tribe and Nerve*, 65 Ford. L. Rev. at 1249–1269 (1997). A similar approach can be seen in Shiffrin, *supra* note 7.

9. Robert H. Bork, *The Tempting of America: The Political Seduction of the Law* (1990).

10. For a cogent critique of Judge Bork's views, *see* Lawrence Levy, *Original Intent and the Framers' Constitution* (1988). Bork addresses Levy's critiques in *The Tempting of America* at 218.

11. Lee C. Bollinger, *The Tolerant Society* (1986).

12. *Whitney v. California*, 274 U.S. 357, 372–373, 380 (1927) (Brandeis and Holmes, JJ. concurring). In *Whitney*, the conviction of a delegate to the Communist Labor Party was upheld under the California Syndicalism Act, a statute aimed on its face at preventing terrorism. Ms. Whitney had claimed that the conviction, for expressing a viewpoint only, rendered the statute unconstitutional as applied to her. The Supreme Court disagreed. Justices Brandeis and Holmes, agreeing with Whitney's constitutional claim, nonetheless found the conviction to be proper because Ms. Whitney had failed to make her objections to the court below, thus preserving them for appeal.

13. *See*, for example, J. M. Balkin, *Agreements with Hell and Other Objects of Our Faith*, 65 Ford. L. Rev. 1703 (1997); Michael J. Klarman, *Fidelity, Indeterminacy, and the Problem of Constitutional Evil*, 65 Ford. L. Rev. 1739 (1997).

accorded an "instrumental fidelity," a conditional allegiance to the system as a means to the real end.[14]

Each of these viewpoints assumes that the judiciary and the legal academy are free to rework the Constitution based upon individual philosophical views of the good without any inherent limitation in serving that good. Proponents of these viewpoints select the lodestar of constitutional interpretation, based upon their own conception of the good, and elevate equality over liberty. Such preference of one social "good" over another does not serve the citizenry because the document does not make the choice for the judge or the scholar, and the citizenry is not consulted.

In a sense, those who urge that the Constitution is a blank check for the judiciary to vindicate norms that they believe to be "good" are missing the very foundations of our legal order: the right of the citizenry to chart the course of the ship of state, limited only by choices made by their predecessors who designed the craft—which can be overhauled, refitted, or even abandoned (to extend the metaphor), provided that the changes are made by popular vote. It is not that the values chosen by these advocates are not important, nor is the problem even that their values are not enshrined in the Constitution. By the enactment of the Civil War amendments, the value of equality has been raised to constitutional stature, and our constitutional history since then has been one of striving (although often failing) to live up to that principle.

Rather, the new school of legal interpretation errs when it assumes that it is for academics or judges to choose which value to favor. These advocates of value-laden interpretation forget that every choice made for the people is one less that can be made by the people.

This school of thought embraces what in this volume is described as a *subjective* reading of the Constitution, the viewpoint that the individual jurist may legitimately weave his or her own views of right and wrong into the warp and woof of the government under the guise of construing the law.

Because of the inherently coercive nature of legal determinations—the Supreme Court tells the people that their will, expressed through their elected representatives, is to be disregarded as illegitimate—this embrace of subjectivity is one that limits the democratic nature of our government. The overriding of the popular will, based solely upon the emotions and convictions of a small body of individuals can act to destabilize the legitimacy of the law, as exemplified by the voiding by the U.S. Supreme Court of many of the basic economic reforms of the first third of the twentieth century. The

---

14. Dorothy E. Roberts, *The Meaning of Blacks' Fidelity to the Constitution*, 65 Ford. L. Rev. 1761 (1997); Catharine A. MacKinnon, *Freedom from Unreal Loyalties: On Fidelity in Constitutional Interpretation*, 65 Ford. L. Rev. 1773 (1997).

Supreme Court's anti-labor decisions (typified by *Lochner v. New York*[15] and its progeny) that struck economic reforms in the name of safeguarding a judicially created "freedom of contract" (which ignored the economic disparity of the parties to the contract) have long been condemned as an abuse of judicial power because they imported into the Constitution principles that were never voted upon or agreed to in any formal way by the electorate.

Another problem with subjective arguments is that they embrace a distorted notion of the Supreme Court's function. If you consider the matter, these nine individuals who are appointed for life, from whose decisions about the Constitution's meaning there is no appeal short of the incredibly difficult process of actually amending the Constitution itself, serve a pretty undemocratic function. They are there, essentially, to prevent the popularly elected representatives of the people—the vox populi itself, according to the central supposition of our form of government—from violating the Constitution's boundaries. There are times, our theory of government states, when the majority *doesn't* rule. In other words, the Court's constitutional decisions limit the right of "We the People" to revise fundamental decisions contained in the Constitution through our state or federal representatives. Indeed, for just such reasons, the Framers of the Constitution rejected a proposed "Council of Revision," the purpose of which was to update and amend the Constitution.[16]

The antidemocratic function of the Supreme Court is a well-established phenomenon, as is the difficulty of the amendment process.[17] It even has a name—the "countermajoritarian difficulty."[18] Some use it to argue that the Supreme Court should not have the power to review state or federal actions at all (this was the principal issue the Court decided in *Marbury v. Madison* in 1803, and some scholars still think John Marshall got it wrong when he wrote the Court's opinion that unconstitutional federal statutes could be declared unenforceable by the federal judiciary).[19]

---

15. 198 U.S. 45 (1905).
16. Charles Evans Hughes, *The Supreme Court of the United States* (1928) at 27–29.
17. Alexander Bickel, *The Least Dangerous Branch: The Supreme Court at the Bar of Politics* (1963) at 16; *see* Lawrence Tribe, *American Constitutional Law* (2d ed. 1988) at 61–66 (listing sources); John Hart Ely, *Democracy and Distrust: A Theory of Judicial Review* (1980); Henry R. Monaghan, *We the People[s]: Original Understanding and Constitutional Amendment*, 96 Colum. L. Rev. 121, 165–173 (1996).
18. Bickel, *The Least Dangerous Branch* at 16 -23 Tribe, in *American Constitutional Law*, calls it the antimajoritarian difficulty, and dismisses it rather lightly. *Id.* at 61–67.
19. *Marbury v. Madison*, 1 Cranch (5 U.S.) 137, 177, 176–178 (1803) (ruling that it "is emphatically the province and duty of the judicial department to say what the law is"). The Court held that the power to review statutes for constitutionality applied to laws passed by the states in *Cohens v. Virginia*, 6 Wheat. (19 U.S.) 264 (1821). *See also Fletcher v. Peck*, 6 Cranch (10 U.S.) 87 (1816); *see also Martin v. Hunter's Lessee*, 1 Wheat. (14 U.S.) 304 (1816).

Without going as far as those who suggest that the legitimacy of judicial review is so murky that the power should be used only in times of acute crisis, it is a well-established, moderate, position that the Court is "concerned only with the power to enact statutes, not with their wisdom."[20] Or, as Justice William O. Douglas put it, "The problem of the judge is to keep personal predilections from dictating the choice and to be as faithful as possible to the architectural scheme" of the Constitution.[21] The justices of the Supreme Court, who are restrained only by their own fidelity to their oaths of office, must keep this limited function in mind, or they could easily succumb to the temptation to rule as, in the pithy expression of Learned Hand, "Platonic Guardians"—that is, absolute, hopefully benevolent, dictators.

Finally, the importation of subjective views into the Constitution renders the Supreme Court's decisions and thus the effective law of the Constitution subject to wild fluctuations based not on principles but on personalities: what seems abhorrent to Justice Thurgood Marshall may not seem at all repugnant to Chief Justice William H. Rehnquist. Absent decisions tightly tethered to neutral reasoning, a personnel change on the Court can transform "the law" into "a historical error" overnight. Although the making of value judgments cannot be altogether avoided, these factors suggest that subjectivity should be minimized, not embraced as a positive good. This is particularly true in terms of regulating speech, where the subjectivity inherent in determining the value of speech can lead to categorizing in an ipse dixit manner, declaring that one form of speech that is logically indistinguishable in terms of neutral principle from another form of speech may be classed as subject to ban "because I say so."

Historically, as well, the Supreme Court gains its right of judicial review not from the enumerations of its functions in the Constitution, but from the implications of the Constitution's status as the "Supreme Law of the Land."[22] Under this analysis, unless the Constitution forbids the passage of a law, the Court has no business striking it. The Court's mission is to interpret the constitutional text, not to create it.[23] While many today would state

---

Those who dispute the legitimacy of judicial review include Raoul Berger, *Government by Judiciary* (1977); L. Lusky, *By What Right?* (1975), and, most famously, Judge Learned Hand, *The Bill of Rights* (1958).

20. *United States v. Butler*, 297 U.S. 1, 78–79 (1936) (Stone, J., dissenting from a ruling striking New Deal legislation).

21. William O. Douglas, *Stare Decisis*, 49 Colum. L. Rev. 735, 739 (1949).

22. U.S. Const. Art. VI§2 (1789); *see generally, Marbury v. Madison*, 1 Cranch (5 U.S.) at 176–178.

23. Although this very "vanilla" vision of constitutional interpretation is the basis for the arguments advanced in this book, more "cutting-edge" scholars advance a variety of techniques of constitutional interpretation. While a review of that literature here would be both exhaustive and exhausting, it would also not be relevant, as I take the historical mainstream position described in the text as an axiom. However, an unusually wide-ranging

that in the process of interpreting so general a provision as the First Amendment one cannot avoid making decisions based on policy grounds,[24] surely a good-faith effort to ascertain the meaning and the scope of the language used, and not to legislate one's prejudices from on high, is the better practice for an unelected judge—or, for that matter, an author of a book on the meaning of the First Amendment.

That is why the question of whether the First Amendment is worth all the sacrifices or whether a less costly doctrine should replace it (through the amendment process) is discussed separately.[25] Once again, my own views should be given in advance: I believe that the First Amendment is vitally necessary, that the costs and risks it imposes are warranted by its benefits, and that, in fact, we would be far poorer without it. Any fair exposition of this point of view, though, must examine the alternatives to our own system, and must answer the questions posed by the challengers to the First Amendment.

In evaluating how judges go about interpreting the Constitution (or at least how they profess to do so), several axioms can be propounded. First, as stated, the Constitution is the document, the solemn compact between previously free and independent states, by which the federal government was created: It literally *constitutes* the federal government. Thus, no power not granted (whether explicitly or implicitly) by the Constitution may be exercised by the federal government, and the state governments are barred only from exercising authority that is actually ceded by the state governments in the Constitution.[26]

The second axiom: The commencing point for interpretation of any document is the language itself. In this regard the Constitution is a law, like any other law, only broader in scope and governing all other laws—in the

---

and comprehensive symposium at Fordham Law School celebrating the publication of Ronald Dworkin's *Freedom's Law* (1996) manages to present most of the contending views about the appropriate approach to constitutional text. *Symposium: Fidelity in Constitutional Theory*, 65 Ford. L. Rev. 1247–1818 (1997), includes papers and dialogues by a wide range of scholars currently active in the field.

24. Indeed, some go further, and argue that "interpretation" of a text—that is, deciding the document's meaning through what they pejoratively term "formalist logic" instead of reaching the just or beneficial result in the context of the individual case—is a futile undertaking in view of the arbitrary and indeterminate nature of language itself. *See* Thomas Streeter, "Free Speech, Language and the Rule of Law" in *Freeing the First Amendment* (Allen & Jensen, eds.) (1995) at 34–38. *See also* Richard Delgado, *First Amendment Formalism is Giving Way to First Amendment Legal Realism*, 29 Harv. Civ. Rights–Civ. Lib. L. Rev. 169 (1994).

25. Thus, many of the "balancing" issues value choices that I argue are for the populace and not for unelected judges to make, but that form the bulk of critical (and, increasingly, conservative) discussions of free speech, are addressed in Chapter 7. For a provocative selection of these critical views, see David S. Allen and Robert Jensen, *Freeing the First Amendment: Critical Perspectives on Freedom of Expression* (1995).

26. Ely, *supra*; Monaghan, *supra*.

words of the Supremacy Clause, "the Supreme Law of the Land."[27] As such, the Court has through the years used many well-established tools designed to help interpreters understand the meanings of statutes of the constitutional text. These tools are useful today.

In teaching Harvard Law School students the basic approach to statutory— and thus constitutional—construction, Felix Frankfurter used to emphasize this point by explaining hyperbolically that there were three steps: read the statute, Read the Statute, and READ THE STATUTE. More realistically, it has frequently been held in construing all kinds of legal instruments—contracts, ordinances, and statutes—that, if there is no ambiguity in the words themselves, there is no need to resort to other means of interpretation to determine their meaning.[28] Thus, as the Supreme Court has held in construing a Congressional enactment, the terms of this statute are unambiguous on their face, or in light of ordinary principles of interpretation, then "judicial inquiry is complete."[29] This is as true for contracts as for constitutions—both are legal instruments. Rather "than rewrite an unambiguous agreement, a court will enforce its plain meaning."[30] This interpretative practice dates back to the very first case in which a statute was struck as unconstitutional.[31]

This rule holds even to honoring omissions through oversight. For example, in an entirely typical contract case, *Firtell v. Crest Builders, Inc.*,[32] the New York State Appellate Division (the state's intermediate appellate court) held that "[t]he quoted provision should be interpreted in accordance with its plain language. It is not for the court to enlarge the meaning of the words in the contract so as to correct seller's admitted oversight." If such fidelity to the instrument is vital in the case of a mere contract, a commercial transaction between individuals, it is even more important in the case of the document from which our government derives all of its authority. Or, as Justice Scalia has put it, courts "are not free to replace" a clear meaning "with an unenacted legislative intent."[33] Unsurprisingly, then, the language of the

---

27. U.S. Const. Art. VI§2; *see also Cooper v. Aaron,* 358 U.S. 1, 18 (1958); *Marbury v. Madison,* 1 Cranch at 177.

28. *Duncan v. Walker,* 533 U.S. 167, 150 L. Ed. 2nd 251, 258 (2001) (construing Federal Antiterrorism and Effective Death Penalty Act of 1996; *CCG Associates I v. Riverside Associates,* 157 A.D.2d 435, 556 N.Y.S.2d 859, 862 (1st Dep't 1990); *see also Matter of Western Union Tel. Co. v. American Commun. Assn. C.I.O.,* 299 N.Y. 177, 184–185 (1949) (contracts).

29. *Connecticut National Bank v. Germain,* 503 U.S. 249, 254 (1992); *Rubin v. United States,* 449 U.S. 424, 430, 431, n.8 (1981). *Duncan,* 150 L. Ed. 2d at 258.

30. *CCG Associates, supra* 556 N.Y.S.2d at 862; *Laba v. Carey,* 29 N.Y.2d 302, 308, 327 N.Y.S.2d 613, 618 (1971) (same doctrine reaffirmed).

31. *Marbury v. Madison,* 1 Cranch (5 U.S.) 137, 174–175 (1803).

32. *Firtell v. Crest Builders, Inc.,* 159 A.D.2d 352, 552 N.Y.S.2d 630, 631 (1st Dep't 1990).

33. *INS v. Cardoza-Fonseca,* 480 U.S. 421, 453, 452–453 (1987) (Scalia, J., concurring) (citing cases). In *Duncan,* the Court made it clear that its function was "to construe what Congress has enacted."

Constitution, where it is unambiguous, must be granted precedence even over the demonstrable intent of the drafters.[34]

The Fourteenth Amendment, for example, was understood by the ratifiers (if not by the drafters) to principally address the legal status of the freed former slaves after the Civil War.[35] Yet the drafters did not confine their terms so. Instead, the Fourteenth Amendment forbids the States to deny "due process of law" or "equal protection of the laws" to "any person," or to "infringe" the "privileges and immunities of citizens of the United States."[36] Although the drafters patently did not intend for this provision to prevent legal differentiation by gender, the Supreme Court has (incontrovertibly, in my view) held that such classifications are inherently suspect as a result of the amendment's sweep.[37]

If anything, it is even more important to rely on the language than on subjective intent with respect to a constitution than with reference to contracts: The record of the intentions of the Framers is far less clear. Only informal notes of the Constitutional Convention survive, and the meaning of the various provisions were hotly debated at the time: the ratifying conventions, the newspaper debates, the Federalists and anti-Federalists who wrote pro- (or anti-) ratification treatises each articulated their separate understandings of the document's meaning, and these understand-

---

34. *Seminole Tribe of Florida v. Florida*, 517 U.S. 44, 76 (1996) ("Nor are we free to rewrite the statutory scheme in order to approximate what we think Congress might have wanted").

35. *See* Lambert Gingras, *Congressional Misunderstandings and the Ratifiers' Understanding: The Case of the Fourteenth Amendment*, 40 Amer. Journ. Leg. Hist. 41 (1996). *See also Insurance Co. v. New Orleans*, 1 Woods 85 (U.S. 1870). Justice Douglas noted that this view of the amendment's scope, based on legislative intent, held sway "for a decade or more" before the Court began to expand it. William O. Douglas, *Stare Decisis*, 49 Colum. L. Rev. 735, 737 (1949) (citing 1 Woods 85). The difficulties that nativist sentiment caused some other ethnic groups may also have played a part in the drafters' intent. For a comprehensive look at the drafters' intent and a good argument that the amendment's meaning *was* more broadly understood at the time of ratification, *see* Michael Kent Curtis, *No State Shall Abridge: The Fourteenth Amendment and the Bill of Rights* (1986).

36. U.S. Const. Amend. XIV.

37. *Frontiero v. Richardson*, 411 U.S. 677 (1973). It should be noted that the Court has failed to apply the equality principle with full rigor to women. Laws which support racial discrimination are presumed to be invidious and must be shown to be justified by a "compelling" state interest. Nondiscriminatory laws by contrast receive the lowest form of scrutiny—the legislature need only have had a "rational basis" to act. However, statutes that discriminate by gender receive "intermediate scrutiny," a less exacting review than the former, albeit far more difficult to meet than the rubber-stamp rational basis test. *See Craig v. Boren*, 429 U.S. 190, 197–199) (1976). With even less justification, the Court simply ducked the issue of the Equal Protection Clause as applied to homosexuals when it upheld state bans on homosexual sodomy—while intimating that *heterosexual* sodomy might well be protected. *Bowers v. Hardwick*, 478 U.S. 186, 188 n. 2, et seq.; *see id.* at 220 (Blackmun, J., dissenting) (1986). That equal protection extends to homosexuals at some level has been made clear in *Roemer v. Evans*, 517 U.S. 620 (1996).

ings differ dramatically. No one set of subjective intentions can claim to be authoritative.[38]

Finally, the worst kind of "interpretation" is that which rewrites the instrument while purporting to "construe" it.[39] Especially disfavored is the erasure through interpretation of language used. As the Court held in *Marbury*, "It cannot be presumed that any clause in the Constitution is intended to be without effect; and, therefore, such a construction is inadmissible, unless the words require it."[40]

For all of these reasons, the lawyer, constitutional scholar, or judge is denied the freedom of the philosopher. To ask, "Why give speech more protection than other forms of behavior?" and "conclude that there is no compelling reason to do so" and accordingly reject "the speech is special position"[41] is to leave entirely the realm of constitutional law for that of political philosophy. In terms of the Constitution, regardless of whether one agrees with that document or not, speech is special because it has a provision directed to its protection. That is enough to set it apart from other forms of conduct that are not similarly advantaged.

Although some scholars—and, unfortunately, some judges who have lost sight of their limited roles in a political society[42]—claim to be advocates of

---

38. Levy, *supra*; Monaghan, *supra*. Jack M. Rakove, *Original Meaning: Politics and Ideas in the Making of the Constitution*, 1996.
39. *See Babbit v. Sweet Home Chapter, Communities for Great Ore.*, 515 U.S. 687, 698 (1995); *Collard v. Incorporated Village of Floral Hill*, 52 N.Y.2d 594, 604, 439 N.Y.S.2d 326, 331 (1981) ("Where language has been chosen containing no inherent ambiguity or uncertainty, courts are properly hesitant, under the guise of judicial construction, to imply additional requirements to relieve a party from asserted disadvantages flowing from the terms actually used"); *see also Goodstein Construction Corp. v. City of New York*, 111 A.D.2d 49, 489 N.Y.S.2d 175, 177 (1st Dep't 1985) (*citing Morlee Sales Corp. v. Manufacturers Trust Co.*, 9 N.Y.2d 16, 210 N.Y.S.2d 516 [1961]); *Benderson Development Company, Inc. v. Schwab Bros. Trucking, Inc.*, 64 A.D.2d 447, 409 N.Y.S.2d 890, 897 (4th Dep't 1978) ("Additional obligations may not be imposed upon a party to a contract under a theory of contractual construction").
40. *Marbury*, 1 Cranch (5 U.S.) at 174. *See Duncan v. Walker*, 150 L. Ed. 2d at 259. *See also United States v. Manasche*, 348 U.S. 528, 538–539 (1955); *Market Co. v. Hoffman*, 101 U.S. 112, 115 (1879) (tracing rule back to Bacon's abridgement, Sect.2. Again, it bears stressing that this rule is no radical pronouncement, but rather a standard principle in interpreting any legal instrument. For example, "in construing a contract, one of a court's goals is to avoid an interpretation that would leave contractual clauses meaningless." *Two Guys from Harrison-N.Y., Inc. v. S.F.R. Realty Corp.*, 63 N.Y.2d 396, 403, 482 N.Y.S.2d 465, 468 (1984). That the same holds true for statutes was recently reaffirmed by the Supreme Court. *Duncan, id.*
41. Robert A. Jensen & Elvira R. Arriola, "Feminism and Free Expression," in Allen & Jensen, *Freeing the First Amendment* (1995) 195, 210. From there, the authors go on to construct a "theory of free speech" based on the precept that "*speech is not special*" (*Id.* at 212, emphasis in original.). *See also* Frederick Schauer, *Must Speech Be Special?*, 78 Northwestern L. Rev. 1284, 1306 (1983) (concluding that it should not be, but accepting precedent and the constitutional text, holding that it must be treated as so despite resultant "intellectual ache").
42. For a particularly egregious example, see Harold G. Rothwax, *Guilty: The Collapse of Criminal Justice* (1996), in which the author, a Justice of the Supreme Court of New York (that

"common sense" and urge judges to, in the name of substantial justice, "re-define" the Constitution by shaping doctrines based upon their views of the social good, such an approach represents the surrender of any semblance of a democratic-republican form of government. In such a government, as has long been understood, "[q]uestions of political expediency belong to the legislative halls, not to the judicial forum."[43] Worse, when the judiciary performs these fundamental revisions under the guise of "interpreting" the Constitution, the people are left out of the mix while remaining deluded that the fundamental book of rules that their ancestors voted on cannot be changed without their consent.

If unelected judges can legitimately refashion, at their whim, the funda-mental role of government without the consent of the governed, we may live in a nicer society, but it is not a democracy or even a republic—it is an oligarchy, where the chosen few decide for the rabble, hopefully to the benefit of the latter. As a member of the rabble, I think I prefer constitu-tionalism, with all of its flaws.

This does not mean that intent, or implication, are irrelevant. They, as well as the values and goals that shaped the Constitution, are helpful in resolving ambiguities in the language (For example, what is the freedom of speech that Congress may not abridge, and does it differ from unmodified freedom of speech?) and disputes about the meanings of the words (For example, is every regulation an "abridgement"?).

WHY?

Normally, books of this scope—examining the entire corpus of the law about free speech—are written for lawyers, law students, and academics. They tend to be thick, imposing volumes that accept the premises that presenting the subject in depth means giving up the lay audience and that writing for the lay audience means a condescending oversimplification of the subject mat-ter. I hope to walk the tightrope between these two dangers, because I be-lieve that law is too important a subject to be left to lawyers. And that the First Amendment especially is a misunderstood creature. Like any other limi-tation on government, it says that we are impotent before admitted social evils. This does not go down well with the American people.

---

    is, a trial court judge) blandly urged that judges abolish such fundamental constitutional provisions as the right to silence (Fifth Amendment) and the restrictions against un-reasonable search and seizure contained in the Fourth Amendment.

43. *Knox v. Lee and Parker v. Davis (The Legal Tender Cases)*, 12 Wall (79 U.S.) 457, 562 (1871) (Bradley, J. concurring).

Many on the moderate right as well as those on the moderate left of the political spectrum have in the last decade or so grown concerned with the apathetic reaction to proposals for censorship in universities and in society at large. From John Leo and Diane Ravitch to Alan Dershowitz and June Callwood, people of strongly diverse views recognize the danger of the stifling of free expression—and just how little stir is caused by abridgments of free speech that would have been roundly condemned twenty years ago.

I personally first experienced this climate in a class on the First Amendment that I took at Columbia Law School in 1988. The professor, Vincent Blasi, was an admirable, even-handed lecturer, and the class was solidly in favor of protecting speech . . . until we came to the writing of Catharine MacKinnon on pornography. Professor Blasi was his usual fair-minded self, but the student commentary changed. Not only were the students who spoke out unanimously in favor of the censorship of pornography as defined by MacKinnon, they treated it as axiomatic that only evil people could oppose such censorship. The climate of the class dropped to arctic levels when I began putting the case against censorship. It was not simply that my class-mates felt I was wrong, it was more that the spirit of intellectual debate was gone, and I was an infidel in the tents of the faithful. I was no longer of the herd, even though my classmates had made all the arguments I was making the week before. Most of the students were silent on both days we discussed MacKinnon, although a few came up to me afterward and said that they were glad I had spoken out. This changed classroom atmosphere was, I think, the reason that nobody dared jump in: Somehow the pro-censorship cohort had the knack of making opposition seem to be an act of oppression.

Similarly, the tearing down of unpopular messages at the law school (in my time at Columbia it was the Young Republicans who were primarily victimized) goes on merrily today. In my undergraduate years at Fordham, I noticed similar behavior: Pax Christi and the so-called Progressive Student Alliance tried to prevent the CIA from recruiting on campus; the Young Republicans struck back by trying to silence the "lefties." Both at Fordham (where, God help them, I was considered a man of the left) and at Columbia (where, God help me, I was considered a good-hearted bumpkin conservative of the Fred Grandy type), nobody seemed to value freedom of speech for its own sake.[44] Both in society at large and in the campus lives of our young people today, that trend of devaluation seems if anything to have accelerated.

---

44. A far more experienced and wise commentator than I has noted that both the right and the left vacillate between accepting and rejecting the use of free speech based upon, seemingly, no other principle than political expediency. Nat Hentoff, *Free Speech for Me—But Not for Thee: How the American Left and Right Relentlessly Censor Each Other* (1992).

This trend, like our ever-declining voting patterns, could over time deprive us of much of the meaning, and of the fun, of freedom. The right of U.S. citizens to read and speak as they will—to challenge the central precepts of our government and even of our culture is itself one of the central precepts of the "American Experiment." This freedom is not just a safeguard against tyranny, but is also a cultural source of the rebellious, admittedly sometimes appalling, but seldom dull, paths the United States wanders down. It provides much of the spirit, and the pleasure, of being an American: For all of our gaucheries, we are able to begin anew, because no issue is ever finally decided.

2

The Road to *Brandenburg*

A Look at the Evolving Understanding of the First Amendment

THE FIRST AMENDMENT has been called the most charismatic provision of the United States Constitution by one eminent scholar[1] and has been enshrined in our cultural morality in a way no other law has been. While law usually at best receives respect (even if only in the breach), the First Amendment commands—and gets—devotion. At some level, this provision, tacked on with nine companions to the federal Constitution at the last minute to ensure its ratification, has become the centerpiece of our civic religion. We celebrate our heritage in terms of our freedom, not from Great Britain—*that* battle was fought and won centuries ago, and at least two "evil empires" have fallen since—but rather in terms of our creation of a "free society."

The platitudes about freedom have become bromides—comforting, but in the end insubstantial. All Americans, of whatever ideological stripe, can say that they favor freedom. And it is hard indeed to find anyone to proclaim that he or she is against freedom of speech, or its guarantor, the First Amendment.[2] Yet each of the various constituencies that claims devotion to the First Amendment, it seems, has a distinct vision of what it means, and what exactly it does and does not protect.

The paradox of devotion to a rule of law whose parameters, and even whose basic meaning, cannot be agreed upon within the legal academy, let alone by the general populace, can be attributed to several factors. It could

---

1. H. Kalven, *A Worthy Tradition* (1988) at xii.
2. Although the secular religion aspect of the First Amendment may well pertain to the Free Exercise and Establishment clauses, which safeguard the right of individuals to worship as they please and prevent the government from worshiping at all, the subject of this discussion is limited to the Free Speech and Free Press clauses.

be claimed that this fact stems from human nature; it is easier to proclaim freedom of speech in the abstract than to champion it for that speech which one finds personally offensive. As Mark Twain once wrote, "[I]t's nobler to teach others, and no trouble."[3] But this factor alone surely does not account for the paradox, or else First Amendment literature would simply consist of charges and countercharges of hypocrisy. A more fundamental cause is implicit in the jurisprudence that has evolved.

In fact, the First Amendment has been assigned numerous functions in our society, functions that range from individual self-fulfillment to the hypothesis that the marketplace of ideas will inevitably lead to the discovery of truths. All of these various concepts that have been used to vindicate, and shape our understanding of, free speech play a role in our current jurisprudence. The warring emphases placed upon these values, and on other values with which these come into tension, have led to an increasing breakdown in the scope given the First Amendment's protections. In the name of equality, for example, various scholars have urged the censorship of speech that has rationally been deemed to reinforce attitudes that contribute to discriminatory and even criminal behavior.[4] Jurists and scholars alike have called for an overt ad hoc balancing by judges of the importance of the speech at issue against speech that the state would protect.[5]

The uncertainty over what the amendment means, and what values it serves, has informed these efforts, and has given them a veneer of respectability. Although no Rosetta Stone for First Amendment jurisprudence exists, such an ad hoc approach is consistent neither with the language of the First Amendment—"Congress shall make *no law* . . . abridging the freedom of speech"—nor with its history, if one goes back to the beginning.

---

3. Mark Twain, *Following the Equator* (1897) at 6.
4. Catharine A. MacKinnon, *Toward A Feminist Theory of the State* (1989) at 139–152; Cass R. Sunstein, *Pornography and the First Amendment*, 1986 Duke L.J. 589, 616–619; *see also* Tracy Higgins, *Giving Women the Benefit of Equality: A Response to Wirenius*, 20 Ford. Urb. L. J. 77 (1992). For my views on the specific issue of pornography in light of the various values served by the First Amendment, see Wirenius, *Giving the Devil the Benefit of Law: Pornographers, the First Amendment and the Feminist Attack on Free Speech*, 20 Ford. Urb. L. J. 27 (1992).
5. See *Winters v. New York*, 333 U.S. 507, 531–532 (1948) (Frankfurter, J., dissenting from opinion striking statute construed by state court to prohibit distribution of magazines, books, and other publications, "made up of news or stories of criminal deeds so massed as to become vehicles for inciting violent and depraved crimes against the person"); *see also Beauharnais v. Illinois*, 343 U.S. 250 (1952) (Frankfurter, J., upholding imposition of criminal liability for defamatory statements concerning minority groups); Higgins, *supra* note 4 at 87.

For most, the "official" history of the First Amendment begins with the World War I Espionage Act cases.[6] Although the Sedition Act and the intent of the Framers of the Constitution are debated, the actual *jurisprudence* prior to these cases is almost never discussed.[7] Even when discussions occur, they tend to be cursory statements of the rule of law that merely show how repressive the bad old days were. What has hitherto been lacking, despite the yeoman work of some constitutional historians, is a focused examination of the evolution of the reasons underlying society's— and for "society's," read "the Supreme Court's"—decisions to protect or not to protect dissent. Such an examination undermines the classic image of a century's silence followed by a repressive, conservative Court that ruthlessly squashed dissent over the protests of the prophetic liberals Oliver Wendell Holmes and Louis D. Brandeis. In fact, the reality was not that simple.

An examination of the evolving jurisprudence shows a gradual refinement of the way in which judges viewed free speech issues. The conservative Espionage Act decisions in fact reflect the dawn of a radical rethinking of the nature of free speech, which the later dissents of Holmes and Brandeis would justify and elaborate. Finally, this rethinking would gain the force of law, after having first been elaborated by the majority, which then backed away from it as its implications became more clear. It is this path, which I contend truly represents the "worthy tradition" justly celebrated by First Amendment scholars,[8] that this chapter explores. Along the way, some of the orthodoxies of our current jurisprudence will be challenged, by reference to seldom-cited views of freedom of speech, and also by viewing some old friends in a new context. That such an exploration is not merely of antiquarian interest seems clear: It is impossible to choose a destination and a route without an awareness of where the journey began.

---

6. *See*, for example, K. Greenwalt, *Speech, Crime, and the Uses of Language* (1989) at 188 ("Substantial Supreme Court development of First Amendment doctrine began with review of convictions under the 1917 Espionage Act"). *See also Dennis v. United States*, 341 U.S. 494 (1951), discussed at text *infra* at note 167 *et seq.*

7. An important exception is David Rabban's *The First Amendment in Its Forgotten Years*, 90 Yale L.J. 514 (1981). Although Professor Rabban cites many of the cases referred to here, he does not attempt to relate them to the emerging tradition as does this discussion; where he sees a sea change in the "conversions" of Holmes and Brandeis, I argue that the evolving views of the two justices, *and of their conservative colleagues*, are an integral part of an essentially coherent progression. Rabban does, however, point to a split between the court-evolved prewar jurisprudence and the thought of many academicians, who were far more protective of speech. *See also* David M. Rabban, *Free Speech in Its Forgotten Years* (1997).

8. *See* Kalven, *supra* note 1.

EARLY VIEWS BEFORE THE CONSERVATIVE REVOLUTION

The Pre–Civil War Understanding

For the initial understanding of the First Amendment's meaning, no better source can be found than Joseph Story, who, over twenty years after his appointment to the Supreme Court, wrote:

> THAT this amendment was intended to secure to every citizen an ab-
> solute right to speak, or to write, or to print whatever he might please,
> without any responsibility, public or private, therefor, is a supposition
> too wild to be indulged by any responsible man. This would be to allow
> to every citizen a right to destroy, at his pleasure, the reputation, the
> peace, the property, and even the personal safety of every other citi-
> zen. . . . It is plain, then, that the language of this amendment imports
> no more, than that every man shall have a right to speak, write, and
> print his opinions upon any subject whatsoever, without any prior re-
> straint, so always, that he does not injure any other person in his rights,
> person, property, or reputation; and so always, that he does not thereby
> disturb the public peace, or attempt to subvert the government. It is
> neither more or less, than an expansion of the great doctrine, recently
> brought into operation in the law of libel, that every man shall be at
> liberty to publish what is true, with good motives and for justifiable
> ends.[9]

Story then went on to say that "to punish any dangerous or offensive writings, which, when published, shall, on a fair and impartial trial, be adjudged
of a pernicious tendency, is necessary for the preservation of peace and good
order, of government and religion, the only solid foundation of civil liberty."[10] Like William Blackstone before him—whom he approvingly quotes—
Story found that this restrictive rule did not limit freedom of thought or
inquiry, because only the dissemination of "bad sentiments," and not their
thinking, was subject to ban.[11]

The Supreme Court did not, however, construe the First Amendment
until a generation after Story wrote. When it did, it did not simply follow
the Blackstonian view he advocated. Rather, it viewed the amendment in
the context of a federalist system, a system in which the states and the fed-

---

9. Joseph Story, *Commentaries on the Constitution of the United States*, § 993 (1833); *see also*
   J. Kent, 2 *Commentaries on American Law* at 18 (1830) ("[I]t has . . . become a constitutional principle in this country, that 'every citizen may freely speak, write, and publish
   his sentiments, on all subjects, being responsible for the abuse of that right.'").
10. Story, *supra* note 9, at § 995.
11. *Id.*, citing, 4 *Commentaries on the Laws of England* 150–152 (1769).

eral government existed in separate spheres of influence, with the balance far more favorable to the states than that which exists today. The jurisprudence of the First Amendment that prevailed in the pre–Civil War era and for some thirty years after it, was predicated on an understanding of the scope of the Bill of Rights that has long since died. The Bill of Rights had been held by the Supreme Court in the very year Story published his treatise, 1833, to inhibit only the exercise of power by the federal government, and to have no impact on the states.[12] This view remained constitutional orthodoxy until the Court began to wrestle with the impact of the Fourteenth Amendment.

In the case of the First Amendment, of course, its very language seems to command such a reading: The amendment states that "Congress shall make no law abridging" the rights it guarantees. Thus, the Supreme Court's extension of the rule that the Bill of Rights did not apply to the states to include free expression clauses of the First Amendment was hardly a great step, although it was not taken until 1875 in *United States v. Cruikshank*.[13] In an opinion by Chief Justice Waite, the Court refused to apply the Free Assembly Clause to state governments. The Court intimated just how dependent that right was for its existence upon the goodwill of the states:

> THE particular amendment now under consideration assumes the existence of the right of the people to assemble for lawful purposes, and protects it against encroachment by Congress. The right was not created by the amendment; neither was its continuance guaranteed, except as against congressional interference. For their protection in its enjoyment, therefore, the people must look to the States. The power for that purpose was originally placed there, and it has never been surrendered to the United States.[14]

Although arrived at ten years after the close of the Civil War, the reasoning of *Cruikshank*, and of its direct antecedent, *Barron v. Baltimore*, was grounded in the doctrine of enumerated powers established by the Marshall Court's decision in *Gibbons v. Ogden*.[15] That doctrine, which limited the fed-

---

12. *See Barron v. Mayor of Baltimore,* 7 Pet. (32 U.S.) 243, (1833).
13. 92 U.S. 542 (1875). *See also Permoli v. First Municipality, City of New Orleans,* 3How. (44 U.S.) 589 (1844) (same; religion clauses).
14. *Id.* at 552.
15. 9 Wheat (22 U.S.) 1, 195 (1824) (upholding exercise of the specifically enumerated power of Congress to regulate interstate commerce, and voiding state effort to grant a monopoly to interstate ferry line) ("The genius and character of the whole government seems to be, that its action is to be applied to all the external concerns of the nation, and to those internal concerns which affect the States generally; but not to those which are completely within a particular state, which do not affect other States, and with which it is not necessary to interfere, for the purpose of executing some of the general powers of the government").

eral government's powers to those specifically enumerated in the Constitution, reflected the same fear that the Bill of Rights itself did: a fear that the size of the federal government would lead it to usurp the prerogatives of the states and become an engine of oppression. The responsiveness of the state governments to the will of their citizens and their ability to safeguard the rights of the individual are an assumption of the Court—and, in view of the First Amendment's own language—of the Framers.

The level of protection afforded free expression by the states is made clear in several key decisions. The classic example of the states' approach to the issue can be found in *Respublica v. Oswald*.[16] In that case, the Supreme Court of Pennsylvania opined, in words reminiscent of Blackstone, that

> THE true liberty of the press is amply secured by permitting every man to publish his opinion; but it is due to the peace and dignity of society, to inquire into the motives of such publications, and to distinguish between those which are meant for use and reformation, and with an eye solely to the public good, and those which are intended merely to delude and defame. To the latter description, it is impossible that any good government should afford protection and impunity.[17]

The states, then, were given plenary power over speech, a power that was not conferred by the federal Constitution, but rather a power that the federal Constitution disabled Congress from affecting, or from exercising itself. The states themselves exercised their power in accordance with the English common law rule delineated by Blackstone. The end result of this was a rule of law in which freedom of speech amounted to little more than a freedom from licensing, the British monarchical practice of requiring all writings to be approved by the government.

The federal lack of involvement in free speech issues postulated in *Cruikshank*, although it aptly reflects the constitutional orthodoxy of the time, was by no means the last word even before the Civil War amendments were brought to the Supreme Court's attention. In *Ex Parte Jackson*,[18] the Court

---

16. 1 Dall. (1 U.S.) 319, 325–326 (Sup. Ct. Pa. 1788) (upholding an adjudication of a libel defendant as being in contempt of court for "addressing the public" in an effort to win popular support for his position in the lawsuit). For the Supreme Court's wrestling with the identical issues, see *Bridges v. California*, 314 U.S. 252 (1941).

17. *Id.* at 326. For other state court views to the same effect from the same period, see *Commonwealth v. Blanding*, 3 Pick. 304, 313–314 (1824). This view was not an aberrational one; indeed, the same analysis lasted into the twentieth century. *See People v. Most*, 171 N.Y. 423, 64 N.E. 175, 178 (1902) ("The punishment of those who publish articles which tend to corrupt morals, induce crime, or destroy organized society is essential to the security of freedom and the stability of the state").

18. 96 U.S. 727 (1877).

upheld regulation by Congress of the content of the federal mails. The Court found in the constitutionally granted power of Congress to determine what can be mailed a necessary corollary power to determine what matter could be excluded, and relied on the fact that the mails were not the only available competitive means of transporting publications. However, in so doing, the Court conceded, "Nor can any regulations be enforced against the transportation of printed matter in the mail, which is open to examination, so as to interfere . . . with the freedom of the press. Liberty of circulating is as essential to that freedom as liberty of publishing. . . . If, therefore, printed matter be excluded from the mails, its transportation in any other way cannot be forbidden by Congress."[19]

Similarly, in *Ex Parte Curtis*,[20] the Court upheld a ban on the solicitation or the giving of political contributions by federal employees. In an opinion that does not even mention the First Amendment, the Court grounded its opinion in the perceived need to protect civil servants from "shakedowns" by superiors. Nonetheless, the decision represents a direct limitation of political speech and organizing by Congress, albeit in a federal enclave— that is, the ban is restricted to those who voluntarily affiliate themselves with the federal government. Perhaps the decision is best viewed in light of Justice Holmes's subsequent distinction (itself long since rejected) that although there is a right to free speech, there is no constitutional right to be a governmental official.[21] In any case, the Court did not even advert to the First Amendment in its opinion.

Enter the Fourteenth Amendment

A new form of analysis of civil liberties questions made its debut, although in the form of a doubt and not of a certainty, in *Spies v. Illinois*.[22] In *Spies*, the Court reaffirmed the doctrine of *Barron v. Baltimore* that "the first ten Articles of Amendment were not intended to limit the powers of the state governments in respect to their own people, but to operate on the National government alone."[23] However, the Court acknowledged the argument that the Fourteenth Amendment had altered that fifty-year-old doctrine.

---

19. *Id.* at 733.
20. 106 U.S. 371 (1882).
21. *See McAuliffe v. Mayor of New Bedford*, 155 Mass. 216, 220, 29 N. E. 517 (1892) ("The petitioner may have a constitutional right to talk politics, but he has no constitutional right to be a policeman").
22. 123 U.S. 131 (1887).
23. *Id.* at 166.

It was contended in argument, that,

> THOUGH originally the first ten Amendments were adopted as limitations on Federal power, yet in so far as they secure and recognize fundamental rights—common law rights—of the man [*sic*], they make them privileges and immunities of the man as a citizen of the United States, and cannot now be abridged by a State under the Fourteenth Amendment. In other words, while the ten Amendments as limitations of power only apply to the Federal Government, and not to the States, yet in so far as they declare or recognize rights of persons, these rights are theirs, as citizens of the United States, and the Fourteenth Amendment as to such rights limits state power, as the ten Amendments had limited Federal power.[24]

The Court did not feel it necessary to decide the validity of this approach, finding that the state constitutional provision that permitted the jury selection method that was being contested on appeal was "substantially the provision" of the federal Constitution, and that no federal constitutional violation could thus have occurred. Although the privileges and immunities clause of the Fourteenth Amendment died an ignominious death in *The Slaughter House Cases*,[25] the impact of the Fourteenth Amendment on First Amendment jurisprudence would be profound, and would grow in the next few decades.

In the meantime, the simple model of jurisprudence under which Congress had no power to regulate speech and the states had whatever power they chose to take was dealt several serious blows. In *Davis v. Beason*,[26] the Court upheld the conviction of a Mormon who registered to vote in violation of a territorial statute that deprived those who practice or teach polygamy of the right to vote. In sustaining the statute against a First Amendment challenge, the Court argued that the "[l]aws were made for the government of actions, and while it cannot interfere with mere religious belief and opinions, they may with practices," but did not draw any distinction between the actual practice and the simple advocacy of such beliefs.[27] Although it marked a new distinction between speech and action, this approach did not necessarily imperil the autonomy of the states. The case involved territories, creatures of the federal government that were under the substantial control of Congress.[28]

---

24. *Id.*
25. 83 U.S. 36 (1872); *see also Id.* at 111–123 (Bradley, J., dissenting).
26. 133 U.S. 333 (1890).
27. *Id.* at 344–345.
28. *See* U.S. Constitution, Article IV, § 3.

The Court returned to the issue of the power of Congress over the mails in *Rosen v. United States*,[29] in which a congressional prohibition of the transportation of obscene materials through the mails was upheld. The Court did not discuss the First Amendment; the issue raised by the defendant on appeal was the sufficiency of the indictment in light of his right to know the charges against him.

In 1897, the Court would, in *Robertson v. Baldwin*,[30] refine its view of the First Amendment, revising the essentially two-tiered structure created in *Cruikshank*. In *Robertson*, the Court explored the impact of the Bill of Rights on the *federal* government. Its conclusions were, perhaps, surprising:

> THE law is perfectly well settled that the first ten amendments to the Constitution, commonly known as the Bill of Rights, were not intended to lay down any novel principles of government, but simply to embody certain guaranties and immunities which we had inherited from our English ancestors, and which from time immemorial been subject to certain well-recognized exceptions arising from the necessities of the case. In incorporating these principles into the fundamental law there was no intention of disregarding the exceptions, which continued to be recognized as if they had been formally expressed. Thus, the freedom of speech and of the press (art. 1) does not permit the publication of libels, blasphemous or indecent articles, or other publications injurious to public morals or private reputation.[31]

Rather than endorse the complete disabling of the federal government from speech regulation implied in *Cruikshank*, the *Robertson* decision declared that Congress is restrained, within its area of competent jurisdiction (itself perhaps broadened by implication in the opinion), only by the common law limitations on the regulation of speech. What limits, if any, the Fourteenth Amendment imposes upon *state* regulation of speech are not hinted at in the opinion.

The sway of the common law, as explicated by Blackstone, over the analysis of the meaning of free speech was clinched just ten years after *Robertson* was decided, when, in *Patterson v. Colorado*,[32] the Court described the "main purpose" of the First Amendment as the prevention of "all such *previous restraints* upon publications as had been practiced by other governments" and flatly

---

29. 161 U.S. 29 (1895).
30. 165 U.S. 275, 280–82 (1897) (upholding statute forcing deserting seamen to live up to their contract against Thirteenth Amendment claim that such constituted "involuntary servitude").
31. *Id.* at 281.
32. 205 U.S. 454 (1907) (upholding criminal contempt statute as constitutionally applied; only error, if any, was one of state law).

stated that the amendment does "not prevent the subsequent punishment of such as may be deemed contrary to the public welfare."[33] The Court went on to elaborate that "[t]he preliminary freedom extends as well to the false as to the true; the subsequent punishment may extend to the true as well as to the false."[34]

Justice Story had argued that the First Amendment guaranteed to the citizen the right to publish free of prior restraint, without differentiating between the power of the state and national governments to regulate; *Cruikshank* had simply written the federal judiciary out of the business of reviewing state regulation. Now, twenty years later, the two approaches would merge: the power of Congress over speech was defined by the common law relied upon by Story, and the states were still, it would seem, absolutely free to approach the matter in their own ways.

Or were they? Despite the ringing endorsement of the common law position in *Patterson* (written by Justice Holmes, already the author of *The Common Law*, but not yet the trailblazer of a liberal First Amendment tradition), *Patterson* explicitly left "undecided the question whether there is to be found in the Fourteenth Amendment a prohibition similar to that in the First."[35] Just as had *Cruikshank*, *Patterson* left the possibility open that the freedom of the states may have been circumscribed by the Fourteenth Amendment. Of course, that limitation of their power would, under either scenario, only require the states to adopt the common law doctrine of free speech—which they had already done, in any case. As late as 1907, the law was clear at least this far: There were no substantive limitations on what either the states or the federal government could suppress or punish *after* publication.

---

33. *Id.* at 462 (emphasis in original).

34. *Id.*

35. *Id.* In his dissenting opinion, Justice Harlan would have answered the question, and in the affirmative, relying upon the Privileges and Immunities Clause of the Fourteenth Amendment. 205 U.S. at 464–465. The failure of Harlan's bold, but I think estimable, effort to command a court, thereby overruling the holding of *The Slaughter House Cases*, 83 U.S. 36 (1873), is one of the great tragedies of civil liberties jurisprudence in general; from *Patterson* on, the Court was doomed to slog through the substantive due process swamp that has marred the jurisprudence into the present. The derivation of substantive liberties from the privileges and immunities clause would have made eminent sense, whereas the notion of "substantive due process" is an oxymoron (as has often been argued by others; *see* J. Ely *Democracy and Distrust* [1980] at 18). This is not to say that incorporation of fundamental rights through the Fourteenth Amendment is improper. Rather, the wrong clause has been used—a clause with no inherent limiting principles—and as a result the Court has given itself carte blanche to legislate its own prejudices.

The Conservative Revolution

Early Noises

With the birth of the twentieth century, the Supreme Court was in a deeply conservative groove, one that would last from the turn of the century until Franklin Roosevelt's Court-packing plan and the famous "switch in time that saved nine." It is one of the paradoxes of history that this conservative, *Lochner*-loving Court[36] would act not only boldly but radically in expanding the protections that were accorded speech. It is an even more amusing paradox that the decisions in which the Court took these bold steps are even today regarded as high points of repression.

The conservative revolution began with a few feeble indications that the eighteenth century's prohibition of prior restraint might not be the full extent to which the Constitution protected speech. In *American School of Magnetic Healing v. McAnnulty*,[37] the Court refused to allow the postmaster general to ban opinions he considered "false" from being disseminated through the mail under a statute that allowed him to prevent the use of the mails to promote fraud. Justice Peckham's opinion for the majority at no time relies on the First Amendment; in fact it relies solely upon the statutory language. Nonetheless, the opinion marks a rare note of tolerance in a hitherto entirely intolerant jurisprudence.

Gompers v. Bucks Stove & Range Company[38] upheld an injunction that restrained as an illegal boycott technique statements that accused the boycottee of unfair practices. The Court found that the First Amendment was not involved on the grounds that the words were used under such circumstances to "become what have been called 'verbal acts' and as much subject to in-

---

36. The Court's allegiance to *Lochner v. New York*, 198 U.S. 45, 64 (1905) (invalidating state maximum hour statute for bakers) and its progeny, which relied upon "substantive due process" (that is, the *substantive* rights guaranteed by the Fourteenth Amendment's *Due Process* Clause) to invalidate pro-labor regulation of work conditions on the grounds that such regulations deprived the laborers of their "liberty of contract," has deservedly won opprobrium for its proponents. *See*, for example, B. Siegan, *Economic Liberties and the Constitution* (1980) at 23. In this line of cases, the Court essentially constitutionalized its economic prejudices, as was pointed out by Justice Holmes in dissent. The irony here is that the very justices who inflexibly vetoed every effort of the Progressive Movement to better the conditions of the working class on the grounds of constitutionality did so without being able to cite a single constitutional provision to support their conclusions. Their line of argument was particularly tenuous in view of the holding in *The Slaughter House Cases*, 82 U.S. 36 (1873).
37. 187 U.S. 94 (1902).
38. 221 U.S. 418 (1911).

junction as the use of any other force whereby property is unlawfully damaged."[39] This ruling is intriguing for two reasons. First, the Court in *Gompers* approved punishment for violation of an order imposing prior restraint, undermining the only protection accorded speech in the common law jurisprudence. More significantly, the ruling was predicated on a distinction between speech and conduct, legitimating the punishment of words not for their communicative content but because they are the equivalent of physical actions. In view of this libertarian stride—for if words are not in any way protected subsequent to their speaking, why distinguish them from conduct at all?—it is tempting to dismiss the actual holding as an example of the result-oriented jurisprudence of its day, typical of the Court of that era in its freewheeling ability to disregard both logic and precedent to reach the desired result.

In view of the decision of the Court in *Turner v. Williams*[40] the temptation becomes irresistible. In *Turner,* a federal statute, the Immigration Act of 1903, which barred the entrance of anarchists to the United States, was upheld against several constitutional challenges, including a First Amendment challenge. The Court found the authority for such a bar in the ability to secure self-preservation "inherent in sovereignty," or, alternatively, in the power of Congress to regulate commerce with foreign nations.[41] The Court described itself as "at a loss" to understand how the law could be violative of the First Amendment, reasoning that

> IT has no reference to an establishment of religion nor does it prohibit the free exercise thereof; nor abridge the freedom of speech or the press; nor the right of the people to assemble and petition the government for a redress of grievances.

"It is of course true," the Court conceded,

> THAT if an alien is not permitted to enter this country, or, having entered contrary to law, is expelled, he is in fact cut off from worshipping or speaking or petitioning in this country, but that is merely because of his exclusion therefrom. He does not become one of the people to whom these things are secured by our Constitution by an attempt to enter forbidden by law.[42]

---

39. *Id.* at 439.
40. 194 U.S. 279 (1904).
41. *Id.* at 290.
42. *Id.* at 292. The long precedential reach of *Turner* can be seen in *Matthews v. Diaz,* 426 U.S. 67, 69 (1976) (upholding federal statute limiting participation in federal medical insurance program to citizens and resident aliens; the Court opined: "In the exercise of its

The Court in the *Turner* decision asserted that it was "not to be understood as depreciating the vital importance of freedom of speech and of the press, or as suggesting limitations on the spirit of liberty, itself unconquerable," but again asserted that "this case does not involve such considerations."[43] In this opinion, itself an agent of repression, one strain seems clear: The Court seemed to believe that the petitioner, *had he been a citizen,* could not have been punished for his expressed anarchist beliefs—else why distinguish this case from one involving a citizen? By implication, then, some limit on the ability of Congress to punish the expression of opinion had been enunciated, in defiance of a century's jurisprudence.

Similarly, in *Fox v. Washington,*[44] the Court, *per* Justice Holmes, in upholding a statute that prohibited the "willful [] printing [or] circulat[ing] . . . of matter advocating . . . crime or . . . disrespect for law," construed the statute narrowly, explicitly to avoid a finding of unconstitutionality.[45] The Court emphasized that "[i]t does not appear and is not likely that the statute will be construed to prevent publications merely because they tend to produce unfavorable opinions of a particular statute or of law in general. In this present case the disrespect for law that was encouraged was disregard of it—an overt breach and technically criminal act."[46] The Court therefore interpreted "disrespect as manifested disrespect, as active disregard going beyond the line drawn by the law."[47]

Again, what is fascinating about this narrow reading of the statute in order to avoid a finding that the statute was violative of the First Amendment—called in constitutional law jargon a "saving construction"—is the fact that it was wholly unnecessary under the Blackstonian approach that ostensibly held sway. In all three cases, the justices were beginning to carve out an area of substantive protection for free speech, even if only by showing where it did not apply.

The Conservative Revolution Redux:
The Birth of Substantive Protection

In moving from these cases to the familiar and execrated Espionage Act cases, the realm of implication is left behind, and the existence of an area

---

broad power over naturalization and immigration, Congress regularly makes rules that would be unacceptable if applied to citizens"). *See also Kleindienst v. Mandel,* 408 U.S. 753, 769–770 (1972) (upholding provision of the 1950 Internal Security Act declaring foreign Communists ineligible to receive visas to enter the United States).

43. 194 U.S. at 294.
44. 236 U.S. 273 (1915).
45. *Id.* at 275–277.
46. *Id.* at 277.
47. *Id.*

of absolutely protected speech becomes explicit. This great though gradual stage in the evolution is largely dismissed, and the Court's opinions written off as a set of repressive decisions, memorable only for their wrongheadedness, and for the initial joining in the repression of Justices Oliver Wendell Holmes and Louis D. Brandeis, who would later defect to the more liberal camp in dissent. Once again, the story was not that simple.

In *Schenck v. United States*[48] the Court upheld the convictions of two defendants, both members of the Socialist Party, for violating the Espionage Act by seeking to cause insubordination in the military and to obstruct recruitment, by circulating antiwar literature among "men who had been called and accepted into military service," that is, conscriptees.[49] The defendants asserted that their conduct was protected by the U.S. Constitution, especially because, as the Court grudgingly conceded, "[t]wo of the strongest expressions are said to be quoted respectively from well known public men."[50] In evaluating this First Amendment claim, the Court overruled—at first only tentatively but then firmly—the *Patterson* decision:

> IT may well be that the prohibition of the laws abridging the freedom of speech is not confined to previous restraints, although to prevent them may have been the main purpose, as intimated in *Patterson v. Colorado* [citation omitted]. *We admit that in many places and in ordinary times the defendants in saying all that was said in the circular would have been within their constitutional rights.* [emphasis added][51]

The Court then began its first effort to construct a jurisprudence that acknowledged substantive limitations (as opposed to limitations regarding the *time, manner,* or *place*) on the ability of Congress to regulate what free citizens could or could not say to each other. Holmes began with the common law proposition that "the character of every act depends on the circumstances in which it is done," opining that "[t]he most stringent protection of free speech would not protect a man in falsely shouting fire in a theatre and causing panic."[52] From this seemingly indisputable and often-quoted extreme, Holmes took an intermediate step that is often forgotten, but vital; his next sentence began "It [freedom of speech] does not even

---

48. 249 U.S. 47 (1919).
49. *Id.* at 48–49.
50. *Id.* at 51.
51. *Id.* at 51–52.
52. *Id.* at 52, *citing Aikens v. Wisconsin,* 195 U.S. 194, 205–206 (1904) (upholding state statute barring malicious mischief inflicted upon business as authority for this "common law proposition.")

protect a man from an injunction against uttering words that have all the effect of force," relying upon *Gompers*.[53]

Holmes thus resurrected a distinction that would haunt the jurisprudence in the future, that between "pure speech" and speech that has the effect of action, with the implication that one is granted a higher level of protection than the other. Holmes was, it seems, edging toward the zone of protection. We can all agree with the example of shouting "fire," he seems to have supposed, and then took a harder example, the labor injunction involved in *Gompers*. It too did not involve an infringement of freedom of speech, Holmes reasoned, because the speech involved was not regulated for its expressive content alone, but for the context in which it was uttered—a context that made the ordinarily protected speech tantamount to action.[54]

Before following Holmes's next step, this passage should be pointed out as the possible birthplace of much libertarian constitutional theory. The distinction between speech and "speech brigaded with action" as one that enhances freedom would become central under the advocacy of Justices William O. Douglas and (although to a lesser extent) Hugo Black. Douglas, as will be seen, constructed a seemingly monolithic jurisprudence in which the regulation of conduct that falls on the action side of this distinction formed one of the only two permissible restrictions on free expression.[55] The distinction Douglas relied on dates back to *Gompers*, but was only given real life here, in Holmes's typically terse opinion.

Holmes, however, did not entirely anticipate Douglas. Rather, he proceeded from these context-based examples to provide a more lax general rule:

> THE question . . . is whether the words used are used in such circumstances and are of such a nature as to create a clear and present danger that they will bring about the substantive evil that Congress has a right to prevent. It is a question of proximity and degree. When a nation is at war many things that might be said in time of peace are such a hindrance to its effort that their utterance will not be endured

---

53. *Id.* citing *Gompers*, 221 U.S. at 419.

54. Although no reasoning is given to explain the propriety of forbidding the false shout of fire, the emphasis Holmes places on the context of speech both before and after the example seems to indicate that it is simply an easier case involving the same precept as the labor injunction example.

55. Indeed, Douglas found the source of his theory in *Schenck*'s example of falsely shouting fire in a crowded theatre. As he wrote, "The example given by Holmes of one who shouts 'fire' in a crowded theatre is of course an utterance, but like a top sergeant's command in the Army, it is so closely brigaded with action as to be part of the instant action that takes place." William O. Douglas, *The Supreme Court and the Bicentennial* (1978) at 23.

so long as men fight and that no Court could regard them as protected by any constitutional right.[56]

Although this rule led the Court to affirm the convictions of Schenck and his codefendant Baer and to the censorship of their views (as the subsequent cases would show), it nonetheless was a great stride forward. First, the ghosts of Blackstone and Story were finally laid to rest, in spite of the then-recent precedent of *Patterson* that reaffirmed their views.[57] Second, the test that replaced those of Blackstone and Story explicitly required that the speech be viewed in its context before it could be censored and that the speech must create by its utterance a real danger—a proximate danger—of some evil result. Finally, that evil must be one that Congress has the right under the Constitution to prevent—no small concession from a jurist who believed that "if my fellow citizens want to go to Hell, I will help them. It's my job."[58] Thus, the right to strive for *lawful* change through such methods as electioneering was now secured, even for those whose views were despised by the conservatives who sat on this Court. Eugene V. Debs, for example, ran for president—from prison—but he was at least allowed to run. In the pre-*Schenck* world that right was by no means safe under the law.

---

56. 249 U.S. at 52.
57. Although Harry Kalven recognized this contribution of *Schenck's*, he did so grudgingly. *A Worthy Tradition, supra* note 1 at 137. The watershed nature of *Schenck* in Holmes's evolution was noted in David S. Bogen, *The Free Speech Metamorphosis of Mr. Justice Holmes*, 11 Hofstra L. Rev. 97, 141–149 (1982) (contending that Holmes underwent a conversion in reading the government briefs in *Schenck* and was thereafter far more speech protective). Where I argue that the Court's overruling of *Patterson*, and the establishment of some level of substantive protection was an eradication of the common law tradition, at least one author, David Yassky, portrays it as a "set of judicially articulated norms" that "drew heavily upon the pre-existing state-centered constitutional structure" in that they "derived almost entirely from common law precepts." David Yassky, *Eras of the First Amendment*, 91 Colum. L. Rev. 1699, 1717 (1991). Yassky's view of *Schenck* seems more apt when applied to the jurisprudence leading up to it, but because his entire analysis of the Espionage Act cases is confined to their results, and not to their methodology, he erroneously treats them as part of the "tradition of indifference to free speech values" that he states extended into the 1930s. *Id.* at 1718–1719. Yassky believes that "Holmes's change of heart came in *Abrams v. United States*", 250 U.S. 616 (1919). That Holmes underwent a conversion comparable to that on the Road to Damascus in *Abrams* is a cliché of the literature. *See*, for example, G. Edward White, *Justice Holmes and the Modernization of Free Speech Jurisprudence: The Human Dimension*, 80 Cal. L. Rev. 391, 412–438 (1992) (dividing Holmes's jurisprudence between his "orthodox" pre-*Abrams* and his subsequent libertarian jurisprudence); Rabban, *The Emergence of Modern First Amendment Doctrine*, 50 U. Chi. L. Rev. 1205, 1208–1209 (1983). Bogen, in placing Holmes's conversion at *Schenck*, is closer to the mark, but is still off the mark. From his wholehearted endorsement of the Blackstonian common law in *Patterson*, Holmes in *Fox* engaged in a saving construction of a statute that was wholly unnecessary under the Blackstonian view and exhibited some doubt in that approach's validity. In fact Holmes's development was *evolutionary*, not revolutionary, so much so that he may not have noticed its occurrence. See text *infra* at notes 122–127.
58. Mark DeWolfe Howe, ed. 1 *Holmes-Laski Letters* 249 (1953).

A week later, the Supreme Court decided Eugene Debs's fate in *Debs v. United States*,[59] and a companion case, *Frohwerk v. United States*.[60] In *Frohwerk* the Court upheld another Espionage Act conviction, this one based on the writing and distribution of an antiwar newspaper. The Court found itself faced with a record far less clear than that in *Schenck*, "owing to unfortunate differences" between the parties that prevented the filing of a bill of exceptions.[61] Expressing "a natural inclination to test every question of law to be found in the record very thoroughly before upholding the very severe penalty imposed," Justice Holmes wrote for a unanimous Court that such testing was impossible on the scanty record before it, and found that "on that record it is impossible to say that it might not have been found that the circulation of the paper was in quarters where a little breath would be enough to kindle a flame and that the fact was known and relied upon by those who sent the paper out."[62]

The Court reaffirmed *Schenck's* dictum that the First Amendment "cannot have been, and obviously was not, intended to give immunity for every possible use of language."[63] This time it gave the illustration of plainly permissible regulation in the form of an expression of confidence that "neither Hamilton nor Madison, nor any other competent person, then or later, ever supposed that to make criminal the counselling of a murder within the jurisdiction of Congress would be an unconstitutional interference with free speech."[64] The Court further explained that *Schenck* did not create a special wartime exception to the First Amendment, explaining that "[i]t may be that all this might be said or written even in time of war in circumstances that would not make it a crime. We do not lose our right to condemn either measures or men because the Country is at war."[65] Whether the minimal review accorded was the true, denuded meaning of the seemingly tremendous advance in *Schenck*, or the result of the peculiarities of appellate review of a flimsy, confused record could only be seen in the context of other cases.

Debs was, on its face, hardly a propitious signal. In that case, the great Socialist leader (who would poll impressively high in his 1920 run for the presidency) was convicted, under the "new and improved" Espionage Act,

---

59. 249 U.S. 211 (1919).
60. 249 U.S. 204 (1919).
61. *Id.* at 206.
62. *Id.* at 208–209.
63. *Id.* at 206.
64. *Id.* Interestingly, this example also falls neatly on the action side of the *Gompers* pure speech/speech-action distinction that Douglas would later rely upon so heavily. *See* text *infra* at notes 241–242.
65. 249 U.S. at 208.

for a speech whose main theme, according to Justice Holmes's opinion for the still-unanimous Court "was socialism, its growth, and a prophecy of its ultimate success."[66] Yet upon closer examination, *Debs* may even have represented another baby step forward. In his opinion, Holmes clung still to the general line expressed in *Schenck* in saying, with regard to the speaker's main theme, "with that we have nothing to do, but if a part or the manifest intent of the more general utterances was to encourage those present to obstruct the recruiting service and if in passages such encouragement was directly given, the immunity of the general theme may not be enough to protect the speech."[67]

Holmes found such "manifest intent" in Debs's statements that he "had to be prudent and might not be able to say all that he thought, thus intimating to his hearers that they might infer that he meant more" and then praising (among other protesters and resisters) three individuals who were convicted for helping another to avoid the draft;[68] in his statement "Don't worry about the charge of treason to your masters; but be concerned about the treason that involves yourselves";[69] and in his statements to the crowd that "you need to know that you are fit for something better than slavery and cannon fodder."[70] A document endorsed by Debs was also introduced that advocated resistance to the war, and Holmes used it as evidence that if Debs's words tended to obstruct recruiting, he intended them to have that effect.[71]

Holmes concluded that the status of Debs's speech under the Constitution turned on the question of whether it was given with intent to obstruct recruitment: If it was "intended and if, in all the circumstances that would be its probable effect, it would not be protected by reason of its being part of a . . . general and conscientious belief."[72] Holmes also noted approvingly that "the jury were most carefully instructed that they could not find the defendant guilty for advocacy of any of his opinions unless the words used had as their natural tendency and reasonably probable effect to obstruct the recruiting service, etc., and unless the defendant had the specific intent to do so in his mind."[73]

---

66. 249 U.S. at 212.

67. *Id.* at 212–213.

68. *Id.* at 213.

69. *Id.* at 214.

70. *Id.*

71. *Id.* at 216.

72. *Id.* at 215.

73. *Id.* at 216. G. Edward White, *supra* at note 57, is able to claim that these three cases were consistent with the common law orthodoxy both by devaluing their importance and by providing the *Patterson* tradition with a limiting concept. White states that the "Espionage Act trilogy" applied the so-called "bad tendency test"—that is, simply required the government

The purpose of this discussion is not to justify the results reached by the Court under Justice Holmes's tutelage. The persecution of dissenters during and immediately after the First World War was a national disgrace, as Holmes himself began to realize.[74] Rather, it is to point out how in one hectic term (one that heard these three hotly controversial cases in one week) the conservative justices substantially revised the law of free speech. In these three cases, the presumption that speech could be suppressed once given an airing was demolished and replaced by a presumption of substantive protection. Moreover, *Debs* strengthened the "clear and present danger" proximity test of *Schenck* by adding an intent—a specific intent—requirement. The convictions may have been affirmed, but the groundwork was also established for a new, libertarian jurisprudence.

The conservative revolution had one last achievement left to it, and that was the resolution of the doubt first raised in *Spies* v. *Illinois*: Did the Fourteenth Amendment render the First Amendment applicable to the states? In *Gitlow v. New York*,[75] the Court, in upholding a conviction for violating New York's statute banning the advocacy of "criminal anarchy," answered the question with a tentative yes. "For present purposes," Justice Sanford wrote for the majority, "we may and do assume that freedom of speech and of the press—which are protected by the First Amendment from abridgment by Congress—are among the fundamental personal rights and 'liberties' protected by the Due Process Clause of the Fourteenth Amendment from impairment by the states."[76] In doing so, the Court explicitly invalidated its own statement a bare three years earlier to the contrary in *Prudential Insurance Company v. Cheek.*[77] In determining the extent to which states could infringe

---

to show "a tendency to prevent or obstruct the war effort." *Id.* at 413–414. The clear and present danger language is dismissed as "dicta." *Id.* at 415–419. He further argues that *Patterson* and *Fox* established a need for a "bad tendency" to be found in the speech to justify its suppression. *Id.* at 400–403. I see no such limit in the cases; *Patterson* reaffirms that the Blackstonian view of the common law requires only that the restraint come after publication. 205 U.S. at 462. White seems to be reading a limiting principle into the Court's purely permissive statement that the state "may" regulate speech if it decides that it is contrary to the public weal. *See* 205 U.S. at 462. *Fox* engages in a saving construction of the state-subversive advocacy statute involved, but did not create a new test. *Supra* text at note 44 *et seq.*

74. *See* Howe, ed. 1 *Holmes-Laski Letters* (1953), *supra* note 58, at 190; Howe, ed. 2 *Holmes-Pollock Letters* 11 (1941).

75. 268 U.S. 652 (1925).

76. *Id.* at 652, 666.

77. 259 U.S. 530, 543 (1922) (in upholding state statute requiring corporation at employee's request to furnish letter setting forth nature and duration of service, as well as cause of departure, the Court rejected corporate free speech claim, opining "as we have stated, neither the Fourteenth Amendment, nor any other provision of the Constitution of the United States imposes upon the States any restrictions about 'freedom of speech'"). The Court cited no authority for this proposition, a wise move, because no such authority existed—the question had, as we have seen, been repeatedly left open.

upon the rights of the speaker, the *Gitlow* court cited a hodgepodge of sources that included Story, *Robertson*, *Schenck*, *Frohwerk* and *Debs*, making no distinction between sources that construed the First Amendment vis-à-vis Congress and those that did not. In *Whitney v. California*, the Court, citing *Gitlow*, treated states as bound by the First Amendment as made applicable to the states through the Fourteenth Amendment as a matter of course.[78]

Common Law by Uncommon Lawyers:
Holmes, Hand, and Constitutional Reasoning

The cases dealt with up until *Gitlow* and *Whitney* represent a consensus of judicial thought that was essentially noncontroversial to the justices themselves, although their results did not command the universal enthusiasm of the academicians of the time.[79] The first three Espionage Act opinions, written by Oliver Wendell Holmes, mark, it seems clear, a midpoint in his development, and not a first stab at the issue.

Holmes's first stab at the matter was taken in *Patterson*, as described above. Interestingly, the only authority he cited for the proposition that the First Amendment's impact was to merely prohibit prior restraint was state court cases—*Respublica v. Oswald*, the 1788 Pennsylvania case, and *Commonwealth v. Blanding*, a Massachusetts case from 1824. He did cite Blackstone as well, but as an afterthought; he appended the reference as part of a string cite.[80] Yet at no time did Holmes cite any constitutional authority—not even Justice Story's opinion to the same effect in the *Commentaries*, or the similar statements in Chancellor Kent's *Commentaries on American Law*.[81] Holmes's use of state law authority and of Blackstone when two eminent commentators upon the Constitution was available demonstrates his initial belief that

---

78. 274 U.S. 357, 371 (1927).
79. See Rabban, *Free Speech in Its Forgotten Years, supra*, note 7, for the more speech protective views of various academics. The repressive consensus, as Rabban himself notes, was not without its defenders. In addition to those he cites, two scholars supported the Blackstonian view: Westel Willoughby, in volume two of his treatise *The Constitutional Law of the United States* (1910) at 843–845 and Henry Wolf Biklé in his article *The Jurisdiction of the United States over Seditious Libel*, 50 American Law Register 1 (1902).
80. *Patterson*, 205 U.S.at 462.
81. Story, *supra* note 9; Kent, *supra* note 9. Although it is possible that Holmes was unaware of Story's views on the subject, it is unlikely. Story's book was used as a textbook at Harvard Law School during the period that Holmes attended. *See* Liva Baker, *The Justice from Beacon Hill: The Life and Times of Oliver Wendell Holmes* at 170–171 (1991). Certainly Holmes was aware of Kent's views; he spent much of the years 1870 to 1873 editing the twelfth edition of Kent's treatise. Baker at 209–211; Mark DeWolfe Howe, *Justice Oliver Wendell Holmes: The Proving Years* at 10–25 (1963); G. Edward White, *Justice Oliver Wendell Holmes: Law and the Inner Self* (1993) at 124–127.

the Constitution had simply codified the common law, as applied to Congress. The same result by inference applied to the states by the effect of the Fourteenth Amendment—if indeed any impact upon the states had been effected, which question *Patterson* left open.

In *Patterson*, Holmes seemingly cleared the way for a uniform application of the Blackstonian view of the First Amendment against both the states and the federal government, a view that was presaged, as explained earlier, by the Court's ruling in *Robertson*. Yet in *Schenck*, a mere twelve years after *Patterson*, Holmes spoke for a unanimous Court when he destroyed the sway of the common law and extended the protection accorded to free speech.

Beyond that, the three Espionage Act cases in which Holmes wrote for a unanimous Court created, tentatively, a new standard of review. It has become a commonplace that the rule of *Schenck* was not one that protected speech. Certainly, the results in these cases bear out that commonplace. But when we compare the rule as enunciated by Holmes in *Schenck*, *Frohwerk*, and *Debs* with its most famous contemporary, the test enunciated by Learned Hand in *Masses Publishing Co. v. Patten*,[82] the rule stands up better than its applications.

The rule, as established in what can be called for convenience' sake the *Schenck* trilogy, requires that for any censorship to pass constitutional muster the utterance of the speech must *first* create a significant risk (a "clear and present danger") that an evil will result; *second*, that evil must be one that Congress has the right to act to prevent; *third* (and finally), the actor must have given tongue to the speech with the specific intent of causing that very evil. The Hand test from *Masses* requires the "direct incitement" or "direct advocacy" of unlawful conduct.[83] It thus contains a specific intent

---

82. 244 F. 535 (S.D.N.Y.), *rev'd* 246 F. 24 (2d Cir. 1917) (holding that left-wing magazine's opposition to First World War and conscription did not violate Espionage Act, because magazine fell short of advocating violation of law).

83. *Id.* at 542. For an illuminating look at how Hand structured his First Amendment test through a construction of the Espionage Act, as well as an account of the correspondence between Hand and Holmes that suggests that Holmes's conversion may have partially been caused through Hand's advocacy of a more libertarian test, *see* Gerald Gunther, *Learned Hand and the Origins of Modern First Amendment Doctrine: Some Pieces of History*, 27 Stan. L. Rev. 719 (1975). Gunther's conclusions are soundly endorsed in Rabban, *The Emergence of Modern First Amendment Doctrine*, 50 U. Chi. L. Rev. 1205, 1210 (1983). Because Gunther relies on the "tendency" prong of *Schenck* alone, and misses entirely the intent requirement of *Debs*, he is able to posit, as does Rabban, that Holmes moved significantly forward in his justly famous libertarian dissents, but that the Hand test was far more speech protective. Gunther, at 734–736; Rabban, at 1210. Gunther concludes that "in its origin clear and present danger reflected neither special sensitivity to free speech values nor special concern for tailoring doctrine to implement those values." Gunther, at 736. *See also* White, *supra* note 57, at 402–403. That this argument is essentially founded on a misunderstanding of the trilogy is argued in the text.

requirement; the speaker must seek to persuade his or her audience to violate the law.

Hand's efforts, through his correspondence with Holmes, to persuade
Holmes to adopt this test led Holmes to reply almost plaintively, "I don't
see how you differ from the test as stated by me."[84] At least one authority,
Gerald Gunther, has referred to this comment as proof of "Holmes' lack of
awareness of distinctions quite plain to more concerned contemporary observers."[85] That Holmes was adverting to the intent requirement in his own
test seems patently clear from the context of the letter; just prior to the
comment that allegedly shows Holmes's obliviousness, he wrote concerning intent, although he backed away somewhat from his opinion in *Debs*,
concluding somewhat defensively, "Even if absence of intent might not be
a defence I suppose that the presence of it might be material."[86]

Bearing the intent requirement of *Debs* in mind, it is easier to understand Holmes's confusion; the chasm between Holmes and Hand is after
all neither so wide nor so deep. This is particularly so in light of Hand's statement that "I haven't any doubt that Debs was guilty under any rule conceivably applicable,"[87] a comment that Gunther wrote off as "an effort to seem
to agree with the result while trying to persuade the master" because "it
differs from the tenor of his remarks to others."[88] It is hard to judge if
Hand's remarks were indeed so disingenuous by merely contrasting two
series of inconsistent, equally casual remarks. This is especially the case
where one can readily envision at least one place where Holmes but not
Hand would protect speech: when such speech was a direct incitement to
unlawful conduct but did not create a "clear and present danger" of such
conduct.[89]

The main flaws in this theoretical defense of Holmes's initial test appear
of course in the test's application—how little sufficed to establish a clear
and present danger, and the ease with which intent could be shown. Both
flaws, while serious, are not fatal to the argument. First, of course, the fact
that the test was not properly applied does not wholly invalidate it as a jurisprudential stride, any more than early bungling in the application of *Brown*

---

84. Holmes's letter is reprinted at full in Gunther, *supra* note 83, 759–760.
85. Gunther, *supra* note 83, at 741.
86. Letter, Holmes to Hand reprinted in Gunther, *supra* note 83, at 759.
87. Letter, Hand to Holmes, reprinted in Gunther, *supra* note 83, at 758–759.
88. Gunther, *supra* note 83, at 739.
89. Indeed, Hand explicitly stated as much in a 1950 letter to Elliot L. Richardson: "I would
make the purpose of the utterer the test of his Constitutional Protection. Did he seek to
bring about a violation of existing law? If he did, I can see no reason why the Constitution should protect him, however remote the chance of his success." Gerald Gunther,
Learned Hand: The Man and the Judge (1994) at 604–605.

v. Board of Education[90] invalidates the importance of that case as a ground-breaking precedent. More fundamentally, however, the two flaws stem from Holmes's allegiance to common law thought processes, although he no longer accepted the common law of free speech.

With regard to intent, Holmes had pioneered the application of objective tests for intent in his 1881 classic *The Common Law.*[91] In the context of criminal law, Holmes had argued that the deterrence theory of punishment (which he advocated) required that liability for criminal acts should not be measured by moral blameworthiness but rather by failure to conform to the external standard of what would be blameworthy in the average citizen.[92] From this, Holmes went on to define intent objectively, in terms of consequences of acts that are themselves neutral.[93] Holmes's analysis of intent in the First Amendment context of *Debs* and the result in that case make far more sense with this concept of intent in mind. Debs was held to the objective standard and found wanting; the results of his speech were foreseeable to the average citizen. Whether or not Debs in fact anticipated them was irrelevant to Holmes.

The proximity requirement also stems from Holmes's concept of foreseeability; the volitional nature of the act and the proximity of the unwanted result together make up intent under common law as defined by Holmes. The requirement of proximity in the trilogy then was not yet the requirement of temporal imminence it would become in later cases, a requirement based upon the insight of Justice Brandeis that the cure for evil speech is not enforced silence, but rather corrective speech, and that suppression is only justified when there is no time for the war of words to run its course.[94] Rather, it was a requirement of foreseeability in the context of an intentional act. Thus, when the unlawful result of speech is foreseeable to the average person, it is irrebuttably presumed to be intended—

---

90. 347 U.S. 483 (1954); *see* R. Kluger, *Simple Justice* (1975) at 744–778.

91. O. W. Holmes, *The Common Law* (1881) at 49–51. Holmes's advocacy of the "external standard" in criminal law is contained in Lecture II.

92. *Id.*

93. *Id.* at 53–56. Rabban, *supra* note 83, at 1267–1274 discusses the impact of Holmes's thought in *The Common Law* on the First Amendment, particularly that portion of the book in which Holmes discusses attempts, in which Rabban sees the dawn of "clear and present danger." Rabban explores the subject of Holmes's thinking in terms of attempts thoroughly, but I do not agree with his readings of the *Schenck* trilogy as a restrictive set of decisions from which Holmes moved in a "transformation." Rabban at 1208–1209. His conclusions are accepted, and expanded upon, by White, *supra* note 57, at 412–419 (*"Schenck, Debs,* and *Frohwerk,* taken together, suggest that Holmes's 'clear and present danger' language was simply a restatement of 'attempts' language in his earlier opinions").

94. *See* text *infra* at notes 154–159.

the question is, as Holmes wrote in *Schenck*, a question of proximity and degree.

It has been suggested by David Rabban that Holmes's approach to the *Schenck* trilogy was based upon his previous work on attempts in *The Common Law*.[95] Although Rabban properly draws support from Holmes's letters to demonstrate the justice's thinking in terms of his earlier work in analyzing the First Amendment, this analysis overemphasizes the cases strictly comparable to attempts. Holmes's thinking on the subject of criminal liability in general provides, in my view, a better means of understanding his approach to *all* of the First Amendment cases at this stage of his development. Holmes's concept of the neutrality of actions in themselves colored both his writings on attempts and his First Amendment jurisprudence.

Attempts for Holmes are acts done either with a specific intent or in such circumstances that such an intent on the part of the reasonable actor can be inferred. Speech can be punished, as Rabban properly notes, when it can be likened to an attempt. But the more general point may well be obscured by so intent-bound an analysis. For Holmes, the context of any action determined its meaning, whether the action was the enunciation of words or the firing of a pistol.[96]

Holmes thus would permit the imposition of punishment for the utterance of words when the circumstances in which they are uttered are *analogous* to a criminal act—for example, an attempt. His discussion of attempts is a specific working out of that general theme of criminal liability that runs through *The Common Law*. That Holmes's paradigm moves beyond attempts, however, is clear.[97] Indeed, it does so in the *Schenck* opinion, albeit in Holmes's elliptical style. Holmes referred in *Schenck* to what he called "the common law doctrine" that the nature of every act depends upon its context, for which he cited his own opinion in *Aikens v. Wisconsin*.[98] In fact, in *Aikens*, Holmes had stated, in language that was strikingly similar to his general discussion of criminal liability in *The Common Law*, that:

> AN act, which in itself is merely a voluntary muscular contraction, derives all its character from the consequences which will follow it under the circumstances in which it was done. . . . The most innocent and constitutionally protected acts or omissions may be made a step in a criminal plot, and if it is a step in a plot neither its innocence nor the Constitution is sufficient to prevent the punishment of the plot by law.[99]

---

95. *See* Rabban, *supra* note 83 at 1267–1274.
96. Holmes, *supra* note 91 at 91.
97. *See infra* note 120.
98. 249 U.S. 47, 51–52, citing *Aikens*, 195 U.S. 194, 205–206 (1904).
99. 195 U.S. at 205–206. *See* Holmes, *supra* note 91, at 31–76.

Thus, in *Schenck* Holmes explicitly relied not on the doctrine of attempts (which requires specific intent for a finding of liability)[100] but on his general theory of liability. In relying upon Holmes's enunciation of the concept of attempts, Rabban neglects those circumstances where such specific intent—subjective intent—might be lacking, but where Holmes, in this common law phase of his development, would permit the imposition of liability.[101]

It is possible with this analysis to again resurrect the "pure speech/speech tantamount to action" distinction previously relied on. When does Holmes say that the government may punish speech? When it fits the common law definition of an intentional crime. Speech, like any other action for Holmes, is neutral. It becomes criminal under certain circumstances, just as the action of crooking one's finger becomes criminal when the finger is nestled against the trigger of a gun pointed at a bystander.[102] It is not the expressive content of speech that permits suppression, according to Holmes, but the foreseeability of a resulting breach of law—an evil that Congress has the right to prevent and has acted to prevent in the statute under review. Speech may be punished when it is an act tantamount to a criminal act as defined in the common law.

This presents a fascinating (to me) parallel with Judge Hand's later First Amendment theory. Just as Holmes turned to the common law definition of criminal intent to find the context in which the neutral act of speech ceases to be protected expression and becomes criminal conduct, so too Hand turned to the common law of torts.[103] In *United States v. Dennis*,[104] Hand upheld the convictions of several defendants (including perennial presidential candidate Gus Hall) under the Smith Act for "'willfully and knowingly' conspiring to organize the Communist Party of the United States as a group to 'teach and advocate the overthrow and destruction' of the govern-

---

100. Although in *The Common Law* Holmes reinterpreted the doctrine of attempts to some extent, and urged that the objective standard be applied there as well, he conceded that for a "class" of attempts "actual intent is clearly necessary, and the existence of this class as well as the name (attempt) no doubt tends to affect the whole doctrine." Holmes, *supra* note 91, at 66. Had Holmes continued to insist upon this analysis, my difference from Rabban would be solely one of method; however, Holmes would subsequently adopt, in free speech cases, the more common notion that an attempt requires specific (subjective) intent. *See* text *infra* at note 122.

101. *See* text *infra* at note 120.

102. This example is given by Holmes in *The Common Law* at 54–55.

103. For my more elaborate comparison of Holmes's and Hand's views of freedom of speech, see Wirenius, *Helping Hand: The Life and Legacy of Learned Hand*, 25 Seton Hall L.Rev. 505, 516–521 (1994) (reviewing Gerald Gunther, *Learned Hand: Man and the Judge* (1994).

104. 183 F.2d 201 (2d Cir. 1950), *aff'd*, 341 U.S. 494 (1951).

ment 'by force and violence.'"[105] Hand's opinion, replete with the anti-Communist rhetoric of the day, explained the constitutional test as "whether the gravity of the 'evil,' discounted by its improbability, justifies such invasion of free speech as is necessary to avoid the danger."[106]

This formulation harks back to Hand's famous economic formulation of tort liability in *United States v. Carroll Towing Co.*[107] In *Carroll Towing*, Hand defined a barge owner's duty "to provide against resulting injuries [a]s a function of three variables: (1) The probability that she will break away; (2) the gravity of the resulting injury, if she does; (3) the burden of adequate precautions. . . . [I]f the probability be called P; the injury L; and the burden B, liability depends upon whether B is less than L multiplied by P."[108] Thus for Hand, the tort-feasor acts at his or her peril when the burden is less than the probability and the magnitude of the likely injury multiplied, just as a speaker speaks at his or her peril when the invasion of free speech (the burden) is less than the magnitude of the injury combined (multiplied?) with its (im)probability. The identical nature of the tests should not be lost, because in *Dennis* Hand described the probability factor negatively—rather than multiplying by probability he "discounts by *im*probability," which is of course the same thing. Hand treated speech as a common law tort situation; Holmes sought to find the presence or absence of common law criminal intent in the circumstances of the speech. Both, however, looked to the common law areas in which they excelled to find guidance in constructing a constitutional standard. Intriguingly, both Holmes (at this stage of his development) and Hand did not see a difference between the two modes of reasoning, or any need for a special level of protection. Holmes would grow beyond common law constitutional reasoning; Hand would not.[109]

---

105. *Id.* at 205.
106. *Id.* at 212.
107. 159 F.2d 169 (2d Cir. 1947).
108. *Id.* at 173.
109. This is not to imply that Hand underwent a conversion from liberal constitutionalist (*Masses*) to crusty old common lawyer (*Dennis*). Two things should be pointed out about *Masses*. First, in *Masses* Hand did not rule that Congress *could* not have prohibited the speech at issue, but only that it did not. The opinion is in fact an exercise in statutory construction, not in constitutional reasoning, although Hand construed the statute in harmony with the values of the constitution. *Masses*, 244 F. at 540; *see* Gunther *supra* 83 at 725; Vincent Blasi, *Learned Hand and the Self-Government Theory of the First Amendment: Masses Publishing Co. v. Patten*, 61 U. Col. L. Rev. 1, 8–11 (1990). Moreover, as already suggested, the *Masses* test is no great improvement over the midpoint reached by Holmes (let alone over the next stage in the elder jurist's evolution), permitting as it does proscription of any speech advocating violation of law, however remote the potential for harm. 244 F. at 540; Gunther, *supra* note 89, at 604–605; Wirenius, *supra* note 103, at 519–520.

The Holmes-Brandeis Dissents

The looseness of the Holmes definition may be explained, but it is a flaw nonetheless. It may be held to be foreseeable that an audience member will violate the law in many circumstances in which the speaker does not in fact foresee the violation, and thus speakers speak at their peril regardless of what it is they say. Moreover, by treating speech like any other action Holmes (and Hand) may be missing the point; not every other kind of action has a constitutional provision to protect it. Should one really speak "at his peril," as Holmes was fond of saying,[110] in light of this protection?

But Holmes's evolving jurisprudence in this area was not quite complete. The next, and final stage, for which Holmes has been hailed as often as he has been vilified for the *Schenck* trilogy, comes in his great dissents in partnership with Justice Louis D. Brandeis. These cases also marked the end of the Court's tradition of unanimity in First Amendment cases.

The Court split first in *Abrams v. United States.*[111] *Abrams* involved yet another Espionage Act prosecution (the Justice Department apparently had a lot of time on its hands), this time of five Russian immigrants who were anarchists, for pamphlets that opposed the sending of American troops into Russia, urging "the persons to whom it was addressed to turn a deaf ear to patriotic appeals in behalf of the government of the United States and to cease to render it assistance in the prosecution of the war."[112] The Court found in the pamphlet direct incitement to "arise and put down by force the government of the United States."[113] In addition, the pamphlet urged a general strike to oppose federal policy toward Russia.[114] In its opinion, the Court rejected the argument that the only intent of the defendants was to prevent injury to the Russian cause and not to obstruct the war against Germany. "Men must be held to have intended, and to be accountable for, the effects which their acts were likely to produce," the Court wrote, drawing from Holmes's "objective" concept of intent.[115] The Court went on to allow that the "primary purpose and intent" may have been to aid Russia, but then held that "the plan of action which they adopted necessarily involved, before it could be realized, defeat of the war program of the

---

110. *See,* for example, *The Common Law, supra* note 91, at 79.
111. 250 U.S. 616 (1919).
112. *Id.* at 621.
113. *Id.* at 620. For the details of the inaccuracy of the translations relied upon by the government, as well as a revealing look at the trial and appellate stages of *Abrams, see* Richard Polenberg, *Fighting Faiths: The Abrams Case, The Supreme Court, and Free Speech* (1988) at 49–55.
114. 250 U.S. at 620.
115. *Id.* at 621.

United States."[116] There was no discussion of the imminence requirement beyond the statement quoted above that the results were "likely," that is, foreseeable.

In Holmes's dissent, joined by Justice Brandeis, the great exponent of the common law of intent emphasizes the statute's specific intent requirement—that the speech be uttered "with intent by such curtailment to cripple or hinder the United States in the prosecution of the war."[117] Holmes explained:

> I am aware of course that the word intent as vaguely used in ordinary legal discussion means no more than knowledge at the time of the act that the consequences said to be intended will ensue. Even less than that will satisfy the general principle of civil and criminal liability. A man may have to pay damages, may be sent to prison, at common law might be hanged, if at the time of his act he knew facts from which common experience showed that the consequences would follow, whether he individually could foresee them or not. But, when words are used exactly, a deed is not done with intent to produce a consequence unless that consequence is the aim of the deed. . . . It seems to me that this statute must be taken to use its words in a strict and accurate sense. They would be absurd in any other. A patriot might think that we are wasting money on aeroplanes, or making more cannon of a certain kind than we needed, and might advocate curtailment . . . yet even if it turned out that the curtailment hindered and was thought by other minds to have been obviously likely to hinder the United States in the prosecution of the war, no one would hold such conduct a crime.[118]

Having so construed the Espionage Act, Holmes then moved on to "a more important aspect of the case," the First Amendment.

Reaffirming his belief that the *Schenck* trilogy had been correctly decided, Holmes restated their premise: "[B]y the same reasoning that would justify punishing persuasion to murder, the United States constitutionally may punish speech that produces or is intended to produce a clear and imminent danger that it will bring about forthwith certain substantive evils that the United States constitutionally may seek to prevent."[119] Interestingly, Holmes bifurcates the standard: *Either* the speech must *actually* produce a clear and imminent danger, in which case the watered-down, common law "objective" form of intent would suffice, *or* specific intent to cause the re-

---

116. *Id.*
117. 250 U.S. at 626. (Holmes, J., dissenting)
118. *Id.* at 626–627.
119. *Id.* at 627.

sult foreseen must be established—a subjective test.[120] From this general principle, he went on to assert, that whether in time of war or of peace, the right survives, although the increased dangers inherent in wartime gave the government greater power to encroach upon free speech in wartime.

Holmes then dismissed the first prong of the test with regard to the leaflet, declaring that, "nobody can suppose that the surreptitious publishing of a silly leaflet by an unknown man, without more, would present any immediate danger that its opinions would hinder the success of the government arms or have any appreciable tendency to do so."[121] Noting that had the act been done with the requisite intent, it would have constituted an attempt,[122] and thus been legally cognizable, Holmes reiterated that he did not "see how anyone can find the intent required by the statute in any of the defendants' words. . . . To say that two phrases taken literally might import a suggestion of conduct that would have interference with the war as an indirect and probably undesired effect seems to me by no means enough to show an attempt to produce that effect."[123]

In *Abrams* Holmes had further refined his thinking, producing not the "conversion" referred to by Professors David Rabban and Gerald Gunther, but rather another evolutionary step. Two changes were noticeable from the *Schenck* trilogy. The first was the newly bifurcated standard, requiring either specific intent or a "clear and present danger" from which common law intent could be found. It is possible that Holmes did not mean to omit the concept from the *Schenck* trilogy—it would further explain the results in those cases, which are far more like attempts than they are like "clear and present danger" cases. It would also explain his puzzlement at Hand's disagreement with him on the standard—direct advocacy of law-breaking and advocacy with the specific purpose of triggering law-breaking overlap considerably. But the concept is not necessarily to be inferred from those opinions.

However, the factual circumstances of the three cases do not negate such a continuity between them and *Abrams*. Debs of course admitted trying to

---

120. *Id.* This is another reason for my emphasis on Holmes's *general* theory of criminal liability (*supra* note 95 and text); only the latter variety of speech corresponds precisely to an attempt, the source of Rabban's analysis.

121. *Id.* at 628.

122. Here, of course, Rabban's reliance on Holmes's letters that emphasize the connection between free speech jurisprudence and the common law of attempt bears fruit. Holmes treats unsuccessful efforts to achieve the unlawful result as failed attempts like any others, done with the specific intent to bring about the proscribed result. However, when *not* spoken with the requisite intent to constitute an attempt, speech was at the time Holmes wrote *Schenck*, as suggested above, an act like any other, to be measured by the external standards of criminal liability. *Abrams* marks Holmes's fullest exposition of as well as his evolution beyond this common law paradigm.

123. 250 U.S. at 628–629.

stir up opposition to the war—an admission of an attempt, perhaps, to Holmes's jaundiced eye. *Frohwerk* is best seen as an instance of the vagaries of appellate review; unsure of his record, Holmes was reluctant to second-guess the trial court. *Schenck* itself could fairly to be said to involve a clear and present danger of the obstruction of recruitment (with or without the presence of specific intent) because the defendant was handing his leaflets to conscriptees that urged them to resist the draft and reminded them of their higher destiny than that of cannon fodder.

The second, and more fundamental, step was Holmes's substitution of an "immediacy" requirement for that of foreseeability in the initial triad of cases. This step further divorced the twentieth-century jurisprudence from its common law roots, and brought the rule within hailing distance of the general rule for subversive advocacy that is in place today.[124] Holmes offered a rationale for this newly tightened requirement. He defined the Constitution as "an experiment, as all life is an experiment," going on to say that "every year if not every day we have to wager our salvation upon some prophecy based upon imperfect knowledge."[125]

Holmes boldly declared that

> [W]HEN men have realized that time has upset many fighting faiths, they may come to believe even more than they believe the very foundations of their conduct that the ultimate good desired is better reached by free trade in ideas—that the best test of truth is the power of the thought to get itself accepted in the competition of the market, and that truth is the only ground upon which their wishes safely can be carried out.[126]

---

124. Compare *Brandenburg v. Ohio*, 395 U.S. 444 (1969). See text *infra* at notes 237–241. The argument in the text above that the test propounded by Holmes in *Abrams* and in his subsequent dissents with Justice Brandeis represents a "further refinement" of his thinking is contrary to the view of another Holmes biographer, Sheldon Novick. *See* Novick, *The Unrevised Holmes and Freedom of Expression*, 1991 Sup. Ct. Rev. 303 (1992). Novick correctly disputes the views of Rabban and Gunther, but denies the existence of any development on Holmes's part. *Id.* at 353–356; 358–361. Such an argument denies not only the subtle changes of vision explained in the text, but also requires that the reader, with Novick, conclude that Holmes could not have "entirely accepted Brandeis's argument" in *Whitney v. California*, 277 U.S. 438, despite the fact that he joined in Brandeis's opinion in that case. Novick at 371.

125. *Abrams*, 250 U.S. at 630 (Holmes, J. dissenting). That this belief was part of Holmes's own philosophy is reflected in his epigram that "to have doubted one's own first principles is the mark of a civilized man." O. W. Holmes, *Collected Legal Papers* (1920) at 307.

126. *Id.* This is not to say, although many have, that Holmes had a simplistic faith that the forces of the market inevitably lead to truth—that the market would take care of itself, so to speak. Rather, Holmes believed that the free expression of ideas, by which ideas may be rejected but not proscribed, was the "best chance" to reach truth. Milton believed

Thus, "we should be eternally vigilant against attempts to check the expression of opinions that we loathe and believe to be fraught with death, unless they so imminently threaten immediate interference with the lawful and pressing purposes of the law that an immediate check is required to save the country."[127] Holmes concluded that only "the emergency that makes it immediately dangerous to leave the correction of evil counsels to time warrants making any exception to the sweeping command" of the First Amendment.[128]

The Holmes dissent in *Abrams* contained one other important feature, in addition to Holmes's stirring rhetoric in defense of the "free trade in ideas." Holmes, the author of *Patterson*, completed his recantation of that case's rule, declaring that "I wholly disagree with the argument of the Government that the First Amendment left the common law of seditious libel on force," citing the historical rejection of the Sedition Act of 1798, and the government's "repentance" of that act, manifested through its repayment of fines imposed pursuant to the act.[129] Finally, in noting that in *Abrams* the Court dealt "only with expressions of opinion and exhortations" Holmes left open the question of how to treat other speech.

Just how far apart the majority was from the dissenters was shown in *Gitlow v. New York*.[130] The majority, in finding that New York's ban of advocacy of violent change was within the First Amendment's purview, pointed out that the "statute does not penalize the utterance or publication of abstract 'doctrine' or academic discussion having no quality of incitement to any concrete action. It is not aimed against mere historical or philisophical essays."[131] The Court also implicitly limited the statute's sweep, exempting such speech as was "too trivial to be beneath the notice of the law."[132]

Up to that point, the *Gitlow* majority was seemingly ready to rely upon the old advocacy-incitement distinction of *Fox*. But then, the Court set out the test for constitutional regulation of free speech: "That a State

---

that truth could not be bested; Holmes knew that the received wisdom of any age was suspect, and that the eradication of "error" overcommitted society to dubious first principles. *See* Wirenius, *supra* note 4, 64–65.

127. *Abrams*, 250 U.S. at 630.

128. *Id.* at 630–631.

129. *Id.* at 630. The impact of the Alien and Sedition Acts upon the jurisprudence is actually minimal; the laws were never tested before the Supreme Court. However, several lower federal courts did uphold their constitutionality. *See*, for example, *Trial of Matthew Lyon* (D. Vt. 1798), in Francis Wharton, *State Trials of the United States* (1849) at 333; *Trial of Thomas Cooper*, (D. Pa. 1800), *Id.* at 659. Other cases are cited in Bikle *supra* note 79, at 19–20.

130. 268 U.S. 652 (1923) (upholding conviction under state law for "criminal anarchy" based on advocacy of violent overthrow of the government).

131. *Id.* at 644.

132. *Id.* at 670.

in the exercise of its police power may punish those who abuse this freedom by utterances inimical to the public welfare, tending to corrupt
public morals, incite to crime, or disturb the public peace, is not open to
question."[133]

In explicating this "bad tendency" test, the Court squarely rejected the
Schenck trilogy's foreseeability requirement, to say nothing of the more stringent imminence requirement of Holmes and Brandeis.[134] *Schenck* was limited
by the Court to cases where the utterances themselves were not proscribed,
but where the use of language is claimed to have had an effect violative of a
statute.[135]

In dissent, Holmes rejected the majority's various premises. Holmes flatly
declared that the *Schenck* test is the appropriate test, acknowledging that "this
criterion was departed from in [*Abrams*], but the convictions that I expressed
in that case are too deep for it to be possible for me as yet to believe that it
... has settled the law."[136] More fundamentally, Holmes rejected the Court's
attempt to differentiate between "theory" and "advocacy":

> IT is said that this manifesto was more than a theory, that it was an
> incitement. Every idea is an incitement. It offers itself for belief and if
> believed it is acted upon unless some other belief outweighs it or some
> failure of energy stifles the movement at its birth. The only difference
> between the expression of an opinion and an incitement in the nar-
> rower sense is the speaker's enthusiasm for the result. Eloquence may
> set fire to reason. But whatever may be thought of the redundant dis-
> course before us it had no chance of starting a present conflagration.
> If in the long run, the beliefs expressed in proletarian dictatorship are
> destined to be accepted by the dominant forces in the community, the
> only meaning of free speech is that they should be given their chance
> and have their way.[137]

---

133. *Id.* at 667.
134. *Id.* at 669 ("And the immediate effect is none the less real and substantial, because the
effect of a given utterance cannot be accurately foreseen. The State cannot reasonably
be required to measure the danger from every such utterance in the nice balance of a
jeweler's scale. A single revolutionary spark may kindle a fire that, smouldering for a
time, may burst into a sweeping and destructive conflagration. It cannot be said that
the State is acting arbitrarily or unreasonably when . . . it seeks to extinguish the spark
without waiting until it has enkindled the flame or blazed into the conflagration").
135. *Id.* at 670–671.
136. *Id.* at 673 (Holmes, J., dissenting) (citations omitted).
137. *Id.* Holmes's oft-quoted willingness to assist his fellow citizens on the road to hell
should they choose to go (*see supra* text at note 58)—a concept of the appropriate
role of the judge—is thus tied to a theory of the state—that the people must be free
to steer the republic in whichever direction they might choose. *See* Blasi, *supra* note
109, at 23–24.

Thus, for Holmes (and Brandeis who joined this dissent), the right to free speech extended beyond that speech that stands no chance of being adopted. Holmes recognized that freedom is risky—the populace may well choose to abandon the fundamental precepts of our society, and to impose new ones. That choice, if made, must be honored, so long as it is a genuine choice, and not itself the product of an "immediate conflagration."

Justice Brandeis Recasts Clear and Present Danger

In *Schaefer v. United States*[138] the split in the Court between the conservative wing and the Holmes-Brandeis liberal wing became more clear. The majority opinion contains not a single reference to clear and present danger. In fact, the majority bluntly stated "Their [the statements involved] effect or the persons affected could not be shown, nor was it necessary. The tendency of the articles and their efficacy were enough for offense—their 'intent' and 'attempt,' for these are the words of the law, and to have required more would have made the law useless. It was passed in precaution. The incidence of its violation might not be immediately seen, evil appearing only in disaster, the result of the disloyalty engendered and the spirit of mutiny."[139]

The Court thus explicitly rejected the imminence and the proximity requirements, enshrining only the meaningless platitude that the speech had a bad "tendency." Although this "bad tendency" test (as it has come to be known) is not quite the open season on prosecution of speech so long as no prior restraint was involved that antedated *Schenck*, it is hardly more protective; it is perhaps comparable to a "rational basis" test of constitutionality. Although some hope was left because of the Court's reference to the speech's "efficacy," the result was incomprehensible because it followed a sweeping declaration that the effect of the speech, or any risk posed by it, need not be proved.

---

138. 251 U.S. 466 (1920). (upholding still more Espionage Act convictions, this time involving the conviction of the staff of a German language newspaper for publishing false information and for statements conveying "sneering" toward and "derision of America's efforts" in the war). Justice Clarke dissented, with regard to several affirmed counts, neither seeing appropriate conduct by the Court below, nor a substantial First Amendment issue. He rested his opinion on the trivial and technical nature of the so-called "false statements," which he explained as errors by the government translators, or as innocuous, and disagreed with the government's theory as to what constituted a false report when a newspaper edited reprinted material. 251 U.S. at 496–501. Justice Brandeis's dissent, in addition to the constitutional arguments detailed *infra* (text at notes 141–144) catalogued these and similar errors of fact mandating, in his view and Holmes's, a reversal. 251 U.S. at 484–493.

139. *Id.* at 479.

The Court's opinion, by Justice McKenna, openly displayed anger at the "curious spectacle" of the invocation of the First Amendment in this case, which the Court described as "a strange perversion of its precepts."[140] This also did not bode well for future claimants.

The dissent of Justice Brandeis, joined by Holmes, hewed closely to the lines of Holmes's *Abrams* dissent, even at one point comparing the "rule of reason" applicable in free speech cases to that obtaining in "the case of criminal attempts and incitements."[141] Most of Brandeis's opinion pointed out the deficiencies in the charges (such as reading mistranslations as "falsifications"),[142] but in his peroration, Brandeis sounded a warning note. Reminding the Court that "[t]he constitutional right of free speech has been declared to be the same in peace and in war," he chided his colleagues, saying that "[i]n peace, too, men may differ widely as to what loyalty to our country demands; and an intolerant majority, swayed by passion or by fear, may be prone in the future, as it has often been in the past to stamp as disloyal opinion with which it disagrees." Convictions such as these, he concluded, "beside abridging freedom of speech, threaten freedom of thought and of belief."[143]

Brandeis's opinion, however, raised at least one concern that was not present in Holmes's writings on the subject: the nature of repression. For Holmes, persecution of those who hold minority opinions was "perfectly logical."[144] But for Brandeis it was a result at best of intolerance, and at worst of fear. This concern with the character of repression would form the underlying theme of Brandeis's great contribution to First Amendment doctrine, his opinion in the 1927 case of *Whitney v. California*.[145]

Much of what needs to be said about *Whitney* has been stated elsewhere, and in detail.[146] The case arose when Anita Whitney, a member of the Cali-

---

140. *Id.* at 477.
141. *Id.* at 482, 486.
142. As does the dissenting opinion of Justice Clarke, who depicted the case as "simply a case of flagrant mistrial, likely to result in disgrace and great injustice, probably in life imprisonment for two old men" because of the Court's pusillanimity in refusing to exercise its power to correct error at the trial level. *Id.* at 501 (Clark, J., dissenting).
143. *Id.* at 495. It is difficult not to find in Brandeis's prophetic warning a hint of the agonies the nation would be subjected to by Senator Joseph McCarthy and his ilk in the name of "loyalty," a process that far outlasted the fall of the demagogue from Wisconsin. *See* Thomas C. Reeves, *The Life and Times of Joe McCarthy* (1982); William O. Douglas, *Points of Rebellion* (1970). While one of Douglas's biographers dismisses the book as seeming "to have been churned out for the quick buck" (James Simon, *Independent Journey: The Life of William O. Douglas* [1980] at 410), his publication of the "inflammatory volume" was one of the grounds asserted by then-Representative Gerald R. Ford in his abortive attempt to impeach Douglas. Simon at 405.
144. *Abrams*, 250 U.S. at 631.
145. 274 U.S. 357, 372 *et seq.* (1927).
146. See Vincent Blasi, *The First Amendment and the Ideal of Civic Courage: The Brandeis Opinion in Whitney v. California*, 29 Wm. & Mary L. Rev. 653 (1988).

fornia branch of the Communist Labor Party who attended several of its organizing sessions and did some committee work for it, was tried and convicted under the state Criminal Syndicalism Act.[147] Ms. Whitney's defense was that "it was not her intention that the Communist Labor Party of California should be an instrument of terrorism or violence, and that it was not her purpose or that of the Convention to violate any known law."[148]

The Court, in rejecting Ms. Whitney's various attacks upon the constitutionality of the act, found it constitutional both on its face [149] and as applied to the speech uttered by Ms. Whitney. The Court gave her free speech claim short shrift, repeating the "bad tendency" language from *Gitlow*. This time, the court summarily opined that the fact that "a State in the exercise of its police power may punish those who abuse this freedom by utterances inimical to the public welfare, tending to incite to crime, disturb the public peace, or endanger the foundations of organized government and threaten its overthrow by unlawful means, is not open to question."[150]

Moreover, the Court decided that the legislature's judgment that such tendency could be found in joining an organization that promoted these values by advocating or teaching the use of force[151] was a "determination [which] must be given great weight."[152] The statute could not be deemed unconstitutional unless "it is an arbitrary or unreasonable attempt to exercise the authority vested in the State in the public interest."[153]

Once again, the Court seemed to have relapsed to the *Robertson v. Baldwin* formulation, treating any speech the state deemed to be harmful to the

---

147. 274 U.S. 365–366. The statute in question was Cal. Stat. 1919 Ch. 188, p.281, § 2. *Id.* at 359–360.

148. *Id.* at 366.

149. *Id.* at 366–371 (rejecting claims that the act violated the Due Process Clause's mandate that criminal statutes be sufficiently definite in their prohibitions as to provide notice as to what conduct is and is not lawful and the Equal Protection Clause of the Fourteenth Amendment).

150. *Id.* at 371.

151. Note that the Court does not in any way reckon with Ms. Whitney's defense that the Communist Labor Party of California had no intent to use terroristic means or to violate any laws.

152. 274 U.S. at 371.

153. *Id.* Again, the Court has so far removed itself from the test announced in the *Schenck* trilogy of cases as to be once again treating free speech cases as just another common law form of regulation. The standard of review—that the state's action must be "arbitrary" or "unreasonable" pretty closely corresponds to the "arbitrary and capricious" or "rational basis" test currently used by the Supreme Court to review economic and social legislation; this most deferential level of constitutional review asks only if the measure adopted bears a rational relationship to a constitutionally permissible goal. See Tribe, *American Constitutional Law* (2d ed. 1988) at 581–584. This "bad tendency" test is claimed by White to be inherent in Holmes's pre-*Abrams* opinions, but that seems to me to be confounding *Patterson's* permissive statement that the state "may" punish such statements that they deem contrary to public order.

public weal as subject to proscription, and with the scales of review firmly weighted in favor of the state on review. Although the Court did not at least backslide all the way to the Blackstonian view that any author or speaker makes his or her views known at his or her peril—there remained, after all the mandate that a statute regulating the speech be in place—it seems fair to say that while Holmes and Brandeis evolved, the Court *devolved*. Indeed, compared to the incremental steps by which Holmes and Brandeis made "clear and present danger" a doctrine that was ever more protective of speech, the Court's abrupt renunciation of the *Schenck* trilogy's rule inexorably leads to the conclusion that the "revolution" that critics find in the cases which split the Court was in the minds of the conservative justices and not in the minds of their more liberal colleagues.

The concurrence[154] that Brandeis wrote and Holmes joined brings to its pinnacle their tradition of dissent and articulated an entirely new theory of free speech in the jurisprudence. After disparaging the Court's failure to articulate a standard by which a danger is to be deemed "clear" or "present,"[155] Brandeis turned to the fundamental business at hand: once again explaining the *whys* of free speech to an unappreciative[156] Court:

> THOSE who won our independence believed that the final end of the State was to make men free to develop their faculties; and that in its government the deliberative forces should prevail over the arbitrary. They valued liberty both as an end and as a means. They believed liberty to be the secret of happiness and courage to be the secret of liberty. They believed that freedom to think as you will and to speak as you think are means indispensable to the discovery and spread of political truth; that without free speech and assembly discussion would be futile; that with them, discussion affords ordinarily adequate protection against the dissemination of noxious doctrine, that the greatest menace to freedom is an inert people. . . .
>
> Believing in the power of reason as applied through public discussion, they eschewed silence coerced by law—the argument of force in its worst form. Recognizing the occasional tyrannies of governing ma-

---

154. The justices concurred in the judgment and cited a technical question of reviewability—the doctrine of "preservation," which requires objection at trial to the precise legal error alleged in the appellate court, so that the trial court has an opportunity to avoid error. 274 U.S. at 372.

155. *Id.* at 373–374.

156. Just how unappreciative can be seen in the off-the-bench remarks of Chief Justice Taft regarding Brandeis, whom he portrayed in distinctly unflattering terms and Holmes, whom Taft dismissed as senile clay in the hands of the master manipulator. Baker, *supra* note 81 at 560.

jorities, they amended the Constitution so that free speech and assembly should be guaranteed.

Fear of serious injury cannot alone justify suppression of free speech and assembly. Men feared witches and burnt women. It is the function of speech to free men from the bondage of irrational fears. To justify suppression of free speech there must be reasonable ground to fear that serious evil will result if free speech is practiced. There must be reasonable ground to fear that the danger apprehended is imminent. There must be reasonable ground to believe that the evil to be prevented is a serious one. . . .

Those who won our independence by revolution were not cowards. They did not fear political change. They did not exalt order at the cost of liberty. To courageous, self-reliant men, with confidence in the power of free and fearless reasoning applied through the processes of popular government, no danger flowing from speech can be deemed clear and present, unless the incidence of the evil apprehended is so imminent that it may fall before there is opportunity for full discussion. If there be time to expose through discussion the falsehoods and fallacies, to avert the evil by the processes of education, then the remedy to be applied is more speech, not enforced silence. Only an emergency can justify repression.[157]

So long an extract from even Justice Brandeis's great rhetoric would need justification were it not for the remarkable revamping of the rationales for the free speech jurisprudence contained in these stirring words. Brandeis was not simply restating Holmes's previous rationales; he was recasting them, endowing them with an ethical component that had been hitherto lacking.

Where for Holmes free speech represented the best chance (iffy though it may be) of attaining truth, for Brandeis it represented far more. As Vincent Blasi aptly points out, Brandeis saw freedom of speech as a means of encouraging the sort of citizen a democracy needs; brave, self-reliant men and women.[158] Moreover, for Brandeis repression was a sign of panic, of weakness. His rhetoric conjured up the image of shifty, sweaty demagogues silencing their opponents in a panic that their machinations will be exposed, as opposed to the calm, rational censors depicted by Holmes in *Abrams*.[159] Brandeis had something new to say about the conflicting natures of freedom and repression.

---

157. 274 U.S. at 375–377.
158. See Blasi, *supra* note 109, at 25; see also Bollinger, *The Tolerant Society* (1986), at 90.
159. 250 U.S. at 630. ("Persecution for the expression of opinions seems to me to be perfectly logical. If you have no doubts of your premises or your power and want a certain result with all your heart you naturally express your wishes in law and sweep away all opposition").

Moreover, he transformed the imminence requirement from a pro-
phylactic rule that protected the admittedly shaky marketplace of ideas
(Holmes's rationale for it once he left behind his foreseeability position)
into a mandate that the democratic process take its course, leaving suppression as a possible option only in those aberrational cases where the rush of
events prevents the populace from deliberating.

One must not overstress the point; Brandeis's new rationales were compatible with those advanced by Holmes, and indeed the elder justice concurred with them.[160] They represent another incremental step, and not a
rejection of Holmes's thoughts on the subject. Brandeis's insistence that the
people are the ultimate sovereigns, and that the state can only act to ensure
sufficient opportunity for deliberation amplified Holmes's flat declaration
that "if in the long run the beliefs expressed in proletarian dictatorship are
destined to be accepted by the dominant forces of the community, the only
meaning of free speech is that they should be given their chance and have
their way," misguided as Holmes thought it to be.[161] What Brandeis did
achieve that Holmes neglected to do in his own opinions was to tie First
Amendment jurisprudence to a democratic theory in a positive, as opposed
to Holmes's more negative, way.

The basic tradition was in place; all that was necessary was for the Holmes-
Brandeis view to command the assent of a majority of the Court.

The Nascent Tradition

The slow death of *Whitney* in the 1930s and the Court's gradual adoption of
the Holmes-Brandeis rule is not itself to the point; suffice it to say that during this period the Court ruled in favor of speakers whose conduct was

---

160. Indeed, in *Schaefer, supra* text at note 138 *et seq.*, Holmes urged that the populace must
    have its way, wherever that might lead the state. Brandeis's view is different, in that
    he grounded it not in a view that the people must be free to plot their course in an
    uncharted, chaotic sea, but in the notion that the dignity of the people and the de-
    sired character of both people and institutions require freedom as a precondition.
    Sheldon Novick's conclusion that Holmes did not fully agree with Brandeis's argu-
    ment in *Whitney* is based on Holmes's disbelief "that the Constitution had in it any
    program of social reform," a statement undoubtedly true. Novick, *supra* note 124, at
    371. However, Novick does not reckon with Holmes's willingness to let the majority
    rule, and in his belief that courage was the supreme virtue; as Novick himself points
    out, "His definition of a gentleman was someone who would die for a point of honor,
    or a feather." *Id.* at 384. The only distinction between Holmes and Brandeis regard-
    ing *Whitney* seems to me to be rooted in Brandeis's faith in the journey's destination,
    something altogether lacking in Holmes.
161. *Gitlow*, 268 U.S. at 673.

essentially indistinguishable from that of Anita Whitney or her equally un-fortunate predecessors.[162] Beyond these rulings, intimations of a new rationale, one weighted more in favor of free speech claims, began to evolve.[163] In the celebrated Footnote 4 of *United States v. Carolene Products,* the presumption of constitutionality attached to statutes, and relied upon by the *Gitlow* and *Whitney* majorities, was stripped from statutes restricting speech.[164] In *Kovacs v. Cooper,* the Court likewise emphasized that freedom of speech has a "preferred position" among the constitution's guarantees.[165] Several cases even adverted to the *Schenck* formulation of clear and present danger, or to the rationales advanced in the Holmes-Brandeis dissents, al-though without explicitly repudiating the majority opinions.[166]

---

162. *See Stromberg v. California,* 283 U.S. 359 (1931); *De Jonge v. Oregon,* 299 U.S. 353 (1937); *Herndon v. Lowry,* 301 U.S. 242 (1937).

163. The case law from this time period is both well known and voluminous. A complete exposition of these decisions would not serve the present project. Thus, only those cases that illuminate the evolution toward *Brandenburg* have been discussed, and other cases, including those that vindicate speech interests but do not involve subversive advocacy, are not discussed, such as *West Virginia Board of Education v. Barnette,* 319 U.S. 624 (1943) (overruling *Minersville School District v. Gobitis,* 310 U.S. 586 (1940), and invali-dating a regulation that mandated that public school students salute and pledge their allegiance to the nation's flag). Further, the evolution of classes of "low-value" speech, speech deemed to be outside of the scope of the First Amendment or to have only marginal protection (*see Chaplinsky v. New Hampshire,* 315 U.S. 568 (1942)), is outside the scope of this chapter, although this unfortunate evolution narrows the extent to which the tests discussed herein are *the* First Amendment tests.

  Although these omissions make it possible to focus on the continued evolution of the First Amendment rationale for or against censorship, they do present an artificially narrow view of the Court's political coalitions, especially of the brief harmony and sub-sequent dissonance of the justices appointed by Franklin D. Roosevelt. After a brief time of cooperation, those justices who were sympathetic with Felix Frankfurter's school of judicial deference to the legislature in cases involving civil liberties found themselves at loggerheads with their colleagues—spearheaded by Hugo L. Black and William O. Douglas—who believed in a more skeptical, independent approach. According to Doug-las, and to his and Black's biographers, the final rupture came with *Barnette. See* James F. Simon, *supra* note 143, at 7; Howard Ball & Philip Cooper, *Of Power and Right: Hugo L. Black, William O. Douglas, and America's Constitutional Revolution* (1992) at 108–109; *see generally,* H. N. Hirsh, *The Enigma of Felix Frankfurter* (1981) at 127–176.

  For a more complete history of the free speech jurisprudence between 1940 and 1970, *see* Kalven, *supra* note 1; Frank Strong, *Fifty Years of Clear and Present Danger,* 1969 S. Ct. Rev. 41 (1970).

164. 304 U.S. 144, 152, n. 4 (1938).

165. 336 U.S. 77, 88 (1949); *see also Thomas v. Collins,* 323 U.S. 516, 530 (1945).

166. *See,* for example, *Thornhill v. Alabama,* 310 U.S. 88, 104–105 (1940) (invalidating state statute prohibiting picketing) ("Abridgment of the liberty of such discussion [of mat-ters of public interest] can be justified only where the clear danger of substantive evils arises under circumstances affording no opportunity to test the merits of ideas by com-petition for acceptance in the market of public opinion"); *Terminiello v. Chicago,* 337 U.S. 1, 4–5 (1949) (reversing conviction for disorderly conduct).

Dennis v. United States: Speech Wins by Losing

Finally, in 1951, the Court explicitly adopted their rationale in *Dennis v. United States*, although the case was itself a blow to free speech, sustaining a conviction under the Smith Act.[167] *Dennis*'s failure to provide protection for speech in the context of the Red Scare of the 1950s[168] simply showed that the tradition was still in the process of refinement, that it had not reached its culmination.

The opinions in *Dennis* represent the next, and penultimate, step in the road to *Brandenburg*, a step that presents a surprisingly strong parallel to the conservative revolution delineated earlier. In *Dennis*, the Court upheld the application of the Smith Act to the organizers of the Communist Party of the United States of America for conspiring to organize "a society, group, and assembly of persons who teach and advocate the overthrow and destruction of the Government of the United States by force and violence,"[169] and for their advocacy of those principles. In reaching this decision, the plurality (the Court split 4–2–2, with Justice Tom C. Clark not participating) took a bold, even a radical, step forward.

Opining that "[n]o important case involving free speech was decided by this Court prior to *Schenck v. United States*,"[170] the Court bluntly stated that "[a]lthough no case subsequent to *Whitney* and *Gitlow* has expressly overruled the holdings in those cases, there is little doubt that subsequent opinions have inclined toward the Holmes-Brandeis rationale."[171] In rejecting the bad tendency test once and for all, the Court adopted the clear and present danger test—but, as in the first libertarian stride, with a catch. In *Dennis*, the catch was that the version of the clear and present danger test that the Court adopted bore little resemblance to any variant written by Holmes, Brandeis, or their colleagues. Instead, the Court accepted the formulation of Learned Hand, that "'[i]n each case courts must ask whether the gravity of the 'evil,' discounted by its improbability, justifies such invasion as is necessary to avoid the danger.'"[172] Thus, the courts must perform

---

167. 341 U.S. 494, 507 (1951); *see also Yates v. United States*, 354 U.S. 298, 320–324 (1957).
168. See Strong, *supra* note 163.
169. 341 U.S. at 497.
170. *Id.* at 494. Earlier, the popular misconception that free speech jurisprudence begins with *Schenck* was adverted to. Its genesis can quite fairly be traced to this statement by Chief Justice Vinson, which is followed by the gross oversimplification that "the summary treatment accorded an argument based upon an individual's claim that the First Amendment protected certain utterances indicates that the Court at earlier dates placed no unique emphasis on that right." *Id.*
171. *Id.* at 507.
172. *Id.* at 510 quoting *Dennis v. United States*, 183 F. 2d 201, 202 (2d Cir. 1950). As explained *supra* text at note 104 *et seq.* Hand's formulation treated conduct protected by

their own utilitarian calculus, balance the harms on an ad hoc basis, and constantly second-guess the state's decision that the balance tips *against* the speaker.

In the *Dennis* case itself, the Court found that free speech cannot mean that "before the government may act, it must wait until the *putsch* is laid."[173] Finding that the right to prevent revolution is not dependent upon the revolution's chance of success, the Court also stressed that the existence of a group "ready to make the attempt" more than nullified the argument that no attempt had been made.[174] Chief Justice Vinson concluded that "this analysis disposes of the contention that a conspiracy to advocate, as distinguished from the advocacy itself, cannot be constitutionally restrained, because it comprises only the preparation. It is the existence of the conspiracy which creates the danger."[175]

The end result of this balancing approach is a loss of that clarity said to be a prerequisite for criminal laws.[176] The fact that the same speech can be protected or proscribable depending on the subjective (and necessarily unprovable) judgment of the authorities that the speech may or may not, at some point of human history, lead to a harm that the legislature is empowered to prevent deprives the speaker of the clear notice that his or her conduct is about to cross the line into criminality that the Constitution mandates.

As before, after some preliminary rumblings, the conservative wing strode boldly forward, claiming to adopt the "Holmes-Brandeis view," but then thought better of it and backed away from the meaning of that bold stride. Just as clear and present danger melted back into bad tendency in the days of the Taft court, under Chief Justice Vinson, clear and present danger was again invoked, but then melted down to a haphazard balancing test.

The explicit affirmance and adoption of Hand's balancing approach grounded the Court's approach in a decidedly *non*constitutional type of analysis. The Court treated free speech as comparable to tortious conduct— a breed of conduct not insulated by any special level of protection.[177] Intriguingly, however, rather than adopt more traditional tort law reasoning,

---

a constitutional provision in just the same way as conduct not so protected, allowing *criminal* liability for speech under the identical circumstances as justify the imposition of *civil* liability for any form of action. The upshot of this is that speech is accorded no special treatment from any other act deemed to be criminal. *Id.*

173. 341 U.S. at 509.

174. *Id.* at 510.

175. *Id.* at 511.

176. *See United States v. Hudson & Goodwin*, 11 U.S. (7 Cranch) 32 (1812) (in reversing conviction of editors for seditious libel, Court rejected existence of common law federal crimes, mandating that federal crimes be legislatively defined).

177. *See* analysis of Hand opinion, *supra* text at note 104 *et seq.*

or criminal law reasoning, as had Holmes in the *Schenck* trilogy, the *Dennis* courts (Hand, and by adoption, Vinson) followed the logic of Hand's pioneering opinion in what has been deemed the first case to employ "Law and Economics" reasoning, *United States v. Carroll Towing.*[178] The adoption by the Supreme Court of essentially economic analysis to determine the scope of constitutional rights is reminiscent of more recent promptings to apply similar methods in non-business law contexts,[179] but its conflation of constitutionally protected conduct (speech) with unprotected conduct (harboring a toxic waste dump) renders it especially unconvincing.

The concurring opinion by Justice Frankfurter reflected a somewhat different understanding of the First Amendment. Frankfurter combined an unusual frankness with a willingness to disregard precedent. He began by candidly admitting that the Court's own prior "pronouncements" regarding clear and present danger "and their cumulative force has, not without justification, engendered belief that there is a constitutional principle, expressed by those attractive but imprecise words, prohibiting restriction upon utterance unless it creates a situation of imminent peril against which legislation may guard."[180] Frankfurter dutifully set out these statements that the usual standard by which the constitutionality of legislation is judged does not apply in free speech cases: "The rational connection between the remedy provided and the evil to be curbed, which in other contexts might support legislation against attack on due process ground, will not suffice."[181]

Denouncing these "uncritical libertarian generalities," Frankfurter conceded that the issue is one that required a careful answer, in view of the Court's prior statements.[182] He began by reviewing the various cases decided by the Court, dividing them into six categories: 1) use of public space for political speech; 2) restrictions on picketing; 3) deportation for expression of political views; 4) taxes on the press alone, and prior restraints on "libel"; 5) the Taft-Hartley Act's requirement that officers of unions who used the services of the National Labor Relations Board sign affidavits that they are not Communists; and 6) statutes prohibiting speech because of its tendency to lead to crime—the very issue involved in *Dennis.*[183]

---

178. *See supra* text at note 107. *Caroll Towing* has been so described by, among others, Posner, *A Theory of Negligence,* 1 J. Legal Stud. 29, 32–33 (1972), in which Judge Posner urges the adoption of economic analysis as a general means of determining tort liability.

179. *See,* for example, Posner, *An Economic Theory of Criminal Law,* 85 Colum. L. Rev. 1193 (1985) (urging adoption of economic analysis to determine substantive content of criminal law).

180. 341 U.S. at 527.

181. *Id.* at 526, *quoting Thomas v. Collins,* 323 U.S. at 530.

182. *Id.* at 527–528.

183. *Id.* at 529–535. Frankfurter reviewed the cases to synthesize what speech had been deemed protected and what had not, a project that led him to a brief survey of *holdings*

In reviewing this last category, Frankfurter recast Holmes's *Abrams* dissent as a difference "on its view of the evidence," failing to recognize any difference in the test applied by the Court from that advocated by Holmes and Brandeis.[184] In *Gitlow* and *Whitney,* Frankfurter did recognize a difference—the immediacy requirement.[185] Declining to reconcile these cases, Frankfurter contended that the Court had erred both in the favor of speech[186] and on the side of suppression.[187] From this grand array of decisions, he derived his own approach. Frankfurter urged that free speech cases were not to be given heightened scrutiny, but rather that the legislative judgment must be deferred to.[188] Frankfurter wistfully looked to *Gitlow,* but acknowledged that the dissent in that case had "been treated with the respect usually accorded to a decision."[189] He thus rejected the case's holding, but not its reasoning of judicial deference to the legislative will.[190] He rejected the clear and present danger rubric as an "oversimplified judgment unless it takes into account also a number of other factors: the relative seriousness of the danger in comparison with the value of the occasion for speech or political activity; the availability of more moderate controls than those which the state has imposed; and perhaps the specific intent with which the speech or activity is launched."[191] Frankfurter invoked the concept, first articulated in *Chaplinsky v. New Hampshire*[192] that not all speech deserves equal protec-

---

and not of rationales. That survey, while useful in its own terms—that is, to buttress Frankfurter's contention that the judicial branch must defer in these matters to the legislative—has little to do with the rationales advanced for the amendment, a process that has been worked out here. To put it more simply, Frankfurter, as a good Legal Realist, sought to demonstrate what courts have allowed; I have endeavored to explain why they have allowed it.

184. *Id.* at 535.
185. *Id.* at 536–537.
186. Frankfurter cited *Bridges v. California,* 314 U.S. 252 (1941) (reversing conviction of newspaper editor for criminal contempt based on harsh editorials urging judge toward particular result in case; the majority deemed strength against such pressure a prerequisite to properly filling a position on the bench, while Frankfurter saw the result as sacrificing the defendant's right to a fair trial to the press's right to free speech, a right Frankfurter deemed less urgent in the circumstances).
187. 341 U.S. at 539.
188. *Id.* at 539–541.
189. *Id.* at 541.
190. *Id.* 541–542.
191. *Id.* at 542–543, *quoting* Paul Freund, *On Understanding the Supreme Court,* at 27–28 (1949).
192. 315 U.S. 568, 571–572 (1949) (holding various categories of speech—"the lewd and the obscene, the profane, the libelous, and the insulting or 'fighting' words—those which by their very utterance inflict injury or tend to incite an immediate breach of the peace"—fall outside of the First Amendment as "low-value" speech and their proscription does not even raise a constitutional question). The decision in *Chaplinsky,* which ruled many classes of speech out of the First Amendment's scope, represents a major change in the jurisprudence, and one that impacts on the amendment's importance.

tion under the First Amendment. Where *Chaplinsky* drew a rough line, according speech either full protection or none whatsoever, Frankfurter applied a sliding scale that involved multiple levels of protection accorded to speech, which varied depending on the level of value accorded that speech by society.[193] Advocacy, Frankfurter stated (relying on *Fox v. Washington*), of violent overthrow of the government ranks low on the scale of valuable speech.[194]

For Frankfurter, then, the test was one of whether Congress, who has "the primary responsibility for reconciling" these conflicting values, did so in a rational manner.[195] Bearing in mind what he saw as the world-threatening danger of communism, Frankfurter found the Smith Act, while unwise and intolerant, to be well within the scope of the powers of Congress.[196] Frankfurter's concurrence is of more than historical interest, as his conception and justification of a balancing test would buttress the viability of the plurality's approach until *Brandenburg*.[197]

At some level, *Dennis* is a victory for free speech—and not only for the seeming resuscitation of clear and present danger and the repudiation of *Gitlow* and *Whitney*. Perhaps the most important result of *Dennis*, however, is that Frankfurter's opinion did not command a court. His subtle and sophisticated scale of values would, even more than the plurality's three-variable standard, have ushered in an age of utter subjectivity, in which "the speech that we hate" could be accorded minimal protection by a stroke of the pen, deeming it "low value," and protect all of it likely to be socially beneficial, and we could reassure ourselves that we value speech. Of course we do.

The *Dennis* Dissents

Justice Black's dissent in *Dennis* was quite short; running to only three pages, it nonetheless packs a punch wholly disproportionate to its size. Black took

---

That *Chaplinsky* disrupts the evolution of this jurisprudence is obvious, but it does so by narrowing the field of protected speech, not by altering the manner in which admittedly protected speech is treated.

193. 341 U.S. at 544–545.

194. *Id.* at 545. Frankfurter also declared that this was especially so as "no government can recognize a 'right' of revolution." *Id.* at 549. This seems peculiar in light of the explicit recognition of such a right in the Preamble to the Declaration of Independence, itself a deliberate act passed by the Continental Congress, and so one of the earliest constitutive documents of the United States. *See Declaration of Independence*, Preamble (1776).

195. 341 U.S. at 550–552.

196. *Id.* at 554–557.

197. Justice Jackson's unusually shrill and unpersuasive concurrence adds really nothing to the debate, treating the case as a criminal conspiracy, in spite of the lack of an overt act, one where the statute mandates no overt act, and that the conspiracy itself is a crime separate from any attempt to bring it to fruition. 341 U.S. at 561–579.

on Justice Jackson as a threshold matter, pointing out that Jackson's treat-ment of the case, based on the alleged conspiracy of the defendants to over-throw the government, was not reflective of the charge: The defendants were charged with conspiring to organize to advocate, and thus Jackson's ques-tion, whether Congress can punish subversive advocacy, was not to the point. The question before the Court was whether Congress may properly punish conspiring to organize with the purpose of eventually advocating—a far more remote danger than Jackson was willing to admit.[198]

Black then moved on to the issue as framed by Jackson and conceded that "a governmental policy of unfettered communication of ideas does entail dangers. To the Founders of this Nation, however," he continued, "the benefits derived from free expression were worth the risk. They embodied this philosophy in the First Amendment's command that 'Congress shall make no law . . . abridging the freedom of speech, or of the press. . . .'"[199] Black thus revived Holmes's notion that free speech is risky, that it is not for the faint of heart. Like Holmes, he asserted that this risk was necessary to "provide the best insurance against destruction of all freedom."[200] Black asserted that freedom and its risks are worth bear-ing for the benefits they bring us, a view reminiscent of Brandeis's view in *Whitney*.

But Black did more than merely rehash the views propounded by Holmes and Brandeis. He asserted that judicial restraint, the concept so reverently invoked by Frankfurter, actually mandated the reversal of Dennis's convic-tion. He denied that the clear and present danger test was a failure of judi-cial humility as Frankfurter asserted, saying that it "does no more than recog-nize a minimum compulsion of the Bill of Rights."[201] Moreover, he regarded the preference for freedom as one *not* left in the hands of the populace, but enshrined in the "command" of the First Amendment.

Finally, Black attacked the application of rational basis review to free speech cases. He observed that Frankfurter's approach "waters down the First Amendment so that it amounts to little more than an admonition to Congress." The amendment so construed, he noted, "is not likely to pro-tect any but those 'safe' or orthodox views which rarely need protection"[202]

Justice Douglas's dissent is interesting more for what it does not say than for what it does say. He did not yet advocate the First Amendment absolutism that has come to be thought of as his greatest legacy; indeed, he referred

---

198. *Id.* at 579.
199. *Id.* at 580.
200. *Id.*
201. *Id.*
202. *Id.*

approvingly to the obscenity doctrine limiting freedom of speech.[203] What Douglas did in *Dennis* was point out the fallacy of the majority that would allow teaching of Communist doctrine by those who do not believe in it, but punish the same teaching when done by a believer.[204] As Douglas pointed out:

> THE crime then depends not on what is taught but on who the teacher is. That is to make freedom of speech turn not on *what is said* but on the *intent* with which it is said. Once we start down that road we enter territory dangerous to the liberty of every citizen. . . .
>
> Intent, of course, often makes the difference in the law. An act otherwise excusable or carrying minor penalties may grow to an abhorrent thing if the evil intent is present. We deal here, however, not with ordinary acts but with speech, to which the Constitution has given a special sanction.[205]

Douglas set out the rationale for the nature of government as a precursor to a Brandeisian reliance on counterspeech wherever possible,[206] and then, in his peroration, began to draw a conclusion:

> THE First Amendment provides that Congress "shall make no law abridging the freedom of speech." The Constitution provides no exception. . . . Seditious conduct can always be punished. But the command of the First Amendment is so clear that we should not allow Congress to call a halt to free speech except in the extreme case of peril from the speech itself.[207]

Douglas was already beginning to move away from the clear and present danger test as propounded in the Holmes-Brandeis dissents, and toward the absolutism of his later years. The rest of the story is how he and Black pulled the majority with them past even the Holmes-Brandeis dissent version of clear and present danger and toward *Brandenburg*.

Yates, Scales, and *Noto*: Justice Harlan's Balancing Act

Dennis marks a turning point in the jurisprudence, but a peculiar one in that it is a way station to further developments. The next three opinions show

---

203. *Id.* at 581. For Douglas's absolutism as his greatest legacy, *see* Ball & Cooper, *supra* note 163 at 146–147; Melvin Urofsky, ed., *The Douglas Letters* (1987) at 196.
204. 341 U.S. at 583.
205. *Id.*
206. *Id.* at 584–586.
207. *Id.* at 590.

Justice John Marshall Harlan striving to apply the *Dennis* test, under increasingly strident fire from Black and Douglas. Along the way, the subjectivity of that test becomes even more clear.

In *Yates v. United States*,[208] Justice Harlan seemingly explicated *Dennis*, but in fact substantially limited its rule. Harlan stated that Chief Justice Vinson in *Dennis* had not meant to erase the "consistently recognized" distinction between advocacy of abstract doctrine and advocacy directed at promoting unlawful action, a distinction Harlan found in *Fox v. Washington* and one that he stated was "heavily underscored" in *Gitlow*.[209] Harlan went on to describe the "heart of *Dennis*":

> THE essence of the *Dennis* holding was that indoctrination of a group in preparation for violent future action, as well as exhortation to immediate action, by advocacy found to be directed to "action for the accomplishment" of forcible overthrow, to violence as "a rule or principle of action" and employing "language of incitement," . . . is not constitutionally protected when the group is of sufficient size and cohesiveness, is sufficiently oriented toward action, and other circumstances are such as reasonably to justify apprehension that action will occur. That is quite a different thing from the view . . . that mere doctrinal justification of forcible overthrow, if engaged in with the intent to accomplish overthrow is punishable *per se* under the Smith Act. That sort of advocacy, even though uttered with the hope that it might ultimately lead to violent revolution, is too remote from concrete action to be regarded as the kind of indoctrination preparatory to action which was condemned in *Dennis*.[210]

Harlan's recasting of *Dennis* is less than accurate; the language Harlan cited came from the *charge* upheld by the Court, and the opinion's own discussion of advocacy leads, as we have seen, to an entirely different conclusion. Harlan did also point out Vinson's statement that there could be no conviction for "advocacy in the realm of ideas."[211] However, the full state-

---

208. 354 U.S. 298 (1956) (reversing conviction under Smith Act for various grounds, including that judge's charge intimated that act banned simple advocacy of communist ideas).

209. *Id.* at 318. In relying on *Gitlow*, Harlan quoted the Court's statement in that case that "the statute [the Espionage Act] does not penalize the utterance or publication of abstract 'doctrine' or academic discussion having no quality of incitement to any concrete action." *Id.* Harlan did concede, however, that the *Gitlow* court took a "narrow view" of the First Amendment. *Id.* In fact, the *Gitlow* court simply used these qualifications to show how moderate the Espionage Act is, and to separate what issues were *not* before it. There is no reason to believe that the bad tendency test of *Schaefer* and *Gitlow* would except advocacy if Congress chose to punish it.

210. *Id.* at 321–322, quoting *Dennis*, 341 U.S. at 511–512.

211. *Id.* at 297, *quoting Dennis*, 341 U.S. at 502.

ment—which also merely described the charge—is that "they [the jury] could not convict if they found the petitioners did 'no more than pursue peaceful studies and discussions or teaching and advocacy in the realm of ideas,'" a statement that shows that the "advocacy" referred to is not that of belief but the bloodless setting out of a concept by a nonbeliever.[212] Moreover, as if there were any doubt, the statement Harlan relied upon follows the blunt statement that the Smith Act "is directed at advocacy, not discussion."[213] Indeed, Justice Clark chided the majority's restatement of *Dennis*, stating that he could "see no resemblance between it and what the respected Chief Justice wrote in *Dennis*, nor do I see any such theory in the concurring opinions."[214] It is difficult not to agree with him.

In *Yates*, then, a new element has been added to the mixture. In addition to the balancing mandated by *Dennis*, the courts must distinguish between "advocacy or teaching of abstract doctrines, with evil intent, and that which is directed to stirring people to action"—even if the action is remote in time.[215] This distinction, admitted by Harlan to be "fine," seems nonexistent. Because the "evil intent" involved is said to be "specific intent to accomplish overthrow,"[216] Harlan was saying that it is different to urge people to overthrow the government while hoping that they will overthrow it than it is to urge people to overthrow the government while hoping that it will be overthrown. Surely this is the sort of logic that leads to cotillions on the heads of pins.

Of course, it can be argued that what Justice Harlan was really trying to do was drag the Court a little further from the subjective, free-floating balancing approach of *Dennis*—that he was seeking a way to retain its flexibility, but to find a means by which patently harmless speech could be protected. Harlan found that method by subtly rewriting *Dennis*, teasing from it a distinction that had been arguably drawn in *Fox*, and that could be used to create a commonsense exception to *Dennis*'s world in which all speech had to be balanced before its status was known.

Certainly the distinction that Harlan drew is one for the protection of speech. In addition to providing the one reversal of a conviction seen so far, by separating "advocacy" from "incitement," Harlan provided a rubric under which to protect antigovernment speech, albeit a murky one.

The concurrence by Black, in which Douglas joined, showed no retreat from their positions in *Dennis*. Black put his absolutist view, not explicated in *Dennis*, quite succinctly:

---

212. 341 U.S. at 502.
213. *Id.*
214. 354 U.S. at 350 (Clark, J. dissenting).
215. *Id.* at 326.
216. *Id.* at 320.

THE Court says that persons can be punished for advocating action
to overthrow the Government by force and violence, where those to
whom the advocacy is addressed are urged "to *do* something, now or
in the future, rather than merely to *believe* in something." Under the
Court's approach, defendants could still be convicted simply for
agreeing to talk as distinguished from agreeing to act. I believe that
the First Amendment forbids Congress to punish people for talking
about public affairs, whether or not such discussion incites to action,
legal or illegal. As the Virginia Assembly said in 1785, in its "Statute
for Religious Liberty," written by Thomas Jefferson, "it is time enough
for the rightful purposes of civil government, for its officers to interfere when principles break out into overt acts against peace and good
order."[217]

In *Yates*, then, the conflict is stark and sharp. Harlan and the majority
tinkered with *Dennis* in the hope of creating a clear and present danger
approach that protected speech enough to allow legitimate dissent but was
flexible enough to allow the government to quell "dangerous" speech. Black
and Douglas on the other side asserted the legitimacy of *all* dissent, even
that which questions the very heart of our political order. They even rejected
clear and present danger—perhaps due to its dilution by the majority.

In *Scales v. United States*,[218] Harlan clarified the impact of *Yates*. "*Dennis*
and *Yates*," he wrote, "have definitely laid to rest any doubt that present
advocacy of *future* action for violent overthrow satisfies statutory and constitutional requirements equally with advocacy of *immediate* action to that
end."[219] In clarifying what constituted such advocacy, as opposed to protected
"abstract advocacy," Harlan stated that the Smith Act offenses, "involving as
they do subtler elements than are present in most other crimes, call for strict
standards in assessing the adequacy of the proof needed to make out a case
of illegal advocacy."[220]

As a threshold matter, this shows a willingness on Harlan's part to admit
that *Yates* was not the mere restatement of *Dennis* that it claimed to be—the
opinion did add, if only implicitly, a higher burden of proof. Moreover, by
distinguishing between "harmless" advocacy of violent overthrow and dangerous advocacy, Harlan added—what? Perhaps an unstated, but real recognition that some subversive advocacy is simply beneath the notice of the

217. *Id.* at 340 (Black, J., concurring in part) (citations omitted).
218. 367 U.S. 203 (1960) (upholding application of Smith Act provision prohibiting knowing membership in organization advocating violent overthrow of government to Communist Party member).
219. *Id.* at 251.
220. *Id.* at 232. Harlan admitted that this view was "not articulated in the [*Yates*] opinion,
though perhaps it should have been." *Id.*

Court or is endemic to the political process. It is perhaps helpful to recall Vinson's (and Jackson's) repetitive use of the conspiracy doctrine against the Communist Party. Harlan may well have been striving to exempt non-conspiratorial, nonactive Communists from the strictures which he felt were properly applied to members of the Communist Party.

Harlan's distinction in *Scales* between active and nonactive members in the Communist Party appears to bear this out. The latter, he writes, may well be "foolish, deluded, or perhaps merely optimistic, but he is not, by this statute, made a criminal."[221] To exempt these individuals, perhaps, or because he genuinely saw the ultrafine distinction between these two forms of advocacy of violent overthrow as weighty, Harlan specified what does *not* in itself constitute sufficient proof to show illegal advocacy:

> THIS category includes evidence of the following: teaching of Marxism-Leninism and the connected use of Marxist "classics" as textbooks; the official general resolutions and pronouncements of the Party at past conventions; dissemination of the Party's general literature, including the standard outlines on Marxism; the Party's history and organizational structure; the secrecy of meetings and the clandestine nature of the Party generally; statements by officials evidencing sympathy for and alliance with the U.S.S.R.[222]

In dissent, Justice Black chided the Court for having "practically rewritten" the statute to require activity and specific intent prior to penalizing membership in the Party. Black argued persuasively that by so doing, the Court impermissibly transformed a provision void on its face into a valid one, in effect itself passing an *ex post facto* law—the defendant's right to be tried under a clearly defined, preexisting law was vitiated.[223] Black then passed to his more fundamental objection to the majority's approach. The majority, he stated, sought to have it both ways. First, it claimed that only when no "direct" abridgement of First Amendment freedoms is involved, the proper test to be applied is the balancing of harms first introduced in *Dennis.* Yet, Black noted, the defendant here had been sentenced to six years' imprisonment for his association with those who "have entertained unlawful ideas and said unlawful things, and that of course is a *direct* abridgment of his freedoms of speech and assembly."[224] Thus, Black doubted that the majority only applied the balancing test to cases not involving direct abridgement.[225]

---

221. *Id.* at 230.
222. *Id.* at 232.
223. *Id.* at 260–261 (Black, J., dissenting).
224. *Id.* at 261 (emphasis in original).
225. This criticism of the majority seems a trifle unfair. Although Black did adduce support for the proposition that the balancing test only is involved in "indirect" cases,

Black strongly rebuked the majority for "balancing away" First Amendment freedoms, arguing that:

> THE question in every case in which a First Amendment right has been asserted is not whether there has been an abridgment of that right, not whether the abridgment of that right was intentional on the part of the Government, and not whether there is any other way in which the Government could accomplish a lawful aim without an invasion of the constitutionally guaranteed rights of the people. It is, rather, simply whether the Government has an interest in abridging the right asserted, and, if so, whether that interest is of sufficient importance, in the opinion of a majority of this Court, to justify the Government's action in doing so. This doctrine, to say the least, is capable of being used to justify almost any action Government may wish to take in suppressing First Amendment freedoms.[226]

Here, surely, Black was correct. Because the "distinction" Harlan drew was elusive at best, and quite possibly nonexistent,[227] it is difficult to deduce any limiting principle save for Harlan's personal judgment that the speech in *Yates* was harmless and that in *Scales* was not.

Douglas's dissent reviewed the evidence, coming to the conclusion that "[n]ot one single illegal act is charged to petitioner. That is why the essence of the crime covered by the indictment is merely belief—belief in the proletarian revolution, belief in the Communist creed."[228] Reviewing the long tradition against punishing belief,[229] Douglas pointed out also that the right to rebel had been long honored, although society's right to prevent armed revolt had also been recognized.[230] He pointed out that the Court, in denying that it was punishing belief, nonetheless "speaks of the prevention of 'dangerous behavior' by punishing those 'who work to bring about that behavior.'"[231] Like Black, he concluded that the whole concept of "balancing" was at fault:

> WE have too often been "balancing" the right of speech and association against other values in society to see if we, the judges, feel a par-

---

Dennis seems quite fairly to stand for its across-the-board application. *See* text *supra* at notes 168 *et seq.*

226. *Scales*, 367 U.S. at 262 [Black, J. dissenting).
227. *See* text *supra* at notes 218–222.
228. 367 U.S. at 265 (Douglas, J. dissenting).
229. *Id.* at 265–268.
230. *Id.* at 269–273 (*citing, inter alia,* Thomas Jefferson and James Madison).
231. *Id.* at 270.

ticular need is more important than those guaranteed by the Bill of Rights.[232]

Balancing, which for Frankfurter and Harlan represented an act of judicial humility, was for Douglas an act of arrogance, a usurpation of the prerogatives of the Framers of the Constitution, who in adopting the First Amendment struck the balance already—struck it in favor of speech.[233]

On the same day that *Scales* was decided, the Court reversed a conviction under the same provision in *Noto v. United States*.[234] In *Noto*, the court found that the membership provision of the Smith Act had not been violated by a Communist Party member who had made inflammatory comments. These comments included the statement that "[s]ometime I will see the time we can stand a person like this S.O.B. against the wall and shoot him."[235] Harlan's treatment of this statement as not advocating future violence, but as mere venom, muddied the already untenable distinction drawn by the Court between lawful and unlawful advocacy. Despite the fact that the defendant's statements, in conjunction with his speeches advocating violent overthrow of the government, fell clearly within the boundaries of proscribable speech under *Dennis*, *Scales*, and *Yates*, the Court reversed the conviction.

Plainly, by this stage, the Court's approach to determining what speech that advocated violence was dangerous and what was not had degenerated to a subjective approach akin to that of Justice Stewart in deciding what is and what is not obscene: It knew it when it saw it.[236]

Brandenburg: Who Shall Claim the Victory?

In 1969 the Court decided *Brandenburg v. Ohio*.[237] The case came from the conviction, under the Ohio Criminal Syndicalism statute that prohibited the advocacy of violent change, of the leader of a Ku Klux Klan group. The speech involved statements such as "bury the niggers" and "if our President our Congress our Supreme Court continues to suppress the white Caucasian race, its possible that there might have to be some revengance [*sic*] taken."[238]

---

232. *Id.* at 270–271.
233. That this view was shared by Black is also evident. *See Dennis, supra* text at note 199; H. L. Black, *A Constitutional Faith* (1968) at 50–51.
234. 367 U.S. 290 (1960).
235. *Id.* at 296. At least one other similar statement by the defendant had been introduced into evidence.
236. *See Jacobellis v. Ohio*, 378 U.S. 184, 197 (1964) (Stewart, J., concurring).
237. 395 U.S. 444 (1969).
238. *Id.* at 446.

The Court reversed the conviction in a short (six-page) per curiam opinion. Admitting that the statute was "quite similar" to that upheld in *Whitney*, the Court reiterated that "*Whitney* has been thoroughly discredited by later decisions," citing *Dennis*.[239] The Court then summarized these "later decisions" in a manner surprising to anyone familiar with them: "The Constitutional guarantees of free speech and free press do not permit a state to forbid or proscribe advocacy of the use of force or of law violation except where such advocacy is directed to inciting or producing imminent lawless action or is likely to incite or produce such action."[240]

At the very least, in *Brandenburg* the Court substantially revised the standard. It eliminated Harlan's efforts to distinguish between "good" advocacy and "bad" advocacy of unlawful conduct. But in fact it did much more. The basic holding of *Dennis* was overruled. The vision of "clear and present danger" adopted was that of the later Holmes and Brandeis dissents, complete with the imminence requirement. Indeed, the specific intent requirement that Holmes flirted with and that Learned Hand enunciated in *Masses* was also read into the standard.

Black and Douglas concurred in the result only, emphasizing that in their view "clear and present danger" had proved to be too amorphous a standard. Douglas emphasized, after pointing out the dilution this standard had suffered in the past, that only those rare cases in which speech and the resulting action are inseparable—cases of "speech brigaded with action"—are properly subject to prosecution.[241] In such cases, it is the overt act which is prosecuted and not the speech save insofar as it is the trigger for that act. The actor under those circumstances, it is fair to say, has become the agent of the speaker.[242]

---

239. *Id.* at 447.
240. *Id.* The Court relied on *Yates* in its decision and quoted *Noto* to the effect that "the mere abstract teaching . . . of the moral propriety or even moral necessity for a resort to force and violence, is not the same as preparing a group for violent action and steeling it to such action." *Id.* at 448, quoting *Noto*, 367 U.S. at 297–298.
241. *Id.* at 445–457.
242. *See* Douglas, *supra* note 55, at 23. Such a requirement was prefigured in *Gompers's* concept of the "verbal act," which could, unlike speech in the ordinary course, be prosecuted. Another preview of Douglas's standard, the standard that I argue the Court has essentially adopted, was presented in *Fox v. Washington, supra* note 44, where the Court stated that the statute in question "lays hold of encouragements that apart from statute, if directed to a particular person's conduct, generally would make him who uttered them guilty of a misdemeanor if not an accomplice or a principal in the crime encouraged and deals with the publication of them to a wider and less selected audience." 236 U.S. at 277–288. Although the *Fox* Court did not use the concept as a limiting principle, it may have acted as a spur to Douglas's analysis, especially as the verbal acts concept was so used in *Gompers*.

Despite Douglas's reservations about the *Brandenburg* rule,[243] the rule seems to indeed encapsulate Douglas's requirement that the speaker-audience relationship be analogous to that of principal and agent. The imminence and specific intent requirement capture that dynamic nicely; liability only attaches when the speaker *knows* the audience will act as a result of the speech, and *intends* that it should do so. Under such circumstances, particularly given the lack of time for the audience to reflect (the imminence requirement), the audience can be truly said to be acting under the direction of the speaker and in fulfillment of his or her will.[244] Despite the Court's refusal to explicitly adopt the Black-Douglas rational, the opinion seems to have done so *sub silentio.*

CONCLUSION

Along the long road to *Brandenburg*, the cause of free speech went through many gains and setbacks, repeatedly receiving lip service in the process of being watered down to uphold a given conviction. From the common law tradition in which the state could punish any publication it chose, provided it first allowed publication (adding a new dimension to "publish or perish") to the Conservative Revolution above described, the First Amendment seemed a paltry thing. With the birth of substantive protection and the evolution of "clear and present danger" a new day seemed at hand. But the Court backed away from its radical stride, leaving Justices Holmes and Brandeis to work out many of the meanings of free speech in dissent. In the 1950s, the Court repeated this sleight-of-hand process, overruling *Whitney* and singing the praises of Holmes and Brandeis, while emptying their standard of virtually all its meaning. Yet again, it took a duet of dissenters' efforts to haul the majority to a standard that protected speech.

That the evolving First Amendment jurisprudence was a Socratic dialogue between the American populace and the Supreme Court was a conceit first postulated by Harry Kalven.[245] Perhaps it is more appropriate to compare this evolution to a Socratic dialogue among the members of the Court itself. Those justices who would afford the protecting of speech a high ranking in our scheme of constitutional values have consistently prodded, ques-

---

243. Douglas's reservations did not decrease over time, but rather grew more profound. In *The Supreme Court and the Bicentennial, supra* note 55, Douglas stated that "[a]ll of the objections to the 'clear and present danger' test are equally applicable to the new *Brandenburg* test." *Id.* at 22.

244. See Douglas, *supra* note 55, at 23; Wirenius, *supra* note 4, at 70–71.

245. Kalven, *A Worthy Tradition, supra* note 1.

tioned, and even fulminated against the more wary of their colleagues, who feared for the stability of a truly free state. By this continual probing of the weaknesses and inconsistencies of the censorial mind, the dissenters were able to bring the majority to their point of view.

It would be foolhardy to postulate that this evolution is at an end, although in which direction the tradition will evolve cannot easily be predicted. All that one can say with certainty is that the dialectic will continue, that both speech and repression will find new champions.

3

The Road Not Taken

The Curse of *Chaplinsky*

FIRST AMENDMENT JURISPRUDENCE has been depicted as a tradition in which the Supreme Court has evolved settled rules of law through case-by-case adjudication in the classic common law manner.[1] However, this notion of a "Socratic dialogue" between either the Supreme Court and the American people[2] or between different blocs of the Court itself,[3] has one very serious flaw; it does not explain the bizarre mess that is current First Amendment jurisprudence.

This characterization may seem at first to be unduly harsh, but a more charitable terminology simply fails to convey the regrettable lack of coherence in the way that First Amendment claims are resolved. The United States prides itself on the centrality it accords freedom of speech, and yet our First Amendment jurisprudence ranges across the broadest possible spectrum. It allows the suppression of some speech without any but the most cursory judicial review, holds the suppression of other kinds of speech up to mild scrutiny, and exposes a third set of speech categories to very exacting scrutiny indeed. This multilayered jurisprudence is ostensibly necessary to fulfil the First Amendment's seemingly simple and uniform mandate that "Congress shall make no law abridging . . . the freedom of speech."[4]

The Supreme Court has established not one test, or even several related tests to measure the degree of protection accorded to speech, but rather a

---

1. *See* Wirenius, *The Road to Brandenburg* 43 Drake L. Rev. 1 (1994). The analogy was best made by Harry Kalven, Jr., in *A Worthy Tradition* (1988), although it also owes something to Thomas Emerson's *The System of Freedom of Expression* (1970).
2. *See* Kalven, *supra* note 1, at xiii.
3. My own notion; *see* Wirenius, *supra* note 1, at 49.
4. U.S. Const., Amend. I (1791).

series of pigeonholes into which various forms of expressive conduct are slotted. The appropriate degree of protection to be extended to the conduct depends upon into which pigeonhole the speech at issue is fitted. The levels of protection range from requiring a compelling state interest and the use of the least restrictive means that will vindicate that interest in order to justify suppression to the bare requirement that the state be able to articulate a rational basis for asserting the expressive conduct to be harmful at some level to some interest that the government involved has a right to protect. Thus, the level of protection mandated by the First Amendment ranges from the most to the least exacting degree of scrutiny of governmental conduct provided under the Constitution.

This incredible range of levels of protection is justified, not by the text of the First Amendment, or by history, but by vague references to the "values" served by the First Amendment, and sometimes to its "core values."[5] The end result is that a given instance of speech is fitted into one of a selection of categories, which are, more or less arbitrarily, deemed to be protected, unprotected, or somewhere in the middle.

These categories—although some have been dropped, and others added—essentially originated in *Chaplinsky v. New Hampshire*, in which the Court declared by fiat, as it were, that "[t]here are certain well-defined and limited classes of speech, the prevention and punishment of which have never been thought to raise any constitutional problem. These include the lewd and obscene, the profane, the libelous, and the insulting or 'fighting' words—those which by their very utterance inflict injury or tend to incite an immediate breach of the peace."[6] The sole rationale offered for this remarkable statement—that some speech is more equal than other speech—was based in a rough functional logic and was not tethered to the constitutional language:

> IT has been well observed that such utterances are no essential part of any exposition of ideas, and are of such slight social value as a step to truth that any benefit that may be derived from them is clearly outweighed by the social interest in order and morality. "Resort to epithets or personal abuse is not in any proper sense communication of information or opinion safeguarded by the Constitution, and its punishment as a criminal act would raise no question under that instrument."[7]

---

5. *See*, for example, *New York Times v. Sullivan*, 376 U.S. 254 (1964).
6. 315 U.S. 568, 571 (1941) (upholding conviction of Jehovah's Witness for calling city marshal "a God damned racketeer" and "damned fascist").
7. *Id.* at 572, quoting *Cantwell v. Connecticut*, 310 U.S. 296, 309 (1940).

What is astonishing about this dictum is the casual ease with which the Court brushed aside the constitutional question, and the breadth of its doctrine. With a single stroke, the Court purported to settle not only the case at hand, but the questions of obscenity, libel, and "lewd" speech.

The impact of *Chaplinsky* can scarcely be overestimated. The slowly maturing and essentially coherent *functional* tradition that was emerging, and had been doing so since the formation of the republic,[8] was at a blow shattered and replaced with a highly subjective jurisprudence that ranked speech by its "value" (in the opinion of the individual justices on the Court at the time). Indeed, subjectivity infected the process at both stages; whether a category of speech has constitutional value is as murky a question as which category a particular sample of speech falls into. Why commercial speech should or should not be accorded "high-value" protection or treated as "low-value" speech is as little subject to rational defense as Justice Stewart's infamous definition of obscenity—the good justice simply knows it when he sees it.[9]

The end result is that categorization—classifying the speech in terms of pigeonholes whose status as "exceptions" to the First Amendment is predetermined—has replaced the *Brandenburg* analysis, which provides a functional examination of the speech in the terms of the values of the amendment and of the role of the speech to be regulated. In short, classifying has replaced thinking. In no area have the justices of the Supreme Court so usurped the positions of Platonic guardians as in interpreting the First Amendment. This chapter will seek to demonstrate the damage caused by *Chaplinsky*'s ever-spreading dominance in the jurisprudence. Although what might be called (with apologies to Immanuel Kant) the *Chaplinsky* categorical imperative began as a means of brushing away pesky questions of law that

---

8. This chapter builds from Chapter 2's contention that the First Amendment's evolution was both simpler and more complex than is usually depicted. The simplicity comes from the depiction of a coherent if gradual evolution from a Blackstonian common law model at the time of the Sedition Act of 1798 (at which time the dominant view was that the First Amendment forbade only prior restraint) to the model of substantive protection currently in force, in which no idea may be banned and only intended concrete harms directly resulting from speech may be made the subject of legal sanction.

The complexity comes from the recognition of the many steps along that path, several of which raise intriguing alternative models of federal-state relations that the evolution of the jurisprudence has choked off. For example, at one point the Court seemed ready to simply withdraw from the business of regulating speech altogether, but declaring that the states had plenary power over the subject. *See United States v. Cruikshank*, 92 U.S. 542 (1875). This approach had the advantage of closely tracking the amendment's language, "*Congress* shall make no law," and of answering the Anti-Federalist's fears that this new government would exercise too much power and would tyrannize over the citizenry, in contrast to the states who could be trusted by virtue of their smaller size to be more receptive to the popular will. *See* Alexander Hamilton, et al., *The Federalist Papers*, Nos. 10, 28, 41, 47, 51.

9. *See Jacobellis v. Ohio*, 378 U.S. 148, 195 (1966) (Stewart, J. concurring).

were thought to be as unimportant as they were vexatious, it has become more and more the centerpiece of the jurisprudence. The context in which this approach was first taken will be examined, and then the evolution (and sometimes the devolution) of the initial categories that have been deemed to be nonspeech for First Amendment purposes can be examined. From there, the more recently created multitiered structure of the jurisprudence can be placed in its proper context. Finally, the validity of the entire *Chaplinsky* approach can be assessed in terms of the First Amendment's language, the values that the amendment has been thought to serve, and the goals purportedly served by suppression of speech.

THE CURSE DESCENDS: *CHAPLINSKY* IN CONTEXT

The Court decided *Chaplinsky* in 1942, the same year in which—indeed, less than a month after—President Franklin Roosevelt signed Executive Order 9066, authorizing the Secretary of War to establish military zones from which Japanese Americans and resident aliens would be excluded.[10] The same month that the Court handed down *Chaplinsky*—March 1942—Congress passed legislation premised upon Order 9066 that authorized criminal penalties for violating military orders, and General J. L. DeWitt began to issue a series of such orders establishing curfews for Japanese Americans, who were ordered to relocation camps.[11] In short, the country was beset with war fever, including the administration that had appointed seven of the Justices—Black (1937), Reed (1938), Frankfurter (1939), Douglas (1939), Murphy (1940), Byrnes (1941), and Jackson (1941).[12] All of these jurists were in one way or another closely affiliated with the president. Black and Byrnes were two key senatorial allies of the president—indeed, Black was one of the few senators to support Roosevelt's Court-packing plan—while the remainder served as members of his administration or as key advisers.[13]

---

10. *See* Roger Daniels, Sandra Taylor, & Henry Kitano, eds., *Japanese Americans: From Relocation to Redress* (1986); Howard Ball & Philip Cooper, *Of Power and Right: Hugo Black, William O. Douglas, and America's Constitutional Revolution* (1992) at 109–110.

11. Ball & Cooper, *supra* note 10, at 110.

12. Paul Freund, et al., *Constitutional Law, Cases and Problems* (1977) at xxxiii; Melvin Urofsky, *Conflict Among the Brethren: Felix Frankfurter, William O. Douglas, and the Clash of Personalities and Philosophies*, 1988 Duke L. J. 71. *See also* Urofsky, *Division and Discord; The Supreme Court under Vinson and Stone, 1941–1953* (1997) at 47–84.

13. Hugo Black's support for the Court-packing plan is set out in Ball & Cooper, *supra* note 10, at 56–57, 73–74. *See generally* Roger K. Newman, *Hugo Black: A Biography* (1994) at 210–214; for Roosevelt's appreciation of Black's loyalty, *see id.* at 228. Felix Frankfurter held no official position save that of Harvard professor of law, but prided himself on his role as one of Roosevelt's advisers in various legal areas, both before and after his ap-

With their former principal or ally leading the nation into an almost apocalyptic conflict against totalitarianism, even the justices were under some pressure—the hydraulic pressure of the times, not unethical influence-peddling—to conform. In fact, Justices Black, Douglas and Murphy would be led in this period to swallow their own beliefs in the name of national morale to vote with Frankfurter on several occasions in the trampling of minority rights.[14] In the context of these major upheavals, the fledgling justices—seven of whom had been appointed within half a decade prior to issuing the *Chaplinsky* opinion—must have viewed the case as very small beer indeed.

Contemporary evidence buttresses this argument; *Chaplinsky* is a remarkably brief opinion, consisting of a mere five pages. Moreover, the opinion's author, Justice Frank Murphy, was no legal craftsman; he believed that substantive results were more important than technical correctness. Normally,

---

pointment to the Court (*see* William Leuchtenberg, *Franklin D. Roosevelt and the New Deal* [1963] at 64; Bruce Allen Murphy, *The Brandeis-Frankfurter Connection* (1981) at 247–341). Robert H. Jackson had served in multiple posts under Roosevelt, including solicitor general and attorney general. Eugene Gerhart, *America's Advocate: Robert H. Jackson* (1958) at 62–229. William O. Douglas had been both a commissioner and the chairman of the Securities and Exchange Commission. *See* Bruce Allen Murphy, *Wild Bill: The Legend and Life of William O. Douglas* (2003); James Simon, *Independent Journey: The Life of William O. Douglas* (1980) at 139–194; Ball & Cooper *supra* note 10 at 45–50. Frank Murphy served as attorney general in 1939 until his appointment to the Court. See J. Woodford Howard, *Mr. Justice Murphy* (1968) at 203–228. Stanley Reed served as solicitor general. Ball & Cooper, *supra* note 10 at 27.

14. In *Minersville School District v. Gobitis,* 310 U.S. 586 (1940) the three justices voted with the majority to compel the children of Jehovah's Witnesses to salute the flag despite their claim that such a salute violated the scriptural prohibition against bowing to graven images, and that the right to free exercise of religion exempted them from the salute and the accompanying Pledge of Allegiance. In 1942, Douglas, Black, and Murphy admitted their error in *Jones v. Opelika,* 316 U.S. 584 (1942). Douglas attributed their joining the *Gobitis* majority to pressure from Frankfurter, who emphasized the need for conformity against the surge in totalitarianism. William O. Douglas, *The Court Years* (1980) at 44–45; *see also* Simon, *Independent Journey supra* note 13, at 205–209 ("Frankfurter's argument had persuaded every Roosevelt appointee"); James Simon, *The Antagonists: Hugo L. Black, Felix Frankfurter and Civil Liberties in America* (1989) at 106–114. That the powerful presentation of Chief Justice Charles Evans Hughes may have helped sway Black (and, also Douglas, who profoundly respected Hughes, the chief justice by whom Douglas would measure all of his successors and find none comparable save for Warren) is contended in Newman, *Hugo Black, supra* note 13, at 284–285.

In any event, these errors of the era surrounding the war did not cease in 1942. Douglas came to bitterly regret his concurrence in *Korematsu v. United States,* 323 U.S. 214 (1944) (upholding involuntary internment of Japanese Americans as potential subversives) and in *Hirabayashi v. United States,* 320 U.S. 81 (1943) (upholding curfew imposed solely on Japanese Americans). *The Court Years* at 39, 280; Ball & Cooper, *supra* note 10, at 115. Douglas acted from his concern that "the disastrous bombing of Pearl Harbor made an invasion of the West Coast a real threat." Simon, *supra* note 13, at 243. Murphy's vote was the result of unremitting pressure from Frankfurter and Reed. Howard, *supra* note 13, at 308.

of course, this approach worked in *favor* of civil liberties, and not against them; as Murphy wrote in cutting through a flurry of technical objections, "the law knows no finer hour than when it cuts through formal concepts and transitory emotions to protect unpopular citizens against discrimination and persecution."[15]

The poor workmanship of the opinion is evident in the very breadth of the statement that has led to the multitiered jurisprudence currently in force. More fundamentally, the statement is pure dictum, in that it is entirely unnecessary to the resolution of the case. *Chaplinsky* involved a Jehovah's Witness who, warned by a city marshal that a crowd hostile to his views was "getting restless," allegedly denounced him as a "God damned racketeer" and a "fascist."[16] Using state court decisions, the Court found that the statute under which Chaplinsky was prosecuted:

> DOES no more than prohibit the face-to-face words likely to cause a breach of the peace by the addressee, words whose speaking constitutes a breach of the peace by the speaker—including "classical fighting words," words in current use less "classical" but equally likely to cause violence, and other disorderly words, including profanity, obscenity and threats.[17]

As a result, the Court concluded, the statute was "a statute narrowly drawn and limited to define and punish specific conduct lying within the domain of state power, the use in a public place of words likely to cause a breach of the peace."[18] Under the basic First Amendment test, that enunciated by Justice Holmes in *Schenck v. United States,* the statute would be found constitutional if it was shown that the speech sought to be proscribed presented a clear and present danger of a substantive evil—such as violence—that the

---

15. *Falbo v. United States,* 320 U.S. 549, 561 (1943) (dissenting from Court's affirmance of Jehovah's Witness's conviction for disobedience of draft board's order to report to local draft board for an assignment as a conscientious objector to "work of national importance"). This attitude stands in sharp contrast to that of Justices Brandeis and Holmes, who, in *Whitney v. California,* 274 U.S. at 357, 372 (1927) (Brandeis and Holmes, JJ. concurring), argued in one of the most impassioned, eloquent opinions in the United States Reports that the conviction of Anita Whitney under a state "Criminal Syndicalism Act" was unconstitutional, and then voted to uphold the conviction on technical grounds.

16. 315 U.S. at 569–570. Chaplinsky's account was different; he admitted directing the insults at the marshal (although he stated that he did not invoke the name of the Deity), but that he did so only after the marshal first cursed him and arrested him after Chaplinsky asked that the people responsible for the disturbance—the "restless" crowd—be arrested. *Id.* at 570.

17. *Id.* at 573, quoting *State v. Brown,* 68 N.H. 200 (1895).

18. *Id.*

state had a right to prevent.[19] Thus, the Court's holding that Chaplinsky's speech was not protected because it consisted of "epithets likely to provoke the average person to retaliation" really amounts to little more than an application of the clear and present danger doctrine, albeit in the context of a speaker who provoked a *hostile* audience reaction as opposed to a desired audience reaction.[20]

Murphy's opinion not only fit the suppression of Chaplinsky's speech comfortably within the confines of the applicable jurisprudence; he then went on to anticipate William O. Douglas's eventual distinction between "speech," which he would state could not be suppressed at all, and "speech brigaded with action," which he would allow to be suppressed if the action of which it formed a part were proscribable under the applicable substantive law.[21] Similarly, Murphy relied upon an earlier version of this concept that he found first enunciated in *Fox v. Washington*,[22] that a "statute punish-

---

19. 249 U.S. 47 (1919). For the complex evolution of the *Schenck* test into the standard used today, and for its status as the operative test at the time *Chaplinsky* was decided, *see* Wirenius, *supra* note 1 at 17.

20. This problem still dogs First Amendment doctrine; Harry Kalven called it the "reflexive disorder" and came reluctantly to the conclusion that such speech could be prosecuted. Kalven *supra* note 1, at 77–106; 116–118. The Court, insofar as it has considered the issue, appears to agree. See *Gooding v. Wilson*, 405 U.S. 518 (1972) (invalidating statute as overbroad as not limited "as in *Chaplinsky*" to words having "a direct tendency to cause acts of violence by the person to whom, individually, the remark is addressed"). *Id.* at 524. For myself, it seems clear that between the two "parties" involved, the nonviolent speaker and the rioting audience, the state's duty is to protect the speaker. *See Nelson v. Streeter*, 16 F. 3d 145, 149–150 (7th Cir. 1994) (Posner, C. J.). Although such protection might, in a genuine riot situation, entail protective custody and thus incidentally involve silencing the speaker, the notion of subsequently prosecuting the speaker is violative of *Brandenburg v. Ohio*, which permits suppression only when a speaker both inflames an audience and *intends* that violence will result. *Brandenburg v. Ohio*, 395 U.S. 444 (1969). This test, more stringent than clear and present danger as understood by the Court in its 1930s and 1950s adoption of it (although not necessarily than Holmes's later understanding), requires the speaker to affiliate him- or herself with the crowd's conduct in order to find it actionable—that is, by his or her words, the speaker must participate in the violence by directing it or precipitating it. The mere refusal to back down and be silent in the face of a hostile crowd does not fulfill this requirement, unless intent is read in its broadest possible sense—that is, that the speaker knows what will occur and carries on regardless, although not desiring the result. In the Model Penal Code, of course, this state of mind is not "intent" but rather recklessness. Compare Model Penal Code §§1.13(12), 2.02(2)(a)(i) with 2.02(2)(c). The *Brandenburg* rule seems to mandate *specific* intent—a conscious decision to bring about a desired result (again to use the Model Penal Code's terms "purposely"). Indeed, Holmes's vision of clear and present danger can be read fairly to impose such a requirement. S *ee Debs v. United States*, 249 U.S. 211 (1919); Wirenius, *supra* note 1 at 17.

21. *See,* for example, *Brandenburg v. Ohio*, 395 U.S. at 455–457 (Douglas, J., concurring).

22. 236 U.S. 273, 277 (1915). In fact, the concept was first enunciated in *Gompers v. Bucks Stove & Range Co.*, 221 U.S. 418, 439 (1911).

ing verbal acts, carefully drawn so as not unduly to impair liberty of expression, is not too vague for a criminal law."[23]

Had *Chaplinsky* simply contained the actual reasoning that leads to the suppression of "fighting words," the case might have successfully revived the *Fox* line of thought well before Douglas became its exponent, and it might have loomed large in the jurisprudence as a further step along the pathway to *Brandenburg*. At the very least, the case would have marked another stage in the developing jurisprudence—a step away from the subversive advocacy cases and their evolution of the clear and present danger rule, and that rule's application in another context.[24] However, the opinion did contain the dictum, and, more than the reasoning of the case, that dictum would come to be Justice Murphy's ironic legacy.

Murphy was at the time the most liberal member of the Court, far more concerned than even Black and Douglas with the rights of individuals and the government's usurpation of power during the war.[25] It is impossible to believe that he, let alone Black and Douglas (who admittedly were not yet First Amendment absolutists), would so cavalierly create whole new exceptions to the First Amendment if they were aware that they were doing so.

Yet that is precisely what they did.

The sea change in the jurisprudence represented by *Chaplinsky* was certainly not comprehended by the Court if their opinions immediately following the case's decision are any guide. In those cases, the Court cited *Chaplinsky* for quite limited purposes, and only gradually does the dictum begin to have an impact on the analysis. The process illustrates how the rearguard tactics of a minority in Supreme Court infighting can be victorious over time—a truth shown most recently by Justice Brennan in his last terms on the Court, during which he achieved majorities even as the Court surged generally to the right.[26]

A mere three months after the decision in *Chaplinsky*, the Court decided *Jones v. Opelika*,[27] in which a city ordinance that required businesses, includ-

---

23. 315 U.S. at 574.
24. The case's application of the rule is at best somewhat quaint in assigning responsibility for violence to the provoking speaker, who is apparently presumed to be aware that the offended violent party is behaving reasonably. *Id.* at 574. This rule harks back to the Old West model of honor. It is also, as indicated at note 20, poor constitutional reasoning, and violative of the logic that legitimates the imposition of punishment of speech under either the *Debs* rule or its eventual successor, the *Brandenburg* rule.
25. Ball & Cooper, *supra* note 10, at 108–109.
26. See David G. Savage, *Turning Right: The Making of the Rehnquist Court* (1992) at 122–123 (describing Brennan's "outmaneuvering" of Chief Justice Rehnquist throughout the 1986–1987 term); *id.* at 306–349 (describing Brennan's last term, and victories for his views in the areas of free speech and affirmative action); Peter Irons, *Brennan vs. Rehnquist: The Battle for the Constitution* (1994).
27. 316 U.S. 584 (1942).

ing "transient merchants" (that is, door-to-door salespeople), to obtain a license and pay a tax could properly be applied to the Jehovah's Witnesses in their door-to-door ministry. The Court upheld the ordinance, and cited *Chaplinsky* twice in so doing. The first proposition for which the case was cited was that the rights guaranteed by the Constitution (which the Court rather sententiously contrasted with the "ethical principles" and "personal liberties" of "the mental and spiritual realm") "are not absolutes."[28] After this groundbreaking revelation, the Court further relied upon *Chaplinsky* as support for the innocuous statement that "[c]onflicts in the exercise of rights arise, and the conflicting forces seek adjustments in the courts, as do these parties, claiming on one side the freedom of religion, speech and the press, guaranteed by the Fourteenth Amendment."[29] The Court, in describing the state's interest in social order that conflicts with individual interests, footnoted not to *Chaplinsky* but to other authority.[30]

Almost a year to the day after the Court had decided *Chaplinsky*, the justices recited their most libertarian understanding of its rule in *Jamison v. Texas*.[31] In that case, the Court opined, the states could constitutionally "punish conduct on the streets which is in violation of a valid law."[32] In contrast, the Court emphasized that the citizen in the street retained his right to "express his views in an orderly fashion."[33] The Court further expounded upon this doctrine in *Giboney v. Empire Storage & Ice Co.*[34] In distinguishing between protected speech and unprotected restraint of trade, the Court stated that:

---

28. *Id.* at 593. In his dissenting opinions, Justice Reed repeatedly cited *Chaplinsky* to support the nonabsolute nature of the rights guaranteed by the First Amendment. *See McCollum v. Board of Education*, 333 U.S. 203, 256 (1948) (dissenting from holding that state program exempting students from secular programs to attend religious instruction provided at public schools by sectarian [though school-approved] teachers was an unconstitutional establishment of religion); *Marsh v. Alabama*, 326 U.S. 501, 511 (1946) (dissenting from opinion that applied First Amendment guarantees to privately owned "company towns").

29. 316 U.S. at 593. *Chaplinsky* was again cited for this proposition—that the Fourteenth Amendment incorporated the First and deemed it applicable to the states—in *Largent v. Texas*, 318 U.S. 418, 422 (1943) (deeming unconstitutional a municipal ordinance which, as construed and applied, forbade the distribution of religious literature except with a permit issued at the discretion of a municipal official as "censorship in an extreme form").

30. 316 U.S. at 593.

31. 318 U.S. 413 (1943) (invalidating city ordinance prohibiting the distribution of handbills as applied to Jehovah's Witnesses handbills, despite allegedly commercial component of handbills—i.e., solicitation of funds for religious purposes).

32. *Id.* at 416.

33. *Id.*

34. 336 U.S. 490, 502 (1949) (upholding state injunction against First Amendment challenge to labor union picketing).

IT is true that the agreements and course of conduct here were as in most instances brought about through speaking or writing. But it has never been deemed an abridgement of freedom of speech or press to make a course of conduct illegal merely because the conduct was in part initiated, evidenced, or carried out by language, either spoken, written, or printed [citing *Fox* and *Chaplinsky*]. Such an expansive interpretation of the constitutional guarantees of speech and press would make it practically impossible to ever enforce laws against agreements in restraint of trade as well as many other agreements and conspiracies deemed injurious to society.[35]

Whatever one thinks of the logic—the First Amendment must not reach this type of speech because such speech is "deemed injurious to society"—the notion leads to an interesting line of thought.[36] By distinguishing between unprotected "conduct" and protected speech, the Court used *Chaplinsky* to harks back to the concept of the "verbal act," strengthening the claim to legitimacy of Justice Douglas's absolutist theory of the First Amendment. Far from serving as an agent of repression, *Chaplinsky* was being used to revisit a potentially libertarian theory of speech which had never quite crystallized.

The point must not be overstressed: *Chaplinsky* was not in fact relied upon in *Jamison* to create a breathtaking new libertarian approach to the First Amendment. The doctrine the Court teased out of the case did, however, bear the seeds of such an approach.

Unfortunately, it is in *Jamison* that the categorization approach to *Chaplinsky* can begin to be seen. The Court differentiated between the religious speech involved in the case and "purely commercial leaflets."[37] The differential treatment of speech that was purely commercial in nature followed hard upon *Chaplinsky* but was effected without citation to Murphy's dictum. With no reasoning or precedential support, the Court baldly declared that "[w]e are equally clear that the Constitution imposes no such

---

35. *Id.* at 502.
36. The Court in *Giboney* also shut down an interesting approach, by rejecting the argument that the picketing should have been separated out "into illegal and legal parts." *Id.* at 502. Such a hybrid approach would have left the labor union a means to achieve its end— to induce the target to join its boycott—by persuasion. Of course, the Court's rejection of this approach was premised on its conclusion that such an effort was properly an unlawful act in itself, on the grounds that the statute forbade restraint of trade, however it was accomplished. *Id.*
37. 318 U.S. at 417. The Court relied not upon the *Chaplinsky* dictum for this distinction but upon *Valentine v. Chrestensen*, 316 U.S. 52, 55 (1942). The Court found in *Valentine* a blanket license for the state to absolutely prevent the use of its streets for the distribution of such "purely commercial leaflets." *Id.* at 54–55. In *Jamison* the Court affirmatively upheld a line of cases mandating a different result when the handbills in question were religious in nature. 318 U.S. at 417–418.

restraint on government as respects purely commercial advertising," as it does on the expression of opinion in the streets, and that "[w]hether, and to what extent, one may promote or pursue a gainful occupation, to what extent such activity shall be judged a derogation of the public right of user, are matters for legislative judgment."[38] In *Jamison*, this doctrine hardened into a distinction between two kinds of speech, one presumptively protected, the other subject to the plenary power of the state.[39] Although the dictum was not the basis for it, this distinction marked the way of things to come.

The Court's early use of *Chaplinsky* had two remaining permutations, both swiftly described. In *Prince v. Martin*[40] the Court delivered its most reductive employment of *Chaplinsky*'s rule, as part of a string cite for the proposition that, although street preaching "cannot be wholly prohibited, it can be regulated within reasonable limits in accommodation to the primary and other incidental uses" of the streets.[41]

The Court also used *Chaplinsky* (and quite rightly) to create a distinction in the *types* of regulation. Although it accepted that, save for in the very narrowest of circumstances, the *substance* of speech is absolutely privileged, the Court recognized that "the manner in which it is practiced at times gives rise to special problems with which the police power is competent to deal."[42] The Court enlarged upon this distinction by the purpose and impact of regulation in *Kovacs v. Cooper*.[43] The *Kovacs* court found the regulation of "loud and raucous" noise—sound trucks—to be within the police power of the state because the ordinance did not grant unbridled discretion to a municipal official to license some speakers and not others.[44] Moreover, the interest the state asserted was not that of protecting the audience from the message the sound truck carried but from the otherwise inescapable and "intolerable" noise.[45]

---

38. 316 U.S. at 54.
39. The regulable nature of purely commercial speech was reiterated in *Murdock v. Pennsylvania*, 319 U.S. 105, 110–111 (1943).
40. 321 U.S. 158 (1943) (upholding application of state statute prohibiting children from selling newspapers, magazines, etc., to pre-adolescent Jehovah's Witnesses).
41. *Id.* at 169.
42. *Murdock v. Pennsylvania*, 319 U.S. 105, 110 (1943) (Invalidating municipal ordinance which, as construed and applied, requires "religious colporteurs"—i.e., the Jehovah's Witnesses—to pay a licensing tax as a precondition to their ministry).
43. 336 U.S. 77 (1949) (upholding municipal ordinance forbidding the use of sound trucks or of any instrument emitting "loud and raucous" noises on the public street).
44. 336 U.S. at 82–83; compare *Saia v. New York*, 334 U.S. 558 (1948).
45. *Id.* at 83. For the evolution of such "content-neutral" regulation, *see* Stone, *Content Neutral Restrictions*, 54 U. Chi. L. Rev. 46 (1987).

Rearguard Strategy: Conquering the Liberals

The process by which Murphy's casual dictum became the constitutional orthodoxy involved a battle that lasted over a decade between the Court's liberal
and conservative wings. The Roosevelt appointees, all chosen for their belief
in judicial restraint with regard to economic questions, split into two camps
on issues involving civil liberties. The liberal, activist side was led by Hugo Black,
ably backed by Douglas and supported by Murphy and Wiley Rutledge.[46]

The conservative wing was led by Felix Frankfurter, ironically once famous
for his devotion to civil liberties, subsequently the Court's leading exponent
of "judicial restraint"—the belief that the Court's deference to governmental choices should not be abandoned in cases that presented civil liberties
questions.[47] Frankfurter drew support from Robert H. Jackson, as well as from
Stanley Reed.[48] The ferocity of this infighting was extreme; Frankfurter referred to Black, Douglas, and Murphy as "the Axis" in correspondence with
Jackson—a far more hate-filled epithet in the 1940s than it is today.[49] Frankfurter's greatest venom was reserved for Douglas, whom he called "one of the
most completely evil men I have ever met,"[50] "the most systematic exploiter
of flattery I have ever known,"[51] and a "hypocrite."[52] Frankfurter revealed an
almost genial contempt for Murphy, bullying him in the Japanese-American
internment cases[53] and referring to him disparagingly as "Saint Frank."[54]
Douglas returned Frankfurter's contempt and teased the elder justice un-
mercifully and baited him with the talent of a natural-born prankster be-
deviling a pedant.[55] More seriously, he described Frankfurter as "divisive,"

---

46. The deep divisions within the Court during this time period, and the resulting personal
    acrimony between the so-called liberal and conservative wings have been well docu-
    mented, and in rehearsing them here, a twice-told tale must be referred to yet again.
    For an engaging and concise account, *see* Urofsky, *supra* note 12, at 71.
47. Fred Rodell, *Felix Frankfurter, Conservative,* 183 Harper's Mag. 449–450 (1941); Urofsky,
    supra note 12, at 89; H. N. Hirsch, *The Enigma of Felix Frankfurter* (1981) at 127–175.
48. For accounts confirming this analysis, see Simon, *Independent Journey, supra* note 13, at
    245–247; Simon, *The Antagonists, supra* note 14, at 115–117; Ball & Cooper, *supra* note
    10, at 84–99; W. O. Douglas, *The Court Years, supra* note 14, at 52–54.
49. See Urofsky, *supra* note 12 at 90; Simon, *The Antagonists, supra* note 14, at 116; Ball &
    Cooper, *Fighting Justices: Hugo L. Black, William O. Douglas and Supreme Court Conflict,* 38
    Am. J. of Leg. Hist. 1 (1994); Urofsky, *Division and Discord* (1997).
50. *See* Ball & Cooper, *Of Power and Right, supra* note 10, at 90; Simon, *Independent Journey,*
    supra note 13, at 217.
51. *Id.*
52. *See* Ball & Cooper, *Of Power and Right, supra* note 10, at 90.
53. Ball & Cooper, *Of Power and Right, supra* note 10, at 56, 98–99; Ball & Cooper, *Fighting*
    Justices, supra note 49, at 13, n. 36; Urofsky, *supra* note 12, at 80.
54. *See* Urofsky, *supra* note 12.
55. Simon, *Independent Journey, supra* note 13, at 218–219; Simon, *The Antagonists, supra* note
    14, at 185–186.

"Machiavellian," and claimed that he craved subservience from all around him.[56]

The tension at the Court was exacerbated by Justice Robert Jackson, who after he failed to be appointed Chief Justice following Stone's death in 1948 publicly accused Black of having (with Douglas's help) connived to deny him the position by threatening to resign from the bench if Truman appointed Jackson.[57] This followed closely upon Jackson's public attack on Black for failing to disqualify himself from a case argued by his former law partner— a case in which Black's vote meant the difference between victory and defeat for his former partner.[58]

In addition, Jackson's year-long leave from the Court to act as Chief American Prosecutor at Nuremberg caused significant tension at the Court, between those who supported him, and those who felt that the trials were not truly "legal" and that the judiciary was sullied by participation in a formalized revenge spree.[59] Even Chief Justice Stone disapproved of Jackson's leave, which left the Court short-handed for an entire term.[60]

These tensions explain the adversarial relationships between the justices in the late 1940s and early 1950s, and are germane in that the Court's bitter division led the justices to view their battle for dominance—philosophical dominance, activists versus conservatives—as a war.[61]

This increased the bitterness of some of the battles, and led to a degree of inconsistency among the Court's results as one faction or the other gained a temporary ascendance.[62] However, closely pressed, and fully committed to the battle, the justices brought a rare degree of passion to their opinions.[63] Frankfurter found himself frequently on the losing side of

---

56. Interview, James Simon with William O. Douglas, *Independent Journey, supra* note 13, at 9–12; *see also* W. O. Douglas, *The Court Years, supra* note 14, at 43 *et. seq.*

57. See Simon, *The Antagonists, supra* note 14, at 157–170; Newman, *supra* note 13, at 336–337, 345–348.

58. *Id.*

59. *See* Simon, *The Antagonists, supra* note 14, at 158–159; Newman, *supra* note 13, at 340. *Id. See also* Eugene Gerhart, *America's Advocate: Robert H. Jackson* (1958) at 436 (quoting Chief Justice Stone describing the trials as "Jackson's high-grade lynching party").

60. *Id.*

61. *See* Bruce Allen Murphy, *The Brandeis-Frankfurter Connection* 267 (1982) (interview with Frankfurter clerk Elliott Richardson, State College Pennsylvania, described Frankfurter declaring "don't you get the idea that this is a *war* we are fighting") (emphasis in original).

62. For example, the two sound truck cases discussed *supra* were in fact not easily reconcilable; the ordinance in *Kovacs* does not specify that the trucks be "loud and raucous" any more than the ordinance invalidated in *Saia v. New York, see supra* note 43–45. *Saia* nonetheless accords sound trucks free speech protection, and prohibits discretionary licensing thereof. Indeed both Black and Jackson—on opposite sides in *Kovacs*—agreed that the two cases were contradictory. 336 U.S. at 97–98 (Jackson, J., concurring); 336 U.S. at 101–103 (Black, J., dissenting).

63. *See* Simon, *The Antagonists, supra* note 14, at 197–215.

battles that split the Court he had once confidently been expected to dominate.[64] Deeply disturbed by what he saw as the improper activism of his colleagues in invalidating state legislative measures because they disagreed with them, he sought to permit the states to set their own rules, interfering only when the state violated precepts of "fundamental fairness."[65] The concept that the rights guaranteed by the First Amendment stood in a "preferred position" to other constitutionally protected rights was anathema to him.[66] To Hugo Black, and to William Douglas, it was the centerpiece of their constitutional worldview.[67] As the host of cases cited by Frankfurter in his concurring opinion in *Kovacs* showed, the preferred position had moreover become a centerpiece in First Amendment jurisprudence.[68]

The first use of Murphy's dictum, the tool with which the conservative wing would break the incipient victory of the liberals on the question of how exactly the Court would scrutinize statutes regulating speech by declaring wide swaths of speech not to be speech for constitutional purposes, came, however, not from Frankfurter, but from Justice Reed. In *Martin v. City of Struthers*,[69] Justice Reed in dissent stated:

> FREEDOM to distribute publications is obviously a part of the general freedom guaranteed the expression of ideas by the First Amendment. It is trite to say that this freedom of expression is not unlimited.

---

64. *Id.; see also* Urofsky, *supra* note 12, at 76–81, 112–113; Hirsch, *op. cit.*
65. See Simon, *The Antagonists, supra* note 14; *see also Winters v. New York*, 333 U.S. 507, 524 (Frankfurter, J., dissenting).
66. *Kovacs*, 336 U.S. at 90–97 (Frankfurter, J., concurring) in which Frankfurter attacks the many cases intimating or even explicitly declaring the primacy of First Amendment freedoms. As Frankfurter wrote, "I deem it a mischievous phrase, if it carries with it the thought, which it may subtly imply, that any law touching communication is infected with presumptive invalidity." 336 U.S. at 90. As Frankfurter accurately notes, the "preferred position" way of expressing just this doctrine, as formulated from the opinions of Justices Holmes and Brandeis, later adopted by the Court, seems to have begun in Chief Justice Stone's dissent in *Jones v. Opelika*, 316 U.S. at 600, 608. Frankfurter asserts that the proper method of resolving these cases is not a presumption of invalidity of such statutes, but a more complex process, which he does not describe in *Kovacs*. In the cases that follow, Frankfurter's position becomes more clear. Rather than set it out here and compare it with the far more libertarian (as I understand them) views of Holmes and Brandeis, its development through the categorization of First Amendment law, and his readiness to go beyond the *Chaplinsky* approach are set out *infra*.
67. *See* H. L. Black, *A Constitutional Faith* (1968) at 44–46; W. O. Douglas, *The Right of the People* (1958) at 21–25, 29–35.
68. *See supra* note 66.
69. 319 U.S. 141 (1943) (invalidating municipal ordinance forbidding door-to-door canvassing as applied to Jehovah's Witnesses distributing religious literature and advertisements of meetings). Frankfurter concurred in striking the ordinance on the ground that it did not ban all canvassing but "merely penalizes the distribution of 'literature.'" *Id.* at 153.

Obscenity, disloyalty and provocatives do not come within its protection. *Near v. Minnesota, Schenck v. United States, Chaplinsky v. New Hampshire.*[70]

Similarly, in *United States v. Ballard*,[71] Chief Justice Stone, relying on *Chaplinsky*, wrote in dissent that the First Amendment does not "afford immunity from criminal prosecution for the fraudulent procurement of money by false statements as to one's religious experiences, more than it renders polygamy or libel immune from criminal prosecution."[72] These dissents that drew from the categorical dictum of *Chaplinsky* did not of their own weight change the course of the jurisprudence, but they signaled that the functional, libertarian views of *Chaplinsky* were not the only ways to read that precedent.

Justice Reed was able to write the first opinion in which the categories established by Murphy were used as a vehicle for censorship. Ironically, he did so in *Winters v. New York*, in an opinion that struck a New York state statute that restricted speech, on the ground that the statute involved was too "indefinite" to provide sufficient notice of what publications would violate its edict.[73] In the course of Reed's opinion, the Court stated that:

THE line between the informing and the entertaining is too elusive for the protection of that basic right [of free speech]. Everyone is familiar with instances of propaganda through fiction. What is one man's amusement teaches another's doctrine. Though we see nothing of any possible value to society in these magazines, they are as much entitled to the protection of free speech as the best of literature. They are equally subject to control if they are lewd, indecent, obscene or profane.[74]

---

70. *Id.* at 155 (citations omitted). Justice Reed's interpretations of the case law is, to be kind, unique. *Schenck v. United States*, 249 U.S. 47 (1919) contained no general exception to the First Amendment for "disloyal" speech, but simply held that an instance of such speech, under certain circumstances adduced at trial, presented a clear and present danger that a violation of law would occur. Reed's other citations are only marginally more accurate. In *Near v. Minnesota*, 283 U.S. 697 (1931), the Court struck as unconstitutional a system of prior restraint for offensive newspapers or magazines, likewise carving out no such general exception, although it did state in dicta that "the primary requirements of decency may be enforced against obscene publications." *Id.* at 716.

71. 322 U.S. 78, 88–89 (1944) (Stone, C. J., dissenting from judgment that federal district court properly withheld from jury issue of truth or falsity of defendant's religious belief as mandated by the First Amendment).

72. *Id.* at 88 (Stone, C. J., dissenting).

73. *Winters v. New York*, 333 U.S. 507 (1948) (striking statute as construed by state court to prohibit distribution of magazines. etc., "made up of news or stories of deeds . . . so massed as to become vehicles for inciting violent and depraved crimes against the person"). *Id.* at 508.

74. *Id.* at 510 (citations omitted).

The Court's statement should not be read as limiting the *Chaplinsky* categories, but rather as discussing the only categories that might be applicable to the true crime magazines involved in *Winters*, which the state had sought to ban as a collation of horror that could blunt the sensibilities and deprave their primarily adolescent readership.[75]

Justice Frankfurter dissented, arguing that the exposure to such materials could erode the reader's (especially the youthful reader's) social inhibitions against violence. The magazines would not do this through outright advocacy, but through the titillating presentation, with gruesome detail, of atrocity after atrocity. The end effect would be to accustom the readers to violence, and to hold it out to them as a means of obtaining glamour and even celebrity in the form of media attention in the same (or similar) magazines.[76]

In *Winters*, Frankfurter urged the Court to apply the "rational basis" test across the board to free speech cases, relying principally on Justice Holmes's substantive due process decisions, opining that the Fourteenth Amendment was not "intended to give us *carte blanche* to embody our economic or moral beliefs in its prohibitions."[77] In determining whether the publications could be deemed to "incite" to violence, Frankfurter declaimed the Court's error in "giv[ing] publications which have 'nothing of any possible value to society' constitutional protection, but den[ying] to the States power to prevent the grave evils to which, in their rational judgment, such publications give rise."[78] Because the state's decision that such publications bore a causal relationship to crime was "not arbitrary," that ended the inquiry about the facial validity of the statute.[79]

In summarizing and defending the logic used by the state, Frankfurter described the effect of the publications as "so massing 'pictures and stories of criminal deeds of bloodshed or lust' as to encourage like deeds in others."[80] In deeming this view reasonable, he adverted to the review of the Court of Appeals of "many recent records of criminal convictions", the holding of similar views by a judge in Australia, and, in the light of the indeterminacy

---

75. *Id.*
76. *Id.* at 529–531 (Frankfurter, J., dissenting).
77. *Id.* at 535–537.
78. *Id.* at 528–529.
79. *Id.* at 530. Nor was Frankfurter impressed with the claim that the statute was too indefinite to provide adequate notice to the defendant of what constituted a violation of its terms. Frankfurter opined that striking the law merely "forbid publications inciting to crime, and as such not within the constitutional immunity of free speech, because in effect it does not trust State tribunals, nor ultimately this Court, to safeguard inoffensive publications from condemnation under this legislation." *Id.* at 540.
80. *Id.* at 529 (quoting *People v. Winters*, 294 N.Y. 545, 550 [1945]).

of psychology as a science, the need to defer to wisdom of the democratically elected legislature.[81]

The state's logic, as endorsed (or at least deferred to) by Frankfurter, was substantially the same as that used by Catharine A. MacKinnon to justify the present-day effort of some feminists to suppress pornography.[82] Like Frankfurter, MacKinnon argues that the nonrational presentation of sex (for Frankfurter, substitute violence) essentially bypasses the brain's cognitive functions, and appeals to—what? Neither Frankfurter nor MacKinnon is terribly clear on the subject,[83] but both believe that the harm found in such a presentation properly merits suppression by the state. The same flaw that undermines MacKinnon's reasoning also undermines Frankfurter's reasoning—communication has never been strictly restricted to appeals to rationality, and neither has the First Amendment.[84]

Frankfurter elaborated and refined his unique vision of the First Amendment in his concurrence in *Dennis v. United States*.[85] Where *Chaplinsky* drew a rough line, according speech either full protection or none whatsoever,

---

81. *Id.* at 528–530.
82. Catharine A. MacKinnon, *Toward A Feminist Theory of the State* (1989) at 134–152.
83. Frankfurter confessed his ignorance, explaining that the science of psychiatry was in its youth, and that his ignorance in fact served as an additional ground for showing deference to the state court determination that harm could result. *Winters*, 333 U.S. at 529–530. MacKinnon does not specify how the portrayal of degrading sexuality influences its audience in a qualitatively different way from portrayals of other facets of life. Indeed, in, *Only Words* (1993), she suggests that her rationale in fact does extend beyond the merely sexual, and that speech that tends to undermine equality of all citizens, or at least that of women, can and should be proscribed. *Id.* at 116. Interestingly, her approach is like Frankfurter's both in her results and in her methodology, a vague balancing test heavily weighted in the state's favor. *See* Wirenius, *Giving the Devil the Benefit of Law: Pornographers, The Feminist Attack on Free Speech and the First Amendment*, 20 Ford.Urb.L. J. 27 at 42–48 (1992).
84. Beyond providing a contemporary application of the logic espoused by Frankfurter in *Winters*, MacKinnon's growing acceptance in scholarly and political circles exemplifies (though by no means constitutes) the growing trend toward explicit subjectivity in assigning value to speech, and thus toward concomitant quantities of protection. As to the stress placed both by Frankfurter and by MacKinnon on the lack of rational appeal in the speech each believes should properly be censored, reasoned discourse is not the only breed of speech long understood to be worthy of protection. Protection of symbolic speech as speech is a classic instance of the extension of First Amendment protection of speech the communicative content of which is not a rational appeal. *See*, for example, *Tinker v. Des Moines School Dist.*, 393 U.S. 503 (1969) (extending First Amendment protection to students' wearing of black armbands to protest the Vietnam War). Many other instances abound, but the more fundamental point is that no distinction between reason-based speech and emotion-based speech has ever been validated by the Court. Nor, I would suggest, should any such distinction be approved. For a discussion of MacKinnon's approach to the pornography issue, and an attempt to rebut her—and Frankfurter's— seeming conclusion that only appeals to rationality merit First Amendment protection, see Wirenius, *supra* note 83, n. 171; *see also* Chapter 7, *infra*.
85. 341 U.S. 494 (1951).

Frankfurter applied a sliding scale involving multiple levels of protection accorded speech, which vary depending on the level of value accorded that speech by society.[86] Advocacy, Frankfurter stated (relying on *Fox v. Washington*), of violent overthrow of the government ranks low on the scale of valuable speech.[87]

For Frankfurter, then, the test is whether Congress, bearing "the primary responsibility for reconciling" the conflicting values of free speech and its policy decisions, did so in a rational manner.[88] In view of the low value of the speech involved, and what he felt to be the world-threatening danger presented by communism, Frankfurter found the Smith Act, while unwise and intolerant, to be a rational act, and thus well within the scope of Congress's powers.[89]

In *Dennis* Frankfurter expanded on his approach in *Winters*, applying the *Chaplinsky* concept of using the value of speech to society as a counterweight to determine whether the legislative judgment was an exercise of rationality. Upon finding that it was, affirmance was for Frankfurter the only possible result. On the one hand, Frankfurter's opinions, by watering down the First Amendment to an "admonition to Congress"[90] seems to at least escape the vagueness of the *Chaplinsky* approach: A uniform test, whether the test uses strict scrutiny (as demanded by the liberals) or rational basis scrutiny, at least has the virtue of avoiding subjective decisions based upon the "value" accorded speech. Yet even this virtue was not to be had in the Frankfurter approach, because a highly subjective inquiry is used to determine the rationality of the legislative judgment

Winters thus represents a watershed in two distinct ways. First, Justice Frankfurter began to articulate his unique, multitiered approach to the First Amendment. This explicit creation of a First Amendment hierarchy based on a general balancing test would not command a majority until *Beauharnais v. Illinois*,[91]

---

86. *Id.* at 544–545.

87. *Id.* at 545. Frankfurter also declares that this is especially so because "no government can recognize 'right' of revolution . . ." *Id.* at 549. As already pointed out in Chapter 2, the explicit recognition of such a right in the Preamble to the Declaration of Independence, itself a deliberate act passed by the Continental Congress, and so one of the earliest constitutive documents of the United States undermines Frankfurter's argument.

88. *Id.* at 550–552.

89. *Id.* at 554–557. Frankfurter's approach was rather more sophisticated than the approach taken by the majority in *Dennis* (a simple balancing test—does the speech cause more harm than good, essentially). For a fuller discussion of both the majority's and Frankfurter's opinions in *Dennis*, their origin, methodology, and historiography, *see* Chapter 2 *supra*.

90. *Dennis*, 341 U.S. at 580 (Black, J. dissenting).

91. 343 U.S. 250 (1952) (upholding "group libel" statute applied to racial epithets published by a white supremacist group in a newspaper advertisement). *See also Dennis*, 341 U.S. 494, 500–502.

but it reached its apogee (or nadir) in *Dennis*. Second, and of more immediate importance, in the *Winters* decision, a majority of the Court first used the categorical approach of *Chaplinsky* as a means to cut analysis short. If the speech in *Winters* had been found to have been "lewd, indecent, obscene or profane," no further thought would have been necessary. The speech would not *be* speech for the purposes of the First Amendment, in that it would have fit into one of the "certain well defined and limited classes of speech, the prevention and punishment of which have never been thought to raise any constitutional problem."[92] Not only would the state have been within its rights, but no First Amendment issue would have been raised.

The Curse Takes Hold:
Five Little Categories and How They Grew

The growth of the *Chaplinsky* categories from "narrow" little exceptions to the ordinary rules of First Amendment analysis into the centerpiece of the doctrine has been gradual. Since the Court's decision in *Chaplinsky*, it has toyed with the list of categories given by Justice Murphy and has supplemented it from time to time. Along the way, the field in which full First Amendment analysis applies has steadily contracted. Today's doctrine is perilously close to the balancing test advocated by Frankfurter—a fact that should chagrin all who care for the right to speak, write, or think freely.

The process has happened in three stages. First, the original *Chaplinsky* categories have been refined, and some added or dropped. Second, the concept of these specific categories as exceptions to a general type of analysis has eroded, and instead the distinction has been reduced to a more vague preference between "high-" and "low-" value speech. Finally, the third step is incipient. Academics have begun to call for, and some judicial authorities to adopt, a variant of the Frankfurterian model, in which the Court establishes its own sliding scale of tests, based upon its ranking of the relative importance of the speech and the interests sought to be advanced through suppression.

Obscenity

The first, and possibly the most litigated, of the *Chaplinsky* categories to take on a life of its own was obscenity. The long and often tortured history of the

---

92. 343 U.S. at 255–256, quoting *Cantwell v. Connecticut,* 310 U.S. at 296 (1940).

obscenity doctrine in the United States is an oft-told story.[93] Although that story need not be repeated here, a few of its salient features are helpful to illustrate the nature of categorical reasoning in a First Amendment context.

The Supreme Court first used the *Chaplinsky* obscenity category in *Roth v. United States*.[94] In an opinion by Justice Brennan, the Court found many expressions in prior opinions to the effect that obscenity was not considered protected speech.[95] In the list of judicial statements to that effect, Brennan relied exclusively on cases that had either not involved obscenity or that had denied obscene materials the use of the federal mails but had not banned them.[96] *Roth* was therefore a case of first impression, yet the opinion was dismissive and settled the central question of whether obscene materials were entitled to constitutional protection within three pages. Brennan's reasoning in this case was deceptively simple. First, the purpose of the First Amendment is "to assure unfettered interchange of ideas for the bringing about of political and social changes desired by the people."[97] This meant that "[a]ll ideas having even the slightest redeeming social importance—unorthodox ideas, controversial ideas, even ideas hateful to the prevailing climate of opinion—have the full protection of the guaranties unless excludable because they encroach upon the limited area of more important interests."[98] Brennan found that obscenity had been deemed to be "utterly without redeeming social importance," as evidenced by the universal ban on it by the states and the federal government as well as by many other nations.[99] Indeed, Brennan found that this was precisely the judgment contained in the *Chaplinsky* dictum.

Having decided that obscene speech fell outside of the ambit of the First Amendment's protection, Brennan found no cause to examine obscene speech in the light of the prevailing test that governed legislation aimed at speech. The entire issue became whether the speech in question fell into the category of obscenity.[100] From that day to this, in every obscenity pros-

---

93. *See* Peter Magrath, *The Obscenity Cases: The Grapes of Roth* 1966 Sup. Ct. Rev. 7 (1967); Edward de Grazia, *Girls Lean Back Everywhere: The Law of Obscenity and the Assault on Genius* (1992); Kent Greenawalt *Speech, Crime, and the Uses of Language*, (1989) at 149–154, 302–309. These works taken together provide a comprehensive account of the evolution of obscenity doctrine both at the trial and at the appellate levels. Magrath provides an especially interesting account of the obscenity doctrine prior to *Miller v. United States*, 413 U.S. 15 (1973), and thus at a time when it was still in a state of flux.

94. 354 U.S. 476 (1957).

95. *Id.* at 481–483

96. *Id.*

97. *Id.* at 484.

98. *Id.*

99. *Id.* at 485. Since Miller, works lacking "serious, literary, artistic, political, or scientific value" are vulnerable to the ban on "obscene" speech.

100. *Id.* at 486–487. The remainder of the *Roth* opinion seeks to distinguish between "prurient" exploitation of sex and legitimate discussion of sexuality as "one of the vital problems of human interest and public concern." *Id.* at 487 *et seq.*

ecution the issue decided has always been whether or not the speech at hand fit into the obscenity pigeonhole.[101]

There are many flaws inherent in the *Roth* formulation. Most fundamentally, *upon what theory obscenity did not qualify for constitutional protection was left completely vague.* If Brennan's social importance theory were to be applied across the board, much of popular culture would cower in fear of the censor. It is difficult to see in what way Harlequin romances or the writings of Agatha Christie or P. G. Wodehouse enrich the debate "for the bringing about of political and social changes desired by the people." Whatever one may think of the respective merits of these authors, their work is fairly classifiable as pure escapism. Yet these works, as well as countless others, are sacrosanct, while materials of equal social relevance—that is to say, none at all—but that are sexually explicit are denied any protection at all.

In *Stanley v. Georgia,*[102] the Court tried to recast *Roth* and its progeny in such a way as to provide both a limiting principle and a distinction between the regulation of obscenity and other First Amendment issues. Justice Marshall quoted *Roth* to the effect that the "door barring federal and state intrusion into this area [First Amendment rights] cannot be left ajar; it must be kept tightly closed and opened only the slightest crack necessary to prevent encroachment upon more important interests."[103] Marshall went on to explain that "*Roth* and the cases following it discerned such an 'important interest' in the regulation of commercial distribution of obscene material."[104] Thus, Marshall concluded, the right to possess obscene materials in one's own home—to read what one chooses, as a function of *thinking* what one will, is more fundamental than the right to disseminate such materials and does not implicate the same "important interests."

---

101. *See,* for example, *Jacobellis v. Ohio,* 378 U.S. 184, 195 (1966) (reversing conviction under state obscenity law because film involved was "not utterly without social importance" and thus not obscene under *Roth*); *Paris Adult Theatre v. Slaton,* 413 U.S. 49 (1973) (reaffirming *Roth*'s holding that obscenity falls outside of the ambit of constitutional protection, and upholding conviction under state obscenity law to audience concededly comprised exclusively of consenting adults); *Miller v. California,* 413 U.S. 15 (1973) (in upholding conviction under state obscenity law for selling "illustrated books," Court revised definition of obscenity, establishing "local community standards" test); *Jenkins v. Georgia,* 418 U.S. 153 (1974) (reversing state court finding that film *Carnal Knowledge* was obscene under *Miller,* Court held that nudity alone was insufficient to establish obscenity); *Hamling v. United States,* 418 U.S. 87 (1974) (in upholding conviction under *Miller* for mailing "illustrated version" of official report on pornography, held that "local community" under *Miller* is not statewide standard but truly local in scope); *United States v. Thomas,* 74 F. 3d 701 (6th Cir. 1996) (applying standard of District of Tennessee to Internet postings originating in California). *See also* Greenwalt, *supra* note 93, at 304 ("The basic constitutional standards have remained those of *Miller*").
102. 394 U.S. 557 (1969) (*per* Marshall, J.).
103. *Id.* at 563 (*quoting Roth* 354 U.S. at 488).
104. *Id.* at 563–564.

This attempt at a theoretical reformulation simply does not pass muster. Two grave flaws undermine the attempt, admirable though it is, to confine Chaplinskyism while retaining its flexibility. First, the statement that a "more important interest" than the First Amendment that is cognizable to the Supreme Court but that is not embodied in the Constitution itself may be used to defeat the First Amendment is violative not only of the Supremacy Clause, but of the entire concept of a written constitution—if subjective value judgments are to be allowed to defeat the Constitution, how does it qualify as "law" at all, let alone as the supreme law of the land? Moreover, on the rhetorical level, Justice Marshall provided no grounds for defining such an "important interest" at the expense of the First Amendment, and did not answer the inevitable question: Who decides what values are important in a democratic republic—the elected representatives of the people or appointed judges who seize the fact of their unreviewable status to make such judgments under the guise of construing the instrument they are supplementing or revising?

The attempted Marshall reformulation fails on a logical level: The First Amendment postulates a right to communicate, to distribute, by its very terms. It is the right to possess a library that is implied from "the freedom of speech" and of "the press", and not the other way around. The idea also fails pragmatically, because what good is the right to possess materials if their distribution (and thus the citizen's ability to acquire the materials he or she has a right to possess) can be banned? Does the First Amendment rely upon failures on the part of law enforcement? Indeed, the distinction makes no sense, because the materials so possessed (and thus unseizable and unprosecutable) are conclusive evidence of a crime (receiving and distributing) for which the citizen is properly punished if caught. Surely this distinction is too flimsy to be of constitutional weight. The First Amendment, if it means anything, cannot merely require the prosecutor to leave out a count for possession in an otherwise valid indictment.

These flaws in the *Stanley* formulation are not evidence of ineptness on Justice Marshall's part, but of the complete impossibility of restraining the subjectivity of Chaplinskyism. Aside from the fundamental question begged by each of the *Chaplinsky* categories—that is, *Why* is this speech unprotected unlike any other?—an extra layer of subjectivity dogs the category of obscenity. Not only is the carving out of the exception done on a "because we say so" or ipse dixit basis, but the definition of what speech falls under the interdict is heavily subjective as well. From *Roth* to *Miller* to the present day, judges and juries have had to wrestle with the distinction between "wholesome" interest in sex and "depraved" interest in sex—that is, between good smut and bad smut. It is scarcely surprising, then, that Justice Stewart threw up his hands in despair and embraced subjectivity, crying "I know it when I see it."[105] Needless to say, this approach provides little guidance to lower courts and even less to publishers and writers.

The *Miller* test, which uses local community standards to determine what constitutes obscenity, is almost as unhelpful as the Stewart approach, in that obscenity law is now balkanized not simply throughout the fifty states but throughout countless communities within these fifty states. The litigation headaches that can result from the application of this test are legion.[106] Not only is the would-be author required to steer clear of offending his own community, she or he must avoid giving offense to even the most parochial township in the nation if she or he wishes to avoid prosecution. Moreover, an additional touch of surrealism is added by the applicability of local community standards to proceedings under federal statutes relevant to obscene materials.[107]

Indeed, the Court has recently recognized the illogical nature of this balkanization of obscenity law, and its unfairness to those who speak to the nation as a whole. In declaring the partial application of the *Miller* standard to the Internet by Congress in the Communications Decency Act (CDA), the Court noted the "breadth of the CDA's coverage is wholly unprecedented."[108] This unhappy and unconstitutional state of affairs, Justice Stevens's opinion for the Court noted, was partially evinced by the fact that applying the "community standards criterion" to the Internet "means that any communication available to a nationwide audience will be judged by standards of the community most likely to be offended by the message."[109] Although the Court is quite right to note this flaw, and to find in it the seeds of unconstitutionality, the logic is every bit as deadly to the logic that underpins *Miller* as it is to the CDA.

The obscenity doctrine thus represents Chaplinskyism at its worst—layers upon layers of subjectivity coating the ugly reality that criminal convictions depend not on an author's conduct but rather upon her or his prose style and political relevance. Although Brennan's appeal to the animating purposes of the First Amendment is not without appeal, it is not grounded in the amendment's language, nor does it recognize that statutes, especially

---

105. *Jacobellis*, 378 U.S. at 197 (1964) (Stewart, J., concurring).
106. *See* Wirenius, *Giving the Devil the Benefit of Law, supra* note 83, at 35 n. 24.
107. *See*, for example, *Hamling v. United States*, 418 U.S. 87, 99 (1974) (upholding 18 U.S.C. § 1461, prohibiting the mailing of obscene materials); *see also United States v. Reidel*, 402 U.S. 351 (1970); *United States v. 12 200-ft Reels of Film*, 413 U.S. 123 (1973) (applying *Miller* test, including contemporary community standards, to federal regulation does not render such regulation unconstitutional); *Sable Communications of California, Inc. v. FCC*, 492 U.S. 115, 125 (1989) (upholding federal regulation of obscene telephone messages, for example, "dial-a-porn").
108. *Reno v. American Civil Liberties Union*, 521 U.S. 844 (1997) [hereafter *Reno v. ACLU*].
109. 521 U.S. at 877–878

constitutional provisions, frequently sweep in a broader fashion than is required to fulfill their narrowest purpose.[110] Thus, the agreed-upon purpose of the amendment, to guarantee political freedom, does not of itself stand as a limiting principle, and does not justify a more narrow reading of the amendment than the scope of its language.

Brennan offered in *Roth* no coherent reason for the obscenity exception other than his subjective belief that such ideas are of "no redeeming social importance." The very point of a Bill of Rights, however, is to protect the individual from the tyrannical excesses of the majority: To interpret those guarantees as the court did in *Roth* and in *Miller* through the will of the majority subverts the whole purpose of the undertaking. Citizens may speak against the popular consensus only when the consensus allows us to do so.

Offensive Speech

The *Chaplinsky* category that is most like obscenity, in that no interest save that of sensibility is at the root of its proscription, is the category of offensive speech. In *Chaplinsky*, of course, the lewd and the obscene were joined together, and the profane did not follow far behind.[111] From this conjoining, a reasonable deduction would be that these variants are closely related. And indeed they are. Materials at common law were repeatedly held proscribable as obscene even when they lacked a sexual component, and Lenny Bruce was prosecuted and convicted in New York (even after the Supreme Court redressed this blurring in *Roth* and further liberalized the standard in *Jacobellis*) under the obscenity statutes despite the general consensus that his act was at most profane, and not salacious.[112]

The fate of profane or simply offensive speech[113] varies widely with the medium of expression selected for its use. Many decisions involving such

---

110. The classic example of such a provision is the Fourteenth Amendment, which, it is broadly agreed, was designed to protect freed African-Americans after the Civil War. The Fourteenth Amendment has come to be the vehicle through which most of the provisions of the Bill of Rights have come to be incorporated against the states and thus guarantees civil liberties to all U.S. citizens. *See,* for example, *Adamson v. California,* 332 U.S. 46 (1947); *Palko v. Connecticut,* 302 U.S. 319 (1937); *Duncan v. Louisiana,* 391 U.S. 145 (1968). For its use for rights not specifically enumerated in the Bill of Rights, *see,* for example, *Roe v. Wade,* 410 U.S. 113 (1973).

111. See text at note 6, *supra*; 315 U.S. at 571.

112. For a passionate account by one of Bruce's attorneys of Bruce's trial in New York, its impropriety under the obscenity statutes then prevailing, and the trial's possible role in Bruce's death, *see* Martin Garbus, *Ready for the Defense* (1971) at 81–141; for a somewhat less involved, but substantially identical, account, *see* deGrazia, *supra* note 93, at 452–474; Ronald K. L. Collins & David M. Skover, *The Trials of Lennie Bruce* (2002).

113. The case law, as one can imagine, is far from well developed in this field. Indeed, the very name of the category is somewhat up for debate; although "profane" was Justice Murphy's term, the word is objectionable as equating traditionally with blasphemy, con-

speech have centered on the use of the radio and television media, and have permitted regulation based on the allegedly public nature of the airwaves. Those decisions, which rest on the quasi-public nature of the medium by which the speech is disseminated, have notably represented a step away from the *Chaplinsky* dichotomy of all-or-nothing protection of speech, and represent a different stage in the development of the categorical imperative.

With regard to the pure category of regulation of offensive but nonsalacious speech, the Court did not treat the issue as one of any importance until the 1971 decision of *Cohen v. California*.[114] In *Cohen*, an anti–Vietnam War protester was arrested for wearing a jacket outside a courthouse bearing the legend "Fuck the Draft."[115] Cohen was prosecuted under a catch-all section of a state statute that proscribed "maliciously and willfully disturbing the peace or quiet of any neighborhood or person . . . by . . . offensive conduct."[116] In reversing Cohen's conviction, the Supreme Court, in an opinion by Justice Harlan, narrowed the issue to review of the constitutionality of the statutory rubric to effectively ban "that word" from public discourse.[117]

The Court first determined what Cohen's conduct was *not*; it was not obscene: It lacked the requisite element of salaciousness. "It cannot plausibly be maintained," Harlan wrote, "that this vulgar allusion to the Selective Service System would conjure up such psychic stimulation in anyone likely to be confronted with Cohen's crudely defaced jacket."[118] Similarly, the case did not involve the original *Chaplinsky* category of "fighting words," because no message was directed at any specific individual.[119] Finally, the Court rejected the notion that the visibility of the jacket to the public raised a "captive audience" problem such as that inherent in the sound truck cases. Because passersby could easily avert their eyes from Cohen's jacket, Justice

---

noting an attack on the sacred. Profane speech, as prosecuted, has run the gamut from political harangues or satirical writings, to conduct deplored as violating traditional, widely shared boundaries of taste. For the purpose of precision, the entire gamut is considered here under the general heading of "offensive speech".

114. 403 U.S. 15 (1971).

115. *Id.* at 16.

116. *Id. quoting* Cal. Penal Code § 415 (ellipses in original). The provision under which Cohen was charged and convicted was the catch-all portion of a statute containing other, more specific definitions of conduct constituting disturbing the peace. *Id.* at n.1.

117. In an amusing counterpoint to the core ruling of *Cohen*, Chief Justice Burger has been described as pleading with Harlan not to use "that word" in reading his opinion from the bench. Burger reportedly assured Harlan that such an utterance "would be the end of the Court." Bob Woodward and Scott Armstrong, *The Brethren* (1979) at 133. Harlan, although he kept the chief justice in suspense, did not deliver the feared death blow. *Id.*

118. 403 U.S. at 20.

119. *Id.*

Harlan argued that *Cohen* was distinguishable from the line of cases that raised the issue of a captive audience,[120] and that "substantial privacy interests" were not infringed by Cohen.

The Court was finally left with the simple *Chaplinsky* category of "profane" speech, characterized by Harlan as "offensive" speech. The Court rejected the appropriateness of such a category, rejecting both grounds proffered by the state for it: the state's power to protect community moral climate and the expressed fear that violence would be inflicted on the obnoxious speaker.[121] The grounds for the rejection are interesting. The antiviolence concern was dismissed, based on the premise that the risk of a crowd taking matters into its own hands and silencing an offensive speaker is not (when the speaker does not intend to provoke that crowd) appropriately averted by allowing the states to "more appropriately effectuate that censorship themselves."[122]

Justice Harlan then conceded that "it is not so obvious that the First and Fourteenth Amendments must be taken to disable the States from punishing public utterance of this unseemly expletive in order to maintain what they regard as a suitable level of discourse within the body politic."[123] However, he opined, "it is largely because government officials cannot make principled distinctions in this area that the Constitution leaves matters of taste and style so largely to the individual."[124] Moreover, the Court relied on the "dual communicative function" of language: "It conveys not only ideas capable of relatively precise, detached explication, but otherwise inexpressible emotions as well. In fact, words are often chosen as much for their emotive as their cognitive force."[125] This second dimension of communicative function the Court deemed as worthy of protection as the first—noting that "practically speaking, [it] may often be the more important element of the overall message sought to be communicated."[126]

Finally, the Court feared the likelihood of suppressing ideas through the banning of specific words, especially in light of the limited social utility of such a ban.[127]

Justice Harlan's opinion in *Cohen* merits the scrutiny given it here because it demonstrates the ease with which an unreasoned *Chaplinsky* category can be made to look absurd. No real rational argument can be adduced in

---

120. *Id.* at 21.
121. *Id.* at 23–24.
122. *Id.* at 23
123. *Id.*
124. *Id.* at 25.
125. *Id.* at 26.
126. *Id.*
127. *Id.*

opposition: If we accept Justice Holmes's description of our system as one that must permit and even protect speech which we "hate" or believe to be "fraught with death," how can we rationally draw the line at speech that we may not believe to be harmful but find vulgar? The dissent in *Cohen*, by Justice Blackmun, certainly fails to respond to this argument, although it is difficult not to sympathize with Blackmun's perplexed statement that "the case appears to me to be well within the sphere of *Chaplinsky v. New Hampshire*" and thus "this Court's agonizing over First Amendment values seems misplaced and unnecessary."[128]

In fact, Blackmun's point is well taken, and evaded by the Court in a somewhat disingenuous statement that "most situations where the State has a justifiable interest in regulating speech will fall within one or more of the various exceptions, discussed above but not applicable here, to the usual rule that governmental bodies may not prescribe the form or content of individual expression."[129] The reason this statement is less than forthcoming should be clear from the exposition of Harlan's opinion: The Court did not address the existence of a category into which Cohen's expression— what Blackmun termed his "absurd and immature antic,"[130] in a phrase more vivid than illuminating—squarely fell. Yet such a category existed, until the Court in *Cohen* quashed it.

That the Court was right to do so, and that Cohen's conduct was not, as the dissent mistakenly decided, "mainly conduct and little speech" will be addressed later; what is significant for present purposes is that the Court in *Cohen* looked beyond the *Chaplinsky* rubric and found, in this one category at least, a very substantial First Amendment problem posed by the censorship that Justice Murphy presumed to be beyond cavil.

Libel

The law of libel was well established at common law at the time of the enactment of the Bill of Rights, and indeed its existence is reflected in the Constitution. For many years libel suits were filed and tried without any thought that the First Amendment might pose a bar to recovery. Only in the instance of seditious libel—libel against political figures or against the country as a whole—was the issue brought up.[131] Prior to the Supreme Court's ruling in *New York Times v. Sullivan*,[132] the Court, when it spoke at

---

128. *Id.* at 27.
129. *Id.* at 24.
130. *Id.* at 27.
131. *See* Henry Wolfe Biklé, *The Jurisdiction of the United States Over Seditious Libel*, 50 Am. Law Reg. 1 (1902).
132. 376 U.S. 254 (1964).

all, merely referred to libel as an instance of unprotected speech.[133] In *Sullivan,* that changed. Confronted with a *New York Times* advertisement that described repression of the burgeoning Civil Rights movement by local law enforcement without naming any names, the Commissioner of Public Affairs of Montgomery, Alabama (whose duties included supervision of the local police force) sued for libel, claiming that he was the target of the advertisement, and that it was libelous.[134] Because the trial court charged the jury that the statements were not privileged, and that the jury need not find actual malice or gross negligence in awarding punitive damages, the failure of the *Times* to verify the advertisement's factual assertions became the base of a substantial verdict in favor of the Commissioner—$500,000.[135]

The Supreme Court, in a landmark opinion, reversed the finding of liability, holding the speech to have been protected by the First Amendment, because it dealt with the conduct of a public official and the *Times* was not found to have acted with "actual malice." The opinion, by Justice Brennan, based its reasoning on the very high place accorded in the constitutional hierarchy of speech of criticism of public officials, reasoning from the United States' "profound national commitment to the principle that debate on public issues should be uninhibited, robust and wide-open, and that may well include vehement, caustic, and sometimes unpleasantly sharp attacks on government and public officials".[136]

What is particularly interesting in the *Sullivan* decision is the neatness with which it tracks the *functional* component of Justice Brennan's earlier opinion in *Roth,* while at the same time it eschews the obscenity case's invocation of the categorical imperative. In *Sullivan,* Brennan denied the

---

133. *See,* for example, *Konisberg v. State Bar of California,* 366 U.S.36, 49, n. 10 (1961); *Times Film Corp. v. City of Chicago,* 365 U.S. 43, 47–48 (1961); *Beauharnais v. Illinois,* 343 U.S. at 250, 266; *Pennekamp v. Florida,* 328 U.S. 331, 348–349 (1946). For a pre-*Chaplinsky* holding to the same effect, *see Near v. Minnesota,* 283 U.S. 697, 715 (1931). None of these cases, save for *Beauharnais,* upheld a libel verdict after constitutional scrutiny, and *Beauharnais* does not fit the paradigm of libel, a tort against individuals, in its typical formulation, involving as it did *group* libel—insults based on race directed not at any individual, but applied across the board to all members of the "defamed" group.

134. 376 U.S. at 255, 281–282.

135. *Id.* at 256, 261–262. Although stingy by the standards of the multimillion-dollar 1980s, this award was quite substantial in 1964. According to Anthony Lewis's splendid account of the *Sullivan* case, *Make No Law: The Sullivan Case and The First Amendment* (1991) at 35, the award "was the largest libel judgment in Alabama history, and enormous by the standards of verdicts anywhere at the time." Because the *Sullivan* case was but one of five suits predicated on the advertisement pending against the *Times* (that totaled $3 million), as well as other suits of a similar nature based on an article by Harrison Salisbury on Birmingham, the newspaper's general counsel was quoted by Lewis as opining that "[w]ithout a reversal of those verdicts there was a reasonable question of whether the *Times,* then wracked by strikes and small profits, could survive." *Id.*

136. 376 U.S. at 270, 280–281.

Chaplinsky categories their "talismanic immunity" from scrutiny.[137] This significant and promising step away from *Chaplinsky* was justly celebrated by Harry Kalven, who called for dancing in the streets in celebration.[138] However, in *Sullivan*, Brennan did not simply jettison his approach in *Roth*, or find it at all inapposite. Rather, he refined it, adopting the functional analysis of obscenity and applying it to libel.

As in *Roth*, in *Sullivan* Brennan found the "central meaning" of the First Amendment to be the promotion of discussion and the debate of ideas that inform political and social choices of the citizenry.[139] Brennan found speech that promoted this ideal to be constitutionally protected; it was, in *Roth* terms, of redeeming social importance.[140] Kalven summarized it with a syllogism:

> THE central meaning of the First Amendment is that seditious libel cannot be made the subject of government sanction. The Alabama rule on fair comment is closely akin to making seditious libel an offense. The Alabama rule, therefore, violated the central meaning of the First Amendment.[141]

By tying the protection of speech to its function, Brennan had both broken free of the *Chaplinsky* framework and unduly limited the definition of which speech is protected. By placing the onus on speech to justify itself, although far less directly or obtrusively than in *Roth*, Brennan opened the way for Robert Bork to opine that the First Amendment's protections were limited to overtly political speech, speech that concerned itself with public affairs.[142] The opinion's freedom from the categorical imperative, however, was a step in the right direction, and a bold one at that.

The subsequent development of libel law, however, has been a story of forgetting—of losing the functional impetus of *Sullivan*, and of simply ghettoizing the *Sullivan* rule to the rule of decision in a *Chaplinsky* category.

---

137. *Id.* at 269.
138. Kalven, *The New York Times Case: A Note on "The Central Meaning of the First Amendment,"* 1964 Sup. Ct. Rev. 191 (1965). Because Kalven's interpretation of the *Sullivan* decision was endorsed by its author, Justice Brennan, the Kalven appreciation is an unusually authoritative analysis of what the Court sought to achieve in the case. *See* Brennan, *The Supreme Court and the Meiklejohn Interpretation of the First Amendment,* 79 Harv. L. Rev. 1, 14–17 (1965).
139. 367 U.S. at 269–270, 291–292.
140. This view found support in the writings of Alexander Meicklejohn. *See Free Speech and Its Relation to Self-Government* (1948). It was adopted (and its inherent limitations pointed out) by Robert H. Bork in 1971. *See* Bork, *Neutral Principles and Some First Amendment Problems,* 47 Ind. L. J. 1, 27 (1971).
141. Kalven, *A Worthy Tradition, supra* note 1, at 66–67.
142. Bork, *supra* note 140, at 27, *et seq.*

Just as the story of obscenity law after *Roth* is a story of definition—what is and what is not obscenity—so too the story of *Sullivan* has become that of the parameters of libel law: Is the privilege *Sullivan* extended limited to statements concerning public officials, or does it extend to public figures?[143] Who is a public figure?[144] What constitutes sufficient recklessness to permit the imposition of liability?[145] Other than the extension of *Sullivan*'s logic to the libelesque case of *Hustler Magazine, Inc. v. Falwell*,[146] which applied *Sullivan*'s requirement of knowing or reckless falsification to an admittedly vicious cartoon and held it to be protected speech because the statements therein were patently not meant to be taken as factual, *Sullivan* has been a sterile propagator outside of its own category.[147]

Fighting Words and the Heckler's Veto

The status of "fighting words" under current constitutional jurisprudence is somewhat confused. In addition to *Chaplinsky*, a flurry of cases reaffirmed the basic doctrine of the decision: that words reasonably understood as provocative of a breach of the peace in a one-on-one situation can result in criminal liability on the part of the speaker. Because this category is so narrowly confined to face-to-face insults that will likely provoke a reasonable person to violence, little need be said about this category, especially in view of recent explications of the jurisprudence of this category, including one compelling (although limited) call for its "interment."[148] Suffice it to say that the category, although strictly limited, still exists in the constitutional jurisprudence.

---

143. *See Curtis Publishing Co. v. Butts*, 388 U.S. 130 (1967) (extending privilege to press reports regarding public figures).

144. *Gertz v. Robert Welch Inc.*, 418 U.S. 323, 339–340 (1974) (defining public figure as an individual of such prominence that he or she is always deemed a public figure, or one who has thrust himself or herself into "the vortex" of a public issue, and is within the context of that issue a public figure). The Court held that private figures need only show negligence to make out a case for liability that will survive constitutional scrutiny. The requirement of negligence was (impliedly) deleted by Justice Powell in *Dun & Bradstreet Inc. v. Greenmoss Builders Inc.* 472 U.S. 249 (1985).

145. *St. Amant v. Thompson*, 390 U.S. 727, 731–732, 734 (1968).

146. 485 U.S. 46 (1988). The case also bears the influence of *Cohen* because the vulgarity of the advertising parody at issue, which portrayed Reverend Falwell recounting incest with his mother in an outhouse in the manner of a Campari advertisement, was extreme both in subject matter and presentation. For a fascinating account of the case's progression through the lower courts to the Supreme Court, and of the decision's significance, see Smolla, *Jerry Falwell v. Larry Flynt: The First Amendment on Trial* (1990).

147. *See also Bond v. Floyd*, 385 U.S. 116 (1966) (defamation, essentially, of United States government protected under *Sullivan* logic).

148. See *Note: The Demise of the Chaplinsky Fighting Words Doctrine: An Argument for Its Interment*, 106 Harv. L. Rev. 1129 (1993). *But see Virginia v. Black*, 538 U.S.—, 155 L.Ed. 2nd 535 (2003) fighting words catagory still viable.

The "heckler's veto" referred to earlier, the existence of which Kalven only reluctantly supported, was typified in *Feiner v. New York*.[149] In *Feiner*, a college student's speech that included "derogatory remarks concerning President Truman, the American Legion, the Mayor of Syracuse and other local officials" also "gave the impression that he was endeavoring to arouse the Negro people against the whites, urging that they rise up in arms and fight for equal rights."[150] The police, tipped off to the growing disputatiousness of the crowd gathered about Feiner by a telephoned complaint, asked Feiner to stop talking, and upon his refusal, and in response to the feeling of the crowd—"at least one threatened violence if the police did not act" against Feiner—arrested him. The Court upheld the conviction as not infringing upon Feiner's First Amendment rights, because his conduct in continuing to address the meeting was tantamount to "incitement to riot"— despite the fact that the putative rioter was *hostile* to Feiner, and intended to silence him by force.

In *Terminiello v. Chicago*,[151] Justice Douglas, writing for a majority of the Court, reversed a conviction in remarkably similar circumstances. In *Terminiello*, a speaker who addressed a crowded auditorium in racist, anti-Semitic terms, and impugned Eleanor Roosevelt (among others) as a Communist, was arrested when the hostile crowd seemed about to erupt. Unlike the *Feiner* conviction, the *Terminiello* conviction was overturned. As Justice Douglas wrote, the court's charge to the jury that offending speech "stirs the public to anger, invites dispute, brings about a condition of unrest, or creates a disturbance" was unconstitutional because "[a] function of free speech under our government is to invite dispute. . . . [S]peech is often disturbing and challenging. It may strike at prejudices and preconceptions and have profound unsettling effects as it presses for acceptance of an idea."[152]

Although the Court in *Terminiello* sidestepped the issue later addressed in *Feiner*, its rhetoric showed little sympathy with the application of the heckler's veto. In *Feiner*, of course, the crowd's anger was imputed to its object. The dissenters in *Feiner* suggested that the duty of the police is to protect the lawful (although noxious) speaker against the crowd—an unobjectionable proposition, surely, until it is no longer objectively possible. What is odd about *Feiner* is that the Court legitimated the subsequent punishment of the speaker, and not simply his being taken into custody and removed from the scene of the incipient riot. Although the protection of the

---

149. 340 U.S. 315 (1951) (upholding, *per* Vinson, C.J., conviction of racially provocative speaker of disorderly conduct based on hostile audience response).

150. *Id.* at 317.

151. 337 U.S. 1 (1949).

152. *Id.* at 4.

speaker might appropriately lead, as a last resort, to his justifiable removal from the scene, (as a sort of ad hoc time, manner, and place restriction), it seems virtually impossible to justify subsequent prosecution of the *victim* of the mob's violence.

Commercial Speech

Although commercial speech is not one of the categories delineated in the *Chaplinsky* opinion, it was created at about the same time.[153] This exclusion from the First Amendment was, at the time it was first enunciated, as absolute as those exclusions provided by *Chaplinsky*. In *Valentine*, the Court provided the states with plenary power to regulate wholly commercial speech. The Court neither completely wrote the category out of the jurisprudence, nor did it simply hew to the *Valentine* rule. Rather, it used the commercial speech category as a prototype for a new breed of categorical analysis. This innovation—the creation of hybrid categories—recognized commercial speech as not wholly outside of the protections of the First Amendment, but did not accord it full protection. By doing so, the Court abandoned the only justification for the *Chaplinsky* categories—that they denied protection only to speech which was so trivial as to be below the dignity of the First Amendment.

In *Virginia State Board of Pharmacy v. Virginia Citizens Consumer Council*,[154] the Court essentially overruled *Valentine*, holding that the First Amendment does provide limited protection to speech of a wholly commercial nature. It rejected the plenary power view as "highly paternalistic," reasoning that "people will perceive their own best interests if only they are well enough informed, and . . . the best means to that end is to open the channels of communication, rather than to close them."[155] In explicating the extent to which the First Amendment applies to commercial speech, the Court found a "'common sense' distinction between speech proposing a commercial transaction, which occurs in an area traditionally subject to government regulation, and other varieties of speech."[156]

In *Orhalik*, the Court opined that the traditional susceptibility to regulation justified the application of a less protective standard of review of state regulation of commercial speech.[157] After acting several times to protect

---

153. See *Valentine v. Christensen*, 316 U.S. 52, 55 (1942).
154. 425 U.S. 748, 771–773 (1976).
155. *Id.* at 770.
156. *Orhalik v. Ohio State Bar Association*, 436 U.S. 447, 455–456 (1978); *see also Bates v. State Bar of Arizona*, 433 U.S. 350, 374 (1977).
157. 436 U.S. at 457.

truthful advertising of lawful activities, however, the Court fouled the waters. In *Central Hudson Gas & Electric Co. v. Public Service Commission*,[158] the Court imposed a balancing test to determine when commercial speech enjoyed constitutional protection and when it could permissibly be banned. Reiterating that the "First Amendment's concern for commercial speech is based on the informational function of advertising," the Court declared that "there can be no constitutional objection to the suppression of commercial messages that do not accurately inform the public about lawful activity."[159]

This seemingly promising holding evaporated quickly, however, as the Court went on to hold that, where the "communication is neither misleading nor related to unlawful activity," suppression was still permissible if the state could "assert a substantial interest to be served by restrictions on commercial speech," and if those restrictions are both directly related to the substantial interest to be served and are the most limited means of achieving that goal.[160] This standard of review, directly equivalent to "intermediate scrutiny" under the Equal Protection Clause, such as is applied to gender discrimination,[161] provides far less protection than the far more exacting standard applied in traditional free speech analysis under *Brandenburg*.

Just how easily this standard can be met was demonstrated in *Posadas de Puerto Rico Association v. Tourism Co.*,[162] in which the Court upheld a ban on casino advertising—which was admittedly not misleading nor did it contain false statements of fact—when directed at residents of Puerto Rico, although similar advertisements directed at tourists were exempted. Moreover, the restrictions were upheld despite the legality of gambling in Puerto Rico, on the theory that the local residents needed protection from the lure of gambling. The government interest asserted—"the reduction of the demand for casino gambling by the residents of Puerto Rico"—was justified as an exercise of the state's police power to protect the "health, safety and welfare" of

---

158. 447 U.S. 557 (1980).

159. *Id.* at 563. *See also First National Bank of Boston v. Bellotti*, 435 U.S. 765, 783 (1978).

160. *Id.* at 564. The Court has recently reaffirmed this articulation of the test for regulation of admittedly truthful, nondeceptive commercial speech. *See Ibanez v. Florida Dept. of Business and Professional Regulation*, 512 U.S. 136, 148–149 (1994) (reversing judgment censuring attorney for use of CPA [Certified Public Accountant] and CFP [Certified Financial Planner] in advertising concerning her law practice, although she was so licensed by the state) (citing other cases).

161. *See Craig v. Boren*, 429 U.S. 190, 202 (1976) (invalidating state statute permitting females to purchase 3.2 percent beer at 18 while limiting males to purchasing said beer after turning 21); *see also Dothard v. Richardson*, 433 U.S 321, 335–336 (1977) (permitting state to decline employing women as "contact guards" in state prisons where record showed prison system suffered from endemic violence with women especially prone to be attacked).

162. 478 U.S. 328, 339–345 (1986).

its people.[163] The restriction was held to directly advance that interest, because preventing the stimulation of demand for casino gambling through advertisement would have the preventive effect of keeping demand down. The Court deferred to the legislative finding that gambling would be more effectively combated by an outright ban on advertising rather than by "promulgating additional speech designed to *discourage* gambling."[164]

The implications of *Posadas* were rather troubling; Chief Justice Rehnquist's opinion for the majority went even further, however. He argued (as he is wont to do)[165] that the power to ban the greater (casino gambling) necessarily includes the power to restrict the lesser, that is, advertisements about the activity.[166] Thus, Rehnquist stated, it would be a "strange constitutional doctrine which would concede to the legislature the authority to ban a product or activity, but deny to the legislature the authority to forbid the stimulation of demand for the product or activity through advertisement on behalf of those who would profit from such increased demand."[167] Justice Brennan in dissent replied correctly, if tartly, that this strange doctrine is called the First Amendment.[168] Moreover, the equal protection and commerce clause implications of *Posadas* are staggering, in that it permits the states to discriminatorily ban speech on the basis of its intended audience—in this case, Puerto Rican residents, but not tourists.

The illusory nature of the protection accorded commercial speech under this highly subjective balancing test should be clear.[169] The moral or finan-

---

163. *Id.* at 341.
164. *Id.* at 344.
165. *See* Lawrence Tribe, *American Constitutional Law* (2d ed., 1988) at 903, n. 84.
166. 478 U.S. at 345–346.
167. *Id.* at 346.
168. *Id.* at 354, n. 4 (Brennan, J., dissenting). In his excellent discussion of *Posadas*, Tribe describes this rejoinder as containing "only slight exaggeration." Tribe, *supra* note 165, at 903. In fact, in view of the fact that the legislature can regulate or ban most activities not specifically enumerated in the Constitution, but cannot under *Brandenburg* ban intentional advocacy of unlawful conduct absent an imminent likelihood of resultant violation of the law, Justice Brennan's response seems not an exaggeration but, if anything, understated.
169. That "illusory" may be too harsh a characterization is shown by the Court's decisions subsequent to that case. In *Rubin v. Coors Brewing Co.*, 514 U.S. 476 (1995), the Court struck (under the *Central Hudson* test), § 5 (e) (2) of the Federal Alcohol Administration Act, prohibiting beer labels from displaying the alcohol content of the beverage. Although the state interest in prohibiting "strength wars" in advertising was found to be substantial enough to pass muster under *Central Hudson*, the fact that the statute in question left alternative means to conduct those "wars" and did not even put a blanket ban on such labeling was found to prevent a finding that the "measure directly advance the asserted government interest." 514 U.S. at 481–482, 488–490. The logic of *Posadas* was explicitly rejected in *44 Liquormart, Inc. v. Rhode Island*, 517 U.S. 484 (1996) (invalidating state's complete ban on advertisement of liquor prices under *Central Hudson* test).

cial harm to Puerto Rican residents from their decision to act (or not act) on the communication directed at them regarding the lawful activity of casino gambling is simply not an objectively ascertainable quantity. To the extent that moral harm forms the basis of this remarkably paternalistic regulation, any moral precept held by a significant segment of the population can then be declared a "substantial" state interest and be permitted to trump the most sacrosanct civil right of all—the right to free speech.[170] Yet this test, first in the form of multiplying semi-*Chaplinsky* categories, and then in the form of a reversion to Frankfurter's balancing approach, has become the standard in all but a limited group of cases. Ironically, the so-called general rule, as encapsulated by the painstakingly evolved *Brandenburg* test, has itself become a *Chaplinsky* category.

TERMINAL STAGES: WINTERS TAKES IT ALL

The proliferation of semi-*Chaplinsky* categories is a story briefly told, as is the marginalization of the *Brandenburg* rule. In the last three decades, the Court has created a series of categories of expression that are accorded intermediate protection, in the tradition of commercial speech. Although the state does not have plenary power to regulate these varieties of speech, it can do so upon a showing of state interest that upon examination is minimal.

The archetypal semi-*Chaplinsky* category, child pornography, was separated from obscenity in *New York v. Ferber*.[171] The Court in *Ferber* upheld the application of child pornography statutes to materials that, although sexually explicit, failed to be obscene. In *Ferber*, the Court explicitly harked back to *Chaplinsky*, approvingly citing Justice Murphy's dictum, and briefly tracing the history of the obscenity doctrine,[172] concluding that "the *Miller* standard, like its predecessors, was an accommodation between the State's interests in protecting the sensibilities of unwilling recipients from exposure to pornographic materials and the dangers of censorship inherent in un-

---

170. There is, of course, nothing new in the state using the police power to safeguard the "moral welfare" of its citizens. The point is that although such vague precepts may be properly used to reflect community standards in questions of public concern, and to protect them, their use in derogation of rights guaranteed to the individual by the Constitution is of far less legitimacy; a vaguely defined, unarticulated moral view shared by some (but not all) citizens should not be more highly valued than the formal provisions of the document by which the government which seeks to impose this moral view is constituted.

171. 458 U.S. 747 (1982).

172. *Id.* at 754–756.

abashedly content-based laws."[173] The Court noted that "[l]ike obscenity statutes, laws directed at the dissemination of child pornography run the risk of suppressing protected expression by allowing the hand of the censor to become unduly heavy."[174] However, the Court found five reasons to justify the application of a looser standard to erotic depictions of children. These reasons range from the "prevention of sexual exploitation and abuse of children," an interest that the Court understandably and justifiably deemed "a government objective of surpassing importance," and various grounds that amplify this concern[175] to the conclusion, that "the value of permitting live performances and photographic reproductions of children engaged in lewd sexual conduct is exceedingly modest, if not *de minimis*."[176] The Court went on define child pornography, in the constitutional sense, in a manner that was both quite broad and more than a trifle disturbing in its vagueness:

> THE test for child pornography is separate from the obscenity standard enunciated in *Miller*, but may be compared to it for the purpose of clarity. The *Miller* formulation is adjusted in the following respects: A trier of fact need not find that the material appeals to the prurient interest of the average person; it is not required that sexual conduct portrayed be done so in a patently offensive manner, and the material at issue need not be considered as a whole. We note that the dis-

---

173. *Id.* at 756 (quoting *Miller*, 413 U.S. at 18–19). It should be stressed that such a justification of *Miller* and of its predecessors is simply untenable, despite the language quoted by the Court. As Justices Douglas and Brennan pointed out in their dissents from that decision, the obscenity doctrine does not require sellers of obscene materials to take reasonable steps to avoid exposing the unwilling and the underage to the materials—indeed, the defendant in *Miller* had taken such precautions, and no evidence was adduced at trial to show that they had failed to be effective. 413 U.S. at 37–48 (Douglas, J. dissenting), 47 (Brennan, J. dissenting). Moreover, even Justice Brennan, who dissented in *Miller*, agreed that the state had the right to protect juveniles and unconsenting adults from exposure to obscene materials. *Paris Adult Theatre*, 413 U.S. at 73 (Brennan, J. dissenting). The *Miller* test, as set out above, likewise in no way requires a showing that the materials could "fall into the wrong hands"; it is sufficient that they are obscene in the eyes of the local community to warrant a ban. *Id.* at 33.

174. 458 U.S. at 756.

175. *Id.* at 756–757, 758–762.

176. *Id.* at 762. The Court justified this *de minimis* status by specifying that "if it were necessary for literary or artistic value" to represent minors engaged in sexual acts, "a person over the statutory age who perhaps looked younger could be utilized." *Id.* at 763. The Court noted the limitations of its ruling by declaring "Nor is there any question here of censoring a particular literary theme or portrayal of sexual activity. The First Amendment interest is limited to that of rendering the portrayal somewhat more 'realistic' by utilizing or photographing children." *Id.* at 763.

tribution of descriptions or other depictions of sexual conduct, not otherwise obscene, which do not involve live performance or photographic or other visual reproduction of live performances, retains First Amendment protection. As with obscenity laws, criminal responsibility may not be imposed without some element of scienter on the part of the defendant.[177]

The breadth of this definition is attested by the Court's own concession that the concern of the New York Court of Appeals, which had found the statute at issue to be overbroad, that "some protected expression, ranging from medical textbooks to pictorials in the *National Geographic* would fall prey to the statute" was understandable, a concern expressed by the Court's own statement that "[h]ow often, if ever, it may be necessary to employ children to engage in conduct clearly within [the statute] in order to produce educational, medical or artistic works cannot be known with certainty."[178]

Under this approach, the works of serious artists or researchers who explore these themes are subject to ban under a statute, presumptively constitutional as applied to their work, that has been explicitly upheld against a facial challenge. Moreover, although the Court hedges on the subject of overbreadth, seeming to state that a category exists of protected sexual depiction of minors,[179] the definition of the unprotected category of child pornography renders the notion that sexual depictions exist that are outside of its scope tenuous at best. Take away the requirements of appeal to prurient interest, offensiveness in that portrayal, and the requirement that the entirety of the work be considered, and what is left is a blanket ban on any explicit sexual portrayal, including, as the Court approvingly cites, "lewd exhibition of the genitals."[180] One could, I suppose, quibble over whether a specific depiction constituted unprotected lewd nudity or protected innocent, fawn-in-Arcady nudity,[181] but the standard fairly read seems to permit the censorship of any depiction of sexuality exhibited on the part of (or suffered by) those under the age of majority. Thus, Sally Mann, a well-regarded photographer who uses her own children as models (with care that they never feel pressured into posing or are exploited), whose photographs explore these areas stands in violation of the

---

177. *Id.* at 764–765 (citations omitted).
178. *Id.* at 773.
179. *Id.* at 766, 774.
180. *Id.* at 765.
181. *Id.* at 765, n. 18 ("nudity, without more, is protected expression," citing *Erznoznik v. City of Jacksonville,* 422 U.S. 205, 213 [1975] (striking down local ordinance against drive-in theaters showing nude scenes if the films could be seen from a public place).

law,[182] as does Ejlat Feuere, a New Jersey part-time art student whose class projects depicting his children precipitated a nightmarish sexual abuse investigation and thoroughly disrupted the lives of Feuere and his entire family.[183] A final example would be a purist's film or stage production of *Romeo and Juliet*; according to the Nurse, Juliet is not yet fourteen when her quite steamy romance with Romeo begins.[184]

The Court by inference found in addition that the merit of these works was no defense (hence the elimination of the context defense of *Miller*), although it formally left the issue open, and in respectively approving and deploring this implication of the opinion, Justices O'Connor[185] and Brennan[186] left the drawing of the inference for another day and were content to give their separate opinions on the issue.

Although a great deal more can be said about the *Ferber* opinion,[187] its great relevance here is in its creation of a new category of unprotected ex-

---

182. For a description of Mann's working methods, as well as of the substantive content of her work and the critical response to it, *see* Mark Mori, *Blood Ties: The Life and Work of Sally Mann* (1993); Richard L. Abel, *Speaking Respect, Respecting Speech* (1998) at 208–209.

183. Doreen Carvajal, "Family Photos or Pornography: A Father's Bitter Legal Odyssey," *New York Times*, 30 January 1995, A1. Abel, *supra* note 182 at 208–209.

184. William Shakespeare, *Romeo and Juliet*, Act I, scene iii, ln. 20–35 (1595). Frederick Schauer points this out, although he leaves it to the Shakespearian knowledge of the reader to recognize just how juvenile the two lovers are, and in how frankly sexual a manner their relationship is depicted. Fredrick Schauer, *Codifying the First Amendment: New York v. Ferber*, 1982 Sup. Ct. Rev. 285, 292 (1983).

185. 458 U.S. at 774–775. O'Connor's opinion on the issue is frankly somewhat schizophrenic, coming down firmly as she does against the creation of "an exception for depictions of serious social value" and in the same breath maintaining that "it is quite possible that New York's statute is overbroad because it bans depictions that do not actually threaten the harms identified by the Court." *Id.* at 775. She then adverts to the examples of medical textbooks and the *National Geographic* brought up by the plurality. What both Justice O'Connor and the plurality seem to miss is that, in the context of the definition of child pornography advanced not by the statute but by the Court itself in *Ferber*, and of the implication seized upon by O'Connor that "serious social value" does not confer a defense upon the material, the issue of overbreadth has already been determined.

186. *Id.* at 775–777.

187. For an interesting look at the *Ferber* opinion, although one that asserts that the categorical approach, if kept within reasonable bounds, can be a valuable tool, *see supra* note 184 at 285. Schauer, Schauer's review of the opinion is especially deft in examining the opinion's methodology, especially the way in which the Court invokes *seriatim* each of the various methods used by it in other situations to conclude that child pornography is a category of unprotected speech. *Id.* at 299–308. Although Schauer concedes that the Court utilizes *Chaplinsky*-like language to describe its result, he maintains (correctly) that the Court does not restrict its methodology to a *Chaplinsky*-style fiat, but rather employs a variety of interpretational techniques, including a *Winters*-style balancing. That the result is the same as Justice Murphy's arbitrary declaration of worthlessness has been shown by the Court's own subsequent characterization of the opinion. *See Waters v. Churchill*, 511 U.S. 661, 671 (1994).

pression. That the speech excepted from the First Amendment's ambit by *Ferber* is one of those categories "so lacking in value that [it falls] outside the protection of the First Amendment" has been recently reaffirmed by the Court, which has breathed new life into the *Chaplinsky* articulation.[188] Notably, if Justice O'Connor's reading of the majority opinion in *Ferber* is correct, speech can now be deemed "low value" even if it possesses "serious social value."

Broadcast speech, whether through the media of television or of radio, the Court has held, is subject to more intrusive governmental regulation than permissibly applied to speech that uses other media.[189] As the Court has repeatedly stated, the basis for the distinction between broadcast media and others is based on the scarcity of broadcast channels: Because the government must regulate and assign the frequencies that individual broadcasters will be permitted to use to prevent airwave Babel or piracy, the Court has consistently reasoned that "[w]here there are substantially more individuals who want to broadcast than there are frequencies to allocate, it is idle to posit an unabridgeable First Amendment right to broadcast comparable to the right of every individual to speak, write, or publish."[190]

The Court has declined to question the validity of this rationale for permitting greater regulation of broadcast speech[191] and has likewise refused to expand the rationale to include the "market dysfunction" that some have argued characterizes the broadcast television market and that allows the rich greater access to speech outlets than the poor, or even those who are simply not wealthy.[192] As a result, the Court limited the sweep of this doctrine, holding in *Turner Broadcasting System, Inc.*, that "[i]n light of [the] fundamental technological differences between broadcast and cable transmission, application of the more relaxed standard of scrutiny adopted in *Red Lion* and the other broadcast cases is inapt when determining the First Amend-

---

188. *Waters v. Churchill,* 511 U.S. at 661; 677–678 (upholding right of government facility as employer to dismiss employee for disruptive speech upon reasonable investigation of evidence of conduct).

189. *Turner Broadcasting System, Inc. v. FCC,* 512 U.S. 622 (1994); comparing *Red Lion Broadcasting Co. v. FCC,* 395 U.S. 367 (1969) (television) and *National Broadcasting Co. v. United States,* 319 U.S. 190 (1943) (radio) with *Miami Herald Publishing Co. v. Tornillo,* 418 U.S. 241 (1974) (print) and *Riley v. National Federation of the Blind of N.C., Inc.,* 487 U.S. 781 (1988) (personal solicitation).

190. *Red Lion, supra* note 189, at 338; *see also Turner Broadcasting System, Inc.,* 512 U.S. at 638–639. For criticism of the scarcity rationale for increased regulation of broadcast speech, see Lee C. Bollinger, *Images of A Free Press* (1991) 87–90, Note, *The Message in the Medium: The First Amendment on the Information Superhighway,* 107 Harv. L. Rev. 1062, 1072–1074 (1994).

191. *FCC v. League of Women Voters,* 468 U.S. 364, 377 (1984).

192. *Id.* at 377; *Austin v. Michigan Chamber of Commerce,* 494 U.S. 652, 657, 658 (1990); *Turner Broadcasting System, Inc.,* 512 U.S. at 639–640.

ment validity of cable regulation."[193] Accordingly, although statutes and regulations that restrict or govern cable transmissions are said to be judged under settled principles of First Amendment jurisprudence, regulations of broadcast television and radio are judged under a relaxed standard.[194]

That standard permits not only regulation of the time, manner, and place of broadcast speech, but also regulation of the speech's substantive content. Thus, the Court has upheld (based on a lesser showing than would suffice under standard First Amendment analysis) restrictions on "indecent" speech, speech that is not obscene and thus is entitled to protection under the First Amendment.[195]

Disparate treatment of speech that has been deemed to be "indecent" has not, however been limited to the broadcasting of such admittedly non-obscene materials. In *Young v. American Mini Theatres, Inc.*,[196] the Court upheld zoning regulations that impacted adult movie theaters, when there was a finding that the films shown there were not obscene, but were merely erotic in their focus.[197] The Court treated the restrictions as "nothing more than a limitation on the place where adult films may be exhibited" and, rather incredibly, one that did not discriminate impermissibly on the basis of the material's content, because the attitude or philosophical content of the films, and their attitude toward the sexuality depicted in the various films shown, was not relevant under the regulation.[198] However, the plurality opinion by Justice Stevens made it quite clear in rejecting the vagueness and the First Amendment and Equal Protection challenges to the regulations, that such films, even when not obscene and thus what one could term "no-value" speech, were of peripheral value, and thus received lesser protection as "low-value" speech:

> [T]HERE is surely a less vital interest in the uninhibited exhibition of material that is on the borderline between pornography and artistic expression than in the free dissemination of ideas of social and political significance. . . . The fact that the First Amendment protects some,

193. 512 U.S. at 639 (citing *Bolger v. Young's Drug Store*, 463 U.S. 60, 74 [1983].)

194. However, in a plurality opinion in *Denver Area Consortium*, 518 U.S. 727, 744, 745 (1996), the Court reversed itself, relying upon the "uniquely pervasive" nature of the cable medium. The Court did not apply traditional "strict scrutiny" but rather assessed whether the restrictions "properly address an extremely important problem, without imposing, in light of the relevant interests, an unnecessarily great restriction on speech."

195. *FCC v. Pacifica Foundation*, 438 U.S. 726 (1978) (upholding, under intermediate scrutiny, regulations prohibiting indecent speech as applied to broadcast of George Carlin's "Seven Dirty Words" monologue).

196. 427 U.S. 50 (1976).

197. *Id.* at 70–71.

198. *Id.*

though not necessarily all, of the that material from total suppression does not warrant the further conclusion that an exhibitor's doubts as to whether a borderline film may be shown in his theater, as well as in theaters licensed for adult presentations, involves the kind of threat to the free market of ideas and expression that justifies the exceptional approach to constitutional adjudication [permitting a covered petitioner to object to a statute on the ground of vagueness]. . . . [199]

Moreover, even though we recognize that the First Amendment will not tolerate the total suppression of erotic materials that have some arguably artistic value, it is manifest that society's interest in protecting this type of expression is of a wholly different, and lesser, magnitude than the interest in untrammeled political debate that inspired Voltaire's immortal comment. Whether political oratory or philosophical discussion moves us to applaud or to despise what is said, every schoolchild can understand why our duty to defend the right to speak remains the same. But few of us would march our sons and daughters off to war to preserve the citizen's right to see "Specified Sexual Activities" exhibited in the theaters of our choice. Even though the First Amendment protects communications in this area from total suppression, we hold that the State may legitimately use the content of these materials as the basis for placing them in a different classification from other motion pictures.[200]

Justice Powell, the swing vote in the case, associated himself only with the time, manner, and place element of this opinion.[201] Nonetheless, as the expression of a plurality view, this analysis (which as the dissent of Justice Stewart aptly noted "stands 'Voltaire's immortal comment' on its head")[202] demonstrates the growing subjectivity of *Chaplinsky* analysis: The plurality did not feel required to tie its views to prior precedent (none of the statements above quoted bear any precedential support) or to the text of the First Amendment. Rather, the Court felt free to read into the

---

199. *Id.* at 61 (rejecting vagueness challenge pursuant to *Dombrowski v. Pfister*, 380 U.S. 479 (1969) [permitting First Amendment vagueness challenge by petitioner plainly within scope of challenged statute]).

200. *Id.* at 70–71. The "immortal comment" of Voltaire, "I disapprove of what you say, but I will defend to the death your right to say it," was quoted earlier in the opinion. *Id.* at 63 (*quoting* S. Tallentyre, *The Friends of Voltaire* (1907) at 199).

201. 427 U.S. at 73–84.

202. *Id.* at 86 (Stewart, J., dissenting). As Justice Stewart goes on to demonstrate, the addition of a "weight" test giving greater protection to speech that the Court finds to be more worthy of protection disregards that which it finds to be of peripheral value empowers the state in a way that even Justice Frankfurter found impermissible: "[w]holly neutral fatuities come under the protection of free speech as fully as do Keats' poems or Donne's sermons." *Id.* at 87 (*quoting Winters v. New York*, 333 U.S. at 528 (Frankfurter, J. dissenting)).

First Amendment its own notions of what speech is worthy or important to society.

This remarkable arrogation of power would truly constitute the Court as the Platonic Guardians feared by Judge Learned Hand.[203] As to the plurality's limiting gloss on the First Amendment, it simply flies in the face, as Justice Stewart so pointedly noted, of the entire point of the Bill of Rights:

> FOR if the guarantees of the First Amendment were reserved for expression that more than a "few of us" would take up arms to defend, then the right of free expression would be defined and circumscribed by current popular opinion. The guarantees of the Bill of Rights were designed to protect against precisely such majoritarian limitations on individual liberty.[204]

One final apparent semi-*Chaplinsky* category of speech should be examined briefly before adverting to the general spread of categorical analysis and its implications. Limits on employer speech—that is, the right of an employer to address his or her unionizing employees—were upheld in *NLRB v. Gissel Packing Co.*[205] In *Gissel Packing Co.* the Court explicitly found that the challenged statute, 29 U.S.C. § 158 (c),

> MERELY implements the First Amendment by requiring that the expression of "any views, argument or opinion" shall not be "evidence of an unfair labor practice" so long as the expression contains "no threat of reprisal or force or promise of benefit" in violation of [§158(a)(1)]. Section [158(a)(1)], in turn, prohibits interference, restraint or coercion of employees in the exercise of their right to self-organization.[206]

This seeming *Chaplinsky* category, however, represents not a categorical imperative founded on fiat but rather a functional analysis, when one applies the reasoning that underlay *Brandenburg*. Even the great First Amendment absolutist Justice Douglas recognized that speech could sometimes form a component of an action, so closely bound up in the action as to be a part thereof.[207] The sort of speech—threats and bribes—included within the proscription at issue in *Gissell Packing Co.* is plainly an example of Justice

---

203. Learned Hand, *The Bill of Rights* (1958) at 73–74; *see also* Gerald Gunther, *Learned Hand: The Man and the Judge* at 659 (1994).

204. 427 U.S. at 86 (Stewart, J. dissenting) (*citing Terminiello v. Chicago*, 337 U.S. 1, 4–5 (1949)).

205. 395 U.S. 575 (1969).

206. *Id.* at 617.

207. *See Brandenburg v. Ohio*, 395 U.S. 444, 454–457 (1969) (Douglas, J. concurring).

Douglas's "speech brigaded with action." In such a case, the speech's message is not censored; rather, the ban falls upon the speech component of the act only incidentally in the process of preventing the action of coercion through threat.

More fundamentally, in *Gissell Packing Co.* the Court treated speech by employers in a unionizing or labor dispute setting as a case of two constitutional rights butting heads—both stemming from the First Amendment (although the employees' right was also further protected by statute)—and ruled that "an employer's rights cannot outweigh the equal rights of the employees to associate freely."[208] Similarly, in *Gentile v. State Bar of Nevada*,[209] an attorney's right to speak freely was held to be regulable only when it clashed with the right to a fair trial enshrined in the Sixth Amendment. Such genuine cases of conflict between constitutional provisions afford, as I have written elsewhere,[210] the only legitimate exercise in "balancing" constitutional rights. Where no such conflict exists, the constitution, as "the supreme law of the land" must prevail over policy decisions, whether those decisions originate with the legislature, the executive, or—least appropriately of all—the judiciary.

By contrast, what links these disparate by-blows of First Amendment jurisprudence is the subtle manner in which their existence subverts the classical *Chaplinsky* paradigm in a way that brings the jurisprudence closer in line with *Winters* and further from the so-called general rule announced by the Court in *Brandenburg v. Ohio*. In the classical paradigm, as has been demonstrated, the *Chaplinsky* categories were conceptualized as speech so inherently lacking in the values recognized by the First Amendment that their censorship left the populace as a whole and public discourse no poorer—and indeed, if anything, richer—for the removal of speech that could only debase the discourse and offend its participants without in any way contributing. In the sliding scale that has instead resulted, speech may have "serious social value" and still be banned upon a lesser showing. Rather than finding such speech to be absolutely outside of the scope of the First Amendment's protection, the Court has watered down the level of protection in these instances by creating a new category, based on the perceived social utility of the speech, with its own distinct level of protection. This result, which Frederick Schauer deems "the inevitable byproduct of broadening the First Amendment,"[211] and which Vincent Blasi so fears that he argues

---

208. *Id.* at 617.
209. 501 U.S. 1030, 1031 (1991).
210. Wirenius, *supra* note 83, at 38–39, n. 38.
211. Schauer, *supra* note 184 at 317 (1983).

for a "lean, mean" First Amendment, is now incipient, is in fact not inevitable. The Court should, as indeed one Justice has called for it to do, simply reject the *Chaplinsky* approach and return to the functional, textually tethered (and thus justifiable) *Brandenburg* jurisprudence that is currently marginalized to one categorical imperative among many others.[212]

R.A.V. AND THE ROAD BACK

In *R.A.V. v. City of St. Paul*,[213] the Court struck down as unconstitutional a city ordinance that made it a misdemeanor to engage in speech that "arouses anger, alarm, or resentment in others on the basis of race, color, creed, religion, or gender."[214] Intriguingly, the Court was unanimous in the result: All nine Justices agreed that the ordinance must be struck. Justice Scalia's opinion for the Court commanded a bare majority; Justice White's concurrence was joined by Justices Blackmun and O'Connor, as well as in part by Justice Stevens, who also filed a separate opinion. The Scalia opinion radically restructured the Court's approach to speech deemed to be within a proscribable *Chaplinsky* category.[215] Where previously such speech had been deemed to be wholly outside of the purview of the First Amendment, Scalia wrote that such speech was merely subject to regulation and not "wholly invisible to the First Amendment."[216] It was not, he continued, that such speech utterly failed to communicate ideas in a manner recognized by the Constitution. Rather, as he quoted from *Chaplinsky*, such speech failed to be "an essential contribution to public discourse."[217] This lack of importance, when weighed against the social ill that defines the category of speech, permitted the state to constitutionally proscribe the speech. However, a proscription based on the underlying message and not on the defining social ill—as the Minneapolis ordinance under which R.A.V. was prosecuted was found by the Court to be—would be unconstitutional.[218] Thus, by focusing on the racist message of R.A.V.'s cross-burning and not on its status as an

---

212. Indeed Schauer even lists "advocacy of illegal conduct"—the *Brandenburg* scenario—as a "distinct" First Amendment category, and not as the general rule. *Id.* at 308.
213. 505 U.S. 377 (1992).
214. *Id.* at 380.
215. Each of the opinions in *R.A.V.* accepted the construction of the ordinance of the Minnesota Supreme Court that limited the ordinance to fighting words as defined in *Chaplinsky.* 505 U.S. at 381. *See also In Re Welfare of R.A.V.*, 464 N.W.2d 507, 510–511 (Minn. 1991).
216. 505 U.S. at 383–384.
217. *Id.* at 384.
218. *Id.* at 385–390.

instance of "fighting words," St. Paul unconstitutionally based its ban on what was protected and not on that element of the speech that permitted suppression.[219] As Scalia put it, the ordinance "is facially unconstitutional in that it prohibits otherwise permitted speech solely on the basis of the subject the speech addresses."[220]

Scalia's opinion, the complexity of which has been neglected in the interests of brevity, has been described as erecting an "ornate conceptual castle."[221] Certainly Scalia was recasting the entire concept of *Chaplinsky*, but not in an entirely rational or supportable way. Indeed, the Scalia gloss on *Chaplinsky* strips away its one claim to legitimacy. If the categories carved out by Justice Murphy over fifty years ago are in fact not so utterly devoid of cognitive value as to fall outside the scope of the First Amendment, we are confronted with a rather frightening doctrine. Rather than Murphy's commonsense (although highly dubious) recognition that some discrete categories of speech are simply of so little importance that the regulation of the speech comprising them does not even pose a First Amendment issue, Scalia stressed that the *Chaplinsky* categories are "no *essential* part of any exposition of ideas."[222] Does this herald a jurisprudence in which the speaker must show that his or her precise articulation forms an essential or at least an important part of the speaker's exposition? As Justice Harlan noted in *Cohen v. California*, "words are often chosen as much for their emotive as for their cognitive force."[223] To permit the government to punish speech based on the word in which an otherwise perfectly legitimate argument is couched is to push the mute button and relegate our purportedly free speakers to uniformity and drabness.

Moreover, to again quote Justice Harlan, "we cannot indulge the facile assumption that one can forbid particular words without also running a substantial risk of suppressing ideas in the process. Indeed, government might soon seize upon the censorship of particular words as a convenient guise for banning the expression of unpopular views."[224] Finally, the cen-

---

219. *Id.* at 386–388.
220. *Id.* at 381. In *Virginia v. Black*, 155 L. Ed. 2d at 552–554 made clear that *R.A.V.* was limited to bans disfavoring one viewpoint or topic of fighting words. Other content discrimination based on the perceived harm caused by specific instances of proscribed speech within the category was deemed constitutional. This holding may substantially vitiate the holding of *R.A.V.*, or reintroduce viewpoint discrimination *sub silentio.*
221. G. Sidney Buchanan, *The Hate Speech Case: A Pyrrhic Victory for Freedom of Speech?*, 21 Hof. L. Rev. 285 (1992). Buchanan's article, which disagrees with Scalia's opinion as both over- and underprotective of speech; on the one hand limiting unduly the government's ability to regulate speech which is concededly outside of the scope of the First Amendment and at the same time permitting the government to regulate speech on the basis of "word-form choice" and not substantive content. *Id.* at 289–292.
222. 505 U.S. at 385 (emphasis in original).
223. *Cohen v. California*, 403 U.S. 15, 26 (1971).
224. *Id.*

sorship of speech based upon its lack of elegance or politesse is an elitist argument in essence, favoring the best educated and thus (normally) the most articulate over those whose points of view may be as valid but who lack the polish of their wealthier competitors in the marketplace of ideas. This onerous requirement, as G. Sidney Buchanan points out, has been rejected by the Court in an unbroken line of cases beginning with *Cohen*.[225] In *R.A.V.*, ominously, the requirement appears to command a court.

Equally ominous is Scalia's revival of the discredited "group libel" decision in *Beauharnais v. Illinois*,[226] the validity of which has been undermined by *Brandenburg v. Ohio*, in which substantially similar speech was held to be protected, and which has been openly rejected by lower federal courts as a precedent as a result.[227] The revival of *Beauharnais* is ominous, not simply because of its extension of the libel category beyond its traditional boundaries (by recognizing a cause of action to inhere in those who have not personally been affected by the speech that they seek to punish through a civil action), or through the use of criminal libel statutes,[228] but in the lax standard of review applied in that case. In the majority opinion in *Beauharnais*, Justice Frankfurter found that the state need only show a rational basis to justify suppression, and further found that the state had met its burden in that "the Illinois legislature may warrantably believe that a man's job and his educational opportunities and the dignity accorded him may depend as much on the reputation of the racial or religious group to which he willy-nilly belongs, as on his own merits."[229] Although Scalia cited *Beauharnais* for a thoroughly innocuous proposition, the mere existence of the defamation category created by *Chaplinsky*, the revival of this extremely broad category that permits censorship on a bare finding of rationality cannot but be greeted with regret.

---

225. Buchanan, *supra* note 221, at 305–308.
226. 343 U.S. 250 (1952) (upholding group libel statute applied to racial epithets published by a white supremacist group in a newspaper advertisement). Scalia used *Beauharnais* in a seemingly innocuous way, merely citing it for the existence of the defamation category. 505 U.S. at 383.
227. For a comparison of *Beauharnais* and *Brandenburg*, see Wirenius, *supra* note 83, at 45–46, n. 65 (1992). For lower court disregard of *Beauharnais*, see *American Booksellers' Association v. Hudnut*, 771 F.2d at 323, 331–332, n. 3 (7th Cir. 1985), *aff'd mem.*, 475 U.S. 1001 (1986) (subsequent decisions have "so washed away the foundations of *Beauharnais* that it cannot be considered authoritative"); *Collin v. Smith*, 578 F.2d 1197, 1205 (7th Cir.), *cert. denied*, 439 U.S. 916 (1978); *see generally* Tribe, *supra* note 165 at 861. Justice Blackmun, joined by Justice Rehnquist, demurred from the devaluation of *Beauharnais*, but to little effect. *See Smith v. Collin*, 439 U.S. 916 (1978) (Blackmun, J. dissenting from denial of certiorari).
228. Notably, *Beauharnais* is the single precedent Catharine MacKinnon relies on in justifying her expansive definition of pornography. However, because she goes beyond even the definition of group libel, even *Beauharnais* does not justify her ordinance. *See* Wirenius, *supra* note 83, at 45–47.
229. 343 U.S. at 258–262, 263.

The most fundamental flaw in Scalia's schema, however, is in its embrace of the *Winters*-style sliding scale approach to the First Amendment, in which the amendment reaches all speech, but to a greater extent when the speech is socially important. Depressingly, one of the keenest critics of Scalia's approach, G. Sidney Buchanan, embraces this aspect of the *R.A.V.* opinion, echoing Frederick Schauer's call for a free-ranging categorical approach to speech questions.[230]

Equally depressing (although in a different way), the concurring opinion by Justice White, preferring to reaffirm the traditional analysis, bemoaned Scalia's reformulation of *Chaplinsky*. Justice White simply found that the ordinance at hand extended beyond the "fighting words" category as defined in *Chaplinsky*.[231] Only Justice Stevens expressed doubts about the continuing viability of the *Chaplinsky* categorical imperative. Sadly, Justice Stevens did so in the process of finding the categorical approach too *protective* of speech, and urged its modification so that the government may more readily censor pernicious and not terribly important speech. In short, Justice Stevens urged the essential adoption of the standard set out by Frankfurter in *Winters*.[232] Most recently, in *Denver Area Consortium*, a plurality of the Court appears to have endorsed just such a naked balancing approach, reviving the discredited "uniquely pervasive" line of argument from *Pacifica*, which later cases have abandoned.[233]

That this line of thought inevitably leads to the devaluing of free speech in favor of other interests, pursuant to the subjective values elevated by the individual scholar or judge has been the lesson painfully taught again and again in the decades since *Chaplinsky*. The Frankfurter-MacKinnon balancing (or cost and effect) approach, which essentially applies a rule of reasonableness to free speech claims, is not considered to be an extreme in the jurisprudence. Indeed, Schauer also has come to adopt (although tentatively) such an overt balancing.[234]

Shying away from "concrete proposals for law reform," Schauer nevertheless argues that free speech law can and should be reformulated to "reallocate costs [of free speech] towards those best able to bear them", by (apparently) separating protected status from civil liability.[235] Without responding in detail to Professor Schauer's interesting and provocative discussion, it seems fundamentally flawed in its assumption that the divorce

---

230. Buchanan, *supra* note 221, at 297–298, n. 77, n. 79.
231. 505 U.S. at 397, 406–407 (White, J., concurring).
232. *Id.* at 417–428.
233. *Supra* note 194.
234. Frederick Schauer, *Uncoupling Free Speech*, 92 Colum. L. Rev. 1321, 1323–1326 (1992).
235. *Id.* at 1324–1326, 1323.

between protected status and civil liability is anything but a fiction; as a far more pragmatic jurist than Schauer knew full well, "the power to tax involves the power to destroy,"[236] and thus eliminates, whatever cosmetic label may remain, the protected status of the speech Schauer seeks to "uncouple." Likewise, Cass Sunstein has joined in the fray, arguing that speech that "costs" can and should be regulated.[237]

Indeed, even *Gentile*, which presented a genuine case in which balancing was inevitable, contains language suggesting that general, holistic balancing is appropriate: "When a state regulation implicates First Amendment rights, the Court must balance those interests against the State's legitimate interest in regulating the activity in question."[238]

What unites all those who advocate this approach, from Frankfurter on, is a dual fallacy: *first*, that only that speech that is cost free is worthy of protection in a free society, and *second*, that the Constitution can be legitimately read to mean whatever we choose it to mean—in short, that judges write on a tabula rasa and can without danger to our freedom inscribe upon the void they would make of the First Amendment whatever rule the judge (or scholar) believes to pitch the proper balance.[239] Justices Holmes and Brandeis, to say nothing of Douglas and Black, saw this usurpation (so often clothed in the guise of judicial humility) for the arrogation it was.[240]

That *R.A.V.* marks a watershed in the jurisprudence is clear. What is not clear is just in what direction the jurisprudence will go from this watershed event. The negative components of *R.A.V.* have been pointed out; its great

---

236. *McCulloch v. Maryland*, 17 U.S. (4 Wheat.) 316 (1819) (Marshall. J.) (invalidating Maryland state statute purporting to levy taxes on federally chartered Bank of the United States).

237. Cass R. Sunstein, *Neutrality and Constitutional Law*, 92 Colum. L. Rev. 1 (1992); *see also* Sunstein, *Pornography and the First Amendment*, 1986 Duke L. J. 589.

238. *Gentile*, 501 U.S. at 1075.

239. In fairness, the "cost and effect" standard in fact originated with Learned Hand's opinion in *United States v. Dennis*, 183 F.2d 201 (2d Cir. 1950) in which Hand, drawing upon his classic "law and economics" opinion in *United States v. Carroll Towing Co.*, 159 F.2d 169 (2d Cir. 1947), applied the same standard of liability to constitutionally protected speech as applied in a garden variety tort action; the test in free speech cases, he wrote in *Dennis*, is "whether the gravity of the 'evil,' discounted by its improbability, justifies such invasion of free speech as is necessary to avoid the danger." For an analysis of Hand's First Amendment jurisprudence in terms of judicial "restraint" and "usurpation," *see* Wirenius, *Helping Hand: The Life and Legacy of Learned Hand*, 25 Seton Hall L. Rev. 505, 516–521 (1994).

240. For Justice Holmes's recognition of the risks of free speech, *see Gitlow v. United States*, 268 U.S. 652, 673 (1925) (Holmes and Brandeis, JJ. dissenting) ("every idea is an incitement"); for a discussion of the institutional arrogance of judicial usurpation clothed as humility, *see Dennis v. United States*, 341 U.S. 494, 580 (Black, J. dissenting); *Scales v. United States*, 367 U.S. 203, 270–271 (Douglas, J. dissenting); *Whitney v. California*, 274 U.S. 357, 375–377 (1927) (Brandeis, J. concurring) (interpreting First Amendment in terms of its explicit language and the Framers' intent).

positive is that it has broken the increasingly improbable fantasy that the *Chaplinsky* (and the semi-*Chaplinsky*) categories are "narrow, clearly defined" exceptions to a generally understood and applicable rule. In fact, the exceptions have come to typify the jurisprudence, leading to the reduction of the general rule—the *Schenck-Debs-Frohwerk-Brandenburg* rule—to just another category of speech.

Although scholars such as Buchanan and Schauer call for the sort of flexible First Amendment applied by the Supreme Court through the categorical imperative that allows a range of constitutional standards to be applied to differing breeds of speech,[241] and other scholars such as Vincent Blasi[242] call for a narrow but strong First Amendment, both suggestions are flawed in the same manner. Either by determining what is "in" or "out" for purposes of the First Amendment (the Blasi approach), or by assigning a given value to speech (the Schauer-Buchanan approach), the person (or persons) who gets to make the determination or the assignment predetermines the outcome of the cases involving those classes of speech.

Both schools of thought (as well as the justices on both sides of the *R.A.V.* debate) seem to believe that the First Amendment permits those who are empowered to enforce it to create their own theory of the desirable meaning of free speech in the context of a democratic republic, untethered to the amendment's language or the history preceding its enactment or subsequent thereto. In view of the monolithic language of the First Amendment, and of the lack of any such tradition of arbitrary selection in the jurisprudence (Frankfurter's opinion in *Winters* was a dissent, after all) the onus should be upon those who promote such a freewheeling approach to constitutional interpretation.

At present, the First Amendment bears a striking resemblance to Julius Caesar as described by Suetonius—"Every woman's man and every man's woman."[243] The exaltation of subjective value judgments to legal principles,

---

241. The essentially political nature of such an "overt" weighing of speech has been recognized and nonetheless endorsed by some advocates of censorship as a means of achieving greater social equality. *See* for example, Tracy Higgins, *Giving Women the Benefit of Equality: A Response to Wirenius*, 20 Ford. Urb. L. J. 77, 87 (1992) (calling for weighing of nature of harm done by speech and "making a judgment about its significance" prior to determining protected or unprotected status of speech, absent issues of intent or remoteness of the causation or likelihood of the alleged harm stemming from that particular speech).

242. Vincent Blasi, *The Checking Value in First Amendment Theory*, 1977 Am. Bar. Found. Res. J. 521; Vincent Blasi, *The Pathological Perspective and the First Amendment*, 85 Colum. L. Rev. 449 (1985) (arguing that the First Amendment's protections should be kept to a limited class of speech, but should be stringent; essentially calling for "a lean and mean" First Amendment).

243. Suetonius, *The Twelve Caesars* (trans. Robert Graves) (revised by Michael Grant) (1989) at 37 (quoting the Elder Curia).

which permits them to determine the outcome of constitutional litigations or to narrow the scope of the amendment itself, eliminates the need for thought, but at a great price. The much vaunted "flexibility" so gained is in fact an anodyne, which disguises under code words ("high value" or "core functions," "low value" or "exceptions") the fact that First Amendment protection is so riddled with exceptions and qualifications that the government has a "legitimate" (that is, acceptable to the courts) argument for censoring virtually anything. Add to this traditional matrix for censorship the relatively recent phenomenon of advocacy of censorship from the left in the name of equality,[244] and the continued evisceration of freedoms to which we all pay lip service as precious seems not paradoxical but inevitable: With so many exceptions to choose from, the American legal community is like an alcoholic staunchly promising to stay sober, but allowing for one glass— or two, at most—of scotch. After all, all things in moderation—including freedom of speech or thought.

---

244. In addition to the examples already cited, *see* Liza Mundy, "The New Critics," *Lingua Franca*, September/October, 1994, 25–33; Marjorie Heins, *A Public University's Response to Students' Removal of an Art Exhibit*, 38 N.Y. Law School L. Rev. 201 (1994).

4

The Road Back

A Unified Field Theory
of the First Amendment

AS THE PRECEDING chapters have hopefully made clear, current First Amendment jurisprudence is simply untenable; based, without any support in the amendment's text, on an ahistorical, illogical and subjective division of speech into "good" speech—protected high-value speech—and "bad" speech—unprotected low-value speech—the present-day understanding of free speech is breaking down before our very eyes. Thus, intermediate categories of speech—semi-high-value speech? or sort-of-low-but-not-quite-nugatory speech?—have been evolved in the contexts of commercial speech, broadcast speech, employer speech (in the context of labor elections or union disputes) and, of course, child pornography. The U.S. Congress, seizing upon the "indecency" standard applied to broadcasting and child pornography, has unsuccessfully tried to extend the rationale to yet another context: the Internet.[1]

In short, the situation is becoming ever more fluid. Increasingly, it is impossible to determine whether an utterance is protected until after it is published and some authority determines or declines to prosecute. We are not far, jurisprudentially, from the state Justice Black feared and so eloquently warned against, "water[ing] down the First Amendment so that it becomes little more than an admonition to Congress."[2] Note that, so far, this state is only reflected in the jurisprudence: Despite the existence of

---

1. For example, the Telecommunications Act of 1996, 47 U.S.C. § 223 is discussed in full at Chapter 6 *infra*.
2. *Dennis v. United States*, 341 U.S. 494, 580 (1950) (Black, J. dissenting). Such a watered-down view of the First Amendment was in fact urged by Judge Learned Hand in *The Spirit of Liberty* (2d ed. 1953) at 278 (describing the First Amendment's prohibitions as "no more than admonitions of moderation").

laws that regulate speech and doctrines that support such laws, in most of the United States materials that are so forbidden are nonetheless readily available. Of course this is more true in some areas (New York City, for example) than in others.

This phenomenon is probably the result of the persistence of the culture of the First Amendment. The old libertarian generalities—the "bromides" of chapter 2—have at least enshrined the *ideal* of freedom of speech and instilled an orthodoxy based on a reluctance to censor. But that culture, under assault from the right and the new left, is flagging. The present political era has transformed *liberalism* into a dirty word; the left rejects it as (at best) well-meaning but ineffective, the right as morally bankrupt. Both of them, of course, profit from liberalism's single greatest contribution to our society: the First Amendment. Like a wounded bear in a bear-baiting, the ideal of freedom of speech is still formidable, but unless it is succored and reinvigorated it will eventually collapse under the weight of its individually puny adversaries. How to provide that succor is the concern of this chapter.

In order to effectively confront its attackers, those who favor free speech must have answers to the difficult questions they pose. But no answers are possible, no defense can be constructed, without a logically coherent understanding of what the First Amendment means. What is frustrating about this position is that such a coherent understanding has been at hand for decades and has unjustifiably been neglected. That coherent understanding involves reassertion of the *Schenck-Debs-Frohwerk-Brandenburg* tradition of free speech as the center of the First Amendment's meaning and scope, and its application as such.[3] *Brandenburg* and its parents must be rescued from the marginalized status that Chaplinskyism has relegated them to.

In order to do this, that center needs to be fleshed out, both in terms of its justifications, and in its application across the board. This means weeding out the false conflicts—discarding the nonsense about "high-" and "low-" value speech in favor of a functional approach to the First Amendment. Then the difficult task must be assayed of examining the amendment's scope in those rare cases of genuine conflicts between constitutional mandates—the only time when the "balancing" advocated by Frankfurter and his modern disciples (most of whom would not recognize themselves as such, in fairness) can be appropriate.

---

3. In the process, of course, we will be revisiting a certain amount of the ground covered in the preceding chapters. Having described the evolution of the jurisprudence in Chapters 2 and 3, I now discard the mask of neutrality, and propose an effort at synthesis.

The Test and Its Origin

The "test," by which is meant the First Amendment standard as evolved in the line of cases from *Schenck v. United States* to *Brandenburg v. Ohio* discussed in Chapter 2, is a hybrid. To unpack the unitary *Brandenburg* standard requires more than just quoting the operative language from the case, that is, the Court's statement that the First Amendment does "not permit a state to forbid or proscribe advocacy of the use of force or of law violation except where such advocacy is directed to inciting or producing imminent lawless action or is likely to incite or produce such action."[4]

If one reads into *Brandenburg* the qualifications expressed as far back as *Schenck* and *Debs*, it permits punishment for speech only under the following circumstances: *first*, when the utterance of the speech creates a significant risk (a "clear and present danger") that an evil will result; *second*, when that evil is one that Congress has the right to act to prevent; *third* (and finally), when the actor has given tongue to the speech *with the specific intent of causing that very evil*.[5] It combines the strictest form of the old "clear and present danger" standard evolved by Justices Holmes and Brandeis with the "direct incitement" required for censorship by Judge Learned Hand in *Masses Publishing Co. v. Patten*.[6]

Because *Brandenburg* on its face speaks only to the case of subversive advocacy, it is less than obvious how its standard applies in different contexts and in what way it encapsulates the prohibition of the First Amendment. That prohibition, and that test, center on the concept of the *verbal act* or

---

4. 395 U.S. at 447, *quoting Noto v. United States*, 367 U.S. 290, 297–298 (1960). The Court relied on *Yates* in its decision and quoted *Noto* to the effect that "the mere abstract teaching . . . of the moral propriety or even moral necessity for a resort to force and violence, is not the same as preparing a group for violent action and steeling it to such action."

5. *See Brandenburg v. Ohio*, 395 U.S. 444 (1969). As set out in Chapter 2, *Brandenburg* represents a culmination of the evolving tradition of a meaningful standard under the First Amendment begun in *Schenck v. United States*, 249 U.S. 47 (1919); *Debs v. United States*, 249 U.S. 211 (1919); and *Frohwerk v. United States*, 249 U.S. 204 (1919) (affirming convictions of antiwar protesters under Espionage Act on ground that such conduct presented a "clear and present danger" that unlawful conduct would occur).

    These cases, properly understood (that is, with a tight temporal framework as mandated by *Brandenburg*, and with a finding of actual subjective intent to cause the harm that is implied in *Debs*, explicit in *Brandenburg*) form a uniform test, which will be referred to as the "*Brandenburg* standard" for the purposes of brevity.

6. 244 F. 535 (S.D.N.Y.), *rev'd* 246 F. 24 (2d Cir. 1917) (holding that left-wing magazine's opposition to First World War and conscription did not violate Espionage Act, as magazine fell short of advocating violation of law). This truism of the literature—that *Brandenburg* reflects the approaches of both Holmes and Hand—is a little misleading; as seen in Chapter 2, Holmes required a finding of specific intent as a prerequisite for liability in *Debs v. United States*, 249 U.S. 211 (1919), one of the initial trio of decisions that created a substantive protection of speech under the United States Constitution.

"speech brigaded with action" that have been at the outskirts of the juris-prudence from the beginning. An examination of the text of the amend-ment, remembering the historical evolution of the test as already explained in Chapter 2, suggests that this restatement of the *Brandenburg* rule quite aptly captures the nature of the First Amendment.

From Federalism to Individualism: Growth of a Guarantee

The text of the Free Speech and Free Press Clauses state in some of the most uncompromising prose contained in the Constitution the simple statement that "Congress shall make no law . . . abridging the freedom of speech, or of the press, or the right of the people peaceably to assemble and to peti-tion the Government for a redress of grievances."[7] In a text-bound analysis, the first question to ask is whether there are any ambiguities here. One can discuss what is meant by "abridging" and what is meant by "the freedom of speech" and whether that limits the amendment's scope, as Holmes initially thought,[8] to protection of the freedom of speech that existed under the common law of the time: that is, the right to be free to publish—and to take the consequences if the government prosecuted and the judicial branch convicted.

This view of the language is certainly not compelled by the words "abridging" or, for that matter by the definite article preceding the words "freedom of speech." It seems a stretch to read such a limitation into the words, particularly when the authors of the first ten amendments to the Con-stitution clearly knew how to protect the scope of a right as defined in the common law. Under the Seventh Amendment, for example, "no fact tried by a jury shall be otherwise re-examined in any Court of the United States, than according to the rules of the common law."[9]

Similarly, the Seventh Amendment also states that "the right of trial by jury shall be preserved,"[10] a word far more redolent of an intention to freeze already existing doctrine than is abridging. An "abridgement" may be of a right newly created, where the "preservation" of a right clearly references a preexisting set of law. This is particularly the case because the First Amend-ment, unlike the Seventh, does not explicitly reference the existing legal concept, that is "the right to" freedom of speech, as opposed to "the free-dom of speech."

---

7. U.S. Const. Amend. I.
8. *See Patterson v. Colorado,* 205 U.S. 454, 462–463 (1907).
9. U.S. Const. amend. VII.
10. U.S. Const. amend. VII.

Despite its endorsement by Justice Story (in his off-the-bench writing), Chancellor Kent,[11] and Holmes (in the short-lived *Patterson* case),[12] the view that the First Amendment merely codified the common law does not derive support from the language of the First Amendment. Under the axioms of constitutional interpretation, the language is, after all, the first place to go in constructing an understanding of any legal instrument,[13] and not the contemporary understanding of it.[14]

The evidence for this so-called intent-based construction of the amendment is in any event quite slim. It rests on the facts that the states widely accepted the common law rule that limited protection of freedom of speech to a prohibition of prior restraint, and that the federal government, under the Alien and Sedition Acts, prosecuted expressions of opinion unfavorable to the ruling Federalist Party.[15] However, the actual *validity* of this course of conduct is far from clear. It was hotly contested at the time, and, as Justice Holmes summed up the evidence in his classic dissent in *Abrams v. United States*, "History seems to me against the notion. I had conceived that the United States through many years had shown its repentance for the Sedition Act of 1798, by repaying fines that it had imposed."[16] The Supreme Court later adopted Holmes's analysis, concluding bluntly that "[a]lthough the Sedition Act was never tested in this Court, the attack upon its validity has carried the day in the court of history."[17]

In any event, the language of the amendment does not support the common law or "Blackstonian" view of the First Amendment, and the practice of the government is unilluminating, because it was not taken to the Supreme Court for scrutiny and evaluation. Such evidence as to contemporary intention can best be deemed equivocal. The remaining question is whether there is an alternative understanding of the First Amendment. In fact, there is.

The First Amendment by its own words expresses an absolute prohibition—like Justices Hugo Black and William O. Douglas, I cannot find the

---

11. Joseph Story, *Commentaries on the Constitution of the United States* § 993 (14th ed., reprint Carolina Academic Press, 1987 [1833]); James Kent, 2 *Commentaries on American Law* 18 (reprint, 1901).

12. *See also* Westel W. Willoughby, *The Constitutional Law of the United States* §§ 450–451, at 842–845 (1910).

13. *See* Chapter 1 at notes 17–23.

14. Although a good case is made for an alternative, and far more expansive, understanding of the First Amendment by academic contemporaries of Story that persisted throughout the pre–World War I period by David Rabban, *The First Amendment in Its Forgotten Years*, 90 Yale L.J. 514 (1981), *Free Speech in Its Forgotten Years* (1996).

15. *See* Levy, *Legacy of Suppression: Freedom of Speech and Press in Early American History* (1960) (revised and modified as *The Emergence of a Free Press* (1985); *see also* David Yassky, *Eras of the First Amendment* 91 Colum. L. Rev. 1699, 1709–1713 (1991).

16. *Abrams v. United States*, 250 U.S. 616, 630 (Holmes, J. dissenting) (1919).

17. *New York Times v. Sullivan*, 376 U.S. 254, 276 (1964) (collecting historical materials).

arrogance to rewrite "no law abridging" into some less sweeping statement. But that prohibition is directed at one place and one place only. It is *Congress* that may not pass any law abridging the freedom of speech. Now, the executive, in the language of the Constitution, does not have any power to pass laws, and the judicial branch is not so empowered, either. Prior to the development of the modern executive pioneered by Theodore Roosevelt, such was (with occasional exceptions) the constitutional practice as well as the theory.[18] The most natural understanding of the First Amendment's language is that it presents an absolute bar to the intrusion on speech—a blanket prohibition—by the federal government. And *only* by the federal government.

This literalist understanding of the amendment is also supported by the available evidence about the general purpose of the Bill of Rights: to prevent the expansion of the more remote and less easily controlled federal government into areas best left to the more local (and thus more directly answerable to the people) state governments.[19] Indeed, the understanding of the Supreme Court, from John Marshall's time until the enactment of the Civil War amendments is that *none* of the protections of the Bill of Rights were applicable against the state governments.[20] As we have seen already,[21] the Supreme Court in *United States v. Cruikshank* held just that:

> THE first amendment to the Constitution prohibits Congress from abridging "the right of the people to assemble and to petition the government for redress of grievances." This, like the other amendments proposed and adopted at the same time, was not intended to limit the powers of the State governments with respect to their own citizens, but to operate upon the National government alone. It is now too late to question the correctness of this construction. As was said by the late Chief Justice [Chase], in *Twitchell v. the Commonwealth*, "the scope and application of these amendments are no longer subjects of discussion here." They left the authority of the States just where they found it, and added nothing to the already existing powers of the United States.[22]

Thus, the complete disabling of the federal government in proscribing speech seems quite clearly to be the effect of the words of the First Amend-

---

18. *See* H. W. Brands, *TR: The Last Romantic* (1997) at 417–418 (concluding that at Roosevelt's accession to the presidency, "the center of American political gravity was still well toward the eastern end of Pennsylvania Avenue").

19. Yassky, 91 Colum. L. Rev. at 1707–1709.

20. *Barron v. Mayor of Baltimore*, 32 U.S. (7 Pet.) 243 (1833); *see* Chapter 2 at notes 12–15.

21. Chapter 2 at notes 13–15.

22. *United States v. Cruikshank*, 92 U.S. 542, 552 (1875), *quoting Twitchell v. Pennsylvania*, 7 Wall. (74 U.S.) 321 (1869) other citations omitted.

ment, and is supported by the understanding of the respective roles of the federal and state governments that motivated the enactment of the Bill of Rights. Thomas Jefferson's understanding of the First Amendment seems also to reflect a disabling of the federal government: "libels, falsehood and defamation, equally with heresy and false religion, are withheld from the cognizance of federal tribunals."[23] For the protection of legitimate interests that conflict with those of speakers, the theoretically more trustworthy states had plenary power to legislate.

However, this dualistic model was thrown out of joint by the enactment of the Fourteenth Amendment. That amendment states that "[n]o State shall make or enforce any law which shall abridge the privileges and immunities of citizens of the United States; nor shall any State deprive any person of life, liberty, or property, without due process of law."[24] The effect of the passage of this amendment was addressed, although not decided, in *Spies v. Illinois*.[25] In *Spies*, the Court summarized the approach that has been, correctly, taken over time with respect to the effect of the Fourteenth Amendment: "[W]hile the ten Amendments as limitations on power only apply to the Federal Government and not to the States, yet in so far as they declare or recognize rights of persons, these rights are theirs, as citizens of the United States, and the Fourteenth Amendment as to such rights limits state power, as the ten Amendments had limited Federal power."[26] Although the Court has always declined to declare at any one point that the passage of the Fourteenth Amendment "incorporated" the guarantees of the Bill of Rights and applied them against the states, each of those guarantees has been found to have been so incorporated, including the First Amendment, as set out in Chapter 2.

This is, of course, a broad-brush statement. The evolution of the jurisprudence concerning the Fourteenth Amendment was rendered problematic by the Court's early and manifestly wrong decision in *The Slaughter-House Cases*,[27] holding that the Privileges and Immunities Clause of the Fourteenth Amendment was essentially without meaning—that it simply reiterated the guarantee of the similar clause of the Fifth Amendment. This ruling, of

---

23. J. Elliot, *Debates on the Federal Constitution* (1876) at 541; William O. Douglas, *The Supreme Court and the Bicentennial* (1978) at 18.
24. U.S. Const. Amend XIV, § 1 (1869).
25. 123 U.S. 131, 166 *et seq.* (1887).
26. *Spies v. United States*, 123 U.S. at 166 (*quoting* petitioner's argument). In *Spies*, the Court found that it did not have to rule on whether this was in fact the effect of the Fourteenth Amendment because the state law in question was constitutional under both the state and federal standards. *Id.* at 170.
27. 83 U.S. 36 (1872). For a critique of this decision that remains, in my view, unanswerable even over 130 years later, *see* Justice Bradley's dissent, which attacks the majority opinion on the grounds of language, logic, the intent of the drafters, and sanity. *Id.* at 111–123.

course, violates one of the principal axioms of constitutional construction —that no provision shall be read in such a manner as to deprive it of meaning. Rather than overrule the decision, the Court has fashioned its understanding of the Fourteenth Amendment's meaning, and the vast bulk of civil rights jurisprudence, on the Due Process Clause. Although the end result has been largely the same as if the Court had simply accepted the petitioner's argument in *Spies*, it is rather difficult to set rational limits to a jurisprudence that finds *substantive* constitutional rights under a clause explicitly directed at the *process* accorded persons by the states.[28]

In any event, both in the cold light of what really happened, and in a commonsense reading of the Fourteenth Amendment as propounded by Justices Harlan and Bradley, it is clear that the First Amendment must be applicable to the states through incorporation. The only question is whether the incorporation applies the amendment at full strength against the states, or whether a denatured First Amendment—free speech lite—is the result of the incorporation. The courts have uniformly held,[29] and the rather mechanistic language of the Fourteenth Amendment suggests, that the result of the process of incorporating the First Amendment is that the same limitations must apply to the states as to the federal government.

The theory animating this reading of the Due Process Clause is that the First Amendment is a liberty which is fundamental in any scheme of ordered liberty[30] and as such is *selected* to be, in its entirety, incorporated into the Fourteenth Amendment (like most of the other provisions of the Bill of Rights, except for the Second, Third, and Seventh Amendments, which somehow don't rate).[31] The problem with this assumption of "jot-for-jot incorporation" under the Due Process Clause is that there is nothing in the Due Process Clause that suggests that the clause *does* uniformly import,

---

28. *See* Chapter 2, note 35. Notably, the first Justice Harlan tried to resurrect the Privileges and Immunities Clause as a source of the substantive rights provided under the Fourteenth Amendment in his dissenting opinion in *Patterson v. Colorado*, 205 U.S. 454, 463–465 (Harlan, J. dissenting).

29. *See* Michael Kent Curtis, *No State Shall Abridge: The Fourteenth Amendment and the Bill of Rights* (1986) at 171–211 (summarizing judicial adoption of incorporation theory).

30. *See Palko v. Connecticut*, 302 U.S. 319, 324–336 (1937) (*per* Cardozo, J.). The specific holding of *Palko*, that the double jeopardy clause does not apply to the states, was overruled in *Benton v. Maryland*, 395 U.S. 784 (1969). In *Benton*, the Court also restructured the inquiry somewhat, asking whether a guarantee was "fundamental to the American scheme of justice" and not whether its presence rendered the state's proceedings violative of "fundamental fairness," as Cardozo had. 395 U.S. at 794–795, *quoting Duncan v. Louisiana*, 391 U.S. 145, 149 (1968).

31. The Third Amendment has not yet been incorporated, but neither the federal nor the state governments have demonstrated much interest in quartering soldiers in private dwellings. Barracks have somewhat mitigated this concern of the Framers. Likewise, the Second Amendment and the Seventh Amendment's protection of jury trials in civil cases has yet to be applied to the states.

unaltered, the provisions of the Bill of Rights. (Or, for that matter, that any substantive rights fall within its scope). That argument is far better based on the Privileges and Immunities Clause, as Justice Black argued in *Adamson v. California* and many subsequent opinions, a conclusion that was shared by Justice Douglas.[32]

By contrast, substantive due process analysis plays right into the so-called countermajoritarian difficulty discussed in Chapter 1. Legal philosopher par excellence Ronald Dworkin disputes this, stating that the substantive constraints that have been imported into due process are legitimately to be found there. He justifies his argument on the ground that "a demand for coherence of principle, which has evident substantive consequences, is part of what makes a process of decision making a legal process."[33]

As an attempt to legitimate "substantive due process" reasoning, however, Dworkin's theory also reduces the error of the *Lochner*-era court to an error of choosing the wrong moral precepts to elevate. Moreover, Professor Dworkin's approach is one that strives to maximize the moral quality of the law—to make of the law the best it can be. But that in a sense usurps the right of the people to decide what the "best" to be enshrined in our law should be. Hence a closer conformity to the body of the Constitution, by reviving the Privileges and Immunities Clause not only makes for a more comprehensible jurisprudence, one that hews more closely to the text, it also blunts the criticism, otherwise fairly strong, that the Supreme Court is in essence antidemocratic.

As suggested above, that long-neglected clause, disregarded because of the *Slaughter House Cases*, makes clear that the federally guaranteed rights of American citizens are not to be infringed upon by the states. There is nothing to suggest that those rights do not include those provided in the Bill of Rights, and so the conclusion seems inevitable that the First Amendment, of its own weight a prohibition directed at the Congress, applies uniformly against the states as well. In other words, despite T. S. Eliot's warning, when the Supreme Court held the states to be subject to the First Amendment, it did "the right deed for the wrong reason."[34]

If the *Cruikshank* meaning of the First Amendment—a complete disabling of the federal government from the regulation of speech—was correct, both in terms of the language and of the intention of the drafters, then its incorporation and effect on the states must likewise be a complete disabling. In

---

32. *Adamson v. California*, 332 U.S. 46, 92–123 (1949) (Black, J. dissenting). *See generally* Curtis, *supra* note 29, at 197–211.

33. Ronald Dworkin, *The Arduous Virtue of Fidelity: Originalism, Scalia, Tribe, and Nerve*, 65 Ford. L. Rev. 1249, 1254, n. 6 (1997); *see also* Ronald Dworkin, *Law's Empire* (1986) at ch. 6.

34. T. S. Eliot, *Murder in the Cathedral* (1935) Act II. "The last temptation is the greatest treason/to do the right deed for the wrong reason."

truth, as Justices Douglas and Black urged, "no law abridging" must in truth mean "no law abridging." Which poses the question: What is "speech" in the terms of the First Amendment?

The Nature of Speech and the Concept of "Verbal Acts"

The question of what is meant by the word "speech" as used in the First Amendment is of critical importance in understanding the amendment's scope, particularly if the absolute nature of the ban against "abridgement" is agreed upon. Indeed, it is by declaring unpopular forms of communication to be "nonspeech" that the entire *Chaplinsky*-based approach was able to have its cake and eat it too—by paying lip service to the stringent tests that are applied to government regulations of speech, the Court has managed to evade applying those tests in the overwhelming majority of cases by declaring that these cases do not involve speech at all in constitutional terms.

This sort of dodge, in addition to the flaws of subjectivity, creates a temptation on the part of the judiciary to cave in to popular pressure in times of trouble—how bad can one more category of "nonspeech" or "low-value" speech be in our already riddled shield? Without any doctrinal limiting factor, any exception may be made with equal legitimacy. Far better, surely, to really plumb the meaning of the "verbal act" concept as it evolved to *Brandenburg*, and then to evaluate the free speech "problem areas" in light of that exploration.

Significantly, the *Brandenburg* test does not encapsulate the only set of circumstances in which a verbal act may be discerned. Rather, it captures the dynamic of when an action performed by an auditor may be imputed to another whose sole contribution to the act takes the form of speech that falls short of a command. Rather, the rule, as Justice Douglas encapsulated it in his dissenting opinion in *Roth v. United States*, "Freedom of expression can be suppressed if, and to the extent that, it is so closely brigaded with illegal action as to be an inseparable part of it."[35]

One of the cases relied upon by Douglas in his *Roth* formulation, *NLRB v. Virginia Electric & Power Co.*,[36] provides an excellent analysis of "speech brigaded with action." In that case, an employer with a long history of anti-union behavior actively resisted its employees' decision to join a local union chapter. The company sought to urge its employees to deal with the company on an individual basis rather than to bring in "outsiders." In ex-

---

35. *Roth v. United States*, 354 U.S. 476, 514 (1957) *citing Giboney v. Empire Storage & Ice Co.*, 336 U.S. 490, 498 (1949) (upholding state court injunction against labor picketing) (*per* Black, J.).
36. 314 U.S. 469, 477–478 (1941).

plaining the impact of the National Labor Relations Act upon the right of employers to speak, the Court stated:

> THE sanctions of the Act are imposed not in punishment of the employer but for the protection of the employees. The employer in this case is as free now as ever to take any side it may choose on this controversial issue. But, certainly, conduct, though evidenced in part by speech, may amount in connection with other circumstances, to coercion within the meaning of the Act. If the total activities of an employer restrain or coerce his employees in their free choice, then those employees are entitled to the protection of the Act. And in determining whether a course of conduct amounts to restraint or coercion, pressure exerted vocally by an employer may no more be disregarded than pressure exerted in other ways.[37]

In applying this concept, the Court held that the finding of the National Labor Relations Board that the employer had "urged its employees to organize and to do so independently of 'outside' assistance, and that it thereby interfered with, restrained and coerced its employees" failed to articulate a proper basis for liability. Because "it does not appear that the Board raised them [the employer's utterances] to the level of coercion by reliance on the surrounding circumstances" and the utterances were themselves were not coercive on their face, the Court vacated the finding against the employer, and remanded the case for further fact-finding.[38]

In a more seminal case involving employer speech that *was* deemed coercive and thus violative of the National Labor Relations Act, *NLRB v. Gissel Packing Co.*,[39] the Court explicitly noted that the challenged statute, 29 U.S.C. § 158(c), "merely implements the First Amendment by requiring that the expression of 'any views, argument or opinion' shall not be 'evidence of an unfair labor practice', so long as such expression contains 'no threat of reprisal or force or promise of benefit in violation of [§ 158(a)(1)]. Section [158(a)(1)], in turn, prohibits interference, restraint or coercion of employees in the exercise of their right to self-organization."[40] The *Gissel* court thus found itself presented with a case of two sets of constitutional rights—the rights of the employer and the rights of the employees (the latter of which was also protected by a statute)—and had sought to mediate between

---

37. 314 U.S. at 477.
38. *Id.* at 479–480.
39. 395 U.S. 575 (1969).
40. *Id.* at 617.

them, concluding that "an employer's rights cannot outweigh the equal rights of the employees to associate freely."[41]

This concept of "speech brigaded with action" advanced by Justice Douglas (and, as suggested in Chapter 2, captured by the threshold for suppression established in *Brandenburg*) harks back to the concept of a verbal act, notably set out in *Gompers v. Bucks Stove & Range Co.*[42] The *Gompers* concept, that speech is not immunized from prosecution when it functions not as a means of communication but rather solely as an integral component in an action that the state (or federal) government has the right to proscribe, is reflected as well in the jurisprudence, as pointed out earlier. Picketing, for example, was described by Justice Douglas as "free speech plus," meaning that it combined expressive elements with regulable conduct, and that the regulable component did not gain immunity because of the entwined expression.[43] Thus, "[t]hough the activities themselves are under the First Amendment, the manner of their exercise or the collateral aspects fall without it."[44]

In *Schenck*, that was the entire point of the classic Holmes analogy that permitted punishment for falsely shouting "Fire!" in a crowded theater. From this clear example of speech that functions as a "verbal act," Holmes moved immediately on to the injunction in *Gompers*, justifying that decision because the First Amendment does not protect "words that may have all the effect of force" in the context in which they are uttered.[45]

The *Brandenburg* test and the concept of verbal acts are not an automatic formula that will magically wave away any difficulty in adjudicating cases. The *Brandenburg* test captures usefully several of the criteria for identifying a verbal act, or when a speaker can appropriately be held liable for actions physically performed by another; it thus recognizes what is or is not functional speech under the First Amendment in such a context. The requirement of temporal imminence serves the purpose of aligning the speaker with the performed action. Like a command that carries along with

---

41. *Id.* The Court expressed itself in terms of "balancing" these conflicting rights, but that concept really only becomes applicable when conduct that is protected by the conflicting rights is present, and the Court's conclusion that the employer's speech was the functional equivalent of a verbal act—was "speech brigaded with action," in other words—renders talk of balancing inapplicable.

42. *Gompers v. Bucks Stove & Range Co.*, 221 U.S. 418, 439 (1911); *see also Fox v. Washington*, 236 U.S. 273, 277 (1915). Both cases are more fully discussed in Chapter 2 at notes 38–39 (*Gompers*) and 44–47 (*Fox*).

43. *Communist Party v. SAC Board*, 367 U.S. 1, 173 (1960) (Douglas, J. dissenting).

44. *Id.* at 173 (Douglas, J. dissenting).

45. 249 U.S. 47, 52 (1919).

the message of "do this" the subliminal or implicit corollary of either "or else" or "on my authority," the temporal imminence requirement personally involves the speaker in the resultant act, and (through the intent requirement) puts his or her imprimatur upon it.

An excellent example of just such a verbal act surfaced in the prosecution of Charles Manson. As Vincent Bugliosi explained in *Helter Skelter*, his account of the investigation and trial of the Manson family murders, Manson's style of ruling his followers presented a problem in holding him accountable for the murders he had instigated:

> MANSON rarely gave direct orders. Usually he'd suggest, rather than command, though his suggestions had the force of commands, rather than of suggestions. . . . *Domination*. Unless we could prove this, beyond all reasonable doubt, we'd never obtain a conviction against Manson.[46]

Because Manson generally used permissive language, Bugliosi had great difficulty showing that he knew that his statements would be regarded as mandatory, and thus in establishing that Manson's mere utterance of the "suggestion" sufficed to impute the murders to him. In other words, Bugliosi needed to show, by adducing evidence of his control over every aspect of his followers' lives, that Manson was not merely spouting off to a collection of zealots who weighed his ideas and, on their own accord, chose to act upon them.

Plenty of writers, from Karl Marx to Andrea Dworkin, have at times made statements suggesting that violence is an appropriate way to address perceived social problems. The distinction between such bloodless advocacy and Manson's statements, although they are in the abstract much alike, requires a showing of something more in order to impose liability, a specific context to tie the resultant act to the words at issue.

The verbal act standard enables construction of a standard of constitutional protection that (1) is not tied to the judge's subjective and idiosyncratic view of the merits of the message conveyed by the speech at issue; (2) respects the constitutional text; and (3) draws a principled distinction between the right to communicate, which is constitutionally protected, and the right to act, which may not be.

Embracing this old-fashioned dichotomy between speech and action may seem simplistic to some; speech is an act, after all, and sometimes has consequences such as (or even worse than) the swinging of a fist. But the distinction is based on a difference. Speech (that is, purely communicative acts

---

46. Vincent Bugliosi, *Helter Skelter* (1974) at 286 (emphasis in original).

that merely convey information and/or images) may cause harm, but solely through the independent action of another person who evaluates the ideas or images received and chooses to act after bringing in an independent component—that person's own judgment. Even if it is foreseeable that someone who comes into contact with the speech will react to it in a particular way—either by performing unlawful conduct in agreement with the message contained within the speech or by performing such conduct in revulsion from the message—that resultant harm depends upon an independent actor's internalization of the speech and arrival at a decision about the appropriate response. This is plainly a different set of circumstances from that addressed by the *Brandenburg* test, or by the verbal act concept from which it derives.

To a great extent, the recognition of this difference underlies the doctrine of "content neutrality" that has long been recognized by the Supreme Court. This doctrine states that for government regulation of speech to pass constitutional muster, such regulation must not be based on governmental disapproval of the message itself. Rather, concrete harm caused by the speech must be the basis of the regulation.[47] This requirement is one of the principal qualifiers applied by the Supreme Court in upholding restrictions on constitutionally protected speech on a showing of a "compelling state interest" served by the regulation, which must not be aimed at suppressing the ideas contained in the expression.[48] How that test would apply in contexts other than those that spawned it, cases involving subversive advocacy, is the final issue as to the test's viability as a replacement for the reign of Chaplinskyism.

APPLICATIONS OF THE TEST

A "test" for a law's constitutionality does not function to provide a mechanistic, guaranteed answer for every legal conundrum. Particularly in the area of constitutional law, which implicates the fundamental values of our society, the potential for good-faith disagreement is too high to be resolved by a self-executing rule of thumb. However, to the extent that a common language can be constructed, and the level of subjectivity minimized, a test for a law's constitutionality serves the purpose of maximizing the rationality of a court's decision and preserving for evaluation the reasoning that supports it. Thus, the mere fact that disagreements will persist does not ren-

---

47. For the content neutrality requirement's evolution and scope, *see* Geoffrey R. Stone, "Content Neutral Restrictions," 54 U. Chi. L. Rev. 46 (1987).
48. *See*, for example, *United States v. O'Brien*, 391 U.S. 367, 376 (1968).

der the creation of a test pointless, but provides a framework that enables the law to be put right (where it has gone wrong) after passions have cooled.

To take but one example, the constitutional guarantee of "equal protection of the law" was assessed under *Plessy v. Ferguson*[49] to permit state-ordered separation of the races. Years later, under the same standard, but in a less racist climate, the erroneous nature of that decision under that standard was more clear, and the Court reversed itself in *Brown v. Board of Education.*[50]

That said, a few specific examples of the application of the *Brandenburg* standard for verbal acts in areas outside of its traditional scope may illuminate its meaning, as long as it is clear that one person's impression of the test's impact in a given context does not mean that no possible argument for the contrary result can be made under the standard.

Antitrust

A good example of the extent to which the verbal act formulation undergirds the law of free speech is contained in the solicitude toward protected speech shown by what has come to known as the *Noerr-Pennington* exception to antitrust law. Antitrust law, as enshrined in the Sherman Antitrust Act,[51] makes illegal restraints of trade that are either effected or attempted by means of a conspiracy, in which case "a plaintiff must allege (1) the existence of a conspiracy (2) affecting interstate commerce (3) that imposes unreasonable restraint of trade,"[52] or through "(1) monopolization; (2) attempted monopolization; and (3) conspiracy to monopolize."[53]

Because of the breadth of the act's prohibitions, the act could be held to penalize efforts to invoke government action against a competitor, such as a lawsuit or a planning commission inquiry. The Supreme Court has limited the reach of this neutral, otherwise valid law regarding verbal acts by repeatedly holding that the protections of the First Amendment extend to the petitioning of government for the redress of grievances

---

49. 163 U.S. 537 (1896).
50. 347 U.S. 483 (1954). For the definitive account of the road from *Plessy* to *Brown, see* Richard Kluger, *Simple Justice* (1975).
51. Codified at 15 U.S.C. §§ 1, 2.
52. *Dillard v. Merrill, Lynch, Pierce, Fenner & Smith,* 961 F.2d 1148, 1158 (5th Cir. 1992) *cert. denied,* 506 U.S. 1079 (1993); *Fort Wayne Telsat v. Entertainment and Sports Programming Network,* 753 F. Supp. 109, 115 (S.D.N.Y. 1990).
53. *Broadcast Music v. Hearst/ABC Viacom Entertainment Services,* 746 F. Supp. 320, 326 (S.D.N.Y. 1990); *see also Telectronics Proprietary, Ltd. v. Medtronic, Inc.,* 687 F. Supp. 832, 837 (S.D.N.Y. 1988).

even when such conduct falls within the scope of prohibitions of antitrust law.[54]

The federal courts, however, have emphasized that not all conduct that may be characterized as advocacy before legislative, administrative, or judicial bodies is automatically protected. As the District Court for the Southern District of New York in *Citicorp v. Interbank Card Association*,[55] noted, "That the objective of perjury, fraud and bribery may be to influence some government action can hardly be considered redeeming."[56] Accordingly, the *Noerr-Pennington* doctrine is not an absolute statement that all resort to government bodies is immune to antitrust attack. When such conduct is "a mere sham to cover what is actually nothing more than an attempt to interfere directly with the business relationships of a competitor . . . application of the Sherman Act would be justified."[57] In order to constitute a "sham," a lawsuit must *both* objectively lack merit—be without probable cause for an "objective litigant to conclude that the suit is reasonably calculated to elicit a favorable result"—*and* be intended to "interfere *directly* with the business relationships of a competitor."[58]

When the objective of the suit or other purported petition for redress is "to harass and deter . . . competitors from having 'free and unlimited access' to the agencies or the courts" it falls outside of the ambit of First Amendment protection.[59]

Indeed, some have suggested that the scope of the "sham" exception should be limited only to that conduct that prevents competitors from gaining access to the courts or government administrative decision makers.[60] The Supreme Court has not so limited the "sham" exception, and neither have the circuit courts been so inclined. In *Litton Systems, Inc. v. American Telephone & Telegraph Co.*, the Court of Appeals for the Second Circuit addressed this notion:

> WE reject the suggestion . . . that the applicability of the sham exception turns on whether a competitor is denied access to administrative

---

54. *California Motor Transport Co. v. Trucking Unlimited*, 404 U.S. 508, 509–511 (1972) (summarizing its opinions in *Eastern Railroad Presidents Conference v. Noerr Motor Freight, Inc.*, 365 U.S. 127 (1961); *United Mine Workers v. Pennington*, 381 U.S. 657 (1965)).
55. 478 F. Supp. 756, 762 (S.D.N.Y. 1979)
56. *See also California Motor Transport*, 404 U.S. at 512–513.
57. *Noerr, supra* 365 U.S. at 144.
58. *Professional Real Estate Investors, Inc. v. Columbia Pictures Industries, Inc.*, 508 U.S. 49, 60 (1993).
59. *California Motor Transport*, 404 U.S. at 515; *see generally Citicorp v. Interbank Card Association*, 478 F. Supp. 756, 762 (S.D.N.Y. 1979).
60. *See*, for example, *BusTop Shelters, Inc. v. Convenience & Safety Corp.*, 521 F. Supp. 989 (S.D.N.Y. 1981).

agencies or the courts. The Supreme Court's opinion in *California Motor Transport* cited access barring as one example of the illegal results that might flow from abuse of the administrative process. . . . More recent Supreme Court decisions have referred to the sham exception's availability without regard to the necessity of "access barring." [61]

Thus, the sham exception, as has been more recently held by the Southern District of New York, "embraces the whole spectrum of activities which abuse and corrupt the administrative process to further anticompetitive objectives."[62]

The Supreme Court clarified the test for a sham litigation in *Columbia v. Omni Outdoor Advertising, Inc.,* holding that it "encompasses situations in which persons use the governmental process—as opposed to the outcome of that process—as an anticompetitive weapon."[63] As the Court went on to note, it applies when, "the conspirators' participation in the governmental process was itself claimed to be a 'sham' employed as a means of imposing cost and delay."[64] In other words, only when the speech is plainly not meant to be of its own weight effective, and is intended to inflict harm through delay or expense (that is, when its incidental effect, and not its substantive content, brings it within the language of the statute) will the Court permit the imposition of liability. This plainly brings the speech within the *Gompers-Brandenburg* framework.

Libel and Slander

In the context of libel, the continued existence of the right to sue civilly for damage caused by false statements that injure the plaintiff's reputation seems consistent with the *Brandenburg* rule, or at least with the concept of verbal acts that is embodied in that rule. The tort of defamation is able to clear each of the three hurdles presented to regulation of speech by government.

The first hurdle poses the question of whether the utterance of the speech creates the requisite significant risk (a "clear and present danger") that a

---

61. 700 F.2d 785, 809, n. 36 (1983) *Citing City of Lafayette v. Louisiana Power & Light Co.,* 435 U.S. 389, 405, (1978); *Vendo Co. v. Lektro-Vend Corp,* 433 U.S. 623, 635, n. 6, (1977) (Rehnquist, J. concurring).

62. *Interstate Properties v. Pyramid Company of Utica,* 586 F. Supp. 1160, 1162 (S.D.N.Y. 1984). Indeed, the court in *Interstate Properties* made it clear that not even a "pattern" of conduct need be established; in appropriate cases, a single act can suffice to bring a course of conduct within the sham exception. 586 F. Supp. at 1162.

63. 499 U.S. 365, 379–380 (1991).

64. *Id.* at 381–382, *citing California Motor Transport,* 404 U.S., at 512 ("It is alleged that petitioners instituted the proceedings and actions . . . with or without probable cause and regardless of the merits of the cases").

particular evil will result. Plainly, this hurdle is easily cleared. As Justice Potter Stewart put it thirty years ago, the individual's right to protect his or her reputation:

> REFLECTS no more than our basic concept of the essential dignity and worth of every human being—a concept at the root of any decent system of ordered liberty. The protection of private personality, like the protection of life itself, is left primarily to the individual states under the Ninth and Tenth Amendments. But this does not mean that the right is entitled to any less recognition by this Court as a basic of our constitutional system.[65]

It is difficult to deny that the harm to an individual caused by spreading false statements about her or him is dramatic. False charges of communism, for example, blighted the media career of John Henry Faulk,[66] to name but one victim of the witch-hunt of that period. Libelous statements can result in exclusion from the community and even in legal sanctions (if the libel is believed). That outlandish and false statements can be believed was recently driven home by the exoneration of Margaret Kelly Michaels of charges of Satan-worshiping child molestation. Ms. Michaels's exoneration *seems* to set the stage for a happy ending, but what can compensate her for the years in prison, the economic devastation she suffered, and the experience of being on the receiving end of the pure venom our society directs at suspected sex offenders? What has been aptly termed the "leaven of malice" can leave a very bitter taste indeed.

Of course, that an evil will result from the utterance of the speech is not the sole criterion for liability under *Brandenburg*. That evil must be one that the Congress—or the states—have the right to act to prevent the second hurdle of the *Brandenburg* test. Again, Justice Stewart's description of the right to private personality in part addresses this authorization issue, by referring the matter to the states, which in fact is easily settled in view of the need to judge the "authorization" to combat the harm *separately* from the First Amendment challenge levied against it. Apart from the protection of the First Amendment, it is clear that "words defamatory of another are still placed 'in the same class with the use of explosives or the keeping of dangerous animals'" with respect to their ability to inflict harm

---

65. *Rosenblatt v. Baer*, 383 U.S. 75, 92 (1966) (Stewart, J., concurring). This statement was adopted by a majority of the Court in *Gertz v. Robert Welch Inc.*, 418 U.S. 323, 341 (1974).

66. *See* Louis Nizer, *The Jury Returns* (1966) at 225–438; Molly Ivins, *Molly Ivins Can't Say That, Can She* (1993) at 263–274. For Ms. Michaels' case, discussed *infra, see Michaels v. State of New Jersey*, 50 F. Supp. 2d 353 (D.N.J. 1999), (summarizing history, including dismissal of charges against Michaels due to tainted evidence; summary judgment granted to prosecutors based upon governmental immunity even for negligent acts). *See also* Debbie Nathan and Michael Snedecker, *Satan's Silence: Ritual Abuse and the Making of a Modern American Witch-Hunt* (1996).

on others.[67] That plainly falls within the state's ability to act to protect the "health, welfare and morals" of its citizens.[68]

Third (and finally), under *Brandenburg*, the actor must have given tongue to the speech with the specific intent to cause that very evil. Now here is where some libel law may be questionable, because in fact this level of intent to libel would not even be met in every case by the "actual malice" standard applied to individuals who are public officials or public figures.[69] That standard requires a finding of actual malice in the utterance or publication of the libel, which the Court defined to include not merely intent to slander but recklessness as to the veracity of the published utterance. Private individuals who are the victims of libel may, by contrast, recover damages upon a showing of negligence.[70] Does this mean that, under a *Brandenburg*-centered analysis all libel law must fall prey to the constitutional headsman?

Tempting as it would be to engender controversy by declaring huge swaths of the law unfounded, the answer is clearly no. Although it *can* support an abolition of libel law as applied to discussions of public officials and actions (and indeed Justices Douglas and Black urged such an abolition),[71] *Brandenburg*, both of its own weight and as an expression of one context in which the verbal act concept finds application, can also be read to support the continued existence of libel law. Indeed, neither Black nor Douglas opposed the continued existence of the tort of libel as applied to wholly private persons in their private capacity, stating baldly that the First Amendment protected free speech by "granting the press an absolute immunity for criticism of the way public officials do their public duty."[72] *Brandenburg*, it must be remembered, deals with the level of intent—of mens rea, to use the criminal law concept—needed to impute the action of one person to another who merely urged that the action take place, and thus find that the speech was so "brigaded with the action" as to form a component thereof. That is why in Chapter 2 the analogy of principal and agent was helpful.

Here, however, the question is whether the speech in question—libel—constitutes a "verbal act" or is "speech" as protected by the First Amendment. Although the argument can be constructed to require perfect adherence

---

67. *Curtis Publishing Co. v. Butts*, 388 U.S. 130, 152 (1967) (*quoting*, Prosser, *The Law of Torts* § 108 at 792).
68. 388 U.S. at 151–152; *New York Times v. Sullivan*, 376 U.S. 254 (1964).
69. *New York Times*, 376 U.S. 254, was held to apply not merely to public officials but also to public figures in *Curtis Publishing Co.*, 388 U.S. at 155.
70. *Gertz v. Robert Welch*, 418 U.S. 323, 339–346 (1974).
71. *See New York Times*, 376 U.S. at 297 (1964) (Black and Douglas, JJ. concurring); *Curtis Publishing Co.* 388 U.S. at 171 (1967) (Black and Douglas, JJ., concurring and dissenting).
72. *New York Times*, 376 U.S. at 295.

to the *Brandenburg* formula, surely it makes more sense to look at the function the utterance performs in order to determine whether or not it is a verbal act.

A verbal act takes place when the very utterance of speech inflicts harm. It is not based on disapproval of the message, but on the incidental effects of the communication in the particular context. As Holmes noted with respect to the verbal act he found to have taken place in *Schenck*, for example, "in many places and in ordinary times the defendants in saying all that was said in the circular [at issue in *Schenck*] would have been within their constitutional rights. But the character of every act depends upon the circumstances in which it is done."[73] Justice Holmes then stated the verbal act principle: "The question in every case is whether the words are used in such circumstances and are of such nature as to create a clear and present danger that they will bring about the substantive evils that Congress has the right to prevent."[74]

In the case of subversive advocacy, or other harms dependent upon the adoption of the speech by others, that can only be answered by determining whether the speaker has managed to deputize the listener. In the case of libel, the question is whether the speaker has *deceived* the listener, or rather, created an impermissible risk that the listener will be deceived, and that the damage resulted. No imputation is needed; the listener need not have acted upon the aspersion, it must merely be broadcast and become known as a putatively true statement that has been made. Indeed, the statement need not always be in fact believed: In cases of libel per se, that is, statements that are so plainly damaging to reputation that if they are false *any* publication of them must cause harm, damage is presumed and the plaintiff need not show that any person in fact believed the statement.[75]

The Court has—almost—related libel to verbal acts. In explaining why libel is not "speech" under the First Amendment in *Hustler Magazine, Inc. v. Falwell*,[76] the Court stated that "[f]alse statements of fact are particularly valueless; they interfere with the truth-seeking function of the marketplace of ideas, and they cause damage to an individual's reputation that cannot easily be repaired by counterspeech, however persuasive or effective." In *Hustler v. Falwell* the Court also reemphasized that "the First Amendment

---

73. 249 U.S. 47, 52 (1919).
74. *Id.*
75. *See*, for example, *Matherson v. Marchello*, 100 A.D.2d 233, 473 N.Y.S.2d 998 (2d Dep't 1984) (where comments attack plaintiff or disparage him or her in profession or trade, damages are presumed); *see also McCullough v. Certain Tweed Products Corp.*, 70 A.D.2d 771, 417 N.Y.S.2d 353 (4th Dep't 1979).
76. 485 U.S. 46, 52 (1988), *citing Gertz*, 418 U.S. at 340, 344 n. 9.

recognizes that there is no such thing as a false idea."[77] In other words, actionable libel does not function as "speech" that is protected by the First Amendment because the *incidental* harm caused by the speech—the injury to reputation caused by the false factual representation and not the underlying communicative message contained in the libelous statement—is the ground for a finding of liability.

Of course, for the constitutional literalist, there is another means of arguing that the Constitution recognizes that libelous statements are not protected speech under the First Amendment. One can point to Article I, section 6 of the Constitution, which provides that senators and representatives, among other privileges, "shall not be questioned in any other Place for any Speech or Debate in either House."[78] As Justice Douglas pointed out in his *Right of the People*, this immunity presumes the existence of the law of libel and slander, and, as a more specific proposition than the general statement of the First Amendment, should not be presumed to have been amended by it.[79]

Douglas's analysis is in accordance with one of the most ancient maxims of statutory or contractual interpretation. The rule that "the general shall be controlled by the particular" exists in several variants: *generalis clausula non porrigitur ad ea quaeantea specialiter sunt comprehensa,* translated freely to state that "a general clause does not extend to those things which are provided for specially," originated with Lord Coke[80] and is itself an application of another ancient maxim: *generalia specialibus non derogant,* that is "general words do not derogate from special."[81] Thus, even if the *Brandenburg* verbal act concept is deemed inapplicable to libel, an argument may be made for the preservation of the tort as the one explicit exception to the First Amendment provided for in the text of the Constitution.

Now, the mere fact that the existence of the tort of libel is consistent with the First Amendment does not mean that the Constitution has nothing to say with respect to the *scope* of the tort. Even in the (now discredited) group libel case, *Beauharnais v. Illinois*[82] the Court made clear that "[w]hile this Court sits, it retains and exercises authority to nullify action which encroaches upon freedom of utterance under the guise of punishing

---

77. *Hustler Magazine, Inc. v. Falwell,* 485 U.S. at 51 (1988). *See also* Rodney A. Smolla, *Jerry Falwell v. Larry Flint: The First Amendment on Trial* (1990) at 245–249 (describing antecedents of this viewpoint).

78. U.S. Const., Art. I, § 6, cl. 1.

79. William O. Douglas, *The Right of the People* (1958) at 36.

80. *Coke's English King's Bench Reports,* part 8 at 154b. The translation used is that from *Black's Law Dictionary* (4th ed. 1968) at 815.

81. *Jenkins' Eight Centuries of Reports, English Exchequer* at 120; *see also* 4 *English Law Reports, Exchequer* (1866–1875) at 226. Again, the translation is that provided by *Black's Law Dictionary* (4th ed. 1968) at 815.

82. 343 U.S. 250.

libel."[83] Indeed, one such policing of the perimeter is exemplified in *Branden-burg's* silent overruling of *Beauharnais*; the case goes beyond the scope of the *Brandenburg* logic (or the textual implication discussed here) by leaving behind the very interest that has long been deemed compelling enough to warrant legislative protection: the *individual* interest in reputation. The Illinois statute that the Court upheld in *Beauharnais* protected against "group" defamation, in that case defamatory stereotyping and racist slurs. No *individualized* defamation was required by the Court to be shown, nor was the speech in *Beauharnais* shown to have impacted upon the individual reputations of the victims. And indeed, the line of cases beginning with *New York Times v. Sullivan* and evolving to the present day involves the Court in the struggle to demarcate the line between protected speech that impinges upon the reputation of individuals and the unprotected verbal act of libel.[84]

Obscenity

A second area of First Amendment law that repays examination in light of the *Brandenburg* test and the verbal act concept enshrined within it is obscenity. Originally conceived as a *Chaplinsky* category of speech "of such slight social value as a step to truth that any benefit that may be derived from [it] is clearly outweighed by the social interest in order and morality,"[85] obscenity law has been primarily concerned with definition, and not with justification. An application of the principles contained in *Brandenburg* explains why—the anti-obscenity rules are simply violative of any logical concept of free speech.

As always, it is good to define the terms before applying the test. When I use obscenity in this chapter I mean just what the Supreme Court does: the traditionally unprotected class of speech that is concerned with sex and has been held since *Roth v. United States*[86] to be outside of the scope of the First Amendment. In *Miller v. California*,[87] the Supreme Court created a new test to determine whether or not given materials were "obscene," a test that required the finder of fact to ascertain (1) whether the average person, applying "contemporary community standards," would find that the work,

---

83. *Id.* at 263–264. *See also Curtis Publishing Co. v. Butts*, 388 U.S. 130, 143–144 (1967).

84. For a look at the current state of the law of defamation, an easily accessible account of the concerns and the evolving case law is contained in Anthony Lewis, *Make No Law: The Sullivan Case and the First Amendment* (1991) at 183–233. For a general, and more practical, guide to defamation law, *see* David A. Elder, *Defamation: A Lawyer's Guide* (Clark, Boardman & Callaghan, 1993, revised 1996).

85. *Chaplinsky v. New Hampshire*, 315 U.S. at 572.

86. 354 U.S. 476 (1957).

87. 413 U.S. 15 (1973).

taken as a whole, appeals to the prurient interest in sex; (2) whether the work depicts, in a patently offensive way, sexual conduct specifically defined by the applicable state law; and (3) whether the work, taken as a whole, lacks serious literary, artistic, or political social value. The *Miller* court explicitly rejected the former constitutional standard that the work be "*utterly* without redeeming social value" established in *Memoirs v. Massachusetts*.[88]

As I discuss the issue of obscenity, therefore, it must be clear that the issue is the role of the state in suppressing immoral (in some eyes) discussion, depiction, and expression of fantasies about sex. The issues of violence against women, and the purported causal (or at least contributory) role that pornography—a somewhat narrower class of materials and depictions than obscenity, as the word has come to be used—is said to play in such violence is a distinct issue from the regulation of obscenity as traditionally (and currently) permitted by the Supreme Court.[89]

In applying the *Brandenburg* criterion, the first question is Does this speech in question present an immediate danger that an evil will result? Because of the breadth of the definition of obscenity, the "evil" so addressed therein cannot be limited to fear of violence against women. Obscenity doctrine, as Catharine A. MacKinnon has pointed out, is about preserving morality.[90] Indeed, in *Roth* and in *Miller*, that point is not merely conceded, it is embraced.

The first question then is whether the publication of obscene materials (assuming we can agree on the obscenity of the materials) presents a clear and present (or immediate in temporal proximity, to use the less colorful modern articulation) danger of harm to morality. The second question is whether the danger that obscenity poses (such as it is) is of a kind that Congress (or the states) is able to act to prevent. Finally, the requisite level of intent needs to be determined.

With respect to temporal proximity, the supporter of obscenity doctrine has a seemingly insuperable difficulty. There is not a single shred of evidence that the reading or viewing[91] of obscene materials *of a sudden* corrupts the

---

88. *A Book Named "John Cleland's Memoirs of a Woman of Pleasure" v. Massachusetts*, 383 U.S. 413 (1966).

89. That issue is further discussed *infra* at Chapter 6.

90. Catharine A. MacKinnon, *Only Words* (1993) at 87; MacKinnon, *Feminism Unmodified* (1989) at 146–163.

91. Certain critics of pornography, notably Catharine MacKinnon, would replace the words "reading" or "viewing" with "consumption" on the theory that the perusal of porn is a subrational, and inherently coercive experience. As shown in Chapter 6, I do not agree. Moreover, "consumption" suggests that the reader merely mentally "ingests" the materials, which then act upon him, eliding the reader's/viewer's role in interpreting the material, as well as suggesting that the pornography is somehow "used up or destroyed." *See*, for example, *Webster's Universal College Dictionary* (1997) at 175 (defining *consume* and *consumption*).

reader's moral framework; the most that has been alleged is that repeated exposure to violent and degrading images in "pornography" can lead some viewers to become desensitized to the violence depicted. In other words, people who repeatedly view or read certain kinds of obscene materials may over time come to adopt some of the viewpoint expressed in the materials as their own. Although this may qualify as evil, depending on the value system through which the obscene materials are viewed, it does not present a temporally imminent danger either of moral decadence or that any given audience member will form a clear and present intention to implement the message of the obscenity.

Obscenity is not a verbal act, moreover, in that it presents, isolated from any active context (that is, any factual context in which the audience is able to in fact become an actor), images of sexuality. It is not the equivalent of force, because the receiving mind can reject these images, and even be repulsed by them, and the harm that is feared thus never materializes. A verbal act, by contrast, takes place in circumstances where its utterance by itself inflicts the harm that should be prevented. Once the speech is issued in a place where there is time for its message to be weighed and accepted and rejected, we are simply beyond the realm of verbal acts, and of *Brandenburg*.

Unsurprisingly then, Justice Douglas, dissenting in *Roth*, distinguished the texts impacted upon by the obscenity doctrine (whose adoption by the Court in that case he deplored) from verbal acts, writing that "I have the same confidence in the ability of our people to reject noxious literature as I have in their ability to sort out the true from the false in theology, economics, politics or any other field."[92]

The temporal imminence hurdle is not the only one to trip up the obscenity doctrine. Obscenity is based on the protection of morality, but whose morality? If it is a religious, Judeo-Christian sexual morality, does not that other provision of the First Amendment, the Establishment Clause, prohibit the enshrinement of such matters of religious doctrine in the civil law? If it is a sort of denatured secular-humanist ethical code, again from what source does the government, federal or state, derive a right to impose value choices upon its citizenry with respect to deeply personal issues, which are bound up in the construction of the self, of the family, and even of one's religious identity?

Of course these questions break down to the fundamental inquiry about to what extent our fellow citizens can tell us how to think, as opposed to how to act. Even in less tolerant days, the government was reluctant to countenance such behavior; in *Davis v. Beason*, the Supreme Court held, as we

---

92. *Roth*, 354 U.S. at 514 (Douglas, J. dissenting).

have seen, that "laws were made for the government of actions, and while it cannot interfere with mere religious belief and opinions, they may with practices."[93]

Insofar as the police power of the states has been held to permit the states to act to protect the "health, welfare, and morals" of its citizens, the "morals" category would seem to provide some justification for holding that the obscenity doctrine falls within the scope of the second hurdle of the *Brandenburg* test: whether the "evil" to be prevented falls within the power of the state to remedy. However, the police power, although it has been read to protect people from impinging upon the moral beliefs of others, does not authorize the state to indoctrinate its citizens, or to impose a set of ethical guidelines on their private interactions. Is this solely because of the free speech and press clauses of the First Amendment? If so, do we not have to leave out that limitation in determining whether the states have a countervailing right to regulate morals? At first glance, one could say yes, but the Establishment Clause suggests that the indoctrination of its citizens with moral and ethical principles and teaching falls afoul of an independent prohibition.

Moreover, if the "clockwork orange" theory of democracy suggested by Douglas in *Roth*—the theory that to be meaningful, a democratic-republican government must be more than a mere form of government, but must rather permit the citizenry to make real and individual choices—is true, then the systematic moral indoctrination which could find support in a broad reading of the police power of the states could violate Article IV, section 2 of the Constitution. That section provides "to every State in this Union a Republican Form of Government." Indeed, in its more recent articulations of the police power, the Court has, in a seeming concession of this point, unobtrusively dropped "morals" from the list, rephrasing the power's scope to extend to the "health, safety and welfare" of citizens.[94]

Regardless of the scope one affords the "morals" provision of the state's police power, it is clear that obscenity law cannot be based on the verbal act concept, whether on one ground (lacking temporal imminence, or intent, for that matter) or on two (as violative of the right of the people to form their own characters, as a corollary to democratic self-rule), as I have suggested. This should be so much the worse, not for the verbal act concept, but for the obscenity doctrine. The obscenity doctrine, a survival of the days when regulation of the novels of Émile Zola could be based upon the unsupported proposition that "the material was of such a leprous nature that it would be impossible for any young man who had not learned

93. 133 U.S. 333, 344 (1890).

94. *Posadas de Puerto Rico Association v. Tourism Co.*, 478 U.S. 328, 341 (1986). *See also Lawrence v. Texas*, 538 U.S.—155 L. Ed—(June 26, 2003) (state law on homosexual sodomy struck as violative of right to primary despite "moral" basis).

the Divine secret of self-control to have read it without committing some form of outwards mischief within twenty-four hours after,"[95] has no place in a legal system in which the ability of the people to form a moral framework for themselves is a core belief.

Verbal Acts II: The Outer Limits and Symbolic Speech

The verbal act formulation stands up, even if the complete *Brandenburg* circumstances are not met, in the case of libel, and in cases of conspiracy where at least one of the conspirators performs an "overt act" that yields an unlawful result (or at least makes an effort to do so). But what about those cases in which nothing but speech is used to violate the law? How can we square the concept of freedom of speech with the law regarding deceit and fraud? Or, for that matter, how can we square the First Amendment with the law of contract that regulates "speech" by requiring people who have entered into agreements to live up to their "word"?

As the First Amendment suddenly swells up, and threatens to engulf the entire legal world, a little common sense (not a quality perpetually at odds with legal reasoning, regardless of the opinion A. P. Herbert)[96] may help restore some perspective.

The whole point of the verbal act concept that has been so stressed in this chapter is to understand that "speech" under the First Amendment is a question of *function* and not one of *form*. The question is not whether words are used (mute cartoons may express ideas too), but rather whether the expressive conduct serves as the functional equivalent of action, or as speech.

A nice theoretical distinction, and one ripe for the legal philosophers, no?[97] It can be even further complicated by the fact that certain forms of conduct contain expressive elements as well: symbolic action can convey thought as strongly as can words. For example, burning the American flag at an antiwar meeting strongly conveys a message about the burner's views toward what that flag represents.[98] Conduct can be speech; speech can be conduct. The question is how to distinguish between the two?

Great legal minds have clashed on the subject, and in fact the question of when expressive conduct is "speech" divided the usually allied Justices William O. Douglas and Hugo L. Black in *Cohen v. California*.[99] As previously mentioned, in *Cohen*, an antiwar protester who wore a jacket stating "Fuck

---

95. *Quoted* in Walter Kendrick, *The Secret Museum* (1988) at 87.
96. A. P. Herbert, *Uncommon Law* (1935) wittily parodies the sometimes tortuous logic used by courts.
97. It has generally not been explored in a fruitful manner. An exception is Kent Greenawalt, *Speech, Crime and the Uses of Language* (1989).
98. *Texas v. Johnson*, 491 U.S. 397 (1989).
99. 403 U.S. 15 (1971).

the Draft" into a California courtroom was arrested and charged with disturbance of the peace.[100] Cohen was convicted, but the Supreme Court reversed the conviction. Neither Douglas nor Black wrote, but they joined diametrically opposed opinions.

The Court split 5–4. Douglas voted with the majority, joining an opinion by John Marshall Harlan. Harlan's opinion found that "the conviction quite clearly rests upon the asserted offensiveness of the *words* Cohen used to convey his message to the public," and concluded that "[t]he only 'conduct' which the State sought to punish is the fact of communication."[101] Black, to the contrary, joined Justice Harry Blackmun's dissenting opinion, which dismissed "Cohen's absurd and immature antic" as "mainly conduct and little speech."[102]

The relevance of *Cohen* is not simply to show that great minds can differ, but rather to provide a clue to how expressive conduct can be judged as either "expressive" or "conduct"; the result varies depending on the lens through which the expression is viewed.[103] This complication underlines the need for a functional analysis of what is speech, because a purely formal analysis (by which any use of *words*, but *only* of words is protected) leads not only to the absurd result of exempting verbal acts, including fraud, but also to the equally absurd result of leaving symbolic speech unprotected.

The *function* served by speech, on the other hand, is distinctly more helpful. When the expressive conduct is "not itself the wrong for which [a defendant] [is] convicted, but [is] merely the means by which he committed the crimes of which he [is] convicted,"[104] the speech component does not immunize the conduct from proscription under a statute that is directed at the underlying conduct or result and *not* at the speech component of the verbal act. In other words, it is permissible for government to target the "act" component, but not the "verbal" or "expressive" component of the action involved. Thus, while, like picketing, Cohen's jacket could be described as "free speech plus," the statute and the conviction were directed not at the regulable component of the conduct but at the substance of the expression. The explanation for the difference between Black and Douglas may simply be that Black did not see the case in such terms.

---

100. *Id.* at 16.
101. *Id.* at 18 (emphasis added).
102. *Id.* at 27.
103. Justice Black saw this; at the end of his career, during the "Pentagon Papers" case, he joked that his law clerks feared he would come down against the *New York Times*' right to publish: "Somehow I'll find a way to call this conduct rather than speech," he said. Bob Woodward & Scott Armstrong, *The Brethren* (1979) at 143.
104. *United States v. Daly,* 756 F.2d 1076, 1082 (5th Cir. 1985).

The various flag-burning cases decided by the Supreme Court provide a useful measure of this distinction. In *Street v. New York*,[105] the Court found that it had before it an insufficient record to tell if the defendant (a veteran who, upon hearing of the murder of civil rights activist James Meredith, burned a flag as an act of mourning and defiance) was prosecuted for his oral statements about the flag as he burned it, for burning a *flag* in order to make his symbolic point, or simply for burning a large cloth object in public. Because at the very least the first option would violate the First Amendment, the conviction was reversed.

In *Texas v. Johnson*[106] and *United States v. Eichman*,[107] the burning of a flag as a symbolic manifestation of disrespect, had been proscribed by (respectively) state and federal governments, and the Court struck both statutes as impermissibly based on the legislative disapproval of the message conveyed by the burning. However, a content-neutral statute that prohibited open fires generally in an urban district would surely pass constitutional muster, even if its effect was to send defendants Street, Johnson, and Eichman to jail.[108]

The Court's present approach to symbolic speech in general, first explicated at length in *United States v. O'Brien*,[109] is a classic example of "verbal act" jurisprudence. In *O'Brien*, the defendant burned his draft card at an antiwar protest. In upholding his conviction under a statute that explicitly stated that anyone who "destroys, knowingly mutilates, or in any manner changes any such certificate" has committed an offense, the Court summed up its logic in language that by now will seem almost drearily familiar:

> [A] GOVERNMENTAL regulation is sufficiently justified if it is within the constitutional power of the government; if it furthers an important

---

105. 394 U.S. 576 (1969).
106. 491 U.S. 397, 411–412 (1989).
107. 496 U.S. 310 (1990).
108. *See* Geoffrey R. Stone, *Flag Burning and the Constitution*, 75 Iowa L. Rev. 111 (1989); *Virginia v. Black*, 538 U.S.—, 155 L. Ed. 2nd 535 (2003) (viewpoint neutral statute restricting symbolic speech as fighting words constitutional). The law with respect to flag desecration prior to *Johnson* and *Eichman* is a bit schizophrenic. On the one hand, two other convictions for flag desecration were overturned by the Supreme Court in 1974. In *Smith v. Goguen*, 415 U.S. 566 (1974), the conviction was overturned because the statute upon which it was founded, which made it a criminal offense to "publicly . . . treat contemptuously the flag of the United States" was "impermissibly vague." In *Spence v. Washington*, 418 U.S. 405 (1974), the conviction of a student for pasting a peace sign on a flag, and hanging it out his window was reversed as violative of the First Amendment. The statute forbade any imposition or appending of other images to the flag, but had only been enforced as to "anti-establishment" viewpoints such as the appellant's.
     On the other hand, in *Radich v. New York*, 401 U.S. 531 (1971), the Court affirmed the conviction of an art dealer who displayed a sculpture of the flag in the shape of a phallus in order to symbolize the aggression of the United States in Vietnam.
109. 391 U.S. 367 (1968).

or substantial governmental interest; if the governmental interest is unrelated to the suppression of free expression; and if the incidental restriction on alleged First Amendment freedoms is no greater than is essential to the furtherance of that interest.[110]

The logic of *O'Brien* matches that of *Brandenburg*, except for the third element, which seems to fulfill, in the factually different context of the case, the same purpose as does the specific intent hurdle of the *Brandenburg* test— it draws a line between the protected communication and the incidental harm that is the only regulable component of state laws that impact on conduct with a message. The results in *Johnson* and *Eichman* were dictated, essentially, by *O'Brien* (which was heavily relied upon in both opinions) and represent another delineation of the concept of the verbal act.

Verbal Acts III: Crimes Effected Solely Through Words

Strangely, the most difficult form of verbal act to construct a rational account of is also the form that we most instinctively know to be outside of the confines of free speech: The words that are used to deceive in criminal (or civil) fraud, or that violate similar criminal statutes. The Supreme Court has not been greatly helpful here; it has restricted itself to blanket declarations that such speech is "outside" of the scope of the First Amendment.

It is a commonplace that deceptive falsehoods used for gain are not within the scope of the First Amendment's protection. As the Supreme Court has put it, "[it] rarely has been suggested that the constitutional freedom for speech . . . extends its immunity to speech or writing used as an integral part of conduct in violation of a valid criminal statute."[111] That is to say, "speech is not protected by the First Amendment when it is the very vehicle of crime itself."[112] Classically, this explains the existence of the crime of conspiracy, and is the quintessence of the verbal act—a usage of words that effects results forbidden by statute whether the results are achieved through words or deeds. Indeed, the *Brandenburg* agency concept can be used effectively in conspiracy cases as it was in cases of subversive advocacy.

Thus, co-conspirators, who may contribute only words to a conspiracy, have not been able to immunize their conduct by resort to the First Amendment. Because conspirators are jointly liable for the acts taken in support

---

110. *Id.* at 377.
111. *New York v. Ferber*, 458 U.S. 747, 761–762 (1982), *quoting Giboney v. Empire Storage & Ice Co.*, 336 U.S. 490, 498 (1949).
112. *United States v. Rowlee*, 899 F.2d 1275, 1278 (2d Cir. 1990), *quoting United States v. Varani*, 435 F.2d 758, 762 (6th Cir. 1970).

of the conspiracy by their co-conspirators,[113] the only acts of any given conspirator may be lawful and still suffice for imposition of liability against them.[114] As the Second Circuit Court of Appeals has noted of such conspirators, "Their conduct was not protected by the First Amendment merely because, in part, it may have involved the use of language."[115] The reason for this stripping away of immunity is nothing more than a recognition that such crimes involve verbal acts.

The Court has long recognized that "when 'speech' and 'nonspeech' elements are combined in the same course of conduct, a sufficiently important governmental interest in regulating the nonspeech elements can justify incidental limitations on First Amendment freedoms."[116] An act of speech by a conspirator may thus be used as a "hook" on which to hang liability for the intended actions of the other conspirators, because where "conduct properly proscribed is coupled with conduct protected by the First Amendment, the latter does not cure the former."[117]

In this context, the rule is clear: The "act" of speech, when it is used to effect a result that is achievable in another way, is no more protected than the other methods of achieving the unlawful result, because speech has not been targeted as such. Rather, it is an act like any other, and punished for the result it contributed to. In fact, it is not the speech that is punished but rather the concurrence in the unlawful action as evidenced by the speech—which falls clearly within the principle-agent dynamic that *Brandenburg* captures in a less formal scenario.

But what of the speech that is the only means of effecting the illegal result? Deception, for example, or fraud? Without the speech, without the conveying of false information through expressive conduct, there is simply no way to commit fraud. In the otherwise admirable *Speech, Crime, and the Uses of Language,* Kent Greenawalt clearly traces the line between fraud and other criminal acts that are performed through speech and speech, but does not

---

113. *See,* for example, *Alco Standard Corp. v. Schmid Bros., Inc.,* 647 F. Supp. 4 (S.D.N.Y. 1986) (elements of a properly pled conspiracy); *State of New York v. Cedar Park Concrete Corp.,* 665 F. Supp. 238, 247–48 (S.D.N.Y. 1987) (complaint alleging agreement and specific overt acts of some defendants is sufficient).

114. *See,* for example, *United States v. Gisehaltz,* 278 F. Supp. 434, 437 (S.D.N.Y. 1967).

115. *United States v. Rowlee,* 899 F.2d at 1278.

116. *United States v. O'Brien,* 391 U.S. 367, 376 (1968); *see also United States v. Daly,* 756 F.2d 1076, 1081–1082 (5th Cir.), *cert. denied,* 474 U.S. 1022 (1985).

117. *Citicorp v. Interbank Card Association,* 478 F. Supp. 756, 762 (S.D.N.Y. 1979) (citing cases) (holding that otherwise illegal antitrust scheme is not legitimated by inclusion of plan to petition government or speak to the press as a component thereof); *see also Michael Anthony Jewelers v. Peacock Jewelry,* 795 F. Supp. 639, 649 (S.D.N.Y. 1992) (same; refusing to find nonsham initial component of lawsuit removed lawsuit in its final form from sham exception to antitrust liability).

provide a rationale differentiating such speech from that protected by the First Amendment. In short, to borrow a phrase from Tim Rice, he's far too keen on where and how, and not so hot on why.

Justice Douglas's analysis of subversive advocacy cases, in which an informal (as opposed to explicit) agency relationship may be imputed, is helpful here. Such speech is classic "speech brigaded with action" as required by Douglas for the appropriate imputation of liability in *Brandenburg* and *Roth.*

To extrapolate Douglas's broad-brush analysis, the connection is this: The "deception" of another for profit involves the creation of an inducement to presently enter into a transaction, and as such is an integral component to such an act. An invitation to enter into a transaction—an offer—is itself a component of the act of entering into business transactions, as is the acceptance of the offer. Indeed, because the third element of a contract, consideration (that is, some bargained-for exchange between the parties) may be a promise to act at a future date,[118] a contract may exist that is wholly embodied in speech acts. Such a contract would be entirely "executory" because both sides have yet to perform,[119] but clearly the First Amendment would not act to bar its enforceability.

Similarly, in cases of fraud or misrepresentation, the words are spoken with the specific intent to induce imminent conduct—essentially the handing over of funds or the provision of services by the victim, whose legitimate expectations of what his or her return will be are doomed to be frustrated. It is nothing more than the functional equivalent of theft—and indeed is legally recognized as such in, to take but one designation, the crime of "larceny by trick" or "larceny by false promise."[120] Thus, the denial of First Amendment protection to such speech, far from being without justification, is entirely consistent with the operating principle discussed previously: The protection of speech stops short of verbal acts.

---

118. *See Weiner v. McGraw-Hill, Inc.,* 57 N.Y.2d 458, 464, 457 N.Y.S.2d 193, 196 (1982). Moreover, consideration need not be of any particular value, nor need it flow directly to the party who has bargained for it. *Id.* (court "will not ask whether the thing which forms the consideration does in fact benefit the promisee or a third party or is of any substantial value to anyone"), *quoting Hamer v. Sidway,* 124 N.Y. 538, 545 (1891); *Rector of St. Mark's Church v. Teed,* 120 N.Y. 583, 587 (1890) (contract where consideration conferred benefit on third party enforceable).

119. *See* 1 *Williston on Contracts* (4th ed., 1990) (Richard A. Lord, ed.) §1.19 at 48–49.

120. *See,* for example, N.Y. Penal Law § 155.05, *et seq.* (defining larceny); *People v. Kirkup,* 4 N.Y.2d 209, 173 N.Y.S.2d 574 (1958) (larceny defined as having been committed when, *inter alia,* a person, "with criminal intent and by false representation of fact relied upon by the seller, obtains more than that to which he knows he would be entitled as a purchaser in his business as retailer were he to tell the truth"); *People v. Luongo,* 47 N.Y. 2d 418; 418 N.Y.S. 2d 365 (1979) ("larceny by false promise" includes Ponzi schemes).

The Concept Applied: Threats

Because of the proliferation of Chaplinskyism, the courts have not had broad scope to apply the verbal act concept, as outlined above. However, these preliminary suggestions for how that concept could be rationally applied are not utterly without foundation, and not simply by their (overall) harmony with many of the specific offenses discussed above. In fact, the courts have shown themselves, in at least one concept, to be quite adept at distinguishing between verbal acts and speech that is protected by the First Amendment.

Congress has enacted two statutes that proscribe threats to kidnap or injure the person of another, one geared to the communication of such threats through interstate commerce,[121] the other proscribing threats directed at the person of the president of the United States.[122] Both statutes have been construed to require the government to prove, in order to distinguish between a threat and constitutionally protected speech, a "true threat."[123]

Prior to 1969, the statute concerning the president was invoked as a means of silencing criticism that was harsh and vituperative but that in no way implicated actual concerns for the president's physical safety.[124] The rationale for such prosecutions was, at best, weak, and highly reminiscent of the "bad tendency" language used by the Supreme Court when it shied away from the Holmes-Brandeis concept of clear and present danger:

> THE expression of such direful intentions and desires, not only indicates a spirit of disloyalty to the nation bordering upon treason, but is, in a very real sense, a menace to the peace and safety of the country. . . . It arouses resentment and concern on the part of patriotic citizens.[125]

---

121. 18 U.S.C. § 875(c).
122. 18 U.S.C. § 871(a).
123. *Watts v. United States*, 394 U.S. 705 (1969); *see Virginia v. Black*, 155 L. Ed. 2d at 551–552.
124. *See*, for example, *United States v. Apel*, 44 F. Supp. 592, 593 (N.D. Ill. 1942) (upholding conviction for displaying posters urging passersby to "hang [Franklin] Roosevelt"); *United States v. Stickrath*, 242 F. 151, 152 (D.C. S.D. Ohio 1917) (upholding conviction based on statement that "President Wilson ought to be killed. It is a wonder some one has not done it already. If I had an opportunity, I would do it myself"); *Clark v. United States*, 250 F. 449 (5th Cir. 1918) (upholding conviction based on statement that "Wilson is a wooden-headed son of a bitch. I wish Wilson was in hell, and if I had the power I would put him there myself"); *see also*, Note, *Threatening the President: Protected Dissenter or Political Assassin*, 57 Geo. L.J. 553, 570 (1969); *Watts*, 394 U.S. at 710–711 (Douglas, J. concurring) (describing similar prosecutions under Sedition Acts as well as under modern statute).
125. *United States v. Jasick*, 252 F. 931, 933 (E.D.Mich. 1918).

Justice Douglas dismissed this line of thought: "Suppression of speech as an effective police measure is an old, old device, outlawed by our Constitution."[126]

However, even prior to the 1969 *Watts* decision, some lower courts read the statutory language to require something more than a mere imagining, wishing, or hoping that the deed would be executed by another; these courts generally expressed the requirement in terms of an avowed present determination or intent to injure presently or in the future.[127] Alternatively, courts required the expression of a "menace of such nature and extent as to unsettle the mind of the person on whom it operates, and to take away from his acts that free and voluntary action which alone constitutes consent."[128]

In *Watts*, the Court clarified the "true threat" requirement, reversing the conviction of an eighteen-year-old recipient of a draft notice who, declaring "if they ever make me carry a rifle the first man I want to get in my sights is LBJ," vowed that he would not "kill my black brothers."[129] The Court reached its conclusion by reading the statute's language "against the background of a profound national commitment to the principle that debate on public issues should be uninhibited, robust, and wide-open, and that it may well include vehement, caustic, and sometimes unpleasantly sharp attacks on government and public officials."[130] As the Court observed in reversing Watts's conviction, "[t]he language of the political arena . . . is often vituperative, abusive, and inexact. We agree with [Watts] that his only offense here was 'a kind of very crude offensive method of stating a political opposition to the President.'"[131] The Court determined that no true threat could be found in Watts's statement, taken in context, in light of its expressly conditional nature, and in view of the reaction of the listeners— which was to join Watts in laughing.

In applying the *Watts* "true threat" standard to § 875 (c), the Second Circuit Court of Appeals, in the leading case to construe the section in

---

126. *Watts*, 394 U.S. at 712 (Douglas, J. concurring).
127. *See United States v. Daulong*, 60 F. Supp. 235 (W.D. La. 1945) (statements that defendant had a "notion" or "felt like" killing the president insufficiently positive to constitute a threat); *see also, United States v. Metzdorf*, 252 F. 933 (D.C. Mont. 1919) (conditional threat that may have been an expression of past intent not sufficient to sustain a conviction); *United States v. Marino*, 148 F. Supp. 75; 77 (N.D. Ill. 1957) (poster stating "There can be slain no sacrifice to God more acceptable than an unjust President" insufficient because it contained no statement of intent to do any act, let alone implement the death of the president).
128. *United States v. French*, 243 F. 785 (S.D. Fla. 1917).
129. *Watts*, 394 U.S. at 706.
130. *Id.* at 708, *quoting, New York Times Co. v. Sullivan*, 376 U.S. 254, 270 (1964).
131. *Id*, quoting petition for review.

the light of the First Amendment, defined a true threat in terms drawn from *Brandenburg*.[132] In *Kelner v. United States*,[133] that court explained that a true threat must be "unequivocal, unconditional, and [exhibit a] specific intention immediately to inflict injury . . . only such threats, in short as are of the same nature as those threats which are . . . 'properly punished every day under statutes prohibiting extortion, blackmail and assault without consideration of First Amendment issues.'"[134] In requiring that an utterance "convey a gravity of purpose and imminent prosepect of execution" in order to constitute a "true threat," the Second Circuit reasoned that such a reading of the First Amendment's impact upon the statute:

> IS, we trust, consistent with a rational approach to First Amendment construction which provides for governmental authority in instances of inchoate conduct, where a communication has become "so interlocked with violent conduct as to constitute for all practices part of the [proscribed] action itself."[135]

In other words, when a threat is a verbal act, it is a "true threat" and the statute may constitutionally be applied to proscribe and punish its utterance.

In a more recent decision, *United States v. Baker*,[136] Judge Cohn of the Eastern District of Michigan applied these principles to dismiss an indictment against Jake Baker and Arthur Gonda, which had been predicated on a series of e-mail communications in which the two lasciviously described their fantasies of murdering young teenage girls. Baker, incidentally, was the same fine young specimen of American manhood who had been previously hauled into court for posting on an on-line bulletin board a story "graphically describ[ing] the torture, rape and murder of a woman who was given the name of a classmate of Baker's at the University of Michigan."[137] The Gonda correspondence came to light during the investigation of the initial complaint, and led to the filing of a superseding indictment that charged that

---

132. The "true threat" requirement of *Watts* has been widely employed, generally in conformity to the approach taken by the Second Circuit. *See*, for example, *United States v. Gordon*, 974 F.2d 1110 (9th Cir. 1992); *United States v. Kosma*, 951 F.2d 549 (3d Cir. 1991) (affirming conviction). However, some case law takes a more expansive position about what is a "true threat." *See*, for example, *United States v. Welch*, 745 F.2d 614 (10th Cir. 1984) (no need to prove intention or apparent ability to carry out threat to support conviction).

133. 534 F.2d 1020 (2d Cir.), *cert. denied*, 429 U.S. 1022 (1976).

134. *Kelner*, 534 F.2d at 1027, *quoting Watts*, 402 F.2d at 690.

135. *Kelner*, 534 F.2d at 1027 *quoting* Thomas Emerson, *The System of Free Expression* (1970) at 329.

136. 890 F. Supp. 1375 (E.D. Mich. 1995).

137. *Id.* at 1379.

the repeated expression of a desire on Baker's and Gonda's part to meet and enact their sanguinary lust constituted a threat under §875 (c).[138]

The dismissal of the indictment was based upon the lack of a "true threat" under the immediacy and specificity grounds of *Kelner,* adopted by the *Baker* court.[139] In so doing, Judge Cohn canvassed the decisions under both statutes, and found the *Brandenburg* analogy drawn by the Second Circuit in *Kelner* to be persuasive.[140] In *R.A.V. v. City of St. Paul,*[141] the Supreme Court had also justified state regulation of expressive conduct—the cross-burning—under circumstances in which such action created a reasonable fear of likely imminent violence, thus reaffirming the "verbal act" content of the "true threat" requirement, a holding the Court has reaffirmed even where specific intent to actually commit the threatened violence is lacking.[142]

WHEN RIGHTS COLLIDE:
BALANCING AND THE FIRST AMENDMENT

This functional approach to free expression seems quite near to First Amendment absolutism, and indeed does have several features in common with it. Like the absolutism professed by Justices Black and Douglas, a jurisprudence based on the verbal act standard must reject the subjectivity of the Court's current, *Chaplinsky*-based approach, and even more so reject the generalized balancing approach called for by Justice Frankfurter in *Dennis* and in *Beauharnais.* This holistic balancing has, as discussed in Chapter 3, come into vogue among many academics today, who feel that by silencing some, the state may empower others who have traditionally been deprived of power in our society.[143] However, because of the lack of any support in the amendment itself for such a subjective and value-laden inquiry, it cannot be grafted onto the constitutional text without doing great violence to not only the text, but also to the legitimate (but limited) role of judges in American society.

As Justices Black and Douglas said so often, the balancing was done by the Framers of the Constitution, and is enshrined within the text of the docu-

---

138. *Id.* at 1379–1380.
139. *Id.* at 1387–1390.
140. *Id.* at 1382–1384.
141. 505 U.S. 377, 388 (1992).
142. *Baker,* 890 F. Supp. at 1385; *Virginia v. Black,* 155 L. Ed. 2d 552–554 (applying strict scrutiny under First Amendment to cross-burning, finding that action under circumstances alleged constituted a threat, and so were outside of First Amendment's scope, relying, in part, on "cross-burning's long and pernicious history as a signal of impending violence").
143. *See,* for example, *Freeing the First Amendment,* Allen & Jensen, eds. (1995).

ment. Thus, they "reject[ed] too the implication that problems of freedom of speech . . . are to be resolved by weighing against the values of free expression, the judgment of the Court that a particular form of that expression has 'no redeeming social importance.' The First Amendment, its prohibition in terms absolute, was designed to preclude courts as well as legislatures from weighing the values of speech against silence."[144]

Does this mean that there is no legitimate place for "balancing" of constitutional rights? Actually, there is such a place. When a conflict arises between two constitutional rights and they cannot be reconciled, then some balancing must take place. However, the only counterweight to a constitutional provision is another constitutional provision. Thus, only such a conflict can legitimate such balancing.

Such a situation is not a desirable state of affairs, however, because it entails a recognition that the Constitution will be infringed in one way or another. The only question is which of the two provisions involved in the conflict will yield. In such a case, to adopt a theological analogy, the court must choose which is "the greater or lesser of two evils, but this does not mean that one of them is any more positive or has more being than the other, for the so-called 'greater' evil is simply that which devastates more."[145]

Over the years, the Court has wrestled with several of these clashes, in circumstances in which free expression has resulted in the deprivation of another constitutionally guaranteed right or in the exercise by the government of a constitutionally mandated function. In these cases, the Court has sought first to reconcile the rights involved, and, failing that, to pitch a balance between the interests asserted. After deciding which interest is paramount in the specific circumstances, the Court will allow infringement of the other by the government, but only to the extent necessary to serve the preferred right. The right to free expression has sometimes had to give way, and on other occasions has been upheld at the expense of other constitutional prerogatives or rights. A few samples of how the Court has fared in this delicate and difficult endeavor will serve to show the quagmires that lurk in the practice of balancing and the importance of minimizing its scope.

Fair Trial

A recurring source of conflict with the guarantees of the First Amendment has been the right of a criminal defendant to a fair trial, guaranteed by the Fifth and Fourteenth Amendments. Saturation press coverage of notorious criminal cases has resulted in the poisoning of the community atmosphere

---

144. *Roth v. United States*, 354 U.S. 476, 514 (Douglas, J., dissenting).
145. John Macquarrie, *Principles of Christian Theology* (2d ed. 1977) at 254–255.

against a defendant, such that the rendering of a verdict based solely on the trial evidence and not upon newspaper reports, which may be fueled by gossip, innuendo, and speculation, becomes impossible. The courts have long recognized this fact, and their gropings toward a just solution of this conflict is a notable instance of constitutional "balancing" logic.

The scope of the right to a fair trial should first be pointed out:

> IN essence, the right to a jury trial guarantees to the criminally accused a fair trial by a panel of impartial, "indifferent" jurors. . . . "The theory of the law is that a juror who has formed an opinion cannot be impartial." It is not required, however, that the jurors be totally ignorant of the facts and issues involved. In these days of swift, widespread and diverse methods of communication, an important case can be expected to arouse the interest of the public in the vicinity, and scarcely any of those best qualified to serve as jurors will not have formed some impression or opinion as to the merits of the case. . . . It is sufficient if the juror can lay aside his impression or opinion and render a verdict based on the evidence presented in court.[146]

The critical impact of press reports on a criminal trial has long been acknowledged by the Supreme Court. Although it normally accedes in the legal fiction that a juror, instructed by a judge, can forget evidence that he or she has heard (A wonderful cartoon depicts the members of a jury, hair standing on end, faces aghast, while the judge blandly informs them, "The jury will disregard that last answer."), the Supreme Court in *Irvin v. Dowd*[147] took a more pragmatic view of the impact of pretrial publicity.

In that case, a suspect charged with committing six murders in Vanderburgh County, Indiana, after which the county prosecutor and local police issued a series of press releases. These releases became extensively publicized, and included headline stories that described the defendant as a "confessed slayer of six," a parole violator, and a fraudulent-check artist. The defendant moved for a change of venue, which was granted, but only to the extent of moving the trial to the next county—where the case had been just as thoroughly publicized. Of the approximately 400 potential jurors, 370 (90 percent of the available jurors) stated that they "entertained some opinion as to guilt—ranging in intensity from mere suspicion to absolute certainty."[148] Of the final panel of 12 jurors, 8 had expressed that they "thought petitioner was guilty."[149] The Court viewed the risk to a fair trial pragmatically:

---

146. *Irvin v. Dowd,* 366 U.S. 717, 722–723 (1961) *quoting Reynolds v. United States,* 98 U.S. 145, 155 (1978).
147. *Id.*
148. *Id.* at 727.
149. *Id.*

WITH such an opinion permeating their minds, it would be difficult to say that each could exclude this preconception of guilt from his deliberations. The influence that lurks in an opinion once formed is so persistent that it unconsciously fights detachment of the average man. . . . Where one's life is at stake—and accounting for the frailties of human nature—we can only say that in light of the circumstances here that the finding of impartiality does not meet constitutional standards. . . . No doubt each juror was sincere when he said that he would be fair and impartial to petitioner, but the psychological impact requiring such a declaration before one's fellows is often its father. Where so many, so many times, admitted prejudice, such a statement can be given little weight. As one of the jurors put it, "You can't forget what you hear and see."[150]

Thus, in *Irvin*, it was established that a conviction that was garnered in an atmosphere poisoned by hostile reportage must be reversed. That such would be its holding had been suggested in several previous decisions. However, such a holding leaves open the question of whether accepting the mistrial or being reversed on appeal is inevitable: Because those who are convicted remain incarcerated during the pendency of their appeals and (frequently) during the retrial, such a "solution" exacts a severe penalty on the very party whose right to a fair trial was concededly violated. Similarly, continuing a trial until the furor surrounding the case dies down can result in a defendant's being held in prison for a lengthy period, rendering meaningless the right to speedy trial.

As a former staff attorney for the Legal Aid Society's Criminal Appeals Bureau, where I spent three years representing indigents on appeal of their criminal convictions, I can personally testify that both prosecutors and defense attorneys are aware of these facts. On those rare occasions when a conviction will almost certainly be reversed, district attorneys will frequently delay filing their briefs on appeal until the last possible moment, seeking adjournments or incurring court orders to file by a certain date to maximize the unofficial punishment the convict will undergo. Because the ordinary appeal can take up to a year to process (and defenders, both private and public, sometimes perfect—that is, file—appeals too slowly, as well), this is no academic balancing of abstract rights: Innocent people can sit in jail for unconscionably long periods of time based on these accommodations.

In *Irvin* the Court did not discuss the possibility of restraining the press in its opinion. The harm, after all, had been done, and no member of the press was a party to the case. Thus, *Irvin* does not shed much light on the thorny question of whether, as Justice Frankfurter put it in his concurring

---

150. *Id.* at 727–728.

opinion, "while convictions must be reversed and miscarriages of justice result because the minds of jurors or potential jurors were poisoned, the poisoner is constitutionally protected in plying his trade."[151]

One striking case, because of its notoriety, its posthumous fame, and the unusual fact that some agreement about the miscarriage of justice has at last been reached, is *Sheppard v. Maxwell*.[152] The *Sheppard* case was a cause célèbre, and remains one to this day. Sam Sheppard, a successful, youngish doctor, was tried for the murder of his wife. Maintaining his innocence throughout, Sheppard insisted that an intruder had committed the crime. At the trial, the atmosphere was that of a "'Roman Holiday' for the news media."[153] Throughout the nine weeks of trial, the courtroom was jammed with reporters, whose movements "caused such confusion that, despite the loudspeakers installed in the courtrooms, it was difficult for the witnesses and counsel to be heard." Outside of the courtroom, the witnesses, counsel, and jurors had to run a gauntlet that consisted of "a host of photographers and television personnel," who photographed their entrances and exits. Worst of all, a constant stream of publicity, often containing information, speculation, and pure guesswork that was never offered into evidence blanketed the area, despite which the jurors were never sequestered until the close of trial, when they began their deliberations.[154]

The Supreme Court, in reversing the conviction, noted that "reversals are but palliatives; the cure lies in those remedial measures that will prevent the prejudice at its inception."[155] What are these remedial measures? The Court opined that the failure of the system in Sheppard's case was directly attributable to the trial judge, who could "easily" have prevented "the carnival atmosphere of the trial" because "the courtroom and the courtroom premises" are subject to his control. Among the trial court's failures, Justice Clark's opinion for the nearly unanimous justices pointed out that the judge should have provided privacy for the jury, insulated the witnesses from the media (rather than permitting them to be interviewed at will), limited the number of reporters permitted in the courtroom at any one time, and prohibited the reporters from examining, handling [!], and photographing the exhibits during recesses.[156]

These measures, however helpful, do not address the fundamental problem raised by the *Sheppard* trial—the feeding to jurors of inadmissible evidence outside of the courtroom. However, in demarcating the more seri-

---

151. *Id.* at 730 (Frankfuter, J. concurring).
152. 384 U.S. 333, 86 S.Ct. 1507, 16 L.Ed.2d 600 (1966).
153. *Id.* at 356 *quoting Sheppard v. State,* 165 Ohio St. 293, 294, 135 N.E.2d 340, 342.
154. *Id.* at 355.
155. *Id.* at 363.
156. *Id.* at 355–357.

ous problems posed by the *Sheppard* case, the Court ran into a problem: It does not square well with our very theory of government

> TO place any direct limits on the freedom traditionally exercised by the news media for "what transpires in the courtroom is public property." . . . The press does not simply publish information about trials but guards against the miscarriage of justice by subjecting the police, prosecutors, and judicial processes to extensive public scrutiny and criticism.[157]

So this First Amendment value limits the admitted "power of the court to control the publicity about the trial" that the Court found vested in the trial court. In attempting to pitch the balance, the Court favored indirect limitations—restrictions not on the press but on the parties:

> THE trial court might well have proscribed extra-judicial statements by any lawyer, party or witness, or court official which divulged prejudicial matters, such as the refusal of Sheppard to submit to interrogation[158] or take any lie detector tests; any statement made by Sheppard to officials; the identity of prospective witnesses or their probable testimony; any belief in guilt or innocence; or like statements concerning the merits of the case. . . .
>
> Being advised of the great public interest in the case, the mass coverage of the press, and the potential prejudicial impact of publicity, the court could also have requested the appropriate city and county officials to promulgate a regulation with respect to dissemination of information about the case by their employees.[159]

Before moving on to the development of the ideas suggested in the *Sheppard* opinion, several observations may or may not be pertinent, but cannot be omitted. First, on retrial, Sam Sheppard was acquitted.[160] However, the

---

157. *Id.* at 349–350 (citations omitted).
158. The late New York State Supreme Court Justice Harold Rothwax, in his controversial, rather ill-tempered screed *Guilty: The Collapse of the Criminal Justice System* (1995) argued that such prejudicial information should be permitted to reach the jury, despite the fact that it only shows that the defendant, at most, recognizes that he or she is no match for a trained interrogator who already has a preconceived result in mind. The *Sheppard* case is an excellent example (as will be seen shortly) of the illogic of Justice Rothwax's position that such silence is a classic indicator of guilt.
159. 384 U.S. at 361–362. For a more extensive discussion of measures that the trial court can permissibly use to diminish the risk of prejudice to the defendant, *see* Note, Robert S. Stephen, *Prejudicial Publicity Surrounding a Criminal Trial: What a Trial Court Can Do to Ensure a Fair Trial in the Face of a "Media Circus,"* 26 Suffolk U. L. Rev. 1063 (1992).
160. *New York Times,* 17 November 1966, p. 1 col. 7.

years in jail, the experience of being a pariah, and the stress of struggling to establish his innocence so undermined his character that he simply could not rebuild his life—especially because his medical license was not automatically restored. After his various legitimate efforts to rebuild his life failed, Sheppard took to drink, ended up on the wrestling circuit, and died young.[161]

Unlike his fictional counterpart, Dr. Richard Kimble of the television program *The Fugitive*, Sam Sheppard never found his wife's killer, and the poisonous cloud of suspicion blighted the life of a man who even the successor of the district attorney who tried him now concedes was innocent.[162] Sadly, the lessons of the Sheppard case sometimes seem as elusive as was justice in this tragedy of the law. In arguing "For an Honest Death Penalty"[163] federal Judge Alex Kozinsky and Sean Gallagher fatuously stated that "[t]he case where the innocent defendant is saved from the electric chair because the one-armed man shows up and confesses happens only in the movies." This careless reference to *The Fugitive* (in its 1994 Harrison Ford incarnation) as though its factual predicate never took place is disquieting. Similarly, the many innocent defendants who have been exonerated during appeals of their death sentences might just possibly disagree—Randall Adams and Larry Hicks to name just two, to say nothing of Jesse DeWayne Jacobs, whose death sentence for a crime that even the prosecutor who secured it now concedes he did not commit was upheld by the federal Court of Appeals for the Fifth Circuit and the United States Supreme Court.[164]

Freedom of speech has its costs, this book opened by assuming. Sam Sheppard paid more than most. In that he was not alone. Leo Frank, the "Scottsboro Boys," Julius and Ethel Rosenberg—disagreement about the innocence of Ethel still rages decades after their executions—all were "tried" in a "carnival" atmosphere. The Court's efforts to prevent future such tragedies are still relatively new.

In striking a balance in *Sheppard* and *Irvin*, the Court hesitated to restrain the press; it preferred to try to ameliorate the problem by denying the press access to information that would enable it to damage the defendant's right

---

161. F. Lee Bailey, *The Defense Never Rests* (1971) at 91–92; Sam Reese Sheppard & Cynthia L. Cooper, *Mockery of Justice: The True Story of the Sheppard Murder Case* (1995).

162. "After Life of Notoriety and Pain, Son Tries to Solve Mother's Murder," *New York Times*, 26 March 1996 at A12 (quoting present-day first assistant county prosecutor Carmen Marino as saying "I don't think Sam Sheppard killed his wife. . . . It seems far-fetched to me now that Sam did it.").

163. *New York Times*, 8 March 1995, Op-Ed page A.

164. *See* Randall Adams, William Hoffer and Marilyn Mona Hoffer, *Adams v. Texas* (1991); Martin Yant, *Presumed Guilty* (1991) at 167–170; *Jacobs v. Scott*, 31 F.3d 1319 (5th Cir. 1994), *cert. denied*, 513 U.S. 1067 (1995) (Stevens, J. dissenting from denial of review of capital murder case where prosecutor took inconsistent positions in two prosecutions of different alleged "murderers").

to a fair trial by placing restrictions on other actors. This principle has, however, its own inherent limitations. These other actors, after all, have *their* First Amendment rights.[165]

With respect to attorneys who are licensed by the state to represent other citizens in disputes, special rules have been deemed applicable, both under the rubric of legal ethics, and under court decisions that apply First Amendment principles in balance with the special roles played by attorneys in the U.S. justice system.

Legal ethics, the set of rules by which lawyers are guided when they represent the interests of their clients, specially delimit the speech of lawyers in the context of ongoing litigation. For example, according to the American Bar Association's 1983 *Model Rules of Professional Conduct,* a lawyer "shall not make an extrajudicial"—that is, an out of court statement—"that a reasonable person would expect to be disseminated . . . if the lawyer knows or reasonably should know that it will have a substantial likelihood of materially prejudicing an adjudicative proceeding."[166] The *Model Rules* define a statement as likely to have that effect "when it refers to a civil matter triable to a jury, a criminal matter, or any other proceeding that could result in incarceration, and the statement refers to matters reflecting on the outcome, the prospects of settlement, or the credibility, character or expected testimony of witnesses to appear at trial." Also deemed prejudicial are statements of "any opinion as to the guilt or innocence of a defendant or suspect."[167] Information that is inadmissible and meets the standards set out in the *Model Rules* is specifically defined as likely to be substantially likely to materially prejudice the outcome of litigation, as is the fact of an accusation when it is not accompanied by "a statement explaining that the charge is merely an accusation and that the defendant is presumed innocent until proven guilty."[168]

The Supreme Court addressed the constitutionality of this provision in *Gentile v. State Bar of Nevada.*[169] In *Gentile,* the Court upheld the "substantial likelihood" standard as constitutionally permissible, "for it is designed to protect the integrity and fairness of the state's judicial system, and it imposes only narrow and necessary limitations on a lawyer's speech."[170] Restrictions

---

165. For a spirited defense of the Court's performance in this one area of First Amendment jurisprudence since *Schenck, see* William O. Douglas, *The Right of the People* (1958) at 51–53.
166. *American Bar Association Model Rules of Professional Conduct,* Rule 3.6 (1983).
167. *Id.*
168. *Id.*
169. 501 U.S. 1030 (1991).
170. 501 U.S. at 1075. Other provisions of the rule that are not discussed in the text were struck as constitutionally vague. *Id.*

on the speech of attorneys cannot take the form of blanket prior restraint. Rather, like all admitted abridgements of First Amendment rights that are mandated by the clash of constitutional imperatives, the restraint must be as narrowly tailored as possible while still preserving the preferred right—that which is more "compelling" in the specific factual context involved, as the Court has phrased it, and must only be adopted after all other means of reconciling the two interests have been tried and have failed.

Gentile is a troubling opinion, and it harks back to the clear and present danger test in a manner calculated to delight the heart of an advocate of the verbal act formulation—and then cast him or her down in despair. Part of the problem is that there is no one opinion of the Court. Rather, three justices joined Justice Kennedy's opinion that reversed the imposition of a disciplinary sanction on attorney Dominick Gentile in its totality, while three joined Chief Justice Rehnquist's opinion that dissented from that reversal. However, Justice O'Connor joined the Chief Justice's opinion with respect to its first and second sections, providing the general analytic framework, but joined Justice Kennedy's opinion with respect to section III (holding that the so-called "safe harbor" provision—which gave exceptions as to when a lawyer can speak about a case and know that she or he is within the law—rendered the statute so confusing as to be unconstitutionally vague) and section VI (the bare statement that the judgment below was reversed). As a result, the opinions are somewhat in tension, and render a uniform approach to them somewhat fictitious.

The basic analysis of the Chief Justice states that:

> WHEN a state regulation implicates First Amendment rights, the Court must balance those interests against the State's legitimate interest in regulating the activity in question. . . . The limitations are aimed at two principal evils: (1) comments that are likely to influence the actual outcome of the trial, and (2) comments that are likely to prejudice the jury venire, even if an untainted panel can ultimately be found. Few, if any, interests under the Constitution are more fundamental than the right to a fair trial by impartial jurors, and an outcome affected by extrajudicial statements would violate that fundamental right.[171]

Rehnquist's opinion in *Gentile* speaks in general, Frankfurterian terms of balancing and suggests that a "substantial" (as opposed to the more usual "compelling") state interest need be shown to trump the First Amendment in a balancing competition. Even worse, the line of cases relied upon by Chief Justice Rehnquist do not support his quoted statement.

---

171. 501 U.S. at 1075 (citations omitted).

After his "balancing" statement, the Chief Justice cites as an example *Seattle Times Co. v. Rhineheart*.[172] However, that case (which involved a protective order against the disclosure before trial to the press by a litigant of any materials produced in the course of litigation under state rules governing disclosure or discovery) found that because the normally private information had been pried from the litigant for the purpose of trying the case: "A litigant has no First Amendment right of access to materials made available only for purposes of trying his suit."[173] Because the information was not itself concealed under the court order, merely the information that was obtained from court-ordered discovery, the right of the litigants to try their case under state law and their resultant disclosure obligations were weighed against an *incidental* limitation on free expression, not a general ad hoc balancing.

The principal case relied upon by the Court in *Seattle Times, Procunier v. Martinez*,[174] makes the point even more clear, because the Court in that case dealt with prison regulation of inmate mail as an "incidental restriction on First Amendment liberties imposed in furtherance of legitimate government activities."[175] Like *O'Brien*, whose four-prong standard the Court relied upon, the case involved not a suppression of words as ideas, but a state interest in ensuring that the act of speech not become a cloak for the acts of insurrection and escape.[176] Notably, in *Procunier* the Court struck the prison regulations involved, stating that they "fairly invited prison officials and employees to apply their own personal prejudices and opinions as standards for prison mail censorship."[177]

Thus, the statement by Chief Justice Rehnquist, as a general matter, is too broad. However, it is far from clear that the Chief Justice meant it so broadly. *Gentile* likewise involved an "incidental" limitation: a restriction that impacted First Amendment values only to the extent necessary to protect a fair trial; was restricted to attorneys, who are agents of the state and officers of the Court; and that "merely postpones the attorney's comments until after the trial."[178]

Regardless of the weight given the various interests to be balanced, this portion of the Chief Justice's analysis is precisely the sort of legitimate balancing that cannot be avoided when two constitutional rights come into an irreconcilable conflict. However, the Chief Justice continued:

---

172. 467 U.S. 20 (1984).
173. *Id.* at 32.
174. 416 U.S. 396, 413 (1974).
175. *Id.* at 409.
176. *Id.* at 412–413.
177. *Id.* at 415.
178. 501 U.S. at 1075–1076.

EVEN if a fair trial can ultimately be ensured through *voir dire*, change of venue, or some other device these measures entail serious costs to the system. Extensive *voir dire* may not be able to filter out all of the effects of pretrial publicity, and with increasingly widespread media coverage of criminal trials, a change of venue may not suffice to undo the effects of statements such as those made by [Gentile]. The State has a substantial interest in preventing officers of the court, such as lawyers, from imposing such costs on the judicial system and on the litigants.[179]

The weighing of the efficient functioning of a state (or federal, for that matter) proceeding against the First Amendment's imperative is simply inappropriate. Chief Justice Rehnquist either impermissibly is blurring the line here, or he is again relying (as he had previously in the opinion) on the attorney's "fiduciary" obligation to the courts, the litigants, and to the state, as well as on a decision *sub silentio* (which is unquestionably correct) that in safeguarding the fairness of judicial proceedings by regulation of their participants, the state is only incidentally impacting free expression. That this latter optimistic conclusion may be correct is supported by the chief justice's conclusion: He justifies the regulation in terms of *O'Brien*'s four-point test, although he does not cite or quote *O'Brien*.

The plurality opinion by Justice Kennedy did not go as far as that of the Chief Justice: Rather, finding the substantial likelihood test to encapsulate and approximate the clear and present danger test (and thus the verbal act formulation), it held the standard to be constitutional, but found that the statements involved by Gentile did not amount to a violation of the standard.[180]

The question of regulating the press in the name of ensuring the right to a fair trial is perhaps the hardest constitutional case of all. That case has been addressed as well. The problem, of course, is that the Court has long recognized that in such circumstances, either of the scale in the "balance of harm" scenario truly yields a bad result. For just as the defendant's interest in not being unfairly tried is of enormous magnitude, so too is the need for press coverage of the exercise of state power through the judicial branch. As the Court phrased it in *In Re Oliver*, the "knowledge that every criminal trial is subject to contemporaneous review in the forum of public opinion is an effective restraint on possible abuses on the part of judicial power. . . . Without publicity, all other checks are insufficient, in comparison."[181]

---

179. *Id.* at 1075 (citations omitted).
180. *Id.* at 1057–1058.
181. 333 U.S. 257, 270–271 (1948); *see also Gentile,* 501 U.S. at 1035 (opinion of Kennedy, J.).

The balance that has been struck with respect to substantive news reportage of criminal trials is almost entirely—and the qualifier could well be dispensed with—in favor of the media. In a series of cases, the Court has held that "trial courts might not constitutionally punish, through use of the contempt power, newspapers and others for publishing editorials, cartoons, and other items critical of judges in particular cases."[182] Such punishments may only be imposed when the publication presents a clear and present danger of "some serious substantive evil which they are designed to avert."[183] In other words, only when the verbal act formulation is met—when press coverage fits the classic speech brigaded with action test—will suppression of it be justified. There is, seemingly, no "give" in the balance at all.

However, there are ways of preventing the press from prejudicing the trial of a defendant that fall short of proscribing reportage of specific facts and views. One such means is by restricting access to the judicial processes. Yet here too the Court has held that the press has a "qualified First Amendment right of access" to judicial proceedings, noting that only where the nature of the proceeding is one that requires secrecy by its very nature (such as the presentation of evidence and resulting deliberations of grand jury), or in a case-specific showing of a risk of prejudice in the form of an unfair trial, may the press be denied access to proceedings or even to transcripts of proceedings.[184]

Interestingly, the inquiry in the context of allegations of a danger of unfairness has been expressed in purely balancing terms: "In such cases, the trial court must determine whether the situation is such that the rights of the accused override the qualified First Amendment right of access."[185]

---

182. *Gentile*, 501 U.S. at 1069, *summarizing Nebraska Press Association v. Stuart*, 427 U.S. 539 (1976); *Bridges v. California*, 314 U.S. 252 (1941); *Pennekamp v. Florida*, 328 U.S. 331 (1946); and *Craig v. Harney*, 331 U.S. 367 (1947).

183. *Bridges v. California*, 314 U.S. at 270. Although the Court in *Bridges* does not use the "clear and present danger" expression, it has been so understood by successor courts. *See*, for example, *Gentile*, 501 U.S. at 1069. This understanding is simply correct, as the *Bridges* Court not only quotes the *Schenck* language we have seen so often, as it is cited in the text, but also relies explicitly upon Justice Holmes's dissenting opinion in *Toledo Newspaper Co. v. United States*, 247 U.S. 402, 425 (1918) (Holmes, J., dissenting) stating that a judicial contempt citation against a newspaper was "wholly unwarranted by even color of law" where "there was no emergency, that there was nothing that warranted a finding that the administration of justice was obstructed." In such a case, Holmes opined, "when there is no need for immediate action, contempts are like any other breach of the law, and should be dealt with as the law deals with other illegal acts." In short, a verbal act is an act. Notably, the case did not even present a First Amendment challenge.

184. *Press-Enterprises Co. v. Superior Court*, 478 U.S. 1, 8–9 (1986) (invalidating court order denying access to transcript of preliminary hearing).

185. *Id.* at 9.

In determining whether the right of access applies to various stages of criminal trials, the Court has looked to "two complementary considerations."[186] First, "because a 'tradition of accessibility implies the favorable judgment of experience' . . . we have considered whether the place and process have historically been open to the public."[187] The second factor is "whether public access plays a significant positive role in the functioning of the particular process in question."[188]

The presumption is generally one in favor of access, and can only be "overcome only by an overriding interest based on findings that closure is essential to preserve higher values and is narrowly tailored to serve that interest. The interest is to be articulated along with findings specific enough that a reviewing court can determine whether the closure order was properly entered."[189]

In discussing preliminary hearings, for example, the Court has adverted to both tradition and functional analysis for justification of the qualified right of access of the press, stating that preliminary hearings in criminal cases were "sufficiently like a trial" that public access was "essential to their proper functioning."[190]

By contrast, the "proper functioning of the grand jury system depends on the secrecy of grand jury proceedings."[191] However, that interest in secrecy is far from absolute: Access may be granted to transcripts when a particularized showing of the need for disclosure is made that outweighs the need for continued secrecy.[192]

A separate issue exists, really, as to whether news media may *broadcast*, as opposed to report, courtroom proceedings. The presence of television cameras in the courtroom can intimidate some witnesses, lead to histrionic behavior on the part of witnesses and attorneys alike, and in many other ways play a prejudicial role in the trial. Additionally, by providing the thrill of watching the net tighten (or fail to tighten) around a defendant in a celebrity case that is broadcast live, such coverage can feed a growing media hoopla.

The trial of O. J. Simpson, unusual though it was in that it mixed issues of race, sex, and celebrity, was not inherently different from that say, of Harry K. Thaw for the murder of Stanford White over Evelyn Nisbet—but

---

186. *Id.* at 8–9.
187. *Id.* at 8 *quoting Globe Newspapers Co. v. Superior Court*, 457 U.S. 596, 605 (1982) (*quoting Richmond Newspapers Inc. v. Virginia*, 448 U.S. 555, 589 [1980]).
188. *Id.* at 9. *See also Richmond Newspapers, Inc. v. Virginia*, 448 U.S. 555, 589 (1980) (Brennan, J., concurring).
189. *Press-Enterprises v. Superior Court*, 464 U.S. 501, 510 (1984).
190. *El Vocero de Puerto Rico v. Puerto Rico*, 508 U.S. 147, 149 (1993) (characterizing *Press-Enterprises v. Superior Court*).
191. *Douglas Oil Co. v. Petroleum Stops Northwest*, 441 U.S. 211, 218 (1979).
192. *Id.* at 222.

saturation coverage now is a great deal more intense than it was in the ragtime era. The action was broadcast live, after all, and people with little or no prior interest in the operation of the criminal justice system became experts on the testimony of Detectives Vanatter and Fuhrman. A "helpful" cadre of lawyers became commentators, and debates about ethics and tactics continued months after Simpson's acquittal,[193] with virtually all of the major players (including the jurors!) writing books on the subject.

On one level, this case represents the First Amendment at its most triumphant. A brutal murder sparked new awareness of police misconduct, raised the consciousness of many with respect to the pervasiveness of domestic abuse through all levels of society, and engaged the attention of the American people in debates about one of their government's most fundamental purposes, preventing and punishing crime.

So why did the case leave such a bad taste in the nation's mouth?

Written nearly two centuries prior to the invention of the news media, of the cult of celebrity, of the talk show, the First Amendment provides little explicit help in deciding how to deal with this phenomenon. The Court has flip-flopped on the issue. In 1965, a plurality of the Court—including Justice Douglas, forced for once to recognize a genuine "balancing" situation to the detriment of the press—held that "televising [a] criminal trial is inherently a denial of due process" to the hapless defendant.[194] In *Chandler v. Florida*,[195] the Court limited its prior decision in *Estes v. Texas* to the particular facts involved in that case—that is, a physically intrusive and clearly visible camera, as well as a cause célèbre that combined to "utterly corrupt" the trial. It did so without overruling *Estes*, by relying on Justice Harlan's opinion in that case that provided the fifth vote necessary to reverse the tainted conviction.

In *Chandler*, the Court rejected the idea of a per se rule that the broadcast of a trial is a violation of the right to a fair trial and required the defendant to show either that the media's coverage—including but not limited to the broadcast—"compromised the ability of the jury to judge him fairly," or "that broadcast coverage of his particular case had an adverse impact sufficient to constitute a denial of due process."[196]

---

193. For example, a furious two-hour debate ensued between Alan Dershowitz and Charles Grodin, televised on Geraldo Rivera's talk show *Rivera Live!* on 15 April 1996, in which Dershowitz attacked Grodin's critical commentary as slipshod and irresponsibly careless with respect to factual assertions, and Grodin claimed that Dershowitz's book on the case unfairly denigrated the prosecutors. *See generally*, Alan M. Dershowitz, *Reasonable Doubts* (1996).

194. *Estes v. Texas*, 381 U.S. 532, 552 (Warren, C. J. concurring) (1965); *see also Id.* at 542–543 (opinion of court to similar effect).

195. 449 U.S. 560 (1981).

196. *Chandler*, 449 U.S. at 581.

Interestingly, with respect to the prospect of broadcasting its own deliberations, the Court has been much less pro-media. As was recently reported, Justice David Souter reacted quite strongly to the prospect of introducing cameras into the Supreme Court. "I think the case is so strong," Justice Souter commented, "that I can tell you that the day you see a camera come into our courtroom, it's going to roll over my dead body."[197] He explained why, in terms that should give all who care about the fairness of trials pause. According to the *New York Times*, "Justice Souter said that when he had been a judge in New Hampshire, camera coverage had affected his behavior on the bench because he had believed that some questions would be taken out of context on the evening news."[198]

The War Power and National Security

Another area in which constitutional imperatives have clashed involves the waging of war and the reportage of activities carried out in prosecuting war. The breadth of the war power is, potentially, enormous; as Chief Justice Stone wrote for the Court in *Hirabayashi v. United States*[199] in the context of freeing a demonstrably innocent (among thousands of others) Japanese-American who was interned during World War II, "the power to wage war is the power to wage war successfully." Thus, actions—such as the internment program—that fly in the face of ordinary limitations on the Government's powers have been upheld as constitutional in time of war.[200]

That the war power may have some impact on the exercise of free speech rights in wartime was accepted as long ago as *Schenck v. United States*,[201] in which Justice Holmes made the fact that the nation was at war a factor in determining the "danger" element of his fledgling clear and present dan-

---

197. *New York Times*, 30 March 1996, p. 24, col. 1.
198. *Id.*
199. 320 U.S. 81, 93 (1943). Justice Black wrote the opinions in *Ex Parte Endo*, 323 U.S. 283 (1944) and *Korematsu v. United States*, 323 U.S. 214 (1944) (approving criminal penalties for violation of Executive Order), legitimating the internment program itself, in which Justice Douglas, to his later regret, joined. William O. Douglas, *The Court Years: The Autobiography of William O. Douglas* (1980) at 279–280.
200. *Korematsu*, 323 U.S. 214, has been subsequently qualified in restatement. As summarized in *Kent v. Dulles*, 357 U.S. 116, 128 (1958), the decision "allowed the Government in time of war to exclude citizens from their homes and restrict their movements only on a showing of 'the gravest imminent danger to public safety.'" The difficulty is that the alleged showing was not individualized, and thus swept up Japanese-Americans in an undifferentiated manner, regardless of whether they posed such a danger or even contributed to such a danger. Also, in *Korematsu* the "danger" was the undifferentiated one presented by war, and not a showing that *any* Japanese-Americans presented a potential "Fifth Column."
201. 249 U.S. 47 (1919).

ger test. Holmes's opinion stated quite explicitly that "[w]hen a Nation is at war, many things that might be said in time of peace are such a hindrance to its effort that their utterance will not be endured so long as men fight and that no Court could regard them as protected by any constitutional right."[202]

As the Court explained that impact in *Near v. Minnesota*:

> NO one would question but that a government might prevent actual obstruction to its recruitment service or the publication of the sailing dates of transports or the number and location of troops.[203]

The limits of this doctrine have proved to be slippery.

In the first place, the language used by the Court in *Near* itself suggested that this ability to act only comes into play when the reportage "must inevitably, directly, and immediately cause the occurrence of an event kindred to imperiling the safety of a transport already at sea."[204]

Moreover, the potential limitation of the doctrine to times of "war" has been used on at least one occasion to protect speech. In *New York Times v. United States*,[205] a government-secured injunction against the publication by the *New York Times* of the purloined "Pentagon Papers" (describing the handling of the Vietnam War through 1968) was voided as unconstitutional "prior restraint." The case was so controversial at the time that each of the nine justices authored a separate opinion. In one of the six opinions that voided the injunction, that of Justice Douglas,[206] the fact that a declaration of war by Congress had not taken place was given great weight. Justice Douglas, it should be noted, did not stand utterly alone on this issue; Justice Black joined in his concurring opinion, and Justice Brennan noted the lack of a declaration of war, although he did not decide what weight should be placed upon it.

In Justice Douglas's opinion, the issue was dispositive. After citing his own previous statement about the scope of the war power, Douglas continued,

> BUT the war power stems from a declaration of war. The Constitution by Art. I, § 8 gives Congress, not the President, the power "to declare

---

202. *Id.* at 52.
203. 283 U.S. 697, 716 (1931) (invalidating statute permitting injunctions of allegedly defamatory statements).
204. *New York Times Co. v. United States*, 403 U.S. 713, 726–727 (1971) (Brennan, J. concurring).
205. *Id.*
206. The remaining five justices, Black, Brennan, White, Stewart, and Marshall, did not reach the issue based on their disapproval of prior restraint, especially in the absence of a statute supporting the government's application. *See also* opinion of Justice Brennan, 403 U.S. at 726, *et seq.*

War." Nowhere are presidential wars authorized. We need not decide therefore what leveling effect the war power of Congress might have.[207]

From there, Justice Douglas found, no imperative of a like dignity to that of the First Amendment had been implicated. Indeed, Justice Douglas wrote, the government's argument "that it has inherent power to go into court and obtain an injunction to protect the national interest, which in this case is alleged to be national security" was "an expansive doctrine" that had long been rejected because "[t]he dominant purpose of the First Amendment was to prohibit the widespread practice of governmental suppression of embarrassing information."[208]

Up to the present, the issue of the existence and scope of Douglas's "leveling effect" has not yet been decided. In fact, such precedent as exists inclines the other way, suggesting that the power of the executive to act to protect national security in peacetime may be concomitant with that extant in wartime.[209] However, the inherent power to act to protect "national security" pressed by the U.S. solicitor general in *New York Times* raises a separate balancing question: What happens when speech may in some manner imperil national security?

In *New York Times*, the issue was complicated by what was in essence a power grab by the executive; without a statutory grant of injunctive power, in the face of congressional rejection of that extensive power (at least one amendment to the Espionage Act of 1917 that sought to confer such authority had failed), the Court was reluctant to legitimize its old bugbear, prior restraint.

Indeed, the swing votes in the case, Justices Stewart, White, and Marshall, each rested their concurrence on separation of powers, as well as what Justice White termed the "extraordinary protection against prior restraints enjoyed by the press under our constitutional system."[210] Justice Marshall, in an opinion that is breathtaking in its simplicity, and yet that makes a point of unquestionable validity, did not see the case in First Amendment terms at all. As he saw it, "The issue is whether this Court or the Congress has the power to make law."[211] Resting on the basic ingredients of the federal sys-

---

207. 403 U.S. at 722.
208. *Id.* at 723–724.
209. *See*, for example, *Haig v. Agee*, 453 U.S. 280, 303 (1981) (rejecting petitioner's contention that "statements of Executive policy are entitled to diminished weight because many of them concern the powers of the Executive in wartime. However, the statute [therein construed] provides no support for this argument. History eloquently attests that grave problems of national security and foreign policy are by no means limited to times of formally declared war").
210. 403 U.S. at 730–731 (Stewart, J. concurring); *id.* at 739–740 (White, J., concurring).
211. *Id.* at 741.

tem, Justice Marshall reminded his colleagues that "[t]he Constitution provides that Congress shall make laws, the President execute laws, and courts interpret laws."[212] Justice Marshall pointed out that the newspapers were not charged with violating any criminal statute, "just as it is a traditional axiom that equity will not enjoin the commission of a crime."[213]

New York Times represents the definitive rejection of a secret regime whereby publication—of virtually anything—could be enjoined on the alleged grounds of national security, prior to publication, in the absence of statutory authority. In vain did Blackmun dolefully say "[w]hat is needed here is a weighing, upon properly developed standards, of the broad right of the press to print and of the very narrow right to prevent."[214]

However, the Court did not address the limits posed by the Constitution to the drawing of such standards by the appropriate branches of the federal government—that is, the legislative branch with the concurrence of, or over the veto of, the president. Indeed, only Justices Black and Douglas squarely held that prior restraint on "national security" grounds was in every case unconstitutional. Justice Brennan left the question open, and the remainder of the majority felt only that it could not be done in the way in which the Nixon administration had tried to impose prior restraint—although Stewart and White left a clear impression that not much in the way of prior restraint was permissible. As an examination of the statutory scheme as it has been played out over the years may attest, the dissenters in *New York Times* were not so soundly beaten as they feared—or as the friends of free speech hoped.

The existence of the government's right to secrecy has long historical antecedents. Without unraveling them completely, it has long been accepted by the judiciary that the "President, both as Commander-in-Chief and as the Nation's organ for foreign affairs, has available intelligence services whose reports are not and ought not to be published to the world."[215] In the context of the treaty-making power the Court elaborated, tracing the principle as far back as the presidency of George Washington, and concluded that the president "has his sources of confidential information. He has his agents in the form of diplomatic, consular and other officials. Secrecy in respect of information gathered by them may be highly necessary, and the premature disclosure of it productive of harmful results."[216]

---

212. *Id.* at 742.
213. *Id.* at 744 (Marshall, J. concurring) (*citing* Z. Chaffee & E. Re, *Equity* 935–937 (5th ed. 1967); 1 H. Joyce, *Injunctions* §§ 58–60a (1909).
214. 403 U.S. at 761 (Blackmun, J., dissenting).
215. *Chicago & Southern Air Lines, Inc. v. Waterman Steamship Corp.*, 333 U.S. 103, 111 (1948).
216. *United States v. Curtiss-Wright Export Corp.*, 299 U.S. 304, 320 (1936).

However, the "First Amendment interest in informed popular government does not simply vanish at the invocation of the words 'national security.' National security is public security, not security from informed criticism."[217] Despite this high-flown language, the suppression of critics is rather
what *has* tended to happen at the invocation of "national security." The Court
has held that "it is 'obvious and inarguable' that no governmental interest
is more compelling than the security of the Nation."[218] Or, as the Court expressed it somewhat more pithily, "while the Constitution protects against
invasions of individual rights, it is not a suicide pact."[219]

Thus, to take the language of *Haig* and its progenitors seriously, the "compelling state interest" in national security allows it to trump the First Amendment. In pure balancing terms—which is how at least one court of appeals
has read the opinion in *Haig*[220]—this loads the dice against free speech. What
limits are there on the exercise of a claim of national security? What constitutes the requisite showing? The cases do not really set it out, because they
involve regulations that impact on persons with a fiduciary relationship to
the government (former employees) who have bound themselves contractually to respect confidentiality, and thus who may be deemed to some extent limited by their own choice the extent of their First Amendment right
to speak. Like lawyers at trial, or litigants in discovery, they have been granted
access to information not normally granted the public and cannot use the
First Amendment to shelter behind their breach of trust.[221]

Notably, though, the issue left open in *New York Times*—the applicability
of criminal sanctions against the disseminator of classified information—
has been resolved by at least one circuit in upholding the conviction of a
former intelligence analyst who disclosed classified information to *Jane's
Defence Weekly*.[222] The upholding of the conviction in that case, *United States v.
Morrison*, was based on the premise that "the Amendment does not reach so
far as to override the interest of the public in ensuring that neither reporter

217. *United States v. Morrison*, 844 F.2d 1057, 1081 (4th Cir. 1988) (Wilkinson, J. concurring).
218. *Haig v. Agee*, 453 U.S. 280, 307 (1981) (*quoting Aptheker v. Secretary of State*, 378 U.S.
     500, 509 (1964).
219. *Kennedy v. Mendoza-Martinez*, 372 U.S. 144, 160 (1963) (striking as unconstitutional
     statutory provision imposing forfeiture of citizenship as punishment for draft evasion).
220. *United States v. Morrison*, 844 F.2d 1057, 1082–1083 (4th Cir. 1988) (Wilkinson, J.,
     concurring).
221. The courts in a series of cases have held federal employees who sign contracts in which
     they agree to keep Governmental information confidential (that is, classified, informa-
     tion that they came upon in the course of their employment) financially liable for their
     breach of their agreements. *See Haig v. Agee*, 453 U.S. at 309 (stating that Agee retains
     his First Amendment rights—"always subject to express limits on certain rights by vir-
     tue of his contract with the Government"); *see Snepp v. United States*, 444 U.S. 507 (1980);
     United States v. Marchetti, 466 F.2d 1309 (4th Cir. 1972).
222. *United States v. Morrison*, 844 F.2d 1057 (4th Cir. 1988).

nor source is invading the rights of other citizens through reprehensible conduct forbidden to all other persons."[223]

This majority opinion, however, begs the question to be resolved, to some extent, by *assuming* that the criminal law that forbids the dissemination of government information (which is subject to neither copyright protection nor proprietary protection) is constitutional as against all citizens, and by treating the defendant's First Amendment claim as a call for special license to violate statutes on the part of the press or of press sources. The straightforward "balancing" approach employed by Judge Wilkerson's concurring opinion at least uses a less suspect methodology than setting up a straw man by assuming the constitutionality of the very enactment under question.

The Wilkerson balancing approach, and the general language of *Haig v. Agee* bring us back to the question of what the compelling state interest test means in the context of the First Amendment (as opposed to the Equal Protection Clause analysis, where it is more typically seen). Take, for example, the facts involved in *Haig*. Philip Agee, a disaffected former agent of the CIA and an author of books critical of the agency, found his passport revoked during a lecture tour in Germany. As was found in upholding the revocation, "[t]he revocation of Agee's passport rests in part on the content of his speech: specifically his repeated disclosures of intelligence operations and names of intelligence personnel."[224] This punishment of speech (or, perhaps more accurately, preventive measure to prevent further speech) was found not to infringe the First Amendment:

> AGEE'S disclosures, among other things, have the declared purpose of obstructing intelligence operations and the recruiting of intelligence personnel. They are clearly not protected by the Constitution. The mere fact that Agee is also engaged in criticism of the Government does not render his conduct beyond the reach of the law.

> TO the extent the revocation of his passport operates to inhibit Agee, "it is an inhibition of *action*," rather than of speech. Agee is as free to criticize the Government as he was when he held a passport.[225]

Justice Brennan's dissent in *Haig* attacked this logic as sophistic (If one is jailed for speaking unfavorably about the government, he reasoned, does the freedom to carp from prison mean that "action" rather than speech has been punished?), and that criticism seems on target, unless what is involved

---

223. *Id.* at 1068 *quoting Branzburg v. Hayes*, 408 U.S. 665, 691–692 (1972).
224. *Haig v. Agee*, 453 U.S. at 308. Notably, both American and other operatives identified by Agee had suffered violence and Agee admitted his intention to name other operatives in future.
225. *Id.* at 309 *quoting Zemel v. Rusk*, 381 U.S. 1, 16–17 (1965).

in *Haig* is *not* ad hoc balancing, but rather a separation of disclosure into a criticism component (protected) and a disclosure component (unprotected). If that is the case, the requirements that the regulation serve a "compelling state interest", and, one would think (although the Court did not explicitly so state), that it be "narrowly tailored to serve that interest," serve to winnow out those cases in which the government genuinely targets the "verbal act" of disclosure of classified information and separates such disclosure from the caustic commentary of an former agent.

Such a reading may not in fact comport with *Haig* as it will be construed over time, but the decision's language—and that of the Court in *Morrison*—suggests that national security cases represent *not* a pragmatic weighing after all, but an extension (and a dilution, or at least a distortion) of verbal act logic into a difficult and untrustworthy area. Although it is difficult, in any event, to call for an unrestricted right to disseminate any and all information regarding government activities, the potential for abuse of the power to make secret has been repeatedly shown, and the Court's formulation in *Haig* does nothing to protect against such abuse.

The real crux of the balance of the national security as against the right to free speech has not yet been established. In our system of case-by-case adjudication, the issue cannot be resolved from the prosecution of a former agent, whose breach of fiduciary duty and of contract muddies the waters, but from the punishment of precisely that conduct committed by the *Times* in publishing the Pentagon Papers. If the prosecution takes the form of accomplice liability for theft, or follows some other verbal act theory, the issue may even then be ducked again. The theoretical question, however, has been answered; the national security interest has been held to trump that of free speech, and the questions that remain are those primarily of limitation and prevention of abuse.

Speech by Government Employees

Another instance where balancing appears to be inevitable is that where the government acts not in a legislative or in a capital *E* Executive manner, but rather as an employer confronted with speech by an employee that threatens disruption of government functions. Such a case presents a conflict of like values—the functioning of the federal, state, or local government through its agents and employees is itself provided for in the Constitution, and is as much a component of constitutional law as is the First Amendment.[226] While an ordinary employee who works for private industry can as

---

226. U.S. Const. Arts. I–III lay out the functioning of the federal government; Art. IV, sec. 4 requires that the "United States shall guarantee to every State in this Union a Republican Form of Government." Article IV, sec. 1 requires that "Full Faith and Credit shall

a general matter be terminated for any reason or for no reason, such carte blanche would jeopardize the values of the First Amendment. Therefore, the Supreme Court has required a balancing of the interests involved.

The test of general applicability to government employee speech was restated by the Supreme Court in *Waters v. Churchill*[227] "[t]o be protected [by the First Amendment], the speech must be on a matter of public concern, and the employee's interest in expressing herself on this matter must not be outweighed by any injury the speech could cause to the "'interest of the State, as an employer, in promoting the efficiency of the public services it performs through its employees.'" Thus a governmental employer "may take unfavorable employment action against an employee for speech—even on a matter of public concern—where the speech has the potential to disrupt the work environment."[228]

When such an employment action is brought before a court for review, even if the speech is conceded to be on a matter of public concern, "the government can prevail if it can show that it reasonably believed that the speech would potentially interfere with or disrupt the government's activities, and can persuade the court that the potential disruptiveness was sufficient to outweigh the First Amendment value of that speech."[229] "Substantial weight" is given the government employer's "prediction that given speech has the potential for disruptiveness, but its prediction must be reasonable."[230]

---

be given in each State to the public Acts, Records, and judicial Proceedings of every other State." Congress is empowered to "prescribe the manner in which such Acts, Records and Proceedings shall be proved, and the Effect thereof." The Tenth Amendment provides that the "powers not delegated to the United States by the Constitution, nor prohibited by it to the States, are reserved to the States, respectively, or to the People." Lawrence Tribe, *American Constitutional Law* (2d ed. 1988), at 378–400, 378 ("It is clear that the Constitution does presuppose the existence of the states as entities independent of the national government"). That the concept of federalism and the role of the states is undergoing radical rethinking by the Supreme Court is shown by recent decisions undermining the expansive reading given the Commerce Clauses of the Constitution since the New Deal was upheld. *United States v. Lopez*, 514 U.S. 549 (1995) (invalidating congressional statute forbidding sale of firearms in proximity to schools as outside Congress's ability to regulate interstate commerce); *Seminole Tribe of Florida v. Florida*, 517 U.S. 44 (1996) (federal constitution's Indian Commerce Clause did not permit Congress to confer jurisdiction over states for suits against states; overruling contrary precedent under Interstate Commerce Clause).

227. 511 U.S. 661, 668 (1994), *quoting Connick v. Myers*, 461 U.S. 138, 142 (1983); *see Pickering v. Board of Ed. of Township High School District*, 391 U.S. 563, 568 (1968).

228. *Heil v. Santoro*, 147 F.3d 103, 108 (2d Cir. 1997); *Sheppard v. Beerman*, 94 F.3d 823, 827 (2d Cir. 1996).

229. *Heil v. Santoro*, 147 F.3d at 109, *citing inter alia Waters v. Churchill*, 511 U.S. 661, 673, 681 (1994) (plurality opinion); *Jeffries v. Harleston*, 52 F.3d 9, 13 (2d Cir.), *cert. denied*, 516 U.S. 862 (1995).

230. *Id.*

In establishing what constitutes a reasonable prediction of potential disruptiveness such that some adverse employment action is justified, the Second Circuit in *Heil v. Santoro* found that "an employer that has received a report of such speech must make a reasonable investigation before deciding to take action against the employee."[231] From these principles the Second Circuit drew a corollary: "in light of the employer's duty, as described in *Waters*, to make a reasonable investigation before imposing discipline on an employee for engaging in protected speech, it is clear that [plaintiffs'] plaint [sic] that defendants conducted an investigation is not a valid First Amendment claim." Where such an investigation is conducted under the procedures generally applicable to cases of suspected employee misconduct and is the entire thrust of the complaints, a plaintiff would fail to state a cognizable claim.[232]

It is a stated prerequisite of the *Pickering-Waters* line of cases that the expressive conduct in question be protected "speech" for the purposes of the First Amendment. However, not all expressive conduct is protected as speech, but only that nonverbal conduct that is intended by the actor to convey a "particularized message" and if the likelihood is great that the message will be understood by those who view it.[233]

The second requirement of employee speech to invoke the benefits of the *Pickering-Waters* balancing test its that the speech relate to a matter of public concern. Whether speech relates to a matter of public concern is "determined by the content, form and context of a given statement, as revealed by the record as a whole."[234] As clarified by the Supreme Court in *Rankin v. McPherson*,[235] that context includes whether the speech in question fits into an ongoing exchange relating to public issues or private concerns.

In *Rankin*, the plaintiff upon hearing of the shooting of President Reagan capped a discussion with her boyfriend in which she had expressed strong opposition to the policies of the Reagan administration with an expression of hope that the next assailant would be more successful. The Supreme Court

---

231. *Id.* at 109–110; *see Waters v. Churchill*, 511 U.S. at 677–678 (employer should proceed with "a certain amount of care," that is, "the care that a reasonable manager would use before making an employment decision—discharge, suspension, reprimand, or whatever else— of the sort involved in the particular case").

232. *Id.* at 110.

233. *Texas v. Johnson*, 491 U.S. 397, 404 (1989) (applying test, finding that burning American flag as political gesture constitutes protected speech protected against statute directed against "dishonoring" the flag); *Cohen v. California*, 403 U.S. 15, 18 (1971) (patch worn on jacket reading "Fuck the Draft" intended to convey message, and message highly likely to be understood); *United States v. O'Brien*, 391 U.S. 367, 376–377 (1968) (while burning of draft registration card could be intended to convey a message and be so understood, statute prohibiting destruction of such cards regardless of the existence of any communicative intent did not impermissibly target the speech content of the expressive act, and was thus constitutional).

234. *Connick v. Myers*, 461 U.S. 138, 147–148 (1982).

235. 483 U.S. 378, 386–387 (1987).

held that the political context of the conversation, as well as the close connection of that discussion with the then-fresh news of the assassination attempt, supported a finding that the speech was of public concern, and therefore was protected speech.

In *Rankin*, the Court found that the plaintiff, a clerical assistant in a local deputy constable's office, had been improperly terminated on the basis of a statement to a co-worker outside of the hearing of any other co-workers or members of the public. After finding the remark about assassination (in the context of a political discussion) to be clearly speech on a matter of public concern, the Court weighed the competing interests of the employer and the government employee, applying the *Pickering* balancing test.[236] In doing so, the Court stated that "the state interest element of the [balancing] test focuses on the effective functioning of the public employer's enterprise. Interference with work, personnel relationships, or the speaker's job performance can detract from the public employer's function."[237]

In *Rankin*, it was conceded by the parties that disturbance of the workplace had not been considered in the employee's discharge.[238] Nor, the Court found, "was there any danger that [the employee] had discredited the office by making her statement in public"; relying heavily on the fact that the speech "took place in an area to which there was ordinarily no public access; her remark was evidently made in a private conversation with another employee."[239] Additionally, the constable had not rendered any determination that the clerk's remark revealed character traits which rendered her unfit for the job she held.[240] In the last analysis, the Court held that in view of the fact that the employee "serves no confidential, policy-making, or public contact role, the danger to the agency's successful functioning from that employee's private speech is minimal."[241]

The nature of the employee's position is as critical to the equation, as the Court noted in *Rankin*, as the public, or the on- or off-duty of the nature of the speech drawn in question. Thus, the Second Circuit has noted in a recent decision, where a public employee "who is paid a salary so that he will contribute to an agency's effective operation but who begins to do or say things that detract from the agency's effective operation," the employer has the right to terminate that employee. In this recent decision, *Lewis v. Cowen*, the court of appeals held, even where "weighty" interest in testifying truthfully and speaking on matters of public concern was involved, the

---

236. *Id.* at 388–389.
237. *Id.* at 388.
238. *Id.* at 389.
239. *Id.*
240. *Id.*
241. *Id.* at 390–391. *See also Lewis v. Cowen*, 165 F. 3d 154 (2d Cir. 1999), discussed *infra*.

employer may terminate a state lottery employee who declined to present employer's plan for a revamped lottery system.[242]

The utterance of speech which cannot but instill a public perception of indifference or hostility on the part of an employee trusted to administer or to publicly represent the law or policy with whom that employee is entrusted must create a potential for disruption which the city cannot be required to ignore. In *Lumpkin v. Brown*,[243] the removal of a San Francisco city commissioner of human rights for speeches condemning homosexuality was found not to violate the First Amendment, as "the City has not only a legitimate but a heightened expectation that its Human Rights Commissioners refrain from speaking publicly in a way that mocks the City's anti-discrimination policy." Similarly, in *Sims v. Metropolitan Dade County*,[244] an African-American male employee of the Miami Department of Community Affairs was found to have been properly disciplined for anti-Hispanic statements. As the Court pithily justified its holding, "The First Amendment does not require that [plaintiff] be allowed to continue his weekday employment drenching the fires of racial animosity for the Department while he fans those flames during his weekend sermons."[245]

Further examples here would only belabor the point; the Court, finding constitutional imperatives genuinely in tension, has sought to weigh the provisions asserted not abstractly but rather pragmatically, with an eye to the underlying values served by the conflicting imperatives. Where possible to resolve this tension without real sacrifice, as in *Rankin*, where departmental functioning was not implicated in any but a symbolic way—it is, after all, highly inappropriate for a law enforcement official to champion a political murder, but where the "official" is a back room file clerk, the state's interest becomes, absent a showing of workplace impact or impairment of agency functioning, attenuated at best—the Court has favored freedom of speech. But where the case has involved a real prospect of damage to the employer, the Court has had the unenviable task of choosing the lesser evil. Generally, suppression of the employee's speech has been the result. One could suggest that the first two prongs prior to the balancing strain out most significant claimants of free speech, or at least act to protect

---

242. The Second Circuit held that the Constitution provides the state with "greater leeway" in regulating employee speech where its functions are implicated, including such "essential public services as public safety." *Id.* at 161. The Court further found that this power was to be exercised within "wide latitude without intrusive oversight by the judiciary." 165 F.3d at 161. The Court further found that where the employee's job involves "policy making, confidentiality, or public contact" the employer's interest was correspondingly greater. *Id.* at 162; *quoting McEvoy v. Spencer*, 124 F.3d 92, 103 (2d Cir. 1997).
243. 109 F.3d 1498, 1501 (9th Cir. 1997).
244. 972 F.2d 1230 (11th Cir. 1992).
245. *Id.* at 1238.

against content-based suppression.[246] At least, with its focus on incidental effect, the balancing test applied to government employer regulations of speech by government employees seems geared to serve the same purposes of the verbal act concept.

CONCLUSION

The difficulty in sketching out how a nascent tradition in law *can* work is the need to draw on cases decided under a different theory. Cases in which "balancing" has been employed, to take the last instance first, do *not* all fit the paradigm that only a constitutional right can outweigh another constitutional right. On several occasions, interests that are not provided for in the Constitution have been deemed sufficiently "compelling" to trump the First Amendment. For example, the danger of trauma caused by news reportage of a sex offense trial at which the principal victim is a juvenile when that interest would be injured by disclosure in a particular case.[247] The decision did not invoke the constitutionally recognized right to privacy, but suggested that the trauma to a minor victim was itself a sufficient interest to permit infringement.

The purpose of this analysis is not to show that every decision by the Court fits into the verbal act framework. Obviously, as Chapter 3 went to great lengths to point out, such is not the case. Rather, it is to point a way to a better analysis than the holistic balancing that a half century of Chaplinskyism has slowly persuaded the academy and even many in the judiciary to adopt. That analysis is provided by the strong but underappreciated legacy of verbal act jurisprudence that draws together so much of the First Amendment's applications in areas that seem disparate on the surface.

If the First Amendment means anything, it means that "because I think it is evil" is not a sufficient ground to ban any idea. That legitimate balancing can exist when the interests are on the same scale does not detract from the norm that only verbal acts fall outside of the amendment, or carve out exceptions to the amendment's scope, because it recognizes that unusual situations can bring about conflicts among different constitutional rights. In such cases, constitutional *Situationethik* is the only option. How to fit—or whether to fit—"compelling state interests" into this framework is an issue that will repeatedly return when these principles are applied.

---

246. Such contact-based suppression in retaliation for speech not based on a reasonable prediction of actual disruption constitutes a violation of the First Amendment. *Sheppard v. Beerman*, 94 F.3d 823, 827 (2d Cir. 1996); *Lewis*, 165 F.3d at 163.

247. *Globe Newspaper Co. v. Superior Court*, 457 U.S. 596 (1982) (striking statute which excluded press in sex offense cases involving juvenile victims in every case on a *mandatory* basis).

5

Brigaded with Action
Undirected Advocacy and the First Amendment

WHEN OLIVER STONE released his 1994 film, *Natural Born Killers,*[1] he probably never imagined that the result would be a lawsuit seeking to hold him liable as an accessory to a real life series of crimes modeled on those committed by the fictitious Mickey and Mallory. The film, a scalding, angry satire of media glamorization of violence, itself employed graphic violence in depicting the titular characters' "reel-life" killing spree. In directing the film, Stone used several cinematic tools, including distancing techniques, the depiction of the patent stupidity of Mickey and Mallory's conduct, and the sheer sleaziness of their associates to reinforce his points that Mickey and Mallory were certainly not admirable, and that their violence was indicative of their spiritual emptiness and their sickness. To further emphasize this point, Stone introduced the character of a Native American wise man, who explains this in words of one syllable to his grandson, who serves as a surrogate for the audience. Although he is the only wholly admirable character in the film, the wise man pays with his life for having offered Mickey and Mallory shelter. His murder, a gratuitous act of cruelty, is too much even for Mallory, and it precipitates her one fight with Mickey. To miss the anti-violence message of *Natural Born Killers,* one would have to be spectacularly obtuse, be focused solely on the most literal and narrow reading of the text, and be wholly impervious to nuance, irony and techniques of subversion. Nonetheless, when Sarah Edmonson and Benjamin Darrus shot Patsy Ann Byers during a convenience store holdup, the resultant civil suit[2] named as defendants Stone, Warner Home

---

1. *Natural Born Killers* (Warner Brothers, Inc., 1994).
2. The suit was filed before Ms. Byers's death in her name by her husband and their three children.

Video, Inc.,[3] Warner Brothers, Inc.,[4] corporate parent Time Warner Entertainment, L.P., and other affiliated corporations.[5] The case brought against Stone and Time Warner alleged several theories of recovery,[6] including a claim that Stone and Time Warner "intended to incite viewers of the film to begin, shortly after viewing the film, crime sprees such as the one that led to the shooting of Patsy Byers."[7] The trial court held that Byers did not state a cause of action.[8] The Louisiana Court of Appeal accepted the complaint's allegation as true for the sake of reviewing the trial court's dismissal of the action, and found that the petition did indeed state a cause of action.[9] The court stated that if plaintiffs could prove their allegations, the First Amendment would not be a bar to recovery.[10]

The facts in *Byers* resemble those in a dramatic Fourth Circuit case, *Rice v. Paladin Enterprises, Inc.*[11] In *Rice,* the defendant was Paladin Enterprises, Inc., a small publishing house catering to supermacho fantasies with an edge of lawlessness. In 1983, Paladin published a slender volume titled *Hit Man: A Technical Guide for Independent Contractors* (*"Hit Man"*).[12] The book provided explicit and detailed instructions on how to establish a career as a contract killer.[13] A decade later, James Perry, at the behest of

---

3. Warner Home Video is the company that released the video rented by Edmonson and Darrus.
4. Warner Brothers is the company that made the film.
5. *Byers v. Edmonson,* 712 So. 2d 681, 681–684 (La. Ct. App. 1998).
6. *Id.* at 685. The causes of action included:
   A) for producing and distributing a film (and marketing same on videotape) which they knew, intended, were substantially certain, or should have known would cause or incite persons such as defendants, Sarah Edmonson, and Benjamin Darrus (via subliminal suggestion or glorification of violent acts) to begin, shortly after repeatedly viewing the same, crime sprees as that which led to the shooting of Patsy Ann Byers;
   B) for negligently and/or recklessly failing to take steps to minimize violent content of the video or to minimize glorification of senselessly violent acts and those who perpetrate such conduct;
   C) by intentionally, recklessly, or negligently including in the video subliminal images which either directly advocated violent activity or which would cause viewers to repeatedly view the video and thereby become more susceptible to its advocacy of violent activity;
   D) for negligently and/or recklessly failing to warn viewers of the potential deleterious effects upon teenage viewers caused by repeated viewing of the film/video and of the presence of subliminal messages therein; and
   E) as well as for other such intentional, reckless, or negligent acts will [sic] be learned during discovery and shown at trial of this matter.
7. *Id.* at 690 (emphasis added).
8. *Id.* at 685.
9. *Id.* at 689.
10. *Id.* at 691–692.
11. 128 F.3d 233 (4th Cir. 1997).
12. Rex Feral, *Hit Man: A Technical Guide for Independent Contractors* (1983).
13. *Id.* at ix.

Motown producer Lawrence Horn, killed Horn's ex-wife Mildred, and Trevor, their severely brain-damaged son.[14] Perry also killed Trevor's nurse, Janice Saunders, seemingly to eliminate her as a witness.[15] Perry had been hired by Lawrence Horn to do the job, so that Horn could inherit the proceeds of a settlement on a malpractice claim stemming from the injury causing Trevor's brain damage.[16] In killing the Horns and Saunders, Perry followed many of the suggestions contained in *Hit Man*.[17] The victims' survivors sued Paladin on the theory that it had been guilty of aiding and abetting the murders.[18] Paladin moved for summary judgment on the theory that the First Amendment served to protect it from liability.[19] It even stipulated, for the purpose of the motion, that it had intended some unknown number of its readers to act upon the suggestions conveyed in the book.[20]

The Fourth Circuit decision in *Rice* was the principle authority upon which the Louisiana Court of Appeal relied in *Byers*.[21] Both decisions found that a representation of violent and unlawful conduct as desirable or beneficial can subject the purveyor of the message to accomplice liability for the acts of those who act upon the representations.[22] Both courts required that in order for the purveyor of images or text to be liable, it must intend that someone, although not necessarily the criminal/tortfeasor in question, act upon the representations.[23] The courts also suggested that there should be some sort of relationship between exposure to the image or text and commission of a criminal or tortious act, but it is unclear whether either court would require any kind of temporal imminence or immediacy.[24]

The cases, *Rice* in particular, have occasioned a blizzard of commentary in the mainstream press and from legal scholarship.[25] Much of the commen-

---

14. *Rice*, 128 F.3d at 239.

15. *Id.*

16. *Id*

17. *Id.*

18. *Id.* at 241.

19. *Id.*

20. *Rice*, 128 F.3d at 241.

21. *Byers*, 712 So. 2d at 690–691.

22. *See Rice*, 128 F.3d at 267; *Byers*, 712 So. 2d at 690.

23. *See Rice*, 128 F.3d at 248–251; *Byers*, 712 So. 2d at 691.

24. *See Rice*, 128 F.3d at 253–254 (declining to impose any kind of time frame as a predicate for liability and holding that intent was a sufficient basis for liability); *see also Byers*, 712 So. 2d at 691. In *Byers*, the court held that the plaintiff's petition alleged sufficient facts to establish an incitement to imminent lawless action exception to First Amendment protection. *Id.* Accordingly, the court ruled that the cause of action was not barred by the First Amendment. *Id.*

25. *See*, for example, *Symposium Issue*, 27 N. Ky. L. Rev. 1 (2000).

tary has applauded the decisions, although a significant number of commentators deplore them.[26] Much of the positive commentary has been from self-styled "friends of the First Amendment," and indeed, two of the counsel involved in *Rice*, Rodney A. Smolla,[27] lead counsel for the plaintiffs, and Professor David Crump,[28] who filed a brief *amicus curiae*, plainly consider themselves guardians of the First Amendment.

Establishing the outer boundaries of free expression cannot be a simple task, and for as long as the jurisprudence has been evolving, the courts and scholars have grappled with the fluctuating parameters of the line. Indeed, some Supreme Court Justices and scholars have argued that bright-line approaches are doomed to fail, and instead suggest a pragmatic weighing of the estimated value of speech to society against the speech's foreseeable potential for harm.[29] But the appeal of bright lines in First Amendment jurisprudence is not easy to deny. The uncompromising language of the Amendment, its function as a bulwark against repression in times of crisis, and the ease with which such repression is rationalized in the face of seeming urgency are all factors that militate against subtle, multi-variable equations, which can be susceptible to manipulation by judges who desire to reach the politically "right"—that is, expedient—result. These multi-variable tests are inherently prone to manipulation when judges yield to the pressure to

---

26. *See* discussion *infra* beginning on page 233.
27. *See supra* note 25. *See also* Rodney A. Smolla, *Free Speech in an Open Society* (1992) [hereinafter Smolla, *Free Speech*] and Rodney A. Smolla, *Jerry Falwell v. Larry Flynt: The First Amendment on Trial* (1988) for examples of outstanding works of scholarship. Professor Smolla has written numerous books celebrating the First Amendment, several of which may attain classic status in free speech jurisprudence.
28. Professor Crump so values his First Amendment credentials that he included his status as a "Recipient of the 'Friend of the First Amendment' Award" from Sigma Delta Chi as part of his *amicus* brief. *Rice*, 128 F.3d at 233. Additionally, it is inserted in his author's biographical footnote in his article titled *Camouflaged Incitement: Freedom of Speech, Communicative Torts, and the Borderland of the Brandenburg Test*, 29 Ga. L. Rev. 1 (1994). Crump's article provided much of the intellectual ballast for the court's approach in *Rice*.
29. *See*, for example, *Dennis v. United States*, 341 U.S. 494, 517, 542–545 (1951) (Frankfurter, J., concurring) (agreeing with Court's ruling to uphold convictions of Communist Party leaders for "criminal syndicalism" and advocating multiple variable, case-by-case balancing test approach to free speech claims); *Beauharnais v. Illinois*, 343 U.S. 250 (1952) (opinion by Frankfurter, J.) (upholding criminal prohibition against "group libel" under balancing approach); *see also Winters v. United States*, 333 U.S. 507, 527–530 (1948) (Frankfurter, J., dissenting) (urging application of rational basis review to free speech claims). Works by present day advocates of a holistic, *ad hoc* balancing approach to speech claims include Richard Delgado, *Toward a Legal Realist View of the First Amendment*, 113 Harv. L. Rev. 778 (2000); Tracy Higgins, *Giving Women the Benefit of Equality: A Response to Wirenius*, 20 Fordham. Urb. L.J. 78 (1992). For a representative selection of viewpoints to this effect, *see* David S. Allen & Robert Jensen, *Freeing the First Amendment: Critical Perspectives on Freedom of Expression* (1995).

conform, thus potentially reducing freedom of speech to a mere empty promise.[30]

In striving to draw bright lines to protect freedom of speech, the Supreme Court has adopted various strategies, some more convincing than others. Perhaps the most viable is the notion of the "verbal act" or "speech brigaded with action," a concept that has persisted in the free speech jurisprudence since its beginning.[31] The verbal act approach to free speech claims avoids many of the difficulties posed by other interpretative approaches to the First Amendment, and is accurately captured in *Brandenburg v. Ohio*,[32] the leading case on the line between advocacy that is protected and advocacy that is proscribed in the depiction of unlawful conduct. In *Brandenburg*, the Supreme Court reaffirmed the principle that:

> THE constitutional guarantees of free speech and free press do not permit a State to forbid or proscribe advocacy of the use of force or of law violation except where such advocacy is directed to inciting or producing imminent lawless action and is likely to incite or produce such action. As we said in *Noto v. United States*, "the mere abstract teaching . . . of the moral propriety or even moral necessity for a resort to force and violence, is not the same as preparing a group for violent action and steeling it for such action."[33]

---

30. *See*, for example, *Minersville Sch. Dist. v. Gobitis*, 310 U.S. 586 (1940) (upholding a rule compelling children to recite the Pledge of Allegiance against claims by the Jehovah's Witnesses that such compulsion required them to violate their understanding of the Biblical admonition against worshipping idols), overruled by *W. Va. Bd. of Educ. v. Barnette*, 319 U.S. 624 (1943); *Dennis*, 341 U.S. at 499 (upholding laws essentially banning the American Communist Party by applying the "clear and present danger" test). This application was radically different from the intent of its creator, Justice Oliver Wendell Holmes). *See generally* Chapter 2 at 56–60.

31. *See Gompers v. Bucks Stove & Range Co.*, 221 U.S. 418 (1911) (upholding labor injunction against boycott on theory that the First Amendment does not afford protection to words used in such circumstances where they "become what have been called 'verbal acts,' and as much subject to injunction as the use of any other force whereby property is unlawfully damaged"); *see also Roth v. United States*, 354 U.S. 476, 514 (1957) (Douglas, J., dissenting) (recasting the verbal act concept as "speech brigaded with action"). *See generally* Chapter 4 at 122–181 (discussing "verbal act" concept as embodying basic First Amendment standard.

32. 395 U.S. 444 (1969).

33. *Id.* at 447–448 (citation omitted). The Court noted that to the extent the criminal syndicalism statute, under which the Ku Klux Klansmen led by Frank Brandenburg had been charged, impacted the right to free assembly, as distinct from that of free speech, the analysis was the same; such statutes "must observe the established distinctions between mere advocacy and incitement to imminent lawless action '[because] . . . [t]he right of peaceable assembly is a right cognate to those of free speech and free press and is equally fundamental.'" *Id.* at 449 n.4 (*quoting DeJonge v. Oregon*, 299 U.S. 353, 364 (1937)). *See also United States v. Cruikshank*, 92 U.S. 542, 552 (1876); *Hague v. CIO*, 307 U.S. 496, 513, 519 (1939); *NAACP v. Alabama ex rel.* Patterson, 357 U.S. 449, 460–461 (1958).

Justice Douglas contended, with cogent logic, that the Court in *Brandenburg* had gone even further than the old clear and present danger test, and that it should avowedly adopt the verbal act formulation.[34] As he put it, the "line between what is permissible and not subject to control and what may be made impermissible and subject to regulation is the line between ideas and overt acts."[35] Taking the infamous example of "the case of one who falsely shouts fire in a crowded theatre," as clearly regulable speech, Justice Douglas described it as a "classic case of speech brigaded with action."[36] Douglas, addressing the "fire" example, explained that the misleading cry and the resultant dangerous chaos were "indeed inseparable and a prosecution can be launched for the overt acts actually caused."[37]

The Court's high level of solicitude regarding violent rabble-rousing might seem strange, but in fact it is at the core of First Amendment jurisprudence. The regulation of speech based on its message, where that message consists of advocacy of unlawful conduct, raises problems which the regulation of other forms of "low value" speech does not. As a matter of history, the regulation of such advocacy, particularly when it is tied to a political message, has consistently implicated the fundamental values of freedom of speech.[38] The historical primacy given to speech encouraging law violation makes logical sense as well, as it encompasses political speech calling for revolutionary change. Thus, the centrality of violent rhetoric and hyperbole to the American traditions of civil disobedience, struggles

---

34. *Brandenburg*, 395 U.S. at 456 (Douglas, J., concurring).
35. *Id.*
36. *Id.* (Douglas, J., concurring) (*citing Speiser v. Randall*, 357 U.S. 513, 536–537 (1958)). The "fire" hypothetical was first employed by Justice Oliver Wendell Holmes in *Schenck v. United States*, 249 U.S. 47, 52 (1919). Holmes employed the hypothetical as a means for cautiously delineating the outer limits of protected speech. *Id.* He then backed into a more controversial, but still (to him) self-evident class of plainly unprotected speech, the "uttering [of] words that have all the effect of force." *Id.* at 52 (citing *Gompers*, 221 U.S. at 419). *See also* Chapter 2 at 27–36.
37. *Brandenburg*, 395 U.S. at 456–457. For confirmation that the Court in *Brandenburg* in essence adopted Justice Douglas's position, *see Hess v. Indiana*, 414 U.S. 105, 107–108 (1973); *Ashcroft v. Free Speech Coalition*, 535 U.S. ___, 152 L.Ed2d 403, 423,122 S.Ct. 1700 (2002).
38. The first three decisions to accord any level of substantive protection to speech, as opposed to merely prohibiting punishment prior to publication, each involved subversive advocacy. In the factual circumstances present in these decisions, the Court found that subversive advocacy presented a "clear and present danger" of resultant lawless action which the government was entitled to prevent, and thus upheld convictions under the federal Espionage Act. *See Schenck*, 249 U.S. at 47; *Debs v. United States*, 249 U.S. 211 (1919); *Frohwerk v. United States*, 249 U.S. 204 (1919); *see also* Chapter 2 at 29–36.

for liberation, and revolution, position such speech at the core of the First Amendment's protections.[39]

Each of the courts and the scholars who have urged a finding of liability in cases of seductive depictions of unlawful conduct has had to attempt to justify itself in terms of the line drawn by the Supreme Court in *Brandenburg*, or to redraw a different line that supplements the *Brandenburg* line. Some scholars have blinked at the question, seeking instead to carve out a new category of "low value" speech. These scholars ignore the fact that the increasing permeability of the First Amendment to such *ipse dixit* approaches dilutes the doctrine and renders it meaningless. More candidly and productively, the basic approach of the Fourth Circuit in *Rice* seeks to situate the advocacy of homicide for hire somewhere between the poles of speech and criminal or tortious conduct. The case demonstrates the persistent difficulty in defining the boundary between speech and conduct.

This chapter examines that boundary, employing both *Rice* and *Byers* as illustrative examples. The position adopted is that the imposition of liability for speech like that involved in *Rice* impermissibly blurs this distinction between speech and conduct, defined here as "verbal acts." These cases clarify this distinction in a manner more precise than has been accomplished previously.

This exploration into the hinterland of free speech jurisprudence leads us through an underconceptualized, uncertain body of legal opinions. The ambiguity of the reasoning in these cases includes a morass of poorly explained case results and of broad dicta. This has left scholars seeking to deduce organizing principles from broad generalities.[40] In seeking to bring some clarity to the discussion, the first step is to explore the nature of advocacy. The various forms of speech that courts and legislators have sought to subject to regulation have been treated as essentially fungible. However, even if the distinctions do not lead to different results, they may help to clarify what rationales are applicable to the distinct variants of advocacy. Each form of advocacy can be measured against the traditional notions of criminal jurisprudence that have been used as justification for subjecting the authors to liability. Addition-

---

39. Many scholars have celebrated the critically important role of dissent in the American tradition and have explicitly tied the protection of dissent to the centrality of the First Amendment to American political views. *See*, for example, William O. Douglas, *Points of Rebellion* (1970). For a more recent dissent-based view of the First Amendment, although one far less speech-protective than that of Justice Douglas, *see* Steven H. Shiffrin, *Dissent, Injustice and the Meanings of America* (1999) and Steven H. Shiffrin, *The First Amendment, Democracy, and Romance* (1990).

40. For an ambitious, comprehensive synthesis of these concepts, see Kent Greenawalt, *Speech, Crime and the Uses* of *Language* (1989); and Thomas Emerson, *The System of Free Expression* (1970) at 401–465. My own effort to explore the ramifications of the verbal act concept and its boundaries in other factual contexts is contained in Chapter 4 at 122–181.

ally, an examination of the role of the speech that supposedly triggered the crimes or tortious acts may help explain the extent to which free speech rationales are either undermined by or consistent with a determination of liability. From there, a study of the policy based arguments deployed in favor of regulation, and a reflection upon their resultant political corollaries, will shed light on the nature of moral agency and of the relationship between the individual and the state embodied in the First Amendment.

THE NATURE OF ADVOCACY AND OF "VERBAL ACTS"

Before addressing the parameters of this First Amendment doctrine, both as it stands currently and as various scholars would have it, some refinement of the notion of advocacy is needed. At its broadest, advocacy can be defined as speech in favor of a given cause or a statement or argument on behalf of a given result. One may advocate on behalf of a client to prevail in a lawsuit, for a political party to win in election, to persuade someone to pursue a given course of conduct, or to obtain a favorable result in any other situation. Styles of advocacy can range from the decorous to the threatening, and the conduct at which the advocacy is aimed can likewise range from the legal or innocuous to the reprehensible or proscribed. Almost every speech or writing relating to public affairs falls within this definition of advocacy. The courts have frequently recognized that different levels of advocacy exist, and have endeavored to distinguish between the variants based on elements, including the intensity with which the speaker exhorts, and the specificity of the desired result.

In the frequently examined context of speech urging overthrow of the government, the Supreme Court has sought to distinguish, in the first instance, between protected "advocacy" and unprotected "incitement," and in the second, between protected "discussion" and unprotected "advocacy."[41] For the present discussion, the distinction between advocacy and incitement can wait.

---

41. *See* Harry Kalven, Jr., *A Worthy Tradition: Freedom of Speech in America* (1988) at 127–129 (discussing the distinction between "direct incitement" and protected speech in *Masses Publ'g Co. v. Patten*, 244 F. 535, 540 (S.D.N.Y. 1917), *rev'd*, 246 F.24 (2d Cir. 1917)); *id.* at 154–156 (discussing *Gitlow v. United States*, 268 U.S. 652 (1925), and the duel between Justices Sanford and Holmes over whether incitement could be meaningfully distinguished from advocacy of ideas in general); *id.* at 215–217 (distinguishing between "discussion" and "advocacy" as used by Justice Harlan in *United States v. Yates*, 354 U.S. 298 (1957), and noting his own preference for the term "incitement" to capture the circumstances involved).

The term "incitement" implies a legal conclusion about the unprotected status of the speech in question, and thus is a result of analysis and not an aid to it. As a threshold matter, it is better to first distinguish the types of advocacy without making assumptions as to their constitutional status.

Three Forms of Advocacy

The first type of advocacy may be called "directed advocacy," which involves speech urging a particular action be taken in a specific situation. Such advocacy is "directed" in that the speaker knows the specific factual context of the occasion calling for action and is thus in a position to assess both the likelihood that her advice will be implemented, and the likely consequences of her advice being followed. This renders the advocate's connection to any resultant conduct more intimate, and less abstract or bloodless. The advocate in a sense is giving her imprimatur to the performance of the deed and is authorizing the specific result. The listener, who is not indulging in philosophic speculation, applies the advocate's general principles to a context that arises independently. Thus, the listener internalizes the advocate's message, independently accepts the message's validity, and decides to implement these principles in the concrete terms of the real world. This process involves three separate intellectual actions: evaluation, acceptance, and implementation, whereby the listener desires a fact-specific result in a given set of circumstances. In directed advocacy, the advocate participates in each of these three actions and approves of the performance of the action advocated. Thus, the listener is far less independent in her decision-making process and the speaker far more involved. Frequently, direct advocacy creates instances where the time between the speech and the resultant act is short. This further links the act with the advocate because the listener has less time to perform the three mental operations and is less able to closely consider the speaker's reasoning.

The second type of advocacy may be termed "undirected advocacy," in which the speaker addresses a hypothetical set of facts or a general course of conduct. When a speaker uses undirected advocacy, she does not have as large a role in two of the three mental operations: application and implementation of the speech to a factual context. In fact, the real life context of time and place are missing entirely, which renders the applicability of the advice or advocacy less tangible. The listener may perceive distinctions between the hypothetical and reality, and may conduct a separate balancing of factors not addressed by the speech. Alternatively, the listener may simply remove the fact situation from the principle advocated altogether.

The third and most subtle form of advocacy would be "indirect advocacy," which is limited to the depiction of a course of conduct or a belief-system in a sympathetic, approving manner, but without explicit exhortation. By using this type of advocacy, the author or speaker may be teaching by example, or by presenting the conduct or beliefs in question in a favorable light.

Narrative commentary can provide further spin and the opportunities to co-mingle undirected and indirect advocacy. For example, in the novel *Atlas Shrugged,*[42] author Ayn Rand uses the actions of the leading character, John Galt, to evoke the reader's admiration and emulation. This is an example of indirect advocacy—the portrayal of action in a manner that seeks to teach a lesson to the reader or audience. In contrast, the long—wearisomely long, to this reader—speech given by Galt is an example of undirected advocacy, in that it is designed to persuade the reader to rationally accept the theory Rand calls "Objectivist Ethics."[43] Such an effort is undirected because it seeks to convince the audience to adopt a conclusion, but does so with no real life context for the reader to apply the conclusion. And, of course, direct advocacy would feature an employment of Rand's principles to a specific context—for example, the argument that prosecution under securities laws against Enron or Tyco would be in the long run contrary to public policy.

More subtle examples of the intermingling of indirect and undirected advocacy can be found in less overtly didactic novels such as Anthony Trollope's *The Last Chronicle of Barset,* where the opinions of the elderly Mr. Harding regarding the proper place of money in the priorities of a young couple have extra weight because of the moral stature Trollope has accorded Harding.[44] Trollope also is famous for giving his own opinions in chatty little asides to the reader. To give a more contemporary example, the insights of the recurring character Dunstan Ramsay in the novels of Robertson Davies are generally to be equated with Davies's own views.[45]

---

42. Ayn Rand, *Atlas Shrugged* (1957).

43. In addition to *Atlas Shrugged,* at 936–999, Rand explicates her belief in the philosophy set out by the fictional Galt, whom she describes as "its best representative," in Ayn Rand, *The Virtue of Selfishness: A New Concept of Egoism* (1964) at 13–35.

44. Anthony Trollope, *The Last Chronicle of Barset* (1867) at 509–510. For Trollope's final estimation of Mr. Harding, *see id.* at 864.

45. Dunstan Ramsay, the protagonist in Robertson Davies, *Fifth Business* (1970), appears not only in its sequels, *The Manticore* (1972) and *World of Wonders* (1975), but in several of Davies's otherwise unrelated novels. *See* Robertson Davies, *What's Bred in the Bone* (1985) at 157–159 (Ramsay sets Francis Cornish, the protagonist, on his artistic path); *The Lyre of Orpheus* (1988) at 319 (Cornish repays Ramsay by including him in a great painting of the Wedding at Cana); *The Cunning Man* (1994) at 73–83 (Ramsay participates in a debate with an aspirant to the priesthood against the moral and philosophical outlook of public schools).

Even less overtly, in Robert Bolt's 1962 play, Thomas More is held up as *A Man For All Seasons*,[46] and as one to be admired and emulated.

Indirect advocacy can be further veiled thorough the use of irony and satire. For instance, in *The Adventures of Huckleberry Finn*, Huck Finn's decisions both not to betray Jim based upon his recognition of Jim's moral worth, and to reject the racist standards of the slaveholding South, are all the more potent because for Huck it represents a sin—and Huck nonetheless concludes, "Alright then, I'll go to hell."[47] Undirected advocacy can also afford the luxury of sarcasm and irony. Jonathan Swift's *A Modest Proposal*[48] masquerades as a tract urging people to eat the children of the poor, but of course advocates very different reforms—the "other expedients" rejected by the persona adopted by the author. The irony is laid on with a trowel, but the point is made. In the context of direct advocacy, such tools can seldom be used because time is generally of the essence and action must be taken before the state of affairs changes and the evanescent opportunity is lost. Thus, direct advocacy tends to adopt a more simple, rhetorical strategy as a function of the need to compel immediate—or at least swift—action.

Liability for Advocacy: The Supreme Court's Exegesis

The distinction between these three forms of advocacy is relevant because the underlying First Amendment values that sometimes permit the imposition of liability on people who advocate harmful conduct through speech apply predominantly—indeed, exclusively—to direct advocacy. The imposition of liability for even the most direct advocacy, however, strongly undermines the values associated with the First Amendment, and particularly undermines the verbal act concept that lies at the heart of First Amendment jurisprudence.

The *Brandenburg* rubric and Justice Douglas's cognate "speech brigaded with action" formulation provide the most philosophically coherent account of the First Amendment principles relating to the Government's prevention of speech and punishment of speakers.[49] Indeed, disregarding the categories of "lesser value" speech, this account resonates on the whole with the Supreme Court's own understanding of the First Amendment.[50] The Court has yet to jettison the verbal act concept, despite the increasing number of speech

---

46. Robert Bolt, *A Man For All Seasons* (1962).
47. Mark Twain, *The Adventures of Huckleberry Finn* (1884) at 207 (Penguin Books ed. 1983).
48. Jonathan Swift, *A Modest Proposal* (1729).
49. *Roth v. United States*, 354 U.S. 476, 514 (1957) (Douglas, J., dissenting).
50. For examples of cases applying verbal act logic to symbolic speech, *see Texas v. Johnson*, 491 U.S. 397 (1989), and *United States v. O'Brien*, 391 U.S. 367 (1968). Such logic has been successfully applied to a variety of contexts. *See* Chapter 4 at 135–156.

categories considered to be "lesser value" and the Court's increasing reliance on balancing tests, which, as a general matter, threaten the existence of a coherent jurisprudence. In applying the verbal act concept, the Supreme Court has long recognized that "when 'speech' and 'nonspeech' elements are combined in the same course of conduct, a sufficiently important governmental interest in regulating the nonspeech elements can justify incidental limitations on First Amendment freedoms."[51]

Distinguishing between protected speech and unprotected conduct in the form of speech brigaded with action is frequently difficult.[52] However, "if the evidence shows that the speeches crossed the line into criminal solicitation, procurement of criminal activity or conspiracy to violate the laws, the prosecution [of such speech] is permissible."[53] In *Rahman*, the Second Circuit described such unprotected words as "ones that instruct, solicit, or persuade others to commit crimes of violence," and found that they might appropriately be prosecuted under statutes of "general applicability."[54]

---

51. *O'Brien*, 391 U.S. at 376; *see also Citicorp v. Interbank Card Ass'n.*, 478 F. Supp. 756, 762 (S.D.N.Y. 1979) (where "conduct properly proscribed is coupled with conduct protected by the First Amendment, the latter does not cure the former"); *United States v. Viehaus*, 168 F.3d 392, 395–396 (10th Cir. 1999) (distinguishing between protected political speech and unprotected threat component of telephone call threatening bombings); *Michael Anthony Jewelers v. Peacock*, 795 F. Supp. 639, 648–649 (S.D.N.Y. 1992) (discussing limitations on freedom of speech of the Noerr-Pennington Doctrine). *See generally R.A.V. v. City of St. Paul*, 505 U.S. 377, 388 (1992) (stating that speech within a class of speech may be regulated for the "very reason the entire class of speech at issue is proscribable," but not based upon disapproval of the viewpoint expressed); *Watts v. United States*, 394 U.S. 705 (1969) (distinguishing between protected political hyperbole in the form of ostensibly threatening statements and unprotected verbal act of "true threat"); *United States v. Dinwiddie*, 76 F.3d 914 (8th Cir. 1996) (distinguishing between "true threats" and First Amendment protected speech in the context of threats against abortion clinic staff); *United States v. Kelner*, 534 F.2d 1020, 1026 (2d Cir. 1976) ("Threats punishable consistently with the First Amendment were only those which according to their language and context conveyed a gravity of purpose and likelihood of execution so as to constitute speech beyond the pale of protected 'vehement, caustic . . . unpleasantly sharp attacks on government and public officials.'" (quoting *N.Y. Times v. Sullivan*, 376 U.S. 254, 270 (1964))); *United States v. Baker*, 890 F. Supp. 1375 (E.D. Mich. 1995), *aff'd*, 104 F.3d 1492 (6th Cir. 1997) (stating that email messages containing sexual violence against women and girls were not an immediate threat and were therefore protected by the First Amendment).

52. *See generally* Greenawalt, *supra* note 40 (endeavoring to chart the permutations of Supreme Court decisions in seeking to draw this line, but unable to discern a bright-line, or even a series of bright-line distinctions to facilitate analysis).

53. *United States v. Rahman*, 189 F.3d 88, 117 (2d Cir. 1999) (upholding conviction of Muslim cleric for his role in terrorist conspiracy against First Amendment speech and free exercise challenges).

54. *Id. (citing Employment Div. v. Smith*, 494 U.S. 872, 879 (1990) (rejecting Free Exercise challenge to anti-drug regulation impacting upon religiously inspired use of peyote)); *see also City of Boerne v. Flores*, 521 U.S. 507, 533–534 (1997).

The applicability of this verbal act analysis has never been limited to the advocacy of violence[55] and did not originate in the subversive advocacy context of *Brandenburg*. In fact, the formulation antedates the 1919 Espionage Act cases in which such speech was first given any substantive level of protection.[56] Well before *Brandenburg*, the Supreme Court declared, through Justice Hugo Black, that "it has never been deemed an abridgment of freedom of speech or press to make a course of conduct illegal merely because the conduct was in part initiated, evidenced, or carried out by means of language, either spoken, written, or printed."[57]

Of Conspiracies and Attractive Nuisances: Grappling with the Limits

The decision in *Rice* would be tempting to write off, as Professor Smolla has suggested, as a unique instance where liability attached only because of Paladin's spectacularly arrogant confession of intent to assist in the fruition of crime.[58] Such a limited view of the case would nonetheless require the

---

55. *See IDK, Inc. v. County of Clark*, 836 F.2d 1185, 1194 (9th Cir. 1988). The court cited as "examples illustrat[ing] that the State does not lose its power to regulate commercial activity deemed harmful to the public whenever speech is a component of that activity:" *SEC v. Texas Gulf Sulphur Co.*, 401 F.2d 833 (2d Cir. 1968) (the exchange of information about securities); *Mills v. Electric Auto-Lite Co.*, 396 U.S. 375 (1970) (corporate proxy statements); *Am. Column & Lumber Co. v. United States*, 257 U.S. 377 (1921) (the exchange of price and production information among competitors); *NLRB v. Gissel Packing Co.*, 395 U.S. 575, 618 (1969) (employers' threats of retaliation for the labor activities of employees); *Paris Adult Theatre I v. Slaton*, 413 U.S. 49, 61–62 (1973) (damage to neighborhood property values by adult movie theatres).

56. *Compare Gompers v. Bucks Stove & Range Co.*, 221 U.S. 418 (1911) (upholding contempt citation for labor demonstrators violating an injunction on theory that boycott was a "verbal act" and as such, subject to regulation), with *Schenck v. United States*, 249 U.S. 47 (1919) (upholding convictions under the 1919 Espionage Act based on written speech). The Court in *Schenck*, however, first enunciated the "clear and present danger" test and the first extension of substantive immunity to some speech, as opposed to previous decisions holding that the First Amendment was in essence only a protection against prior restraint. *Schenck*, 249 U.S. at 51 (*citing Patterson v. Colorado*, 205 U.S. 454 (1907)).

57. *Giboney v. Empire Storage & Ice Co.*, 336 U.S. 490, 502 (1949) (upholding as constitutional an injunction barring labor picketing deemed to be coercive); s*ee New York v. Ferber*, 458 U.S. 747, 761–762 (1982) (upholding a New York law prohibiting persons from knowingly promoting a sexual performance by a child under the age of 16); *see also Sanitation and Recycling Indus., Inc. v. City of New York*, 107 F.3d 985, 999 (2d Cir. 1997) ("When a trade organization becomes so closely brigaded with illegal activity as to become inseparable from it, the government is justified in withholding benefits based on association with such an organization"); *United States v. Rowlee*, 899 F.2d 1275, 1278 (2d Cir. 1990) (advisor's counseling tax fraud in advancing agenda of anti-tax society). The *Rowlee* court stated that "[s]peech is not protected by the First Amendment when it is the very vehicle of crime itself." *Id.* (quoting *United States v. Varani*, 435 F.2d 758, 762 (6th Cir. 1970)); *IDK, Inc.*, 836 F.2d at 1194 (escort service asserting associational rights).

58. *See* Rodney Smolla, *Deliberate Intent: A Lawyer Tells the True Story of Murder By the Book* (1999) at 266–277 [hereinafter Smolla, *Deliberate Intent*].

artificial harmonization of two countervailing streams of cases in which the courts have struggled with the breadth of the verbal act concept.

In the first set of decisions, various circuit courts have seemingly applied the verbal act doctrine when considering instructional materials that provide assistance in the commission of unlawful activity. The courts have found a sufficient linkage between these instructions and resultant acts so as to establish liability under several theories, ranging from attempt, to accessory liability, to conspiracy. These cases were resolved on several different grounds, but as the Second Circuit has rightly perceived, some could have been resolved on verbal act grounds. In *Rowlee,* [59] the Second Circuit upheld the conviction of a tax protestor who conducted "tax seminars" under the aegis of an anti-taxation organization known as the "New York Patriot's Society for Individual Liberty Association."[60] At the seminars, class members were instructed and assisted in the preparation of false and evasive tax returns, and were taught how to set up frivolous but purportedly effective defenses against an audit.[61] At trial, the defendant was convicted of conspiracy. The Second Circuit noted that the conspiracy was partly proven through the verbal acts of the defendant and that in addition, "Appellants were convicted of the act of conspiracy. . . . Their act was not protected by the First Amendment merely because, in part, it may have involved the use of language."[62] Such logic, the Court held, rendered appropriate the finding of aiding and assisting liability.[63] The Second Circuit conceded that the theories upon which aiders and assistants in tax evasion could be convicted were not consistent from circuit to circuit, but noted that the "consensus of this and every other circuit is that liability for a false or fraudulent tax return cannot be evaded by evoking the First Amendment."[64]

In explaining its conclusion, the *Rowlee* court found that the District Court had over-complicated the analysis by discussing the First Amendment and

---

59. 899 F.2d at 1275.
60. *Id.* at 1276–1277.
61. *Id.*
62. *Id.* at 1278 (*quoting Ferber,* 458 U.S. at 747; *United States v. O'Brien,* 361 U.S. 367 (1968)).
63. *Id.* at 1278–1279.
64. *Id.* at 1279. The Court went on to canvass the rationales employed by the various circuits to justify the conclusion that "the preparation of tax returns does not implicate the First Amendment at all." *Id.* (*citing, inter alia, United States v. Kelley,* 864 F.2d 569 (7th Cir. 1989) (holding that under a balancing test of the individual rights weighed against the need of the government to collect revenue, the government interest prevails); *Hudson v. United States,* 766 F.2d 1288 (9th Cir. 1985); *Kahn v. United States,* 753 F.2d 1208, 1217 (3d Cir. 1985)). Regarding the rationale employed by the District Court in *Rowlee* that the seminar could be divided into protected advocacy and unprotected "counsel[ing] and participat[ion] in the actual preparation of returns so as to become part of the crime itself," the court held that a First Amendment defense rested on words alone. *Rowlee,* 899 F.2d at 1280 (*citing, inter alia, United States v. Freeman,* 761 F.2d 549 (9th Cir. 1985)).

the temporal imminence requirement of *Brandenburg*. The Court found that "to the extent that the concept of 'imminence lawless action' has any role to play in this non-syndicalism case, it is incorporated *sub silentio* in the tax evasion statute itself."[65] The court concluded that if the defendants did not violate the statute, "the restrictions imposed by that statute did not violate their First Amendment rights," and that, "if they did violate [the statute], they were not protected by the First Amendment."[66] The court further explained that, "Insofar as Rowlee commented generally on the tax laws during his seminars without aiding, assisting, procuring, counseling, or advising the preparation or presentation of the alleged false or fraudulent tax documents, he did not violate [the statute]. Accordingly, as to those comments, the question of First Amendment protection was redundant and irrelevant."[67] The Court stated that the converse applied to actual participation and assistance in the preparation of specific documents.[68] Thus, the Second Circuit concluded, the trial court's charge on the First Amendment "simply required the jury to consider a duplicative and unnecessary issue and would better have been omitted."[69]

Most intriguingly, the Second Circuit found these arguments equally effective with respect to the mail fraud charges. The court squarely rejected that the application of the "'incitement to imminent lawless action' required by *Brandenburg* can be applied in any reasonable manner to violations of the mail fraud statute."[70] As the Court described it:

> MAIL fraud cases often involve long-term, slowly-developing wrongs, not "imminent lawless action." Imminence of mailing likewise is not essential to a mail fraud violation. Indeed, the scheme to defraud need not even contemplate use of the mails as an essential element. "Where one does an act with knowledge that the use of the mails will follow in the ordinary course of business, or where such use can reasonably be foreseen, even though not actually intended, then he 'causes' the mails to be used." Thus, in tax fraud cases, the mailing required by the statute may not take place until the Government sends out refund checks, a procedure that some tax payers look upon as "long-term" indeed.[71]

Thus, in terms of assessing liability, the Circuit suggested that the requirement of temporal imminence contained within *Brandenburg* is specific to the

---

65. *Rowlee*, 899 F.2d at 1280.
66. *Id.* at 1280.
67. *Id.*
68. *Id.*
69. *Id.*
70. *Id.*
71. *Rowlee*, 899 F.2d at 1280–1281 (citations omitted).

factual scenario involved there: the context of "syndicalism," or the advocacy of political change through lawless, especially violent, action.

Like the Second Circuit in *Rowlee*, the Fourth Circuit in *Rice* concluded that the imminence prong of *Brandenburg* "generally poses little obstacle to the punishment of speech that constitutes criminal aiding and abetting, because 'culpability in such cases is premised, not on defendants' "advocacy" of criminal conduct but on defendants' successful efforts to assist others by detailing to them the means of accomplishing the crimes.'"[72] The Fourth Circuit concluded that the "question of whether criminal conduct is 'imminent' is relevant for constitutional purposes only where, as in *Brandenburg*, the government attempts to restrict advocacy, as such."[73]

The second series of cases, seemingly more analogous to *Byers* than to *Rice*, involves "copycat" behavior. In a series of lower court decisions, a general consensus has evolved that representations or discussions of risky conduct do not subject publishers to liability for imitative behavior. In perhaps the most pointed case in this genre, *Herceg v. Hustler Magazine*,[74] an adolescent died after following a description of the practice of "autoerotic asphyxiation" contained in an article in *Hustler* magazine.[75] Both the text of the article and a prefatory disclaimer warned that the practice was "neither healthy nor harmless" and stated that "it is a serious—and often-fatal—mistake to believe that asphyxia can be controlled."[76] The article also described the "thrill" and the "high" those who engage in the practice seek to achieve.[77] The disclaimers in the two-page article were not enough to eliminate the allure of the "intense physical pleasure" obtained by successful practitioners of this "dangerous, self-destructive and deadly" practice in the mind of one 14-year-old boy, who imitated the practice, lost consciousness, and died of strangulation—just as the article warned might happen.[78] The mother of the hapless boy sued, as did one of his closest friends who found him hanging dead in the closet with the article opened at his feet.[79]

---

72. *Rice*, 128 F.3d at 246 (*quoting* U.S. Department of Justice, *Report on the Availability of Bombmaking Information, the Extent to Which Its Dissemination is Controlled by Federal Law, and the Extent to Which Such Dissemination May Be Subject to Regulation Consistent with the First Amendment to the United States Constitution* (Apr. 1997) at 37 [hereinafter Department of Justice Report]).

73. *Id.* (quoting Department of Justice Report, *supra* note 72).

74. 814 F.2d 1017 (5th Cir. 1987).

75. *Id.* at 1018 (the article was charmingly entitled "Orgasm of Death").

76 *Id.*

77. *Id.* at 1018–1019.

78. *Id.* at 1019.

79. *Id.*

The district court dismissed all the claims except those based on the theory that the article served to incite the youth's experiment, and that the magazine should be held accountable because the result was foreseeable.[80] After a jury trial, damages were awarded to both plaintiffs.[81] The district court found that the "crucial element to lowering the First Amendment shield is the imminence of the threatened evil" when evaluating whether an article or book may be deemed an "incitement."[82] Moreover, finding that "[t]he root of incitement theory appears to have been grounded in concern over crowd behavior," the court intimated doubts, but did not deem impossible, that "written material might ever be found to create culpable incitement unprotected by the First Amendment."[83] On appeal, the Fifth Circuit Court of Appeals reversed, finding that the First Amendment operated to shield the article.[84]

Perhaps part of the analytical difficulty here is that many of the acts described fall within the class of criminal activities known as "inchoate crimes."[85] In criminal law, these crimes are not easily defined. Glanville Williams, however, in his masterful survey of the common law, divides inchoate crimes into three related offenses: incitement, attempt and conspiracy.[86] The concept of incitement incorporates the rubric of liability applied in *Rice*, because the difference between an accessory before the fact and an inciter "is that in incitement the crime has not (or has not necessarily) been committed, whereas a party cannot be an accessory in crime unless the crime has been committed. An accessory before the fact is party to consummated mischief; an inciter is guilty only of an inchoate crime."[87]

The Supreme Court has, without much analysis of the effect of the First Amendment, accepted that such doctrines are unaffected by its sweep. With respect to the Second and Fourth Circuits' circumscribed view of the applicability of the *Brandenburg* temporal imminence requirement, the Supreme Court has addressed the nature of agreements and solicitations of participation in specific unlawful acts:

> ALTHOUGH agreements to engage in illegal conduct undoubtedly possess some element of association, the State may ban such illegal

80. *Herceg*, 814 F.2d at 1019.
81. *Id.*; *see Herceg v. Hustler Magazine*, 565 F. Supp. 802 (S.D. Tex. 1983) (the district court's reasoning is set out in its opinion on the motion to dismiss).
82. *Herceg*, 814 F.2d at 1022.
83. *Id.* at 1023.
84. *Id.*
85. *See* Glanville Williams, *Criminal Law: The General Part* (1953) at 466.
86. *Id.*
87. *Id.* at 469.

agreements without trenching on any right of association protected by the First Amendment. The fact that such an agreement necessarily takes the form of words does not confer upon it, or the underlying conduct, the constitutional immunities that the First Amendment extends to speech. Finally, while a solicitation to enter into an agreement arguably crosses the sometimes hazy line distinguishing conduct from pure speech, such a solicitation, even though it may have an impact in the political arena, remains in essence an invitation to engage in an illegal exchange for private profit, and may properly be prohibited.[88]

In the instance of conspiracy, the archetype of such inchoate offenses, it is the formation of the agreement itself that is the offense—the creation of an association with the goal of committing the criminal act.[89] Many lower courts have opined that using speech as a means to effect ends prohibited by otherwise valid laws does not cause these laws' application to become unconstitutional. However, such application may lead to a blurring of the line between speech and conduct. In *Jews for Jesus, Inc. v. Jewish Community Relations Council, Inc.*, the Second Circuit applied anti-discrimination law to impose liability based upon boycotts "with the objective of coercing the [boycott target] to deny plaintiffs accommodations for reasons prohibited by the anti-discrimination statute."[90] The Second Circuit opined that "if discrimination engaged in by 'primary' actors using words can be constitutionally outlawed," so too can discrimination engaged in by third parties who use speech or other expressive conduct to coerce a 'primary' actor to violate an anti-discrimination statute."[91]

Similarly, in *United States v. Kufrovich*, the United States District Court for the District of Connecticut rejected a First Amendment challenge to federal statutes that prohibited the use of any means of interstate commerce "to persuade a minor to engage in sexual activity for which anyone may be prosecuted," or "travel in interstate commerce to engage in a sexual act with a minor."[92] The court, following *Rowlee*, found such persuasion unprotected because it was a component of the interrupted act of child molestation,

---

88. *Brown v. Hartlage*, 456 U.S. 45, 55 (1982) (upholding state statute prohibiting the sale and purchase of votes (citing *Vill. of Hoffman Estates v. The Flipside, Hoffman Estates, Inc.*, 455 U.S. 489, 496 (1982); *Cent. Hudson Gas & Elec. Corp. v. Pub. Serv. Comm'n*, 447 U.S. 557, 563–564 (1980); *Pittsburgh Press Co. v. Human Relations Comm'n*, 413 U.S. 376, 388 (1973))).
89. Williams, *supra* note 85, at 512.
90. 968 F.2d 286, 296–297 (2d Cir. 1992).
91. *Id.* at 295–297.
92. 997 F. Supp. 246, 254 (D. Conn. 1997).

rather than mere speech.[93] This result may be influenced by the fact that it, and others like it, target expression that is directed at minors—those who, in the eyes of the law, are not deemed fully accountable for their own behavior, and are considered to be especially vulnerable to such blandishments. The result may alternatively be justified by interpreting the communication in question as an attempted act of child molestation in that it is a "substantial step" towards the efficacy of the deed, or as bringing the illegal action "dangerously close to fruition," in violation of the penal law.[94]

The results in these cases may have turned on the coercive nature of the boycott in *Jews for Jesus,* or in the presumptively less fully developed moral agency of minors as compared to adults in *Kufrovich.* But if they were not decided on these points, then the "verbal act" concept could swell up to obliterate the very protection it distinguishes. If efforts to persuade others in a non-coercive way are deemed to fall on the "conduct" side of the dividing line, then the law of attempt, or the law of incitement, is on a collision course with the protection of speech advocating illegal conduct that stands at the heart of the First Amendment doctrine.

In *Rice* and in *Byers,* the criminal and tort law concepts that generally have been seen as unexceptional boundary lines demarcating protected speech from unprotected conduct were applied in a manner that upset expectations and highlighted the lack of a clear boundary between the two. A look at the rationales undergirding these decisions is helpful to an effort to distinguish speech as conduct.

FOR THE WRONG REASON: THE DISTRICT COURT OPINION IN *Rice*

The district court in *Rice* focused on the practical impact of *Hit Man*'s concrete suggestions on the crime committed by Perry on Horn's behalf.[95] In-

---

93. *Id.* at 254; *see People v. Foley,* 94 N.Y.2d 668, 709 N.Y.S.2d 467 (N.Y. 2000) (upholding a state statute criminalizing Internet communications of a sexually explicit nature, which were deemed "designed to lure children into harmful conduct." Such communications were defined as those consisting of an "invitation or an enticement" or an effort to "solicit" or "procure," as opposed to "pure speech"); *see also United States v. Wilson,* 154 F.3d 658, 666–667 (7th Cir. 1998) (stating that those who conspire to violate the law can be held liable, despite First Amendment concerns).

94. *Compare People v. Hernandez,* 93 N.Y.2d 261, 689 N.Y.S.2d 695 (N.Y. 1999) (noting that the phrase "substantial step" in the definition of criminal attempt has been "supplanted" and is a "disfavored phrase"), and *People v. Slater,* 705 N.Y.S.2d 777, 778 (N.Y. Gen. Term 2000), with *United States v. Porter,* No. 99–1235, 2000 U.S. App. LEXIS 1865 (2d Cir. Feb. 1, 2000). (2d Cir. 2000) (stating that Federal law definition of criminal attempt involves committing an act constituting a "substantial step" toward the commission of the actual crime).

95. *Rice v. Paladin Enters., Inc.,* 940 F. Supp. 836, 839–840 (D. Md. 1996).

deed, the district court's brief factual summary consists largely of a correlation of *Hit Man*'s "how-to" suggestions and the methods adopted by Perry in committing the murders:

> "What other basic equipment will the beginner need as essential tools of his trade?" An AR-7 rifle.

> (James Perry used an AR-7 rifle to commit the murders of Mildred Horn and Janice Saunders.)

> "The AR-7 rifle is recommended because it is both inexpensive and accurate. The barrel breaks down for storage inside the stock with the clip. It is lightweight and easy to carry or conceal when disassembled."

> (After the murders, James Perry disassembled the AR-7 rifle as instructed by the Defendants.)

> "The AR-7 has a serial number stamped on the case, just above the clip port. This number should be completely drilled out. The hole left will be unsightly but will not interfere with the working mechanism of the gun or the clip feed."

> (James Perry drilled out the serial number of the AR-7 rifle exactly as instructed by the Defendants.)

> "The directions and photographs that follow show in explicit detail how to construct a silencer for a Ruger 10/22 rifle. The same directions can be followed successfully to construct a silencer for any weapon, with only the size of the drill rod used for alignment changed to fit the inside dimension of the barrel."

> (James Perry used a homemade silencer which he used to silently kill Mildred Horn and Janice Saunders.)

> "Close kills are by far preferred to shots fired over a long distance. You will need to know beyond any doubt that the desired result has been achieved. When using a small caliber weapon like the 22, it is best to shoot from a distance of three to six feet. You will not want to be at point blank range to avoid having the victim's blood splatter you or your clothing. At least three shots should be fired to ensure quick and sure death . . . aim for the head—preferably the eye sockets if you are a sharpshooter."

> (James Perry shot Mildred Horn and Janice Saunders from a distance of three feet. He shot them each three times in the eyes.)

> "Use a rat tail file, alter the gun barrel, the shell chamber, the loading ramp, the firing pin and the ejector pin. Each of these items leaves its own definite mark and impression on the shell casing, which if any shells happened to be left behind, can be matched up to the gun under

a microscope in a police laboratory. . . . Of primary importance now too, is changing the rifling of the murder weapon. This should be done even before you leave the crime scene. That way, even if you get picked up or stopped with the weapon in your possession, its ballistics will not match the bullets you left behind in the mark."

(James Perry filed down the parts of the AR-7 Rifle.) [96]

The district court adduced further instances of the extent to which Perry had employed techniques suggested by *Hit Man* including:

> HOW to solicit for and obtain prospective clients in need of murder for hire services; requesting up-front money for expenses; how to register at a motel in the vicinity of the crime, paying with cash and using a fake license tag number; . . . reminding to clean up and carry away the ejected shells; breaking down the gun and discarding the pieces along the roadside after the murders; and using a rental car, a stolen tag on the rental car and the discarding of the tag after the murders. [97]

The district court also found that "Paladin engaged in a marketing strategy intended to attract and assist criminals and would-be criminals who desire information and instructions on how to commit crimes." [98] Reciting the stipulations of the parties, the Court concluded that, "In publishing, marketing, advertising and distributing *Hit Man* . . . Paladin intended and had knowledge that their publications would be used, upon receipt, by criminals and would-be criminals to plan and execute the crime of murder for hire, in the manner set forth in the publications." [99] The district court, however, concluded its factual recitation by stating that:

> ALL parties agree that Paladin's marketing strategy is intended to maximize sales to the public, including authors who desire information for the purpose of writing books about crime and criminals, law enforcement officers and agencies who desire information concerning the means and methods of committing crimes, persons who enjoy reading accounts of crimes and the means of committing them for purposes of entertainment, persons who fantasize about committing crimes but do not thereafter commit them, and criminologists and others who study criminal methods and mentality. [100]

---

96. *Id.* (citations omitted).
97. *Id.* at 840.
98. *Id.*
99. *Rice,* 940 F. Supp. at 840.
100. *Id.*

The district court proceeded to analyze whether the plaintiffs had stated a cause of action. Acknowledging that the imposition of tort liability against a publisher constituted state action sufficient to implicate the First Amendment, Judge Williams concluded that "if the court finds that *Hit Man* is protected by the First Amendment, the Plaintiffs [sic] are barred from maintaining tort claims against Paladin."[101] Judge Williams found the task of "balancing society's interest in compensating injured parties against the freedom of speech guaranteed by the First Amendment" to be "both novel and awesome" in the factual circumstances of this case.[102] Judge Williams then set out his template for First Amendment analysis:

> THE First Amendment bars the imposition of civil liability on Paladin unless *Hit Man* falls within one of the well-defined and narrowly limited classes of speech that are unprotected by the First Amendment. Those classes of speech which receive limited or no First Amendment protection include: (1) obscenity (2) fighting words (3) libel (4) commercial speech, and (5) words likely to incite imminent lawless action.[103]

The district court proceeded to examine whether the speech at issue fit into any of these categories of speech receiving "limited or no First Amendment protection."[104] Before examining the district court's reasoning, however, a discussion of some underlying principles may shed some light on this examination. Judge Williams' reasoning reflects an understanding of First Amendment jurisprudence, which is growing in the academic commentary, but which is antithetical to any kind of free speech protection not dependent upon the subjective whim of the judiciary. Judge Williams assumed in his opinion that the only type of speech subject to government regulation was speech deemed to be low value, and that the categories of low value speech, among others, included speech likely to incite imminent lawless action. In fact, this is not the case.

The categorization analysis is, as a general matter, applied only to discrete classes of speech that the Supreme Court has deemed to be of such minimal social value that "the prevention and punishment of which have never been thought to raise any Constitutional problem."[105] Those classes,

---

101. *Id.* In support of its conclusion, the court cited *N.Y. Times v. Sullivan*, 376 U.S. 254, 265 (1964) ("The test is not the form in which state power has been applied but, whatever the form, whether such power has . . . been exercised.").
102. *Rice*, F. Supp. at 840.
103. *Id.* at 840–841 (citations omitted).
104. *Id.* at 841.
105. *Chaplinsky v. New Hampshire*, 315 U.S. 568, 571–572 (1942).

as Justice Murphy stated in *Chaplinsky v. New Hampshire*, were subject to proscription because "such utterances are no essential part of any exposition
of ideas, and are of such slight social value . . . as a step to truth . . . that any
benefit that may be derived from them is clearly outweighed by the social
interest in order and morality."[106] The Supreme Court in recent years has
pointed to nothing but tradition in justifying these exceptions carved out
of the Amendment's scope, but has reasserted that "a limited categorical
approach has remained an important part of our First Amendment jurisprudence."[107] The rule protecting speech advocating lawless behavior, by
contrast, is the descendant of the "clear and present danger" test, and is the
basic test applied to speech concededly at the core of the First Amendment's
protective scope.[108]

Judge Williams' error in deeming categorization to be the universal approach to speech cases is attributable to two sources, but is still potentially
dangerous. First, in *Chaplinsky*, the Court, in an inherently confusing manner, explained the classes of speech subject to regulation as: "those which
by their very utterance inflict injury or tend to incite an immediate breach
of the peace."[109] However, this language modifies the original list of categories, and is offered, in context, as an explanation of why these so-called
narrow and well-defined categories may be proscribed without creating a
First Amendment concern. The category to which the "incitement" language
refers is "fighting words," generally understood to refer to face-to-face-
insults that would provoke a reasonable person to violence.[110]

Moreover, the *Chaplinsky* decision was rendered in 1942, 27 years before
Brandenburg, at a time when the status of politically inflammatory speech was
still governed by the loose "bad tendency" test, or by a watered-down version of the "clear and present danger" test, which allowed the Court to

---

106. *Id.* at 572.
107. *R.A.V. v. City of St. Paul*, 505 U.S. 377, 382–383 (1992).
108. *See* Chapter 2 at 17–71 (describing evolution of standard); Chapter 4 at 122–156 (applying "verbal act" formulation as touchstone of First Amendment jurisprudence). Even
among scholars who are not hostile to the "multi-tier" theory, as the *Chaplinsky* analysis
has come to be known, the centrality of the *Brandenburg* verbal act analysis is widely
conceded. *See,* for example, Harry Kalven, Jr., *A Worthy Tradition: Freedom of Speech in
America* (1988) at 119–124 (In a chapter titled, "Subversive Advocacy: The Core Issue
and the *Brandenburg* Answer," Kalven describes the issue as "the ultimate battleground
for free speech theory"); Smolla, *Free Speech, supra* note 27, at 50–51 (describing the
Brandenburg version of the "clear and present danger" principle as the "rigorous causation rule" upon which the "integrity" of the three main principles of government regulation of speech is dependent).
109. *Chaplinsky*, 315 U.S. at 571.
110. *See R.A.V.*, 505 U.S. at 397, 401 (White, J., concurring) ("Fighting words are not a means
of exchanging views, rallying supporters, or registering a protest; they are directed
against individuals to provoke violence or to inflict injury.").

employ a holistic balancing test to decide whether it felt the harm posed by speech was outweighed by the value of the speech.[111] Indeed, this variation of the clear and present danger test, modeled on a formulation created to measure a ship owner's liability for damages caused when a ship broke free of its moorings, analogized constitutionally protected speech to a garden variety tort claim.[112]

Another factor that could have led Judge Williams to conflate the *Chaplinsky* categorization approach with the mainstream test is that other courts had done so previously. In *Simon & Schuster Inc. v. Crime Board*,[113] Justice Kennedy wrote an opinion deploring the Court's application of the "compelling state interest" standard from equal protection law to the First Amendment context on the ground that such an application could lead to wider interpretation of content-based restriction:

> THERE are a few legal categories in which content-based regulation has been permitted or at least contemplated. These include obscenity, defamation, incitement, or situations presenting some grave and imminent danger the government has the power to prevent. These are, however, historic and traditional categories long familiar to the bar, although with respect to the last category it is most difficult for the

---

111. For the development of the *Brandenburg* test, *see* Chapter 2 at 17–71. See also Frank Strong, *Fifty Years of Clear and Present Danger*, 1969 Sup. Ct. Rev. 41 (1970), for a discussion on the status of the "clear and present danger" test between 1930 and 1950. *See also Dennis v. United States*, 341 U.S. 494, 505, 507–510 (1951) (reaffirming the "clear and present danger" formula as the standard for evaluating content-based restrictions on speech, but watering it down to a holistic balancing test as suggested by Judge Learned Hand at the circuit level (quoting *United States v. Dennis*, 183 F.2d at 212 (2d Cir. 1950), *aff'd*, 341 U.S 494 (1951))). *See also* Chapter 2 at 56–62 for further discussion of *Dennis*.

112. *Compare Dennis*, 183 F.2d at 212 (balancing test for free speech claims in which "gravity of the evil, discounted by its improbability" is weighed to determine if "invasion of free speech" inherent in finding liability is justified), *with United States v. Carroll Towing*, 159 F.2d 169 (2d Cir. 1947) (balancing test for common law tort claims, the so-called "Learned Hand formula," in which the probability that vessel will break away and the magnitude of damage likely to result are measured against the burden of preventing the ship's breaking away to determine if owner was negligent, and thus should be liable).

   At the risk of riding a well-worn hobby horse, I reiterate that a comparison of these two cases establishes that Judge Hand's formulation in *Dennis*, mirroring his *Carroll Towing* approach, is unworkable because it gave an unprotected tortious act the same standard of protection as core First Amendment speech. This formula effectively erased the First Amendment from the Constitution, or at best, reduced it to a codification of common law practice. This is in itself ahistorical, as Judge Hand's analysis of tort liability was an innovation from common law and of the state practice. *See* Chapter 2 at 36–42; *see also* John F. Wirenius, *Helping Hand: The Life and Legacy of Learned Hand*, 25 Seton Hall L. Rev. 505, 516–521 (1994).

113. 502 U.S. 105 (Kennedy, J., concurring) (1991).

government to prevail. While it cannot be said with certainty that the foregoing types of expression are or will remain the only ones that are without First Amendment protection, as evidenced by the proscription of some visual depictions of sexual conduct by children, the use of these traditional legal categories is preferable to the sort of ad hoc balancing that the Court henceforth must perform in every case if the analysis here used becomes our standard test.[114]

Judge Williams, therefore, had reason to believe that the First Amendment status of speech turned on whether it had social value. However, the discussion did not end on this point. After examining *Hit Man* with respect to the *Chaplinsky* categories, Judge Williams found that the book did not fall within any of the *Chaplinsky* categories and was therefore entitled to protection, thus defeating the plaintiffs' claim for compensation.[115] Easily dismissed were the obscenity, fighting words and libel classes of lesser value speech.[116] The Court then turned to commercial speech, a category of speech deemed to be intermediate, and thus afforded a lesser quantum of protection.[117] On

---

114. *Id.* at 127 (citations omitted). A similarly flawed analysis was applied by the court in *Herceg v Hustler Magazine*, 814 F.2d 1017 (5th Cir. 1987). As in the case of the District Court opinion in *Rice*, employment of this *Chaplinsky* analysis did not result in a finding that regulation was appropriate. *Herceg*, 814 F.2d at 1020. In each case this was a result of delimiting the classes of speech that can be regulated to those which the Supreme Court has explicitly established.

   Leaving aside the question of conflation of the *Brandenburg* scenario with a *Chaplinsky* category, Justice Kennedy has remained vigilant to the harmful nature of the application of the terms evolved in Equal Protection analysis to the First Amendment context, which suggests "that content-based limits on speech can be upheld if confined in a narrow way to serve a compelling state interest." This is contrary to the First Amendment's complete disabling of the government as censor—with the exception of the *Chaplinsky* categories. *Burson v. Freeman*, 504 U.S. 191, 211–214 (1992) (Kennedy, J., concurring).

115. *Rice*, 940 F.Supp at 849.

116. Judge Williams rejected application of the obscenity doctrine to *Hit Man* on the incontrovertible ground that "it does not depic[t] or describ[e], in a patently offensive way, sexual conduct." *Id.* (*quoting Miller v. California*, 413 U.S. 15, 25 (1973)). The fighting words category was rejected on the basis that "the words in the book do not, by their very utterance inflict injury or tend to incite an immediate breach of the peace." *Id.* (*quoting Chaplinsky*, 315 U.S. at 572). *Hit Man* "is clearly not libelous since it does not tend to injure the reputation of any particular individual." *Id.* (*quoting N.Y. Times. v. Sullivan*, 376 U.S. 254, 267 (1964)).

117. *See 44 Liquormart v. Rhode Island*, 517 U.S. 484 (1996). The exact level of protection that commercial speech receives is somewhat unclear, as is perhaps not surprising for a doctrine created out of whole cloth by the judiciary. The notion that commercial speech was subject to a different standard of protection than other speech originated as an exclusion under *Chaplinsky*. *Valentine v. Chrestensen*, 316 U.S. 52, 55 (1942). Since *Central Hudson Gas & Elec. Corp. v. Public Serv. Comm.*, 447 U.S. 557 (1980), a balancing test has been applied to even truthful advertising where the state could "assert a substantial interest to be served by restrictions on commercial speech," if those restrictions

the ground that "commercial speech is speech which does no more than propose a commercial transaction," Judge Williams found this category to be inapplicable.[118] He stated that although *"Hit Man* is published for profit, the book itself cannot be considered an effort to achieve the type of commercial result that an advertisement is designed to achieve."[119] This conclusion is well in accord with mainstream First Amendment jurisprudence, which holds that the mere fact that a work is written for profit does not render it commercial speech, and therefore subject to a lesser level of protection.[120] Accordingly, Judge Williams determined that the "only cat-

---

are directly limited to the substantial interest, and are the most limited means of achieving that goal. For example, In *Posadas de Puerto Rico Ass'n v. Tourism Co.,* 478 U.S. 328, 340–345 (1986), this test was applied with a level of deference to the legislature as to suggest that the protection afforded commercial speech could be described as "illusory." *See* Chapter 3 at 105. Cases subsequent to *Posadas* have been substantially more protective of speech, and a plurality of the Court in *44 Liquormart* rejected the "greater-includes-the-lesser" approach of *Posadas,* which argued that the ability to ban the transaction proposed justified regulation of the advertisement. *44 Liquormart,* 517 U.S. at 509–510 (Stevens, J., plurality opinion); Chapter 3 at 105, n.169 (discussing these cases). Justice O'Connor's concurring opinion did not go so far as to declare *Posadas* wrongly decided, but did opine that "the closer look we have required since *Posadas* comports better with the purpose of the analysis set out in *Central Hudson,* by requiring the State to show that the speech restriction directly advances its interest and is narrowly tailored." *44 Liquormart,* 517 U.S. at 531–532. While redressing some of the imbalance of the *Posadas* approach, Justice O'Connor's approach retains the subjectivity and *ad hoc* nature of the *Central Hudson* test. For today at least, the Justices agree that so great a deference to the legislative will as was invoked in *Posadas* was excessive. *See Greater New Orleans Broad. Ass'n. v. United States,* 527 U.S. 173, 182 (1999) (reaffirming disavowal of logic underlying *Posadas*).

118. *Rice,* 940 F. Supp. at 844 (*quoting Pittsburgh Press Co. v. Pittsburgh Comm'n on Human Relations,* 413 U.S. 376, 385 (1973); *citing Va. State Bd. of Pharmacy v. Va. Citizens Consumer Council, Inc.,* 425 U.S. 748 (1976)).

119. *Id.*

120. *See,* for example, *Joseph Burstyn, Inc. v. Wilson,* 343 U.S. 495, 501 (1952). However, while the classic definition of commercial speech limits this intermediate class of speech to "speech which does no more than propose a commercial transaction," the Supreme Court has referred to this as the "core notion" of commercial speech, and has stated that under certain circumstances, speech which combines elements of commercial and noncommercial speech may be regulated as commercial speech. *Bolger v. Youngs Drug Prods.,* 463 U.S. at 60, 66 n.11 (1983) (*quoting Va. State Bd. of Pharmacy,* 425 U.S. at 62); *Bad Frog Brewery v. N.Y. State Liquor Auth.,* 134 F.3d 87, 97 (2d Cir. 1998). This rule has led some courts to consider speech that seems rather far from the notion of advertising to be susceptible to interpretation as commercial speech. For example, in *In re Orthopedic Bone Screw Prods.,* 193 F.3d 781, 793–794 (3d Cir. 1999), the court refused to hold as a matter of law that seminars on the use of orthopedic bone screws were not commercial speech, on the ground that the information regarding medical treatment provided may be "inextricably intertwined" with endorsement of the products made by the seminars' sponsors, the companies manufacturing the screws. Nonetheless, *Hit Man* seems far enough from any notion of commercial speech that Judge Williams was correct to dismiss this theory.

egory of unprotected speech under which *Hit Man* could conceivably be placed is incitement to imminent, lawless activity under *Brandenburg*."[121]

Before examining the viability of any conceivable regulation of *Hit Man* under *Brandenburg,* Judge Williams looked to the various theories of recovery propounded by the plaintiffs. The first theory was that *Hit Man* constituted an act of aiding and abetting, and could be punished as such.[122] Judge Williams's answer to this claim was perhaps the weakest section of his opinion. He asserted that, in "the absence of any reported decision suggesting that Maryland extends the tort of aiding and abetting to the circumstances of this case," such extension would violate the rule that "a federal court sitting in diversity cannot create new causes of action."[123] It is a weak and unconvincing argument that the application of an established cause of action to a new set of factual circumstances constitutes a "new cause of action" or a "new theory" such that a federal court sitting in diversity must decline to rule upon the viability of a cause of action, or, worse, must dismiss an otherwise meritorious cause of action because it requires the federal court to apply settled legal principles to new constellations of facts. Such is the inherent nature of case-by-case adjudication.

The district court glossed over the tax seminar cases and the PCP instruction manual cases relied upon by the plaintiffs. The court noted that in the tax seminar case, "the defendants' speech went beyond mere advocacy to incitement of lawless activity" under *Brandenburg,* and that the PCP instruction manual case was a criminal case and not one in which the imposition of civil liability for a criminal act was involved.[124] These distinctions were not fully developed by Judge Williams's opinion, but the latter is not especially convincing. In fact, the issue of whether Maryland law permitted the imposition of civil liability for an aider and abettor of a criminal act was convincingly addressed by the plaintiffs, and the court of appeals rightly rejected this holding on the part of the district court. Likewise, the applica-

---

121. *Rice,* 940 F. Supp. at 841.
122. *Id.*
123. *Id.* at 842 (*citing Guy v. Travenol Labs., Inc.,* 812 F.2d 911 (4th Cir. 1987); *Tarr v. Manchester Ins. Corp.,* 544 F.2d 14, 15 (1st Cir. 1976); *Woods v. Interstate Realty Co.,* 337 U.S. 535, 538 (1949)). Judge Williams also flatly declined to "create another category of unprotected speech, that is, speech that aids and abets murder." *Id.* In so declining, Judge Williams displayed an appropriate sensitivity to his role as a district judge and to First Amendment values.
124. *Id.* at 842–843 (discussing *United States v. Barnett,* 667 F.2d 835 (9th Cir. 1982) (upholding criminal conviction on aiding and abetting theory based on publication of manual instructing how to manufacture PCP) and *United States v. Buttorff,* 572 F.2d 619 (8th Cir. 1978), *cert. denied,* 437 U.S. 906 (1978) (upholding criminal conviction based on aiding and abetting persons filing fraudulent tax returns)).

bility of the First Amendment analysis developed in the criminal context to the civil claims brought by the plaintiffs was conceded by Judge Williams at the very outset of his discussion of the First Amendment.[125]

The district court was on more solid ground in rejecting the plaintiff's effort to analogize the case to *New York Times v. Sullivan.* The plaintiff argued that if the lesser interest in reputation could support liability on the part of a defendant acting with knowledge or recklessness, "then of course the First Amendment must permit parallel liability in tort when publications cause physical injury and death."[126] The Court rejected this argument as lacking precedential support, and distinguished *Times* on the basis that the speech involved in that case "tend[ed] to injure the reputation of a particular individual."[127] Judge Williams likewise declined to follow *Weirum v. RKO General, Inc.,*[128] a California case. In *Weirum,* a disc jockey, who offered a cash reward for the first person to find him, "actively and repeatedly encouraged listeners to speed to announced locations" during the course of his broadcast.[129] The California court imposed liability "on the broadcaster for urging listeners to act in an inherently dangerous manner."[130] Judge Williams concluded that, regardless of the merits of the decision, there was immediate, real-time urging involved in *Weirum,* and "no such urging occurred in this case."[131]

Having cleared away all of this jurisprudential underbrush, Judge Williams moved on to the critical question: whether the speech contained in *Hit Man,* was protected by the First Amendment under the standard articulated in *Brandenburg.*[132] Judge Williams concluded that the speech was protected, likening the case to many reported decisions relating to "copycat" crimes where courts had generally found no cause of action.[133] Judge Williams rejected plaintiff's efforts to distinguish the copycat cases from *Hit Man* on the grounds that Paladin intended the book to be used for the purpose of killing. Judge Williams shakily relied on Paladin's "clarifi-

---

125. *Id.* at 840 ("The imposition of tort liability constitutes state action, so the First Amendment is applicable in this case. 'The test is not the form in which state power has been applied but, whatever the form, whether such power has in fact been exercised'") (*quoting N.Y. Times, Co. v. Sullivan,* 376 U.S. 254, 265 (1964)).

126. *Id.* at 843 (*citing N.Y. Times,* 376 U.S. at 279).

127. *Rice,* 940 F. Supp at 841.

128. 539 P.2d 36 (Cal. 1975).

129. *Rice,* 940 F. Supp. at 844 (describing *Weirum,* 539 P.2d at 36).

130. *Id.*

131. *Id.*

132. *Id.* at 845–846 (Judge Williams rejected plaintiffs' effort to argue that the *Brandenburg* standard applied only to speech which advocated illegal conduct in the context of urging or advocating political reform or change.).

133. *Id.* at 846.

cation" of its stipulation regarding intent and, more plausibly, on the ground of immediacy:[134]

> THERE is no evidence that Defendants intended imminent lawless activity. Secondly, the Court has read the book and concludes that, although morally repugnant, it does not constitute incitement or "a call to action."
>
> Nothing in the book says "go out and commit murder now!" Instead, the book seems to say, in so many words, "if you want to be a hit man, this is what you need to do." This is advocacy, not incitement. . . . The Court finds that the book merely teaches what must be done to implement a professional hit. The book does not cross that line between permissible advocacy and impermissible incitation to crime or violence. The book does not purport to order or command anyone to any concrete action at any specific time, much less immediately.[135]

Judge Williams also found that *Hit Man* did not have a tendency to incite violence, noting that "out of the 13,000 copies of *Hit Man* that have been sold nationally, one person actually used the information over the ten years the book has been in circulation."[136] The Court also pointed to Paladin's disclaimer that the book was "[f]or information purposes only," a disclaimer reiterated within the book itself.[137] Additionally, the nature of the book— the time it would take to read and its "advocacy of illegal action at some indefinite future time"—were deemed to exclude the book from the category of "incitement to imminent lawless action."[138] In short, Judge Williams concluded that, while "the books have been proven to contain information which, when it makes its way into the wrong hands, can be fatal, First Amendment protection is not eliminated simply because publication of an idea creates a potential hazard."[139]

"STEELING TO ACTION": *Rice* ON APPEAL

On appeal, the Fourth Circuit reversed. The opinion for the Court was authored by Judge Michael Luttig, who opened with a long excerpt from

---

134. At oral argument, Paladin maintained it had "intended" such use only to the extent that it knew that a cross-section of readers would buy the work, and would use it for all of their varied purposes. *Id.* at 846.
135. *Rice*, 940 F. Supp. at 847 (citations omitted).
136. *Id.* at 848.
137. *Id.*
138. *Id.*
139. *Id.*

Hit Man.[140] Much of the opening part of the opinion consists of selections from *Hit Man's* "recipes" for murder—the sort of "how to" materials that were not quoted verbatim by Judge Williams, but that the district court acknowledged and linked to the murders.[141] The material excerpted by the court of appeals had a different tone:

> *To Those Who Think,*
> *To Those Who Do,*
> *To Those Who Succeed.*
> *Success is nothing more than taking advantage of an opportunity.*
>
> A woman recently asked how I could, in good conscience, write an instruction book on murder.
>
> "How can you live with yourself if someone uses what you write to go out and take a human life?" she whined.
>
> I am afraid she was quite offended by my answer.
>
> It is my opinion that the professional hit man fills a need in society and is, at times, the only alternative for "personal" justice. Moreover, if my advice and the proven methods in this book are followed, certainly no one will ever know.
>
> Almost every man harbors a fantasy of living the life of Mack Bolan or some other fictional hero who kills for fun and profit. They dream of living by their reflexes, of doing whatever is necessary without regard to moral or legal restrictions. But few have the courage or knowledge to make that dream a reality. . . .
>
> [After you killed your first victim,] you felt **absolutely nothing**. And you are shocked by the nothingness. You had expected this moment to be a spectacular point in your life. You had wondered if you would feel compassion for the victim, immediate guilt, or even experience direct intervention by the hand of God. But you weren't even feeling sickened by the sight of the body. . . .
>
> The people around you have suddenly become so aggravatingly ordinary. You start to view them as an irritating herd of pathetic sheep, doing as they are told, doing what is expected, following someone, anyone, blindly. You can't believe how dumb your friends have become, and your respect diminishes for people you once held in awe.
>
> You too have become different. You recognize that you made some mistakes, but you know what they were, and they will never plague you

---

140. *Rice v. Paladin Enters.*, 128 F.3d 233, 235–239 (4th Cir. 1997).
141. *Id.* at 236.

again. Next time (and you know there will be a next time), there will be no hesitation, no fear.

Your experience in facing death head-on has taught you about life. You have the power and ability to stand alone. **You no longer need a reason to kill . . . .**

You are a man. Without a doubt, you have proved it. You have come face to face with death and emerged the victor through your cunning and expertise. You have dealt death as a professional. You don't need any second or third opinions to verify your manhood.[142]

Port of Departure

After recounting the murders, and setting out at some length the parallels between them and the instructions contained within *Hit Man*,[143] the court admitted:

> THAT such a right to advocate lawlessness is, almost paradoxically, one of the ultimate safeguards of liberty. Even in a society of laws, one of the most indispensable freedoms is that to express in the most impassioned terms the most passionate disagreement with the laws themselves, the institutions of, and created by, law, and the individual officials with whom the laws and institutions are entrusted.[144]

As Judge Luttig further stated, "Without the freedom to criticize that which constrains, there is no freedom at all."[145] Yet he continued, "speech which, in its effect, is tantamount to legitimately proscribable nonexpressive conduct may itself be legitimately proscribed, punished, or regulated incidentally to the constitutional enforcement of generally applicable statutes."[146] Judge Luttig spent the rest of the opinion seeking to justify the court's conclusion that *Hit Man* falls within the latter, and not the former, principle.

After discussing the cases exploring this distinction, Judge Luttig placed the case within the tort doctrine of aiding and abetting, because "*every* court that has addressed the issue, including this court, has held that the First Amendment does not necessarily pose a bar to liability for aiding and abet-

---

142. *Id.* at 235–239 (emphasis in Court's opinion).
143. *Id.* at 239–243.
144. *Id.* at 243.
145. *Id.*
146. *Rice,* 128 F.3d at 243 (*citing Cohen v. Cowles Media Co.,* 501 U.S. 663, 669 (1991)) ("[G]enerally applicable laws do not offend against the First Amendment simply because their enforcement against the press has incidental effects on its ability to gather and report the news."); *Giboney v. Empire Storage & Ice Co.,* 336 U.S. 490, 498 (1949).

ting crime, even when such aiding and abetting takes the form of the spoken or written word."[147] After examining cases in which aiding and abetting theory was applied to speech, the court moved on to conclude that the imminence requirement of *Brandenburg*:

> GENERALLY poses little obstacle to the punishment of speech that constitutes criminal aiding and abetting, because "culpability in such cases is premised, not on defendants' 'advocacy' of criminal conduct, but on defendants' successful efforts to assist others by detailing to them the means of accomplishing the crimes."[148]

Judge Luttig then[149] moved on to apply the Maryland aiding and abetting law and, after considering certain factors including Paladin's stipulations of fact, found that the suggestions in *Hit Man* qualified it as aiding and abetting.[150] The court then examined whether, and in what manner, the *Brandenburg* standard should be applied to *Hit Man*.

Freedom to Speak Vaguely?

Judge Luttig's opinion proceeds on two separate but intertwined analytical tracks, of varying import for First Amendment jurisprudence. The first is the court's conclusion that *Hit Man* constitutes "aiding" of murder, as defined by the lower courts to fall within the speech act doctrine, because it provided such detailed technical information that it lost its protected status as purely informational speech. The second is the applicability of *Brandenburg* to *Hit Man* and the court's conclusion that its rule is limited to "abstract advocacy." The court said that *Hit Man* is not "abstract," and instead falls within a class of non-protected speech that the court styles "steeling to action" or, less floridly, "incitement." Both of these tracks present difficult questions as to the nature of speech and verbal acts, but the former is by far the less controversial.

---

147. *Rice*, 128 F.3d at 244.
148. *Id.* at 246 (citation and quotation marks omitted).
149. In fact, the opinion then raises in capsule form two notions discussed at greater length subsequently in the opinion. First, the court examined and rejected the notion that the First Amendment "superimpose[s] upon the speech-act doctrine a heightened intent requirement in order that preeminent values underlying that constitutional provision not be imperiled." *Id.* at 247. Second, the court suggests that the First Amendment "might well (and presumably would) interpose the same or similar limitations upon the imposition of civil liability for abstract advocacy, without more, that it interposes upon the imposition of criminal liability for such advocacy." *Id.* at 248–249.
150. *Id.* at 250–255.

The notion that the provision of raw data, absent editorial analysis or any other "message," presents a series of First Amendment concerns different than those encapsulated by mainstream First Amendment jurisprudence, is not inherently implausible. One can imagine a First Amendment analysis following Judge Luttig's lead, in which a showing that a party intentionally provided data and that it intended a reader to act upon it would be deemed tortious. If such an analysis came to being, a reviewing court could further ensure First Amendment protections by applying the "viewpoint neutrality" requirement of public forum and public funding doctrine,[151] or by treating the speech, somewhat paradoxically, under the four-point test applied to the regulation of expressive conduct, which originated that requirement.[152] It is even possible that that such an approach could be squared with *Brandenburg*.

However, Judge Luttig's second track is far more problematic. In narrowing the scope of the rule in *Brandenburg* to the protection of only "abstract advocacy," Judge Luttig seized upon language in that short opinion reciting the Court's prior holdings in *Noto v. United States*[153] and *Scales v. United States*.[154] Judge Luttig, on the strength of this historical summary, claimed that the *Brandenburg* Court required reviewing courts to draw a distinction between "'the mere abstract teaching . . . of the moral propriety or even moral necessity for a resort to force or violence' on one hand, and the 'prepar[ation] [of] a group for violent action and steeling it to such action' on the other."[155] Only the former, the judge noted, would be protected speech, whereas the latter falls on the side of unprotected verbal acts.[156]

Judge Luttig's reading of *Brandenburg* is highly problematic, for three reasons. First, it assumes a consistency between the *Noto, Scales,* and *United States v. Yates*[157] cases cited by the Supreme Court in *Brandenburg*, which the actual ruling in *Brandenburg* strongly negates. Thus, as an instance of precedent-reading, Judge Luttig ignores the fact that the Court overruled *Yates, Scales* and *Noto sub silentio*. While the Court did reference earlier language in *Noto* concerning "abstract advocacy," it did not reaffirm the distinctions set out in that case between abstract advocacy and advocacy of non-imminent violence subject to proscription and punish-

---

151. *See*, for example, *Legal Servs. Corp. v. Velasquez*, 531 U.S. 533 (2001) (public funding context) (collecting cases describing viewpoint neutrality doctrine). *See generally Rosenberger v. Rector and Visitors Univ. of Va.*, 515 U.S. 819 (1995) (public forum).

152. *See United States v. O'Brien*, 391 U.S. 367 (1968); *Texas v. Johnson*, 491 U.S. 397 (1989).

153. 367 U.S. 290 (1961).

154. 367 U.S. 203 (1961)

155. *Rice*, 128 F.3d at 264.

156. *Id.*

157. 354 U.S. 298 (1957).

ment.[158] Rather, the rule set out in *Brandenburg* states clearly that "[t]he Constitutional guarantees of free speech and free press do not permit a state to forbid or proscribe advocacy of the use of force or of law violation except where such advocacy is directed to inciting or producing imminent lawless action and is likely to incite or produce such action."[159]

Second, by reinvigorating those earlier decisions, Judge Luttig replaced the bright-line rule of *Brandenburg* with an interlocking set of distinctions so illogical as to inspire the prior comment that "this is the sort of logic that leads to cotillions on the heads of pins,"[160] undermining the predictive value of the constitutional standard set out in *Brandenburg*. Finally, the distinction between "abstract advocacy" and "steeling to action" as drawn by Judge Luttig not only is unsupported by the verbal act logic he invokes to justify it, but undercuts any meaningful notion of freedom of speech.

A Limiting Interpretation: Judge Luttig's Legerdemain

As a matter of precedent, Judge Luttig acknowledged that the rule set forth in *Brandenburg* is at tension with the language quoted in that opinion from *Noto*.[161] Judge Luttig assumed that either this proposition must be reconciled with the prior decisions, because they were not explicitly overruled, or that the *Brandenburg* Court was affording some level of protection to "preparation and steeling." Judge Luttig added that if the latter was true, then the Court may have been implicitly limiting its holding to "the context of *advocacy*—speech that is part and parcel of political or social discourse— which was the only type of speech at issue in *Brandenburg*, *Noto*, and the cases relied upon by the Court."[162] Judge Luttig sought to justify his interpretation of *Brandenburg* by stating that *Brandenburg* was limited to the context of political speech. As support, Judge Luttig cited to a plurality opinion by Justice Stevens in *44 Liquormart* describing *Brandenburg* as setting forth the "test for suppressing political speech."[163]

---

158. For a discussion on the development from *Dennis* through *Yates*, *Scales* and *Noto* (each of which seek to draw distinctions between harmful and protected advocacy of non-imminent violence) and the decision in *Brandenburg*, explicitly requiring temporal imminence connecting any advocacy to resultant harm for the imposition of liability, *see* Chapter 2 at 56–70.

159. *Brandenburg v. Ohio*, 395 U.S. 444 (1969).

160. *See* Chapter 2 at 64 (characterizing Justice Harlan's efforts to distinguish between harmless and harmful advocacy for purposes of determining constitutionally protected status).

161. *Rice*, 128 F.3d at 264.

162. *Id.* at 264.

163. *Id.* at 264 (*quoting 44 Liquormart v. Rhode Island*, 517 U.S. 484, 498 (1996)).

However, this reliance on *44 Liquormart's* casual dictum is in fact strikingly misleading. Far from suggesting that the *Brandenburg* test could be pigeonholed into a small category related to political speech in the narrowest sense, the *44 Liquormart* Court's reference to *Brandenburg* reinforces the contention that, in cases where a tier of so-called lesser value speech is not involved, the *Brandenburg* rule states the norm:

> OUR early cases uniformly struck down several broadly based bans on truthful, nonmisleading commercial speech, each of which served ends unrelated to consumer protection. Indeed, one of those cases expressly likened the rationale that *Virginia Pharmacy Bd.* employed to the one that Justice Brandeis adopted in his concurrence in *Whitney v. California.* There, Justice Brandeis wrote, in explaining his objection to a prohibition of *political* speech, that "the remedy to be applied is more speech, not enforced silence. Only an emergency can justify repression."[164]

Judge Luttig's out-of-context quotation of a snippet of Justice Stevens's characterization of *Brandenburg* in *44 Liquormart* completely obscures Justice Stevens's point that, while the *Brandenburg* rule does not apply of its own weight to regulations of commercial speech intended to protect consumers from fraud, it does so apply to truthful commercial speech involving transactions that are legal. The intermediate level of protection applied to commercial speech, traditionally deemed outside the scope of the First Amendment, and only latterly brought within its scope, distinguished it from "other forms of protected speech."[165]

The decisions cited by Justice Stevens in *44 Liquormart* undermine even further Judge Luttig's characterization of *Brandenburg* as an isolated class of speech subject to a *sui generis* level of protection that can be disregarded in other contexts. In each of these cases, the lesser protection afforded commercial speech (which is considered a *sui generis* area of speech, one of the traditional categories of "lesser-value" speech) was construed in accordance with the values underlying the *Brandenburg* test, in order to minimize the scope of suppression.[166] In *Linmark Associates v. Township of Willingboro,* the

---

164. *44 Liquormart,* 517 U.S. at 497–498 (emphasis in original) (*citing Virginia Bd. of Pharmacy v. Virginia Citizens Consumer Council, Inc.,* 425 U.S. 748 (1976); *Whitney v. California,* 274 U.S. 357 (1927)).

165. *Id.* at 498 ("At the same time, our early cases recognized that the State may regulate some types of commercial speech more freely than other forms of protected speech.").

166. Even in the context of categories of speech held to be entitled to no constitutional protection, as opposed to the intermediate level of scrutiny afforded to regulations of commercial speech, the Court has required that such regulations be limited to that factor which brings the speech outside of the First Amendment's scope and otherwise has applied the rationale of *Brandenburg. See R.A.V. v. City of St. Paul,* 505 U.S. 377 (1992).

Court followed Justice Brandeis' counterspeech rationale, quoted by Justice Stevens in *44 Liquormart*.[167] That rationale is the basis for the imminence requirement in *Brandenburg*.[168] In *Carey v. Population Services International*,[169] Justice Brennan's opinion for the Court affirmed a lower court decision striking down a ban of advertising of contraceptives as unconstitutional.[170] The Court rejected the argument that such advertisements did not fall within the *Brandenburg* rubric of unprotected incitement.[171] Far from rejecting the applicability of the *Brandenburg* test, the Court explicitly found that it had not been established that the advertisements "directly incited illicit sexual activity among the young," as opposed to providing truthful information concerning legally available products, and thus did "not justify the total suppression of advertising concerning contraceptives."[172] Thus, Judge Luttig's effort to distinguish *Brandenburg* into an intellectual and political ghetto not only fails, but is contradicted by the very sources upon which it relies.

"Every Idea Is an Incitement"

Beyond the question of precedent, Judge Luttig's effort to distinguish between "abstract advocacy" and "steeling" was persuasively rejected by Justice Holmes in his dissenting opinion in *Gitlow v. New York*:[173]

> IT is said that this manifesto was more than a theory, that it was an incitement. Every idea is an incitement. It offers itself for belief and if believed it is acted on unless some other belief outweighs it or some failure of energy stifles the movement at its birth. The only difference between the expression of an opinion and an incitement in the narrower sense is the speaker's enthusiasm for the result. Eloquence may set fire to reason. But whatever may be thought of the redundant discourse before us it had no chance of starting a present conflagration. If in the long run the beliefs expressed in proletarian dictatorship are destined to be accepted by the dominant forces of the community, the

---

167. *Linmark Assocs. v. Township of Willingboro*, 431 U.S. 85, 97 (1977) (following Justice Brandeis' opinion in *Whitney*).
168. *See* Chapter 2 at 68–70; *see also Brandenburg*, 395 U.S. at 448–449 (explicitly rejecting and overruling *Whitney* and distinguishing "mere advocacy, as opposed to abstract advocacy, from "incitement to imminent lawless action").
169. 431 U.S. 678 (1977).
170. *Id.* at 701.
171. *Id.* at 681.
172. *Id.* at 701–702.
173. 268 U.S. 652 (1925).

only meaning of free speech is that they should be given their chance and have their way.[174]

Justice Douglas made the same point in *Brandenburg* itself, stating that "[t]he quality of advocacy turns on the depth of the conviction; and government has no power to invade that sanctuary of belief and conscience."[175] Likewise, the Court, through Justice Jackson in *West Virginia State Board of Education v. Barnette*,[176] has eloquently indicated the centrality of the freedom of belief, even as to matters which are fundamental, declaring:

> WE can have intellectual individualism and the rich cultural diversities that we owe to exceptional minds only at the price of occasional eccentricity and abnormal attitudes. When they are so harmless to others or to the State as those we deal with here [Jehovah's Witnesses contesting a policy mandating their children to recite the Pledge of Allegiance], the price is not too great. But freedom to differ is not limited to things that do not matter much. That would be a mere shadow of freedom. The test of its substance is the right to differ as to things that touch the heart of the existing order.
>
> If there is any fixed star in our constitutional constellation, it is that no official, high or petty, can prescribe what shall be orthodox in politics, nationalism, religion, or other matters of opinion or force citizens to confess by word or act their faith therein.[177]

Judge Luttig's efforts to revive the *Noto* notion of "steeling to action" would also work a fundamental change of First Amendment doctrine, and would punish the speech in *Rice* for reasons that are contrary to the best-established rationales of freedom of speech. Judge Luttig himself admits that the "right to advocate lawlessness is, almost paradoxically, one of the ultimate safeguards of liberty."[178] Behind this familiar doctrine can be found Justice Jackson's wise words in *Barnette*. Yet Judge Luttig draws his notion of what constitutes "steeling" from Rex Feral's efforts to persuade the reader that the career of contract killer is useful or valid, and to glorify it:

---

174. *Id.* at 673 (Holmes, J., dissenting). *See also Dennis v. United States,* 341 U.S. 494, 507 (1951) (As even Chief Justice Vinson noted in *Dennis,* 341 U.S. at 507, "there is little doubt that subsequent opinions [to *Gitlow* and *Whitney*] have inclined toward the Holmes-Brandeis rationale.")

175. *Brandenburg,* 395 U.S. at 457 (Douglas, J., concurring).

176. 319 U.S. 624 (1943).

177. *Id.* at 641–642 (1943). *See also Scales v. United States,* 367 U.S. 203, 262–263 (1961) (Douglas, J., dissenting) (applying *Barnette* doctrine).

178. *Rice v. Paladin Enters.,* 128 F.3d 233, 243 (4th Cir. 1997).

AS Hit Man instructs, it also steels its readers to the particular violence it explicates, instilling in them the resolve necessary to carry out the crimes it details, explains and glorifies. Language such as that which is reprinted in the prologue to this opinion, and similar language uncanny in its directness and power, pervades the entire work . . . . Speaking directly to the reader in the second person, like a parent to a child, Hit Man addresses itself to every potential obstacle to murder, removing each, seriatim, until nothing appears to the reader to stand between him and his execution of the ultimate criminal act. To those who are reluctant because of the value of human life, Hit Man admonishes that "life is robust and precious and valuable" and that "everything you have been taught about life and its value was a fallacy, a dirty rotten lie."[179]

Similarly, Judge Luttig detailed specific passages aimed to assuage the concerns of those who, afraid of guilt or ghosts, "fear their cold-bloodedness," and even "those who fear only that they will be caught . . ."[180] And, of course, in setting out and relying on the passages used as an epigraph to the opinion, Judge Luttig assailed the author's claim that the career of a contract killer was one of value and social utility.[181] In short, the Fourth Circuit imposed liability on Paladin in large part because it found that *Hit Man* persuasively advocated a vision of the personal and social good, although the means of presentation did nothing to undermine the reader's ability to evaluate and weigh the options presented in the text.

This rationale should be deeply troubling to anyone who cares about freedom of speech. It is especially disturbing that Professor Smolla, who is generally conscious of the value of free speech, could advocate such a ruling. Additionally, it is difficult to understand how any federal judge could so rule, in light of eighty years of jurisprudence in which the Supreme Court has repeatedly acknowledged that, "The First Amendment demands a tolerance of 'verbal tumult, discord and offensive utterance,' as 'necessary side effects of the process of open debate.'"[182] Supporters of the *Rice* decision also ignore the fact that, "Under the First Amendment there is no such thing as a false idea, the fitting remedy for evil counsels is good ones."[183]

---

179. *Id.* at 261.
180. *Id.* at 261–262.
181. *See* "For the Wrong Reason: The District Court Opinion in Rice," *supra.*
182. *Waters v. Churchill,* 511 U.S. 661, 672 (1994) (O'Connor, J., plurality opinion) (*quoting Cohen v. California, 403* U.S. 15, 24–25 (1971)); *see also Terminiello v. Chicago,* 337 U.S. 1, 4–5 (1949) (free speech prevents against "standardization of ideas either by legislature, courts or dominant political or community groups").
183. *Waters,* 511 U.S. at 672 (internal quotation marks and citations omitted) (*quoting Gertz v. Robert Welch, Inc.,* 418 U.S. 323, 339 (1974) and *Whitney v. California,* 274 U.S. 357, 375 (1927) (Brandeis, J., concurring)).

In their defenses of *Rice* and its results,[184] neither Judge Luttig not Professor Smolla delineates between the very amorphous "steeling" concept of *Noto* and the concept of protected advocacy of unlawful behavior that would survive the *Rice* court's relegation of *Brandenburg* to a jurisprudential pigeonhole. The very expansive and inherently vague contours of the definition of steeling employed by the *Rice* court would nullify these well-established foundation stones of First Amendment theory, in the absence of some limiting principle not evident on its face. Seemingly, civil or criminal liability could be imposed in any case in which (1) the advocacy of unlawful conduct took place; (2) the speaker or writer intended that the advocacy be taken seriously (or should have known it was likely to be so taken—watch out, Jonathan Swift!); and, (3) someone in fact acted and implemented, or at least endeavored to implement, the suggestions.[185]

Of course, this tension between the reasoning in *Rice* and First Amendment precedent does not itself establish that the result in *Rice* fails to comport with the First Amendment any more than the flawed reading of the cases by Judge Williams renders the result in the district court incorrect. Rather, the conflict between the concept of a "steeling" theory of liability and the fundamental principles of First Amendment jurisprudence must be resolved beyond determining whether such a theory is consistent with precedent. To resolve the conflict, it is necessary to look at the speech involved in *Rice* in the context of verbal act jurisprudence and to draw independent conclusions.

Verbal Acts Applied: The Limits of Speech Brigaded With Action

At the risk of re-stating the obvious, the defenders of the Fourth Circuit's opinion in *Rice*, including Professor Smolla, have embraced a form of First Amendment jurisprudence that accords a wide range of discretion to the government in determining whether speech is protected "advocacy" or unprotected "steeling to action." By allowing the imposition of liability on Paladin for actions based on the methods set out in *Hit Man*, the Fourth

---

184. *See* Smolla, *Deliberate Intent, supra* note 58.
185. For the imposition of civil liability, resultant damages would need to be shown; no such requirement attaches as a prerequisite for criminal liability. Of course, the State cannot impose liability of either kind to speech that is constitutionally protected. *See N.Y. Times Co. v. Sullivan*, 376 U.S. 254 (1964).

Circuit has left open to question the status of any advocacy of unlawful conduct. Indeed, as more than one commentator has suggested, the Fourth Circuit has revived the long-discredited "bad tendency" test, under which any speech may be punished upon a showing that it has a tendency to lead to some level of harm. Beyond the poor argument for the viability of this approach as a matter of precedent, discussed above, its consonance with the First Amendment is independently subject to question.

In discussing these matters, one should not lose sight of the general structure of First Amendment jurisprudence. As it was summarized in *Terminiello v. Chicago*,[186] "freedom of speech, though not absolute, is nevertheless protected against censorship or punishment, unless shown likely to produce a clear and present danger of a substantive evil that rises far above public inconvenience, annoyance, or unrest."[187] Despite the jettisoning of the "clear and present danger" language in *Brandenburg*, the rule of the *Terminiello* case is still good law, and the dominant paradigm of First Amendment jurisprudence is that speech is protected unless it fits within that rule, or falls within the so-called low-value categories enumerated by the Court in *Chaplinsky*.[188] While these categories have been supplemented by additional categories that have been given an intermediate level of protection, including commercial speech or broadcast speech, the Court has consistently accepted that the default setting of First Amendment jurisprudence is the line of cases culminating in *Brandenburg*. Justice Scalia summarized the present status of the First Amendment in *R.A.V. v. City of St. Paul*:

> THE First Amendment generally prevents government from proscribing speech, or even expressive conduct because of disapproval of the ideas expressed. Content-based regulations are presumptively invalid. From 1791 to the present, however, our society, like other free but civilized societies, has permitted restrictions upon the content of speech in a few limited areas, which are "of such slight social value as a step to truth that any benefit that may be derived from them is clearly outweighed by the social interest in order and morality." We have recognized that "the freedom of speech" referred to by the First Amend-

---

186. 337 U.S. 1 (1949).
187. *Id.* at 4 (internal citation omitted) (*citing Chaplinsky v. New Hampshire*, 315 U.S. 568, 571–572 (1942); *Bridges v. California*, 314 U.S. 252, 262 (1941); *Craig v. Harney*, 331 U.S. 367, 373 (1949)).
188. *Compare* Chapter 2 at 59, n.192, 72–112 *with* Rodney A. Smolla, *Should the Brandenburg v. Ohio Incitement Test Apply in Media Violence Tort Cases*, 27 N. Ky. L. Rev. 1, 14 (2000) [hereinafter Smolla, *Media Violence Tort Cases*] (arguing that *Brandenburg* should be conceptualized as a decision limited to political advocacy). Although Smolla does not provide the misleading citation support that Judge Luttig deploys, his arguments are, in the last analysis, equally flawed.

ment does not include a freedom to disregard these traditional limitations. Our decisions since the 1960's have narrowed the scope of the traditional categorical exceptions for defamation and for obscenity, but a limited categorical approach has remained an important part of our First Amendment jurisprudence.[189]

Thus, there are two paths open to those who would argue that a proposed substantive regulation is consistent with the First Amendment: to fit it within an extant or proposed *Chaplinsky* category, or to fit it in the *Brandenburg* framework, or some variant thereof. Both approaches, we have seen, were employed in *Rice*.

Arguments in favor of this sort of regulation, however, do not end with these rules relating to substantive proscriptions. Another approach involves the presentation of the regulation as nonsubstantive. For an example of an attempt at this argument, one can look to *Reno v. American Civil Liberties Union*,[190] where the Justice Department sought to justify the proposed limitations on purportedly "indecent" speech on the Internet contained within the Communications Decency Act as "a sort of 'cyberzoning' on the Internet."[191] This effort was unsuccessful because, as the Court stated, "the CDA applies broadly to the entire universe of cyberspace. And the purpose of the CDA is to protect children from the primary effects of 'indecent' and 'patently offensive' speech . . . ."[192] Thus, the effort to characterize the CDA's restrictions as analogous to "time, manner and place" restrictions was deemed to be a flawed analogy: the result would have been a total ban in effect, not a limitation on when speech may take place.[193]

Moreover, the "time, manner and place" approach cannot be employed by those advocating the assignment of tort liability on the basis of a reader's response to the advocacy. Such regulations are required to be content-neutral and, as the Court has repeatedly stressed, "Listeners' reaction to speech is not a content-neutral basis for regulation."[194] Since the very basis of tort liability is just this—the listener's reaction—the application of tort liability to a speaker cannot be judged as a content-neutral regulation. Therefore, the only remaining arguments in favor of tort liability for an advocate

---

189. 505 U.S. 377, 382–383 (1992).
190. 521 U.S. 844 (1997).
191. *Id.* at 868.
192. *Id.* at 867–868.
193. *Id.*; *see also* Chapter 6 at 263–268.
194. *Forsyth County v. Nationalist Movement*, 505 U.S. 123, 134 (1992); *see also Boos v. Barry*, 485 U.S. 312, 321 (1988) (stating that "[r]egulations that focus on the direct impact of speech on its audience" are not properly held to the standard for content-neutral restrictions); *Reno*, 521 U.S. at 868.

are content related. An examination of such content-related restrictions delineates the very narrow circumstances in which such liability does not constitute censorship.

Verbal Acts and Inchoate Crimes

Of the two prongs of the *Brandenburg* test, the imminence requirement is the prong most clearly inapplicable to the portrayal of violence as desirable. In defending the result in *Rice,* Professor Smolla makes two arguments that are calculated to overcome this barrier. First, Smolla claims that the imminence requirement can be met by

> TREATING the detailed instruction, written with intent to assist in crime, as itself a form of "lawless action," a deliberate *en mass* aiding and abetting of crime, that in effect satisfie[s] *Brandenburg's* imminence standard *instantly,* for the very providing of such detailed instruction with such intent to aid and abet [is] *itself* lawless action.[195]

This theory requires a rather curtailed reading of the First Amendment. If any advocate who speaks with the hope that her words are effective could be held liable for consequences that occur without her knowledge, then the right to advocate lawless conduct is reserved to those who in fact do not believe in the desirability of their speech. Such a neutering of the First Amendment would reject the above-quoted insight of Justice Holmes that every idea is an incitement.[196]

Indeed, Smolla does not state that the provision of the information itself should be alone a ground for liability. Rather, he states, it is this provision plus the intent that the reader act upon it that is dispositive. This theory, however, ignores the message of Justice Douglas's dissent in *Dennis v. United States* that a cause of action is dangerous when it subjects one to liability for a creed and:

> REQUIRES the element of intent that those who teach the creed believe in it. The crime then depends not on what is taught but on who the teacher is. That is to make freedom of speech turn not on *what is said* but on the *intent* with which it is said. Once we start down that road we enter territory dangerous to the liberties of every citizen.
>
> There was a time in England when the concept of constructive treason flourished. Men were punished not for raising a hand against the

---

195. *See* Smolla, *Media Violence Tort Cases, supra* note 188, at 43 (emphasis added).
196. *See supra* note 174 and accompanying text.

king but for thinking murderous thoughts about him. The Framers of the Constitution were alive to that abuse and took steps to see that the practice would not flourish here. Treason was defined to require overt acts—the evolution of a plot against the country into an actual project. The present case is not one of treason. But the analogy is close when the illegality is made to turn on intent, not on the nature of the act. We then start probing men's minds for motive and purpose; they become entangled in the law not for what they did but *for what they thought;* they get convicted not for what they said but for the purpose with which they said it.

Intent, of course, often makes the difference in the law. An act otherwise excusable or carrying minor penalties may grow to an abhorrent thing if the evil intent is present. We deal here, however, not with ordinary acts but with speech, to which the Constitution has given a special sanction.[197]

Justice Douglas's argument that intent alone fails to raise speech to the level of conduct is further buttressed by the two classic limiting concepts of the inchoate crime of conspiracy: the existence of an agreement and the performance of an overt act. As Justice Douglas expressed it in another dissent, this time in *Scales v. United States,* "Conspiracy rests not in intention alone but in an agreement with one or more others to promote an unlawful project."[198]

Similarly, the inchoate crime of aiding and abetting may include a "counseling" element, but also traditionally includes an element of specificity, which neither Smolla nor the court in *Rice* even mention. To employ an older articulation:

> "COUNSELING" to come up to the definition, must be special. Mere general counsel, for instance, that all property should be regarded as held in common, will not constitute the party offering it accessory before the fact to larceny; "free love" publications will not constitute their authors technical parties to sexual offenses which these publications may have stimulated. Several youthful highway robbers have said that they were led into crime by reading Jack Sheppard; but the author of Jack Sheppard was not an accessory before the fact to the robberies to which he thus added an impulse. Under the head of "counsel" may be included advice and instruction as to the modes of committing particular offenses, *e.g.,* pocket picking. General instruction, it is true, could not be "counseling" in the sense before us; though

197. 341 U.S. 494, 583 (1951) (Douglas, J., dissenting) (emphasis in original).
198. 367 U.S. 203, 262–263 (1961) (Douglas, J., dissenting).

it is otherwise with special instructions as to the management of a particular case. Persuading and tempting to a particular crime fall under this head.[199]

In prose almost explicitly directed at the case of media depictions of violence or other crime, Glanville Williams writes:

> IT seems that the crime instigated must have an element of particularity. D exhorts E to commence a life of crime and recommends burglary as affording a good opening. It is hard to believe that D thus becomes accessory to every burglary thereafter committed by E. The more satisfactory view appears to be that D is guilty of the inchoate crime of incitement, but does not become a party to the various burglaries.[200]

The required element of specificity in terms of the crime to be committed does not mandate knowledge of the minutiae of the criminal act executed.[201] On the contrary, as Williams goes on to describe, the supplier of information or equipment used to perform illegal acts must know that a specific crime is envisioned by the purchaser, and must intend that it take place in order to be held liable.[202] Williams approvingly cites the language of a British judge in a 1928 case:

> A CRIME must be a specific intentional act, and I know of no case saying that a man can be an aider and abettor if he knows nothing of the act or the date or the person against whom the criminal offence is committed. It will not do to say: "You gave the means of doing it."[203]

The stress on this requirement of particularity, or specificity, is not to suggest that the state law doctrines of criminal or of tort liability define the appropriate limits of the protections of the First Amendment or that Professor Smolla or Judge Luttig have misread the law of accessorial liability (which in any event differs subtly in the civil from the criminal context). Rather, the point is to stress that the legal doctrines that allow for such liability draw a distinction between advocate and accessory. This distinction, like that between principal and agent, or that of conspirators acting in concert, carries with it recognition of two facts relating to human conduct. The

---

199. Francis Wharton, *A Treatise on Criminal Law* § 265, n.3 (11th ed. 1912).
200. Williams, *supra* note 85, at 190.
201. *Id.*
202. *Id.* at 190–203.
203. *Id.* at 198 (*quoting Bowker v. Premier Drug Co.,* 1 K.B. 217, 230–31 (1927)).

first is that it is easier, and far less significant, to extol a course of conduct that is totally lacking a context ("kill the capitalists!") than it is to connect that sentiment to a specific object ("kill Kenneth Lay!"). Even then, the context in which the words are spoken may greatly influence their significance, and the blameworthiness of the speaker. For First Amendment purposes, the specificity and finality of a resolution do not exist in terms of general theorizing, or even in the advocacy of the act, absent a context for its application. This is precisely the difference between verbiage and a verbal act.

A verbal act, surely, must be the equivalent of a physical act in that it has consequences on its own. A conspiracy, for example, involves at least two people in an agreement to perform an act—a specific criminal or tortious act. With conspiracies, resolutions are formed. Just as a legal contract carries with it the legal consequences of enforcement, an unlawful contract, or conspiracy, carries with it the legal consequence of punishment. The meeting of the minds is identical in these mirror images. Similarly, in aiding and abetting cases, the provider of the aid knows that she has left the comfortable world of armchair strategy and entered the real world of action. Real consequences to real people necessarily attend her actions. The speaker has affiliated herself with the action's completion and ratified it as her own.

In *Rice*, there was no knowledge on the part of the publisher or author that any crimes would take place. Therefore, the verbal act formulation that allows for the distinction between advocacy of unlawful conduct, and its constitutional protection, and aiding and abetting through words does not apply. The *Rice* court, in blurring this distinction "makes speech do service for deeds."[204] By so doing, the nature of the verbal act concept was expanded beyond all rational limit. Rather than tethering what might otherwise collapse into a bald restriction of speech to a flow of real-world conduct, the *Rice* court used the verbal act concept as a catch-all method to avoid the dictates of the First Amendment.

Incitement and Imminence

In *Rice*, the imminence requirement was avoided by the finding of an analogous requirement, that the materials provide sufficiently detailed coaching. As Professor Smolla puts it:

> *RICE* may be most centrally grounded in what might be called a "detail for imminence trade," a judgment that materials intended to pro-

---

204. *Dennis v. United States*, 341 U.S. 494, 584 (1951) (Douglas, J., dissenting). This logic was reaffirmed by the Court in *Ashcroft v. Free Speech Coalition*, 152 L.Ed2d at 423.

vide detailed training instruction for planning and executing crimes deserve no First Amendment protection even though there may be a gap in time between the provision of the assistance and the perpetration of the crime because the detailed training provides a causal nexus to lawless action that serves as a substitute for the nexus normally required in time.[205]

This "detail for imminence trade" begs a very significant question, however, involving the nature of the causal nexus constructed by the imminence requirement. Professor Smolla states a rather bare-bones version of it:

> ONE of the theories behind the imminence requirement is that when time passes, other competing ideas have a chance to work their influence on the audience. We should count on the marketplace of ideas in situations in which there is time for the marketplace to operate. The marketplace metaphor, however, simply does not resonate at all in the context of a detailed criminal instruction manual, *which by its very nature and express terms is encouraging the criminal to carefully and meticulously plan the future crime.* A manual that says "Go out and blow up the building now!" is actually *less* lethal than a manual that says "Carefully plot and prepare and train and go out and blow up the building in three months."[206]

Smolla endeavors to render the marketplace of ideas metaphor inapposite, and thus, he suggests that the imminence requirement can be eliminated. This is splendid rhetorical strategy, but rests upon an unprovable notion of causation, and impoverishes the roots of the requirement; it is not a persuasive effort.

First, Professor Smolla assumes that the amassing of detail concerning technique somehow acts to render the imminence requirement irrelevant. He contends that Rex Feral has gone from being a participant in the marketplace of ideas, to a principal of crime because of the amount of data he has provided. Such an argument seeks to convince through inflammation. In fact, the provision of detail by no means coerces the reader to act and can, in fact, repulse. The relatively bloodless and tidy murders in the writings of Agatha Christie are far less appalling than the painful and far more graphic murders in the works of P.D. James, or even more so, those of Thomas Harris. The idea that the reader is passive clay in the hands of an author may be flattering to the authorial ego, but is simply contrary to experience. For example, the voluminous literature rejecting allegedly seductive

---

205. Smolla, *Media Violence Tort Cases, supra* note 188, at 43.
206. *Id.* (emphasis in original).

works that contain readers' stringent criticisms makes the point clear. Andrea Dworkin's scathing descriptions of pornography show that she has been able to reach an independent evaluation of it, different from that which an author would desire.[207]

Smolla identifies nothing inherently coercive about reading a book. The reader remains free to close the volume, annotate it, or to take a break from it in order to think through the moral and philosophical ramifications. As a reader, I do all of these and have even been known in extreme cases to discard books. Whereas a face-to-face presentation or a training seminar can be coercive in that one faces group disapprobation if one leaves, a book read in the privacy of one's own home is at the mercy of the reader. Moreover, a reader's reaction to a book is an interaction between an author and a pre-existing self who experiences the text. Common human experience supports such a dynamic—what readers bring to the text plays a role in their interpretation of and reaction to a text. One need not follow the deconstructionists to acknowledge that an author may provoke hostility as well as acceptance, depending on the pre-existing value structure, beliefs, and biases of any individual reader.[208]

What Smolla seems to have overlooked is the underlying reasoning of the imminence requirement that has been expressed by Justices from Holmes and Douglas to Brennan and Stevens: a faith that the people can be trusted to choose between right and wrong, and between good or bad ideas. Justice Douglas, in his dissenting opinion in *Roth v. United States*, best articulated this faith, "I have the same confidence in the ability of our people to reject noxious literature as I have in their capacity to sort out the true from the false in theology, economics, politics, or any other field."[209]

---

207. *See* Andrea Dworkin, *Pornography: Men Possessing Women* (1980).
208. Author Rex Stout and his fictional detective Nero Wolfe are legendary for truly passionate negative assessments by readers of works not to their taste. *See* for example, Rex Stout, *Gambit* (1962) at 2 (Wolfe is first described by the narrator, his assistant Archie Goodwin: "on a chair too small for him, tearing sheets out of a book and burning them. The book is the third edition, of *Webster's New International Dictionary*, published by the G. & C. Merriam Company of Springfield, Massachusetts. He considers it subversive because it threatens the integrity of the English language."); Rex Stout, *Death of a Doxy* (1966) at 58 (Wolfe suffers a similar reaction to Sir Thomas More's depiction of King Richard III: "the young princes had been dead for five centuries, and Wolfe had once spent a week investigating that case, after which he removed Thomas More's *Utopia* from his bookshelves because More had framed Richard III.") (*citing* More, *Utopia* [1516]).
   Stout playfully attributed many of his own views to Wolfe. According to the president of the Richard III Society, Stout was an honorary member and on one occasion placed an "In Memoriam" advertisement in the *New York Times* on the anniversary of the Battle of Bosworth, mourning Richard as a "great king and true friend of the rights of man." Jeremy Potter, *Good King Richard?* (1983) at 261.
209. *Roth v. United States*, 354 U.S. 476, 514 (1957).

In part, the meaning of free speech involves just such a leap of faith. John Stuart Mill asserted in *On Liberty* that truth could not be put to flight by falsehood in an open contest.[210] Holmes declared, from his skeptic's heart, that "the best test of truth is the power of the thought to get itself accepted in the competition of the market."[211] The literature surrounding the First Amendment, and the various rationales proffered in support of it, presuppose this ability on the part of the citizenry to gauge the desirability of representations offered to them by artists, scholars, and advocates of all forms of alternative lifestyles, ranging from the Christian Brothers to the Church of Satan.[212] In a very real sense, the First Amendment codifies this leap of faith, so radically different from the faith of Hitler and Goebbels in "the Big Lie."

In that sense, the idea bruited by Smolla that the reader can be taken outside the "marketplace of ideas" model because the time for other ideas to bring themselves to bear is somehow cancelled out by detailed instruction is simply without foundation. The rationale for imminence provided by Brandeis in *Whitney v. California*[213] resonates in addressing the moral choice of the auditor, and the opportunity for him or her to internalize the argument of the speaker and to decide whether or not to act upon those ideas. Only when the peculiarities of group dynamics act to eliminate the time for reflection can the imminence requirement be omitted from the analysis. Smolla has simply not carried his burden by any fair measure.

The Supreme Court has, rightly, long rejected the approach of *Rice*. In terms of causation, the Court has repeatedly refused to find that the persuasive effect of speech on illegal conduct serves as a content-neutral ground for regulation. The court has found that any resultant violence is a "secondary effect" of the speech. In the context of a "fighting words" ordinance, the Court noted in *R.A.V. v. City of St. Paul* that, "Listeners' . . . reactions are not the type of 'secondary effects'" which may be regulated, and emphasized its prior statements that "[t]he emotive impact of speech on its audience is not a 'secondary effect.'"[214] As the Court explained in the opinion:

> THE only reason why such expressive conduct would be especially correlated with violence is that it conveys a particularly odious message; because the chain of causation thus *necessarily* runs through the persuasive effect . . . of the conduct, [and thus] the St. Paul ordinance

210. John Stuart Mill, *On Liberty* (1869).

211. *Abrams v. United States*, 250 U.S. 616, 630 (1919) (Holmes, J., dissenting).

212. For a brief survey of this literature, *see* Chapter 8 at 380–385.

213. 274 U.S. 357 (1927).

214. 505 U.S. 377, 394 (1992). Again, this concept was reaffirmed emphatically in *Ashcroft v. free Speech Coalition*, 152 L.Ed.2d at 423.

regulates on the basis of the primary effect of the speech—i.e., its persuasive (or repellent) force.[215]

Thus, only under the circumstances captured in *Brandenburg* may they be the grounds of an imposition of liability.

Holmes spoke vehemently about the protection of speech that we believe to be "fraught with death."[216] In contrast to this robust approach, Smolla's equation of speech's protected status with its innocuous nature suggests a decline in modern commitment to the First Amendment. Smolla erroneously assumes that the tying of any kind of serious danger to speech suffices to render the speech outside of the Amendment's scope. This is not and must never become the case, unless freedom of speech is to be reduced to a mere luxury item, protected only when the speech poses no threat to the settled order of things. Rather, it is those dangers captured by the verbal act formulation, which involve the author in a specific crime or wrongful act, that are properly chargeable to the author.

Techniques of Subversion and Steeling to Action

Similarly, Smolla's suggestion that a better framed manual, one which suggests the reader should prepare over an extended period of time rather than attempt a criminal act on the spur of the moment, is somehow "more deadly" and therefore more susceptible to regulation, is overbroad. Should counsel fall outside the scope of the First Amendment because its pragmatic nature makes it more deadly? In this regard, Smolla is surprisingly able to score a telling point. He cites the opening lines of Justice Douglas' dissent in *Dennis v. United States*:

> IF this was a case where those who claimed protection under the First Amendment were teaching the techniques of sabotage, the assassination of the President, the filching of documents from public files, the planting of bombs, the art of street warfare and the like, he wrote, I would have no doubts. The freedom to speak is not absolute; the teaching of methods of terror and other seditious conduct should be beyond the pale. . . .[217]

---

215. *Id.* at 394 n.7 (internal quotation marks omitted) (emphasis in original); *see also Kingsley Int'l Pictures Corp. v. Regents,* 360 U.S. 684, 688–689 (1959).

216. *Abrams,* 250 U.S. at 630 (Holmes, J., dissenting).

217. Smolla, *Deliberate Intent, supra* note 58, at 116 (*quoting Dennis v. United States,* 341 U.S. 494, 581 (1951) (Douglas, J., dissenting)).

It may not be quite fair to hold Justice Douglas to these opening words of his great dissent. After all, they were written in the midst of his evolution to the absolutist position he came to hold in reference to the First Amendment's protections—an evolution triggered by what he saw as the Supreme Court's acquiescence in government repression of dissident speech in the 1950s and 1960s.[218] As indicated previously, a "dangerous data" doctrine of limited scope could be engrafted onto the First Amendment without necessarily diminishing the Amendment's functions of preventing government abuses, fostering spirited debate and allowing for self-expression. Perhaps, after all, some data is too inherently dangerous, too prone to misuse. Certainly, the scope of such an exception would be difficult to define, and its contours could well be misused like other instances of balancing governmental need to control inherently dangerous data, such as national security cases.[219] Nonetheless, in the wake of the terrorist attacks on the World Trade Center and the Pentagon, the potential impetus for such an approach should be acknowledged, if not necessarily embraced.

However attractive this notion may be, it is not the basis of the decision in *Rice*, nor is it founded within the law. Judge Luttig's and Smolla's reliance upon the Supreme Court's decision in *Noto*, and its allowance of the suppression of speech guilty of "steeling to action," suggests that there is some intermediate category between abstract advocacy and the sort of incitement to imminent violence delineated in *Brandenburg*. This category, however, is inherently subjective and efforts to explain it, like previous efforts to define obscenity, tend to collapse into a string of pejorative synonyms:

> SO that if all *Hit Man* did was preach, all that I would do is preach back. But *Hit Man* also teaches. The book not only preaches and teaches, it exhorts, cajoles, encourages, steels, incites. And in that combination, in that evil alchemy of nihilistic philosophy, calculating instruction, and black exhortation, *Hit Man* forfeited the protections of the U.S. Constitution. Freedom of speech is not freedom to kill. *Hit Man* causes murder. Perhaps not in a direct, literal and immediate sense. . . . But its blend of incitement, justification and training in the dark arts of murder does result in the real slaughter of real innocents.[220]

This summary of what Smolla considers steeling, similar to Judge Luttig's reliance on *Hit Man*'s philosophy, makes clear exactly why Justice Douglas

---

218. *See,* for example, William O. Douglas, *Points of Rebellion* (1970) at 1–34; William O. Douglas, *The Right of The People* (1958) at 49–59.
219. *See* Chapter 4 at 170–176.
220. Smolla, *Deliberate Intent, supra* note 58, at 270.

withdrew his notion of steeling expressed in *Dennis* by the time of his concurrence in *Brandenburg*. The question is one of vehemence in presentation and "belief—belief in the" ideas being advocated, surely an impermissible basis for liability.[221] Of course, Paladin's use of a first time novelist to write the book—a woman with no such background and experience as that postulated for the fictional Rex Feral—suggests that the author did not believe in the acts advocated, rather that the belief was faked. Nonetheless, the presentation of feigned passionate advocacy does not lend itself to a distinction that can be drawn with either safety or certitude.

While Smolla acknowledges (as does Judge Luttig) the importance of protecting "abstract advocacy" he does not distinguish this term from "steeling." Apparently, Smolla considers the distinction to be self-evident. However, as Justice Holmes made clear, no such clear distinction exists:

> IT is said that this manifesto was more than a theory, that it was an incitement. Every idea is an incitement. It offers itself for belief and if believed it is acted on unless some other belief outweighs it or some failure of energy stifles the movement at its birth. The only difference between the expression of an opinion and an incitement in the narrower sense is the speaker's enthusiasm for the result. Eloquence may set fire to reason.[222]

Unfortunately, eloquence may also be subject to civil liability—at least in the Fourth Circuit.

The fact that much violent speech and provocative rhetoric could fit the "steeling" rubric should illuminate that the "test" is emotive not logical. If the adjectives used in the context of *Hit Man* can be banned, speech seeking political and social changes on the part of oppressed groups using similar language also could be subject to a ban. This type of speech is plainly at the core of the First Amendment's protection by even the most restrictive definition. For example, Valerie Solanas's *S.C.U.M Manifesto* similarly urges, incites, advocates—choose your own term—the murder of men by women as a means of ending sexist oppression.[223] Solanas's rhetorical strategies are very similar to the passages adverted to by Smolla and Luttig as "steeling." She endeavors to erode inhibitions against violence, justifies resort to such violence, and provides suggestions as to how to execute said violence, along with other unlawful actions. In terms of intent, of course, Solanas's own attempted murder of Andy Warhol suggests that she intended her thoughts

---

221. *Scales v. United States,* 367 U.S. 203, 265 (1961) (Douglas, J., dissenting).
222. *Gitlow,* 268 U.S. at 673.
223. Valerie Solanas, *S.C.U.M. Manifesto* (1967).

to be taken seriously.[224] Yet, such radical pronouncements are commonplace to radical political discourse, which both Smolla and Luttig acknowledge must be protected. It is hard to escape the conclusion that both Smolla and Luttig allowed their revulsion at Paladin's message to color their application of First Amendment doctrine to the *Hit Man* text.

The Tort-Criminal Distinction

One final effort to square the circle presented by the academics who wish to clear the way for regulation of materials such as *Hit Man* is to distinguish between tort formulations of liability and criminal liability. The argument is premised on the notion that civil liability for speech conflicts in lesser measure with the First Amendment than does criminal liability, with its punitive aspects. Several commentators have argued that such a notion should result in liability on the part of publishers or other speakers, essentially conceptualizing the award of damages as the cost of a speaker's exercise of her right to free speech in lieu of punitive consequences.[225] Such a notion is vulnerable on two grounds. First, as current doctrine makes clear, speech that cannot be criminally punished is equally immune to civil sanction. Second, the nature of causation applied in tort law cases that find a speaker liable based upon an actor's independent decision to follow his or her promptings violates the logic inherent in any concept of free expression.

As a matter of hornbook law, it has been clear since at least 1964 that, where a claim of First Amendment immunity challenges any state law, "it matters not that that law has been applied in a civil action. . . . The test is not the form in which state power has been applied but, whatever the form, whether such power has in fact been exercised."[226] This ruling, as the Court noted in *Sullivan*, merely applied principles long established in other realms of constitutional law to the First Amendment context.[227] Since then, the Court has zealously applied the principle even in the contexts of taxation or government subsidies of speech,[228] holding that neither granting of bene-

---

224. *See* John de St. Jorre, *Venus Bound: The Erotic Voyage of the Olympia Press and its Writers* (1994) at 277–278 (*quoting* Solanas to the effect that her motives were "very involved, but best understood if you read my manifesto").

225. *See* Frederick A. Schauer, *Uncoupling Free Speech*, 92 Colum. L. Rev. 1321 (1992); L. Lin Wood & Corey Fleming Hirokawa, *Shot By the Messenger: Rethinking Liability for Violence Induced by Extremely Violent Publications and Broadcasts*, 27 N. Ky. L. Rev. 47, 50 (2000). (applying Schauer's thesis in arguing that *Rice* was correctly decided).

226. *N.Y. Times Co. v. Sullivan*, 376 U.S. 254, 265 (1964).

227. *Id.* (*citing Ex parte Virginia*, 100 U.S. 339, 346–347 (1879); *Am. Fed'n. of Labor v. Swing*, 312 U.S. 321 (1941)).

228. *Nat'l Endowment of the Arts v. Finley*, 524 U.S. 569, 587 (1998).

fits or imposition of costs[229] may be "manipulated" to "drive certain ideas or viewpoints from the marketplace."[230]

Thus, to the extent that commentators such as Frederick Schauer urge the Court to "uncouple" free speech protection from tort liability, they are urging a new and radical deviation from the constitutional norm.[231] Indeed, Schauer himself explicitly states this and urges a paradigm shift, not a re-interpretation.[232] However, such a shift should not be undertaken either in the form Schauer proposes or in the simpler form at issue in *Rice* the decision to impose liability upon the speaker.

Schauer suggests that either the speaker be held liable, or that a public compensation scheme, analogous to workers' compensation, should be imposed to compensate victims of speech torts or crimes where the First Amendment immunizes speech. He presents his theory as a "Law and Economics"— inspired means of reallocating social costs, and not as punitive. Relying in large part on Schauer's painstaking efforts to separate cost allocation issues from First Amendment protection, Wood and Hirokawa argue for imposition of cost upon the party who profits from the speech; in this case, Paladin. [233]

As a matter of precedent, the Court has declined to perform just the sort of cost-shifting that Schauer, Wood and Hirokawa would advocate. In *Forsyth County v. Nationalist Movement*,[234] the Supreme Court struck down as unconstitutional a local ordinance which permitted the county clerk to vary a permit fee on the basis of the anticipated cost of providing police protection to the speakers applying for the permit.[235] The Court explicitly rejected the state's argument that the recoupment of such cost represented a content-neutral regulation aimed at the "secondary effects" caused by the speech or the cost of providing extra police protection.[236] In so doing, the Court reiterated that "listeners' reaction to speech is not a content-neutral basis for regulation."[237] In the context of a hostile reaction to such speech, the Court held that, "Speech cannot be financially burdened, any more than it can be punished or banned, simply because it might offend a hostile mob."[238] The

---

229. *Simon & Schuster, Inc. v. Members of the N.Y. State Crime Victim's Bd.*, 502 U.S. 105, 116 (1991).
230. *Legal Services Corp. v. Velasquez*, 531 U.S. 533, 552 (2001) (*citing Nat'l Endowment of the Arts*, 524 U.S. at 587).
231. Schauer, *supra* note 225 at 1331–1332.
232. *Id.* at 1321–1322.
233. Wood & Hirokawa, *supra* note 225, at 60–61.
234. 505 U.S. 123 (1992).
235. *Id.* at 126–127.
236. *Id.* at 134.
237. *Id.*
238. *Id.*

basic principle at stake in *Forsyth County*—that the state may not burden speech by requiring that a speaker must shoulder its costs—was made long ago in *Schneider v. Irvington*.[239] In *Schneider*, the Court struck down as unconstitutional a ban on public leafleting based on the burden of cleaning up the discarded leaflets. The court stated: "Any burden imposed upon the City authorities in cleaning and caring for the streets as an indirect consequence of such distribution results from the constitutional protection of the freedom of speech and press."[240]

Schauer has frankly disagreed with this principle, while his successors have failed to address it. However, it points to a valuable truth that is relevant here: the protection of free speech is predicated on a series of value judgments standing for the proposition that the creation of a free society is worthwhile in itself and is even worth social costs. Justice Holmes pointed this out in the context of speech "fraught with death" and Justice Douglas celebrated speech causing controversy and turbulence. The Justices were not merely relying on the formalistic (though cogent) argument that a right ceases to be a right when its possessor may be taxed for its use. Rather, they are making a leap of faith based on the notion that enlightenment may come from the least anticipated sources and that free people, used to deciphering the babble of conflicting messages, have the best hope of steering the ship of state. Schauer and his adherents have disagreed with this principle, but have interposed no contrary theory of free speech and its role. Commendably exercised by speech that they see as wounding or leading to harmful conduct, they postulate no limiting principle that delineates the scope of free speech. At the end of the day, they offer only a simulacrum of freedom: speak if you can pay for the privilege.

The First Amendment's leap of faith, by contrast, allows for one to find value in the least likely of places. Indeed, such has been the case. Justice Holmes, with his hatred of "proletarian dictatorship" (as he termed it)[241] would perhaps be shocked at the extent to which a "mixed economy" has evolved, employing policies drawn from socialist thought consciously drawn to "save capitalism from itself" by politicians such as Theodore and Franklin Roosevelt.[242] While the social utility of individual instances of speech are not an appropriate measure of the utility of free speech, violent rhetoric

---

239. 308 U.S. 147 (1939).
240. *Id.* at 162.
241. *Gitlow v. New York*, 268 U.S. 652, 673 (1925) (Holmes, J. dissenting).
242. *See*, for example, Edmund Morris, *Theodore Rex* (2001) at 72–74, *et seq.*; Nathan Miller, *Theodore Roosevelt: A Life* (1992) at 335–356, 365–370; Peter Collier & David Horowitz, *The Roosevelts: An American Saga* (1994) at 265–266; Ted Morgan, *FDR* (1985) at 367–412.

can nonetheless illuminate the depth of disaffection and alienation from the dominant culture that motivates dissidents, and can vindicate the values served by the First Amendment.[243] Thus, the often violent, intemperate speech of figures such as Malcom X and Louis Farrakhan has a value that enriches the debate.

But Judge Luttig's opinion seems to conclude that *Hit Man* is merely a recipe book for getting away with murder, and that it has no social value and cannot be said to advance discourse in any measurable way. This argument, however, is suspect. First, the book does advocate a point of view— that the "personal justice" provided by a hit man performs a valuable social service, and that a career as a hit man may be a valid and satisfying one for the reader.[244] Despite Judge Luttig's and Smolla's anger at this view and its contradiction of the very foundations of the nation's founding principles, their use of the author's viewpoint as justification for censoring the book is deeply troubling in the face of the core principle of content neutrality. Notably, Smolla unwittingly picks up on the fact that the very attributes of the book that are being used to justify a finding of liability are those that militate most favorably for protection. He describes Judge Luttig as having found the book *Hit Man* "so profoundly fraught with death,"[245] that memorable phrase lifted from Justice Holmes, who urged that "we should be eternally vigilant against attempts to check the expression of opinions that we loathe and believe to be fraught with death, unless they so imminently threaten immediate interference with the lawful and pressing purposes of the law that an immediate check is required to save the country."[246]

Moreover, the question of social value allows Professor Smolla to shift the burden of proving that speech should be outside of the Amendment's protection to one where a speaker must prove that the speech should fall within it. Requiring the speaker to justify the worthiness of his speech for inclusion is a very worrisome rhetorical move. Professor Smolla, however, explicitly lists two of the "wonderful and grandiloquent purposes that undergird the First Amendment" and asks "how does the murder manual *Hit Man* stack up when measured against them?"[247] Requiring the speaker to show that her speech serves these purposes imposes a content-based threshold requirement of utility that disserves the relationship between the citizen and the government by allowing the former's expression only on approval of the latter, and only to serve the purposes of the latter.

---

243. For a discussion of those values, *see* Chapter 8 at 380–393.
244. Smolla, *Deliberate Intent, supra* note 58, at 268–270.
245. *Id.* at 216.
246. *Abrams,* 250 U.S. 616, 630 (1919).
247. Smolla, *Deliberate Intent, supra* note 58, at 271.

Moreover, *Hit Man* may even pass this test. Professor Smolla himself notes that the plaintiffs stipulated that:

> PALADIN'S "marketing strategy was and is intended to maximize sales of its publications to the public, including sales to (i) authors who desire information for the purpose of writing books about crime and criminals, (ii) law enforcement officials and agencies who desire information concerning the means and methods of committing crimes, (iii) persons who enjoy reading accounts of crimes and the means of committing them for purposes of entertainment, (iv) persons who fantasize about committing crimes but do not thereafter commit them, and (v) criminologists and others who study criminal methods and mentality."[248]

These functions all are indubitably of social value.

Byers v. Edmonson and Hidden Costs

While little has been said about *Byers*, the decision stands as an example of the perils of a rule such as that engrafted by the Fourth Circuit in *Rice.* The suit, filed in 1996, was dismissed on March 12, 2001, following half a decade of litigation. Thus, a cost was imposed upon the publishers regardless of their eventual legal victory.[249] This, in part, is inherent in the nature of pleading complaints under the Federal Rules of Civil Procedure and cognate "notice pleading" systems in effect in most states, including Louisiana. It is well-established that, where a defendant seeks to dismiss a complaint prior to discovery taking place, the court is "required to assume the truth of the detailed—but as yet untested —factual allegations of the complaint."[250] Thus, artful pleading—asserting each of the elements of a cause of action—can guarantee a plaintiff the opportunity to obtain discovery even where, as in *Byers*, the court openly expresses skepticism as to the plaintiff's ability to establish the elements thus pleaded.

Because the plaintiffs pleaded the appropriate level of intent specified in *Rice,* they would withstand a motion to dismiss regardless of whether it could be borne out at trial. However, the pretrial process itself works a burden on speech that is by no means negligible. Before the trial court even-

---

248. *Id.* at 122.
249. Stephanie A. Stanley, "Filmmaker Cleared in Shooting Trial: Natural Born Killers Protected, Judge Rules," *Times-Picayune* (New Orleans), March 13, 2001, at 1.
250. *Clinton v. Jones,* 520 U.S. 681, 685 (1997).

tually dismissed the case, the plaintiffs were able to compel Stone to testify concerning his artistic intentions, and to obtain and examine internal memos and Time-Warner market research documents in their efforts to establish that "Stone and the company targeted young males and intended to 'push their buttons.'"[251] Despite the court's final ruling, Stone and Time-Warner were forced to cooperate in this pretrial discovery at their own expense, including attorneys fees, thus imposing a sizable cost on the allegedly "free" speech represented by the film. That cost will continue to rise, as the plaintiffs announced their intention to appeal.[252]

Smolla views the defeat at the motion to dismiss stage in *Byers* as an example of poor defense tactics. In *Deliberate Intent*, he describes an exchange with a student who cites the decision as proof that "other courts, in other cases, will take this principle you have ordained and use it as a license to censor and suppress speech."[253] Smolla, admitting that, "The *Natural Born Killers* case was a defeat for the First Amendment, and thus a victory for Paladin, enabled them to crow 'I told you so.' This was precisely what Paladin and its numerous amici in our suit had warned against."[254] Smolla, endeavoring to rebut his student's claim that he has "damaged the First Amendment," places the blame squarely where he feels it belongs—on the media:

> I THINK the *Natural Born Killers* case is frivolous," I said. "The producers of *Natural Born Killers* deserve to win, and I'm sure they eventually will win. But the defendants in the suit took the wrong procedural step. They tried to get the case dismissed on the pleadings, which means they were stuck with the allegations that they knew and intended that the movie would be emulated. If they'd instead moved for summary judgment, on the grounds that there was absolutely no credible proof of any such intent, I'm sure they would have won. The difference between their movie and our murder manual is that it is utterly implausible that Oliver Stone or Warner Brothers intended to encourage or assist crime. But that's exactly what we believe Paladin and Lund knew they were doing and intended to do.[255]

Smolla's defense is less than compelling, as it rather disingenuously elides the fact that in order to get to summary judgment, a defendant must first go through discovery, and that process itself can wreak havoc on the media

---

251. Stanley, *supra* note 249.
252. *Id.*
253. *Id.*
254. *Id.*
255. *Id.* at 265–266.

outlet in question. [256] Indeed, Smolla's silence on this point is especially telling in view of his own awareness of the risk of self-censorship caused by a desire to avoid punitive processes such as pretrial discovery and motion practice. In describing the costs of defending media tort suits, Smolla wrote in 1986, "The time, energy and money consumed is enormous, and its tendency to reduce the aggressiveness and courage of the media in pursuing significant issues of social concern is very real."[257] When Smolla wrote *Suing the Press,* he focused on cases of libel and invasion of privacy—both torts resolved in civil litigation.[258] However, Smolla's analysis applies just as powerfully to the variant of tort litigation championed by Smolla in *Rice:* "[I]f the plaintiff's primary motive is vindication through punishment of the media defendant, it is no longer necessary to win in order to win. If the suit can be prolonged sufficiently the mere ticking away of the defense lawyer's clock will be enough to extract the pound of flesh."[259]

Particularly when it comes to local outlets or smaller producers of content, the "threat of libel or invasion of privacy litigation may be severely crippling to the exercise of First Amendment rights. Such small outlets are not only financially unable to sustain the costs of litigation, but the physical process of mounting a defense may consume so much manpower that the publication or broadcast of news may literally have to stop."[260] Among the most serious contributors to that cost is pretrial discovery. As Smolla aptly pointed out in *Suing the Press,* pretrial discovery can serve as a "weapon for intimidation":

> IN the *Herbert v. Lando* litigation, Barry Lando's deposition alone continued intermittently for a year, and consumed *over 3,000 pages of transcript.* This huge expenditure of money and effort, however, would come to be dwarfed by the discovery process in cases such as those later brought by Ariel Sharon and William Westmoreland. The discovery

---

256. Under federal law, as is also the case under Louisiana law applicable to *Byers,* summary judgment should only be granted if, after discovery, the "nonmoving party has failed to make a sufficient showing on an essential element of its case with respect to which it has the burden of proof. The nonmoving party must have had the opportunity to discover information that is essential to his opposition to the motion for summary judgment. Only in the rarest of cases may summary judgment be granted against a plaintiff who has not been afforded the opportunity to conduct discovery." *Hellstrom v. U.S. Dept. of Veterans Affairs,* 201 F.3d 94, 97 (2d Cir. 2000) (internal quotations and citations omitted) (*citing, inter alia, Anderson v. Liberty Lobby, Inc.,* 477 U.S. 242, 250 n.5 (1986); *Celotex Corp. v. Catrett,* 477 U.S. 317, 323 (1986)).

257. Rodney A. Smolla, *Suing the Press* (1986) at 79.

258. *Id.*

259. *Id.* at 76.

260. *Id.* at 78.

process in suits like Sharon's or Westmoreland's may cost many millions of dollars before they are completed. In *Westmoreland v. CBS* the attorneys for both sides examined over 300,000 documents, and interviewed hundreds of witnesses all over the globe.[261]

For Smolla in the year 2000 to blithely suggest that Stone and Warner Brothers should have waited to move for summary judgment at the close of discovery is for him to forget his own practicality and wisdom in 1986. Now as then, pretrial discovery can be a very expensive proposition—and attorney's fees have risen in the past 16 years. These hidden costs suggest that Smolla's efforts to distinguish the two cases is untenable on the practical front, if not as a matter of law. More likely, it is untenable on both levels. As Chief Justice John Marshall noted, "[T]he power to tax involves the power to destroy," and the imposition of significant costs on what is a legal right constitutes an abridgment of that right.[262] Such is the danger when factual issues, such as subjective intent, form a component of the constitutional status of speech.

Conclusion

The application of verbal act logic, as delineated above, suggests that the jurisprudential leaps taken by the Courts in *Rice* and *Byers* are without warrant. Moreover, these decisions are hurtful both to the coherence of First Amendment jurisprudence and to the security of those who publish ideas that challenge the mainstream. If, as happened in *Byers*, an artistic work that satirizes the very "culture of violence"[263] and promoters of this violence

---

261. *Id.* at 71 (emphasis in original) (footnote and citation omitted). Notably, Smolla does not conclude that the press should be categorically protected from these perils; indeed, he notes the success of plaintiffs in libel suits throughout the 1980s as proof that "America in recent years seems to have been growing increasingly convinced that freedom of speech does not deserve the level of preeminence that the *New York Times* case suggested." *Id.* at 79.

262. *McCulloch v. Maryland*, 17 U.S. 316, 431 (1819). For the application of this logic in a First Amendment context, *see Forsyth County v. Nationalist Movement*, 505 U.S. 123, 135–137 (1992) (forbidding the passing on of police costs attributable to public reaction to unpopular speaker's message to speaker by way of sliding-scale fee); *N.Y. Times Co. v. Sullivan*, 376 U.S. 254 (1964). The Court's decision in *Forsyth County* would seem, as described previously, to effectively undermine the arguments of Professor Schauer and his adherents that the "cost-shifting" approach of civil law does not conflict with the First Amendment.

263. Smolla, *Deliberate Intent, supra* note 58, at 272 ("We have struck a blow against the culture of violence.").

become victims of these culture wars, perhaps the wisdom of the entire enterprise should be rethought, independently of the unconstitutionality of such a course of conduct. For instance, when Canada adopted the definition of pornography as a violation of the civil rights of women long urged by Andrea Dworkin, Dworkin's own works were among the first to fall subject to the ban.[264] The experience of *Natural Born Killers* is similar and a reminder of one of the key dangers of political censorship: censors have a tendency to devour their own young.[265] More fundamentally, reliance on the disapproval of the speech's message as an element of the proof of liability contradicts what has been repeatedly described as the "lodestar" of the First Amendment: the notion that "there is no such thing as a false idea."[266] When Professor Smolla speaks of the "blow" he has struck against the "culture of violence," he admits violating this core precept of free speech.

The Supreme Court has recently rejected just such arguments as made by Professor Smolla and Judge Luttig in reaffirming its commitment to the highest quantum of protection for indirect advocacy, and reasserting the centrality of the verbal act concept in First Amendment jurisprudence. In *Ashcroft v. Free Speech Coalition,* [267] the Court struck down as unconstitutional the Child Pornography Protection act of 1996. In ruling that the statute violated the First Amendment, the Court rejected the Government's claim that "virtual child pornography whets the appetites of pedophiles and encourages them to engage in illegal conduct."[268] As the Court explained:

> THE mere tendency of speech to encourage unlawful acts is not a sufficient reason for banning it. The government "cannot constitutionally premise legislation on the desirability of controlling a person's private thoughts. First Amendment freedoms are most in danger when the government seeks to control thought or to justify its laws for that impermissible end. The right to think is the beginning of freedom, and speech must be protected from government because speech is the beginning of thought.[269]

---

264. Nadine Strossen, *Defending Pornography* (1995) at 237.

265. *See,* for example, Alan Dershowitz, *The Best Defense* (1982) at 191 (recounting that twenty years ago, when he asked the Rev. Tom Michel, the leader of the Moral Majority in New England who welcomed Dworkin as a fellow anti-pornography crusader, whether his organization would seek to enforce such a ban against her writings, Rev. Michel replied, "We would surely ban such ungodly writings.").

266. *Gertz v. Robert Welch, Inc.,* 418 U.S. 323, 339 (1974).

267. 535 U.S. 234, 152 L.Ed.2d 403 (2002).

268. *Id.,* at 423.

269. *Id., quoting Stanley v. Georgia,* 394 U.S. 557, 566 (1969).

The *Ashcroft* opinion goes on to explain that to "preserve these freedoms, and to protect speech for its own sake, the Court's First Amendment cases draw vital distinctions between words and deeds, between ideas and conduct."[270] The Court deemed the promulgation of attractive images of sexuality involving minors did not constitute "more than a remote connection between speech that might encourage thoughts and impulses and any resulting child abuse," and concluded that, "Without a significantly stronger, more direct connection, the Government may not prohibit speech on the ground that it may encourage pedophiles to engage in illegal conduct."[271] While the Court did not provide a comprehensive, definitional account of precisely what linkage is required beyond this description, it distinguished the CPPA from the general bar on child pornography upheld in *Ferber v. New York* on the ground that in "contrast to the speech at issue in *Ferber*, speech that itself is the record of sexual abuse, the CPPA prohibits speech that records no crime and creates no victims by its production."[272]

The Court's decision in *Ashcroft v. Free Speech Coalition* stands as a rebuke to the holding in *Byers*, and at the very least, to the logic advanced in support of the Fourth Circuit's ruling in *Rice*. These holdings, still so new, may be already destined to be swept aside as "a derelict on the waters of the law."[273] More fundamentally, the decision in *Ashcroft* it is a powerful reassertion of the primary rule of free speech: that, as a general proposition, speech may only be deemed to constitute part of an illegal action under very narrow factual circumstances in which a specific relationship

---

270. *Id.; Kingsley International Pictures Corp.*, 360 U.S. 684, 689 (1959); *Bartnicki v. Vopper*, 532 U.S. 514, 529 (2001).

271. 152 L.Ed. 2d at 423.

272. *Id.* The Court explained that it is this rationale that legitimizes the laws forbidding possession of child pornography, upheld in *Osborne v. Ohio*, 495 U.S. 103 (1990). Where materials that are simply obscene may be freely possessed in the home while their dissemination may be banned, *Stanley, supra*, mere possession of child pornography may be criminalized, the Court held in *Osborne* and reaffirmed in *Ashcroft*, on the theory that such materials are themselves the fruit of an unlawful act, known to be such by the possessor, and thus impute accessorial liability after the fact. This concept is supported by the common law maxim that no "one shall be permitted to profit from his own fraud, or to take advantage of his own wrong . . . The maxim [is] *volenti non fit injura*." *Riggs v. Palmer*, 115 N.Y. 506, 511–512, 514 (1889); *New York Mutual Life Insurance Co. v. Armstrong*, 117 U.S. 591 (1886); *Egelhoff v. Egelhoff*, 532 U.S. 141, 152 (2001) (describing *Riggs* principle as "well established in the law"). The application of this concept to include "fruits of crime" that might otherwise fall within the First Amendment's ambit has been upheld, although it presents questions of the appropriate scope. *Simon & Shuster v. Crime Victim's Board*, 502 U.S. 105 (1993) (striking as unconstitutional New York's Son of Sam statute forfeiting memoirs by criminals, as targeting expressive conduct alone).

273. *Lambert v. California*, 355 U.S. 225, 232 (1957) (Frankfurter, J., dissenting); *see also Rose v. Rose*, 481 U.S. 619, 639 (O'Connor, J. concurring) (1987).

between speaker and actor correlates the speaker's expression to the fact-specific crime in question.

The exploration of verbal act logic involves more than a rejection of the reasoning in a brace of bad decisions. The exploration of the outer limits of the First Amendment—unpacking what Justice Douglas meant in his terse phrase "speech brigaded with action"—is by no means easy. Both Judge Luttig and Professor Smolla's yielding to the temptation to censor what affronted them at the most visceral level, despite their own sincere beliefs in the importance of free speech, is evidence of this difficulty. However, the easy gibe that "hard cases make bad law"[274] does not sum up the lessons learned in these media advocacy cases. Rather, a few observations about verbal act logic are in order.

First, as suggested at the beginning of this chapter, the presumption that speech is inviolate is a precondition to such verbal act analysis. It is only upon a showing that the speech is the functional equivalent of a physical act that proscription and punishment are permitted. Second, some kind of specific connection to the illegal conduct that resulted from the speech is needed—the causal chain must be sufficiently tight that the line between protected persuasion and unprotected verbal act remains as sharp as possible. Thus, in *Brandenburg*, and Justice Brandeis' *Whitney* concurrence, the requirement of both the imminence of the resultant act and a specific context in which the act takes place creates a lack of opportunity for reasoned deliberation and the temporary ascendancy of the speaker over the audience. This is similar to an agency relationship that fairly imputes the listener's act to the speaker.

In fact, the relationship of the audience to the speaker is critical in distinguishing a verbal act from advocacy. A classroom professor who instructs her class from the writings of Valerie Solanas, and urges action on the abstract level is not the same as a speaker who is aware that prompt obedience is likely because of a different relationship context. For example, Professor James Moriarity, known as the "Napoleon of Crime," instructs his direct subordinate, Colonel Sebastian Moran, to kill Sherlock Holmes.[275] The power relationship between the two make it expected that Moriarity will be obeyed; violent action on the part of Moran at the behest of Moriarity is within the scope of their relationship as negotiated by them, and as practiced. Moran's act is attributable to Moriarity even if attempted after Moriarity's death.[276] Where the relationship is an explicit one, one agreed

---

274. *N. Sec. v. United States*, 193 U.S. 197, 400 (1904) (Holmes, J., dissenting).
275. *See* A. Conan Doyle, "The Adventure of the Empty House," *Strand Magazine*, October, 1903.
276. *Id.*

upon by the parties and acknowledged by them, the lack of imminence alone does not absolve the speaker. The equation is simply that a relationship plus a command equals causation. A relationship where a command takes place with both parties having reason to believe that the command will be obeyed, makes the speaker liable for the resultant act.

Another example may be helpful. Henry II, at dinner with his loyal barons, fatefully muses about his political conflict with the Archbishop of Canterbury, Thomas Becket, asking "will no one rid me of this turbulent priest?"[277] Four of his knights take the king's angry exclamation as an instruction, and butcher Becket in his own cathedral, while at the altar: Henry disavows any intent that they should have so acted.[278] This case posits an interesting question regarding intent: what is meant by a command? If Henry was just letting off steam, and did not intend his knights to act upon his passionate language (an interpretation much in keeping with the king's well-known rages), Henry might persuasively claim that, despite the relationship, his knights did not reasonably take his remark as a command. That is, Henry might claim either that his statement was not intended to be a command, or simply that the knights unreasonably so interpreted it, regardless of the king's subjective intention at speaking. The latter theory plainly exonerates Henry: If the statement is misunderstood in an objectively unreasonable manner, then the relationship does not act to impute liability to the king. If, however, the king was in the habit of commanding his knights to execute political opponents, and habitually expressed his will so elliptically, the agency relationship might still bind the king, despite Henry's lack of specific intent on that occasion.[279]

In both of these paradigm cases, immediacy is not required to establish liability because the pre-existing relationship creates a context whereby the speaker knows that the command, if spoken, will be acted upon. Speaker and actor are in a power relationship that supports such a conclusion. The *Brandenburg* rule likewise captures an unspoken power dynamic: The audience may be swept up in the feeling created by the speaker, directed at that moment at a specific target. In short, a temporary ascendancy due to group feeling and manipulated emotion has created a power relationship such that the causal chain is established. Power, not reason, links speaker and actor.

Thus, direct advocacy, under certain circumstances, crosses the line to verbal act status. Thus too, indirect advocacy—Henry II's wishing for the death of the "turbulent priest" to those who feel it their duties to anticipate and fulfill his needs—can also cross this line, under the right set of circum-

---

277. W. L. Warren, *Henry II* (1973) at 508.
278. *Id.* at 508–511.
279. Francis Wharton, *A Commentary on the Laws of Agency and Agents*, §§ 459–60 (1876).

stances. However, undirected advocacy—like *Hit Man* or the *S.C.U.M. Manifesto*—can only appeal to reason. No power dynamic between reader and speaker exists to attribute the causation of an act to the following of advocacy that is abstract—in that it is untethered to a specific factual context, not that it is bloodless. The mind of the reader remains free to evaluate, to weigh, to accept or to reject the arguments presented. The acts that result, therefore, are not attributable to the speaker, but solely to the actor. The speaker may be the spreader of error and evil counsel, but she is not herself an actor. To hold otherwise is not only to blur the lines between speech and act—even verbal act—but to reject the central tenet of any notion of free speech: that individuals are capable of receiving and evaluating various messages, and choosing between them. Such a doctrine also undermines our polity's commitment to individual responsibility, and to moral autonomy that undergirds the system of both civil and criminal law.[280] While such doctrines do not of themselves spell the end of freedom, they do show a disturbing ambiguity toward it. Freedom of speech, Judge Luttig and Smolla seem to say, except when there is a price to pay. Perhaps advocates, judges and academics cannot accept the notion that the speech they find truly heinous can with impunity be uttered, even when it is found persuasive. How different from Holmes, who acknowledged the risks of free speech, and acknowledged that the happy ending might not come—that freedom of speech, just like freedom in general, allows us to build both Milton's Pandemonium as well as Bunyan's Celestial City.[281] But only when there is freedom of choice between the highest and the lowest does choosing matter.

---

280. *See* Chapter 8 at 389–393; *see also* Lon Fuller, The Morality of Law (1964).
281. *See* John Milton, *Paradise Lost* (1667), Bk. I, ln. 756 reprinted in *The Poetical Works of John Milton* (Oxford University Press, H. C. Beeching, ed.) (1938) at 199; John Bunyan, The Pilgrim's Progress (1678).

6

Caught in the Net
Cybercensors in Cyberspace

MARSHALL MCLUHAN'S "the medium is the message"[1] may be of dubious validity as a matter of communications, and seems to be utterly fallacious as a question of epistemology. However, there is no doubt that it has substantial validity as a predictive norm in constitutional law. New media have repeatedly presented challenges to the First Amendment that have clouded the jurisprudence, and diminished only as society (and thus the members of that subset of society, the legal system) has grown familiar and more accepting of them. Familiarity may breed contempt, but it also brings about admission to the First Amendment's protective zone.

Like the erosion of the First Amendment under the proliferation of *Chaplinsky*-style categories, the initial distrust of new media of communications has been a means of avoiding the application of First Amendment principles to cases where these principles suggest that the subject speech is protected but a strong emotional impulse to censorship exists. In the cases of obscenity, or of the crude, disgust provides that impetus; in the case of hate speech, the impetus is anger; with new untried media of unknown— and possibly undreamt of—power to persuade, the impetus is fear. In each case, the result is the sacrifice of free speech principles to the adrenaline rush.

The twentieth century, as it limped to a somewhat anticlimactic end, had been one of change on an ever-increasing scale, of an accelerating progression (or slide, if one does not approve of the direction) from a world in which most people lived in a manner not wholly removed from the lives of their ancestors—communicating through the spoken (or, less frequently, the

---

1. Marshall McLuhan, *Understanding Media* (1964) pt. I, chap. 1.

printed) word, carried by horses or by their feet, with the horizons of their lives bounded by the power of the human or the equine body. A world, in short, very different from that of the Stuarts in custom and organization, but recognizably the same world in essence.[2]

The industrial age devoured that world, and created by the twentieth century a wholly different one: a world of ever-increasing pace, noise, and stink. Full-scale industrialized wars such as those of 1914 and 1939 have come and (we hope) gone in a single century, in two moderate lifetimes. My grandfather, who lived to see my majority, served in the waning days of that first war, and I am still reckoned a young man.[3] In the process, communications were revolutionized more fundamentally than at any time in the half millennium since Gutenberg invented the printing press. The popularization of literacy, the creation of recorded sound, of film, and of the broadcast media, have changed the way people experience their world more than any phenomenon since the spread of Christianity. Taking them as an emblem, John Lennon may have had a point when he suggested that the Beatles were bigger than Christ.

Each of these changes in communication has undermined the underside of freedom of speech—the unspoken, but often-implied assumption that free speech was a safe form of indulgence: The "best" in society could be trusted to wander the groves of daring radical thought because the "mob" was excluded in its illiteracy and denied exposure to "harmful" thought that only their betters could brave with impunity.[4] The nervousness of the "elite" toward the growing availability of speech, and the spread of ideas through the entire political structure, was felt in the law. Interestingly, this fear of free speech resonates even in the opinions of its defenders, who combat it by, as a rhetorical tactic, deploying the argument that the speech at issue is not of great moment. Justice Holmes, for example, argued in his soul-stirring dissent in *Abrams* that "nobody can suppose that the surreptitious publishing of a silly leaflet by an unknown man, without more, would present any

---

2. *See* R. F. Delderfield, *The Avenue* (1964) at 11. For a more serious and scholarly assessment to the same effect, *see* C. S. Lewis, "De Descriptione Temporum" in *They Wanted a Paper* (1962) at 20–23 (describing impact of mechanization on Western European society).

3. The rapidity of change in the present day is hardly a novel perception; for an unusually poetic relation of the brevity of this nation's entire existence, *see* Charles L. Black, Jr. *Further Reflections on the Constitutional Justice of Livelihood*, 86 Colum. L. Rev. 1103, 1104 (1986).

4. For distrust of the populace in the framing of the Constitution *see* Jack M. Rakove, *Original Meanings: Politics and Ideas in the Making of the Constitution* (1996) at 202–204, 221–227, 235–237, *et seq.*; Henry P. Monaghan, "We the People[s], Original Understanding and Constitutional Amendment," 96 Colum L.Rev. 121 (1996). The explosive spread of literacy, and the very different world that it has created, are discussed by Robertson Davies in *A Voice from the Attic* (2d ed. 1990) and *Reading and Writing* (1994).

immediate danger that its opinions would hinder the success of the government arms or have any appreciable tendency to do so."[5]

The traditional judicial reaction to new modes of communication is to distrust them, to assume that they are possessed of an atavistic power beyond the paradigm of the First Amendment, and to, accordingly, subject them to a level of censorship beyond that imposed on more established media.[6] Moreover, the vehicle of analysis-proof categories of somehow "lesser" speech, which may be denied protection on purely subjective grounds, provides just enough of a smokescreen that the entire process may be passed off as being in service to the First Amendment, or at least as consistent with it.

That initial reactions to the "newest" medium of speech, the Internet, fit this syndrome can help to evaluate current proposals for what regulation of speech over the Internet should be permitted, and to apply First Amendment principles in this new technological context. The initial results have been interesting to say the least: At least one of the judges, in order to hold Congress to the highest level of scrutiny in regulating on-line speech, applied verbal act logic, while the Supreme Court handed the supporters of free expression a victory, but one founded on somewhat troubing logic.

FAMILIARITY BREEDS CONTENT: DECREASING REGULATION OF MEDIA OVER TIME

The recurring evolution of the legal system's perceptions of strange new media of expression from that of a hostile, volcanic force to be regulated and, if possible, disdained, has taken place several times in this century, but seldom as clearly as in the case of motion pictures. Possibly this is because the development of the motion picture took place just before the "conservative revolution" described in Chapter 2, the birth of substantive protection under the First Amendment. Indeed, the very first decisions of the Supreme Court to apply the concept of freedom of speech to motion pictures were rendered *before* this development; the Court ruled on the constitutionality of state regulation of motion pictures a solid decade prior to the application of the First Amendment's protections to the states in *Gitlow v.*

---

5. *Abrams v. United States*, 250 U.S. 616, 628 (1919) (Holmes, J. dissenting).
6. At the risk of baiting Professor Catharine MacKinnon further than I do in Chapter 7, her depiction of pornography as a subrational means of communication somehow empowered to reduce its "consumers" to dogs that attack on cue is reminiscent of this phenomenon, a result of personal discomfort and not of any objectively reasonable distinction between the distrusted medium of speech and the accepted medium of speech.

New York.[7] The experience of films under the First Amendment presents the exemplar par excellence of the treatment of new media by Congress and the courts; a little detail may shed some light.

In *Mutual Film Corporation v. Industrial Commission of Ohio*[8] and its companion cases,[9] the Court rejected challenges under the applicable state constitutions to state statutes that required films to be approved by local boards as "of a moral, educational, or amusing and harmless character" prior to their exhibition (rejecting without comment the challenges predicated on the First and Fourteenth Amendments to the United States Constitution).[10]

Film exhibitors filed suits in the federal district court seeking injunctions against the enforcement of these statutes. The resulting decision, ostensibly based solely on the state constitution, was rendered in an era when the Court (in determining the constitutionality of the Ohio and Missouri statutes) was able to determine the contents of state law without being governed by state court decisions.[11] Thus, the Court could predicate the decision under the Missouri constitution on the reasoning in *Mutual Film Corporation v. Industrial Commission of Ohio*, decided under the Ohio state constitution.[12]

---

7. 268 U.S. 652 (1925).
8. 236 U.S. 230 (1915).
9. *Mutual Film Co. v. Industrial Commission of Ohio*, 236 U.S. 247 (1915) and *Mutual Film Corporation of Missouri v. Hodges*, 236 U.S. 248 (1915).
10. The only indication that the First Amendment claims were even raised in the *Mutual Film Company* troika of cases is in the statement of the case by Justice McKenna and in the summary of the arguments raised by counsel 236 U.S. at 237–238, 248, 249, 251, 255–256. The district court had rejected those claims on the ground that the First Amendment was not binding on the states, only on the federal government—a result that was mandated by the Supreme Court decisions then in effect. 215 F. 138, 141 (D.C., N.D. Ohio 1914). As framed by the Court (also by Justice McKenna), the argument against the regulation was "direct[ed] to three propositions: (1) The statute in question imposes an unlawful burden on interstate commerce; (2) it violates the freedom of speech and publication guaranteed by § 11, article 1 of the constitution of the state of Ohio; and (3) it attempts to delegate legislative power to censors and to other boards." 236 U.S. at 239.
11. *See Swift v. Tyson*, 16 Pet (41 U.S.) 1, 10 L.Ed. 865 (1842); *Gelpecke v. City of Dubuque*, 1 Wall. (68 U.S.) 175, 17 L.Ed. 520 (1863). Only after *Erie Railroad Co. v. Tompkins*, 304 U.S. 64 (1938), did the Court abandon its self-awarded power to "interpret" as a matter of federal general common law what state law should mean, independently of the state's own decisions.
12. *Mutual Film Corp. of Missouri v. Hodges*, 236 U.S. at 258. However, it should be noted that Justice McKenna's opinion in *Hodges* does not specifically base its holding purely on the state constitution as does his opinion in *Mutual Film Corp. v. Industrial Commission*, 236 U.S. 239. Indeed, the *Hodges* opinion's reference to "the liberty of opinion" is ambiguous, and could be taken to mean that protected by the First Amendment. However, this reading is extremely implausible because (1) no substantive level of protection guaranteed by the First Amendment had been declared by the Court at that time; (2) such protection as the amendment provided had been held to *not* apply to state statutes; and (3) the reasoning of the Ohio case, to which McKenna's opinion explicitly made reference, was *not* based on the First Amendment. 236 U.S. at 258.

In any event, in *Mutual Film Corporation* the Court spoke warmly of freedom of speech, and of the fledgling medium. Of the former, the Court stated that "the freedom of opinion and its expression, whether by speech, writing or printing" are "of such conceded value as to need no supporting praise. Nor can there be any doubt of their breadth, nor that their underlying safeguard is, to use the words of another, that 'opinion is free, and that conduct alone is amenable to the law.'"[13] However, the Court went on to pose the question and imply its negative answer in a single breath:

> ARE moving pictures within the principle, as it is contended they are? They indeed, may be mediums of thought, but so are many things. So is the theatre, the circus, and all other shows and spectacles, and their performances may be thus brought by the like reasoning under the same immunity from repression or supervision as the public press— made the same agencies of civil liberty.[14]

However, silent films had previously been analogized by the Court to novels, in a copyright suit over the (unlicensed) silent film adaptation of *Ben Hur.*[15] In that earlier case, Justice Holmes had written that "action can tell a story, display all the most vivid relations between men, and depict every kind of human emotion, without the aid of a word. It would be impossible to deny the title of drama to pantomime as played by masters of the art."[16] Comparing moving pictures to a pantomime displayed through a mirror, Holmes stated that "[t]he essence of the matter in the case last supposed is not the mechanism employed, but that we see the event or story lived."[17] Thus, he concluded, "moving pictures may be used for dramatizing a novel."[18]

The Court denied that this amounted to a finding that films were entitled to protection under the liberty of opinion, or that it impelled such a finding. Moreover, it went on to assert, motion pictures could cause a new kind of harm. In expanding on the potential harms of motion pictures, especially the "manner of exhibition," the Court made its concerns more clear:

> THEIR power of amusement, and, it may be, of education, the audiences they assemble, not of women alone, nor of men alone, but together, not of adults alone, but of children, make them the more

---

13. *Id.* at 243.
14. *Id.*
15. *Kalem Co. v. Harper Bros.,* 222 U.S. 55, 61–62 (1911) (Holmes, J.) (finding that film adaptation of novel constituted infringement on novel's copyright).
16. *Id.* at 61.
17. *Id.*
18. *Id.* at 62.

insidious in corruption by a pretense of worthy purpose or if they should degenerate from worthy purpose. Indeed, we may go beyond that possibility. They take their attraction from the general interest, eager and wholesome it may be, in their subjects, but a prurient interest may be excited and appealed to. Besides, there are some things which should not have pictorial representation in public places and to all audiences.[19]

The Court relied on these concerns in deciding whether or not motion pictures fell within the purview of the state constitution's protection of freedom of speech or freedom of opinion:

THE first impulse of the mind is to reject the contention. We immediately feel that the argument is wrong or strained which extends the guaranties of free opinion and speech to the multitudinous shows which are advertised on the billboards of our cities and towns, and which regards them as emblems of public safety . . . and which seeks to bring motion pictures and other spectacles into practical similitude to a free press and liberty of opinion.[20]

Of course, the Court had to explain and justify this "first impulse of the mind." Its attempt to do so is enlightening:

THEY are mere representations of events, of ideas and sentiments published and known; vivid, useful, and entertaining, no doubt, but, as we have said, capable of evil, having power for it, the greater because of their attractiveness and manner of exhibition. It was this capability and power, and it may be in experience of them, that induced the state of Ohio, in addition to prescribing penalties for immoral exhibitions, as it does in its Criminal Code, to require censorship before exhibition, as it does in the act under review. We cannot regard this as beyond the power of government.[21]

So the Court found that the state had plenary power to regulate motion pictures, this new and potentially dangerous mode of expression. That holding remained in force until 1952, when the Court disavowed it in *Joseph Burstyn v. Wilson.*[22] In *Burstyn,* the Court noted that, because *Mutual Film*

---

19. *Mutual Film Corp.,* 236 U.S.
20. *Id.* at 243–244.
21. *Id.* at 244–245.
22. 343 U.S. 495 (1952). It should be noted, however, that the Court (*per* Justice Douglas) had already articulated the contrary conclusion in dictum in an antitrust case, *United States v. Paramount Pictures, Inc.,* 334 U.S. 131, 166–167 (1948), stating that "We have no doubt that moving pictures, like newspapers and radio, are included in the press whose

Corporation was decided under the Ohio state constitution, "the present case is the first to present squarely to us the question whether motion pictures are within the ambit of protection which the First Amendment, through the Fourteenth, secures to any form of 'speech' or the 'press.'"[23]

In answering that question, the Court first conceded that "it cannot be doubted that motion pictures are a significant medium for the communication of ideas." The Court stated that "[t]hey may affect public attitudes and behavior in a variety of ways, ranging from direct espousal of a political or social doctrine to the subtle shaping of thought which characterizes all artistic expression."[24] The Court went on to reject the profit motive of filmmaking as grounds for excluding motion pictures from the First Amendment, noting that such was indeed the case for books, newspapers, and magazines.[25]

The concerns that animated the opinion in *Mutual Film Corporation* were addressed by Justice Clark's opinion in *Joseph Burstyn, Inc.*:

> IT is further urged that motion pictures possess a greater capacity for evil, particularly among the youth of a community, than other modes of expression. Even if one were to accept that hypothesis, it does not follow that motion pictures should be disqualified from First Amendment protection. If there be capacity for evil it may be relevant in determining the permissible scope of community control, but it does not authorize substantially unbridled censorship such as we have here.[26]

For these reasons, the Court found that films were within the scope of the First Amendment, and overruled *Mutual Film Corporation* "to the extent that language in [that opinion] it is out of harmony with the views here set forth."[27] However, this marked the beginning of the analysis for the Court, not its end. The Court stated that the extension of First Amendment protection to films does not create a license to exhibit any kind of film at all times and all places, as "is evident from the series of decisions from this Court with respect to other media of communication of ideas."[28]

---

freedom is guaranteed by the First Amendment." However, the Court found in *Paramount Pictures* that the government's claim that the defendant exercised a monopoly of showings at first-run theaters in a specific geographical zone "bears only remotely, if at all, on any question of freedom of the press, save only as timeliness of release may be a factor of importance in specific situations."

23. 343 U.S. at 501.
24. *Id.* at 501.
25. *Id.* at 501–502.
26. *Id.* at 502.
27. *Id.*
28. *Id.* at 502–503. The authority cited by the Court for this pronouncement is curious, listing as it does *Chaplinsky v. New Hampshire* (a case that involved speech deemed to be *outside*

More ominously, the Court stated that its conclusion that the First Amendment protects speech did not mean "that motion pictures are necessarily subject to the precise rules governing any other method of expression. Each method tends to present its own peculiar problems."[29] However, "the basic principles of freedom of speech and the press, like the First Amendment's command, do not vary," and those principles make freedom the rule.[30] Thus, the Court found that the New York statute that required prior approval of the content of films for their exhibition and provided no standards by which they were to be judged was unlawful as prior restraint—a direct nullification of *Mutual Film Corporation*'s holding. The Court in *Burstyn* split the baby neatly in half—*yes*, films receive some level of First Amendment protection and blanket prior restraint is unconstitutional; but *no*, they are not necessarily subject to the same rules that govern any other particular method of expression—which "allowed" the Court to ratify measures that are directed at the unique harms caused by motion pictures.

Burstyn's impact was not at first clear. In an encouraging sign of greater freedom for motion pictures, the Court summarily reversed a general censorship scheme in 1954.[31] Concurring in the brusque, one-sentence judgment that merely announced that the lower court's approval of the censorship scheme was reversed, citing *Burstyn*, Justice Douglas (joined by Justice Black) squarely rejected the notion that motion pictures were somehow different from other forms of speech:

> MOTION pictures are of course a different medium of expression than the public speech, the radio, the stage, the novel, or the magazine. But the First Amendment draws no distinction between the various methods of communicating ideas. On occasion one may be more powerful than another. The movie, like the public speech, radio or television, is transitory—here now and gone in an instant. The novel, the short story, the poem in printed form are permanently at hand to re-enact the drama or to retell the story over and again. Which medium will give the most excitement and will have the most enduring effect

---

the First Amendment); *Feiner v. New York*, 340 U.S. 315 (1951) (an application of the *Chaplinsky* "fighting words" doctrine); and two cases in which the Court upheld what were purely restrictions of the time, manner, and place of admittedly protected speech, *Cox v. New Hampshire*, 312 U.S. 569 (1941) (upholding state requirement that a permit be obtained for a parade on a public street) and *Kovacs v. Cooper*, 336 U.S. 77 (1949).

To the extent that the Court's language is meant to suggest that substantive limitation on the content of protected speech is defensible, its citations simply do not support its premise.

29. 343 U.S. at 503.
30. *Id.*
31. *Superior Films v. Department of Education*, 346 U.S. 587 (1954).

will vary with the theme and the actors. It is not for the censors to determine in any case.[32]

The Court, in a very narrow decision, seemed to undermine the *Burstyn* compromise in *Times Film Corp. v. Chicago.*[33] In that decision, the Court rejected a challenge to the facial validity of a Chicago city ordinance that required the submission of motion pictures to a board of censors prior to their public exhibition. Like the standards disapproved by the *Burstyn* court, the general licensing scheme was upheld in *Times Film Corp.* The Court refused to invalidate this classic instance of prior restraint—the essence of the *pre*-Constitutional immunity that was afforded freedom of speech.[34] The Court, in support of its upholding of the broad censorship of motion pictures,[35] recast the opinion in *Burstyn* to suggest that the decision had gone the other way:

> WE recognized in *Burstyn* that capacity for evil may be relevant in determining the permissible scope of community control, and that motion pictures were not necessarily subject to the precise rules governing any other method of expression. Each method, we said, tends to present its own peculiar problems.[36]

Chief Justice Warren pointed out the extent to which this paraphrase of *Burstyn* distorted the phrases that were drawn from it and strung together by the Court:

> OUR prior decisions do not deal with the *content* of the speech; they deal only with the conditions surrounding its delivery. *These* conditions "tend to present the problems peculiar to each method of expression." Here the Court uses this magical phrase to cripple a basic principle of the Constitution.[37]

Despite this unanswerable rejoinder, the Court concluded with a generalization that resembles Frankfurter's overall approach to the First Amend-

---

32. *Id.* at 589 (Douglas, J. concurring).
33. 365 U.S. 43 (1961).
34. The dissenters in *Times Film Corp.* pressed this very argument, but to no avail; *see id.* at 51–53 (Warren, C. J., dissenting); 78, 81–84 (Douglas, J.).
35. Just how broad censorship of motion pictures had been under the kind of statute upheld by the Court in *Times Film Corp.* is demonstrated in the dissenting opinion of Chief Justice Warren, joined by Justices Black, Douglas, and Brennan. 365 U.S. at 69–72 (detailing censorship of films from Chaplin's *The Great Dictator* to the "innocuous comedy of fifty years ago" *Brewster's Millions*).
36. *Id.* at 49.
37. *Id.* at 78 (Warren, C. J., dissenting).

ment, but no other, "It is not for this Court to limit the State in its selection of the remedy it deems most effective to cope with such a problem, absent, of course, a showing of unreasonable strictures on individual liberty resulting from its application in particular circumstances."[38] Justice Black's fear of a watered-down First Amendment had, in the context of new media, at any rate, finally come to pass.

Fortunately, the balance swung the other way again, beginning in *Freedman v. Maryland.*[39] In that decision, the Court (*per* Justice Brennan) pointed out the sharply limited nature of the holding in *Times Film Corp.* That decision had held (as opposed to its more sweeping analysis, as set out above, that the mere requirement of a license did not violate the First Amendment. Indeed, the Court stated, the actual holding, based on its extraordinarily narrow question presented, could not even be understood as vindicating the Chicago ordinance, the challenge to which was rejected.[40] In Justice Brennan's opinion, the general "heavy presumption" against the validity of prior restraint was reasserted and certain minimal procedural protections laid down: that the censor must bear the burden of proving that "the film is unprotected expression," and that a speedy judicial determination must follow the censor's determination that the film in question be denied a license.[41]

The trend continued in *Interstate Circuit v. Dallas,*[42] in which the Court reverted to the original conception of *Burstyn,* to the extent that it struck down a statutory scheme that authorized an administrative board to classify motion pictures as "not suitable for children" based on the vagueness of the standard that the board was to use in determining that classification.

Burstyn, Times, and *Interstate Circuit* can actually be rather easily reconciled; *Burstyn* and *Interstate Circuit* voided particular schema on the grounds that they failed to provide the censor with appropriate guidance in determining on which side of the protected line particular films would fall; *Times* nonetheless vindicated the general proposition that such standards could permissibly be drawn with greater laxity in the case of motion pictures than in the case of, say, the novels upon which films are based.

By 1975, when the Court decided *Erznozik v. City of Jacksonville,*[43] motion pictures were being treated as the same as more traditional texts for the purpose of determining the impact of the First Amendment. In *Erznozik,* the Court voided a statute that prohibited the showing of motion pictures that

38. *Id.* at 50.
39. 380 U.S. 51 (1965).
40. *Id.* at 54.
41. *Id.* at 58–59.
42. 390 U.S. 676 (1968).
43. 422 U.S. 205 (1975).

included nudity at drive-in theaters. Because the City "concede[d] that its ordinance sweeps far beyond the permissible restraints on obscenity," it "thus applies to films that are protected by the First Amendment."[44] The Court, in applying general First Amendment overbreadth principles[45] to strike the statute, stated that "[s]peech that is neither obscene as to youth nor subject to some other legitimate proscription cannot be suppressed solely to protect the young from ideas or images that a legislative body thinks unsuitable for them."[46] Interestingly, not even the dissent tried to argue that movies were somehow different from other speech, and, just like the majority opinion, drew its analogies from a variety of contexts.[47] Indeed, by *Young v. American Mini Theatres, Inc.*,[48] Justice Powell was able, in his concurring opinion, to summarize the jurisprudence thus:

> MOTION pictures, the medium involved here, are fully within the protection of the First Amendment. In the quarter century since *Burstyn*, motion pictures and an analogous medium, printed books, have been before this Court on many occasions, and the person asserting a First Amendment claim often has been a theater owner or a bookseller. Our cases reveal, however, that the central concern of the First Amendment in this area is that there be a free flow from creator to audience of whatever message a film or book might convey. Mr. Justice Douglas stated this core idea succinctly: "In this Nation, every writer, actor, or producer, no matter what medium he may use, should be free from the censor."[49]

A similar evolution has taken place with respect to broadcast media as well, with governmental regulation of the new media at first rather broad, but narrowing over time, although levels of governmental control over the broadcast media are still dramatically greater than is permissible in the print context.[50]

---

44. *Id.* at 208, *citing Burstyn.*
45. *Overbreadth* is the concept in constitutional review that a statute that is facially void as sweeping beyond the pale of constitutionally permissible regulation may be struck even if the conduct at issue in the particular case is not within the ambit of protection. Thus, an admittedly obscene film could have served as a vehicle to challenge the statute at issue in *Erznozik* (although this was not in fact the case), even though it could have been prosecuted under an appropriate, narrower statute. *Id.* at 212–213.
46. *Id.* at 213.
47. *Id.* at 218–224 (Burger, C. J., dissenting).
48. 427 U.S. 50 (1976) (upholding time, manner, place, zoning regulations as to adult theaters).
49. *Id.* at 77, *quoting Superior Films v. Department of Education*, 346 U.S. 587, 589 (Douglas, J., concurring) (1954) (citations omitted).
50. *See* Lawrence Tribe, *American Constitutional Law* (2d ed. 1988) at 1001–1010 (discussing Supreme Court approval of regulation of radio and television from 1943–1988, noting

As seen in Chapter 3, most regulations on broadcast media are justified by what has been termed by the Supreme Court the "scarcity rationale."[51] This rationale was held to completely obviate any First Amendment claim to justify the denial or removal of radio licenses from operators that the Federal Communications Commission (FCC) deemed to be "not in the public interest," as long as such action was rational. Likewise, admittedly protected speech has been banned from the airwaves without any effort to justify the result in terms of the First Amendment.[52]

In vain did Justice Murphy argue that the unique nature of radio militated in favor of greater scrutiny of the FCC's use of its authority:

> [B]ECAUSE of its vast potentialities as a medium of communication, discussion and propaganda, the character and extent of control that should be exercised over radio is a matter of deep and vital concern. Events in Europe show that radio may readily be a weapon of authority and misrepresentation, instead of a means of entertainment or enlightenment. It may even be an instrument of oppression. In pointing out these possibilities, I do not mean to intimate in the slightest that they are imminent or probable in this country, but they do suggest that the construction of the instant statute should be approached with more than ordinary restraint and caution, to avoid an interpretation that is not clearly justified by the conditions that brought about its enactment, or that would give the commission greater powers than Congress meant to confer.[53]

That plea, repeated in stronger terms by Justices Douglas and Brennan, has yet to meet with a response. However, it is clear that the FCC no longer wields its authority over broadcast media with anything like its former strictness. The success of "shock jock" Howard Stern in fending off the FCC's efforts to moderate his daily programs and the steamy *NYPD Blue* bear witness to the decreasing urge to regulate. The general proposition of William O. Douglas that censorship stems from fear is reflected by the trend that as a

---

expansion of First Amendment protection to broadcast media, although still far short of the quantum of protection accorded print media).

51. *See generally, Turner Broadcasting System, Inc. v. FCC,* 512 U.S. 622 (1994).

52. *National Broadcasting Co. v. United States,* 319 U.S. 190, 226–227 (1943) (*per* Frankfurter, J.). The Court did, however, state that such deprivations should not be based upon disagreement with viewpoint, suggesting that the new medium was not entirely invisible to the First Amendment; *see also Federal Radio Commission v. Nelson Bros. Bond and Mortgage Co.,* 289 U.S. 266, 277 (1933) (upholding redistribution of licenses that deprived broadcaster of outlet as long as FRC action not "arbitrary and capricious"); *compare FCC v. Pacifica Foundation,* 438 U.S. 726 (1978) (permitting regulation of George Carlin's "Seven Dirty Words" monologue based on "uniquely pervasive" nature of medium).

53. *National Broadcasting Co.,* 319 U.S. at 228 (Murphy, J. dissenting).

medium becomes less revolutionary and more ubiquitous, the fear impulse declines and regulation diminishes. The importance of this proposition in understanding the unique position of the Internet is to underscore the critical need to segregate this fear component of regulation from the peculiarities of the Internet. Only then can the new medium's impact upon the First Amendment's operation be evaluated.

THE NET'S SPREAD

If literally hundreds of books have been written discussing the Internet, and monthly/weekly/daily magazines regarding it are pumped out all over the country, the nature of this new medium is very much in flux. Operating through modem communications over telephone lines, the Internet, briefly, is "not a physical or tangible entity, but is rather a giant network which interconnects innumerable smaller groups of linked computer networks. It is thus a network of networks."[54] The idea of linking computers for communication purposes, ranging from the transmitting of hand-entered e-mail to accessing a broader file base, is, of course, nothing new. Even within relatively low-tech offices, such computer link-ups have been available for decades. The Internet is the logical evolution of such technology, writ large.

The Internet originated in 1969 as an experimental project of the Advanced Research Projects Agency (known by the acronym ARPA) that linked computers and computer networks that were owned by the military, defense contractors, and university laboratories that conducted defense-oriented research.[55] At that stage, it was known as the ARPANET. From there, the linked series of networks gradually expanded to include other academic specialties, as well as other communities; it began to incorporate private citizens, corporations, and other universities. The end result—known first as the DARPA Internet, and then finally as the Internet[56]—was (and is) an ever-expanding series of discrete computer networks that permit the global exchange of ideas in an almost chaotic frothing.

Although a description of the Internet is best left to those who are expert in its use and development, and can become in itself a distraction (in two judicial opinions reviewing the federal statute regulating Internet speech, a description of the Internet alone took up a major portion of the

---

54. *American Civil Liberties Union v. Reno,* 929 F. Supp. 824 (E.D.Pa.) (12 June 1996), *American Library Ass'n v. Department of Justice,* 96 Cv. 1458 (consolidated), 929 F. Supp. 824, 830 (hereinafter cited as *ACLU v. Reno*).
55. *Shea on Behalf of American Reporter v. Reno,* 930 F. Supp. 916, 925–926 (S.D.N.Y. 1996) (hereinafter cited as *Shea v. Reno*); *see also ACLU v. Reno,* 929 F. Supp. at 831.
56. *Shea v. Reno,* 930 F. Supp. at 926; *ACLU v. Reno,* 929 F. Supp. at 831.

opinions), the growing ubiquity of this form of communication is breath-taking: in 1996 it was estimated that as many as 40 million individuals had access to the Internet, and that figure was expected to grow to 200 million by the end of the century.[57]

Moreover, the evolution of the technology—in increasing the speed of communication and amount of data which can be sent from one computer to another—has been such that the information that can be accessed is now different in kind, not merely in degree, from that available a mere two decades ago. Realistic sound and video images can now be processed, permitting interactive functioning between computer user and file, and between users. While some of the uses to which this new wave of technology have been put could be considered frivolous, almost no restrictions exist on the Internet: The imposition of any restrictions would require a radical rethinking of the entire medium.

Decentralization is almost the essence of the Internet: The ability to access files and to engage in electronic discussion creates an atmosphere of opportunity and great freedom. One's ability to do research on the Internet is limited only by one's growing knowledge of the almost infinite resources. The ability to create fora for discussion is, quite literally, unlimited: Anyone can send e-mail to thousands of like-minded (or un-likeminded, for that matter) people, or create a Web site, that is, a self-edited, easily found "place" on the super-network known as the World Wide Web to promulgate messages on any subject one wishes—from aardvarks to Zoroastrianism.[58] According to its proponents, the Internet, as long as it remains cheap and uncensored, bids fair to render, through on-line self-publishing, the individual speaker an equal competitor with the largest multinational conglomerates in the marketplace of ideas.[59]

One need not take so euphoric a view of the Internet to realize that its capacity is indeed enormous. Moreover, the technology is still in flux. As has been noted by at least one panel of judges who were trying to come to grips with the nature of the Internet and the impact of the new medium on constitutional guarantees of freedom of expression[60]:

> IN seeking to describe the range of tools and opportunities for Internet users to speak, we recognize the categories we delineate are far from clean, and the technology is far from static. Indeed, by all indications, the way that we conceptualize various media that we have tradition-

---

57. 930 F. Supp. at 926.
58. *See* 930 F. Supp. at 927–930; *ACLU v. Reno*, 929 F. Supp. at 831–838.
59. 929 F. Supp. at 842–844.
60. It is just this cart-before-the-horse view of the First Amendment–new medium interplay that has led, I argue, to the loss of coherence in First Amendment jurisprudence.

ally viewed as distinct—such as cable television, telephones and computer networks—will change dramatically as these media "converge" into common forms of communication.[61]

There has not actually yet evolved a juridical[62] consensus as to how the First Amendment immunizes (or fails to immunize) speech on this new and somewhat intimidating medium. A few decisions, accompanied by a spate of law review articles and books have, it is true, come forward, but the issues are still so new that no distinct "majority" view has had time for its views to set in the public imagination, let alone to be integrated into our increasingly rickety constitutional consensus.

As has been noted "[t]he scope of permissible government limitations on 'cyberspeech' will depend in part on the level of First Amendment scrutiny applied by courts to laws that regulate on-line communications."[63] However, the analysis that will be used is not self-evident. One commentator, fairly accurately, has opined that "the level of scrutiny will in turn depend on the type of communications media to which the courts analogize online networks."[64] The greatest First Amendment protection has been applied to print media—the classic newspaper-book paradigm, media that existed in much the same form today as they did at the time the First Amendment was ratified. If "courts find that electronic media are most similar to such media, a government regulation restricting online speech will have to be narrowly tailored to serve a compelling state interest in order to pass constitutional muster."[65]

This assessment is true at the *initial* stage of review, but is not necessarily dispositive of any given case. Should any particular on-line utterance fall into the category of a wholly—or even partially—unprotected *Chaplinsky* category, the mere fact that it is disseminated over the Internet does not somehow act to miraculously immunize it from proscription and pun-

---

61. *Shea v. Reno*, 930 F. Supp. at 930 (*citing Denver Area Educ. Telecommunications Consortium v. FCC*, 518 U.S. 727, 776–777 & n. 4, (1996) (Souter, J., concurring); Jerry Berman & Daniel Weitzner, *Abundance & User Control: Renewing the Democratic Heart of the First Amendment in the Age of Interactive Media*, 104 Yale L.J. 1619, 1619 n. 1 (1995).

62. Because of the overlap between "judicial" and "juridical," words that are frequently used, even in legal academic parlance, to mean the same thing, I should perhaps pause to note that, throughout this book, "judicial" means simply what judges decide or will do—the law, in Holmes's bleakest sense of what judges say or do. Juridical I take as a broader term, denoting the view or opinions among the informal community of scholars and practitioners—all who study jurisprudential issues.

63. Charles L. White, "Censorship," in Alan Bomser, *et al.*, *A Lawyer's Ramble Down the Information Superhighway*, 64 Ford. L. Rev. 700, 805–806 (1995).

64. *Id.* at 806.

65. *Id.*

ishment.[66] Thus, to some extent, the issues of Internet regulation have been framed in a misleading manner. The question is not whether speech on the Internet is subject to any regulation, but rather whether the means of transmission should render speech liable to additional regulation.

Of course, how these standards will in practice apply to speech over the Internet is by no means self-evident. To take but one example, the application of "contemporary community standards" in determining the obscenity (or indecency) of any given communication requires the determination of what is the appropriate meaning of a "community" in the context of communications through the Internet between individuals in distant geographical regions, which might present widely diverging community standards. [67] The result of the magazine-film-video–oriented jurisprudence that arose in *Miller v. California*,[68] and that was restated in *Hamling v. United States*[69] "as a matter of constitutional law and federal statutory construction, is to permit a juror sitting in obscenity cases to draw on knowledge from the community or vicinage from which he comes in deciding what conclusion the 'average person applying contemporary community standards' would reach in a given case."[70]

According to the Court in *Miller*, three reasons justified this reliance on *local* community standards. First, the determination was deemed one of "fact," not of "law," and thus the commonsense approach of jurors was simply more appropriate, and necessarily involved their bringing with them their own ideas about what was obscene, presumed to be typical of their community.[71] Second, the alternative, erection of a national standard, was deemed to be "futile." This futility argument was predicated on the assumption that a national standard would require that jurors, who the Court questionably stated have been "traditionally" permitted "to draw on the standards of their community, guided always by limiting instructions on the law,"[72] extrapolate a consensus that does not exist about what is not obscene.[73] Finally,

---

66. *See*, for example, *United States v. Thomas*, 74 F.3d 701, 710–712 (6th Cir. 1996) (upholding conviction under general federal obscenity statute for promulgation of obscene materials through the Internet). *See also* Ruth Hill Bro, "The Role of the First Amendment Online," in Thomas J. Smedingoff, ed., *Online Law* (1996) at 305–313 (summarizing categories). *See also Mainstream Loudoun v. Board of Trustees of the Loudon County Library*, 24 F. Supp. 2d 552 (E.D. Va., Alex. Div. 1998) (applying general standard of rights of access, forbidding removal of library books, to libraries' blocking of access to Internet sites).

67. *See*, for example, Richard Coglianese, *Sex, Bytes and Community Entrapment: The Need for a New Obscenity Standard for the Twenty-First Century*, 24 Cap. L. Rev. 385 (1995).

68. 413 U.S. 15 (1973).

69. 418 U.S. 87 (1974).

70. *Hamling*, 418 U.S. at 105. Oddly, this result is somehow equated by the Court as the functional equivalent of the "reasonable person," although no authority has ever tethered the "reasonable person" standard to local prejudices or viewpoints. *Id.* at 104–105.

71. *Id.* at 103 (explicating *Miller v. California*, 413 U.S. at 31–32).

72. *Miller v. California*, 413 U.S. at 30.

73. Of course, this rationale suggests that obscenity *deserves* protection—both because it raises the existence of substantive disagreement as to the worth or social utility of so-called

"People in different States vary in their tastes, and this diversity is not to be strangled by the absolutism of imposed uniformity."[74]

This final rationale is the only one of the three that carries any weight, as it at least plays into what the Court has deemed to be the "legitimate state interests in stemming the tide of commercialized obscenity."[75] As the Court explained in *Paris Adult Theatre I v. Slaton*:

> [E]VEN assuming it is feasible to enforce effective safeguards against exposure to juveniles and to passersby. . . . The interest of the public in the quality of life and the total community environment, the tone of commerce in the great city centers, and, possibly, the public safety itself is implicated.[76]

The Internet presents a conflict about what the local community standard should mean, because its self-contained nature sets two of these three concerns at odds with the third. If, on the one hand, the principal reason to use a geographic locality as the basic hallmark is to prevent the obscenity determination from becoming an abstract issue of law, as suggested by the first two grounds, then the "community standard" to be applied plainly should be that of the district in which the case is tried, as the Court found in *Hamling*. On the other hand, if the question is one of "quality of life," "tone," or risk of exposure to juveniles or unconsenting adults, it simply makes no sense to refer to a geographic community, as only those who deliberately join the Internet community *can* be exposed to the materials. The application of geographically based community standards in the Internet context fails to serve the very interests it was created to protect. Additionally, the dilemma of Internet posters who may be haled into court in communities of which they have never heard, let alone knowingly directed materials to, is even more severe than in the case of film producers who at least are in a contractual relationship with those who distribute their films. The Internet user who chooses to go on-line joins a specific and discrete community in which the potential for exposure to offensive materials is limited to those who are on-line—and bears no relationship to geographical proximity.

---

obscene speech, and because it highlights the risk that the regulation of such speech is a classic instance of the "tyranny of the majority" against which the First Amendment is intended to guard.

74. *Miller*, 413 U.S. at 33. Again, the argument that "taste" should be respected and not dictated seems to me a strange argument to support censorship. The impact of this factor upon on-line "obscenity" is briefly discussed in Ruth Hill Bro, "Sexually Explicit Materials in a Digital World" in Thomas J. Smedinghoff, ed. *Online Law* (1996) at 321–323.

75. *Paris Adult Theatre I v. Slaton*, 413 U.S. 49, 57–59 (1973).

76. *Id.* at 58–59.

Such courts as have discussed the Internet in general terms, or in libel actions, have tended to apply the more stringent tests applied in the context of printed media, and not to relate the Internet to the more heavily regulated broadcast media.[77] As one such court explained, in *Cubby, Inc. v. CompuServe, Inc.*,[78] "a computerized database is the functional equivalent of a more traditional news vendor, and the inconsistent application of a lower standard of liability to an electronic news distributor such as CompuServe than that which is applied to a public library, book store or newsstand would impose an undue burden on the free flow of information." However, with the onset of federal regulation as a component of the Telecommunications Act of 1996, that picture began to change.

The Problem of Federal Regulation: "Indecency" and the CDA

The basic issue of what level of scrutiny will be applied to regulations imposed specifically on on-line speech has been presented squarely. The Supreme Court has only recently rendered its first decision concerning the quantum of First Amendment protection to be applied to the Internet. However, in view of the newness of the issue, the lower court opinions are of considerable interest as well. The Supreme Court can, after all, reverse itself. Although a negative decision binds the lower courts, and it is the law of the land unless and until it is overruled, the Court has no monopoly of wisdom. As Justice Robert H. Jackson once memorably put it, the Court is not final because it is infallible, but rather is infallible only because it is final.[79] As we have repeatedly seen, even the greatest jurists refine their ideas over time, and constitutional jurisprudence is rather like a shark—it dies if it stops moving.

As a component of the Telecommunications Act of 1996,[80] Congress passed what is known as the CDA, the Communications Decency Act of 1996.[81] The CDA adds restrictions on the promulgation of "indecent" speech through the Internet to the previously extant prohibitions of the use of the telephone lines for obscene communications. Already, three-judge panels in two districts have reviewed the CDA and both have found it to be unconstitutional.[82] As it amends Section 223(a)(1)(B) of title 47 of the U.S. Code,

---

77. *See*, White, *supra* note 63, at 806–807 (collecting cases).
78. 776 F. Supp. 135, 140, S.D.N.Y. (1991).
79. *Brown v. Allen*, 344 U.S. 443, 540 (1953) (Jackson, J. concurring).
80. Pub.L.No. 104–104, 110 Stat. 56, 133–135 (1996).
81. 47 U.S.C. sec. 223(a)(1)(B), (a)(2), and (d), as amended or added to by Title V, § 502 of the Telecommunications Act of 1996.
82. *ACLU v. Reno*, 929 F. Supp. at 849, *et seq.*; *Shea v. Reno*, 930 F. Supp. 923, *et seq.*

the CDA provides that "any person in interstate or foreign communications who by means of a telecommunications device knowingly makes, creates or solicits and initiates the transmission of any comment, request, suggestion, proposal, image or other communication which is obscene or *indecent*, knowing that the recipient of the communication is under 18 years of age, shall be criminally fined or imprisoned."[83]

Section 223(d)(1) as amended by the CDA criminalizes the use of "an interactive computer service to send or display in any manner available to a person under age 18, any comment, request, suggestion, proposal, image or other communication that, in context, depicts or describes, in terms patently offensive as measured by contemporary community standards, sexual or excretory activities or organs, regardless of whether the user of such service placed the call or initiated the communication."[84]

Additionally, the CDA makes it a crime "for anyone to knowingly permit any telecommunications facility under his or her control to be used for any activity prohibited in sections 223(a)(1)(B) and 223(d)(1)."[85] The expansive sweep of this law is not, perhaps, clear on its face. As a result of the CDA, Internet providers have, essentially, three choices. They can seek to prevent minors from accessing the Internet at all, thereby grossly restricting its educational value, or they can limit its content to what is fit for children—a ban that would be tremendously difficult to enforce. The third option is that actually hinted at in the CDA, which provides for so-called "safe harbor" defenses.

In order to invoke these defenses, Internet providers are required to devise a means by which indecent materials may be screened away from children, whether by requiring the use of a credit card or other verification of age and identity. The erection of such access barriers "in good faith," according to the statute, need only be "effective";[86] according to the Conference Report, a barrier "does not require an absolute 100 percent restriction of access to be judged effective."[87]

In evaluating the constitutionality of the CDA, it is helpful to know first what it is *not*. The CDA, according to its framers, is not an application of the

---

83. *ACLU v. Reno*, 929 F. Supp. at 828 (emphasis in original, internal quotation marks and ellipses omitted). The text of the CDA is available as well in H.R. Rep. 104–458, the Conference Report accompanying § 652, the final version of the Telecommunications Act of 1996, and is set out in part in *Shea v. Reno*, 930 F. Supp. at 923–924.

84. *ACLU v. Reno*, 929 F. Supp. at 829 (internal quotations omitted) (summarizing 47 U.S.C. §223(d)(1) as amended by the CDA).

85. *Id.* (internal quotations omitted) (summarizing 47 U.S.C., §§ 223 (a)(2) and 223(d)(2).

86. 47 U.S.C. § 223(e)(5)(A).

87. H.R. Rep. 104–458 at 190, reprinted at 104 Cong., 2d Sess. (Vol. 4) *U.S. Code Cong. & Admin. News* at 200, 202–205 (1997).

"variable obscenity" concept endorsed by the Supreme Court in *Ginsberg v. New York.*[88] Under that concept the obscenity of a communication varies as to its audience. Thus, a communication that is protected when directed to and read by adults may not be protected if marketed to or (and here is the difficulty) even simply received by minors. The Conference Report accompanying the CDA makes quite clear, however, that this controversial and little invoked provision is not at the heart of the CDA:

> THE conferees considered, but rejected, the so-called "harmful to minors" standard. [ ] The proponents of the "harmful to minors" standard contended that that standard contains an exemption for material with "serious literary, artistic, political and scientific value," and therefore was the better of the two alternative standards. ("Harmful to minors" laws use the "variable obscenity" test and prohibit the sale, and sometimes the display, of certain sexually explicit materials to minors.)[89]

Rather than seeking to ground its prohibitions on the slippery (and somewhat suspect) foundation of "variable obscenity," Congress chose instead to codify the indecency test as approved by the Court in its application to broadcast media and telephone communications. According to the Conference Committee:

> THE gravamen of the indecency concept is "patent offensiveness." Such a determination cannot be made without a consideration of the context of the description or depiction at issue. It is the understanding of the conferees that, as applied, the patent offensiveness inquiry involves two distinct elements: the intention to be patently offensive, and a patently offensive result. [ ] Material with serious redeeming value is quite obviously intended to edify and educate, not to offend. Therefore it will be imperative to consider the context and the nature of the material in question when considering its "patent offensiveness."[90]

Congress's belief in these two propositions is integral to its conclusion that "use of the indecency standard poses no significant risk to the free-wheeling and vibrant nature of discourse or to serious, literary, and artistic works that currently can be found on the Internet, and which is expected to continue and grow."[91] Moreover, the report notes, citing *Pacifica*, "pro-

---

88. 390 U.S. 629, 640–641 (1968).
89. H.R.Rep. 104–458 at 189 (*citing Ginsberg v. New York*, 390 U.S. at 641–643).
90. *Id.* (*citing In the Matter of Sagittarius Broadcasting Corp., et al,* 7 F.C.C. Rcd. 6873, 6875 [1992]; *In the Matter of Audio Enterprises, Inc.,* 3 F.C.C. Rcd. 930, 932 [1987]).
91. *Id.*

hibiting indecency merely forces speakers to re-cast their message into less offensive terms, but does not prohibit or disfavor the essential meaning of the communication."[92] Accordingly, the syllogism concludes, "requiring that access restrictions be imposed to protect minors from exposure to indecent material does not prohibit or disfavor the essential meaning of the indecent communication, it merely puts it in its proper place: away from children."[93]

The explanation of Congress of its use of the indecency standard, whether one accepts or rejects its value judgments, is predicated on several errors as to the law of indecency. First and foremost, the assumption of Congress that works with "serious literary artistic political and scientific value"—works that are not obscene, in other words—are ipso facto not indecent because they are not intended to offend is just wrong.

To the extent that the conferees acted under the assumption that an *intent* to offend a specific audience is built into the indecency standard, the report simply reads into both the *Pacifica* decision and its progeny an element that is lacking both in the constitutional standard and in the statutes upheld by the Court in those cases. Although an intent to publish the comment later deemed to be indecent may be found in (at least) the upheld statutes, there is nothing in *Pacifica* and its progeny to suggest specific intent to offend any audience, hypothetical or actual.

Additionally, the standard in fact *does* permit the censorship of materials of "serious literary, artistic, political, or scientific value." In another indecency context, that of child pornography, the Court opened the doorway to prosecution of just such materials if sexually explicit depictions of children were involved.[94]

Moreover, the indecency standard, in addition to being greatly subjective, has not been granted general applicability to materials in society at large, but has been confined to certain contexts. In the seminal indecency case, *FCC v. Pacifica Foundation*,[95] after adverting to the "aptly sketched" lowly place of indecent speech in the "hierarchy of First Amendment values,"[96] the Court stated that "[a]lthough these words ordinarily lack serious literary, political or scientific value, they are not entirely outside of the protection of the First Amendment." In the context of radio, the Court found two factors that

---

92. *Id.*
93. *Id.*
94. *New York v. Ferber*, 458 U.S. 747, 773 (plurality opinion); 774–775 (O'Connor, J. concurring and dissenting) (1982).
95. 438 U.S. at 746.
96. Again, the blithe assumption that such a hierarchy exists and is legitimately to be found in the simple command of the First Amendment is the continuing legacy of *Chaplinsky*—which was explicitly relied on by the Court in its opinion in *Pacifica*.

permitted the imposition of a time, manner, and place regulation, proscribing indecent speech from being broadcast at hours when children would likely be exposed to it.[97]

The first factor was the Court's conclusion that "the broadcast media have established a uniquely pervasive presence in the lives of all Americans," and that "[p]atently offensive, indecent materials confront the citizen, not only in public, but also in the privacy of the home, where the individual's right to be left alone plainly outweighs the First Amendment rights of an intruder."[98] Because the ongoing nature of a broadcast renders the efficacy of warnings to the unknowing audience impossible, this right to be left alone was thought by the Court to be extremely important.

The second factor militating in favor of the Court's decision in favor of the FCC was based on its conclusion that "broadcasting is uniquely accessible to children, even those too young to read."[99] The Court feared that, unlike written indecency, which children might fail to understand, "Pacifica's broadcast could have enlarged a child's vocabulary in an instant."[100] Unlike broadcasting, "[o]ther forms of expression may be withheld from the young without restricting the expression at its source."[101]

Subsequent to the Court's holding in *Pacifica*, however, the principal rationale advanced in support of the limited level of protection of broadcast speech has been the scarcity rationale, as discussed in Chapter 3.[102]

---

97. *Pacifica*, 438 U.S. at 748, 750.
98. *Id.* at 748.
99. *Id.* at 749.
100. *Id.*
101. *Id.*
102. That *Pacifica* has been relegated to a backseat in the jurisprudence as the "scarcity rationale" distinguishes broadcast media from others is made clear in the cases qualifying it, from *Bolger v. Youngs Drug Products Corp.*, 463 U.S. 60, 74 (1983) (refusing to extend *Pacifica* to statute unrelated to broadcasting, noting that broadcasting is "*uniquely* pervasive" and "*uniquely* accessible to children") (emphasis in original) and *Sable Communications v. FCC*, 492 U.S. 115, 127–128 (1989) (same; "dial-a-porn" telephone communications) to *Turner Broadcasting Corp.*, which grounded the *Pacifica* formulation squarely in the scarcity rationale. 512 U.S. 622, 637–641.

However, the plurality opinion in *Denver Area Consortium*, 518 U.S. 727, 744–745 (1996) cast some doubt on this evolution, in upholding a federal statutory provision *permitting* cable operators to prohibit indecent communications on "leased access channels" (that is, channels reserved under federal law for commercial lease by unaffiliated third parties) and in invalidating a provision *requiring* cable operators to either block and segregate such programming should they permit its broadcast as well as a provision granting cable operators the power to prohibit indecent programming on "public access channels" (that is, channels reserved under local franchise agreements for public, educational or governmental purposes). In that case, the plurality revived the "uniquely pervasive" argument in *Pacifica*, which has been largely marginalized since that decision.

Clearly, then, the application by Congress of the indecency standard is flawed in that it (1) did not provide the level of protection that the drafters assumed it did, on the basis of either intent or social value; and (2) it assumed that Internet is more like broadcast speech than printed speech. This assumption that the analogy to broadcasting is an apt one disregards the scarcity rationale, harking back to *Pacifica*'s most general phrasing. In discussing the constitutionality of the CDA, this first error must be borne in mind. The second, the congressional presumption that *Pacifica* created another full-bore *Chaplinsky* category, will be examined en route.

The CDA Before the Courts

The drafters of the CDA knew that their product raised serious constitutional issues. Rather than the normal time-consuming process by which individual district court judges deal with challenges in the first instance, the only guaranteed review comes from the federal courts of appeal for each circuit, and the Supreme Court is free to decline to review even conflicting decisions, Congress enacted an expedited means of securing judicial review in a civil proceeding. First, Congress provided that in any civil action in which a party makes a facial challenge to the constitutionality of the CDA, the challenge would be heard before a three-judge panel acting as the district court.[103] Any decision, whether a final judgment or an interlocutory judgment (that is, a nonfinal judgment entered that affected the issue of constitutionality) by the district court panel would be appealable as a matter of right to the Supreme Court, bypassing the courts of appeals, taking the challenge out of the certiorari process, and thus eliminating the Supreme Court's ability to decline to entertain the appeal.[104]

Notably, the Congress did not extend such grace to those prosecuted under the CDA. These unfortunate "malefactors" could not avail themselves of the expedited appeals process, or of the right to Supreme Court review, but had to follow the traditional slower appeals process—which could, in view of the relatively short jail sentences provided for by the CDA, result in an Internet provider serving his or her entire sentence only to have the statute under which he or she was prosecuted struck as unconstitutional.[105]

Similarly, only a challenge to the facial validity was so advantaged; a challenge that the law was being applied in an unconstitutional manner as against the particular party was relegated to the slower appeals process and could

---

103. 47 U.S.C. § 561 (1996); *see* H.R. Rep. 104–458 at 196–197.
104. 47 U.S.C. § 561(b).
105. H.R. Rep. 104–458 at 197.

only reach the Supreme Court by its exercise of discretion under the certiorari process.[106]

Fortunately, neither of these problems became a reality. Instead, lawsuits that challenged the facial validity of the CDA were brought on 8 February 1996—the very day the CDA was signed into law as part of the Telecommunications Act.[107] Additionally, in the litigation that was decided first, the federal government stipulated that it would not bring any criminal prosecutions until the validity of the act was resolved.[108]

In what became the first action decided, two lawsuits were filed in quick succession in the Eastern District of Pennsylvania by the American Civil Liberties Union and numerous co-plaintiffs, and by the American Library Association, again with numerous co-plaintiffs. These litigations were consolidated and were decided together by the three-judge panel on 11 June 1996.[109] The second action to be decided, filed in the Southern District of New York, was likewise filed on the day the law was signed.[110] That action was decided by the panel on July 29, 1996.[111]

Because the Pennsylvania litigation was briefed and decided on a more expedited basis than was the New York litigation, the New York panel had the earlier opinion before it to focus its findings and to draw upon. The court did so, incorporating certain of the Pennsylvania court's findings and rejecting others.

Both courts found the CDA to be violative of the First Amendment. Although the panel entered a single detailed set of findings of fact, each judge in the *ACLU v. Reno* case rendered a separate opinion. Each opinion focused on a distinct facet of the question of constitutionality. By contrast, the panel in *Shea v. Reno* issued one opinion. Although their reasoning overlaps, the respective panels differed with respect to one of the two grounds to invalidate the Act. Both courts found that the CDA was unconstitutionally overbroad—that is, that although the CDA serves the compelling governmental interest of protecting "the physical and psychological well being of a minor,"[112] it does not do so in a manner "narrowly

---

106. *Id.*
107. Edmund L. Andrews, "Communications Bill Signed, and the Battles Begin Anew," *New York Times*, 9 February 1996, p. A1; *ACLU v. Reno*, 929 F. Supp. at 827; *Shea v. Reno*, 830 F. Supp. at 924.
108. *ACLU v. Reno*, 929 F. Supp. at 827.
109. *Id.* at 824, 827–828.
110. *Shea v. Reno*, 930 F. Supp. at 923–924.
111. *Id.* at 916.
112. *ACLU v. Reno*, 929 F. Supp. at 852 (opinion of Sloviter, Chief Circuit Judge) (*quoting New York v. Ferber*, 458 U.S. at 756–757); *Id.* at 882 (Dalzell, J.); *Shea v. Reno*, 930 F. Supp. at 941 (assuming arguendo that this interest extends to "restricting minors' access to all (or virtually all) 'patently offensive' material").

tailored" to serve this interest without unnecessarily infringing upon protected expression.[113]

The Question of Overbreadth

In the Pennsylvania litigations, each member of the panel wrote a methodical, painstaking opinion that outlined why the author believed that the CDA infringed upon freedom of expression. Chief Judge Sloviter, who principally addressed the issue of overbreadth, first set out the statutory provisions, noting that the statute did not itself equate, as the government urged the Court to do, "indecent" (as used in section 223(a), dealing with materials conveyed by "means of a telecommunications device") with "patently offensive," the actual terms used by the Court in *Pacifica*. Noting that the failure to define "indecent," especially coupled with the requirement that a "patently offensive" communication be judged in context (a requirement *not* extended to "indecent" communication), Chief Judge Sloviter argued that the failure to define and qualify the meaning of "indecency" might be viewed as a "negative pregnant," and provide a ground of distinction between the sections.[114] Because both the plaintiffs and the government were content to construe the sections *in pari materia*, however, the chief judge used the terms in that manner, noting that if the distinction became relevant later in the litigation, she would revisit the ruling.[115]

This step in the opinion significantly points out that, for all the ostensible care put into drafting the CDA, in fact at least one tantalizing ambiguity exists. Because one of the principal grounds urged to invalidate the CDA is the claim that it is unconstitutionally vague, the existence of such a negative pregnant (with the potential to untether the standard by which the indecent expression is to be judged from that created by the Court in *Pacifica*) powerfully reinforces the prospects of that claim's success. On the other hand, it is a fair reading of the understanding of the Conference Committee (if not of the entire House or Senate) to read the two sections as enacting the *Pacifica* standard. The Supreme Court is, at present, divided about whether an enactment should be read to effectuate its plain terms (the position of Justices Scalia and Thomas, and, occasionally, Rehn-

---

113. *ACLU v. Reno*, 929 F.Supp. at 855–857 (opinion of Sloviter, Chief Circuit Judge); *Id.* at 859 (opinion of Buckwalter, D. J.); *Id.* at 882–883 (Dalzell, D. J.) (related vagueness conerns); *Shea v. Reno*, 930 F. Supp. at 939–940, 949–950.

114. 929 F. Supp. at 849–850. A "negative pregnant" is a significant omission that conveys meaning about the intent of the drafters of whatever instrument is to be construed. As aptly quoted by the chief judge "an express statutory requirement here, contrasted with statutory silence there, shows an intent to confine the requirement to the specified instance." *Id.* at 850; *quoting Field v. Mans*, 516 U.S. 59 (1995).

115. 929 F. Supp. at 850–851.

quist), or to effectuate the specific policy intentions of the drafters, as gleaned from the legislative history (an understanding favored by Justices O'Connor and Stevens).[116] The question posed by Chief Judge Sloviter was therefore one that, on Supreme Court review, could be revived; doing so would add extra weight on the scale in favor of a finding that the CDA is void for vagueness.

Chief Judge Sloviter, under the unitary interpretation posed by both plaintiffs and defendants, methodically proceeded to set out the standards applicable for the relief sought by the plaintiffs, a preliminary injunction.[117] A preliminary injunction is appropriately entered if the party seeking the order can establish *first*, that that party is likely to prevail on the merits; *second*, that the party seeking interlocutory relief will be irreparably harmed unless the injunction is granted; and *third*, that the equities between the parties tilt in favor of issuing the injunction. Additionally, the issuance of the injunction must be in the public interest (or, more commonly, must not be against the public interest).[118] Chief Judge Sloviter then pared the issues down to one: Did the plaintiffs carry their burden of establishing a likelihood of success on the merits? If they did, she reasoned, there could hardly be a public interest in enforcing an unconstitutional law, and the irreparable injury of being improperly prosecuted and of being deprived of constitutionally guaranteed freedom of speech were well-established in the jurisprudence.[119]

---

116. For an overview of Justice O'Connor's principles of interpretation, *see* Kermit L. Hall, ed. *The Oxford Companion to the Supreme Court* (1992) at 604–605; for an overview of Justice Stevens', *see id.* at 836–837. For a powerful critique of Justice O'Connor's performance, *see* Jeffery Rosen, "A Majority of One," *New York Times Magazine,* June 3, 2001 at 32 *et seq*; Alan M. Dershowitz, *Supreme Injustice* (2001).

117. *ACLU v. Reno,* 929 F. Supp. at 851; *see generally, Elrod v. Burns,* 427 U.S. 347 (1976); *Amarant v. D'Antonio,* 197 A.D.2d 432, 602 N.Y.S.2d 837, 839 (1st Dep't 1993) (same elements under state law).

118. 929 F. Supp. at 851.

119. *Id.* Chief Judge Sloviter's confidence that these questions of irreparable harm and public interest are redressable and are well-established is fully supported by the Supreme Court's First Amendment jurisprudence. For example, the Court stated in *Elrod v. Burns,* 427 U.S. 347, 373 (1976) stated that "the loss of First Amendment freedoms, for even minimal periods of time, unquestionably constitutes irreparable injury."

Likewise, the Court has recently reiterated that the public interest is served by the protection of free speech, because "our political system and cultural life rest on this ideal." *Turner Broadcasting System v. F.C.C.,* 512 U.S. at 641.

That criminal prosecution itself can constitute irreparable injury, even if the defendant is acquitted or the statute under which the prosecution takes place is later struck down on appeal, has its roots in the rationale underlying the void-for-vagueness doctrine: It is unjust that a citizen should speak in the belief that his or her speech is protected by the First Amendment without clear notice about whether or not his or her conduct violates a statute. The injustice of such a situation compounds the risk that the regulation of speech, which may violate the First Amendment, will impermissibly discourage—"chill" to invoke the metaphor long favored by constitutional lawyers—

From discussing the applicable standard for an award of interlocutory relief, and concluding that the single issue to be resolved was whether the plaintiffs had established a likelihood of success on the merits, the Chief Judge turned to that issue: Had the plaintiffs persuaded her that the likely outcome of the litigation was a declaration of facial unconstitutionality? Like most of the other judges who have considered the quantum of protection, Judge Sloviter found that strict scrutiny must be applied to the CDA, and that it "will only be upheld if it is justified by a compelling government interest and if it is narrowly tailored to effectuate that interest."[120] In so doing, she rejected the analogy to broadcast speech governed under *Pacifica*, not merely on the basis that the scarcity rationale did not apply (an argument explicated by her concurring colleague Judge Dalzell)[121] but on another difference between broadcast media and the Internet: the fact that "an Internet user must act affirmatively and deliberately to retrieve specific information online."[122] The opinion explains:

> EVEN if a broad search will, on occasion, retrieve unwanted materials, the user virtually always receives some warning of its content, significantly reducing the element of surprise or "assault" involved in broadcasting. Therefore, it is highly unlikely that a very young child will be randomly "surfing" the Web and come across "indecent" or "patently offensive" material.[123]

Accordingly, Chief Judge Sloviter concluded, "to the extent the [Supreme] Court employed a less than strict scrutiny standard of review in *Pacifica* and other broadcasting cases, there is no reason to employ a less than strict scrutiny standard of review in this case."[124]

Although the interest in protecting children from harm is concededly compelling, the mere fact that Congress acted in the name of protecting that interest does not foreclose judicial review.[125] Moreover, a broad variety

---

protected speech. In such cases, "a man may the less be required to act at his peril, because the free dissemination of ideas may be the loser." *Smith v. California,* 361 U.S. 147, 151 (1957).

120. *ACLU v. Reno,* 929 F. Supp. at 851. Interestingly, despite a half-hearted effort to argue in its papers that the lower standard applicable to broadcasting applies to the Internet, at the hearing stage, the government conceded that it must meet the strict scrutiny test. *Id., citing* Tr. of Preliminary Injunction Hearing at 121 (May 10, 1996). As will be seen *infra*, the government's shifting and somewhat desperate effort to preserve the CDA strongly reinforced the judgment that the act was unconstitutional—and shows the difficulty of preserving this statute from any but perfunctory review.

121. *Id.* at 874–877.

122. *Id.* at 851–852.

123. *Id.* at 852.

124. *Id., citing Red Lion Broadcasting Co. v. FCC,* 395 U.S. 367 (1969).

125. *Id.* at 852–853.

of explicit but nonthreatening materials are swept up within the CDA's ban—materials such as the Pulitzer prize-winning play "Angels in America" or potentially lifesaving materials regarding HIV transmission posted on the Web by plaintiff Critical AIDS Project, as well as *National Geographic* photographs (shades of the 1950s!) and the materials promulgated by plaintiff Stop Prisoner Rape, could all fall under the interdict of the CDA—yet the government, Chief Judge Sloviter concluded, "has made no showing that it has a compelling interest in preventing a seventeen-year-old minor from accessing such images."[126] This conclusion was buttressed by the fact the legislative findings relied upon by the government constituted "primarily testimony and statements by legislators about the prevalence of obscenity, child pornography and sexual solicitation of children on the Internet"—all of which are reachable under extant, more narrow laws.[127]

Independent from, and more important to the Chief Judge than, the government's failed effort to establish a compelling interest in "regulating the vast range of online material covered or potentially covered by the CDA," the statute's terms swept broadly, inclusive of speech "subject to the full protection of the First Amendment, at least for adults," belying the government's argument that the statute was principally directed at commercial purveyors of pornography.[128] That the CDA would impact upon adults was inherent in the Court's finding "that there is no realistic way for [Internet] providers to ascertain the age of those accessing their materials. As a consequence," Chief Judge Sloviter concluded, "we have found that many speakers who display arguably indecent content on the Internet must choose between silence and the threat of prosecution."[129] In light of these findings, the CDA could hardly be found to have used the least restrictive means to achieve its arguably compelling governmental interest.

---

126. *Id.* at 853. Chief Judge Sloviter also explored perceptively the First Amendment rights of minors under existing Supreme Court doctrine. 929 F. Supp. at 852–853.

127. 929 F. Supp. at 853.

128. *Id.* at 853, 855, 854–855. As the opinion stated at greater length: "In questions of the witnesses and in colloquy with the government attorneys, it became evident that, even if 'indecent' is read as parallel to 'patently offensive,' the terms would cover a broad range of material from contemporary films, plays and books showing or describing sexual activities (*e.g., Leaving Las Vegas*) to controversial contemporary art and photographs showing sexual organs in positions that the government conceded would be patently offensive in some communities (*e.g.,* a Robert Mapplethorpe photograph depicting a man with an erect penis)." *Id.* at 855.

129. *Id.* at 855, *quoting*, Findings of Fact, 929 F. Supp. at 849, at paragraph 122. Indeed, the Court found as a whole that "the CDA's defenses—credit card verification, adult access codes, and adult personal identification numbers—are effectively unavailable for non-commercial, not-for-profit entities." *Id.* at 849. Ironically, the latter are arguably the most valuable Internet speakers, and certainly are those for whose use the Internet originally was developed.

Without repeating at length the similar reasoning in *Shea v. Reno*, the three-judge panel in that case likewise invalidated the statute on the ground that it was overbroad: It arguably addressed an interest that was admittedly "compelling" but failed to be "narrowly tailored" to do so by using "the least restrictive means."[130]

In arguing against the weight of the evidence in both cases that the CDA was nonetheless so "narrowly tailored," the government relied upon the so-called safe harbor defenses. In *ACLU v. Reno*, Chief Judge Sloviter's opinion skillfully disposed of the use of these defenses, first pointing out that, in view of the expense of defending a criminal prosecution and the "risk of public obloquy," a "successful defense to a criminal prosecution would be small solace indeed."[131] Moreover, the specific defenses that were proposed within the text of the CDA—credit card and adult verification services are "not technologically or economically feasible for most providers."[132]

As to the "good-faith" defense that a provider had taken "effective" action under present technology to prevent access by minors, the present-day lack of any such technology renders such a defense a dead letter, despite the Conference Committee's qualification of *effective* to mean "reasonably effective." One such technology suggested by the government—"tagging" (a scheme under which any arguably indecent material would have a string of characters attached to it by the provider to prevent access) is simply ineffective. First and foremost, tagging itself does not prevent minors from accessing the materials, "because it depends upon the cooperation of third parties to block the material on which the tags are embedded. Yet these third parties, over which the content providers have no control, are not subject to the CDA."[133]

More fundamentally, even if (1) such a program currently existed (it doesn't) and (2) the government agreed that tagging sufficed to discharge the provider's burden under the CDA (it didn't), tagging places a burden on providers to review all postings promulgated on their services—and "for the many not-for-profit entities which currently post thousands of Web pages, this burden would be one impossible to sustain."[134] Likewise, the alternate suggestions put forward by the government in the *Shea* litigation either are not generally available, or are ineffective at screening out a minor who represents that he or she is of age.[135]

---

130. *Shea v. Reno*, 930 F. Supp. at 941–943.
131. *ACLU v. Reno*, 929 F. Supp. at 856.
132. *Id.*
133. *Id.*
134. *Id.* For an elaborate, helpful discussion of "tagging" and its inherent difficulties, *see also* *Shea v. Reno*, 930 F. Supp. at 944–946.
135. 930 F. Supp. at 946–948.

The Question of Vagueness

The second ground for invalidation of the CDA, its vagueness as a criminal statute, was asserted by Judge Buckwalter in his opinion. That conclusion rests on the well-established principle of constitutional criminal law that "[n]o one may be required at peril of life, liberty or property to speculate as to the meaning of penal statutes," and has been deemed to apply with especial force in the context of statutes that impact on freedom of expression.[136]

The vagueness found by Judge Buckwalter in the CDA (with the concurrence of Chief Judge Sloviter) lies in its use of the "community standards" to define what is "indecent" or "patently offensive."[137] In response to the congressional reliance on *Pacifica,* Judge Buckwalter noted that the Court did not in that case uphold a specific definition of indecency, but rather found that the George Carlin "Filthy Words" monologue at issue could be restricted from the time slot in which it had been played. Again, in *Sable Communications of California, Inc. v. FCC,*[138] the Court found that a complete ban of indecent material in the "dial-a-porn context" violated the First Amendment because it was not narrowly tailored to serve the purpose of limiting children's access to commercial pornographic telephone messages. As Judge Buckwalter summarized, "Once again, the Court did not consider a challenge to the term 'indecent' on vagueness grounds, and indeed has never directly ruled on the issue."[139]

The government's tactics in defending the CDA against the claim of vagueness in *ACLU v. Reno* were, to put it mildly, ham-fisted. Initially claiming that "strict scrutiny" need not be applied to the CDA, the government conceded at oral argument that it must. Moreover, the government attempted to defend the CDA by relying on the "variable obscenity" standard of *Ginsberg v. New York*— a standard explicitly rejected by Congress, as revealed by the conference report. Finally, the government's ultimate argument on the subject of vagueness was that "the court should trust prosecutors to prosecute only a small segment of those speakers subject to the CDA's restrictions, and whose works would reasonably be considered 'patently offensive' in *every* community."[140]

---

136. *ACLU v. Reno,* 929 F. Supp. at 860 (opinion of Buckwalter, D. J.) (*quoting, inter alia, Lanzetta v. New Jersey,* 306 U.S. 451, 453 [1939]).

137. Like the Chief Judge, Judge Buckwalter points out that the statute does not in fact necessarily require that these two terms be construed *in pari materia.* Indeed, he notes, the undefined term "indecent" is elsewhere defined in the federal criminal code as "includ[ing] matter of a character tending to incite arson, murder or assassination." *Id.* at 861, *quoting* 18 U.S.C. at § 1461.

138. 492 U.S. 115 (1989), discussed by Judge Buckwalter with *Pacifica* at 929 F. Supp. at 862.

139. *ACLU v. Reno,* 929 F. Supp. at 862.

140. *Id.* at 864 (chararcterizing government argument) (emphasis in original). For the Government's effort to invoke "variable obscenity," both at the District Court and at the Supreme Court levels, *see* 929 F. Supp. at 863, compare n. 89, *supra* (District Court); *Reno v. ACLU,* 521 U.S. 844, 871 & n. 37 (rejecting argument).

As Judge Buckwalter explained in rejecting this argument, "[s]uch un-fettered discretion to prosecutors is precisely what due process does not allow. . . . Well intentioned prosecutors and judicial safeguards do not neu-tralize the vice of a vague law."[141] The identical effort to justify the law against the claim of overbreadth was similarly rejected in *Shea v. Reno.*

The case law that exists to support the use of "indecency" against a vague-ness challenge stems from lower court decisions in the telephone and cable television context in which "the FCC had defined indecent as patently of-fensive by reference to the contemporary community standards *for that par-ticular medium.*"[142] Judge Buckwalter drew the distinction between such me-dia-specific community standards and the lack of any such consensus among Internet users and providers.[143] The government's argument that the CDA's purpose was to act as a supplement for the obscenity laws exacerbates the problem of this lack of a consensus—because the definition of obscenity expands or collapses from geographical community to community, the mean-ing of the "residual category of 'indecency'" likewise expands or collapses.[144] This reflection of the term in the jurisprudence to date conflicts with the avowed intention of Congress to provide in the CDA "a uniform national standard of content regulation."[145] This conflict in turn "leaves the reader of the CDA unable to discern the relevant 'community standard' and will undoubtedly cause Internet users to steer far wider of the unlawful zone than if the community standard to be applied were clearly defined."[146] As Judge Buckwalter concluded, this "is precisely the vice of vagueness."[147]

The flaw in Judge Buckwalter's logic is apparent. If the case law that ap-plies indecency to specific media based on a media-specific community stan-dard is valid, how can the Supreme Court's definition of what is "indecent" as expanding and contracting with the geographic locality's definition of obscenity be correct? The answer, of course, is that it cannot.

Under just that logic, Judge Dalzell dissented from the finding that the CDA was unconstitutionally vague. Relying on the Conference Committee's bald declaration that the act was intended to codify the *Pacifica* definition of indecency, Judge Dalzell relied on the Supreme Court's statement in that decision that the context of *both* medium and community were relevant, and found no bar to such a locality-based definition of "indecency." If, he rea-

---

141. 929 F. Supp. *quoting Baggett v. Bullitt,* 377 U.S. 360, 373–374. (1964) (internal quota-tion marks omitted).
142. 929 F. Supp. at 862 (citing cases) (emphasis in original).
143. *Id.* at 863.
144. *Id.* quoting *Sable,* 492 U.S. at 132 (Scalia, J. concurring).
145. 929 F. Supp. at 863, *quoting* H.R. Rep. 104–458 at 191.
146. *Id.* (internal quotation omitted).
147. *Id.*

soned, the *Miller* test for the creation of contemporary community standards by obscenity was not impermissibly vague, even though the relevant standard varied from geographic region to region, how could the elimination of unrelated elements render the otherwise identical formulation of a test in the CDA unconstitutionally vague?[148]

The three-judge panel in *Shea v. Reno*[149] reached the same result, declining to hold the CDA unconstitutionally vague for the reasons set out by Judge Dalzell. The New York court was, if anything, even more firm than was Judge Dalzell in rejecting the notion that the interplay of the media-specific standards in the lower court cases that were relied on by Judge Buckwalter somehow conflicted with *Pacifica*; the New York District Court found "no authority discussing the significance of the definition's reference to the" specific medium involved as a requirement that such a contextual media-specific standard exist.[150]

Although the paradox in Judge Buckwalter's logic does exist, and the *Shea* court is more accurate in its reading of *Pacifica*, that does not foreclose the matter. If, as the Supreme Court opined in *Miller*, the erection of a national standard of what is "patently offensive" is doomed to be "futile," then the Conference Committee's statement that the CDA is an avowed attempt to create just that kind of national standard draws into question at least the act's efficacy and possibly its validity on vagueness grounds, as Judge Buckwalter would have it. In other words, although Judge Buckwalter may have been mistaken in thinking that precedent *compelled* a finding of vagueness, such a finding might nonetheless have been in part predicated upon his reasoning.

Calling the Question: Why a Special Standard?

Nonetheless, Judge Dalzell concurred that the CDA was unconstitutional. After a detailed exploration of the level of protection extended to the various media of mass communication and a detailed exposition of the limited reach of the Court's decision in *Pacifica* and its subsequent erosion by the "scarcity rationale," Judge Dalzell concluded that the Court could not "simply assume that the Government has the power to regulate protected speech over the Internet, devoting our attention solely to the issue of whether the CDA is a constitutional exercise of that power. Rather, we

---

148. 929 F. Supp. at 868–869 (*citing, inter alia, Hamling v. United States*, 418 U.S. 87, 118–119 (1974) (upholding criminal prosecution for obscenity under *Miller* definition of obscenity against void-for-vagueness challenge).
149. *Shea v. Reno*, 930 F. Supp. at 935–938.
150. *Id.* at 938.

must also decide the validity of the underlying assumption as well, to wit, whether the Government has the power to regulate protected speech at all."[151] As Judge Dalzell pointed out, this question was one for which no helpful authority could be gleaned from the principal lines of mass communications jurisprudence:

> THAT decision must take into account the underlying technology, and the actual and potential reach of the medium. . . . *Pacifica*'s holding is not persuasive authority here, since plaintiffs and the Government agree that Internet communication is an abundant and growing resource. Nor is *Sable* persuasive authority, since the Supreme Court's holding in that case addressed only one particular type of communication (dial-a-porn) and reached no conclusions about the proper fit between the First Amendment and telephone communications generally. Again, plaintiffs and the Government here agree that the Internet provides content as broad as the imagination.[152]

Thus, Judge Dalzell would have the Court begin with the basic question: Should the Internet be subject to greater or lesser regulation than that applied to the "classic" media of print or oral speech in the village green?[153] Judge Dalzell's logic in fully answering this question takes into account the nature of the Internet as a functional matter, and is instructive.

Judge Dalzell first examined four factors that are characteristic of the Internet. These factors are that:

> [F]IRST, the Internet presents very low barriers to entry. Second, those barriers to entry are identical for both speakers and listeners. Third, as a result of these low barriers astoundingly diverse content is available on the Internet. Fourth, the Internet provides significant access to all who wish to speak in the medium, and even creates a relative parity among speakers.[154]

Each of these factors, with the exception of the fourth, has been summarized in this chapter, and so Judge Dalzell's detailed analysis of how the CDA would undermine these valuable aspects of the Internet need not be summarized here. However, the fourth factor addresses one of the most provocative critiques of current First Amendment doctrine: the notion that the "marketplace of ideas" is so skewed in favor of the wealthy and powerful that to permit them to speak under the same standards as the poor and

---

151. *ACLU v. Reno*, 929 F. Supp. at 877.
152. *Id.*
153. *Id.* at 877, *et seq.*
154. *Id.* at 877.

disenfranchised is to make a mockery of the spirit that animates the First Amendment.[155]

The rationale for this argument rests in the fact that the mass media outlets are concentrated in the hands of a few entities—mostly corporations—that enjoy a virtual monopoly of the technology and resources that are necessary to communicate effectively in an era of mass communications.[156] Because "most people lack the money and time to buy a broadcast station or create a newspaper, they are limited to the role of listeners, *i.e.*, as watchers of television or subscribers to newspapers."[157]

This criticism of the First Amendment, although it is increasingly more popular in academic circles, has fallen on deaf ears in the Court and was firmly rejected as a reason for curtailing the free speech of cable television providers by the Court as recently as 1994 in *Turner Broadcasting System v. FCC*.[158] This rejection, and the previous rejection of "market dysfunction" as a justification for "government-imposed, content-based speech restrictions" is rooted in a recognition that the proposed cure is "almost always worse than the disease."[159] However, in the case of the Internet, this difficulty is obviated:

> IT is no exaggeration to conclude that the Internet has achieved, and continues to achieve, the most participatory marketplace of mass speech that this country—indeed, the world—has yet seen. The plaintiffs in these actions correctly describe the "democratizing" effects of Internet communication: individual citizens of limited means can speak to a worldwide audience on issues of concern to them. Federalists and Anti-Federalists may debate the structure of their government nightly, but these debates occur in newsgroups or chat rooms rather than in pamphlets. Modern-day Luthers still post their theses, but to electronic bulletin boards rather than the door of the Wittenberg Schlosskirche. More mundane (but from a constitutional perspective, equally important) dialogue occurs between aspiring artists, or French cooks, or dog lovers, or fly fishermen.[160]

---

155. *See*, for example, Jerome Barron, *Access to the Press—A New First Amendment Right*, 80 Harv. L. Rev. 1641 (1967).

156. *Id.; ACLU v. Reno*, 929 F. Supp. at 879–880.

157. *ACLU v. Reno* at 880, *summarizing Miami Herald Publishing Co. v. Tornillo*, 418 U.S. 241, 251 (1974).

158. For academic enthusiasm for regulation that is designed to address "market dysfunction," *see*, for example, Owen M. Fiss, *Free Speech and Social Structure*, 71 Iowa L. Rev. 1405, 1410–1411 (1987). For a recognition of the existence of market dysfunction but without the same enthusiasm for regulation, *see* Susan M. Gilles, *Images of the First Amendment and the Reality of Powerful Speakers*, 24 Cap. Univ. L. Rev. 293 (1995). The Supreme Court's rejection of this theory as a ground for regulation in *Turner* is found at 512 U.S. at 663.

159. *ACLU v. Reno*, 929 F. Supp. at 881.

160. *Id.*

Indeed, Judge Dalzell emphasized, the government's argument that the Internet is too chaotic a place to *not* be subject to some regulation "rests on the implicit premise that *too much* speech occurs in that medium, and that speech there is *too available* to the participants."[161] This argument is, as Judge Dalzell aptly pointed out, "profoundly repugnant to First Amendment principles."[162]

In view of the unique qualities of the Internet, Judge Dalzell firmly rejected the analogy to broadcast media. Indeed, the judge found that "[i]f the First Amendment erects a virtually insurmountable barrier between government and the print media, even though the print media *fails* to achieve the hoped-for diversity in the marketplace of ideas, then that insurmountable barrier must also exist for a medium that *succeeds* in achieving that diversity."[163] Likewise, the interest in "individual dignity and choice" that the Supreme Court has recognized that the First Amendment serves by "putting the decision as to what views shall be voiced largely into the hands of each of us," requires that "we should be especially vigilant in preventing content-based regulation of a medium that every minute allows individual citizens actually to make those decisions."[164]

Acknowledging the compelling interest that the government has in protecting children, Judge Dalzell nonetheless noted that to pose the question was not to answer it: Not every medium could be neutered in the interest of protecting children. Judge Dalzell's conclusion to this effect is supported by Justice Frankfurter's oft-quoted aphorism that the First Amendment does not permit "reducing the adult population . . . to reading only what is fit for children."[165] Judge Dalzell gave the hypothetical examples of a Novel Decency Act, a Village Green Decency Act, and a Postal Decency Act, drafted in the same terms as the CDA, and pointed out that sanitization of these forms of communication of "indecency" in the interest of protecting the innocence of children would plainly not pass constitutional muster.[166] Because the Internet "is a far more speech-enhancing medium than print, the village green, or the

---

161. *Id.* (emphasis in original).
162. *Id.*
163. *Id.* (emphasis in original) (internal quotation marks and citation omitted), *citing Miami Herald Publishing Co. v. Tornillo*, 418 U.S. at 259 (White, J. concurring).
164. 929 F. Supp. at 881–882, *quoting Leathers v. Medlock*, 499 U.S. 439, 448–449 (1991) (internal quotation marks omitted).
165. *Butler v. Michigan*, 352 U.S. 380, 383, 77 (1957). In language paraphrased by Judge Dalzell, such a result is "to burn the house to roast the pig." *Id.*; 929 F. Supp. at 882. ("Any content-based regulation of the Internet, no matter how benign the purpose, could burn the global village to roast the pig"). The Supreme Court, on appeal, endorsed this conclusion, 521 U.S. at 882.
166. 929 F. Supp. at 882, *citing Butler*, 352 U.S. at 383 (novels); *Perry Educational Ass'n v. Perry Local Educators' Ass'n*, 460 U.S. 37, 45 (1983) (village green); *Bolger v. Youngs Drug Products Corp.*, 463 U.S. 60, 73 (1983) (postal communications).

mails," he concluded, and would be adversely impacted in a manner that would "necessarily reduce the speech available for adults on the medium," the same result must apply to the Communications Decency Act.[167]

The district court opinions that have analyzed the validity of the CDA have been described at unusual length here because of their status as a first impression review of the issues presented by censorship of the Internet. Interestingly, the various opinions exemplify two very different types of First Amendment jurisprudence. Chief Judge Slovitzer's "overbreadth" analysis, and that adopted by the Southern District panel in *Shea v. Reno,* are classic examples of the formalist *Chaplinsky*-influenced doctrine, in that it fits the speech at issue into a pigeonhole that determines what level of protection the Internet receives, which in turn determines the result. In striving to find the CDA unconstitutionally vague as well as overbroad, Judge Buckwalter took formalism even further, and created a seeming paradox, which the *Shea* court and Judge Dalzell were able to show is a false paradox.

Judge Dalzell, however, to the extent presently possible (bearing in mind the existence of the *Chaplinsky* categories), eschewed the easy shortcut of categorization and adopted precisely the sort of functional analysis urged in Chapter 4. By examining the reasons advanced for censorship (government disapproval of the ideas propounded, tinged with a legitimate concern that some minors may be exposed to these ideas before their time) in light of the extent to which the speech is functioning as speech, rather than as a verbal act (the highest degree permissible), Judge Dalzell declined to apply a watered-down First Amendment test, but applied the best test of those that have been deemed applicable to regulations: Will this regulation deprive adults of their right to enjoy (or loathe) this message?

By treating the Internet as speech, plain and simple, Judge Dalzell did not reach a conclusion different from the most speech-restrictive of his colleagues. Like them, he found the CDA to be unconstitutionally overbroad, but not void for vagueness. Unlike his colleagues, Judge Dalzell's reasoning makes sense, not just in the context of the present-day rules, but in terms of the First Amendment's meaning and message.

The CDA and the Supreme Court

In 1997, the United States Supreme Court reviewed the decision in *ACLU v. Reno.*[168] Adopting the overbreadth portion of the panel ruling, the

---

167. 929 F. Supp. at 882. Judge Dalzell also explains that the ability of persons abroad, and thus not subject to the CDA, to post on the Internet (making up nearly one-half of all such postings) further demonstrates that the CDA will not be effective in accomplishing the government's interest; 929 F. Supp. at 882–883.

168. *Reno v. American Civil Liberties Union,* 521 U.S. 844 (1997).

Supreme Court found the CDA to contravene the First Amendment. The opinion is a remarkably staid one, written by the least staid of the moderate-liberal wing of the Court, Justice Stevens. In a painstakingly careful opinion, Justice Stevens summarized the factual findings of the panel in *ACLU v. Reno*, noting that they were based upon "356 paragraphs of the parties' stipulations and 54 findings based on evidence received in open court."[169] He then summarized the three opinions below, and proceeded to deal with the challenges brought by the government to the panel's ruling of overbreadth.[170]

These challenges were, in the first instance, based on precedent. The government pointed to three decisions that, it claimed, clearly legitimated the CDA. The first challenge to the ruling below was the government's contention that *Ginsberg v. New York*,[171] in which the Court first created the pernicious doctrine of "variable obscenity" (which held that materials that were obscene as to minors but not as to adults could be proscribed when sale to minors was at issue) legitimated the CDA. The Court in *Ginsberg*, rejected the defendant's "broad submission" that "the scope of the constitutional freedom of expression secured to a citizen to read or see material connected with sex cannot be made to depend on whether the citizen is an adult or a minor."[172] That holding was based both on a *parens patriae* analysis (that is, an assertion of the government's interest in protecting children) and also on the Court's "consistent recognition of the principle that the parents' claim to authority in their own household to direct the rearing of their children is basic to the structure of our society."[173]

However, the *Reno* court noted, that decision did not, as the government's overly mechanistic reliance on precedent seemed to suggest, compel the affirmance of the CDA. In fact, the CDA was in several aspects broader than the statute that was upheld in *Ginsberg*. Unlike that statute, the CDA (1) did not permit parents to authorize their children to view materials otherwise within its scope; (2) was not limited to commercial transactions; (3) lacked the "utterly without redeeming social importance" component of the definition of variable obscenity; and (4) included minors over 17 years of age within its protected class.[174] In short, the CDA was broader in its sweep both as to the minors whose perusal of sexually based materials was forbidden and it limited their access to materials with social value *even to the minors themselves*. Moreover, the CDA did not serve the secondary purpose of the vari-

---

169. *Id.* at 849, n. 2.
170. *Id.* at 861–864.
171. 390 U.S. 629 (1968) (upholding statute prohibiting the sale to minors under the age of 17 material that was obscene as to them).
172. *Reno v. ACLU*, 521 U.S. at 864–865, *quoting Ginsberg*, 390 U.S. at 636.
173. 521 U.S. at 865, *quoting Ginsberg*, 390 U.S. at 639 (internal quotation marks omitted).
174. 521 U.S. at 865–866.

able obscenity concept—that is, empowering parents, who, as the Court pointed out "could face a lengthy prison term" if the government disagreed with their exercise of parental judgment.[175]

The second analogue rejected by the Court was *Pacifica*. The Court rejected the notion that the *Pacifica* ruling that George Carlin's "Filthy Words" monologue could be proscribed from the radio airwaves during the afternoon hours. It cited the *Pacifica* court's reliance on the lesser protection given hitherto to broadcast speech and upon the localized time-specific nature of the *Pacifica* ruling—in effect, it treated *Pacifica* as a time, manner, or place decision.[176] Additionally, the Court distinguished between the administrative sanction levied on the broadcaster in *Pacifica* and the criminal prosecution authorized by the CDA.[177]

Finally, the Court moved on to the government's third "binding" precedent: time, manner, or place restrictions themselves, in the context of zoning. The government cited *Renton v. Playtime Theatres* as an applicable instance of such a time, manner, or place restriction and claimed it was dispositive with respect to the CDA.[178]

Although a full discussion of time, manner, or place restrictions would be a distraction here, the *Renton* court applied a line of cases that are clearly compatible with the verbal act formulation. In time, manner, or place cases, the statute or ordinance at issue is

> AIMED, not at the content of the films shown in the theaters, but rather at the "secondary effects"—such as crime and deteriorating property values—that these theaters fostered. It is the secondary effect which these zoning ordinances attempted to avoid, not the dissemination of "offensive speech."[179]

The Court rejected the analogue because the CDA did not take aim at such secondary effects but rather explicitly targeted the spread of offensive speech; the Court refused to treat it as a "content neutral" regulation.[180]

Finding the CDA not clearly within the ambit of its prior decisions, the Court proceeded to examine the statute under general principles of First Amendment jurisprudence. First, the Court declined to apply the reduced level of scrutiny that had been applied in the case of broadcast speech. It explicitly refused to apply the scarcity rationale, and pointed out that, un-

---

175. 521 U.S. at 878, 865.
176. *Id.* at 866–867.
177. *Id.*
178. *Id.* at 864, 867–868, discussing *Renton*, 475 U.S. 41 (1986).
179. *Id.* at 867, *quoting Renton v. Playtime Theatres*, 475 U.S. at 49 (internal quotations edited).
180. *Id.* at 867–868, 871–872, *citing* authorities with respect to the time, manner, place doctrine.

like broadcast speech, there was no "extensive history" of regulation.[181] Although the Court's continued distrust for the scarcity rationale—including an approving nod to its questioning in *Turner Broadcasting System, Inc. v. FCC*[182]—is refreshing, the suggestion that a historical tradition of repression with respect to a given medium might be a sufficient basis for continuing the tradition disregards the wise words of Oliver Wendell Holmes that "it is revolting to have no better reason for a rule of law than that so it was laid down in the time of Henry IV."[183]

In any event, the Court found that neither of these factors are present in cyberspace. Neither before nor after the enactment of the CDA "have the vast democratic forums of the Internet been subject" to such pervasive government regulation, nor has the Internet the kind of limited accessibility that justified the government's entrance as a referee to ensure maximal social benefit from its exploitation as a limited resource.[184] Accordingly, the Court decided, "our cases provide no basis for qualifying the level of First Amendment scrutiny that should be applied to this medium."[185]

The Court criticized the CDA for its poor drafting, especially for the use of the term "indecent" from Supreme Court broadcasting/child pornography jurisprudence, without a statutory definition. However, the statute was not struck on Fifth Amendment vagueness grounds, because the Court was able to strike it exclusively on the grounds of overbreadth.[186] However, its vagueness, as well as its status as a criminal statute, served to further undermine the statute's First Amendment underpinnings, because the lack of precision increased the likelihood of protected speech being caught up within its ambit.[187]

The government had tried to save the statute by adverting to its recitation of "patently offensive" element of the constitutionally approved definition of obscenity in *Miller v. California*.[188] The Court soundly spurned this effort. First, it noted that speech was not "patently offensive" under *Miller* in a vacuum, but had to be "specifically defined [as such] under applicable state law." More important, the Court noted:

> THE Government's reasoning is also flawed. Just because a definition
> including three limitations is not vague, it does not follow that one of

181. *Id.* at 867, 868–869.
182. 521 U.S. at 868 (citing 512 U.S. at 637–638).
183. O. W. Holmes, "The Path of the Law," in *Collected Legal Papers* (1921) at 187.
184. *Reno v. ACLU*, 521 U.S. 868–869 and n. 33. Nor did the court find that the Internet was like broadcast media in terms of invasiveness or ubiquity. *Id.*
185. *Id.* at 870.
186. *Id.* at 870–874; 874–881.
187. *Id.* at 870–871.
188. *Id.* at 872–874; *comparing* CDA with statutory framework endorsed in *Miller v. California*, 413 U.S. 15 (1973).

those limitations, standing by itself, is not vague. Each of *Miller's* additional two prongs—(1) that, taken as a whole, the material appealed to the "prurient" interest, and (2) that it "lack serious literary, artistic, political, or scientific value"—critically limits the uncertain sweep of the obscenity definition.[189]

Noting that without these further limitations—especially the second, which imposes a nonlocal, and thus less subjective standard than the other *Miller* elements—protected speech can hardly help but be swept within the purview of the CDA, the Court found the statute to lack "the precision that the First Amendment requires when a statute regulates the content of speech."[190] Even though the Court accepted the "compelling" nature of the CDA's efforts to protect children from indecent materials, the "burden on adult speech is unacceptable if less restrictive alternatives would be at least as effective in achieving the legitimate purpose that the statute was enacted to serve."[191] Finding this to be the case, the Court deemed the statute unconstitutional. However, it did apply a saving construction that limited the statute's scope to its constitutional limits by permitting its unchallenged obsenity provision, "which can be banned totally, as it enjoys no First Amendment protection."[192]

CONCLUSION

The CDA is not the only form of regulation this new medium has faced. Several states have likewise tried to censor "indecency" over the Internet, usually following the lead of the CDA to justify the censorship to protect minors. That the Internet, far from being feared, should be embraced by the First Amendment, as Judge Dalzell presciently proclaims, seems unassailable, but it will almost certainly be assailed until we have assimilated it into our culture. This truth of the regulation of new media reflects the persistent failure of our legal culture to put its money where its mouth is. Or perhaps, like St. Augustine, the legal system cries out "give me chastity—but not yet."[193] Just as the Court in *Mutual Film Commission* could sing the praises of freedom of speech, but firmly reject the notion that anything as novel as film could be ensconced within, or could in *Pacifica* and *Denver Area Consortium*

---

189. 521 U.S. at 873, 873–874.

190. *Id.* at 874.

191. *Id.* at 874, 874–882 (affirming District Court rejection of government's defense).

192. *Id.* at 882–883. The Court declined to rewrite the law to any further extent, thereby declining the invitation to explore the fringes of constitutional protection. *Id.* at 883–884.

193. St. Augustine, *Confessions* bk. viii, ch. 7.

take protection away from the media through which most Americans get their news (a true slap in the face for the Free Press clause), so Congress has placed the Internet on the fringe of the constitutional order, in a kind of special limbo reserved for "indecent" speech. As George Carlin, the first denizen of First Amendment indecency limbo, used to describe theological limbo: It's not heaven, but it's not hell either. The reassertion of the broader rationale of *Pacifica* by a plurality of the Supreme Court in *Denver Area Consortium* reminds us that, unlike this unlamented theological analogue, First Amendment limbo is still very much with us. However, the failure of the Communications Decency Act to gain judicial approval suggests that perhaps the increasing pace of change encompasses legal culture as well as new media. To go from distrusted stranger to accepted member in the family in as brief a time as the Internet may do (as the opinions in the CDA cases seem to suggest) could well portend that our legal culture is (in this sphere at least) preparing to grow up, to reach the time when, at last, the medium is *not* the message.

This is not to say, however, that the Supreme Court's resolution of the CDA lays all fears to rest.[194] In its concluding paragraphs, the Court rejected the final argument the government advanced to justify the CDA, the assertion of a new interest purportedly served by the statute; that is, the fostering of the growth and development of the Internet. The argument, as summed up by a patently unimpressed Justice Stevens, was based on the assumption that "the unregulated availability of 'indecent' and 'patently offensive' material on the Internet is driving countless citizens away from the medium because of the risk of exposing themselves or their children to harmful material."[195] The Court rejected this claim in language that suggested that the Internet may provide some empirical backing for those who believe in the marketplace of ideas metaphor, most memorably spun by John Milton:

> THE dramatic expansion of this new marketplace of ideas contradicts the factual basis of this contention. The record demonstrates that the growth of the Internet has been and continues to be phenomenal. As a matter of constitutional tradition, in the absence of evidence to the contrary, we assume that governmental regulation of the content of speech is more likely to interfere with the free exchange of ideas than to encourage it. The interest in encouraging freedom of expression

---

194. Since the publication of this work, several Internet-related decisions have maintained the high level of constitutional scrutiny applied to restrictions of on-line speech. *See* Chapter 9, *infra*.

195. *Reno v. ACLU*, 521 U.S. at 885. This argument, Justice Stevens noted in passing, had not been raised prior to the appeal to the Supreme Court, and thus, technically, had been waived. *Id.*

in a democratic society outweighs any theoretical but unproven benefit of censorship.[196]

All very stirring, no doubt, and a fine refutation of the specific result argued for by the new generation of adherents of Frankfurter. But does the Court mean to imply that proof that censorship *may* foster the "socially valuable" uses of a new medium could lead to a different result? Is the Court accepting a balancing act, not as a major premise, but rather as an idea that seeps into jurisprudential thought to such an extent that it colors judicial opinions even when is not adopted? Today's victory is reassuring, but its terms suggest that the Legal Realists of free speech are beginning to have an impact after all. A few more such victories, and we may yet be undone.

---

196. *Id.*

7

When the Devil Turns
Why Tolerate Intolerance?

WORDS ARE SUCH fragile weapons; they are able to pierce and wound in the evanescent moments in which they exist. So few written words capture the attention for more than a fleeting moment or two, and spoken words "die away, and flow off like water—leaving no taste, no color, no smell, not a trace."[1] Yet the results of words can be tremendous; they can inflict psychological trauma or foment violence or feed centuries-old hatreds.

The present legal trend is to recognize the power of words, at least in terms of discussions of what has come to be called "hate speech." Hate speech is normally used to denote speech that expresses bigotry based on a person or group's race, religion, gender, or sexual orientation. Although academic discussions commonly include sexual orientation, the law has been grudging (to put it kindly) in recognizing the claims to equal citizenship of gays and lesbians.

A mere seventeen years ago, the Supreme Court upheld a statute that criminalized consensual "sodomy" (defined as sex between members of the same sex) on the flimsy grounds that the Constitution did not explicitly recognize "a fundamental right to homosexual sodomy." This holding, recently overruled, was based on a distortion of the petitioner's claim, which in fact urged the application of the fundamental right to privacy in the sexual sphere delineated in the line of cases from *Griswold v. Connecticut* to *Roe v. Wade,* and which was simply ignored by the Court.[2] The recent voiding of a

---

1. Alexander Solzhenitsyn, *Nobel Lecture* (1972), *quoted in Collin v. Smith,* 578 F.2d 1197, 1210 (7th Cir. 1978) (Harlington Wood, J. concurring). *Texas v. Lawrence,* 534 U.S.—, 155 L.Ed.2d (June 26, 2003) (overruling *Bowers* on privacy grounds).
2. *See Bowers v. Hardwick,* 478 U.S. 186 (1986); *compare Griswold v. Connecticut,* 381 U.S. 479 (1965) (right of married couple to use birth control based on "sacred precincts" of marital bedroom); *Eisenstadt v. Baird,* 405 U.S. 438 (1972) (extending same right to

statute aimed at partially disenfranchising the gay and lesbian population[3] shows that this hostility has its limits—or that a decade of social activism has not been utterly without effect.

The trend in academia seems to be in favor of the notion that hate speech should be regulated, as somehow outside of (or undeserving of) the protections of the First Amendment. As an examination of the jurisprudence shows, this notion has some support in older cases, but has weakened steadily as the *Brandenburg* standard has come to express the essential meaning of the First Amendment. Thus far, the Supreme Court has regularly rejected claims to carve out a new *Chaplinsky* category of hate speech. How long this obdurate defense of the First Amendment will continue in the face of the growing fashionableness of suppression of hate speech is unclear.

One particular variant of the logic used to urge both that hate speech falls within the ambit of state power to regulate, and that it should be regulated, deserves especially close attention. It is the argument advanced by some feminists that pornography (defined as sexually explicit material that tends to denigrate the equal status of women) should be subject to legal restriction as hate speech. The theoretical justifications that urge censorship with respect to this variant of speech are especially well developed and explicit, having been urged over a nearly twenty-year period by the articulate and politically active feminist advocates Catharine A. MacKinnon and Andrea Dworkin. In this team, MacKinnon provides the legal "scholarly" legitimacy, while Dworkin provides the passionate polemics. Their efforts to construct a civil right of action—in less technical terms, a right to sue—on behalf of women who feel that such materials have had a deleterious impact upon their lives merit extended attention for several reasons.

First, MacKinnon and Dworkin (in their writings addressed to a more sympathetic audience) make clear their grounds for urging regulation in an unusually frank way. They are explicit about what they believe the harms inflicted by pornography are, and what their notion of state power to address those harms is.

Also, like those who urge suppression of hateful speech directed at minority racial groups, MacKinnon and Dworkin call into question the fundamental nature of the state and its relation to the individual citizen, stress-

---

unmarried persons—the "Sex and the Single Girl" of constitutional law); *Stanley v. Georgia*, 394 U.S. 557 (1969) (right to possess obscenity in the privacy of the home) and *Roe v. Wade*, 410 U.S. 113 (1973) (right to privacy extends to control over one's own body, and thus guarantees right to abortion).

3. *Romer v. Evans*, 517 U.S. 620 (1996) (attempting to distinguish *Bowers* on basis of statutory disfavoring of a segment of the population's access to the political process).

ing the collective over the individual and equality over liberty. This represents a sea change in the jurisprudence, should it be adopted by the judiciary and legal academia.

Finally, historical primacy and political influence mandate a focus on MacKinnon's thought especially. The arguments advanced by MacKinnon and Dworkin have been used by a new group of critical legal theorists and advocates of the regulation of hate speech to justify censorship of speech that is pervaded with bigotry, whether it be racial or religious in nature. As the originator of many of these concepts, MacKinnon is of great interest. As the only such advocate to win major concessions—the passage of local ordinances and state statutes, the introduction of a federal statute to Congress, the defeated Pornography Victims' Compensation Act, and the adoption of her reasoning by the Supreme Court of Canada—MacKinnon has influenced the dialogue more than any other advocate of suppression of hate speech.

Hate speech is a troubling issue for several reasons. First, the speech that libertarians are frequently called on to defend is especially vile; the visceral reaction to it is to *want* it suppressed. Somehow obscene materials (as opposed to most "pornographic" speech) do not stir the same depths of revulsion. Possibly this ties into the second troubling aspect of hate speech—that it offends the American ideal of equality, that other great component of our civic religion. Enshrined in the Thirteenth and Fourteenth Amendments, equality is as lofty a goal as freedom, and as necessary to the creation of a just society. Many, including Cass Sunstein, Owen Fiss, or Catharine MacKinnon, would urge that for equality to be given meaning, freedom of speech must, in this unique area, be curtailed.

The concern of this chapter is whether these calls for censorship may constitutionally be adopted. The question is, put differently, whether the First Amendment's language, or judicially created and recognized exceptions or categories, or even the interplay of other constitutional provisions, such as the Civil War amendments, permit the suppression, or the punishment, of hate speech. To put it differently, whether the regulation of hate speech may fit within our constitutional order can be looked at in two contexts: first, does such regulation fit within the broad but extant contours known as First Amendment jurisprudence; and second, if it does not, should that order be revised? This chapter addresses the first question. The American constitutional protection of hate speech is one of the principal examples used in arguing that the First Amendment places too high a value on freedom of speech and devalues other equally important social imperatives. This forms part of a larger argument for First Amendment restructuring, and will be addressed in the concluding chapter. Here, as in the previous chapters, the concern is what *is* the U.S. Constitution, not what it should be.

The Jurisprudence of Hate Speech

The jurisprudence of hate speech is a mid- to late-twentieth-century phenomenon. The popularity of ideals of equality and the social changes that began to give this idea flesh are themselves essentially twentieth-century phenomena. The popular culture of the nineteenth century was explicitly and sometimes brutally racist. Rarities such as Mark Twain's sympathetic and complex portrayal of Jim in *Huckleberry Finn* aside,[4] most portrayals of African-Americans in literature in the last century were at best one-dimensional stereotypes.

Jews also fared poorly. Charles Dickens's portrayal of the utterly wicked Jew Fagin in *Oliver Twist*, or the almost equally sickening Riah, the "good Jew" in *Our Mutual Friend* (a sycophant who addressed the other characters as "Generous Christian Master" or "worshipful Christian Mistress") are characteristic. Even novelists who are remembered for their creation of fully fleshed characters fell occasionally into this cultural morass. Anthony Trollope's wicked Rev. Emilius and Augustus Melmotte[5] are not as one-dimensional as Fagin, but they are cut from the same cloth.[6]

Women, of course, regularly fell into the virgin/whore dichotomy, and were often portrayed as stick figures. Dickens' Nancy in *Oliver Twist*, Thackeray's Amelia Sedley (who is admittedly counterbalanced by the fascinating Becky Sharp), and any one of James Fenimore Cooper's wooden heroines far outnumber the Hester Prynnes, Glencora Pallisers, or Isobel Archers of fiction. Politically, the persecution of Margaret Sanger and of Victoria Claflin Woodhull are examples of the potent social forces which acted to keep women in their places.[7] Moreover, even the more complex portrayals of women were based on a vision of them as less suited than men for the rigors of life outside the home sphere.[8]

---

4. Antislavery literature such as Harriet Beecher Stowe's *Uncle Tom's Cabin* (1852) also present their characters in a favorable, if stereotyped, light. Twain addressed racial injustice in several other works such as *The Tragedy of Puddin'head Wilson* (1894) and "A True Story" (1879). For legal articulation of racist norms, *see Dred Scott v. Sandford*, 19 How. (60 U.S.) 393, 401 (1857) (Taney, C. J.).

5. Rev. Emilius appears in *The Eustace Diamonds* (1872) and *The Prime Minister* (1876), in which he is matched by the equally malevolent Jew, Ferdinand Lopez. Augustus Melmotte appears in *The Way We Live Now* (1875).

6. In fairness to Trollope, his ability to create characters who transcend stereotype should be noted. In *The Way We Live Now*, Ezekiel Breghert is a three-dimensional sympathetic character who is Jewish, and Phineas Finn (a Catholic hero in an era when "Papists" were still largely despised and disenfranchised) marries the Jewish (at least by marriage) Marie ("Madame Max") Goesler. *See Phineas Redux* (1874).

7. *See* David M. Rabban, *Free Speech in Its Forgotten Years* (1997) at 29–30, 67–69; Kenneth Andrews, *Nook Farm: Mark Twain's Hartford Circle* (1980) at 7; Andrew Hoffman, *Inventing Mark Twain* (1997) at 205–206.

8. *See*, for example, the fawning concluding speech of Katherine in *The Taming of the Shrew*, Act V, sc. ii, ll. 137–162, set to music by Cole Porter in *Kiss Me Kate*. For legal articulation of sexist norms, *see Bradwell v. Illinois*, 16 Wall. (83 U.S.) 130, 141–142 (1873) (Bradley, J., concurring).

These portrayals continued into the present century, as evinced by D. W. Griffith's *Birth of A Nation,* hailed for its authenticity by no less a figure than President Woodrow Wilson. *Gone With the Wind,*[9] a love letter to the antebellum South and the Ku Klux Klan, took the same path as Griffith, but focused less on the awful spectacle of free blacks and more on the "good Negroes" who, knowing their places, stayed loyal to "Miz Scarlett."

Asians—known as "Orientals"—were fair game as well, nastily caricatured in portrayals ranging from Sax Rohmer's inscrutable, evil supervillain Fu Manchu to the comic monsters of Arthur Train's once-popular *Tutt and Mr. Tutt.*[10]

Politically, racism was respectable, and the Ku Klux Klan was politically potent until well into this century—demonstrated by the election of Senator (later Justice) Hugo Black, who relied on its support, and indeed held office as the "Kladd of the Klan."[11] Eugenics was in the air culturally, intriguing no less a figure than Oliver Wendell Holmes, as well as the many who supported Nazi ideology in the United Kingdom and the United States.[12]

In sum, the only way to ban racist, anti-Semitic, sexist, or other hate speech prior to World War II would have been to do away with mainstream culture as a whole.

However, the rise of Hitler drew the attention of the Supreme Court to the consequences of racial or religious bigotry in a way never before seen. Indeed, the first "fighting words" cases in the 1940s were tinged with such an awareness; they often explicitly adverted to the dangers of fascism to justify the suppression of racist speech. This awareness was held in check by the Court's simultaneous awareness of the loss of freedom in Europe, which generated a greater awareness of the importance of protecting free speech.

The Mainstream Cases

In *Cantwell v. Connecticut,*[13] the Court reversed the conviction of Jesse Cantwell, a member of the Jehovah's Witnesses, for breach of the peace. Cantwell

---

9. Margaret Mitchell, *Gone With the Wind* (1937).

10. Arthur Train, *Tutt and Mr. Tutt* (1920) at 43–88

11. Roger Newman, *Hugo Black: A Biography* (1994) at 91–100 (describing the extent of Black's activities as a Klansman), 101–103 (describing the Klan's role in Black's Senate nomination).

12. *See* G. Edward White, *Justice Oliver Wendell Holmes: Law and the Inner Self* (1993) at 407–408 (describing *Buck v. Bell,* 274 U.S. 200 (1927) and Holmes's views on eugenics); James Bishop Peabody, ed. *The Holmes-Einstein Letters* (1964) at 267 (O. W. Holmes letter of 19 May 1927, describing *Buck*); J. David Smith & K. Ray Nelson, *The Sterilization of Carrie Buck* (1989) at 241–253 (describing persistence of eugenic thought in the scientific community through the 1980s).

13. 310 U.S. 296 (1940).

had politely accosted two passersby and had asked if he could play a record on his portable Victrola for them. The passersby agreed, and Cantwell played a record titled "Enemies," which included an attack on the Roman Catholic Church. The record, as summarized by the opinion of Justice Roberts for a unanimous Supreme Court, "singles out the Roman Catholic Church for strictures couched in terms which would naturally offend not only persons of that persuasion, but all others who respect the honestly held religious faith of their fellows."[14]

Unfortunately for Cantwell's evangelistic efforts, his auditors were themselves Roman Catholics, and took umbrage at the slurs contained in the record. The auditors "were tempted to strike Cantwell unless he went away. On being told to be on his way he left their presence."[15] As the Court's opinion carefully noted:

> WE find in the instant case no assault or threatening of bodily harm, no truculent bearing, no intentional discourtesy, no personal abuse. On the contrary, we find only an effort to persuade a willing listener to buy a book or to contribute money in the interest of what Cantwell, however misguided others may think him, conceived to be true religion.[16]

Finding that no "resort to epithets or personal abuse" had taken place, the Court deemed that Cantwell's action "raised no such clear and present menace to public peace and order as to render him liable to conviction on the common law offense" of breach of the peace.[17] Despite its reversal of Cantwell's conviction, the Court noted that "there are limits to the exercise of these liberties. The dangers in these times from the coercive activities of those who in the delusion of racial or religious conceit would incite violence and breaches of the peace in order to deprive others of their equal right to the exercise of their liberties is familiar to all. These and other transgressions of these limits the states appropriately may punish."[18]

In *Cantwell*, the players in the hate speech debate all made their debut. The splitting off of "epithets" and "abuse" as a category of low-value speech that is entitled somehow to less than full protection was present in embryonic form in *Cantwell*, as was the restriction of the proscription of hate speech to epithets or abusive words, to "fighting words" or to the inherently "coercive." The subsequent jurisprudence would explore what is and is not in-

---

14. *Cantwell v. Connecticut*, 310 U.S. at 309.
15. *Id.* at 303.
16. *Id.* at 310.
17. *Id.* at 311.
18. *Id.* at 310.

herently "coercive," but over time the dominant thrust has been to stress the connection with fighting words.

In *Terminiello v. Chicago*,[19] Justice Douglas struck the balance that, to the present, is typical of the Supreme Court's approach to hate speech. In his opinion, Justice Douglas did not address the nature of the defendant's speech, or its content. Rather, he glossed over the facts and focused on the ordinance at issue. In fact, the decision turned on whether the definition of breach of the peace, which the jury heard as part of the trial judge's instructions, was too broad. Did it include constitutionally protected speech within the scope of breach of the peace?

The Court found that this indeed was the case; it excoriated the lower court's inclusion of speech that "stirs the public to anger, invites dispute, brings about a condition of unrest or creates a disturbance."[20] As Justice Douglas stated:

> [A] FUNCTION of free speech is to invite dispute. It may indeed best serve its high purpose when it induces a condition of unrest, creates dissatisfaction with conditions as they are, or even stirs people to anger. Speech is often provocative and challenging. It may strike at prejudices and preconceptions and have profound unsettling effects as it presses for acceptance of an idea.[21]

For this reason, Justice Douglas explained, "freedom of speech, although not absolute, is nevertheless protected against censorship or punishment, unless shown likely to produce a clear and present danger of a serious and substantive evil that rises far above public inconvenience, annoyance, or unrest."[22]

This opinion, although it expressly disavowed the absolutism by which Justice Douglas would subsequently become known, nonetheless tracked in this context the verbal act requirement that has become the essence of substantive, non-*Chaplinsky*-based (or first-tier) First Amendment protection. In striking contrast to the more procedurally oriented jurisprudence of his predecessor Louis Brandeis (who affirmed Anita Whitney's professedly unconstitutional conviction), Douglas issued this opinion striking the ordinance as unconstitutionally broad in its application to Terminiello, despite the fact that Terminiello had not presented this ground for the reversal of his conviction to the trial court.[23] Indeed, disagreement with this procedural

---

19. 337 U.S. 1 (1949).
20. *Id.* at 4 (*quoting* lower court's instruction to the jury).
21. *Id.*
22. *Id.*
23. *Id.* at 5. The contrast with Brandeis and Holmes is, of course, a reference to *Whitney v. California*, 274 U.S. 357, 380 (1927) (Brandeis and Holmes, JJ. concurring), in which

aspect of the case was the principal reason that Chief Justice Vinson dissented; he agreed with the majority as to the issue decided, and which also formed a reason for the dissent of Justice Frankfurter, who was also joined by Justices Jackson and Burton.[24]

A ringing endorsement of the centrality of freedom of speech, a notation that the statute or ordinance involved would proscribe protected speech, and a downplaying of the facts—that has indeed been the basic pattern in cases of hate speech. Indeed, Douglas drew the contrast between the American system of justice and more restrictive governments, stating that "the right to speak freely is therefore one of the chief distinctions that sets us apart from totalitarian regimes."[25]

Justice Jackson's dissent also sounds the main themes of those who would argue for repression of hate speech, reveling at length in the offensive and anti-Semitic speech made by Terminiello and charging Terminiello with "following, with fidelity that is more than coincidental, the pattern of European Fascist leaders."[26] Sizable chunks of verbatim reportage of Terminiello's speech—several pages at a stretch—lard Jackson's opinion, but serve to establish the parallel. Moreover, Justice Jackson asserted that this speech would cause "harm"; he quoted the strategy of "mastery of the streets" used by the Nazis in their rise to power, and asserted that "the present obstacle to mastery of the streets by either radical or reactionary mob movements" is "the authority of local governments which represent the free choice of democratic and law-abiding elements of all shades of opinion."[27]

The harm found by Justice Jackson is not merely the potential riot that Terminiello's unleashed invective could have brought forward (indeed, contrary to Justice Jackson's statements, the majority found that that was relatively unlikely in view of the police presence at the scene). Rather, the "drive by totalitarian groups to undermine the prestige and effectiveness of local democratic government is advanced whenever one of them can win from this Court a ruling which paralyzes the power of these officials."[28]

Jackson relied on three separate rhetorical strategies to find that Terminiello was properly convicted. First, he argued that the clear and present danger test *was* satisfied in this instance. He opined that a "trial court and

---

the First Amendment "liberals" *concurred* in affirming Anita Whitney's conviction despite their conclusion that the conviction violated the First Amendment, on the basis that the issue had not been raised below—that is, "preserved" for appeal.

24. 337 U.S. at 6–8 (Vinson, C. J. dissenting), 8–13 (Frankfurter, J. dissenting).
25. *Id.* at 4.
26. *Id.* at 22.
27. *Id.* at 24 (Jackson, J. dissenting).
28. *Id.* (Jackson, J. dissenting).

jury has found only that in the context of violence and disorder in which it was made, this speech was a provocation to immediate breach of the peace and therefore cannot claim constitutional immunity from punishment."[29] Using rioting as the substantive evil to be avoided, Jackson asserted that the "danger of rioting and violence was clear, present and immediate."[30] The second rhetorical strategy Jackson invoked was the *Chaplinsky* "fighting words" category, noting that use of such epithets as "slimy scum," "snakes," and "bedbugs" by Terminiello were below the notice of the First Amendment and were also "likely to provoke the average person to retaliation."[31] Finally, Jackson did explicitly what many of the present-day defenders of regulation of hate speech do implicitly: He called for a special standard of regulation. Where Jackson differs from most present-day advocates of increased regulation is in his rejection of a special category for hate speech. Rather, Jackson called for a generally lower standard of review, at least of state regulation; he insisted that the power of the states over speech (while no longer plenary in light of the Fourteenth Amendment) should not be construed as identical to the disabling of Congress.[32] He argued that the "cryptic phrase" "freedom of speech" is not specifically defined in the First Amendment, and should be defined to permit liability for "the abuse of that liberty."[33]

In any event, Jackson argued that the effort of a speaker to exhort a mob to violence (actually, as Jackson himself stated it, the violence took place *before* the speech, as Terminiello was guided by the police to the hall in which he spoke and was directed against him—another instance of the "reflexive disorder") is simply unprotected by the First Amendment, but the excoriating of any racial or ethnic or religious group is protected.[34]

In fairness, Jackson's expressions of concern that the power to regulate violence may lead to courts becoming "organs of popular intolerance" unless they are vigilant to prevent their being used "in bad faith, as a cover for

---

29. *Id.* at 25 (Jackson, J. dissenting).
30. *Id.* at 26 (Jackson, J. dissenting).
31. *Id.* at 26 (Jackson, J. dissenting).
32. *Id.* at 28–29 (Jackson, J. dissenting).
33. *Id.* This line of thought represents a rejected, but respectable tradition. I have indicated why I believe that Justice Jackson's interpretation of the amendment's language is incorrect, but because Jackson does not develop just what his standard would be (presumably along the lines of that applied by Justice Frankfurter in *Winters v. New York*) it is difficult to assail or defend his approach further. However, the recognition that the Due Process Clause of the Fourteenth Amendment is simply the wrong basis for incorporation of the First Amendment as against the states and that the long-neglected Privileges and Immunities Clause is the only appropriate source of incorporation theory suggests that Jackson's bifurcation alternative is not viable, and his "precatory possibility" (to coin a phrase) is belied by the language of the First Amendment.
34. *Id.* at 32–33.

censorship or suppression"[35] ring sincere. However, he did not explain how courts are to address this concern, nor did he permit this concern to form part of his proposed rule. Indeed, Jackson's opinion somewhat improbably hailed local authority, and not appellate tribunals, as the true guarantors of constitutional liberty.[36]

Jackson correctly pointed out that liberty cannot be provided by judicial fiat; Terminiello could not have reached the hall without police protection, let alone have expressed his views. To the extent that he noted that the other branches of government bear a coordinate responsibility to enforce constitutional guarantees, he provided a valuable reminder that the Court and its rulings are not Delphic oracles who deliver self-fulfilling prophecies. To the extent that he urged that the Court cannot demand the physically impossible, Jackson interjected a valuable note of realism into the discussion. However, to the extent that he stated that the willingness of law enforcement officials to execute decisions and local passions must be factored into the scope of the First Amendment's protections,[37] he mistakenly disavowed the wise maxim of Chief Justice John Marshall that it "is emphatically the province and duty of the judicial department to state what the law is."[38]

But what does this have to do with the hateful nature of Terminiello's speech? Later cases will show that hate speech is typically attacked through one of Jackson's three strategies: fitting it within the *Brandenburg* test, using a *Chaplinsky* category, or (most radically) erecting a new category. To the present, none of these three strategies has led to a successful assault on hate speech, however, and those who support such a ban have enjoyed only fleeting success.

Most of the Supreme Court cases that involve hate speech—and virtually all of the cases that permit regulation of such speech—have invoked the "fighting words" doctrine of *Chaplinsky*, or have limited themselves to "breach of the peace." Indeed, Justice Jackson tried to wedge *Terminiello* within that framework, an effort that was unsuccessful because the doctrine was formulated to permit the regulation of (as even Jackson conceded) face-to-face encounters between individuals.[39] However, on at least one occasion, a conviction for breach of the peace was upheld because an alleged fomenter of racial hostility was held to have gone beyond advocacy to incitement.[40] *Feiner v. New York* was, in fact, another instance of the reflexive disorder—a case in which an onlooker's hostile reaction was held to justify the actions

---

35. *Id.* at 33–34 (Jackson, J., dissenting).
36. *Id.* at 31–32 (Jackson, J., dissenting).
37. *Id.* at 33 (Jackson, J. dissenting).
38. *Marbury v. Madison*, 5 U.S. (1 Cranch) 137, 177 (1803).
39. 337 U.S. at 26 (Jackson, J. dissenting).
40. *Feiner v. New York*, 340 U.S. 315 (1951).

of the police in silencing an admittedly lawful speaker who urged blacks "to rise up in arms" and secure justice. Subsequent cases indicated that the Court was somewhat ashamed of the *Feiner* decision; throughout the turbulent 1960s and 1970s, the Court repeatedly found that the speech under review did not fit within the rule of *Feiner*, instead it adverted increasingly to Justice Douglas's opinion in *Terminiello*.[41] Indeed, in those tumultuous decades, the "fighting words" doctrine was held to *not* justify the conviction of a citizen for using "opprobrious language" toward a law enforcement officer; Justice Powell (concurring in the judgment) made the refreshing comment that "a properly trained officer may reasonably be expected to 'exercise a higher level of restraint' than the average citizen, and thus be less likely to respond belligerently to 'fighting words.'"[42]

Finally, it should be reinforced that the ultimate verbal act case, which rejected out of hand the notion that speech could be regulated without a close causal connection to imminent, specifically intended law-breaking, *Brandenburg v. Ohio*,[43] was a "hate speech" case that involved the Ku Klux Klan and its venomous (and subliterate) hints of "revengeance" to be taken on behalf of "White America." In short, the historical trend of the Court has been to stand firmly against content-based regulation of hate speech, a trend that was solidly followed in *R.A.V. v. City of St. Paul*, in which a city ordinance that banned the burning of crosses as a method of expressing racial animosity was struck down as unconstitutional.[44] However, in *Wisconsin v. Mitchell*,[45] the Court did uphold a penalty enhancement of a criminal act based on racist intent.

The tension between *Mitchell* and *R.A.V.* has been adeptly explored by Lawrence Tribe, who suggests that the cases can in fact be reconciled; *R.A.V.* erases the concept that *Chaplinsky* categories are wholly invisible to the First Amendment because it limits regulation such that the categories cannot be banned for their ideological content.[46] *Mitchell* permits a censoring not of

---

41. *See*, for example, *Gregory v. City of Chicago*, 394 U.S. 111 (1969) (peaceful demonstrators could not be charged with unruly behavior of hostile onlookers, and had not been charged with refusing to disperse when police so instructed them); *Gooding v. Wilson*, 405 U.S. at 518 (1972) (rejecting fighting words argument in reversing conviction); *Hess v. Indiana*, 414 U.S. 105 (1973) (reversing conviction under disorderly conduct statute rejecting fighting words argument); *Norwell v. Connecticut*, 414 U.S. 14 (1973) (same; applying *Terminiello* to strike ordinance proscribing behavior "with intent to annoy").

42. *Lewis v. City of New Orleans*, 415 U.S. 130, 135 (1974) (Powell, J. concurring).

43. 395 U.S. 444 (1969).

44. 505 U.S. 377 (1992). *R.A.V.* is more fully discussed in Chapter 3.

45. 508 U.S. 476 (1993); *see also Virginia v. Black*, 538 U.S.—, 155 L.Ed.2d 535 (2003) (crossburning when performed in context analogous to a "true threat" could be made subject of criminal statute).

46. Lawrence Tribe, *The Mystery of Motive, Private and Public: Some Notes Inspired by the Problems of Hate Speech and Animal Sacrifice*, 1993 Sup.Ct. Rev. 1 (1994).

the racist *message* of the underlying violent crime, but the enhanced punishment of the racist *motive* behind independently illegal actions. He explains that:

> MOTIVE-BASED inquiries such as the one upheld in *Mitchell* should not be confused either with restrictions on ideology or viewpoint, or with message-based restrictions. The traditional First Amendment objections to restrictions of that sort have no relevance where the government merely identifies an external, objectively discernible fact about a situation and makes the culpability of an act turn on whether the actor was directly aware of this fact and acted because of it, or in spite of it. But it ordinarily is *not* compatible with traditional First Amendment protections for freedom of thought for the government to identify as the key to an actor's culpability something *purely internal* to the actor's thoughts and beliefs, even when that internal mental state has indirectly led to what the actor ultimately chose to do.[47]

Tribe's distinction seems overfine. It could be argued that the enhancement of the penalty itself acts to punish not the *external* act but the hatred that animates it. However, this argument fails to recognize that the Thirteenth and Fourteenth Amendments protect all "persons" against being deprived of their citizenship rights, and permit the adoption of necessary laws to protect these rights. As will be seen, this principle has its limitations, but preventing acts that *by themselves* effect these very deprivations does not appear to be among them. In short, the distinction in *Mitchell* between harms that are inherent in the expressive acts under the circumstances at issue—the direct harm—and those harms that are attributed to the persuasive power of the speech upon its auditors may arguably uphold penalty enhancement. The failure to draw this distinction, or to understand the differing natures of these harms, undermines arguments for regulation of hate speech. Before this distinction can be set out more fully, however, the one jurisprudential prop to support regulation of hate speech must be examined.

Fleeting Success: Group Libel

The Supreme Court has at least once endorsed the notion that words that devalue members of groups and their role in society are actionable in a context that would permit civil and criminal liability. The case in which the Court adopted that rule, *Beauharnais v. Illinois*,[48] has surfaced several times

---

47. Tribe, *supra* note 46, at 11.
48. 343 U.S. 250 (1952).

in this volume, and its dubious status as a precedent has been pointed out, including its outright flouting by lower courts[49] and its possible overruling *sub silentio* in *Brandenburg*. Again, that *Beauharnais might* rise from the dead has been suggested by occasional squawks from Justice Harry Blackmun (in his earliest years on the Court) that it is still binding precedent and by a bland citation by Justice Scalia (citing the decision in *R.A.V.*) for the innocuous proposition that libel may be proscribed.

Having repeatedly encountered the jurisprudential weaknesses of *Beauharnais*, the reader will not be surprised to find in the decision a classic example of the Frankfurterian sliding scale of First Amendment "analysis" that reduces the amendment, as Justice Black so memorably termed it, to an "admonition to Congress" of moderation.[50]

Another notable feature of *Beauharnais* is its brushing aside of the fact that the "speech" complained of was in the form of a leaflet that solicited signatures for a petition to the mayor and city council of Chicago.[51] Thus, as Justice Black so aptly pointed out, the majority opinion in *Beauharnais* denied segregationalists not merely the right to express their vitriolic views, but also the right to "petition the Government for a redress of grievances."[52] Despite the Court's blithe assurances that the First Amendment was not violated by the statute and its application to Beauharnais's speech, this extra fillip to the case has never really been looked into by the Court.

More to the point here, however, is the Court's analysis of hate speech and its implications. As Justice Frankfurter wrote:

> IT is not within our competence to confirm or deny claims of social scientists as to the dependence of the individual on the position of his racial or religious group in the community. It would, however, be arrant dogmatism, quite outside the scope of our authority in passing on the powers of a State, for us to deny that the Illinois legislature may warrantably believe that a man's job and his educational opportunities and the dignity accorded him may depend as much on the reputation of the racial and religious group to which he willy-nilly belongs, as on his own merits.[53]

49. *See*, for example, *Collin v. Smith*, 578 F.2d 1197, 1205 (7th. Cir. 1978) *citing Tollett v. United States*, 485 F.2d 1087, 1094, n. 14 (8th Cir. 1973); *Anti-Defamation League of B'nai B'rith v. Federal Communications Commission*, 403 F.2d 169, 174, n. 5 (D. C. Cir. 1968) (concurring opinion), *cert. denied*, 394 U.S. 930 (1969).
50. *Dennis v. United States*, 341 U.S. 494, 580 (1951) (Black, J. dissenting).
51. 343 U.S. at 276 (Appendix to the opinion of Black, J. dissenting) (reprinting in full the petition and request for signatures).
52. *Id.* at (Black, J. dissenting) (quoting the First Amendment).
53. *Id.* at 263.

The dimensions of this statement are twofold: On the one hand, the Court recognizes some of the very real effects that racist, sexist, or (for that matter) heterosexist speech may have. Notably, these effects are *not* of the emotional kind that the law is traditionally reluctant to grant redress for, on the basis that such effects are unquantifiable and subjective.[54] Rather, the Court turned to the concept of *group libel* (somewhat, but not unrecognizably, distorting the Illinois statute at issue), and found inherent in the defendant's racial agitation the kind of *economic* damages that are classically redressed by libel suits, as well as the perennial fear of inciting mob violence.[55]

The second significant aspect of *Beauharnais* is the qualifier, however: The opinion only endorses regulation of hate speech under the rational basis test, the lowest standard of scrutiny, and ignores the heightened scrutiny to which regulation of free speech has been subject (theoretically) since *Schenck v. United States* and certainly since the famous footnote four of Chief Justice Stone in *United States v. Carolene Products*.[56] As Frankfurter's opinions in *Winters* and *Dennis* showed, this was no fluke, but an inherent component of Frankfurter's First Amendment jurisprudence. Only in *Beauharnais* (where its implications are, frankly, less obvious than in the other cases) did this approach command a court. By and large, Frankfurter's view was rejected.

---

54. For example, under New York law, the few cases on record that have imposed liability for the tort of intentional infliction of emotional distress have only done so where the plaintiff could establish: i) extreme and outrageous conduct; (ii) intent to cause, or disregard of a substantial possibility of causing, severe emotional distress; (iii) a causal connection between conduct and injury; and (iv) severe emotional distress. *Howell v. New York Post Co., Inc.,* 81 N.Y.2d 115, 121, 596 N.Y.S.2d 350, 353 (1993).

In applying these elements, the courts have required proof that defendant both committed highly outrageous conduct and that malicious intent animated that conduct. For example, where "severe mental pain or anguish is inflicted through a deliberate and malicious campaign of harassment or intimidation," then a cause of action may be deemed to have been made out. *Doe v. American Broadcasting Companies, Inc.,* 152 A.D.2d 482, 483, 543 N.Y.S.2d 455 (1st Dep't 1989), *app. dismissed,* 74 N.Y.2d 945, 550 N.Y.S.2d 278 (1989) *quoting Freihofer v. Hearst Corp.* 65 N.Y. 2d. 135, 143 (1985), *Roberts v. Pollack,* 92 A.D.2d 440, 461 N.Y.S.2d 272 (1st Dep't 1983) (same). The courts have imposed liability when conscience-shocking callousness has been shown. *See,* for example, *Rotundo v. Reves,* 153 Misc.2d 769, 583 N.Y.S.2d 739 (Sup. Ct. Wayne Co. 1992), *modified on other grounds,* 192 A.D.2d 1086, 596 N.Y.S.2d 272 (4th Dep't), *app. dismissed,* 82 N.Y.2d 706, 601 N.Y.S.2d 585 (1993) (parents and grandparents of deceased child who were falsely informed by coroner that mutilated corpse of pet rabbit was that of child made out cause of action).

55. 343 U.S. at 262–263; for an analysis of how the majority opinion's premise that the statute addresses the same concerns as the well-established offense of criminal libel rests upon a distortion of libel law, *see id.* at 272–273 (Black, J. dissenting); that the statute did not provide the same safeguards and limiting features contained within libel law was argued by Justice Jackson in dissent. *Id.* at 299–305.

56. 304 U.S. 144 (1938).

Beauharnais Bites the Dust: The Lessons of Skokie

The rejection of this view was made clear in the context of a planned march by the National Socialist Party of America through the Chicago suburb of Skokie, Illinois, whose large Jewish population included at that time "as many as several thousand survivors of the Nazi holocaust in Europe before and during World War II."[57] As can be imagined, the prospect of these "Illinois Nazis" goose-stepping their way through such a community was both a moral affront and an act of harassment (in common parlance if not in law) of the survivors and their families. As the village put it when it sought an injunction against the march, "the Jewish community in and around Skokie feels that the purpose of the march 'in the heart of the Jewish population' is to remind the two million survivors 'that we are not through with you' and to show that 'the Nazi threat is not over, it can happen again.'"[58]

Two related litigations ensued from these plans. First, the Illinois state courts enjoined the Nazis from marching in uniform, displaying the swastika, or distributing Nazi propaganda. This order was modified on appeal to the state's intermediate appellate court, to a mere prohibition on the display of the swastika.[59] The state supreme court reversed the order in its entirety, holding that the grounds for an injunction—the classic instance of heavily disfavored prior restraint—had not been met, following the United States Supreme Court's rationale in a series of cases. First, the rationale of *Cohen v. California* was cited to establish that offensive speech is not unprotected speech per se, and mere offensiveness does not of its own weight constitute "fighting words" under *Chaplinsky*.[60] Then the Court found that hostile audience response was not sufficient ground for suppression—a result supported by *Terminiello*, but not by cases such as *Feiner* and the other "reflexive disorder" cases.[61]

Notably, the state courts did not address the harm inflicted by the words, nor did they (save briefly) address the interests of the community:

> WE do not doubt that the sight of this symbol is abhorrent to the Jewish citizens of Skokie, and that survivors of the Nazi persecutions, tormented by their recollections, may have strong feelings regarding its display. Yet it is entirely clear that this factor does not justify enjoining the defendants' speech.[62]

---

57. *Collin v. Smith*, 578 F.2d at 1199 (a federal companion case to the state court action described in the text).
58. *Village of Skokie v. National Socialist Party of America*, 69 Ill. 2d 605, 611, 373 N.E.2d 21, 22 (Sup. Ct. Ill. 1978).
59. *Id.*
60. *Id.* at 23–24.
61. *Id.* at 24–25.
62. *Id.* at 24.

The state supreme court based this conclusion on *Cohen*, quoting that decision's analysis (and eradication of) the *Chaplinsky* category of offensive speech. The court did not explore, let alone discern, any meaningful difference between the forms of offense suffered by an observer to the word "fuck" in conjunction with the draft and the dramatically greater pain of a Holocaust survivor confronted with the symbol under which the extermination policy was enacted.

The village reacted to the state supreme court's decision by passing three ordinances. The first required that a permit be issued for all parades or assemblies of more than fifty people and required the applicants to obtain insurance.[63] The ordinance likewise required that, prior to the issuance of a permit for a demonstration, the appropriate officials find that the assembly

> WILL not portray criminality, depravity or lack of virtue in, or incite violence, hatred, abuse or hostility toward a person or group of persons by reason of reference to religious, racial, ethnic, national or regional affiliation.[64]

The ordinance further required that the assembly be found not to be for "an unlawful purpose," but permitted any of its requirements to be waived by unanimous consent of the village board of trustees.[65] The other two ordinances forbade the "dissemination of any materials within the Village of Skokie which promotes or incites hatred against persons by reasons of their race, national origin, or religion, and is intended to do so,"[66] and prohibited public demonstrations by members of political parties while wearing "military style uniforms."[67]

The Nazi party dutifully filed an application for a permit to march on 4 July 1977. In applying for the permit, the party stated (as summarized by the Court of Appeals for the Seventh Circuit)

> THAT the march would last about half an hour, and would involve about 30 to 50 demonstrators wearing uniforms including swastikas and carrying a party banner with a swastika and placards with statements thereon such as "White Free Speech," "Free Speech for the

---

63. Village of Skokie Ordinance 77-5-N-994 §§ 27–54, *quoted in Collin v. Smith*, 578 F.2d at 1199.
64. *Id.*
65. Village of Skokie Ordinance 77-5-N-994 §§ 27–56(i), 27–64. The ordinance further exempted from its scope any governmental activities.
66. Village of Skokie Ordinance No. 77-5-N-995, *quoted in Collin v. Smith*, 578 F.2d at 1199.
67. Village of Skokie Ordinance No. 77-5-N-996, *quoted in Collin v. Smith*, 578 F.2d at 1200.

White Man," and "Free Speech for White America." A single file side-
walk march that would not disrupt traffic was proposed, without
speeches or the distribution of handbills or literature.[68]

Notably, according to its own counsel, the village did "not maintain that . . .
the NSPA will behave other than as described in the permit application(s)."[69]

That these ordinances were aimed at the National Socialist Party of
America was so patent that the village itself did not even contest on appeal
the trial court's finding to that effect.[70] The inability of the Nazis to get a
permit under a statute that specifically intended to prevent their march is
hardly surprising, any more so than is the fact that the party brought suit in
the federal district court to have the ordinance struck as unconstitutional.

In the federal action (brought by the local Nazi party through its leader,
Frank Collin), each of the three ordinances was struck because it impermissibly burdened protected speech.[71] Unlike most court decisions that deal
with hate speech, the district court addressed head-on the argument that
"to permit an idea to be advocated is to concede its legitimacy and impliedly
accept the possibility that it may be accepted and implemented as a social
policy, and that there are some policies whose implementation would be so
completely unacceptable in a democratic society that their advocacy should
not be permitted."[72]

The Court rejected this alternative to the oft-stated dictum that to the
First Amendment "there is no such thing as a false idea."[73] In so doing, it
opined that such a view of the "marketplace of ideas" rationale set up a straw
man only to knock it down. As Judge Decker explained, after quoting the
"civic courage" language from Justice Brandeis's concurrence in *Whitney*:

> THE question, then, is not whether there are some ideas that are com-
> pletely unacceptable in a civilized society. Rather the question is which
> danger is greater: the danger that allowing the government to punish
> "unacceptable" ideas will lead to suppression of ideas that are merely
> uncomfortable to those in power; or the danger that permitting free
> debate on such unacceptable ideas will encourage their acceptance
> rather than discouraging them by revealing their pernicious quality.
> This question is one of the fundamental dilemmas of free speech, and
> it is certainly open to public debate, but for the purposes of this case,
> the question has been definitively settled by the Supreme Court.[74]

---

68. 578 F.2d at 1200.
69. *Id.*
70. *Id.* at 1199, n. 3.
71. *Collin v. Smith*, 447 F. Supp. 676 (N.D. Ill. 1977).
72. *Id.* at 687, *summarizing* Alexander Bickel, *The Morality of Consent* 70–77 (1975).
73. *Id.* at 687, *quoting Gertz v. Robert Welch, Inc.*, 418 U.S. 323, 339 (1974).
74. 447 F. Supp. at 688.

After a quick tour of the development from *Schenck* to *Brandenburg*, Judge Decker rejected the notion, proffered by the village, that "some ideas are too dangerous to permit their advocacy."[75] He then turned to whether the regulations could nonetheless be sustained, rejecting the applicability of the various *Chaplinsky* categories to the Nazi Party's speech. This finding was upheld on appeal.[76] It should be noted that the decision to reject these arguments was facilitated by the village's concession that "it does not rely on a fear of responsive violence to justify the ordinance, and does not even suggest that there will be any physical violence if the march is held."[77] Coupled with the earlier concession of the village that the marchers themselves were not expected to be physically violent, this second concession had the effect of removing the case "out of the scope of *Brandenburg v. Ohio*, and *Feiner*," as well as from the fighting words category. After *Cohen*, it would be difficult to see just how a lower court *could* have supported the village without defying binding precedent.[78]

However, before seizing upon the notion that even the *Chaplinky* regime under which we live permits no room for the regulation of hate speech per se, the Court's words in that seminal decision should be examined again. When it set out the categories of unprotected speech the Court included "insulting or 'fighting' words—those which by their very utterance inflict injury *or* tend to incite an immediate breach of the peace."[79] In other words, those who seek to reframe the hate speech argument may legitimately ask, Why cannot such speech be regulated, not merely as tending to lead to violence as "manly men" square off, but as words that by their very nature inflict harm?[80] And here, advocates of such regulation would argue, the tort of intentional infliction of emotional distress may provide some guidance.

Because the entire approach of *Chaplinsky* is a target of this book, the extension of the principles of that case to another subset (or rather, the exponential expansion of one subset) cannot be welcome here. However, although the new principle would present an enormous set of interpretational problems, that is, determining how much candor may be used in public discussion and where "injury" takes place, such an extension does not work any violence upon *Chaplinsky*'s literal words. What it would do, however, is

---

75. *Id.*
76. 578 F.2d at 1203–1204.
77. *Id.* at 1203.
78. *Id.* at 1197.
79. *Chaplinsky v. New Hampshire*, 315 U.S. 568, 571–572 (1941) (emphasis added) (upholding conviction of Jehovah's Witness for calling city marshal "a God damned racketeer" and "damned fascist").
80. For a review of the decline and, perhaps, the fall of the "injury" prong of *Chaplinsky*, *see* Note, *The Demise of the Chaplinsky Fighting Words Doctrine: An Argument for Its Interment*, 106 Harv. L. Rev. 1129 (1993).

jeopardize its rationale: that the suppression of such speech is unrelated to legitimate public debate.

In *Collin v. Smith*, Judge Decker articulated the stark dilemma faced by the judges who are confronted with the question of whether to censor bigotry. Noting (and quoting Justice Jackson's eloquent words in dissent regarding) the pain caused by such "missiles" of venom, Judge Decker noted the counterweight:

> ON the other hand, it is equally clear that discussion of race and religion will often involve the exposition of ideas and positions that are inherently offensive to many, but which are nevertheless protected by the First Amendment. We live in a society that is very conscious of racial and religious differences, in which open discussion of important public issues will often require reference to racial and religious groups, often in terms which members of these groups, and others, would consider insulting or degrading. To choose an obvious example, discussion of the use of mandatory quotas in affirmative action programs cannot help but touch upon characteristics perceived to be shared by members of particular groups. The First Amendment does not permit the government to restrict discussion of such sensitive and emotion charged public issues to the sanitary prose of legal and social sciences technical jargon.[81]

That such a prospect is in fact a realistic reading of hate speech regulation is exemplified by *Doe v. University of Michigan*,[82] in which a student-cum-teaching assistant of biopsychology expressed fears that the campus hate speech code would be violated by his discussion of theories relating to alleged sex differences in mental operation. After examining the legislative history of the code, and the university's own explanatory texts regarding it, the Court concluded that "the ideas discussed in Doe's field of study bear sufficient similarity to ideas denounced as 'harassing' in the Guide to constitute a specific and realistic fear of prosecution."[83] Moreover, the spotty record of U.S. law enforcement in the use of blanket powers to suppress dissident speech in times of civil strife—what have been called by Vincent Blasi "pathological periods"—does not exactly provide a ringing endorsement to grant them a "tool that governmental officials may use and have used to harass minority groups and to suppress dissident speech."[84]

---

81. *Collin v. Smith*, 447 F. Supp. at 691.
82. 721 F. Supp. 852, 860 (E.D. Mich 1989).
83. *Id.*
84. Note, *supra* note 80, at 1141.

Finally, as a jurisprudential matter, it should be noted that in *R.A.V.* the Supreme Court explicitly rejected this notion that the injuries inflicted by hate speech differ in kind (rather than in degree) from other verbally inflicted harms. As the Court stated:

> WHAT makes the anger, fear, sense of dishonor, etc. produced by [hate speech] . . . distinct from the anger, fear, sense of dishonor, etc. produced by other fighting words is nothing other than the fact that it is caused by a distinctive idea, conveyed by a distinctive message. The First Amendment cannot be evaded that easily.[85]

In other words, the principle obstacle to the resurrection of this branch of the *Chaplinsky* definition of "fighting words" to permit regulation of hate speech is that the Court seems to have repented of the whole idea. Although this seems to be the right result—the Court's logic is difficult to answer: What *is* the difference in kind in the injury inflicted by hate speech and other, protected, speech?—it is not the end of the debate on hate speech.

Like so many courts in the cases of hate speech, in *Collin* both Judge Decker and the Seventh Circuit adduced their own feeling that "if any philosophy should be regarded as completely unacceptable to civilized society, that of plaintiffs, who, while disavowing . . . genocide, have nevertheless deliberately identified themselves with a regime whose record of brutality and barbarism is unmatched in modern history, would be a good place to start."[86] Like the Supreme Court of the United States in *R.A.V.*, the district and circuit courts in *Collin* expressed loathing of the philosophy whose right to speak they found themselves vindicating—not unlike antislavery judges "forced" to enforce the Fugitive Slave Act, which returned human beings to a bondage the pernicious nature of which they were well aware.[87] Is this ritual baring of judicial teeth anything more than a rhetorical device? Perhaps. After all, if the First Amendment requires us to defend "speech that we hate," surely we are permitted at least to note when we live up to that very hard saying.

---

85. *R.A.V.* 505 U.S. at 392.
86. 447 F. Supp. at 687; 578 F.2d at 1203.
87. *See generally* Robert Cover, *Justice Accused* (1975) at 119–147 (describing perceived limitations of judicial power to serve moral rightness in the face of contrary law, Cover's excellent study as a whole examines this judicial dilemma in the context of antislavery judges confronted with cases under the Fugitive Slave Act); *see also* Paul Finkelman, *Story Telling on the Supreme Court: Prigg v. Pennsylvania and Justice Joseph Story's Judicial Nationalism*, 1994 Sup. Ct. Rev. 247 (1995) (detailing Justice Story's rather disingenuous recasting of history and expansion of national power by writing an unnecessarily proslavery decision in the *Prigg* case).

Sex, Status, and Violence: Pornography as Hate Speech

Since the publication of Andrea Dworkin's *Pornography: Men Possessing Women*,[88] a faction of the women's movement has labored unceasingly for the enactment of laws that would regulate explicitly erotic materials that contribute, in their view, to the degradation of women. Catharine A. MacKinnon, who co-authored the prototypical ordinance[89] with Dworkin, has been one of the most vocal and influential advocates of this faction's position. Described by Professor Cass Sunstein as the most original and important voice behind feminism and law,[90] MacKinnon has gone far to legitimate her view and win adherents to her cause. Indeed, in a 1992 criminal case, the Supreme Court of Canada essentially adopted the arguments set forth by MacKinnon.[91]

The growing acceptance of this viewpoint raises serious questions for First Amendment jurisprudence, questions whose resolution is fraught with peril. Although the enactment of the MacKinnon-Dworkin ordinance and its upholding by the U.S. Supreme Court would not, of course, cause the constitutional sky to fall, the arguments that are winning converts and are acquiring an air of scholarly legitimacy are inimical not only to the Constitution but to the premises underlying democratic-republican government. Both the premises upon which MacKinnon proceeds and the direction in which she hopes to direct the law are utterly foreign to our concept of constitutional liberty within a political form of government. Moreover, because MacKinnon seeks to edit the materials presented to the electorate, including whether or not their support for the ordinance works a change in the constitutional order, the end result of her endeavors, however well inten-

---

88. Andrea Dworkin *Pornography: Men Possessing Women* (1980).

89. The ordinance's text is set out and explained *infra*, text at notes 100–107.

90. Cass R. Sunstein, *Feminism and Legal Theory* 101 Harv. L. Rev. 826, 829 (1989).

91. In *Butler v. Her Majesty the Queen*, 1 S.C.R. 452 (1992), the Canadian Supreme Court held that the harm caused by "the proliferation of materials which seriously offend the values fundamental to our society is a substantial concern which justifies restricting the otherwise full exercise of the freedom of expression." In determining that pornography as described by MacKinnon fell afoul of that rather elastic standard, the Court relied on MacKinnon's arguments that "if true equality between male and female persons is to be achieved, we cannot ignore the threat to equality resulting from exposure to audiences of certain types of violent and degrading material. Materials portraying women as a class as objects for sexual exploitation and abuse have a negative impact on the individual's sense of self-worth and acceptance." *Id.* In explicating the materials that violated the standard the Court declared "[d]egrading or dehumanizing materials place women (and sometimes men) in positions of subordination, servile submission [*sic*] or humiliation. They run against the principles of equality and dignity of all human beings." As MacKinnon has long advocated, consent is no defense, but rather "makes the acts more degrading or dehumanizing." Moreover, the decision is grounded not in morality, but in the public perception that pornography is "harmful to society, particularly to women."

tioned, is not merely a substantive dilution of First Amendment protections, but a subversion of democratic process.[92]

Because the feminist arguments against pornography as made by MacKinnon have recently been used to support censorship of other hate speech and have been redeployed by more rigorous academics,[93] an understanding of these prototypical arguments concerning the values served and disserved by the regulation of hate speech is in order.

In explicating MacKinnon's views, primary importance should be given to the expositions contained in *Feminism Unmodified*[94] and *Toward a Feminist Theory of the State*.[95] MacKinnon's more recent book, *Only Words*,[96] is a passionate defense of her theories, but its brevity and (even by MacKinnon's standards) inflated rhetoric render it more useful as a supplement to these earlier, more disciplined works. Likewise, her 1984 Francis Biddle Memorial Lecture, "Pornography, Civil Rights, and Speech"[97] (revised and reprinted in *Feminism Unmodified*), and the ordinance itself are not as frank about the values they serve: The ordinance is a proposed law that requires popular support to secure passage, while the lecture is, in MacKinnon's own words, "an argument for the constitutionality of the ordinance"[98] that was first given to an audience not entirely sympathetic to her views. Where the two conflict with her more theoretical utterances and those directed at her supporters, I give credence to the latter as being more representative of her genuine views. Without any imputation of lack of candor to MacKinnon (whatever one may think of her views, she certainly does not hide them), it seems clear that the thinker and scholar has a freedom denied the advocate, who can only press for as much change as the legal culture at the present time will permit. This advocate piece has a worth of its own, however, in that it sets out "the vision of the First Amendment with which our law is consistent."[99]

---

92. Although "politics" and "political" have been used to connote anything pertaining to government—the sense in which MacKinnon uses them—they specifically denote the forms of government that rely on the building of public consensus and the making of decisions by a free electoral process. As Bernard Crick has written: "politics represents at least some tolerance of differing truths, some recognition that government is possible, indeed best conducted, amid the open canvassing of rival interests." Bernard Crick, *In Defence of Politics* (2d ed. 1972) at 18.

93. *See*, for example, Cass Sunstein, "A New Deal for Speech," in Allen & Jensen, *Freeing the First Amendment* (1995); Sunstein, *supra* note 90.

94. Catharine A. MacKinnon, *Feminism Unmodified* (1987).

95. Catharine A. MacKinnon, *Toward a Feminist Theory of the State* (1989). (Hereafter cited as *Feminist Theory*).

96. Catharine A. MacKinnon, *Only Words* (1993.)

97. Catharine A. MacKinnon, *Pornography Civil Rights and Speech*. 20 Harvard Civil Rights—Civil Liberties L. Rev. 1 (1985).

98. *Id.*

99. *Id.* at 2.

The Proposed Ordinance

The MacKinnon-Dworkin ordinance defines pornography as:

> THE graphic sexually explicit subordination of women through pic-
> tures and/or words that also includes one or more of the following:
> (i) women are presented dehumanized as sexual objects, things, or
> commodities; or (ii) women are presented as sexual objects who
> enjoy pain or humiliation; or (iii) women are presented as sexual ob-
> jects who experience sexual pleasure in being raped; or (iv) women
> are presented as sexual objects tied up or cut up or mutilated or
> bruised or physically hurt; or (v) women are presented in postures
> of sexual submission, servility or display; or (vi) women's body parts—
> including but not limited to vaginas, breasts, and buttocks—are ex-
> hibited, such that women are reduced to those parts; or (vii) women
> are presented as whores by nature; or (viii) women are presented
> being penetrated by objects or animals; or (ix) women are presented
> in scenarios of degradation, injury, torture, shown as filthy or infe-
> rior, bleeding, bruised or hurt in a context that makes these condi-
> tions sexual.[100]

No doubt to pass muster under the Equal Protection Clause, the ordinance
extends as well to men and transsexuals in the place of women.

The practice of pornography under the MacKinnon-Dworkin ordinance
renders the pornographer liable to civil suit under several sets of circumstances. First, women who are coerced, intimidated, or fraudulently induced
into performing for pornography "shall have a cause of action."[101] Second,
any assault or physical attack attributable to pornography gives the victim of

---

100. *Id.* at 1.

101. Donald Alexander Downs, *The New Politics of Pornography* (1989) at 45.

102. *Id.* at 46. This particular provision is part of the failed Pornography Victim's Compensation Act (PVCA) (S. 1521) (102d Cong. 1991), which was killed by the Senate. Although it was unsuccessful, the bill marks the high-water mark of the anti-pornography
movement, and is thus worthy of some study. Like the MacKinnon-Dworkin ordinance
that can fairly be said to have inspired it, the bill created a dramatic shift of responsibility for sexual violence from the rapist to the publisher who allegedly "inspires" the violence. One distinction between the PVCA and the MacKinnon-Dworkin ordinance is
that the PVCA was limited to speech that is "obscene" where the ordinance is not. This
approach was applied by the Supreme Court of Canada in *Butler v. the Queen*, 1 S.C.R.
452 (1992) in which the MacKinnon-Dworkin approach was wedded to Canada's admittedly "unconstitutional" (that is, violative of the Charter of Rights) obscenity definition as a saving construction of the statute.

    The approach of limiting the scope of the ordinance to materials within the class of
obscene speech with a "pornographic" viewpoint was specifically rejected as a means
to preserve constitutionality under the First Amendment in *R.A.V. v. City of St. Paul*,
505 U.S. 377 (1992). The Senate version, a *Butler*-influenced version of the MacKinnon-

the assault a cause of action against the pornographer.[102] Third, "forcing pornography on a person" in "any place of employment, in education, in a home, or in any public place" creates "a cause of action against the perpetrator and/or institution."[103] Finally, under the model ordinance, the production, sale, exhibition, or distribution of pornography is discrimination against women by means of trafficking in pornography, against which "any woman has a cause of action hereunder as a woman acting against the subordination of women"[104] regardless of any proof of individual harm. Notably, this civil rights ordinance is also *entirely* civil in its impact. There is no effort to impose criminal sanctions under any of the four provisions.

Why an Ordinance: The Harms of Pornography

The ordinance, like MacKinnon's other writings, targets two discrete types of harm that are caused by pornography. The first kind, which can be called "direct,"[105] consists of the coercion of models or actresses into participation in the generation of pornographic materials. This type of harm MacKinnon claims to be endemic in the pornography industry, and MacKinnon provides ample support for its existence.[106] The best-known example cited by MacKinnon among her largely anecdotal, but nonetheless telling, evidence

---

Dworkin ordinance, thus could have passed constitutional muster if the ordinance itself had. The House version, the Pornography Victim's Protection Act (H. 1768) (102d Cong. 1991), dealt with the issue of women and children who are "coerced" into pornography. This bill contained no definition of coercion, and worse, explicitly provided that proof of various facts including "consent to commercial distribution" of the materials on the part of the plaintiff would not prevent a finding of coercion.

103. *Id.* 46–47. This provision is essentially a broader version of Title VII protections against sexual harassment, extending that act's protections beyond the workplace and educational facilities, expanding the reach of the statute to any public place and the home. *Compare* 42 U.S.C.§§ 2000e-2(a)(1)(1976); *see*, for example, *Hawley v. Town of Stratford*, 217 F.3d 141 (2d Cir. 2000) (superior officer denigrating female subordinate as, *inter alia*, having gained her position through sexual favors); *Kracunas v. Iona College*, 119 F.3d 80 (2d Cir. 1997) (student compelled to hear professor's sexual fantasies and to read erotic poetry aloud); *Robinson v. Jacksonville Shipyards, Inc.*, 760 F. Supp 1486 (M.D. Fla. 1991) (female welder belonged to protected class under Title VII; co-workers' conduct in posting pictures of nude and partially nude women in workplace sexualized workplace, constituting actionable sexual harassment).

104. *Id.* I use Downs's *supra* note 101 discussion of the ordinance only because it is slightly less diffuse than MacKinnon's various discussions of it. *See*, for example, MacKinnon, *Only Words.* Downs's account is brief and accurate.

105. MacKinnon, who deplores the use of a solely linear form of causality, would be most unwilling to accept this distinction. For her, one of the great weaknesses of obscenity law and other First Amendment jurisprudence is its reliance upon "John hit Mary" causality. *See Feminist Theory,* 206–207. But *see* H. L. A. Hart & A. M. Honoré, *Causation in the Law* (1959) at 79–103.

106. *See*, for example, *Feminism Unmodified,* 127–134.

of coercion is that of Linda Marchiano, who, according to her own account, has survived the most profitable commercialized rape in history.[107]

What can be called "direct injury"—because it is suffered in the very making of the pornographic product—is not restricted by MacKinnon to actual violent coercion or even to actual intimidation. She includes as coercion into pornographic activity the situation of women who are desperate for funds and, in MacKinnon's view, marginalized by society into accepting such degrading, low-paying jobs. Such women are forced, MacKinnon postulates, by socially imposed circumstances to turn to pornographers for funds.[108] Although these women are not victims in the conventional sense—they are not forced into their situations by pornographers, but are rather exploited by them—their consent is not meaningful in that they have no other real option. Moreover, women's position in society is determined, according to MacKinnon, in no small part by the social attitudes pornography fosters, the view that women are objects whose sexual nature is accessibility to the male.[109] Accepting this view for the sake of argument, it no longer seems outré to view "consent" to appear in pornographic materials because of economic duress as coercion by pornographers as a group. Nonetheless, it is useful to distinguish between actual coercion or intimidation of models/actresses by some producers or pornographers (chilling instances of which are given by MacKinnon) and this allegedly prevalent inability to meaningfully consent to the activities involved.

Not even the most fanatical advocate of First Amendment absolutism would argue that those cases of actual coercion or intimidation should not form the grounds of a civil action or a criminal prosecution. Indeed the films—or photographs thus created—may properly be declared to be forfeit and turned over to the victim for destruction if that is her wish, based on the common law doctrine that one may not profit from one's crimes.[110]

---

107. Although Linda Marchiano's account of being coerced into the filming of *Deep Throat* has been disputed by others, including her co-star on that film, Harry Reems, it nonetheless seems more useful to accept her view, for the sake of discussion. Even if it did not happen to her, it plainly has happened to many others. For Reems's account *see* Alan Dershowitz, *The Best Defense* (1982) at 180–182.

108. *Feminist Theory* at 214, 242–243; *Feminism Unmodified* at 136, 205. The logic used by MacKinnon to explore the coercive effect of capitalism on pornography is irresistibly reminiscent of George Bernard Shaw's explanation of prostitution, "Mrs. Warren's Profession," in *Plays, Pleasant and Unpleasant* (1905) at 200–206.

109. *Feminist Theory* 139–152.

110. "No one shall be permitted to profit by his own fraud, or to take advantage of his own wrong . . . or to acquire property by his own crime. . . . The maxim [is] *volenti non fit injura.*" *Riggs* v. *Palmer*, 115 N.Y. 506, 511–512, 514 (1889). *See also New York Mutual Life Insurance Co.* v. *Armstrong* 117 U.S. 591 (1886) (Field, J.); *Egelhoff v. Egelhoff,* 532 U.S. 141, 152 (2001); *Barker* v. *Kallash* 63 NY2d 19 (1984). Surprisingly, MacKinnon never relies upon this well-established doctrine in support of the ordinance's forfei-

Because films or photographs are the record of a crime as well as its products, it is wholly consonant with the First Amendment to say that such a record may not be sold for the profit of the rapist.

In its most recent utterances on the subject, *Simon & Schuster v. Crime Victims Board*,[111] the Supreme Court struck down New York State's so-called Son of Sam law that forfeited to the Crime Victims Board the proceeds of any memoirs or other writings by the criminal with the goal of providing compensation to the victims. However, the statute was struck on the ground that it was overly broad—its reach extended to writings that were not the fruit or instrumentality of crime as well as to those that were. The Court also found the statute singled out protected conduct—writing—for such forfeiture, and did not extend to other fruits of the crime. With respect to the general principle, however, the Court explicitly held that "the State likewise has an undisputed compelling interest in ensuring that criminals do not profit from their crimes."[112] The Court struck the provision specifically directed at literary retellings of the life story of the criminal that included his/her crime, but it approvingly cited New York's general statutory enactment directed at fruits of crime.[113]

To the extent that she claims that women who are coerced into pornography are without legal redress in the face of the sale of the films of their rapes, MacKinnon is setting up a straw man when she writes that *Deep Throat* is protected speech: "The film apparently cannot be reached *by her* [Linda Marchiano] any more than by anyone else, no matter what was done to her in making it. The fact that Linda was coerced makes the film no less protected as speech, even though the publication of *Ordeal* makes clear that the film documents crimes, acts that violate laws in all the fifty states."[114] MacKinnon bases this argument on the fact that *Deep Throat* has frequently

---

ture and liability provisions, a lapse on her part that unfortunately deprives (in my view) the best provision of the ordinance of a useful doctrinal anchor.

111. 502 U.S. 105 (1993).

112. *Id.* at 119, *citing with approval Children of Bedford v. Petromelis*, 77 N.Y.2d 713, 727 (1991); *Riggs*, 115 N.Y. 511–512.

113. *Id.*

114. *Feminism Unmodified* at 129. MacKinnon's footnote for the statement "*Deep Throat* is protected speech" provides references to an earlier note listing cases ruling on the obscenity or nonobscenity of the film. Some of the decisions in which *Deep Throat* was found not to be obscene include: *United States v. Various Articles of Obscene Merchandise*, 709 F.2d 132 (2d Cir. 1983); *State v. Aiuppa*, 298 So.2d 391 (Fla. 1974); *Keller v. State*, 606 S.W.2d 931 (Tex. Cr. App. 1980). She also gives several examples of cases that hold the film to be obscene, including *United States v. Battista*, 646 F.2d 237 (6th Cir. 1981) (upholding conviction under federal obscenity statute for transporting *Deep Throat* in interstate commerce); *United States v. One Reel of Film*, 360 F. Supp. 1067 (D. Mass. 1973); *State v. Diversified Theatrical Corporation*, 59 Mich. App. 223, 229 N.W.2d 389 (1975); *rev'd*, 396 Mich. 244, 240 N.W. 2d 460 (1976); *People v. Mature Enterprises*, 73 Misc.2d 749, 343 N.Y.S.2d 911 (N.Y. Crim. Ct. 1973); *aff'd* 76 Misc.2d 660, 352 N.Y.S.2d 346 (App. Term 1st Dept. 1974).

been held to be not obscene under the *Miller* test,[115] but coercion was not at issue in the cases that so ruled. Those cases dealt exclusively with the question of whether the film was subject to suppression solely on the basis of its communicative content and not on the basis of any incidents involved in filming.

In a system of case-by-case adjudication, a ruling on the single question of obscenity that is adverse to MacKinnon's position does not at all reflect on how the courts would rule on an entirely separate claim, that of coercion. MacKinnon caustically writes that "[w]hen a woman speaks for herself, her violation becomes an atrocity and is therefore a lie. So *Deep Throat*

---

115. The constitutional status of *Deep Throat* is actually quite murky. In *Miller v. California*, 413 U.S. 15 (1973) the Supreme Court created a new test to determine whether or not given materials were "obscene," a test that required the finder of fact to ascertain (a) whether the average person, applying "contemporary community standards" would find that the work, taken as a whole, appeals to the prurient interest in sex; (b) whether the work depicts, in a patently offensive way, sexual conduct specifically defined by the applicable state law; and (c) whether the work, taken as a whole, lacks serious literary, artistic or political social value. *Id.* at 25–26. The Court explicitly rejected the former constitutional standard that the work be "*utterly* without redeeming social value" established in *Memoirs v. Massachusetts*, 383 U.S. 413 (1966). *Id.* at 24. The resulting balkanization of obscenity law, which requires publishers or filmmakers to be conversant with the obscenity laws of each state into which their work may eventually stray, allows material that is constitutionally protected in one state to be censored in another, under the national Constitution. For example *Deep Throat* goes from protected expression to unprotected filth depending on which court the defendant finds himself—compare *Various Articles*, 709 F.2d 132, affirming the Southern District of New York's finding that the film is not patently offensive to the community of the "New York Area" and *Mature Enterprises*, 73 Misc.2d 749, 343 N.Y.S. 2d 911 finding the same film offensive in New York City. The impact of this balkanization of the definition of obscenity on the Senate's Pornography Victims Compensation Act, is nothing short of staggering. The Senate bill was limited in its scope to reach only materials which are constitutionally deemed obscene. Under *Miller*, the local community is not statewide, but regional—a town or perhaps a county (*see Hamling v. United States*, 418 U.S. 87 (1974)). Thus, in a federal cause of action, under a federal statute, in a federal court, the threshold question of whether the act even applies must be answered with reference to a local community in which that court may not even sit, depending on the vagaries of venue. Moreover, *which* communities' standards apply? Those of the community in which the materials are distributed by the publisher (those currently applicable), those of the community where the rapist or sexual assailant acquires the materials (if he buys them not from a direct distributor, but acquires them secondhand) or those where the crime giving rise to the suit took place? In either of the latter two eventualities, the publisher is held to the standards of a community into which he or she may never have intended to distribute his or her materials, and with which he or she may have absolutely no connection. The end result could well be that no publisher, even a small local press, would ever publish materials that could be found to be obscene even in the most parochial community because the publisher could well be judged by that community's standards years after publishing (the bill's statute of limitations [section 3(e)] relates to the date of the crime, not of publication) even after the materials have been removed from the stream of commerce, and have been in the eventual criminal's hands for years—theoretically, even decades.

is protected speech and *Ordeal* is sued for libel."[116] The fact that a libel suit was brought over Ms. Marchiano's book, *Ordeal*, while perhaps unfortunate, hardly indicts the justice system; surely those whom she accused in print of suborning her violation should have the right to endeavor to contest such accusations in court.

That is not to say that our law goes far enough in protecting coerced or intimidated women; it does not. The numbers of criminal prosecutions and civil forfeiture actions based on directly coercive behavior are woefully inadequate in our society,[117] and should be encouraged by all possible means, including statutory reform. An act based on the doctrine that one may not profit from one's crime that would allow victims positioned as Linda Marchiano describes herself to be in *Ordeal* to sue for destruction of the materials created through such means and for forfeiture of the profits to date would be a valuable tool, so long as it was limited to cases of direct coercion, that is, coercion by force, or fear stemming from implicit threat.[118]

As previously mentioned, MacKinnon does not so limit her definition of coercion: She argues that economic duress also forces women to appear in pornographic materials, and that pornographers as a group are exploiting women by taking advantage of the situation. If this economic duress theory can be supported empirically through statistics or other quantifiable data, which MacKinnon fails to do, it is nevertheless impossible to imagine a legal remedy. MacKinnon's complaint here is not merely with the adult entertainment industry, but with the inherent nature of capitalism—those with money induce those without it to do jobs which they might otherwise refuse to do. MacKinnon has already been criticized for failing to distinguish the plight of these women from that of anyone else who performs a job con-

---

116. *Feminism Unmodified* at 11.

117. Because the *Riggs v. Palmer supra* note 110 forfeiture hearing that I recommend would be a civil and not a criminal proceeding, as indeed are all the proceedings contained in the model ordinance, the plaintiff would enjoy the advantage of a lower burden of proof.

118. The Pornography Victims Protection Act (102d Cong. H. 1768) seems not to have been so limited. First, although it required "coercion" for models/actresses to establish a claim for relief, it set up a series of roadblocks to a defendant who seeks to resist the plaintiff's claim. Among the many types of evidence specifically listed as not negating coercion (others include a contract and monetary remuneration), *consent* to commercial distribution of the materials is included. If consent, apparently untainted by coercion itself, does not serve to negate coercion (which the act does not define) then it is difficult to imagine what would. If the act is simply refusing to allow subsequent consent to negate prior coercion, the result is simply the creation of severe evidentiary problems for the defendant (how can one defend against such a claim?). But it is possible to read the act as saying that a consent apparently full and free at the time it is given does not preclude a jury from later finding coercion, and that all makers of "pornographic" materials act at their constant peril.

sidered to be unpleasant or undesirable.[119] She also fails to explain how blanket prohibition would benefit this proportion of adult film workers and what provision should be made for them other than removing their liveli-hood—a flaw Nadine Strossen has effectively pointed out.[120]

As interviews with women in the adult film industry have shown, not all of them feel that their work is degrading.[121] Yet MacKinnon's hostility toward such sex industry figures as Veronica Vera, her behind-the-scenes role as the inspi-ration if not the instigator in the suppression of the work of Carol Jacobson, belies her claim to stand for the workers. Jacobson's contractually agreed upon participation in a school-funded (though student-run) forum on "Prostitution: From Academia to Activism" at the University of Michigan was first reduced and then eliminated by MacKinnon's students with the surprising imprimatur of First Amendment authority Dean Lee Bollinger.[122] Perhaps more charita-bly, MacKinnon stands for the workers, and speaks for them—so long as they do not seek to speak for themselves. As will be seen later, marginalizing mem-bers of her theoretical constituency who do not accept her evaluation of their lives and experiences is a recurrent MacKinnon trait.

The second form of harm caused by pornography in MacKinnon's analy-sis can be described best as "attitudinal."[123] This harm is done to women at large throughout society. It encompasses a wide range of injuries, from that of having pornographic materials forced upon them, whether in the intimacy of the home or in the workplace, to sexual violence encouraged or caused by the eroticization of the violence that is a pronounced fixture of much por-nography and the objectification of women that occurs in all pornography. MacKinnon and Dworkin argue that such desensitization to violence and re-sulting emulation of violently sexual materials form only a small part of such a harm, claiming that sexist attitudes are further reinforced by pornography.[124] Pornography further reinforces the male image—and thus that held by society—of women as objects and not as people in their own right, as inferior beings to be acted upon. This in turn leads to the legitimization of such atti-tudes, to the spreading of sexist attitudes and thus contributes to the perpetu-

---

119. Nadine Strossen, *Defending Pornography: Free Speech, Sex, and the Fight for Women's Rights* (1995) at 189–191. For a critique of other anti-pornography writers' handling of the same point, *see* Alan Soble, *Pornography: Marxism, Feminism, and the Future of Sexuality* (1986) at 34–37.

120. Strossen, at 189–191.

121. *Id.* at 184–188. According to Strossen, women such as Veronica Vera, Candida Royalle, and Nina Hartley have said they find it fulfilling, even empowering, or a positive part of their personal growth.

122. *Id.* at 212–215.

123. Again, it should be noted that these terms are not MacKinnon's and that she would surely object to their usage.

124. *Feminist Theory* at 134–152.

ation of male dominance in forms much less crude than actual rape.[125] The battle cry of "porn is the theory, rape is the practice" is one MacKinnon believes, but it oversimplifies her view of the harms pornography causes.

Although MacKinnon would claim that both forms of harm are equally attributable to pornography,[126] the attitudinal harms are distinguishable because they result from audience's use of the material and its accompanying ideas or attitudes. The direct harms, in contrast, are inflicted in the very manufacture of the pornography and are not dependent upon the reactions of readers or viewers to the materials. This distinction that I have previously drawn has been criticized by Fordham law professor Tracy Higgins, who wrote that "this characterization suggests at the outset that the specific harms outside of coercion in the production of pornography are derivative, attenuated, indirect."[127]

I do not mean to imply that one harm is of lesser magnitude, but that the two harms are different in kind. Attitudinal harms are certainly "indirect" or "derivative" in the sense that they do not necessarily result from the production of the pornography alone, but require at least two other steps. The pornographic material must be read or viewed, *and* the reader or viewer must accept the portrayed dynamic of relationships between the sexes as desirable. "Indirect harms" could not result were pornography produced by the carload but kept in warehouses; the direct harms could.

Under the ordinance, or, indeed, any schema that penalizes pornographers for these indirect harms, the use to which the materials are put by third persons is attributed to the author regardless of whether he[128] intended, anticipated, or could have foreseen the particular results. For example, if a woman is harassed by the practice of her co-workers of leaving copies of *Playboy* magazine at her work station repeatedly, MacKinnon would hold *Playboy* liable, despite the absence of any *mens rea* on the part of the magazine's publishers. Whether desirable or not, this result is certainly a new departure in tort law, and should be recognized as such.

One can argue that sexual assault is a foreseeable consequence of exposure to "pornographic" materials. Tracy Higgins has endeavored to do just

---

125. *Id.* at 134–138.
126. *Id.* at 206–207.
127. Tracy Higgins, *Giving Women the Benefit of Equality: A Response to Wirenius*, 20 Ford. Urb. L. J. 77, 78, n. 7 (1993).
128. Although MacKinnon assumes that pornography is "not women's speech," it should be noted that more women such as Annie Sprinkle, Marilyn Chambers, and Candida Royalle are becoming involved in producing and writing erotic materials and films. Ms. Royalle especially directs her films toward a mixed or female audience. Also, collections of erotica such as the *Kensington Ladies' Group Book of Erotica* (1991) show a growing interest of women in erotica. Such widespread interest increasingly includes the "pornographic" themes of dominance and submission. *See* Madonna, *Sex* (1992); Nancy Friday, *Women on Top* (1991).

that, suggesting that the products liability tort law definition of a "dangerous product" might be expanded to include pornographic materials.[129] Such an enormous expansion of tort law reflects a fundamental change; altering the nature of another's beliefs and desires by presenting an alternative has not generally been likened to selling that person an exploding Pinto.

Moreover, it is not simply a new analogy or an example of case-by-case adjudication taking (as it sometimes does) a surprisingly long time to draw a clear parallel. Rather, the Higgins-MacKinnon concept of pornography as "dangerous product" blurs the notion of causation undergirding not only tort but criminal law. Traditionally, the interposition of another actor "but for" whose actions a harmful consequence would not have been produced is sufficient to exempt the actor who admittedly set the ball rolling.[130] Likewise, in the case of indirect harms stemming from pornography, the self-determined response of the audience is a "but for" cause that breaks the chain of causation.

Although the captive audience problem should be actionable, surely it is the person who inflicts the pornography upon the unwilling viewer against whom redress lies, as Title VII already provides in the workplace or in educational facilities.[131]

The MacKinnon-Dworkin Worldview

Contrasting Views: Free Speech Jurisprudence and MacKinnon

A significant premise underlying MacKinnon's scheme is that the class of materials unprotected by the First Amendment extends much further than

---

129. Higgins, *supra* note 127 at 79, n. 8.
130. *See*, for example, *Palsgraf v. Long Island Rail Road Co.*, 248 N.Y. 339 (1928). The same concept applies in English law. H. L. A. Hart & A. M. Honoré, *Causation in the Law* (1959) at 85 *et seq.* In the context of criminal liability, even, it is well established that an assault in which the victim subsequently dies becomes murder—unless the victim's medical care, extended as a result of the attack, had the effect of killing the victim, who would not otherwise have died. *See*, for example, *People v. Kane*, 213 N.Y. 260 (1915); *People v. Bowie & Thompson*, 200 A.D.2d 511, 607 N.Y.S.2d 248 (1st Dep't 1994) (reaffirming rule of *Kane* regardless of presence or absence of gross negligence on part of treating physician). But *see Rice v. Paladin Enterprises, Inc.* 128 F.3d 233 (4th Cir. 1997), *cert den.*, 523 U.S. 1074 (1998) (adopting tort/crime liability analysis; rev'g *Rice v. Paladin Enterprises, Inc.*, 940 F. Supp. 836 (D.M.D. 1996)(declining to adopt tort model).
131. *See*, for example, *Harris v. Forklift Systems, Inc.*, 510 U.S. 17, (1993) setting out standard for "hostile work environment" claim under Title VII; for a provocative and intersting commentary on *Harris* and the perceived erosion of First Amendment workplace rights, *see* Richard H. Fallon, *Sexual Harassment, Content Neutrality and the First Amendment Dog that Didn't Bark*, 1994 Sup. Ct. Rev. 1 (1995). Nadine Strossen has likewise expressed her concern that the hostile work environment standard under Title VII has become a Trojan horse in which censorship has sneaked into the workplace. Nadine Strossen, *Defending Pornography* at 119–140.

that presently recognized by the Supreme Court. Because MacKinnon rejects the Court's obscenity doctrine,[132] the exact parameters of her vision of the First Amendment remain cloudy, and of uncertain parameters. Constitutional obscenity doctrine has its roots, as seen earlier, in the 1942 case *Chaplinsky v. New Hampshire*.[133] In *Chaplinsky*, the Court opined that "there are certain well-defined and narrowly limited classes of speech, the prevention and punishment of which have never been thought to raise any constitutional question. These include the lewd and obscene, the profane, the libelous and the insulting or 'fighting' words—those which by their very utterance tend to inflict injury or tend to incite an immediate breach of the peace."[134] The *Chaplinsky* dictum was reaffirmed in *Roth v. United States*.[135] In *Roth*, the Court found that the *Chaplinsky* category of obscenity was indeed not protected by the Constitution.[136] From *Roth* to the present, the basic question of obscenity jurisprudence has not been whether obscenity is protected by the First Amendment but rather whether the materials at issue are obscene.[137] As a result of MacKinnon's rejection of this rubric, and her expansion of the definition of pornography beyond what has been deemed to constitute obscenity, this categorical exception cannot be used to justify the ordinance.

That MacKinnon's approach does not rely on the ipse dixit approach of obscenity law is its one great doctrinal strength (certainly as the *Brandenburg*-based analysis employed in the previous chapters bears out), but it is accidental. Or, rather, it is instrumental. MacKinnon deplores the effort to impose the traditional Judeo-Christian morality upon women that obscenity law dictates, and rejects obscenity law for its reaffirmation of the virgin/

---

132. *See*, for example, *Feminism Unmodified* at 150 ("The law of obscenity, the state's primary approach to its version of the pornography question, has literally nothing in common with this feminist critique. Their obscenity is not our pornography"). In Chapter 13 of *Feminism Unmodified*, "Not a Moral Issue," MacKinnon discusses at length why the obscenity exception to the First Amendment does not provide a valid basis for regulation of speech in the interest of protecting women, based as it is upon a patriarchal standard of morality which it seeks to perpetuate.

133. 315 U.S. 568 (1942) (upholding conviction for use of "fighting words" directed at city marshal in public speech).

134. *Id.* at 571–572.

135. 354 U.S. 476 (1957).

136. *Id.* at 484–485.

137. *See*, for example, *Jacobellis v. Ohio*, 378 U.S. 184, 197 (1964) (opinion of Stewart, J., who cannot define obscenity, but declares "I know it when I see it"); *Paris Adult Theatre v. Slaton*, 413 U.S. 49 (1973) (reaffirming *Roth*); *Miller v. California, supra* note 115 (establishing "local community standards" test); *Jenkins v. Georgia*, 418 U.S. 153 (1974) (nudity alone insufficient); *Hamling v. United States*, 418 U.S. 87 (1974) ("local community" is not statewide standard but truly local in scope); *see also* Kent Greenawalt, *Speech, Crime and the Uses of Language* (1989) at 304 ("The basic constitutional standards have remained those of *Miller*").

whore dichotomy.[138] It is not constitutional analysis but political analysis that leads her to assail the obscenity standard as detrimental to the status of women.

Regardless of her motive, MacKinnon's term "pornography" cannot be used interchangeably with "obscenity" with any accuracy. This rejection of the "Victorian" doctrine of obscenity (not accorded constitutional status until 1951) is reflected in the impact of MacKinnon's analysis, as well as in its theoretical base. That MacKinnon's approach sweeps far more broadly than *Miller* is clear; MacKinnon's ordinance does not provide protection for materials with social value and does not require that pornographic materials be looked at in their context:

> THE requirement that the work be considered "as a whole" legitimizes something very like that on the level of publications such as *Playboy*, even though experimental evidence is beginning to support what victims have long known: legitimate settings diminish the injury perceived to be done to the women whose trivialization and objectification it contextualizes. Besides, if a woman is subjected, what should it matter that the work has other value? Perhaps what redeems a work's value among men enhances its injury to women. Existing standards of literature, art, science and politics are, in feminist light, consonant with pornography's mode, meaning, and message.[139]

The implications of this passage are to allow for the suppression of a wide range of work, broader, perhaps, than that which seems to fall under the strict letter of the ordinance, which was, after all, written in the hope of gaining political support. It is not clear from the text of the ordinance that the context defense currently built into the law of obscenity would not be viable. However, the ordinance as written certainly does not provide for such a defense.[140]

---

138. *Feminist Theory* at 199–201; *see also Id.* at 175 (in the context of anti-rape laws, criticizing categorization of women by availability for sex, condemning virgin-whore dichotomy).

139. *Feminist Theory* at 202.

140. In the most recent version of the ordinance to be approved by MacKinnon, Massachusetts's proposed Act to Protect the Civil Rights of Women and Children (H. 5194) (1992), it is explicitly stated that "[i]solated parts [of the work] shall not be the sole basis for complaints" under the trafficking provision, which allows women to sue on behalf of women as a class absent any showing of individualized injury. (H.B. 5194 Mass. 177th General Court, 192 Sess. Section 2[e]). Two observations apply to this resurrection of the context defense. First, it applies only to the trafficking provision, and not to the rest of the bill, thus allowing isolated passages to serve as a basis for suit under the other provisions. Also, this modification is contrary to her writings against a context defense, and thus can only be deemed to have been made for political expediency. Plainly, this defense of context, while proposed in Massachusetts, is not desired, and is only sparingly extended.

The elimination of the context defense is no mere technical change in the law. Allowing even a single passage deemed pornographic to result in the suppression of the work on trial would result in the bowdlerization or loss of many works currently hailed as classics. James Joyce's *Ulysses,* for one, could not pass muster, nor could much of the works of D. H. Lawrence, to say nothing of Milton's *Paradise Lost.*[141] Although it is perhaps instructive to list works that would fall prey to censorship under MacKinnon's narrowed view of the First Amendment, it is also repetitive, and has been amply done.[142] Indeed, public concern over the possibility of censoring works of literary value has wrung token concessions from MacKinnon and her supporters in at least one state.[143]

More significantly, the reasons that to MacKinnon justify the withdrawal of constitutional protection from materials within the ordinance apply equally to materials that are not within the narrowest reading of it that can be advanced: Why is *explicit* sexual portrayal necessary to permit the censorship of materials thus leaving protected other materials (Ambrose Bierce's fiercely misogynistic but asexual writings leap to mind) that can lead to the same attitudinal harms as such explicit materials? After all, if writing or depiction leads, through means other than explicit portrayals of sex, to the creation of attitudes that tend to the subordination of women, how is the harm it does any different from a pornographic novel, which by definition cannot involve direct harm, and yet falls prey to the ordinance? One suspects that such a line of demarcation represents only a concession to political reality, or is subject to broader interpretation that would lead to its extension beyond portrayals of sexual intercourse to portrayals that are socially degrading to women as well.

"Our Vision of The First Amendment"

Even a pragmatic activist such as MacKinnon who seeks to use the courts as her field of activism must articulate a vision of the First Amendment

---

141. Milton's description of Eve as deeply sexual and "not equal as [her] sex not equal seemed . . . .yield[ing] with coy submission" is just one of the passages to which I advert. *Paradise Lost* in *The Complete Poetry of John Milton,* H. Beeching, ed. (1938); Book IV at page 254.

142. Most recently and exhaustively by Nadine Strossen, *supra* note 119 at 199–217.

143. The Massachusetts Act to Protect the Civil Rights of Women and Children, *supra* note 140 has also limited the trafficking provision to "pornography made using live or dead human beings or animals," effectively (one would hope!) limiting the bill's reach to visual materials (section 2(e)). This was done, according to MacKinnon, in order to end the debate about whether the works of Norman Mailer or Henry Miller might be suppressed. Tamar Lewin, "Pornography Foes Push for Right to Sue," *New York Times,* 15 March 1992, p. A16. However, because of the liability for assaults inspired by or committed in imitation of materials consisting solely of text, the prospect that mainstream publishers will be held liable for sexual assaults cannot be dismissed.

when she perceives traditionally conceived speech to be a major stumbling block to the achievement of her social goals. MacKinnon argues that the First Amendment protects speech only insofar as no harm can result.

Throughout her writings, MacKinnon has acted under the assumption that the problem with First Amendment law is that it is too obtuse to perceive the harm of pornography, or that the harms inflicted on women through pornography are so endemic in our culture that the Court does not perceive their extent. As she has memorably put it, "What unites many cases in which speech interests are raised and implicated but not, on balance, protected is harm, harm that counts."[144] That image is coupled with her critique of linear causation logic:

> THE idea is that words or pictures can only be harmful if they produce harm in a form that is considered an action. Words work in the province of attitudes, actions in the realm of behavior. Words cannot constitute harm in themselves—never mind libel, invasion of privacy, blackmail, bribery or most sexual harassment. But which is saying "kill" to a trained guard dog, a word or an act? Which is its training? How about a sign which reads "whites only"? Is that the idea or the practice of segregation? Is a woman raped by an attitude or a behavior? Which is sexual arousal?[145]

As the case law that led to *Brandenburg* makes clear, however, the Court—and especially Holmes, Brandeis, and Douglas—were aware that much protected speech may cause harm. Protection of that speech is a choice made not in ignorance of that fact, but in the name of what is deemed (and deemed rightly, I believe) a greater good—creating a kind of relationship between the individual and the state in which the individual is not subordinated.

Even more significantly, for present purposes, MacKinnon does not distinguish between the harm done by the communicative content of the material to the values and attitudes of the audience and harms that are incidental in nature, in that they are caused by circumstances surrounding the communication. The harm done by the adoption of the beliefs propounded by the communication at issue, the attitudinal harms, and the result of the auditor's eventually acting on his changed attitudes are distinct from the harms that may be called contextual. These incidental harms are not inherent in the nature of the communication but rather are tied to the specific context in which the communication is made.

---

144. *Feminism Unmodified* at 179.
145. *Feminism Unmodified* at 156; *see also Only Words* at 30, 30–33 ("Speech acts"; giving examples of how speech regarding those in positions of social inequality impacts upon their status).

The classic case of falsely shouting "fire" in a crowded theater,[146] for example, is based not upon the inherent nature of the message, but rather upon the factual context that makes a reasoned reaction to the false message unlikely. An audience in the dark that is given a frightening buzzword in a situation that suggests impending doom is likely to panic, not think. Shout "Fire!" in a sunlit, uncrowded meadow, say, and you may cause puzzlement, but panic is less likely. The evil to be prevented is not the substance of the communication, a false message that there is a fire, but the chaos that would ensue in the darkened theater. MacKinnon rejects this requirement that regulation of speech be content neutral, seeming to fall back on the proposition that speech that exhibits a tendency to lead to unfortunate attitudes or practical results should be subject to the censor—a viewpoint that has long been discredited.[147]

MacKinnon relies heavily upon *Beauharnais*, in which Justice Frankfurter's opinion for the majority found libel of a group as unprotected as libel of an individual. Frankfurter required only that the state be able to show a rational basis for the prohibition of speech, which he found in the possibility that "the dignity accorded [a citizen depends] as much on the reputation of the racial and religious group to which he willy-nilly belongs, as on his own merits."[148] As Justice Black wrote in dissent, the *Beauharnais* approach "degrades First Amendment freedoms to the 'rational basis' level."[149] MacKinnon's reliance upon this case (which was largely discredited and possibly overruled by *Brandenburg*, which involved much the same sort of speech as did *Beauharnais* and found it constitutionally protected) shows just how far outside the mainstream of First Amendment jurisprudence she

---

146. Posited by Justice Holmes in *Schenck v. United States*, 249 U.S. 47 (1919) (upholding convictions under Espionage Act for obstructing recruitment of soldiers during World War I on grounds that the speech that was involved, though normally protected, presented a "clear and present danger" of causing a substantive evil that Congress was empowered to prevent; that is, the spreading of disaffection and resistance to conscription in the ranks).

147. See *Feminism Unmodified* at 178. MacKinnon suggests that any harm suffices, and does not specify the degree or the imminence of the requisite harm. The history of the "bad tendency" test and its eventual rejection is discussed not only in Chapter 2, but in Rabban, *Free Speech in Its Forgotten Years, supra* note 7, at 320 *et seq.* The "bad tendency" test was most famously endorsed by the Supreme Court in *Gitlow v. New York*, 268 U.S. 652, 669 (1925) and in *Whitney v. California*, 274 U.S. at 357 (1927). The Court renounced the approach in *Dennis v. United States*, 341 U.S. at 494, 507 (1951), although the version of the "clear and present danger" test that that court erected was none too speech protected.

148. 343 U.S. 250, 263 (1952).

149. *Id.* at 269 (Black, J., dissenting) Justice Douglas dismissed the Frankfurter opinion contemptuously: "It is a warning to every minority that when the Constitution guarantees free speech it does not mean what it says." *Id.* at 287 (Douglas, J., dissenting).

is, whether for weal or for woe.[150] Indeed, the Seventh Circuit Court of Appeals reaffirmed its belief that subsequent cases have "so washed away the foundations of *Beauharnais* that it could not be considered authoritative" in striking the MacKinnon-Dworkin ordinance as unconstitutional, in *American Booksellers Association v. Hudnut*, a decision that was (in a highly unusual procedure) summarily affirmed by the Supreme Court.[151]

MacKinnon thus cannot claim that the ordinance reaches only speech excluded from First Amendment protection under the *Chaplinsky* categories of libel or obscenity. Indeed, even conceding the continuing validity of *Beauharnais*, this remains the case. As the Seventh Circuit noted in invalidating the MacKinnon ordinance, in not permitting context as a defense the ordinance ignores the requirement that "[w]ork must be an insult or a slur for its own sake to come within the ambit of *Beauharnais*, and a work need not be scurrilous at all to be 'pornography' under the ordinance."[152] Pornography as defined by MacKinnon also does not fit into the fighting words category of *Chaplinsky* because such words must be directed at a single individual to fall under that case's doctrine.[153]

Because MacKinnon is either inviting the creation of a new *Chaplinsky* category or trying to shoehorn pornography within the *Brandenburg* formulation, a testing of her proposed category in the light of the First Amendment's basic standard is an ideal way to see if the speech's suppression serves or does not serve the purpose of a verbal act.

---

150. In *Brandenburg* the speech held to be protected under the First Amendment was a call for political marches to persuade "our President, our Congress, our Supreme Court" to cease from "suppress[ing] the white race," threatening that should the "suppression" continue "it's possible that there might have to be some revengance [sic] taken." 395 U.S. at 445–446. In *Beauharnais*, the speech held to be unprotected was a call for the mayor and city council of Chicago to "halt the further encroachment, harassment and invasion of white people, their property, neighborhoods and persons, by the negro— through the police power." 343 U.S. at 276 (Appendix to opinion of Justice Black). In view of the nearly identical nature of the speech involved in the two cases, it has long been believed that *Brandenburg* gutted *Beauharnais* of any precedential weight. *See also* Tribe, *American Constitutional Law* (2d ed. 1988) at 861. *Contra: Smith v. Collin*, 439 U.S. 916, 919 (Blackmun, J., dissenting from denial of certiorari) ("*Beauharnais* has not been overruled or formally limited").

151. *American Bookseller's Ass'n. v. Hudnut*, 771 F.2d 323, 331 n. 7 (7th Cir. 1985) *aff'd mem.* 475 U.S. 1001 (1986) (invalidating ordinance as viewpoint descrimination).

152. *Id.* at 332.

153. 315 U.S. at 571–572. Indeed, even accepting pornography as "low-value speech" under *Chaplinsky*, the Supreme Court has recently held that "these areas of speech can, consistently with the First Amendment, be regulated *because of their constitutionally proscribable content* (obscenity, defamation, etc.)—not that they are categories of speech entirely invisible to the Constitution, so that they may be made vehicles for content discrimination unrelated to their distinctly proscribable content. Thus, the government may proscribe libel; but it may not make the further content discrimination of proscribing only libel critical of the government." *R.A.V.*, 505 U.S. at 383 (emphasis in original). This

Although MacKinnon does allege that the harm done by pornography is clear and present, it is unclear whether she accepts the clear and present danger test.[154] However, by failing to establish either an intent or an imminence requirement, MacKinnon's definition is simply not within the constitutional framework. At times, she seems to recognize this, and presses for the creation of a new *Chaplinsky* category for pornography.[155] As there is no case law on this innovative point save *Hudnut*, and that ruling has not ended the debate, it is worthwhile to consider the rest of MacKinnon's underlying suppositions, and what her approach would mean to constitutional jurisprudence if it were to be adopted.

"The Personal Is the Political": MacKinnon and Privacy

MacKinnon's extreme variance with most of First Amendment jurisprudence derives from her hostility to the very concept of limited government. This basic disagreement leads her to reject the privacy doctrine. The right of privacy, memorably described as "the right to be let alone," has been considered "the most comprehensive of rights and the most valued by civilized men."[156] MacKinnon's rejection of the doctrine is somewhat unusual, as the doctrine is the foundation of one of the shining victories of the women's movement, *Roe v. Wade*.[157] Moreover, privacy and autonomy rhetoric conventionally pervade the writings of feminists, and have been the source of much of their ideological appeal.[158]

---

aspect of *R.A.V.* survives the recent ruling in *Virginia v. Black*, 155 L.Ed.2d at 553–554. By declaring that even low-value speech is entitled to neutrality in regulation, the Court has substantially reworked *Chaplinsky*, which was itself predicated on the *exclusion* of low-value speech categories from First Amendment strictures, declaring that regulation did not present a First Amendment problem. The same analysis that has been used to invalidate regulation of racist hate speech—a subset of the "fighting words" category—in *R.A.V.* would appear to invalidate the Pornography Victim's Compensation Act. Just as did the invalidated St. Paul ordinance, the PVCA targeted some proscribable (because obscene) speech, but not all, and the distinction is drawn not on the basis of obscenity's "distinctly proscribable content," but on the impermissible criterion of the material's viewpoint.

154. *Feminism Unmodified* at 179, 193–195.

155. *See Feminism Unmodified* at 166–167 ("Substantively considered, the situation of women *is not really like anything else.* . . . Doing something legal about a situation that is not really like anything else is hard enough in a legal system that prides itself methodologically on reasoning by analogy.").

156. *Olmstead v. United States*, 277 U.S. 438, 478 (1928) (Brandeis, J. dissenting). *See generally Whalen v. Roe*, 429 U.S. 589 (1977); *Lawrence v. Texas*, 538 U.S.—, 155 L.Ed.2d— (June 26, 2003) slip op. at 6.

157. 410 U.S. 113 (1973).

158. For an example of "more traditional feminism" as above cited, *see* Virginia Woolf *A Room of One's Own* (1928). Professor Higgins has chided me for this example, saying that "Shakespeare's sister was not silenced by the state but by social constraints enforced by men under patriarchy," and that "[t]hus, Mr. Wirenius's citation to Woolf as a counterpoint

MacKinnon conceives of the privacy doctrine as enunciated in *Roe* as a trap, a seductively liberating doctrine that in fact strengthens male dominance by guaranteeing it an isolated sphere in which to operate. By sanctifying the home, where women's abuse is most pervasive, MacKinnon writes, this liberal doctrine gives men a legal carte blanche to abuse "their women" and "whip them into shape" behind closed doors:

> FOR women the measure of the intimacy has been the measure of the oppression. This is why feminism has had to explode the private. This is why feminism has seen the personal as the political. The private is public for those for whom the personal is political. In this sense, for women there is no private, either normatively or empirically. Feminism confronts the fact that women have no privacy to lose or to guarantee. . . . The doctrinal choice of privacy in the abortion context thus re-affirms and reinforces what the feminist critique of sexuality criticizes: The public-private split . . . [t]he right to privacy looks like an injury presented as a gift, a sword in men's hands presented as a shield in women's.[159]

This rejection, however, seems to be premised on a rather gross misunderstanding of the privacy doctrine. Indeed, if there is any constitutional doctrine that MacKinnon should find objectionable on these grounds, it is not the privacy doctrine but rather the Fourth Amendment's requirement of probable cause to support a search by the police of the home of a citizen.

---

to MacKinnon seems misguided." Higgins *supra* note 127 at 84. Woolf took her title from the most onerous constraint faced by the fictional Judith, an absolute lack of privacy in which to construct and explore an autonomous self. Another striking example of the need for privacy may be seen in the life of Eleanor Roosevelt, whose struggle for autonomy against her domineering mother-in-law Sara was furthered by her renting of a Manhattan apartment, and even more by Franklin Roosevelt's gift of a "cottage" at Val-kill to escape from Sara's incursions, which Eleanor used to create and foster the dynamic persona that made her so effective in the public sphere. *See* Blanche Wiesen Cook, *Eleanor Roosevelt, vol. I* (1992) at 332–335.

159. *Feminist Theory* at 191; *Feminism Unmodified* at 102 ("The right of privacy is a right of men 'to be let alone' to oppress women one at a time"). MacKinnon, it should be noted, does support the right of a woman to have an abortion on the grounds of sexual equality, although the reasoning is to me somewhat murky. Presumably, the right grants women a measure of power and any thing that empowers women in any way helps lead toward sexual equality. Oddly, McKinnon further asserts that the status of the fetus is irrelevant. The choice "must be *women's*, but not because the fetus is not a form of life. . . . I cannot follow that. Why should women not make life and death decisions?" (*Feminism Unmodified* at 94; *Feminist Theory* at 186), she writes, blithely ignoring the fact that it is *never* considered legitimate for anybody, male or female, to decide to end another's life *in the interests of the decider*. Even a military officer, who makes life-and-death decisions, is not permitted to make them on the basis of his or her selfish interests. *See* Glanville Williams *The Sanctity of Life And the Criminal Law* (1957) at 197–205; *United States v. Dykes*, 6 M.J. 744 (N.C.M.R. 1978).

The Fourth Amendment prevents forced entry of a private dwelling place by police unless they have probable cause to believe a crime is in progress. Thus, in cases where probable cause is absent, the Fourth Amendment could be said to prevent police interference in situations where abuse *is* going on behind closed doors. *Roe*, however, simply establishes the right of each person to control his or her body free of state interference as a fundamental liberty which can only be infringed upon a showing of a compelling state interest.[160]

MacKinnon assumes that the privacy doctrine protects spouse abuse in the home, but this is not so. Meaningful, voluntary consent is a necessarily implicit prerequisite for any application of the privacy doctrine. *Roe* and *Griswold v. Connecticut*[161] are based upon the protection of the consensual intimacy of married couples (a protection later extended to heterosexual lovers).[162] It is not based upon the nature of the *home* as sacred (although Justice Douglas's language about the "sacred precincts of the marriage bed" can be read out of context to support such a notion); it is not *where* the state seeks to intervene that creates the right enshrined in *Griswold*, but rather *what* occurs there.[163]

The home can be, and frequently is, a place of domestic abuse, but such abuse is not in any way protected by the right to privacy. The right to privacy belongs to *each* individual, female or male, and is:

> WITHIN the meaning of the term "liberty" as used in the Fourteenth Amendment. *First is the autonomous control of the development and expression of one's intellect, interests, tastes, and personality. . . . Second is freedom of choice in the basic decisions of one's life respecting marriage, divorce, procreation, contraception and the education and upbringing of children. . . . Third is the freedom to care for one's health, freedom from bodily restraint or compulsion, freedom to walk, stroll or loaf.* [emphasis in original][164]

Without a meaningful consent, one formed without fear or undue influence, to whatever activity the state seeks to regulate, privacy interests are not in any way implicated. The fact that privacy-implementing doctrines may not provide sufficient protection for an unconsenting party in a presumptively private setting does not impact on the doctrine's fundamental pre-

---

160. But *see Planned Parenthood v. Casey*, 505 U.S. 833 (1992), (majority opinion analyzing *Roe* treats abortion right as less than fundamental).

161. 381 U.S. 479 (1965).

162. *Eisenstadt* v. *Baird* 405 U.S. 438 (1972). But *see Bowers v. Hardwick*, 478 U.S. 186 (1986) (declining to extend *Griswold's* privacy analysis to homosexual conduct).

163. *See* William O. Douglas, *The Right of the People*, (1957) at 87–93.

164. *Roe v. Wade*, 410 U.S. 113, 211–213 (Douglas, J. concurring). *See Lawrence v. Texas, supra*, for a ringing endorsement of Douglas's logic in his *Roe* concurrence.

cept that the individual should have autonomy over her body and psyche. Indeed, this concept, properly applied, can provide remedies for women whose autonomy is violated.

Interestingly, the right to privacy as elucidated by Douglas provides an alternate basis to the civil right of action under *Riggs v. Palmer* for models whose consent was not meaningfully given. For example, New York State's Civil Rights Law § 51 permits an individual to recover damages if another uses the plaintiff's "name portrait or picture" for commercial purposes without first obtaining consent. This statute has been held to create "a right of privacy" and a corresponding "right of publicity" based upon the right to privacy's doctrine of each individual's right to autonomy over his or her self.[165] The privacy formulation may even be preferable to the "one may not profit from one's wrong" approach suggested earlier, in that it need only be shown that the model did not consent to the distribution of the film commercially, a lower showing than that of coercion or intimidation required to establish a "wrong." MacKinnon's assertion that the right of privacy is inimical to women's interests, as evinced through the pornography debate, is therefore contradicted by the very doctrine she deplores, but apparently does not know the contours of.

MacKinnon's rejection of the right to privacy carries with it interesting consequences, but only one that is important to First Amendment jurisprudence is relevant here. By removing the only precedential basis for protecting sexual conduct in the home, and by declaring that "feminism has had to explode the private,"[166] MacKinnon leads inexorably to the conclusion that there is no sphere of the individual's life that the state may not touch. If the personal is the political to the degree that MacKinnon asserts, then the personal is subject to the regulation of the state. In MacKinnon's schema, therefore, there is no point at which the individual may cry "hands off."

In the absence of a right of privacy, any activity not explicitly mentioned in the Constitution may be regulated or prohibited outright if the state can rationally claim it leads to a harm that the state is empowered to prevent.[167]

---

165. *Stephano v. News Group Publ.*, 64 N.Y.2d 174 (1984) (construing New York Civil Rights Law § 51); *see also Ippolito v. Ono-Lennon*, 139 Misc.2d 230, 238, 526 N.Y.S. 2d 877, 883 (Sup. Ct. N.Y. Co. 1988) *See* Warren and Brandeis, *The Right to Privacy* 4 Harv. L. Rev. 193 (1890), *Prosser and Keeton on Torts* 5th ed. 850 (1984).

166. *Feminist Theory* at 191.

167. Under this logic, and over sixty years of extreme deference to "rational" decisions, for example, the Supreme Court's decision in *Bowers v. Hardwick*, 478 U.S. 186 (1986) that consensual homosexual intercourse may be rendered criminal is patently correct. This is because the states have long been deemed to exercise a "police power" which extends to "morals," including the "tone" of society. *See, Id.* at 192, 196–197. In the face of no constitutional privacy right, or other textual protection, such moral decisions are constitutional, a result that, paradoxically, most of MacKinnon's supporters (if not

And indeed, that is exactly MacKinnon's analysis supporting state regulation of putatively private conduct.[168] The First Amendment notwithstanding, MacKinnon applies the same treatment to thoughts and ideas as she does to actions. As before mentioned, for MacKinnon the state is free to regulate any speech that causes "harm, harm that counts"[169]—a very different proposition from our current jurisprudence, which recognizes only the intentional and direct spurring on to imminent lawlessness as sufficient harm to vitiate the protection of speech gathered within the First Amendment's ambit.[170]

Holding the pornographer liable for the uses to which men put his or her product clearly can be distinguished from holding him or her liable for contributing to a social atmosphere conducive to the subordination of women. Both provisions of the ordinance do, however, violate the same dignitary concern, that expressed by Milton in his metaphor of the schoolboy:

> WHAT advantage is it to be a man over it is to be a boy at school, if we have only escaped the ferula to come under the fescue of an Imprimatur, if serious and elaborate writings, as if they were no more than the theme of a grammar lad under his pedagogue, must not be uttered without the cursory eyes of a temporising and extemporising licenser? He who is not trusted with his own actions, his drift not being known to be evil, and standing to the hazard of law and penalty, has no great argument to think himself reputed in the Commonwealth, wherein

MacKinnon herself) would, it seems, find objectionable. In *Neutrality in Constitutional Law*, 92 Colum. L. Rev. 1 (1996), Cass Sunstein condemns *Bowers*, but likewise rejects the privacy argument in both the pornography and abortion contexts.

168. *Feminist Theory* at 140–43 (analyzing heterosexuality, homosexuality, and lesbian sadomasochism as victim-victimizer relationships, reaffirming the dominance-submission social model); *Feminism Unmodified* at 60–61 (heterosexuality not a choice but "the structure of the oppression of women"), 85–92 (characterizing rape as "very little different from what most men do most of the time and call it sex"), 15 (lesbian sadomasochists "would sacrifice all women's ability to walk down the street in safety for the freedom to torture a woman in the privacy of one's basement without fear of intervention in the name of everyone's freedom of choice"). As shown, MacKinnon believes that harmful conduct of whatever stripe can and should be regulated by the state, without reference to the First Amendment or the right to privacy.

169. *Feminism Unmodified* at 178.

170. The *Chaplinsky* categories are traditionally held to be outside of the First Amendment's scope, constituting "low-value" speech that the state may proscribe upon a rational finding that they are detrimental to the health, morals, or welfare of the populace. This explanation should not be confused with an endorsement; I feel that the categorical approach is insufficiently protective of speech, and, far worse, is without logical foundation because it never indicates why the chosen categories differ from protected speech, and has no support in the constitutional text. In *R.A.V. v. St Paul,* Justice Stevens in dissent also indicated discomfort with the *Chaplinsky* categorical formulation. That pornography as defined by MacKinnon must be judged as falling outside of the *Chaplinsky* categories is argued above.

he was born, for other than a fool or a foreigner. . . . If, in this the most consummate act of his fidelity and ripeness, no years, no industry, no former proof of his abilities can bring him to that state of maturity, as not to be still mistrusted and suspected . . . [unless he] appear in print like a puny with his guardian, and his censor's hand on the back of his title to be his bail and surety that he is no idiot or seducer, it cannot be but a dishonor and derogation to the author, to the book, to the privilege and dignity of Learning.[171]

Like Milton's schoolboy, we are presumed to be irrevocably sullied and forced into acting in manners we would normally be proof against by exposure to ideas. Such logic has been the principal motivation of the censor for as long as there has been censorship.

MacKinnon endeavors to dodge the *Brandenburg* test by a peculiar, if persistent, rhetorical move. She argues that "Law's proper concern here is not with what speech says, but with what it does."[172] The distinction sounds at first reminiscent of the verbal act concept, but in fact MacKinnon is not so doctrinally clear. Where verbal act analysis looks for illegality in the very utterance of the speech, MacKinnon conflates depiction with emulation in a mechanistic cause and effect relationship.

MacKinnon, in short, associates pornography and its consumption with the ultimate sex act itself. She does so by flat, unsupported declarations: "Pornography is masturbation material," she writes. "It is used as sex. It therefore is sex."[173] To prove this, she baldly states, "Men know this," and cites several ancient—Greco-Roman to be precise—statements to the effect that "having sex is antithetical to thinking."[174] Ejaculation, she adds (as though her point were not yet clear), "is a behavior, not a thought or an argument."[175]

It has some base in physiology, in that a male orgasm can with great trouble be triggered in a purely mechanical manner, but such is not normally the case. In real life, the evocation of desire is a cognitive response—mental processing of a visual, auditory, or even olfactory stimulus—the association of a stimulus with pleasure and desire. And these associations are close to the root of the individual soul—perhaps the most vexing and sub-

---

171. Milton, *Areopagitica* (1644), H. B. Cotterall, ed. (1952), at 27.
172. *Only Words* at 29.
173. *Id.* at 17.
174. *Id.*
175. *Id.* On the message of pornography, *see Id.* at 21 ("This message is addressed directly to the penis, delivered through an ejaculation, and taken out on women in the real world").

jective experiences a human being has. Hence the differences of sexual preferences and practices among humankind, and the sometimes wildly improbable choice of partners.

With no sensitivity to the extent to which individuals form and are formed by sexuality, MacKinnon would have the law plunge into full-fledged regulation. Although involving some of the most delicate and misunderstood corners of the human soul, where so many of the traumas of life cluster, and even poets speak in metaphor and euphemism, MacKinnon would extend the ham-handed reach of the state.

Regardless, MacKinnon's erasure of any distinction between sex and the mental processes that produce sexual desire—reminiscent of the disdain for all but the most innocuous thought that led to Bernard Shaw's despairing cry, "Is the Devil to have all the passions as well as all the good tunes?"[176]— fits well with her technique of equating all sex with the most extreme misogynist sexual behavior.[177] It fits far less well with reality.

MacKinnon has constructed her notion of the state in accordance with her reductive view of human (or at least male) nature. The subordination of government to the individual citizens who created it, extending to it only those powers that they deem absolutely necessary to preserve social order with the maximum amount of liberty—all of these quaint notions are discarded in MacKinnon's jurisprudence. Instead we have a state with the authority to regulate every component of the individual's life, from the forms of sexual intimacy they may conduct[178] to the attitudes that they are to have.

Victims of Love: MacKinnon and Women's Speech

MacKinnon repeatedly emphasizes that pornography "is not speech for women"[179] a declaration that is profoundly significant. It should not be simply written off with the flip (although true) reply that not only women's speech deserves constitutional protection, but that of men as well. This easy

---

176. G. B. Shaw, "Man and Superman" (1903) Act I, in *The Collected Plays of Bernard Shaw* (1934) at 346.
177. Many critics have accused MacKinnon of equating all sex with rape, a charge she has recently denied. Although she has never, to my knowledge, made so blanket a declaration as her critics claim, MacKinnon has made statements that can reasonably be taken to that effect. *See,* eg. *Feminist Theory* at 174.
178. *See supra* note 168.
179. *Feminism Unmodified* at 193–196; *Feminist Theory* at 205, 208, 209–211; *Only Words* at 40–41.

answer misses the most interesting feature of MacKinnon's claim. She is not just adverting to the fact that the speaking done in pornography is not that of the models or actresses, although that is certainly a part of her meaning.[180] Nor is she referring to the fact that the vast bulk of pornography is written by and aimed at men, also a part of her observation.[181] Rather, she asserts that women who write pornographic materials themselves are not engaged in women's speech, nor are those women who defend the right to create pornography:

> WHEN women are aroused by sexual violation, meaning we experience it *as* our sexuality, the feminist analysis is . . . not contradicted, it is *proved*. The male supremacist definition of female sexuality as lust for self-annihilation has won. . . . Sexism would be trivial if this were merely exceptional. (One might ask at this point not why some women embrace sadomasochism, but why many women do not).[182]

For MacKinnon, women's speech is not simply the exercise of a woman's right to free speech, whatever it is she chooses to say. Rather, it is speech that is in the interests of women as a group, which is feminist speech. Feminist speech has a definition for MacKinnon: "[Y]ou will notice that I equate 'in my view' with feminism,"[183] she once said in an unusual burst of self-perception. Those women who do not share MacKinnon's view have been tamed by the system:

> WOMEN who oppose the civil rights law against pornography are simply conservative about other things [than are traditional conservatives]. When they defend the life they identify with, it is the sexual status quo they defend. . . . Acknowledging civil rights for women in pornography suggests that they are victims of restricted options on the basis of their sex and that some are directly coerced. This demeans as victims women who choose to survive through sexual sale through pure free will. . . . These women sense a judgement on their lives: that they have gone along with and sometimes even enjoy inequality in the sexual sphere. They would rather live that way forever and make sure other women do too, than face what it means, in order to change it. They recommend appeasement. Enforce the bargain, the bargain with *their* men. They may one day explain why women

---

180. *Id.*
181. *Feminism Unmodified* at 194.
182. *Id.* at 160–161 (emphasis in original).
183. *Id.* at 49. *See also Feminist Theory* at 117 ("radical feminism is feminism"). That MacKinnon is not always—or has not always been—so dogmatic should be noted: "I speak as a feminist although not all feminists agree with everything I say." *Feminism Unmodified* at 21.

and children must be tortured and abused or no one can freely think, write or publish.[184]

These women, like animals in behavioralists' experiments, have accepted a stake in the system; they are "collaborators," or "appeasers."

It is important to note that the argument that pornography is not women's speech, but rather silences women, has two components. Beyond MacKinnon's argument that pornography terrorizes women into silence and that counterspeech cannot be effective (of which more later), the concept that the speech of a woman is anything but women's speech shows her exaltation of the collective over the individual in stark relief. MacKinnon sets apart that speech which—in her judgment—benefits women as a group. Only when a woman conforms to MacKinnon's orthodoxy is her speech women's speech. Anne Rice's three novels, published under the pseudonym of A.N. Rocquelaure, do not constitute women's speech, exploring as they do sadomasochistic sex in various manifestations,[185] as does her novel *Exit to Eden*.[186] Similarly, Pat Califia's or Laura Antoniou's writings about lesbian sadomasochism would be held unprotected. But it is more than the mere holding of such works unprotected that is disturbing. It is the fact that they are not considered "women's speech"; by not fitting the orthodoxy of feminism as defined by MacKinnon, Rice, Antoniou, and Califia (and others, but three examples will suffice) are seemingly drummed out of their sex.

It is odd that MacKinnon, who writes movingly of the social costs paid by Andrea Dworkin and especially by Linda Marchiano in coming forward with their experiences,[187] does not even address the question of whether any grace should be extended to the serious artist (Rice) or the sincere representative of a sexual minority (Antoniou or Califia). Although of course the same questions are presented with regard to their male counterparts, such as Robert Mapplethorpe, it is especially poignant that these women face censorship in the name of feminism.

---

184. *Feminism Unmodified* at 226.
185. *The Claiming of Sleeping Beauty, Beauty's Punishment,* and *Beauty's Release,* all published by Dutton Publishing Co. (New York) between 1983 and 1985, have been revealed to be her work; *see* Katherine Ramsland, *Prism of the Night: A Biography of Anne Rice* (1991) at 213–238.
186. "Anne Rampling," *Exit to Eden* (1985). For Pat Califia's writings as cited by MacKinnon see *Feminist Theory* at 142; Califia has also published a collection of avowedly pornographic short stories with a revealingly candid introduction under the title of *Macho Sluts* (1989). Laura Antoniou has published a series of novels including *The Marketplace* (1993), *The Slave* (1994), and *The Trainer* (1995). I emphasize these examples as being the most stark and favorable to MacKinnon, but others (Anaïs Nin, for example) exist.
187. *Feminism Unmodified* at 132–133.

For whatever reasons, Rice's artistic vision[188] frequently recurs to what MacKinnon would term pornography, and Califia too had to decide whether to be an honest writer or a politically correct one. As Califia phrased the dilemma, "We live in fear of being known, and such fear stifles the nascent erotic wish before the image of what is wished for can be fully formed. We know we are ugly before we have even seen ourselves and the injustice of this, the falsehood, chokes me. . . . I could keep my sexuality private. . . . That involves telling a lie of omission—becoming invisible as a pervert; assuming an undeserved mantle of normalcy and legitimacy."[189] MacKinnon, in the name of women, would choose for women—by the blunt instrument of the law. The individual woman is silenced in the name of providing free speech for women—a paradox if ever I have encountered one.

Paradoxical or not, MacKinnon seeks to empower some vague, uniform collective called women by silencing not just men but individual women who are not in tune with this collective spirit.[190] In our system of jurisprudence where dissent is at least in theory honored,[191] for MacKinnon it is an evil to be crushed. This viewpoint does not go directly to the constitutional validity of the ordinance but provides a chilling vision of the goal that MacKinnon hopes to reach through its enactment and enforcement.

MacKinnon and Dissent

Perhaps the most disturbing aspect of MacKinnon's thought is her belief that silencing all opposition is the correct method to liberate women. She claims that pornography tyrannizes women and silences them:

> I LEARNED that the social preconditions, the presumptions, that under-
> lie the First Amendment do not apply to women. The First Amend-
> ment essentially presumes some level of social equality among people
> and hence essentially equal social access to the means of expression.
> In a context of inequality between the sexes we cannot presume that

---

188. Use of sadomasochistic imagery can be found in Rice's Vampire Trilogy as well; see, for example, *Interview with a Vampire* (1976) at 238, 245; see also *The Vampire Lestat* (1985) and especially *The Queen of the Damned* (1988). Although all three volumes were popularly successful (the first two especially), they have also received high esteem from critics. See Ramsland, *supra* note 185, at 314–315.

189. Califia, *supra* note 186, at 9.

190. In *Feminist Theory* at 40, MacKinnon writes: "Liberal feminism takes the individual as the proper unit of analysis and measure of the destructiveness of sexism. For radical feminism, although the person is kept in view, the touchstone of analysis and outrage is the collective (group called women) . . . In radicalism, women is a collective whole, singular noun . . . in radical feminism the [personal comprises the collective].

191. For an enlightening view of the American tradition of honoring dissenters, see Steven Schiffrin, *The First Amendment, Democracy and Romance* (1991).

that is accurate. The First Amendment also presumes that for the mind
to be free to fulfill itself, speech must be free and open. . . . [P]or-
nography contributes to enslaving women's minds and bodies. As a
social process and as a form of "speech," pornography amounts to terrorism and promotes not freedom but silence. Rather, it promotes
freedom for men and enslavement and silence for women. . . . Under
conditions of sexual dominance, pornography hides and distorts truth
while at the same time enforcing itself, imprinting itself on the world,
making it itself real.[192]

Thus, silencing their oppressors will liberate women. The way to promote
equality is not counterspeech, as Justice Brandeis would have it,[193] but the
oppressing of the oppressor. For MacKinnon, the conditions under which
counterspeech can be effective do not exist because pornography undermines women's credibility when they do speak, and terrorizes them into not
speaking at all.[194]

This logic creates a "slippery slope" approach under which not only pornographers should be silenced, but any speaker whose message is deemed
by MacKinnon to be harmful to the interests of women as well. In the First
Amendment jurisprudence and literature, by contrast, dissent is honored.
Indeed, Steven H. Shiffrin has gone so far as to suggest that dissent should
be the touchstone of First Amendment theory.[195] MacKinnon and Dworkin
have demonstrated their hostility toward dissent, displaying a willingness
to silence those who merely advocate the rights of pornographers. In the
political process of passing the Minneapolis ordinance, for example,
MacKinnon and Dworkin manipulated the hearings and the procedure by
which the ordinance was passed in such a way as to totally disable dissent.[196]

It is this contempt for the political process, evidenced by her manipulation of her role as a consultant and her willingness to disenfranchise
political opposition, which render MacKinnon subject to charges of totalitarianism. Not only does she, simply put, reject the notions of free speech
and that the individual must have some area in his or her life free from
government intrusion, she is willing to short-circuit the democratic process
in such a way that only her view is aired.

---

192. *Feminism Unmodified* at 129–130.
193. *Whitney* 274 U.S. at 375 (Brandeis, J., concurring).
194. *Feminism Unmodified* at 132.
195. Steven H. Shiffrin, *Dissent, Injustice and the Meanings of America* (1999).
196. *See* Downs, *supra* note 101, at 65–87. Downs gives many examples to this effect, including neglect by the ordinance's proponents of concerns of black political action groups,
liberal feminist groups, etc. Although some opposing voices were heard, they were
unable to prepare thoroughly due to the unprecedented speed with which the ordinance was pushed through, and the difficulty of acquiring a copy of it. According to

For MacKinnon, democratic self-rule, political rule, has no value of its own.[197] By any standards, the elimination of privacy, the disenfranchisement of all potential opposition,[198] and the emphasis on attitude correction by the state can only be regarded as totalitarianism. The allegedly benevolent nature of the totalitarians, who seek to create a society in which equality and mutual respect would be at a premium, but liberty would be a thing of the past, does not alter the nature of the society which they seek to build.

THE RENEWED ACADEMIC ATTACK ON HATE SPEECH

In the last two decades, legal academicians have exchanged blows on this very issue—whether a special category of unprotected or at least less protected speech should be carved out to facilitate the regulation of hate

---

Matthew Stark, "until about a day before the city council voted on it [nobody ever] gave us a copy of [the ordinance]. We asked for it but [they] kept playing games . . . for a period of a month or more we didn't have anything." *Id.* at 85 The selection of witnesses and their questioning were ceded to MacKinnon and Dworkin, who made sure that witnesses were properly guided, as was Edward Donnerstein, a leading researcher on pornography's social effects, who was discouraged from qualifying his remarks. *Id.* at 84. MacKinnon shifted roles from that of advocate to that of expert hired by the council whenever it suited her purpose. *Id.* at 79–80, 84–85. Needless to say, because the questioning was left to the authors of the ordinance, no cross-examination was permitted. *Id.* at 80–83. Finally, when any of the unprepared, uninvited opposition *did* get to testify they "were drowned out by the antics of the selected audience." *Id.* at 82. It is not difficult to guess by whom the audience was selected. Shouting down opponents is a favorite tactic of MacKinnon's and Dworkin's supporters; Harvard Professor Alan Dershowitz described the difficulty he encountered when, in the course of a debate with Dworkin, her supporters sought to shout him down whenever he spoke. (Alan M. Dershowitz, *The Best Defense* (1982) at 190–191).

197. *Feminist Theory* at 157–160.
198. Indeed, even liberal feminists are discredited by MacKinnon, *Feminist Theory* at 117 ("radical feminism is feminism"). That liberal feminists, such as June Callwood, felt their concerns were ignored by the Dworkin-MacKinnon group in the Minneapolis political process, *see* Downs, *supra* note 101, shows what happens when you are not with MacKinnon one hundred percent: your opinion becomes irrelevant, something to be brushed aside. To be less than a total supporter is to be a collaborator, or traitor as shown above. For liberal feminist views against censorship *see* Varda Burstyn, ed, *Women Against Censorship*, (1985) and Nadine Strossen, *The Convergence of Feminist and Civil Liberties Principles in the Pornography Debate*, 62 N.Y.U. L.Rev. 201 (1987). For perhaps the most appealing, and gentlest, critique of MacKinnon, *see* Ruth Culker, *Feminist Consciousness and the State: A Basis for Cautious Optimism*, 90 Colum. L.Rev 1146 (1990). While Professor Culker is (in my view) unduly laudatory of MacKinnon, her critique of her conclusions within a shared feminist perspective, as distinguished from my own liberal, pro-feminist framework, is hard to resist. Culker also valuably points out the dangers of intolerant, disrespectful rhetoric on both sides of this debate.

speech.[199] Many of the arguments raised are those addressed in discussing the radical feminist critique of First Amendment law as it relates to pornography. This is hardly surprising; MacKinnon broke the older, obsolete "obscenity" mold, a mold based on traditional moral standards, by analogizing pornography to hate speech. Thus some of the best known rationales for regulating hate speech are precisely those advanced by MacKinnon in favor of suppressing pornography. A survey of the rationales advanced in favor of regulation of hate speech would be, at this stage of the game, a twice-told tale. However, certain distinctive themes (or themes that emerge even more clearly in this context than in a review of the pornography issue) should be noted.

Search for a Text

First, one argument that has been advanced is that the goal of securing equality, a constitutional imperative enshrined in the Thirteenth and Fourteenth Amendments, justifies incursions on the province of the First Amendment if the incursions genuinely advance the cause of equality.[200] This theory is the best argument yet advanced for the regulation of hate speech, because it can be justified both by the language of the Civil War amendments and with general theories of interpretation. However, this theory requires a leap of constitutional faith that seems to me, on balance, unjustified.

The textual base for this argument stems from Section 2 of the Thirteenth Amendment and Section 5 of the Fourteenth Amendment, which may be read as essentially identical. The Thirteenth Amendment states that "Congress shall have power to enforce this article by appropriate legislation," the

---

199. Examples of those for such regulation: Richard Delgado, *Words That Wound: A Tort Action for Racial Insults, Epithets, and Name Calling,* 17 Harv. C.R.-C.L. L. Rev. 133 (1982); Owen Fiss, *The Irony of Free Speech* (1995); *The Supreme Court and the Problem of Hate Speech,* 24 Cap. U. L. Rev. 281 (1995); Mary E. Gale, *Reimagining the First Amendment: Racist Speech and Equal Liberty,* 65 St. John's L. Rev. 119 (1991); Mari J. Matsuda, *Public Response to Racist Speech: Considering the Victim's Story,* 87 Mich. L. Rev. 2320 (1989); N. Douglas Wells, *Whose Community? Whose Rights?—Response to Professor Fiss,* 24 Cap. L. Rev. 319 (1995). *See generally,* Laura Lederer & Richard Delgado, eds., *The Price We Pay: The Case Against Racist Speech, Hate Propaganda and Pornography* (1995).

    Against: Joseph W. Bellacosa, *The Regulation of Hate Speech by Academe vs. the Idea of a University: A Classic Oxymoron?* 67 St. John's L. Rev. 1 (1993); G. Sidney Buchanan, *The Hate Speech Case: A Pyrrhic Victory for Freedom of Speech,* 21 Hofstra L. Rev. 285 (1992); Susan M. Gilles, *Images of the First Amendment and the Reality of Powerful Speakers,* 24 Cap. L. Rev. 293 (1995); Gerald Gunther, *Good Speech, Bad Speech—Should Universities Restrict Expression that is Racist or Otherwise Degrading?* 24 Stan. Lawyer 4, 7 (1990); Peter Linzer, *White Liberal Looks at Racist Speech,* 65 St. John's L. Rev. 187 (1991); Nadine Strossen, *Regulating Racist Speech on Campus: A Modest Proposal?* 1990 Duke L.J. 484.

200. *See* Owen M. Fiss, "The Right Kind of Neutrality," in David S. Allen & Robert Jensen, eds., *Freeing the First Amendment: Critical Perspectives on Freedom of Expression* (1995) at 79, 84–85 (summarizing the argument).

Fourteenth that "the Congress shall have power to enforce, by appropriate legislation, this article."[201] If one reads "appropriate" legislation to mean any legislation that may be effective, then those who value equality over liberty do indeed have a textual basis for their argument.

Moreover, that textual basis for the carving out of an area of substantive nonprotection does not do violence to the democratic functions of the Constitution, and may even be said to enhance them, by showing that, on those rare occasions when a supermajority exists, it may successfully revise the fundamental first principles of our democratic compact.

Those who support such a position reason that the rejection of regulation of hate speech "is saying that debate on all public issues must be uninhibited and wide-open, even when it puts a constitutional value such as equality in jeopardy. The First Amendment is first."[202] As summarized by Owen Fiss, the critics of this line of reasoning

> HAVE insisted that such an ordering of constitutional values remains unjustified—in the conflict between liberty and equality, it is not clear why liberty should prevail. Such an ordering of values may well accord with classical liberal philosophy, with its exclusive devotion to individual liberty, but contemporary liberalism, especially as forged by the civil rights struggles of the 1960s, is defined by a duality of commitments—to both liberty and equality.[203]

As Fiss himself notes, however, "those who criticized *R.A.V.* on this ground are no more secure in their premises than Scalia; in the conflict between liberty and equality, they assert the priority of equality without much more by way of justification."[204]

The weakness of this approach is patent. Fiss, like MacKinnon, like Sunstein, like Frankfurter, offers a vision of a socially activist judiciary, able to construct the meaning of the First Amendment by privileging one set of preferences. That this is done in the name of equality does not provide a principled reason for so doing. If one rejects the "blank slate" view of the Constitution—that is, that it means whatever we wish it to mean—then the experience of contemporary liberalism, encompassing the 1960s civil rights struggle, may have a great deal to say to us as social philosophers, but does

---

201. The temptation of exploring the entertaining, if frivolous, notion that the slight variations in wording mean that one amendment is of more limited scope than the other I leave to others; more likely, the three years between the passage of the Thirteenth Amendment and passage of the Fourteenth Amendment accounts for these classic "distinctions without a difference."

202. Fiss, *The Right Kind of Neutrality,* at 84–85; Fiss, *The Supreme Court and Hate Speech,* 24 Cap. L. Rev. 281, 286–287 (1995).

203. *Id.*

204. *Id.* at 84. A classic example of just this sort of blanket assertion with respect to the primacy of equality is contained in Wells, *supra* note 199.

not resolve the innately legal question posed by the scope of the Fourteenth Amendment.

That experience may, however, incline us to answer the question in a way that most faithfully encompasses the lessons of that social experience and philosophy. And, if the word appropriate may be given the meaning that would legitimate the First Amendment's bowing to the virtue of equality, then the proponents of hate speech may yet have a constitutional argument. However, that reading seems to deprive the term "appropriate" of any independent significance. When construing instruments from contracts to constitutions, "[w]ords and phrases are given their plain meaning."[205] Under the present jurisprudence of the Supreme Court, Congress's power has been limited to allow regulation "that reaches a somewhat broader swath of conduct than that which is not forbidden by the Amendment's text" as long as such regulations exhibit "congruence and proportionality between the injury to be prevented and the means adapted to that end."[206]

The very concept that a statute must be "appropriate" suggests limitation. So too does logic; the Fourteenth Amendment cannot be read as legitimating any and all possible state action that may advance the cause of equality. If the First Amendment is expected to bend the knee to legislation that promotes equality, then why, for instance, should not also the Cruel and Unusual Punishment clause of the Eighth Amendment? Yet no argument that a statute that provides for the death by impalement of those convicted of depriving African-Americans of their civil rights would be constitutional seems possible, despite the fact that such a deterrent might really give racists some pause. This is, of course, an example of reductio ad absurdum, and as such, inherently unfair, but it does make the point clear: Whatever the meaning of Section 5 of the Fourteenth Amendment, a complete suspension of all other constitutional provisions in favor of any legislation that can be alleged to advance the amendment's goal of guaranteeing equality before the law of all citizens cannot be among them.

The use of "appropriate" seems to suggest an inherent limiting principle, which I would suggest is that no statute that is independently unconstitutional may be passed by Congress. In contrast to the previous constitutional order of *Barron v. Baltimore* and the strictly limited powers on the part of the federal government to interfere with the states in issues of civil liberty doctrines, the

---

205. *American Express Bank, Ltd. v. Uniroyal, Inc.*, 164 A.D.2d 275, 277, 562 N.Y.S.2d 613, 614 (1st Dep't 1990), *app. den.*, 77 N.Y.2d 807, 569 N.Y.S.2d 611 (1991) (contracts). *See, generally, Duncan v. Walker* 150 L. ed 2d 251, 258 (2001) (statutes).

206. *Nevada Dept. of Human Resources v. Hibbs*, 538 U.S.—, 155 L.Ed.2d—, May 27, 2003, slip op. at 4–5. The Supreme Court has inconsistently construed Section 5 of the Fourteenth Amendment, at sometimes analogizing Congress's power thereunder to the expansive powers provided under the Commerce Clause, but has more recently limited its scope to enforcement of judicially articulated rights. Compare *Ex Parte Virginia* 100 U.S. 339, 345–346 (1880) and *City of Boerne v. Flores*, 521 U.S. 507, 518–520 (1997).

federal government became the guarantor of the rights of all persons, especially, although not exclusively, the newly freed slaves.

This reading has two pronounced advantages: It mirrors the language of
the amendment and (for devotees of other interpretational strategies) it
conforms with the original intention of its drafters, to the extent that something so ephemeral and so subjective may be discerned.[207] Additionally, the
aspect—one can hardly call it a principle—of *fit*,[208] a pragmatic recognition
that constitutional theorists do not write on a tabula rasa, and that the historical evolution of the constitution provides a loose framework with which
proposed interpretations and refinements should harmonize, stands for this
more limited reading of "appropriate."

Although one can (and should) reject the throttling of the rights of the freed
slaves and their defendants that followed upon the *Slaughter-House Cases*,[209] the
fact that the Supreme Court has consistently read the Fourteenth Amendment
to require adherence to the other, more substantive provisions of the Constitution, suggesting that "appropriate" is a word of limitation (although disputes
about the appropriate scope of that limitation have raged consistently) and is
weighty evidence that so it was meant.[210] Language, precedent, and logic all
combine to suggest that the First Amendment is not abrogated or vitiated by
the Civil War amendments. As a result, the effort to find a textual basis for the
regulation of hate speech in the Constitution itself is at best problematic.

---

207. *See* Michael Kent Curtis, *No State Shall Abridge: The Fourteenth Amendment and the Bill of
Rights* (1986) at 54–56, 62–92 (describing debates in Congress regarding amendment's
meaning); Richard Kluger, *Simple Justice* (1975) at 43–50 (same; detailing struggle
between Congress seeking to secure freedmen's rights and President Johnson to block);
see also Loren Miller, *The Petitioners: The Story of the Supreme Court of the United States and
the Negro* (1966) at 85–101.

208. *See, inter alia*, Ronald Dworkin, *The Arduous Virtue of Fidelity: Originalism, Scalia, Tribe and
Nerve*, 65 Ford. L. Rev. 1249, 1254–1256 (1997) (discussing notion that historical evolution of constitutional law may not be entirely discarded in interpretation of
document's meaning); *see generally* Ronald Dworkin, *Freedom's Law: The Moral Reading
of the American Constitution* (1996).

209. For an account of this grim history, *see* Kluger, *supra* note 207, at 51–91. *See also* Miller,
supra note 207 at 102–182.

210. *Nevada Dept. of H.R. v. Hibbs, supra.* The concept of "fit" is not a slavish adherence to
precedent, it should be noted. To take one example, in Chapter 2, the illegitimacy of
the Supreme Court's decision in *The Slaughter-House Cases* (essentially deleting the Privileges and Immunities Clause of the Fourteenth Amendment) was argued. In advocating that cases's overruling, one consideration advanced was that the piecemeal incorporation of each of the guarantees of the Bill of Rights against the states through the
Due Process Clause made for a less coherent jurisprudence than a yielding to the historical imperative embodied in the gradual broadening of the *Palko* line of cases. In
short, "fit" argues that *Slaughterhouse* was an error, because the developments which the
Court tried to prevent through that decision were so inherent in the Constitution that
they came about in any event. "Fit" requires that a historically aberrant decision, in-
compatible with the main thrust of constitutional development, can and should be
rejected. Dworkin, *supra* note 208.

Robbing Peter to Pay Paul: Silencing the Oppressors

Another line of argument raised in support of regulating hate speech is rather reminiscent of the old Vietnam War cliché of "bombing the village to save it." This is the argument that, as Owen Fiss has recently refined a rather well-worn notion, such regulation may be conceived "as a protection of speech."[211] As Fiss went on to explain, using the example of *R.A.V.*:

> THIS approach is predicated on the view that cross-burning does not merely insult blacks and interfere with their right to choose where they live. It also interferes with their speech rights. It discourages them from participating in the deliberative activities of society. They feel less entitled and less inclined to voice their views in the public square and more inclined to withdraw into themselves. *They are silenced as effectively as if the state intervened to silence them.* [emphasis mine][212]

That last sentence is a big step. In fact, lacking as it does empirical or logical support, it must be treated as a leap of faith. Still, it is not so far from the experiences of many Americans. Who has not known of the crushing pressure to conform suffered by members of minority groups? If they have not felt it themselves, most people surely have heard a friend, a sibling or an acquaintance articulate this feeling. Although it is easy to say, "life's tough," or to urge the virtues of a thick skin, the fact is that life is tougher for others than for some and some need to develop the hide of a rhinoceros to get by. But does this really constitute the functional equivalent of state suppression?

Surely the existence of African-American and gay and lesbian culture (to pick three discrete minorities), and the growing impact each has had on the mainstream, suggest strongly that the answer is no. Moreover, the reaction to hate speech today more often seems to be revulsion, not adoption.[213]

The prompt objection will come that the mere survival of such cultures, in the context of struggle, ghettoization, and condescension from mainstream culture does not destroy the salience of Fiss's critique. But to the extent that that critique depends on the equation of popular pressure to remain silent or closeted with government extirpation of the speech on the

---

211. Fiss, *The Right Kind of Neutrality, supra* note 200, at 85. This notion is nothing new; Fiss himself acknowledges his debt to Robert Post and Harry Kalven, Jr., and similar arguments were made on behalf of the MacKinnon-Dworkin ordinance.
212. *Id.*
213. *See* Susan Gellman, *Hate Speech and a New View of the First Amendment*, 24 Cap. L. Rev. 309–310 (1995).

basis of its content, it in fact does. Prejudice is ugly and costly and cruel. It means that, in the initial run at least, only the brave members of its target class are heard. That such heroic figures have been heard is the lesson of both the civil rights movement and the women's movement. When the government jails speakers for saying their message, nobody, however heroic, gets heard. Or at least nobody, however heroic, gets heard more than once.[214]

Moreover, as has been shrewdly pointed out by Susan Gellman, "to the extent hate speech does appear to silence others, perhaps it is actually the structure and climate of racism, not specifically the shock of hate speech, that is truly the inhibiting factor."[215] Gellman's point is well taken, in that it is not the mere existence of any one sample of hate speech that causes the "silencing" but the feeling that this speech represents the actual working of the mainstream mind, beneath the veneer of politeness. Indeed, the argument made for regulation in Skokie made that clear—the message being sent was described by the Court as "we are not done with you"; that is, that the message of hate would be acted upon. It is the implicit message of hate speech that despite present-day lip service to equality, the discredited historical regime may return or even may persist under a more subtle facade, that carries weight.

Fiss's theory does not, of course, disappear in a puff of smoke because he has overstated his conclusion. What is left is his notion that the government acts, in silencing one speaker in order to encourage or facilitate another speaker, as a parliamentarian of our national town meeting that tries to "end a pattern of behavior that silences one group and thus distorts or skews public debate."[216] Fiss concludes that in so doing "the state is not trying to usurp the public's right of self-determination, but rather to enhance the public's capacity to properly exercise that right."[217] As for the speakers who have been silenced, Fiss offers the rather cold comfort that

> [I]N favoring the speech rights of blacks in this way, the state is not making a judgment—constitutional or other—of the views each side is likely to express, through fighting words or otherwise, but only that this sector of the community must be heard from more fully if the

---

214. Truly heroic figures can overcome imprisonment and even write from the jail cell. Mohandas K. Gandhi, Eugene V. Debs and Martin Luther King all did so (of course, so did Adolf Hitler, showing that defiance is not limited to the virtuous). The point is not that nobody can buck the stiffest of odds; rather, the point is that such unusual fortitude should not be a prerequisite to participation in our polity.

215. Gelman, *supra* note 213, at 311.

216. Fiss, *The Right Kind of Neutrality, supra* note 200, at 85.

217. *Id.*

public is to make an informed choice about an entire range of issues on the national agenda, from affirmative action, to education, to welfare policy.[218]

This comfort is not only cold, it is illusory. In making the decision which speech should be favored in order to open up the public dialogue, an inherent judgment regarding the value of the speech is implicit, unless the state is literally going to canvass every conceivable viewpoint. This presupposes a weighing of the speech of various groups and a finding that some speech is germane—that of blacks, to take Fiss's example—and that other speech is not germane (that of the militia movement, for example). Moreover, the difficulty in finding a way to permit the "proportional" representation of each segment presents a mind-bogglingly complex and subjective utilitarian calculus,[219] and one that is singularly subject to corruption in its application.

Additionally, Fiss's argument that the state has a legitimate role as a parliamentarian misses the whole purpose of that position: to guide and control discussion so that, in the limited time available, a group meeting can get through the agreed-upon agenda. Both the limitation of time and topic are not applicable in society at large. Especially as mass communication technology grows more available to minority groups or individuals, the limitations that could justify the presence of a parliamentarian break down, and the analogy grows more strained.

What then of the general argument—that the effect of the silencing of hate speech rises to the level of invoking the First Amendment to protect the speech that would take place. N. Douglas Wells, suggesting that the United States adopt the International Covenant on Civil and Political Rights,[220] would have us acknowledge that there is an equally compelling right not to be confronted with hate speech (as a function of the Equal Protection Clause) and would have the balance of these rights tip in favor of the right to be protected against hate speech. He further justifies this view by pointing out that hate speech is of limited value, and that its harms outweigh its negligible value.[221]

There are only two problems with this approach. Both problems suggest that Professor Wells seeks not to read a constitution whose independent existence he acknowledges, but rather to fit, under compulsion, his beliefs within a frustrating set of rules that he is willing to subvert if need be.

---

218. *Id.*
219. These notions are more fully explored in Gellman, *supra* note 213.
220. Wells, *Whose Community? Whose Rights?*, 24 Cap. L. Rev. at 324–326.
221. *Id.* at 326–328.

First, it is self-defeating to try to say, if interpreting the document is the real goal, that a right that does not appear in it can outweigh one that is explicitly created by the document's terms. Moreover, the right not to be confronted by hate speech is not created by the Civil War amendments, which merely (by their terms) end slavery or involuntary servitude, and forbid the States to abridge "the privileges and immunities of citizens of the United States," or to fail to provide "due process of law" or "equal protection of the laws" to any person. A right to be free of the expression of private hatred can by no means fairly be inferred from these admittedly broad, but not infinite provisions.

The second weakness of Wells's approach is that his conclusion that any harm that results from free speech is grounds for regulation is, like that of Catharine MacKinnon, proof that he believes in free speech only when it is cheap and easy. Far from being willing to protect the speech he believes to be "fraught with death," in Justice Holmes's memorable phrase, Wells is not even willing to protect speech fraught with inconvenience.

This is not the only case in which the compelling emotional pull of international human rights law has conflicted with the mandates of the U.S. Constitution. The holding of individual participants in an aggressive war accountable for the resultant "crimes against humanity" set a new precedent which had no prior basis when the victorious Allies convened the Nuremberg Trials. That proceeding, many legal scholars, including several justices of the Supreme Court, believed violated the prohibition against *ex post facto* laws.[222]

Wells and many other proponents of the regulation of hate speech further urge that the damage done to the self-perception of those within the "hated" class justifies regulation. This point can be accepted even if the harm done is conceded to fall short of silencing. The question of whether that harm is somehow distinguishable from other forms of negative self-perception that can be inculcated answers itself: in degree, perhaps, but not in kind. In short, hate speech as hate speech alone, and not as an element of a verbal act or in the context of otherwise illegal activity, seldom if ever rises to the level of conduct such that the First Amendment does not protect it.

This is not to say that one may burn a cross on a black neighbor's lawn with impunity; of course not. That is an action that may be regulated, as the Court properly noted in *R.A.V.,* so long as the regulation is not based upon the message, but takes aim only at the medium. So the same can be said

---

222. William O. Douglas, *The Court Years* (1980) at 28–29 (listing Douglas, Black, Stone and Murphy as doubting the constitutionality of the trials); Eugene Gerhart, *America's Advocate: Robert H. Jackson* (1958) at 437–440 (discussing controversy). As Gerhart notes, the prohibition against *ex post facto* laws forms part of the common law of the United Kingdom, as well as of continental legal systems.

for the well-recognized offenses of harassment, assault, or even the tort of intentional infliction of emotional distress—although the looseness of this last rubric could pose grave dangers. The plasticity of these formulations present problems of definition that bid fair to dwarf the speech-protective principle, as modern problems are squeezed into the traditional tort formulations, or, alternatively, the analogy to such formulation of conduct previously deemed to be outside of the realm of legal redress is discovered.[223] However, the "bright line" rule discerned in the more in-depth examination in Chapter 5 holds true with hate speech as well. As in the case of pornography, attitudinal harms caused by hate speech may not be protected against by the law; incidental or direct harms may be.

Case in Point: Campus Speech

The treatment of unpopular speakers, or disapproved ideas, by a university poses several difficult questions that deserve some consideration here, because so often these issues arise in the context of hate speech. The responsibilities of a university are complicated by several factors, including the threshold question of whether the First Amendment is applicable at all. The First Amendment applies only to the governments, state and federal, and their instrumentalities. Only where a finding of "state action" can be made does the First Amendment kick in—private actors, so the theory runs, have the right to express themselves, and the corollary right to screen out the speech of others as they see fit.

Drawing the line of what is and is not state action can be difficult in this era of state and federal funding of the arts and universities. As the Supreme Court has put it, "a multitude of relationships might appear to some to fall within the Amendment's embrace, but that, it must be remembered, can be determined only in the framework of the particular facts and circumstances present."[224] This case-by-case approach represents a cautious, pragmatic approach to the tension between encouragement of such public funding of private endeavor and recognition that at some point such public support can color the private actor's endeavors, more closely affiliating her or him with the state.

---

223. *See*, for example, Cynthia Grant Bowman, *Street Harassment and the Informal Ghettoization of Women*, 106 Harv. L. Rev. 517, 543–545 (1993) (advocating the enactment of legal cause of action for spectrum of sexualized behavior of men toward women on public streets, ranging from catcalls to lascivious comments, including more threatening conduct; analogizing speech to assault/intentional infliction of emotional distress, fighting words, obscenity, and low-value speech).

224. *Burton v. Wilmington Parking Authority*, 365 U.S. 715, 726 (1961).

It has been decided that regulation and subsidization of a private entity does not alone convert private action into that of the state. Rather

> A STATE normally can be held responsible for a private decision only when it has exercised coercive power or has provided such significant encouragement, either overt or covert, that the choice must in law be deemed to be that of the State. Mere approval of or acquiescence in the initiatives of a private party is not sufficient to justify holding the State responsible for those initiatives.[225]

The courts have discerned several factors that help determine "whether the state was responsible for the decision of a private entity."[226] These include "(1) extensive regulation, (2) receipt of public funds, (3) type of function involved and (4) presence of a symbiotic relationship."[227]

Simply put, a public university—one owned and operated by the state—acts as a state agent in imposing discipline upon its students, including (although not limited to) cases in which it directly suppresses speech.[228] Thus, universities have a duty to afford their students due process as it is constitutionally understood before imposing discipline on them.[229] Indeed, the students of a public university may themselves, in the appropriate context, become state actors. So, for example, student-run newspapers may be state instrumentalities as well, unless they are insulated by independence from the direct interference of the university.[230]

In the context of a public university, it is clear that regulation of hate speech, unless it can be justified in concrete terms as preventing the disruption of the university's educative mission, may not pass constitutional muster simply because the arm of the state that effects the suppression is a university any more than it may be by the government at large. Courts that have examined campus speech codes promulgated by public universities have therefore applied the same First Amendment analysis as would be

---

225. *Blum v. Yaretsky*, 457 U.S. 991, 1004 (1982) citations ommitted.
226. *Sinn v. Daily Nebraskan*, 638 F. Supp. 143, 149 (D. Neb. 1986), *summarizing Rendell-Baker v. Kohn*, 457 U.S. 830 (1982) and *Blum*.
227. *Id.*
228. *Gay and Lesbian Students Association v. Gohn*, 850 F.2d 361, 365 (8th Cir. 1988).
229. *See*, for example, *Paine v. Board of Regents of University of Texas*, 355 F. Supp. 199 (W.D.Tex. 1972) (invalidating suspension of student on ground that due process not afforded him); *Jones v. Board of Governors of University of North Carolina*, 557 F. Supp. 263 (W.D.N.C. 1983) (granting nursing student's request for preliminary injunction because her claim that her expulsion was premised on violation of due process stood reasonable chance of success on the merits).
230. *Compare Sinn v. Daily Nebraskan*, 638 F. Supp. at 149 with *Gay and Lesbian Students Association v. Gohn*, 850 F.2d at 365–366.

applied to any other forms of state regulation of speech and have generally found such speech codes to unconstitutionally infringe on the rights of student speakers.[231]

To give one example of this distinction between the university and its students acting on its behalf, and the resulting attenuation of state interest, in October 1992, editors of the *Michigan Journal of Gender and Law*, a student publication at the University of Michigan Law School, removed a video series by Carol Jacobsen from an art exhibit that they had commissioned as a counterpart to a pro-censorship symposium that presented arguments for the regulation of pornography.[232] The video display, which took a sex-positive perspective, offended several participants in the symposium, notably John Stoltenberg and the ubiquitous Catharine MacKinnon, and, upon MacKinnon's advising the students of the existence (at least) of a complaint to her by Stoltenberg, the display was removed. In her interesting (although necessarily partisan) article that discussed the legality of this conduct, Marjorie Heins (Jacobsen's lawyer) focussed largely on the role of MacKinnon in securing the removal of the video display, on the ground that, as a professor at the school, MacKinnon's actions would be more fairly considered state action than would be the same action if taken by the students without her prompting.[233]

However, Heins noted, the fact that the students entered into the contract with Jacobsen with university funding and in the name of a university publication was a factor that supported a finding that their actions—without MacKinnon's prompting or the subsequent ratification of their action by the university, including law school dean Lee Bollinger—were as follows. Bollinger, as dean, entered into a settlement agreement with Jacobsen and the artists included in her display when they threatened to sue, but "publicly took the position that the students had been at worst rude, that they had simply exercised their First Amendment rights and that the university had no responsibility in the matter."[234] This argument overlooks the conceded breach by the students of a contract signed by the *Journal* on their behalf, and elides the question of whether censorship took place, regardless of whether it was actionable.

---

231. *See Doe v. University of Michigan*, 721 F. Supp. 852 (E.D. Mich. 1989) (striking speech code on grounds that it was both overbroad and so vague that its enforcement would violate due process); *UWM Post, Inc. v. Board of Regents of the University of Wisconsin*, 774 F. Supp. 1163 (E.D. Wisc. 1991); *Saxe v. State Area School Dist.*, 240 F. 3d 200, 206–207 (3d Cir. 2001) (same).

232. The following account is based upon Marjorie Heins, *A Public University's Response to Students' Removal of an Art Exhibit*, 38 N.Y. Law School L. Rev. 201 (1993).

233. *Id.*

234. *Id.*

The scope of the potential impact of the First Amendment on private universities is less clear than it is for public universities. Although as a general matter the private university is free to encroach on the speech of its students in a manner that would be insupportable if it were done by a public university, the receipt of state funding and accreditation provides a potential inroad for the First Amendment.[235] Moreover, theoretically a university could be deemed (although it has not been, to my knowledge) to create a privately owned public forum; in which case the normal right of an owner to regulate the conduct of his or her guests is drastically limited. The public forum doctrine originated in the context of so-called company towns, in which employers provided their employees with a place to live—not just individual dwellings, but an entirely company-owned and company-governed town, with parks, stores, and all the other hallmarks of a town, including places to meet and gather. The companies frequently relied on traditional property law rights to govern the lives of their employees in these towns, preventing them (among many other things) from unionizing.[236]

Although the scope of exactly what may constitute a privately owned public forum has expanded and contracted over the years, it is still eminently clear that a private facility may be treated as a quasi-government when it serves as the functional equivalent of a municipality, as evidenced in the seminal decision that applied the First Amendment to these company towns, *Marsh v. Alabama*.[237] A university may be the functional equivalent of a company town, under certain circumstances at least—an all-encompassing environment, in which the residents live and work. In such an environment, the First Amendment may be applicable despite the private ownership of the university.

In the context of university speech codes, the First Amendment has been held to legitimate the regulation of "fighting words" but not to stretch be-

---

235. *See The Dartmouth Review v. Dartmouth College*, 889 F. 2d 13, 21 (1st Cir. 1989) ("[I]f discriminatory conduct is viewpoint-based or infrigidates First Amendment freedoms, then remedies may exist as against state actors or in connection with federally funded programs"; dismissing suit because Dartmouth College not a state actor, and claim pleaded because anti–racial discrimination claim found to be merely one of violation of freedom of expression by purely private college).

236. Life in a company town has been strikingly (if partisanly) described by Clarence Darrow's admiring biographer Irving Stone, *Clarence Darrow for the Defense* (1940) at 40–42.

237. 326 U.S. 501, 502–503 (1946). Subsequent cases applied the doctrine to shopping malls, an application that was later overruled. *Compare Amalgamated Food Employees Union v. Logan Valley Plaza* 391 U.S. 308 (1968) (extending *Marsh* to prevent union picketing of grocery store in a privately owned shopping center) with *Lloyd v. Tanner* 407 U.S. 551 (1972) (permitting ejection of antiwar demonstrators from shopping mall). Although *Lloyd* purported to distinguish *Logan Valley Plaza*, the court subsequently admitted that it in fact had been effectively overruled, in *Hudgens v. NLRB*, 424 U.S. 507 (1976). However, in none of the three cases was the underlying validity of *Marsh* called into question—they turned instead on whether the analogy of a mall to a "central business district"—a traditional public forum—was so inherently compelling as to invoke *Marsh*'s rule.

yond that. Efforts to engraft a Title VII-type protection against a "hostile study environment" have been rejected on the ground that, unlike employees who may be deemed to act as agents of the employer (thereby permitting an inference that the employee's actions at the job site will be directed by the employer), the students of a university are instead the "consumers" and are not, in their role as students, its agents.[238] Likewise, by requiring that universities tailor their hate speech codes within recognized *Chaplinsky* categories, the lower courts have—thus far—refused to engraft special university-based levels of protection, or new categories.[239]

Moreover, whether or not the university *can* censor, it is surely unseemly for it to do so. The very purpose of a university is to explore ideas, to train minds to be flexible, to be able to choose to evaluate and accept or reject ideas. A thoroughgoing regime of censorship hardly seems to be the ideal environment in which to do so. Particularly because race, gender, and sexual orientation are such sore spots, closing off debate or discouraging it save when necessary to preserve the ability of the university to teach is simply unwise. As the Supreme Court once wisely reminded:

> TO impose any straitjacket on the intellectual leaders in our colleges and universities would imperil the future of our Nation. No field of education is so thoroughly comprehended by man that new discoveries cannot yet be made. Particularly is that true in the social sciences, where few, if any, principles are accepted as absolutes. Scholarship cannot flourish in an atmosphere of suspicion and distrust. Teachers and students must always remain free to inquire, to study and to evaluate, to gain new maturity and understanding; otherwise our civilization will stagnate and die.[240]

In short, whether or not any given speech code promulgated by any given university is unconstitutional, the punishment of disruptive behavior alone and not the ideas that are so frequently debated to, or beyond, their logical extremes by the minds being forged, is more consonant with the mission of a university.

CONCLUSION

After a rousing chapter that defends the constitutional right to speak freely, however pernicious the content, an author or advocate can perhaps be for-

---

238. *UWM Post, Inc.* 774 F. Supp. at 1177.
239. *See*, for example, *Doe v. University of Michigan*, 721 F. Supp. at 864–867.
240. *Sweezy v. New Hampshire*, 354 U.S. 234, 250 (1957); *see also Keyishan v. Board of Regents of the University of the State of New York*, 385 U.S. 589, 603 (1967).

given for feeling as if he or she should head to the pithead bath. That much of this stuff is viscerally repugnant and upsetting is clear—but that does not mean that we have to accept the conclusion of Robin West that the regulation of hate speech is "a good idea," and that the fact that such a good idea may well be unconstitutional, means that "at least from a progressive perspective, the First Amendment is morally flawed."[241] Instead, I would urge the reader to think of the Holocaust Museum in Washington, D.C., another viscerally powerful and disturbing experience.

Although many of the displays were moving to those with whom I toured the museum, I found most of it sad, but not immediate. Rather, the great bulk of the exhibits were powerful, but spoke of their own era, finite and over. But the displayed propaganda, including caricatures of Jews as seen by the Nazis, and the poster "How to Distinguish a Jew," as well as newsreels of rallies—only in seeing Hitler in color did I realize how distancing black and white can be—all that was immediate, potent, and somehow foreboding. Likewise, a display in another facility of "Americana" including anti-black depictions—degrading caricatures of African-Americans on household objects—brought home to me the stupid, dirty nature of racism more than any tracts, pamphlets, or consciousness-raising meetings could ever have done.

A general ban on hate speech would not permit such use of these materials, and one that permitted *only* such a use cannot be squared with viewpoint neutrality, the most basic requirement of the government's regulation of speech. Unless we are to falsify our history, our culture—who we were, and what we must grow away from if we are to become who we aspire to be—we need these reminders of the past, and of those who would bring it back upon us if they could. Moreover, how does it benefit us to jail or fine the would-be fomenters of racial hatred? The ideas are all too present for them to be soon suppressed. As martyrs, these hatemongers could attain some degree of credibility. Out in the open, in the cleansing light, they can be held up to the scorn they so deserve.

Because MacKinnon and the other advocates of regulation of hate speech do not offer any replacement for the rejected standards, they are left arguing for nakedly partisan results—that deciding legal disputes should be founded explicitly upon policy preferences, and not grounded in some neutral theory. MacKinnon justifies this by declaring that "anyone with an ounce of political analysis should know that freedom before equality, freedom before justice, will only further liberate the powerful and will never free what is most in need of expression."[242] Beyond the fallacy of her assump-

---

241. Robin West, *Constitutional Skepticism*, 72 B.U. L. Rev. 765, 768 (1992).
242. *Feminism Unmodified* at 15.

tion that justice and equality are static goals that can be achieved at a finite time, and so the sacrifice of freedom is only "for the duration" and may one day be rebated, MacKinnon is in essence demanding a blank check.

Because she offers no overarching rationales except that of achieving equality for women, MacKinnon leaves unasked, let alone unanswered, the question of what society will look like once equality is achieved. MacKinnon explicitly argues for the reaching of equality by, to quote Malcom X, "any means necessary," cutting down traditional notions of free speech, individual autonomy, of due process, and representative democracy. Like Thomas More's son-in-law William Roper in Robert Bolt's drama *A Man for All Seasons*, she is willing to cut down the entire forest of the law to get at the Devil; like "son Roper" she has yet to answer the question posed by More in reply: "And when the last law was down, and the Devil turned round on you, where would you hide, Roper, the laws all being flat?"[243] Bolt's pointed question is relevant to the hate speech debate: "This country's planted thick with laws—man's laws, not God's—and if you cut them down, d'you really think you could stand upright in the winds that would blow then?"[244]

Huey Long once said that if fascism were to come to America, it would come disguised as a quest for equality.[245] This apt warning is not the last word on which to leave Catharine MacKinnon, the feminist movement to ban pornography, and the related new assault on hate speech. Rather, Justice Brandeis's more tolerant and wise words seem apposite:

> Experience should teach us to be most on our guard to protect liberty when the Government's purposes are beneficial. Men born to freedom are naturally alert to repel invasion of their liberty by evil-minded rulers. The greatest dangers to liberty lurk in insidious enroachment by men of zeal, well meaning but without understanding.[246]

---

243. Robert Bolt, *A Man for All Seasons* (1960) at 38.
244. *Id.*
245. *See* Seldes, *The Great Thoughts* (1987) at 249. "Fascism will come to the United States in the guise of Americanism."
246. *Olmstead* v. *United States*, 277 U.S. 438, 479 (Brandeis, J. dissenting) (1927).

8

The Road Goes Ever On
The Case for the First Amendment

AFTER ALL THE invocation of case law, the furious waving of precedents for and against the functionalist interpretation of the First Amendment urged here, and in support of the (so far) occasionally steadfast rejections by the Supreme Court of invitations to tailor the Constitution to the perceived priorities of the day, a time must come when the argument ceases to be one of what a scrap of paper, however hallowed, may say. For the Constitution can, of course, be changed, and the amendment process, difficult though it is to satisfy, has been successfully invoked in the past to urge reversal of constitutional precedent.[1] That change—even fundamental change—has a respected place in the history of our Constitution, and even in its theology has been clear from the very beginning. No less a figure than Thomas Jefferson went on record on several occasions as favoring even violent revolution on a periodic basis, stating of Shays's Rebellion, to take but one example, "God forbid we should ever be twenty years without such a rebellion."[2] Jefferson's further thoughts are worth quoting:

> WHAT country before, ever existed a century and a half without a rebellion? And what country can preserve its liberties, if its rulers are not

---

1. For an illuminating review of Article V of the Constitution, its original purposes and development, as well as current understanding of its history, *see* Henry Paul Monoghan, *We the People[s], Original Understanding, and Constitutional Amendment*, 96 Colum. L. Rev. 121 (1996). Professor Monoghan, in the course of a fascinating and controversial exegesis of the antidemocratic limits built into the amendment process, takes on contemporary efforts to limit the power to amend as well as those who would impeach the slowing of fundamental change built into the process.
2. Thomas Jefferson, Letter to Col. William S. Smith, 1787, *quoted in* George Seldes, *The Great Thoughts* (1985) at 209.

warned from time to time, that his people preserve the spirit of resistance. Let them take arms. The remedy is to set them right as to facts, pardon and pacify them. . . . The tree of Liberty must be refreshed from time to time, with the blood of patriots and tyrants. It is their natural manure.[3]

Without sharing Mr. Jefferson's somewhat sanguinary acceptance of violent slaughter, one can draw from his words, and from the chain of circumstances that gave rise to the First Amendment—the American Revolution, the failure of the Articles of Confederation, and the need of amendments to the Constitution itself in the form of a Bill of Rights to secure passage of the Constitution—a powerful reminder of the fact that change is possible. In defending the document as it exists, this volume has not sought to deny this, merely to stress that fundamental change should be done at the will of the people, acting in full knowledge of the nature of the changes that are occurring in the political order.

Such rewriting should not be done by judges who follow the advice of academics who fail to perceive that the rewriting of the Constitution by unelected officials under the guise of interpreting the document is not just a violation of their oaths of office, but far more important, is a confidence trick played on the populace at large. This is true however noble the cause in which it is attempted. Whether the rewriting is done in the name of democracy, equality, or God, such a rewriting is based on a lie: that such drastic change can be imposed by an elite without effectively disenfranchising the people.

Nonetheless, while deploring the tactics used to secure fundamental changes in the constitutional rubric, no scholar can but acknowledge that our poor beleaguered First Amendment has been subjected to some fairly severe criticism, and that not all of it is trivial. The surging tide of agitation in support of victims' rights, the very real suffering of the targets of racial or religious or sexual bigotry—all of these have raised profound questions about whether the U.S. Constitution, while purporting to guarantee liberty for all, in fact only acts to reinforce the dominant social power elites.

Plainly, some of those who urge fundamental change may be employing Machiavellian (by which I only mean that for them the end justifies the means) tactics, but their fundamental criticisms must be addressed, outside of the scope of extant First Amendment doctrine. At some point, the short-term answer that "the Constitution says so," however correct before the judiciary, must give way to the question of what is right, and the issue laid before the people.

---

3. *Id.*

Because so much of what is written about the new challenges to freedom of speech falls within the context of accusations and counteraccusations of what can or cannot be squared within the logic of the amendment, a look at these challenges solely on the merits of what the proposals themselves are—that is, what kind of society Americans should adopt or cling to—requires a less legalistic, more holistic review than that used in the preceding chapters, and than most of the advocates of these alternative viewpoints have themselves used. Or, in plain English, because I have already argued (with or without success) that most of these new "readings" are not consistent with the First Amendment, the focus now changes to whether the ideas in and of themselves are good ideas, presenting a viable alternative to the system of freedom of expression embodied in the First Amendment.

In so doing, two principal arguments beyond those already invoked under the First Amendment need to be addressed: first, the concept that freedom of speech needs to be reconceptualized in our age of media saturation, where multinational megalithic corporations can outspend any individual, and second, the notion that the First Amendment and the liberal state are a failed experiment, and that greater government involvement is needed to create the equality that liberalism has failed to deliver.

The first argument misconceives the target. Although some argue that wealthy individuals are able to speak more freely than those without such resources, the brunt of the assault is that corporate resources so dominate the market that the individual is drowned out in the cacophony of corporate speech. Attacking freedom of speech indiscriminately, the advocates of regulation in the marketplace of ideas perceive the crushing of individuals in a landscape of corporate juggernauts with essentially limitless resources.[4] In short, the hostility to the First Amendment is misdirected, based on a notion that the speech of corporations and that of individuals must be subject to the same rules.

The second argument is even more ill conceived. The failure of the liberal state to bring about equality of status and of opportunity is a well-worn platitude of the critical legal theory movement. That liberal First Amendment theory is a vehicle of subordination is alleged not only by Catharine MacKinnon, Sunstein, and their sympathizers but by other scholars such as Owen Fiss[5] or Richard Abel.[6] Such views seem rooted in an ahistorical view of history; they seem to expect fifty years of semiliberal interpretation of the

---

4. *See, for example,* Cass Sunstein, "A New Deal for Speech," in David S. Allen & Robert Jensen, *Freeing the First Amendment* (1995) at 54 *et seq.*
5. Owen Fiss, "The Right Kind of Neutrality," in Allen & Jensen, *Freeing the First Amendment* (1995) at 79–89.
6. Richard L. Abel, *Speaking Respect, Respecting Speech* (1998).

First Amendment to wipe away centuries of oppression and classism, and then blame one of the principal tools of evolution for the frustratingly slow pace at which dramatic change is being effected.

Both arguments for abandoning allegiance to the First Amendment merit examination, but must be in the end rejected. Finally, the notions of the relationship between the state and the individual and of the moral agency of individuals in our society support a strong First Amendment, militating in favor of self-determination, a value of which the First Amendment revisionists all too frequently lose track.

The Drowning-Out Argument

Perhaps the most successful argument, in academia, if not yet before the courts, is the claim that we cannot afford unregulated speech because the huge multinational conglomerate can outshout the individual or even the smaller collective. In a world where *only* corporations, or the occasional superrich Atlanta tycoon can afford to saturate the marketplace with their ideas, the First Amendment must be reinterpreted to permit a sort of affirmative action in the marketplace of ideas, or else the underlying social purposes that it was meant to serve will be irrevocably lost.

This argument has been made by a growing number of scholars, sometimes in the exact pattern given above, sometimes urging that the ideas of feminists, African-Americans,[7] or other minority groups be given favorable treatment to make up for their oppression at the hands of corporate America.[8] Others advance a somewhat more nuanced argument, focusing on specific contexts such as the workplace, where the employees are hampered by their status, especially in the context of "at-will employment," which permits termination of an employment relationship at any time for any reason or no reason at all.[9]

---

7. I do not subscribe to the idiocy that there is one feminist or one African-American or one gay/lesbian view, but this articulation reflects the monolithic views of the perspectives of these groups used in support of these "silencing" arguments—the most detailed example being that of Catharine MacKinnon as set out in Chapter 6.

8. *See*, for example, Cass Sunstein, *supra* note 4, at 54–78; Robert Jensen & Elvira R. Arriola, "Feminism and Free Expression," in Allen & Jensen at 195, 208–209.

9. *See*, for example, Victoria Smith Holden, "Effective Voice Rights in the Workplace," in Allen & Jensen at 114–139. Although Holden does not address the doctrine of at-will employment, her claim that workers are disempowered in the workplace gains even more cogency from the fact that, in many states, unless an employment contract provides a term for the duration of employment, it is terminable at will by either party for any reason or for none— a fact that gives employers (in a labor-plentiful market) the whip hand over their workers. *See Porras v. Montefiore Medical Center*, 185 A.D.2d 784, 588 N.Y.S.2d 135, 137 (1st Dep't

To the extent that these arguments take the position that the "oppressors" (that is, the socially dominant groups) must be silenced, or the "victims" will not feel free to speak, this argument is simply untenable: The law cannot create a "respectful" discussion environment because respect cannot be compelled. This argument seems to wholly invalidate the notion of Richard Abel that apologies can be appropriately coerced from those "victimized" by speech which has devalued them.[10] Such apologies would be a hypocritical exercise, at best, and present, at worst, the unedifying spectacle of an individual being forced to mouth words she or he may be choking on. As Justices Black and Douglas wrote over 50 years ago, "Words uttered under coercion are proof of loyalty to nothing but self-interest."[11] In the same case, Justice Murphy acidly rejected the value to be gained "by forcing him to make what is to him an empty gesture, and recite words wrung from him contrary to his . . . beliefs," as "overshadowed by the desirability of preserving freedom of conscience to the full."[12]

The law—whose essence, after all, is that it is mandatory, that disobedience results in compulsion, cannot create at all. It can carve out and distinguish and protect, but the essential negativity of legal compulsion must not be overlooked. Even "best efforts" contracts, in which one party promises to devote themselves to the goals of the contract at issue, a simple example of the law trying to be positive, end up viewed by reviewing courts in their negative light—that is, the question becomes what is the *minimum* required to satisfy the agreed-to condition.

Moreover the lack of elegance, of subtlety, in legal processes must not be overlooked. Law is not a surgeon's scalpel. It is a blunt instrument, capable of inflicting crushing damage, but not of exploring fine nuances. Although it is easy for the advocates and the judge to explore fine legal distinctions, using scholastic logic, every lawsuit ends up in a judgment, and every judgment must be simple enough to be enforced without triggering a new lawsuit.

As it creates such simple resolutions to complex problems, the legal system must award victory to one party or the other, and the process by which that determination of which party should win frequently is long, drawn out, and expensive. Thus, both civil and criminal litigations wreck

---

1992), *app. denied*, 81 N.Y.2d 704, 595 N.Y.S.2d 399 (1993) (discussing at-will employment doctrine); *Doynow v. Nynex Publishing Co.*, 202 A.D.2d 388, 608 N.Y.S.2d 683, 684 (2d Dep't 1994), *Weiner v. McGraw Hill, Inc.* 57 N.Y. 2d 458, 457 N.Y.S. 2d 193 (1982).

10. Abel, *supra* note 6 at 245–282. For a more detailed evaluation of Abel's apology remedy, *see* Wirenius, "The Last Word: Status, Conflicts, Individual Autonomy and Freedom of Speech" 23 Hamline L. Rev. (2000) at 395–426.

11. *West Virginia Board of Education v. Barnette*, 319 U.S. 624, 644 (1942) (Black and Douglas, J J. concurring) (invalidating compulsory flag salute ordinance).

12. *Id.* at 646 (Murphy, J. concurring).

lives, cost fortunes, and polarize people into further extremes. This is particularly true of criminal law, involved in so many free speech issues. The problems of discretion and of administrative inefficiency deprive the system of the theoretical rigor for which it strives.[13]

In other words, not only *should* the law not try to pick sides between contending philosophies in order to foster amity and good will, but it cannot. The legal system is hard-pressed enough to determine facts, let alone be equipped to evaluate the worldview of the parties sucked into its maw. Exposing someone to a coercive system that combines the worst features envisioned by Kafka and Lewis Carroll is not the way to make friends and influence people.

However, the proponents of regulation of speech to prevent "drowning out" of minority viewpoints are rightly concerned about power disparity and the ability to manipulate the most effective means of communication. Some suggest limiting the extent to which the powerful may urge their views; others would suggest mandating that the elite subsidize the messages of those who are less able to seize the public ear. The Supreme Court, most recently in finding that Congress "must carry" regulations applied to cable television to be unconstitutional, has equated these two approaches, with good reason.[14]

To the extent that such arguments have urged that certain specific messages be controlled, as tending to reinforce extant power structures—MacKinnon's argument, essentially—it rests on a futile approach, because it calls for limitations that impact on both powerful individuals or corporations and the powerless who wish to discuss that same subject—either with an ironic viewpoint, or perhaps that most dreaded of phenomena, a new perspective. So, in discussing the effort by MacKinnon to impose a "pro-woman" orthodoxy on speech, we saw that MacKinnon ended up striving to crush the speech of individual women, such as Anne Rice or Sara Adamson. The end result is that both the socially dominant and the socially disadvantaged are forced to carry an equal burden—leaving the advantage of power right where it was to begin with, a fact evidenced by the radical right's embrace of Catharine MacKinnon.[15]

A more interesting, and deeper, approach to some of the same concerns is the argument that socially dominant or advantaged institutions, such as

---

13. For a study of the application of discretion, both prosecutorial and judicial, in the criminal justice system, *see* Wirenius, *A Model of Discretion: New York's Interest of Justice Dismissal Statute*, 58 Alb. L. Rev. 175 (1994). For two first-person views of how the system works, one from the prosecution viewpoint, one from the defense, *see* David Heilbroner, *Rough Justice: Days and Nights of a Young DA* (1990); Seymour Wishman, *Confessions of a Criminal Lawyer* (1981). Systemic failure is dealt with in Martin Yant, *Presumed Guilty: When Innocent People Are Wrongly Convicted* (1991).
14. *Turner Broadcasting System v. FCC*, 512 U.S. 622 (1994).
15. *See* Nadine Strossen, *Defending Pornography* (1995) at 217–246.

corporations, are too heavily weighted in the marketplace of ideas, and that somehow the First Amendment must yield to government regulatory power in order to correct this potential monopoly. The origin of this line of thinking can be traced back at least as far as 1967, when Jerome Barron urged the creation of a new "contextual" right to access to the press.[16] In this seminal work, Barron argued that the "romantic" view of the First Amendment, which permits media barons to urge only their own views on public issues, must give way to a "contextual view, one under which both the states and federal government could compel the media to subsidize dissenting views. This argument would be seen as in essence *a market corrective*[17] (although this is not Barron's term), and would seek to serve the policy functions undergirding the First Amendment.

So far, the Supreme Court has rejected the so-called market dysfunction argument. Most recently, in *Turner Broadcasting Co. v. FCC*[18] it rejected an effort to extend such an argument. The "scarcity rationale" that permits regulation of television and radio could be discerned, but it was not caused by the inherent limits of the medium.

Despite this rejection to date, the market dysfunction concept sounds fairly reasonable, except that the reformers urge us to dilute the First Amendment in order promote the values of active discourse it serves. A more activist state that balanced "good" speech against "bad" speech, or acted as a parliamentarian in the realm of ideas to determine when speech furthers debate and when it tends to discourage others from joining in, would be making very context-specific, fact-intensive determinations.[19]

Such a standard is not a standard at all in any meaningful sense, especially when it is applied in the context of criminal liability. Even in the case of civil penalties, which require a speaker to face the risk that a Monday morning quarterback will rule his or her contribution to the discourse out of order is bound to be a chilling factor. To say that one speaks at his or her peril is the exact opposite of a doctrine of freedom of speech.

These proposed moderators of the social debate perhaps do not realize the extent to which power over the order and structure of debate has a substantive impact, a lesson not lost on any Speaker of the House of Represen-

---

16. Jerome L. Barron, *Access to the Press—A New First Amendment Right*, 80 Harv. L. Rev. 1641 (1967).
17. The Supreme Court, in *Turner Broadcasting Co. v. FCC*, 512 U.S. at 634–640, in characterizing these arguments made in many cases and scholarly works over the thirty years since the publication of Barron's article, as one of "market dysfunction," also squarely rejected it for the reasons set out in the text.
18. 512 U.S. at 638–639.
19. *See*, Owen Fiss, *The Supreme Court and the Problem of Hate Speech*, 24 Cap. L. Rev. 281 (1995); Tracy Higgins, *Giving Women the Benefit of Equality: A Response to Wirenius*, 20 Ford Urb. L. J. 77, 87 (1992); Cass Sunstein, *The Irony of Free Speech* (1995); Richard Abel, *Speaking Respect, Respecting Speech* (1998).

tatives. Likewise, the proposals for creating a "New Deal" for speech forget the extent to which the New Deal, and the resultant administrative state, have led to micromanagement through government regulation. Such all-encompassing management is at worst salutary for the environment, wholesome for employment discrimination, and a damned nuisance for business, if free marketeers are to be believed. But when it comes to the question of what ideas may vie for the attention of the polity, how the people debate what will serve as the lodestar du jour, then micromanagement—what Higgins calls the "activist state"—is an inherently elitist concept that strikes at the heart of the notion of self-rule. More pressingly, for present purposes, the argument wrongly assumes that such a regime is the only way of addressing the problem.

Perhaps it really is a question, as Nat Hentoff suggests, of whose ox is gored.[20] Certainly, the hypothetical idea that feminist journals will be required to support the nascent men's rights movement as a condition of spreading their own views, or that *The Amsterdam News* will be compelled to print rebuttals from racist groups of articles in previous editions gives one pause. (Who today has been more successfully marginalized, after all, than the extreme right?)[21] The immediate surety of wrongness evoked by such a prospective scheme carries with it an instinctive revulsion at the prospect of forcing people to themselves communicate ideas that they oppose. It is at best unseemly to mandate through force of law that individuals behave as though they adhere to what they oppose—a sort of intellectual indentured servitude, as the Supreme Court recognized as far back as *West Virginia Board of Education v. Barnette*.[22]

And, of course, these proponents of balance would reply, here goes the liberal equating everything to the oppression of individuals, like the schoolchildren in *Barnette* forced to "pledge allegiance" to the American flag in defiance of their Jehovah's Witness faith. Microsoft is hardly going to invoke the same dignitary concerns—yet is far more likely to sway the debate than are the Barnettes of the world.

In fact the difficulty is not merely a matter of liberal insistence that persons be equated with corporations, but the fact that most of these proposals to silence some speakers or messages in the name of giving others more voice have made that very mistake.

---

20. Nat Hentoff, *Free Speech for Me—But Not for Thee* (1995).
21. For a condescending, humorous—and apparently accurate—view of one segment of the radical right, and its scapegoating of former President Bill Clinton, whom it blames for this increasing marginalization, *see* Philip Weiss, "The Clinton Haters," *New York Times Magazine*, 23 February 1997 p. 34 *et seq.*
22. 319 U.S. 624 (striking as unconstitutional requirement that schoolchildren salute flag, against challenge brought by Jehovah's Witnesses; reversing *Minersville School District v. Gobitis*, 310 U.S. 586 [1940]).

The reformists who seek to water down First Amendment protections in the name of "equalizing" the voices of individuals to corporations, or of minority to majority groups, completely elide the extent to which the spread of new technology, such as the Internet, is already beginning to redress the balance. As already discussed, however, the impact of that new technology is only beginning to be felt, and is predicted to render, through on-line self-publishing, the individual speaker an equal competitor in the marketplace of ideas with the largest multinational conglomerates.[23] Thus, to a great extent, this concern of access may be growing obsolete before the constitutional corrective called for has been administered.

More fundamentally, the reformers have begged the question of whether the First Amendment applies to corporations in the precise way it does to individuals. Assuming that it does, the reformers then point out what a lopsided advantage this gives corporate speakers, and conclude that a Frankfurterian balancing test, or a proportional representation test, must be applied to rules that purport to redress that advantage. A rule that limits speech and alters outcomes is chosen, because corporations are assumed to be indistinguishable from the individual.

Those who urge greater regulation of the marketplace of ideas have some justification to seek to distinguish between individuals and corporations for constitutional purposes, but not to try to restrict *everybody's* speech rights in the interest of actively promoting the exercise of those rights by a few. The application of the First Amendment to corporate speech is, historically speaking, a recent development, and one that raises questions of federalism as well as of the nature of constitutional interpretation—questions which have gone largely unasked or unanswered, to date.

In addressing these questions, the nature of a corporation must be recollected. A business corporation, as law school texts have made clear, is a device to limit liability.[24] Somewhat less breezily, a corporation is a legal "fiction that is recognized to protect the shareholders from the risk of personal liability for the obligations of the corporation."[25] The policy was designed "as a means of encouraging corporate investment by minimizing the investor's risk."[26] In short, the purpose of corporate structure is to insulate individuals

23. *See ACLU v. Reno*, 929 F. Supp. 824, 843–844.
24. *See*, for example, Larry E. Ribstein, *Business Associations* (1983) at 1–4– 1–5.
25. *Algie v. RCA Global Communications, Inc.*, 891 F. Supp. at 875, 888 (S.D.N.Y. 1994), *aff'd*, 60 F.3d 956 (2d Cir. 1995); *see also Barge v. Jaber*, 831 F. Supp. 593, 601 (S.D. Ohio 1993) (describing corporation as "artificial entity"); *Lowell Staats Mining Co. v. Pioneer Uravan, Inc.*, 878 F.2d 1259, 1262 (10th Cir. 1989) (same; applying Colorado law).
26. *Algie v. RCA Global Communications, Inc.*, 891 F. Supp. at 888 (*citing Labadie Coal Co.v. Black*, 672 F. 2d 92, 96 (D.C. Cir. 1982); Hackney & Benson, *Shareholder Liability for Inadequate Capital*, 43 U. Pitt. L. Rev. 837, 872 [1983]).

from the adverse consequences of their actions. Indeed, because most corporations are managed by a board of directors who act on behalf of the shareholders,[27] it might well be said that the business corporation is organized so that one group of individuals may be immunized for the actions of others taken with the sole purpose of turning a profit for their principals.

Thus, it is a commonplace of mainstream capitalist economic thought that "there is one and only one social responsibility of business—to use its resources and engage in activities designed to increase its profits so long as it stays within the rules of the game, which is to say, engages in open and free competition, without deception and fraud."[28] Milton Friedman emphatically rejects any other role for corporate management, asserting that "[f]ew trends could so thoroughly undermine the foundations of our free society as the acceptance by corporate officials of a social responsibility other than to make as much money for their stockholders as possible."[29] Indeed, Friedman goes so far as to say of charitable contributions by corporations that "[s]uch giving by corporations is an inappropriate use of corporate funds in a free-enterprise society."[30]

Accordingly, corporate sponsorship of the arts, or other charitable giving by corporations, is of at best questionable propriety, generally saved from being declared an *ultra vires* act (an act outside of the corporate charter, and thus one which the corporation cannot legally undertake) by the somewhat slender argument that the advertisement value or good will thereby incurred is "at least of some incidental benefit to the corporation"; if such an argument can be made, and the gift "was not very large in relation to the corporation's assets," then the gift will probably be upheld as proper.[31]

Of course, Friedman's point of view, although it is seminal and heavily relied on by free market purists, is not the only mainstream one—far from it—and a great degree of socially useful activity can be traced back to corporations, regardless of the advertising revenue that could be so generated. The point is not that corporations are evil, and must be abolished (indeed, one could argue that the officer who causes corporate giving is salving his or her conscience with someone else's money), but rather that, as should

---

27. Ribstein, *Business Associations* at 1–3.
28. Milton Friedman, *Capitalism and Freedom* (1962) at 133 (*citing* Adam Smith, *The Wealth of Nations*); *see also* Dennis Arrow, *Social Responsibility and Economic Efficiency*, Pub. Pol. 303, 304–305 (1973); *see generally*, Ribstein, *Business Associations* at 5–3–5–8 (summarizing exponents of "the Friedman view").
29. Friedman, *Capitalism and Freedom* at 133–134; *see* Ribstein, *Business Associations* at 5–6.
30. *Id.* at 135–136.
31. Ribstein, *Business Associations* at 6–24, *citing A. P. Smith Manufacturing Co.*, 13 N.J. at 145, 98 A.2d 581, *app. dismissed*, 346 U.S. 861 (1953); Philip C. Blumberg, *Corporate Social Responsibility and the Social Crisis*, 50 B.U. L. Rev. 157 (1970); Carter, *The Limits of Corporate Social Responsibility*, 33 Mercer L. Rev. 519 (1982).

be obvious, corporations aren't like people. Human beings can be idealistic unto martyrdom, they can be emotional—passionate even—they can be selfless as well as selfish. This plane of existence is denied to corporations.

Moreover, to give a corporation full First Amendment protection is in essence to give its decision makers and/or shareholders *two* levels of insulation, whereas the individual speaker has only one, the First Amendment itself. Under the doctrine of limited liability, a shareholder is not liable for the conduct of the corporation unless the corporate form has been rendered an empty shell—that is, the formalities of corporate existence have been allowed to lapse and the corporation can be deemed the "alter ego" of the defendant shareholder—a process whose very name, "piercing the corporate veil," suggests how rare it is.[32]

Likewise, an officer or director who does not him- or herself engage in unlawful or wrongful conduct can almost never be held liable for the wrongs of the corporate entity.[33] Thus, for a corporate director or shareholder, there is not one but two defenses to punishment for speech: the First Amendment and the doctrine of limited liability. This gives the shareholder/officer an added layer of insulation, and thus a greater degree of freedom to speak through the corporation, than has the individual speaker.

A strong argument may be made that these pragmatic differences—although legally cognizable, as created by the law—may not impact on the activities of the federal government, because the First Amendment states that Congress shall pass "no law abridging . . . the freedom of speech" without specifying *whose* freedom of speech is so protected. The argument that the states must provide the same level of protection for all corporate speech stands on far weaker ground. The states, it must be remembered, are forbidden to deny to any "person" the rights guaranteed by the First Amendment by a process of incorporation through the Due Process Clause of the Fourteenth Amendment, or, if we go back and ignore the plainly muddleheaded reasoning of *The Slaughter-House Cases*, through the agency of the Privileges and Immunities Clause of the Fourteenth Amendment. There are plenty of reasons—the differences set out above, just to name a few—why those rights should not be deemed to run to "artificial persons."

As will be seen, however, the present-day Court does not so distinguish; justices as far apart on the ideological spectrum as Brennan and Rehnquist

---

32. *See* Ribstein, *Business Associations* at § 2.04.
33. *See Rosenberg v. Pillsbury Co.*, 718 F. Supp. 1146, 1151 (S.D.N.Y. 1989) (applying Massachusetts law); *see generally Mills v. Polar Molecular Corp.*, 12 F.3d 1170, 1177 (2d Cir. 1993) ("A director is not personally liable for his corporation's breaches of contractual breaches unless he assumed personal liability, acted in bad faith or committed a tort in connection with the performance of the contract.").

have applied similar standards to the federal government and to the states, holding that at a minimum the rights of free speech of corporations must be protected to the extent necessary to enable corporations to carry out their charters. This consensus of opinion is not clearly wrong, nor is it ludicrous to say that the broader the First Amendment's sweep, the safer from governmental tyranny we all are. Nonetheless, logic, history, and even today's practice better support a Fourteenth Amendment argument that corporations cannot claim the same right to free speech as individuals than they do a whittling down of those freedoms to protect against corporate lung power.

A Brief Look Back: Early Views of Corporate Personhood

In fact, that was the Supreme Court's initial take on the matter. The Supreme Court has emphasized the unique nature of corporations in its jurisprudence for almost as long as it has sat. In *Bank of the United States v. Deveaux*[34] the Court confronted the issue of whether a corporation could be deemed a citizen for the purposes of determining whether the federal courts had jurisdiction in a civil case between natural persons and a corporation. Under the constitutional grant of jurisdiction to the federal courts, one way in which federal courts may entertain cases is if *complete diversity* of citizenship between the parties exists—that is, all of the plaintiffs are citizens of different states from all of the defendants. In holding that corporations could not be considered as citizens, and that the residence to be looked to was that of the shareholders,[35] Chief Justice Marshall's opinion for the Court reflected on the nature of a corporation:

> THAT invisible, intangible, and artificial being, that mere legal entity, a corporation aggregate, is certainly not a citizen; and, consequently, cannot sue or be sued in the courts of the United States, unless the rights of the members, in this respect, can be exercised in their corporate name. If the corporation be considered as a mere faculty, and not as a company of individuals, who, in transacting their joint concerns, may use a legal name, they must be excluded from the courts of the Union.[36]

---

34. 5 Cranch (9 U.S.) 61 (1809).
35. *See also Hope Insurance Co. of Providence v. Boardman*, 5 Cranch (9 U.S.) 57, 60 (1809) dismissing that case, also a diversity action on the grounds of *Deveaux's* holding that "a body corporate as such cannot be a citizen, within the meaning of the Constitution" and thus the jurisdictional requirement of complete diversity between the parties was not met.
36. *Bank of the United States v. Deveaux*, 5 Cranch (9 U.S.) at 86.

In so holding, the Chief Justice canvassed the English cases, citing an unbroken chain of precedent extending to the reign of Henry VIII. Thus, only because the federal courts would look behind that "mere incorporeal legal entity" of a corporation to the citizenship of its members were corporations able to defend their interests before the federal courts.[37] In *Trustees of Dartmouth College v. Woodward*[38] (a case more famous, perhaps, for Daniel Webster's oratory than for its holding), Chief Justice Marshall was able to expand on the doctrine set out in *Deveaux*:

> A CORPORATION is an artificial being, invisible, intangible, and existing only in the contemplation of law. Being the mere creature of the law, it possesses only those properties which the charter of its creation confers upon it, either expressly or as incidental to its very existence. These are such as are supposed best calculated to effect the object for which it was created. Among the most important are immortality, and, if the expression may be allowed, individuality; properties by which a perpetual succession of many persons are considered as the same, and may act as a single individual. . . . It is chiefly for the purpose of clothing bodies of men, in succession, with these qualities and capacities, that corporations were invented, and are in use.[39]

The same doctrine was restated in *Bank of Augusta v. Earle*,[40] in which the Court rejected an effort to apply the Privileges and Immunities Clause of the Fifth Amendment to permit that a bank that was incorporated in Georgia had a constitutional right to make purchases in Alabama, under (at that time) a theory that prevented the entity from doing business or being sued in a state in which it was not incorporated—the equivalent of physical presence (at that time considered the prerequisite of state court jurisdiction). The Court emphasized that to extend the *Deveaux* doctrine's principle that the citizenship of corporate members would confer upon the corporation an unfair advantage under the Privileges and Immunities Clause:

> IF it [the *Deveaux* doctrine] were held to embrace contracts, and . . . the members of a corporation were to be regarded as individuals carrying on business in their corporate name, and therefore entitled to the privileges of citizens in matters of contract, it is very clear that they must at the same time take upon themselves the liabilities of citizens, and be bound by their contracts in like manner. . . . The clause of the

---

37. *Id.* at 90, 91–92.
38. 4 Wheat (17 U.S.) 518 (1819).
39. *Trustees of Dartmouth College v. Woodward*, 17 U.S. at 636.
40. 13 Pet. (38 U.S.) 519, 586 (1839).

Constitution referred to certainly never intended to give to the citizens of each State the privileges and immunities of citizens in the several States, and at the same time exempt them from the liabilities which the exercise of such privileges would bring upon individuals who were citizens of the State.[41]

In short, the Court declined to construe the Privileges and Immunities Clause in such a way as to grant corporations an advantage over natural persons. This holding was reaffirmed in *Paul v. Virginia*,[42] in which the Court flatly declined to apply the clause to permit corporations that were organized under the laws of one state to operate in another.[43] The ground for the decision is of interest: Because a corporation is a creature of one state's law, application of the clause to afford corporations the constitutional protections natural individuals claim would in effect "grant the laws of one state operation in" all others.

The early jurisprudence under the Fourteenth Amendment is internally inconsistent. In *Santa Clara County v. Southern Pacific Rail Road Company*[44] the issue was "settled" in terms of a brief statement outside of the opinion of the Court (written by the first Justice Harlan) in an "Announcement by Mr. Chief Justice Waite." The text of the announcement is sparse, to say the least, reading "The court does not wish to hear argument on the question of whether the provision in the Fourteenth Amendment to the Constitution, which forbids a State to deny to any person within its jurisdiction the equal protection of the laws, applies to these Corporations. We are all of the opinion that it does."[45] That is the extent of the analysis, and no citation is given to authority, nor is any logic. The Court had decreed, and counsel was not even given the chance to argue the point.

Likewise, in *Covington v. Lexington Turnpike Road Co.*,[46] the Court, in an opinion by Justice John Marshall Harlan, reaffirmed the *Santa Clara* holding, stating baldly that "[it] is now settled that corporations are persons within the meaning of the constitutional provisions forbidding the deprivation of property without due process of law, as well as a denial of equal protection of the laws."

That the question of applicability of the Fourteenth Amendment's guarantees had not been finally, albeit brusquely, settled as Chief Justice Waite's "Announcement" indicated was the upshot of the Court's 1906 opinion in

---

41. *Bank of Augusta v. Earle*, 38 U.S. at 586.
42. 8 Wall. (75 U.S.) 168 (1869).
43. *Paul v. Virginia*, 75 U.S. at 180; 177–179; 180–182.
44. 118 U.S. 394 (1886).
45. *Id.*
46. 164 U.S. 578, 592 (1896).

Northwestern National Life Insurance Co. v. Riggs.[47] In upholding a state regulation on the contractual capacity of insurance companies, the Court found the Due Process Clause inapplicable to corporations. Justice Harlan, writing again for a unanimous Court, described as "without foundation" "the contention that the statute, if enforced, will be inconsistent with the liberty guaranteed by the 14th Amendment."[48] He dismissed the contention with the superbly simple explanation that "The liberty referred to in that Amendment is the liberty of natural, not artificial, persons."[49]

Thus, with Justice Harlan writing on both sides of the issue, the Court found that corporations were "persons" under the Fourteenth Amendment for equal protection purposes, but were not persons under the Due Process and Privileges and Immunities Clauses, a fact that elucidates Oliver Wendell Holmes's comparison of Harlan's mind to "a powerful vise the jaws of which couldn't be got nearer than two inches to each other!"[50]

However these pirouettes were performed, the Court seemed happy to continue in them, as demonstrated in *Western Turf Association v. Greenberg,*[51] in which the Court yet again recast its Fourteenth Amendment analysis with respect to corporations:

> OF still less merit is the suggestion that the statute abridges the rights and privileges of citizens; for a corporation cannot be deemed a citizen within the meaning of the clause of the Constitution of the United States which protects the privileges and immunities of citizens of the United States against being abridged or impaired by the law of a state.
>
> The same observation may be made as to the contention that the statute deprives the defendant of its liberty without due process of law; for the liberty guaranteed by the Fourteenth Amendment against deprivation without due process is that of natural, not artificial, persons.[52]

Such inconsistency litters the case law of the Fourteenth Amendment between 1874 and 1978. Justice Sutherland, in *Grosjean v. American Press Co.,*[53] endeavored to reconcile these disparate lines of precedent, opining

---

47. 203 U.S. 243 (1906).
48. *Northwestern National Life Insurance Co. v. Riggs,* 203 U.S. at 255.
49. *Id.* at 255. The Court also found that the statute passed muster under the Equal Protection Clause, because both domestic corporations and corporations organized in different states fell within its scope. *Id.*
50. *See* Edward J. Brander, ed., *Justice Holmes Ex Cathedra* (1966) at 235. Of course, against this odd brace of holdings must be measured Harlan's prescient and honorable dissent in *Plessy v. Ferguson,* 163 U.S. 537 (1896).
51. 204 U.S. 359 (1907).
52. *Western Turf Association v. Greenberg,* 204 U.S. at 363.
53. 297 U.S. 233, 244 (1936).

that the contention that the Fourteenth Amendment does not apply to corporations "is only partly true." Sutherland elaborated:

> A CORPORATION, we have held, is not a "citizen" within the meaning of the privileges and immunities clause. But a corporation is a "person" within the meaning of the equal protection and due process of law clauses. . . .[54]

In Justice Sutherland's own phrase, this articulation is only "partly true," and creates an artificially tidy line that in fact the Court had not followed, either up to the decision in *Grosjean,* or even, with perfect fidelity, after.

Although the discrepancy between the meaning of "persons" as applied in the Equal Protection Clause (extending to corporations) and in the rest of the amendment (where it did not) may not make much textual sense, it was certainly a line that the Court felt comfortable enforcing for a considerable period.[55] As recently as 1943, the Court held that the power of both the states and the federal government to enforce their laws implied a power on the part of these governments to compel corporations to produce their records, "with the privilege against of self-incrimination being limited to its historic function of protecting only the natural individual from compulsory incrimination through his own testimony or personal records."[56]

Corporate Speech under Today's Fourteenth Amendment

This is not to suggest, of course, that such is the understanding of the Court today. What is interesting about the Court's present approach is that the Court simply ducked the question of whether the Fourteenth Amendment's incorporation of the First Amendment applied to corporations in precisely the way that it did to natural persons, a question decided (in part) *against* corporations by the Massachusetts Supreme Judicial Court, which applied a

---

54. *Grosjean v. American Press Co.,* 297 U.S. at 244.
55. *See Selover, Bates & Company v. Walsh,* 226 U.S. 112, 126 (1912) ("[I]t is well-settled that a corporation cannot claim the protection of the clause of the Fourteenth Amendment which secures the privileges and immunities of citizens of the United States against abridgment or impairment by the law of a state"); *Pierce v. Society of Sisters,* 268 U.S. 510, 535 (1925) ("Appellees are corporations, and therefore, it is said, they cannot claim for themselves the liberty which the Fourteenth Amendment guarantees. Accepted in the proper sense, this is true"); *Liberty Warehouse Co. v. Burley Tobacco Growers' Co-Operative Marketing Association,* 276 U.S. 71, 89 (1928) (in view of doctrine announced in *Western Turf* and *Selover,* "[t]he allegation concerning deprivation of corporate life is unimportant"); *Hemphill v. Orloff,* 277 U.S. 537, 548–549 (1928) (*citing Deveaux* and *Bank of Augusta*).
56. *United States v. White,* 322 U.S. 694, 700–701 (1944) (discussing constitutional privilege in federal context, dictum with respect to state context).

"material interest" test to determine if the speech at issue fell into the narrower protective zone extended to corporations:

> WE believe that the court posed the wrong question. The Constitution often protects interests broader than those of the parties seeking their vindication. The First Amendment, in particular, serves significant societal interests. The proper question therefore is not whether corporations "have" First Amendment rights and, if so, whether they are coextensive with those of natural persons. Instead, the question must be whether [the challenged statute] abridges expression that the First Amendment was meant to protect. We hold that it does.[57]

The Court backed this analysis with a simple explanation: the speech that was regulated (campaign contributions by banks and business corporations) was quintessentially First Amendment material—political speech. This holding extended the Supreme Court's earlier decision in *Buckley v. Valeo*,[58] which struck down campaign finance reform laws as unconstitutional violations of the rights of the contributors to exert themselves on behalf of their political standard bearers. At election time, the *Buckley* Court ruled, there is a constitutional right to put your money where your mouth is.

In fact, the expenditure of money is at best an act impregnated with speech implications—action coupled with speech. Under the "verbal act" jurisprudence, a message-neutral campaign finance law like the one struck down in *Buckley* would stand a far better chance of passing muster—a useful fact in view of recent campaign finance scandals, and the helplessness of the elective branches of government to address them in the face of equal obloquy on the part of both parties.[59] Because the statutes at issue in *Buckley* and in *Bellotti* involved statutes that are applicable to all political candidates and parties, and were directed solely at the incidental effects of the act-with-speech-overtones, it seems clear that both decisions are simply wrong.

But leaving aside the question of whether cutting a check as a gesture of financial support is entitled to the same level of constitutional protection as printing a manifesto—pure speech—the decision in *Bellotti* presupposes that there is no difference between the First Amendment as applied to the states through the Fourteenth Amendment and the original enactment. The majority's logic would have had a certain power to it, if *Bellotti* had involved

---

57. *First National Bank of Boston v. Bellotti*, 435 U.S. 765, 776 (1978).
58. 424 U.S. 1 (1976). *See also Nixon v. Shrink Missouri Government P.A.C.*, 528 U.S. 377, 386–395 (clarifying *Buckley*).
59. *But see* the more nuanced position taken by Justice Douglas in *The Right of the People* (1958) at 31–32, arguing for regulation of corruption, publicization of amounts, and denouncing limits on amount or any theory that such would be an "undue" influence.

a congressional regulation. The argument would go: Congress shall pass no law abridging, the First Amendment says, the freedom of speech. The text does not distinguish between the rights of citizens and noncitizens, of natural and artificial persons. It is merely a prohibition, in language that is absolute, against Congress passing a law that impacts upon a particular freedom.

By contrast, the Fourteenth Amendment specifically limits the class of entities—"persons"—whom the states were barred from denying equal protection, depriving of liberty without due process of law, and infringing the privileges and immunities afforded by the federal constitution. If "persons," as used by the amendment is not expanded to include "artificial persons" then a rational ground of distinction between the federal guarantee of freedom of expression as against federal action and that applicable to state action can be drawn.

Such a distinction is supported by the language of the amendment (when I say "I met a person", most people do not ask "IBM?"), the understanding in effect at the time, and the legislative intent and objects—to protect newly enfranchised citizens especially and the rest of us humans incidentally against arbitrary and tyrannical action by the states.[60] Each of these factors, of course is considered to be a key determinant in parsing the meaning of legal instruments, from contracts through statutes to constitutional provisions.[61] And each of these can be used to find that a corporation is not a person—as in fact the Supreme Court recently demonstrated when it held that a corporation is not entitled to proceed in federal courts without prepayment of fees under a statute that extends that grace to poor "persons!"[62]

Another factor in favor of such a reading of the Amendment is that it "fits" into our federalist system.[63] The dispute between "bare bones" and "jot-for-jot" incorporationists described at a very superficial level in Chap-

---

60. *See* Michael Kent Curtis, *No State Shall Abridge: The Fourteenth Amendment and the Bill of Rights* (1986) at 57–91 (analyzing congressional enactment and understanding of members at the time); *Id.* at 131–153 (summarizing state ratification and views of amendment's goals and meanings at the state level).

61. *See,* for example, *Asgrow Seed Co. v. Winterbor,* 513 U.S. 179, 187 (1995) (applying "ordinary meaning" construction, a variant of the well-established "plain meaning" rule, but one hopefully without the sort of superliteral quality that has brought the latter into some disrepute; consulting *Oxford Universal Dictionary* (3d ed. 1955); *Webster's New International Dictionary* [1950]); *United States v. X-citement Video,* 513 U.S. 64, 68–71 (1994), applying legislative history, avoidance of absurd results, where ordinary meaning unclear).

62. *See Rowland v. California Men's Colony,* 506 U.S. 194, 199–202 (1993) (applying legislative purpose and history, plain meaning interpretive techniques to find that corporation is not a "person" as used in 28 U.S.C. S 1915, permitting a "person" to proceed *in forma pauperis*).

63. *See* Ronald Dworkin, *The Arduous Virtue of Fidelity: Originalism, Scalia, Tribe, and Nerve,* 65 Ford. L.Rev. 1249, 1253–1255 (1997) (discussing concept of "fit" in constitutional law).

ter 1 is a fascinating one, and one worthy of more space than is available here. Indeed, Michael Kent Curtis's work, cited in the notes, is especially revealing, as are the opinions of Justices Black and Douglas (on the jot-for-jot side) and Justices Cardozo, Frankfurter, and, especially, the second Justice Harlan (on the bare bones or "fundamental rights" side). What can be said here, though, is that the interpretation of the Fourteenth Amendment suggested here addresses the concerns of both sides of that dispute with respect to the different roles of the federal and state governments in our federalist statement, the text of the amendment (it is, to steal from John Marshall, a constitution we are expounding, and not policy we are setting), and the fear of giving unelected judges too much discretion to overrule the popularly elected branches.

At the moment, the reader who believes in a free press is getting, perhaps, a bit nervous. Corporations own and operate much of the media, after all. Does that mean that the states have carte blanche to limit the *New York Times*'s coverage of events? Not at all. As the Court reminded us in *Pierce v. Society of Sisters*, a corporation may assert the constitutional rights of others, so long as the violation of those rights "have business and property for which they claim protection" and that are "threatened with destruction through the unwarranted compulsion which the [state authorities] are exercising" on those others—in *Pierce*, on the "present and prospective patrons of their schools," whose right to study in private school were wholly outlawed; in the world of publishing, the authors and editors without whom journalism of any kind is impossible.[64] (The Court's requirement of threatened harm or, as the *Pierce* opinion states, "threatened destruction" neatly tracks the requirement of an allegation of "injury in fact" necessary for a party to assert standing to challenge a law under the Court's understanding of Article III's "case or controversy" requirement.)[65] Where a publisher is the classic middleman, presenting Susan Howatch's novel, Andrea Dworkin's polemic, or Maureen Dowd's columns, the speech of a corporate officer is that of the corporation acting through its agents. Corporate advertisements and tracts are understood to speak with the voice of the corporation, not that of the copywriter.

Even assuming that corporations have speech rights under the Fourteenth Amendment, it is not self-evident that such rights are coextensive with those of natural persons. As then-Justice Rehnquist suggested in his dissent in *Bellotti*, one should determine the speech rights of a corporation by reference to the purposes for which it was created under state law. All cor-

---

64. *Pierce v. Society of Sisters*, 268 U.S. at 535, 69 L.Ed. at 1078.
65. *See*, for example, *Valley Forge Christian College v. Americans United for Separation of Church and State*, 454 U.S. 464, 471–476 (1982) (summarizing case law).

porations, after all, are limited by their charters in terms of what they may appropriately do (any act outside of the charter is voidable as an *ultra vires* act). The significance of these limitations should be recognized, according to Justice Rehnquist:

> [CORPORATIONS] either were created by the [state] or were admitted into the [state] only for the limited purposes described in their charters and regulated by state law. Since it cannot be disputed that the mere creation of a corporation does not invest it with all the liberties enjoyed by natural persons, our inquiry must seek to determine which constitutional protections are "incidental to its very existence."[66]

In exploring this avenue, Rehnquist first looked to due process, and felt that the right to be free of deprivation of property without due process of law was a necessary adjunct to the creation of a corporate entity in part defined by the right to acquire and hold property.[67] Likewise, he continued, "when a State charters a corporation for the purpose of publishing a newspaper, it necessarily assumes that the corporation is entitled to the liberty of the press essential to the conduct of its business.[68]

Although Rehnquist does not rely as heavily as the argument suggested above on the federalist interpretation of the Fourteenth Amendment, he argues convincingly that:

> IT cannot be so readily concluded that the right of political expression is equally necessary to carry out the functions of a corporation organized for commercial purposes. A State grants to a business corporation the blessings of potentially perpetual life and limited liability to enhance its efficiency as an economic entity. It might reasonably be concluded that these properties, so beneficial in the economic sphere, pose special dangers in the political sphere.[69]

Rehnquist accepts that a corporation has a right of free speech corresponding to its needs to fulfil its state-created purposes; that is, a right to engage in commercial speech and speech related thereto. But, he quite reasonably asks, why must we be guided in our political realm by entities who cannot suffer the consequences of unjust laws?

---

66. *Bellotti*, 435 U.S. at 823–824 (Rehnquist, J. dissenting) (citation to *United States v. White, supra* note 56, omitted) (*quoting Dartmouth College, supra* note 38 at 636).

67. *Bellotti*, 435 U.S. at 824.

68. *Id.* (Rehnquist, J. dissenting). Rehnquist then goes on to cite *Grosjean* for that proposition, a dramatic narrowing of that decision's actual language, as was made plain by the quotation from Justice Sutherland's opinion above.

69. *Id.* at 825–826 (Rehnquist, J. dissenting).

The Rehnquist view has much to commend it, in its functional approach, and its accommodation between protecting the rights of the press and the historic distinction between natural and real persons. However, it elides some of that history, and artificially tidies a very messy jurisprudential backwater. Finally, it is unclear that the approach creates a comprehensible Fourteenth Amendment jurisprudence. Nonetheless, as a means of escaping the "what about the mainstream press?" dilemma, Rehnquist's *Bellotti* dissent provides further support for the argument that corporations may be treated differently from the natural persons without neutering the very press the First Amendment was enacted, in part, to protect.

The view that corporations should be treated differently from other speakers was taken up by the other dissenters in *Bellotti.* Justices White, Brennan, and Marshall (interestingly, the three best friends to freedom of speech on the Court at that time), were plainly uncomfortable with an all-or-nothing protection of corporate speech, and argued that although corporate speech was entitled to some First Amendment protection, a lesser quantum should be applicable.[70] They justified this sliding scale level of protection on two grounds, first asserting that "what some have considered to be the principal function of the First Amendment, the use of communication as a means of self-expression, self-realization, and self-fulfillment is not at all furthered by corporate speech."[71] The second ground urged by Justice White in dissent is that the shareholders of the corporation remain free to express their views, and so the impingement to free expression is much less, especially in view of the status of a corporation as a specially favored entity under the law.[72]

Chief Justice Burger's concurring opinion deserves mention, because he cogently undermined any attempt to draw too firm a distinction between the Free Speech and the Free Press Clauses as they impact upon corporations, noting that the "institutional" press was not the sole intended beneficiary of the First Amendment, that the occasional tract could form just as important a contribution to public discourse as the regular newspaper. Because the First Amendment arose in an era shaped by pamphlets, tracts, and occasional pieces—Thomas Paine's *Common Sense* being the best known of a voluminous literature—the Chief Justice's contention is hard to dispute.[73]

More recently, Justice Thurgood Marshall, in *Austin v. Michigan Chamber of Commerce,*[74] spoke for a majority of the Court in upholding a state statute that prohibited corporations from using corporate treasury funds for inde-

---

70. *Id.* at 802–822 (White, J. dissenting, joined by Brennan and Marshall, JJ.).
71. *Id.* at 804–805.
72. *Id.* at 807.
73. *Id.* at 795–802.
74. 494 U.S. 652, 654–655 (1990).

pendent expenditures in support of, or in opposition to, any candidate in elections for state office. The statute, Justice Marshall was careful to note, allowed corporations to "make such expenditures from segregated funds used solely for political purposes."[75] Although the Court found that the statute did burden expression, it was upheld as serving a compelling state interest, and as being narrowly tailored to serve that interest. The Court found that the interest in preventing corruption in government took on a special urgency in view of the advantages extended by state law to those who do business through the corporate form:

> STATE law grants corporations special advantages—such as limited liability, perpetual life and favorable treatment of the accumulation and distribution of assets—that enhance their ability to attract capital and to deploy their resources in ways that maximize the return on their shareholders' investments. These state-created advantages not only allow the corporations to play a dominant role in the Nation's economy, but also permit them to use "resources amassed in the economic marketplace" to obtain "an unfair advantage in the political marketplace."[76]

In the last analysis, the fact remains that despite the campaign finance cases, a strong argument can be made for differentiating between natural and artificial persons under the Fourteenth Amendment. Both Chief Justice Rehnquist's formalistic argument and Justice White's functionalist approach strike powerful blows at the notion that the First Amendment is a monolith in its applicability to the states.

As noted above, long-dormant principles of federalism can also be given scope in this reading of the interplay between the First and Fourteenth Amendments. In an era where federalism is again a player in constitutional theory,[77] this cannot be altogether unwelcome. Finally, the concerns that the press will

---

75. 494 U.S. at 654–655.

76. *Austin v. Michigan Chamber of Commerce,* 494 U.S. at 658–659 (*quoting FEC v. Massachusetts Citizens for Life,* 479 U.S. 238, 257 (1986) [striking a statute banning corporate election expenditures despite market dysfunction finding by legislature]).

77. *See Printz v. United States,* 521 U.S. 898 (1997) (striking Brady Act imposing on state law enforcement officials duty to "make a reasonable effort" to determine whether certain pending firearm purchases would be illegal; such imposition "commandeers" state officials in violation of Tenth Amendment). *See United States v. Lopez,* 514 U.S. 549 (1995) (striking federal statute prohibiting the carrying of a gun in a school zone as beyond the scope of the power granted Congress under the Commerce Clause); *Seminole Tribe v. Florida,* 517 U.S. 44 (1996) (striking as unconstitutional as violative of Eleventh Amendment provisions of Indian Gaming Regulatory Act that required states to negotiate legality of Native American–operated gambling establishments with tribes). For further federalism developments, *see also, New York v. United States,* 505 U.S. 144, 174–177 (1992) (striking as unconstitutional congressional enactment requiring states to dispose of low level radioactive waste on grounds that statute "commandeered" states into service of federal regularoty purposes); *Board of Trustees of Univ. of Ala. v. Garret,* 531 U.S. 356 (2001) ap-

be gutted as a result of such an approach appear to be unduly alarmist. Both under the *Pierce* application of standing and the Rehnquist "necessary adjuncts" doctrine enunciated in *Bellotti*, the press may assert its traditional immunities.

Finally, does not the distinction between the Free Press and the Free Speech Clauses—provisions that are so often interpreted as so identic as to suggest that one or the other is redundant—also suggest that this view of the First and Fourteenth Amendment's interplay should be at least considered? The White and Rehnquist dissents may even provide an argument applicable on the federal level, in that if the right of "freedom of speech" is one adhering only in natural persons, but the right of the "press" is determined by the nature of *what* is published and not *who* publishes it, the potential redundancy of the clauses may be avoided. In any event, the access dilemma, to the extent that it is based on the fear of corporate juggernauts, is a false one—a straw man that is set up to justify substantive regulation, which is not the most direct solution to the problem posed. Before we subject ourselves to the censor's regime, surely that direct approach should be weighed.

"THIS DANCE WILL NO FURTHER GO": THE FALLACY OF FREEDOM'S FAILURE

In all of the critical attacks on the First Amendment there is an undercurrent of frustration, a frequently unspoken sense that the ideal of free speech as an engine of social change has been given a long-term chance and failed. It is taken as a given that the chain of justification for expansive protection of speech from John Stuart Mill to Hugo Black to William O. Douglas has proved to be based on false foundations, because it has not proved to be anything more than a reinforcement of the existing social order.[78] This, frankly, reflects a grossly ahistorical viewpoint. If this volume has shown nothing else, it must have made clear that First Amendment jurisprudence has been evolving: The birth of the bare *notion* of substantive protection for speech did not win judicial adherence until 1919, in what I have called the conservative revolution represented in *Schenck, Debs,* and *Frohwerk.* As we saw,

plication of Americans with Disabilities Act to state employees is beyond Congress' power under the Tenth Amendment); *Kimel v. Florida Bd. of Regents,* 528 U.S. 62 (2000) (same; Age Discrimination in Employment Act); *Nevada Dept. of Human Resources v. Hibbs,* 538 U.S. (May 27, 2003) (upholding Family Medical Leave Act as applied to states). For commentary, *see* Matthew Adler & Seth Kreimer, *The New Ettiquette of Federalism: New York, Printz & Yeskey,* 1998 Sup. Ct. Rev. 71 (1999).

78. This sense of frustration, for example, is present in Catharine A. MacKinnon's *Only Words* (1993) from the very first sentence: "Imagine that for hundreds of years your most formative traumas, your daily suffering and pain, the abuse you live through, the terror you live with, are unspeakable—not the basis of literature." *Id.* at 3.

it took another decade, the entirety of the 1920s, for that notion to translate itself into something more than lip service, and by the 1940s the battle was on. Through the 1950s and well into the 1960s it was held by many who cared about civil liberties that the fledgling First Amendment could well be strangled in its cradle.[79]

Even now, in the years since *Brandenburg*, the jurisprudence is still evolving, shaping itself toward greater coherence and a realization of the prescient insights displayed in the verbal act cases, and the pioneering opinions of Justice Douglas. In that time, society has undergone a sea change: Demands for equality have become more strident, more uncompromising, and more successful. The same First Amendment rights that Lenny Bruce fought to vindicate until he died are now exercised routinely by his successors.[80]

Whether for society's weal or its woe, the proprieties of the Victorian and Edwardian ages, as assaulted by a gallery of antagonists from Radclyffe Hall to Larry Flynt, have collapsed, and a frank explicitness has permeated society to an extent unparalleled in this nation's history. One of the few hardy growths of the postwar era has been a meaningful First Amendment. In short, the triumph of free speech is a far more recent phenomenon than the view of a settled, unchanging legal order that has failed to advance the cause of equality with that of freedom would have us believe.

The critics of the First Amendment seem to miss the fact that, historically speaking, the dramatic change that they rightly deem to be insufficient has been accomplished under free institutions in the twinkling of an eye. In a period of time that is shockingly brief, the world order in which every man knew his place (and women were barely permitted a place) has been forced on the defensive. Although it has not been completely overthrown, that world has utterly lost the ideological battle, and defends itself by resisting the extension of "special privileges" to women and minorities, while paying lip service (if nothing else) to the virtue of equality.[81]

Lest the scope of this historical recantation be missed, consider a statement of the United States Supreme Court, our oracle in previous chapters, regarding the status of African-Americans at the time of the adoption of the U.S. Constitution:

---

79. *See* Robert W. Haney, *Comstockery in America: Patterns of Censorship and Control* (1960) (describing cases, many of which never reached the Supreme Court); Corliss Lamont, *Freedom Is as Freedom Does: Civil Liberties Today* (1956) (a passionate account of and polemic against McCarthyism and its spread beyond the scope of government); William O. Douglas, *America Challenged* (1960) (describing "America at the Crossroads" and the growing stifling of dissent).

80. *See* Martin Garbus, *Ready for the Defense* (1971) at 81–140; Edward deGrazia, *Girls Lean Back Everywhere: The Law of Obscenity and the Assault on Genius* (1992) at 444–479.

81. *See,* for example, *Romer v. Evans,* 517 U.S. 620 (1996) (overturning state statute effectively seeking to disenfranchise homosexuals, rejecting state's contention that statute merely sought to prevent extension of "special privileges" to homosexuals).

THEY had for more than a century before been regarded as beings of an inferior order and altogether unfit to associate with the white race, either in social or political relations; and so far inferior, that they had no rights which the white man was bound to respect; and that the negro might justly and lawfully be reduced to slavery for his benefit. He was bought and sold, and treated as an ordinary article of merchandise and traffic, wherever a profit could be made by it. This opinion was at that time fixed and universal in the civilized portion of the white race. It was regarded as an axiom in morals as well as in politics, which no one thought of disputing, or supposed to be open to dispute.[82]

Or again, forty years later, despite the passage of the Fourteenth Amendment, in upholding a statute *requiring* segregation of the races on railway cars:

IF the two races are to meet upon terms of social equality, it must be the result of natural affinities, a mutual appreciation of each other's merits and a voluntary consent of individuals. . . .

LEGISLATION is powerless to eradicate racial instincts or to abolish distinctions based upon physical differences and the attempt to do so can only succeed in accentuating the difficulties of the situation. If the civil and political rights of both races be equal, one cannot be inferior to the other civilly or politically. If one race be inferior to the other socially, the Constitution of the United States cannot put them on the same plane.[83]

Never mind that this seemingly neutral logic was invoked to uphold a state law prohibiting the sort of "mutual appreciation of each others merits" and "voluntary consent" that the Court held to be the only basis for social integration! Fifty-eight years later, the Court disavowed this logic in *Brown v. Board of Education*, and, as the civil rights movement got under way, African-Americans exercised their First Amendment rights and were able to change the discourse such that racial equality has gone from not being merely the law of the land (as after *Brown*) but, increasingly, a fact of life. Were Chief Justice Taney to write *Dred Scott* now, he would be hooted at in the street.[84]

---

82. *Dred Scott v. Sandford*, 19 How. (60 U.S.) 393, 407 (1857) (*per* Taney, C. J.).

83. *Plessy v. Ferguson*, 163 U.S. 537, 551–552 (1896) (*per* Brown, J.).

84. If it is any consolation, at the end of his life Taney *was* "shunned and hated by the men of the new time of storm and struggle for the principles of freedom and nationality." J. A. Logan, *Thirty Years in Washington* at 413, *quoted* in William H. Rehnquist, *The Supreme Court: How It Was, How It Is* (1987) at 149. Chief Justice Rehnquist also quotes Senator Charles Sumner's memorable statement (made in opposition to appropriating funds for the traditional memorial bust in honor of the deceased Chief Justice) that "Taney will be hooted down the halls of history." *Id.* at 149–150.

This is not to say that sufficient progress has been made, but merely that after centuries without progress, a quantum leap has taken place—a leap in part fostered by the First Amendment.

Similarly, although a majority of the Supreme Court was able to deny Myra Bradwell's claim that she be admitted to the bar by ducking the issue, at least one justice obligingly spoke on the subject of women:

> THE natural and proper timidity and delicacy which belongs to the female sex evidently unfits it for many of the occupations of civil life. The constitution of the family organization, which is founded in the divine ordinance, as well as in the nature of things, indicates the domestic sphere as that which properly belongs to the domain and functions of womanhood. . . .

> THE paramount destiny and mission of woman are to fulfill the noble and benign offices of wife and mother. This is the law of the Creator. And the laws of civil society must be adapted to the general constitution of things, and cannot be based upon exceptional cases.[85]

When Justice Brennan, a century later, circulated an opinion declaring classification by sex "inherently suspect," an opinion that became law in *Frontiero v. Richardson*,[86] at least one justice, Lewis Powell, refused to join Brennan's plurality opinion because "he didn't like Brennan's draft, which read at times like a Woman's Liberation tract, calling sex discrimination in statutes 'romantic paternalism' that put 'women not on pedestals but in a cage.'"[87] And in fact, Powell was right—Brennan's language *was* drawn from the literature of the women's movement—further proof of the efficacy of free speech to change the content of the dominant culture, as was the contumely (justifiably) heaped by Brennan on Justice Bradley's fostering of "gross, stereotyped distinctions between the sexes."[88]

The fact that change has happened at a precipitous rate since the birth of substantive protection for free expression does not, of course, establish that the First Amendment is the sine qua non of such change. But, at least

---

85. *Bradwell v. Illinois*, 16 Wall (83 U.S.) 130, 141–142 (1873) (Bradley, J. concurring). Notably, Justice Bradley's was not an isolated opinion, but was joined by Justices Field and Swayne. Only Chief Justice Chase dissented, albeit without a published opinion.

86. 411 U.S. 677 (1973). *See also Nevada Dept. of Human Resources v. Hibbs, supra* note 77 (summarizing legalized oppression of women in the 19th and 20th centuries).

87. Bob Woodward & Scott Armstrong, *The Brethren* (1979) at 254–255, *quoting Frontiero*, 411 U.S. at 684; *see also* John C. Jefferies, Jr., *Justice Lewis F. Powell, Jr.: A Biography* (1994) at 508–510 (describing Brennan's efforts to build, and Powell's refusal to join, a majority in *Frontiero*). Powell, it should be noted in fairness, concurred in the striking of the army regulations at issue in *Frontiero*.

88. *Frontiero*, 411 U.S. at 685.

inferentially, it suggests that equality is best achieved, not when imposed from above as Catharine MacKinnon or Cass Sunstein would have the Solons of the Supreme Court impose it, but when it is taken from below, when the culture is changed by speech.

That has been the American experience. Gains that are imposed from above in response to a vocal minority—Prohibition, for example—have a terrible way of withering in a hostile public climate. Once the initial moral impetus that fueled the crusade is spent, the principles that have been foisted on an indifferent or hostile majority become a subject of mockery or disregard. A law that is not the product of a climate of opinion, but is merely an imposition by the well-organized few is simply less likely to succeed in its goal of changing how people relate to each other than a consensus that is formed over time. This is not to say that public opinion cannot be manipulated, or that systematic propaganda cannot drive targeted ideas out of the marketplace, but it cannot do so without imposing a terrible cost, that of creating a docile citizenry.

One can take an even broader historical view, and contrast post-Enlightenment thought and government with that holding sway over most of the planet throughout most of human history. The conclusion then becomes inevitable that we have come closer to achieving equality and freedom in tandem then either goal has been achieved by itself. One only has to see instances of freedom without equality—Roman Law, for example, or the Greek city-states, both of which made great noise about protecting the rights of citizens, but extended these benefits to the mere handful of its denizens who could claim that exalted status.[89]

MacKinnon might reply—and in fact has argued—that freedom without equality merely further empowers the already dominant forces in society. And of course she is right. However, to uncouple equality from freedom renders the achievement of equality a pyrrhic victory. In the twentieth century, of course, we have seen egalitarianism without freedom, and how quickly that becomes corrupted, in the instances of the Soviet Union and Communist China. The lesson is that equality and freedom are *both* critical and that neither can be safely sacrificed in the pursuit of the other.

The brutal fact remains that throughout all of history, human beings have organized almost all of their societies hierarchically, using devices such as

89. J. B. Moyle, trans., *The Institutes of Justinian* (5th ed. 1913) at Titles III–VII, pp. 6–11 (status of slaves under Roman Law after Christianity adopted); 1 W. Blackstone, *Commentaries on the Law of England* (1754) at *423–*424 (same). *See also,* Aristotle, *The Politics,* trans. T. A. Sinclair, rev'd Trevor J. Saunders (1981) at Book I, ch. iii-vii (status of slaves in classical Greek thought). The editors provide historical background as to actual conditions of slaves, as a supplement to Aristotle's account and theory. Particularly revolting to modern readers is ch. vii, "Slavery as Part of a Universal Natural Pattern."

serfdom or chattel slavery. Leaving aside the questions of racism and of the African slave trade, even so-called Western society, until the Enlightenment, conceived of itself as a "Great Chain of Being" with divinely appointed stations that linked in a set of dominance and submission the highest king and the medieval peasant.[90] Such a hierarchical conception dogged at least English society until well within the twentieth century; the notion of an elite by blood did not collapse until then.[91] These notions were not simply held by the elite themselves; Victorian novelists, themselves predominantly members of the middle classes, were fascinated by "upstarts" looking to marry outside of their rightful spheres in life.[92]

Although class as well as race or gender played a powerful, determinative role in life—it was better from any point of view to be Eleanor of Aquitane than Piers Ploughman—all of these limiting factors on egalitarian thought were assailed through speech, and freedom in the individual sense became a political goal at the same time and through the same process. No wonder that liberal thinkers such as Nadine Strossen display a very human impatience with those who would uncouple freedom and equality! Their interdependence has been the source of the great gains made by those on the "unprivileged" side of the ledger—at first white men born without "breeding," then men born without money or land, and, increasingly, more people of both sexes of any race. But the fermenting that has made this possible has taken place under the aegis of the First Amendment, and has striven for both goals, refusing to sacrifice one to the other. Of what comfort is it to the serf to reflect that nobody is free?

Without belaboring the point, it seems a more reasonable assumption that, in the brief period in which it has evolved, free speech has led to enhanced freedom *and* equality. Certainly, the burden of proof must be upon those who would challenge such an assumption because the two ideals have grown up together, and come closer, though far from all the way, to realization together. Yet the ahistorical radicals have not carried that burden:

---

90. *See* E. M. W. Tillyard, *The Elizabethan World View* (1974); C. S. Lewis, *English Literature in the Sixteenth Century* (1954) at 39–40 (discussing religious belief), 46–50 (discussing Natural Law theory, and prevailing notions of sovereignty); *see also* Charles Ross, *Richard III* (1981) at xxiii–xxviii (describing historians Thomas More and Polydore Vergil's shaping of events to fit cosmological moral drama).

91. *See generally*, David Cannadine, *The Decline and Fall of the British Aristocracy* (1990).

92. *See*, for example, Jane Austen, *Emma* (1816), in which lower middle class Mr. Elton gives great offense by proposing marriage to the heroine, herself solidly middle class, or Anthony Trollope's *The Way We Live Now* (1874), in which likable but common (and, worse, American) Mrs. Hurtle sets her cap at higher-born Paul Montague, to his and her own great misery. Even *The Great Gatsby* (1925) contains an element of this attitude—Daisy Buchanan represents an effete, corrupt elite, yet one which Gatsby forever strives to join, and Fitzgerald cannot bring himself utterly to reject.

Assuming that free speech has "always" been there,[93] they assert that it has thus been proven to be the enemy of equality, which has "never" been there. To explode so fallacious a notion could take an entire book in its own right. Suffice it to say here that such a dance can no further go.

In Praise of Freedom of Speech

A defense of the First Amendment cannot simply react to the criticisms raised over the years; rather there must be a positive defense as well. Freedom of speech, as suggested in previous chapters, is both a good in itself as well as a frontline defense against tyranny. All well and good, and familiar ground, of course, but why, the critics will ask, must the quantum of freedom of speech be so great that the freedom tramples other values of equally great worth? Particularly in view of the uniqueness of the American view of the priority of freedom of speech, as evidenced by the international human rights agreements such as the Universal Declaration of Human Rights and the 1965 Convention on the Elimination of All Forms of Discrimination, where do we Americans come off with our near-absolutist take on freedom of speech? Or, as one author has recently (and snippily) put it, is this unique American veneration of freedom of speech "but an example of the un-enlightened state in which the rest of the world exists, waiting for Americans to carry the white man's burden by introducing advanced American ideas to an unadvanced and largely uncivilized planet?"[94]

Frederick Schauer's condescending hit at Manifest Destiny (which after all appears to be making a sudden comeback in certain quarters) aside, the question of whether the American approach to freedom of speech is the only "civilized" approach begs the question, and loads the dice against free-dom of speech in a manner one can only term sneaky. The argument runs: (1) Great Britain and Germany and France are perfectly civilized, nice, friendly places; (2) they don't get all het up over this free speech stuff, but adopt a decent balancing approach, just as Frankfurter said we should; (3) this allows them to address the evils of hate speech, and all the other evils we have seen that the First Amendment requires us to tolerate. The problems of subjectivity inherent in such an approach have already been

---

93. In addition to the precedents described in Chapter 2, *see* David M. Rabban, *Free Speech in Its Forgotten Years* (1997) (setting out the social, legal, and scholarly context of early Supreme Court decisions, noting that freedom of speech claims were regularly rejected by the courts prior to World War I); Leonard W. Levy, *Legacy of Suppression: Freedom of Speech and Speech in Early American History* (1960).

94. Frederick Schauer, "The First Amendment as Ideology," in David S. Allen & Robert Jensen, eds., *Freeing the First Amendment* (1995) at 10, 14.

fully discussed, and need not be rehashed at this stage. However, one factor should be pointed out to those who, like Catharine MacKinnon or Cass Sunstein or Tracy Higgins, believe an "activist state" is worth the risk because it can always be altered by the people.

Revolutions are always troublesome, and, speaking historically, precious few have enjoyed lasting success. Even when they do, as Bernard Shaw said—himself a revolutionary, in doctrine—"[R]evolutions never get rid of the burden of tyranny—they simply shift it from one shoulder to another."[95] The changing technology has altered once and for all the balance between rebels and the Establishment. As the novelist, civil servant, and scientist C. P. Snow warned as long ago as 1947:

> TWO hundred years ago determined citizens with muskets were almost as good as the King's armies. Now the apparatus is far more complex. A central government which can rely on its armed forces can stay in power forever. So far as I can see . . . revolution is impossible from now on, unless it starts among those who hold the power.[96]

Although this *may* be an overstatement—the collapse of the government of Afghanistan before Taliban force prior to American intervention could be viewed as an example of a successful revolution[97]—it reflects a fundamental change that erases Jefferson's trust in the ability of citizens to revolt when government becomes too oppressive. We now find ourselves in a situation, in short, in which freedom of speech has become a "use it or lose it" proposition.

But freedom of speech is grounded in more than the oft-derided "slippery slope" argument that emphasizes the difficulty in enforcing whatever lines one wishes to draw—even if this argument has taken on new urgency. Freedom of speech involves a choice that we as a society must make, a choice about the nature of the relationship between the individual and his or her government.

---

95. G. Bernard Shaw, "The Revolutionist's Pocket Handbook and Companion," Appendix to *Man and Superman* (1903).

96. C. P. Snow, *The Light and the Dark* (1947) at 192. The speaker of these words is Reinhold Schader, a young Nazi who is engaged in a political debate circa 1938 with Lewis Eliot, the narrator of the novel and (here) Snow's stand-in. Eliot reflects in the narration, when Schader asks him if Eliot disagrees, "I thought he was right, appallingly right: it was one of the sinister facts of the twentieth century scene." *Id.*

97. *See* "Afghan Army Retreats Before Islamic Forces," *New York Times*, 16 February 1997 at p. A1. Of course, as the *Times* made clear, the disarray of the Afghan central forces was in part due to infighting among various factions, thus negating the one condition posited by Snow—reliability of the government forces. Likewise, the collapse of the Soviet Union, directed as it was from above in the face of a complete systemic collapse that included rumblings of disloyalty from the armed forces, fits Snow's paradigm.

Definitions of the speech that is protected by the First Amendment have been based on the function of speech in a free society. Eminent scholars and judges have posited varying scopes for the First Amendment based on the perceived purposes served by the amendment. These purposes include the notions that free speech leads to the elucidation of truth,[98] that it promotes and serves democratic participation in governmental decision making,[99] and that it develops the sort of citizenry that we desire.[100] Any defense of free speech that is not content to rest on slippery slope grounds must presume that people as individuals are competent to rule themselves, that they are able to reach rational decisions. And for that to be true, they must be able to distinguish truth from falsehood.

All of the various articulations of a single rationale for free speech have in this sense fallen short of the mark. It has been argued—though with differing doctrinal results—that the speech with which the First Amendment is concerned is that speech that forms a part of political discourse. Both Alexander Meiklejohn and former Judge Robert Bork have advanced this rationale, which leads strongly to the conclusion that only speech on explicitly political subjects is protected by the First Amendment. Although Meiklejohn sought to bring artistic or literary speech into the ambit of this rationale because it shapes the attitudes that citizens carry with them into the voting booth,[101] Bork correctly pointed out the weakness of this view, noting that "other human activities and experiences also form personality, teach and create attitudes just as much as does the novel but no one would . . . [bar] regulations of economic activity, control of entry to a trade, laws about sexual behavior, marriage and the like."[102] Harry Kalven, Jr., tended to agree with Bork and Meiklejohn, but hedged his bets: He declared the abolition of the crime of seditious libel to be the "core function" of the First Amendment, but did not rule out existence of other values it may serve.[103] He also acknowledged the difficulty of the position and sought to extend protection beyond solely political speech.

---

98. *See* John Milton, *Areopagitica* (1644), H. B. Cotterill, ed. (1952); *Abrams v. United States*, 250 U.S. 616, 628 (Holmes, J. dissenting); John Stuart Mill *On Liberty* 22–30 (Norton Critical Edition, 1975).

99. *See* Robert H. Bork, *Neutral Principles and Some First Amendment Problems*, 47 Ind. L.J. 1 (1971); Alexander Meiklejohn, *Free Speech and Its Relation to Free Government* (1948); Harry Kalven, Jr., *The New York Times Case: A Note on the Central Meaning of the First Amendment*, 1964 Sup. Ct. Rev. 191 (1965).

100. Vincent Blasi, *The First Amendment and the Ideal of Civic Courage: The Brandeis Opinion in Whitney v. California*, 29 Wm. & Mary L. Rev. 653 (1988); Lee C. Bollinger, *The Tolerant Society* (1986).

101. Meiklejohn, *supra* note 99, at 99–100, *et seq.*

102. Bork, 47 Ind. L.J. at 27 (1971).

103. Kalven, 1964 Sup. Ct. Rev. at 208–209.

Another major strain in First Amendment theory has asserted that freedom of speech helps mold the citizenry's character in a desirable fashion, whether by inculcating courage (as desired by Justice Brandeis) or tolerance (the virtue adverted to by Dean Lee Bollinger). In either case, the character-building rationale is subject to various criticisms, the most fundamental of which has been made by Vincent Blasi: "[T]he premise that government should try to shape the 'intellectual character' of the citizenry has disturbing overtones. . . . It is the ambitious and comprehensive catechism that Bollinger wants taught that gives one pause. For he seeks an education experience that will influence the way persons conduct themselves across a wide range of social interaction. He speaks not of lessons or precepts but of character formation."[104] The same charge is applicable, though to a lesser extent, to Brandeis.

Even without such a comprehensive scheme of instruction, the notion that the First Amendment's value is anchored to a notion that individuals need to experience the tutelage of the state is contrary to the common-sense understanding that most people share that freedom is a good thing in itself. People do not seek freedom, people do not revolt against tyranny, because they want a substitute teacher. There is something deeply anarchic in humanity that longs to be answerable to no will but its own. This streak is balanced by the countervailing need to find not only security but reinforcement in others. The effort to accommodate these inconsistent—indeed contrary—needs makes up much of political thought. Even the most conformist of us yearns to be perceived as an individual; even the most independent seeks some degree of community. Moreover, neither theory sufficiently differentiates speech from other forms of conduct. No doubt the setting of a good example is a helpful side effect of the First Amendment, but it will hardly do as a primary purpose.

The third major strain involves the search for truth. Free speech, Milton alleged, will invariably lead to the discovery of the truth, for "who ever knew Truth put to the worse in a free and open encounter?"[105] This justification was also used by John Stuart Mill in his classic *On Liberty*.[106] It was used in a very different form by Justice Oliver Wendell Holmes in *Abrams v. United States*.[107] In perhaps the most famous passage in the United States Reports, Holmes wrote:

> BUT when men have realized that time has upset many fighting faiths, they may come to believe even more than they believe the very foundations of their own conduct that the ultimate good desired is better

---

104. Vincent Blasi, *The Teaching Function of the First Amendment*, 87 Colum. L.Rev. 387, 414 (1987).
105. Milton, *Areopagitica, supra* note 98, at 181.
106. Mill, note 98, *supra*.
107. 250 U.S. at 624–631 (Holmes, J. dissenting).

reached by free trade in ideas—that the best test of truth is the power of the thought to get itself accepted in the competition of the market, and that truth is the only ground upon which their wishes safely can be carried out. That at any rate is the theory of our Constitution.[108]

Not for Holmes the somewhat naive faith that "truth will out" that Milton and Mill place such reliance in. Indeed, in Milton and Mill, this faith in truth seems to indicate lack of awareness of the frequently compelling power of error, especially when seductive but incorrect views are held by the majority and thus bear down on the fledgling dissenter with all the power of the human herd instinct to conformity; nor do they seem to be aware of the power of nonlegal forms of social coercion such as ridicule and ostracism. Holmes's thought seems to many to be rooted in an absolute skepticism in the experience of truth.[109] But perhaps he is saying rather that free speech, which allows both points of view to go on the record and be preserved, is the only means of ensuring that any errors we do make can be rectified in time.

C. P. Snow reminds us that "it is an error, of course, to think that persecution is never successful. More often than not, it has been extremely so . . . [for example, Manicheism] would not have been known to exist except for the writings of its enemies. It was as though communism had been extirpated in Europe in the 1920's and was only known through what is said of it in *Mein Kampf*."[110] The successful suppression of any viewpoint or theory, however abhorrent, is in a sense an editing of the past. The sanitized recollection that is left behind makes not only the re-creation of the lost belief difficult or impossible, but hampers an understanding of the time in which that belief flourished.

The anti-pornography movement seems to have just that sort of oblivion in mind if Cass Sunstein's thinking is any indication: "[W]e could imagine a society in which the harms produced by pornography were so widely acknowledged and so generally condemned that an anti-pornography ordinance would not be regarded as viewpoint-based at all."[111] In other words, the general acceptance of an orthodoxy does not simply legitimate it, it reaches a critical mass and eliminates opposing perspectives—which Sunstein appears to welcome.

---

108. *Id.* at 630.
109. *See,* for example, David M. Rabban, *The Emergence of Modern First Amendment Doctrine,* 50 U. Chi. L. Rev. 1205, 1310–1311 (1983); Gerald Gunther, *Learned Hand and the Origins of Modern First Amendment Doctrine: Some Fragments of History,* 27 Stan. L. Rev. 719, 733 (1975); Yosal Rogat, *The Judge as Spectator,* 31 U. Chi. L. Rev 213 (1964).
110. C. P. Snow, *The Light and the Dark* at 39.
111. Cass Sunstein, *Neutrality in Constitutional Law,* 92 Colum. L. Rev. 1, 29 (1992).

Insights that may benefit humanity, whether from positive or negative examples, can be forever lost, making it difficult if not impossible to trace errors and to set them right. Indeed, the loss of such insights could make the detection of more subtle errors impossible. Thus, to allow for the possibility that one of our experiments will fail, and that we may have to retrace our steps, Holmes defended the right of free expression even of thoughts that we believe to be "fraught with death."

The search-for-truth rationale can be undermined, as it lacks backing as an empirical proposition. It also seems to seriously underestimate the power of propaganda and social duress that falls short of legal compulsion. And in Holmes's "safety catch" form it certainly lacks the emotional sweep to justify what Harry Kalven called the First Amendment: the most charismatic provision of the Constitution.[112] The same critique can be made of entirely negative justifications, such as distrust of government power and the slippery slope argument.[113] The individual autonomy argument, as Bork showed, proves too much, leaving no rational grounds to distinguish between speech and other actions that provide self-gratification.[114] What, one begins to ask in desperation, is left to justify our almost intuitive perception that free speech is a good thing to have, and that the First Amendment—leaving aside all doctrinal questions of limit and interpretation for just a moment—is a worthwhile enactment?

All of the rationales advanced above.

That no one of these rationales provides a completely satisfying justification for freedom of speech is hardly surprising; nothing so basic to our society can be summed up so easily. Each of the rationales offered provides at least one key value served by the First Amendment, but not its complete raison d'être. Despite the undermining of each rationale that has occurred in academic circles, they have all been a part of the discussion since Milton's *Areopagitica*. This fact, and the passionate allegiance each of the justifications has commanded from sharp intellects throughout the evolution of the jurisprudence, points, as does Janus, in two directions. Either the First Amendment serves a host of discrete although not inconsistent values, and of which no synthesis is possible—even desirable—or all of these value claims can be harmonized. The quest for such harmony is worthwhile.

It seems plain that Justice Douglas's vision of the individual's primacy over the government and of his or her right to self-rule is derived from the "self-

---

112. Kalven, *A Worthy Tradition* (1988) at xii.
113. Vincent Blasi, *The Checking Value in First Amendment Theory*, 1977 Am. Bar Found. Res. J. 521 (more than a mere slippery slope argument, but an essentially institutional view of the First Amendment, arguing that its purpose is in preventing abuse of official power) and *The Pathological Perspective and the First Amendment* 85 Colum. L. Rev. 449 (1985).
114. Bork, *supra* note 99, at 27.

evident truths" upon which our government is based: "that all men [!] are created equal, that they are endowed by their Creator with certain unalienable rights. . . . That to secure these rights Governments are instituted among Men [!], deriving their Just powers from the consent of the governed." As Justice Douglas commented on this provision of the Declaration of Independence, its theory grounds legitimate government "not from on high, not from a king, but from the consent of the governed."[115] Thus, the single overarching rationale of the First Amendment must be a statement of the nature of the relationship between government and citizen.

The very nature of a democratic-republican form of government is that the people are presumed—irrebutably presumed, if you like—to be capable of self-rule. And in order to be capable of self-rule, a people must be able to distinguish between good and evil, true and false, wisdom and imprudence. If the people—as individuals—are not able to make personal decisions about reading or viewing, how can they be assumed to be able to choose representatives and in thus choosing make difficult and key policy decisions. Privacy doctrine, part of which is embodied in the First Amendment in that it denies the government access to a zone of self that each individual retains, is required by the very notion of democratic-republic government.

For "we the people" to be sovereigns in any sense of the word, the government must be bound to respect the dignity and right of every citizen to rule over his or her own life. If the state need not honor the dignity of the individual by acknowledging his or her right within broad contours to control his or her own life, how can we be said to enjoy self-rule? It is the failure of Bork and Meiklejohn to perceive this that leads them into an unnecessarily narrow view of the First Amendment's scope.

Does this really mean that the most rigorous form of First Amendment doctrine is a prerequisite of democratic government? After all, critics could retort, it is plainly not some nameless, faceless government that imposes laws upon the citizenry, but rather the citizenry itself, or at least representatives of a majority of them. Why cannot the people themselves democratically decide to delimit the areas of permitted debate? As long as democratic process is observed, and each citizen can vote, surely there is nothing undemocratic about regulation of available ideas by the democratically elected majority, whatever else might also be wrong with such regulation. Such is clearly not the case.

Certainly, the electorate can pass such laws by invoking the amendment process, if all else fails. Such a change would constitute a restructuring so fundamental that it would no longer be accurate to describe the resultant system as a democratic republic. The citizenry whose government can limit

---

115. W. O. Douglas, *Anatomy of Liberty* (1964) at 2–3.

its exposure to ideas that are acceptably orthodox and agreeable to the government no longer can be said to exercise ruling power but rather simply rubber-stamps the actions of the government that shapes its views, its morals, its aesthetics, and its agenda. Although it would be democratic-republican in *form*, in fact such a system would be oligarchical, with the role of the governed limited to that of selecting between alternatives that were acceptable to the ruling class. Such a government would be but a hollow mockery both of democracy and of republicanism. (Although arguably our two-party system is moving us toward, if we have not already arrived there, its functional equivalent. Certainly, however one looks at it, such a movement is deplorable to those who are seriously committed to the Constitution). The notion that we can govern ourselves requires that we be free to explore, question, and challenge the status quo in every walk of life. It is for this reason (and, to be frank, the very nature of the circumstances giving rise to the document) that the Declaration of Independence, solemnly passed by the Continental Congress and the initiatory action of what is called by some "the American experiment," *explicitly* provides for the right to rebel against a government that no longer suits the needs of the people.[116]

So too the people have the right to annul the Revolution by amending the Constitution or altering the system in any other way they see fit. That right includes the replacement of a democratic government with a more authoritarian one. But such an alteration should be done in the open, with the consent of the people, as required by the amending process, and not by "interpreting" the Constitution in such a way as to change the system's fundamentals *sub silentio*. More than that, however, such new glosses on freedom of speech attack the very premises of a democratic form of government, such as this country purports to cherish.

The fundamental tenet of politics in a democratic-republican sense (and indeed of academic exercises such as this volume) is that human beings are capable of rational thought, and of choosing right from wrong. If this is not true with regard to the most intimate and basic of human relations, and the people in their sexual relations must be schoolboys and schoolgirls under the state's tutelage, how can it be true of federal-state relations, or of foreign relations, or of any of the other realms in which the people are assumed to be fit to rule?

If the people are in fact not fit to rule themselves as individuals as well as collectively, to govern their own lives, then self-government is impossible and

---

116. This line of thought, and the notion of the continuing precedential power of the Declaration of Independence, owes much to Charles L. Black, "On Reading and Using the Ninth Amendment" in *The Humane Imagination* (1986) at 196–199. *See also* Black's *Structure and Relationship in Constitutional Law* (1969; reprinted 1983).

we had better abandon the whole hypocritical enterprise of giving them the vote and institute a full-scale regimen of social conditioning based on the most humane, psychologically effective, and cost-effective technology. We will be with B. F. Skinner, *Beyond Freedom and Dignity*. After all, pornographic materials are not the only ones that inculcate on a subrational level harmful attitudes that lead to violence or other harms.[117] *Rambo, Birth of a Nation*, most of Wagner, and the collected works of Friedrich Nietzsche (just look at Leopold and Loeb) inculcate values that most progressive people— including feminists and Marxists—would consider to be abhorrent, and they do it in a way that is similar to pornography's: they slip it in while we are emotionally engaged, whether in the rapture of music, or caught up in the narrative swirl of a "cracking good yarn."

The First Amendment is not without costs. Ideas *do* present a danger to the status quo.[118] Justice Holmes was deadly serious when he wrote that "every idea is an incitement."[119] He recognized that in ideas are tremendous force, potential for good and for destruction. Was a man who had spent his entire life as a devotee of philosophy likely to protect free speech only because it came without serious risks? Although always delighted to point out, as he did in *Abrams*, the tendency of those empowered by the status quo to hysterically exaggerate the dangers posed by dissent, Holmes, in the last analysis, firmly believed that ideas wield the greatest might:

> THUS only can you gain the secret isolated joy of the thinker, who knows that, a hundred years after he is dead and forgotten, men who never heard of him will be moving to the measure of his thought— the subtle postponed power which the world knows not, but which

---

117. Dershowitz, *Taking Liberties* at 293–295. Indeed, many crimes have been attributed to the "inspiration" of popular media presentations; the attempted assassination of then-President Ronald Reagan by John Hinckley, Jr. was based upon the youth's obsession with Martin Scorsese's film *Taxi Driver*; Nathaniel White based his first murder on a scene from the film *RoboCop II*; the well-regarded film *The Deer Hunter* contained a Russian roulette scene said to have inspired similar incidents. Similarly, a 1987 shooting and subsequent attempted suicide by a department store employee was derived from an episode of *Star Trek* (*see* "Imitators Under the Influence of Art," *New York Newsday*, 10 August 1992, p. 38). All of these people emulated actions portrayed in the media with lethal results, yet no cry to ban *Star Trek* or to sue Gene Roddenberry for "causing" the fatality has resulted; so too with Michael Cimino, director of *The Deer Hunter. See also* Richard L. Abel, *Speaking Respect, Respecting Speech* (1998) at 226–232. Seemingly, Americans believe that there is something about sex, as opposed to violence, that makes it special—a distinction premised more on a hangover of Victorian prudery, I suspect, than on any reasonable grounds.

118. Indeed, even MacKinnon writes "Pornography is ideas; ideas matter." *Feminism Unmodified* at 223.

119. *Gitlow* v. *New York*, 268 U.S. 652, 673 (1925) (Holmes, J. dissenting).

to his prophetic vision is more real than that which commands an army.[120]

Holmes, give him his due, believed that if proletarian dictatorship was to win the assent of the majority, it should have its way, much as he despised it.[121] For he recognized that our revolutionary system, one whose very base was in armed revolution, could scarcely be credible if it denied the people the right to change the course of society.

If we posit, with Sunstein or MacKinnon, that the receiving mind is without power to evaluate, to reject or oppose ideas, then in truth democracy is itself a sure path to destruction. If we do not, then the fact that a man or men may act upon abhorrent doctrines or attitudes cannot, in a democratic republic, form the basis for attributing liability for such actions to the preacher of these doctrines outside of the most narrow of circumstances, the circumstances captured in the verbal act concept.

The notion of the state that censorship postulates is a related but no less chilling factor. To take but one topic covered in this book, obscenity provides the starkest instance of the distrust of the people that, just under the surface, motivates censorship. How can we be free if sexual orthodoxy and images are to be prescribed by law? If the state can reach into our bedrooms and tell consenting adults (unlike children who have the blanket protection of the *parens patriae* role of the state) what constitutes proper forms of sexual intimacy, then there is no truth to Theodore Roosevelt's description of an American as *The Free Citizen*.[122] The establishment by law of such a sexual orthodoxy turns us from self-ruled individuals to creatures of the state, with our every move subject to that state's pleasure. That the state is comprised of our neighbors alters this not a jot but adds to the ignominy of our position. We are not asked to give up authority to some wise Solon or to Platonic Guardians, but rather to people no wiser or more inherently virtuous than ourselves. The result of this denial of individual sovereignty is that even our sexual identities and intimacies become the property of our neighbors, just as the stomach contents of the ant are resources for the group to feed off.

If we are not in some spheres of our lives beyond the state's reach, however benevolent its purposes, then we exist for the state, not it for us. One would think that at least those who attack the First Amendment from the left, such as MacKinnon, who advocate for the rights of some sexual minorities (homosexuals and lesbians), would know better than to seek the perse-

---

120. O. W. Holmes, *Collected Legal Papers* (1921) at 32.
121. *Gitlow*, 268 U.S. at 673 (Holmes, J., dissenting).
122. T. Roosevelt, *The Free Citizen*, H. Hadegorn, ed. (1958).

cution of others (sadomasochists) and the regulation of the sexual majority (heterosexuals).

Similar concerns exist in other forms of censorship: the "reflexive disorder" described under fighting words, the fear of the powerful new media we have seen, all boil down to a fear that the audience cannot be trusted to evaluate the worth of the various messages with which we are increasingly bombarded in this era of information overload. And perhaps that fear has some validity: Words can inflict pain.

However, the fear that animates the censor is more radical than most will admit. It is not simply the fear that the unfortunate gull will make a wrong moral decision, or will be swayed into a single deviant act. Condescending though such a view is, it falls short of the view of those who assail freedom of speech on the theory that the characters of audience members will be warped by "bad" speech. That view removes all moral agency from the auditor, and so subjects the auditor to the "protective" whims of the censor. Just what protects the censor from being so warped is never quite clear because it is never clear why the censor is somehow morally superior to the rest of us.

The ramifications of the censorial thesis, that people cannot parse materials and themselves interpret and evaluate them, not only undercut our theory of government but undermine the moral agency of each citizen. Indeed, unlike the more discreet of her supporters, MacKinnon has explicitly avowed this in the case of the impact of pornography on the guilt of the rapist himself. If the rapist cannot help being influenced by pornography and is powerless to reject its message, is not his culpability diminished almost down to nothing? He is a mere tool of the pornographer as well as a victim in his own right. MacKinnon's assertion that rape is endemic—that all but 7.8 percent of women have been raped or otherwise sexually harassed (a figure that she does not break down, which is unfortunate in light of the broad spectrum of conduct covered by MacKinnon's definition of sexual harassment) becomes even more troubling than it is in its own right.[123] Is our society truly ruled by a form of mind control that leads systematically to the brutalization of half of the population? Worse yet, are we to be treated to the "Penthouse defense" in addition to the Twinkie defense?[124]

Apparently, yes. When the Seventh Circuit rejected just such a claim advanced as a mitigating factor by Thomas Schiro a capital defendant, seeking a new hearing on whether his rape and murder conviction warranted

---

123. *See* Catharine A. MacKinnon, *Feminism Unmodified* (1987) "On Collaboration," 198–205.

124. The defense proffered by Dan White for his assassination of Harvey Milk, the "Twinkie Defense" was that consumption of the Hostess confection in bulk had altered his body chemistry to the extent that he was no longer responsible for his actions.

execution,[125] Catharine MacKinnon, in *Only Words*, argued that indeed, under the present-day standard of criminal law, which requires moral responsibility as a prerequisite for punishment, Schiro should have been acquitted of his vicious rape-murders. MacKinnon, claiming that the decision was a tactical evasion of the harmful effect of pornography as recognized by the same Court in *Hudnut*, opined that both the perpetrator and the pornographer should be held liable, but that could only be effected by "by changing the rape law so that it turns on what the perpetrator did rather than on what he thought *and* holding the pornographers jointly liable."[126]

As Nadine Strossen points out, this approach is characteristic of MacKinnon's rejection of the traditional presumption of the moral agency of each individual that undergirds the criminal law.[127] Notably, however, this moral agency is the principal value of most of the rationales that justify punishment under criminal law. Deterrence (both specifically of the actor involved and of others), retribution, and rehabilitation each assume that an actor is able to choose to conform his or her conduct to the requirements of the law.[128] Only one rationale, incapacitation—the removal of the transgressor from the law-abiding society so that he or she cannot continue his or her depredations—is not grounded in a presumption that human beings make moral choices with a rational basis. In other words, MacKinnon denudes the criminal law of almost all of its legitimating authority, yet insists on imposing its consequences as though the foundation was untouched.

To support the imposition of death as a sentence—the effect of rejecting a mitigating factor in a capital case (as MacKinnon seems to argue, conceding that exposure to pornography *should* be a mitigating factor under the present standard, and then urging the amendment of the law to change that result) on purely utilitarian grounds that would have the impact of upholding a death sentence while conceding that the actor is not morally culpable involves a cold-bloodedness reminiscent of Holmes in *The Common Law*, which is not a compliment, for all of the justice's greatness in developing the law of free speech.[129]

MacKinnon's greatest theoretical weakness is showcased by this example, and that is her insistence on the traditional elements and results of law when they suit her agenda, and then casting them away when they do not. She is

---

125. *Schiro v. Clark*, 963 F.2d 962, 972–973 (7th Cir. 1992), *affirmed*, 510 U.S. 222 (1994) (citing MacKinnon, *Feminist Theory* at 195–214).
126. *Only Words* at 96, 95–96 emphasis in original.
127. Nadine Strossen, *Defending Pornography* at 271.
128. *See*, for example, Herbert L. Packer, *The Limits of the Criminal Sanction* (1968) at 35–61 (describing the various rationales and justifications for the imposition of punishment; characterizing them as retribution, deterrence [specific and general], incapacitation, and rehabilitation).
129. O. W. Holmes, *The Common Law* (1881) at 38–51.

happy to dispose of the moral element of the criminal law, but offers no rationale with which to replace it. Having gutted the rationale of criminal law to fit her argument, she then doubles back to act as though the gutting never took place. But MacKinnon is not alone in this elimination of moral agency from her view of human nature. Many of those who advocate the suppression of materials they deem socially harmful urge it on the ground that the materials at issue will "poison the atmosphere"—that is, that the prejudices and dislikes of audiences sympathetic to the message contained in the materials will be strengthened and reinforced by them.[130]

If our synergistic development of freedom and equality together is not to be abandoned, the age-old concept of moral agency must be clung to. We suppose in our criminal justice system that free will exists, if only within the confines of unalterable circumstances and accidents and subject to the impact of other wills that are similarly free. Such a supposition can after all be challenged, but does not that challenge run aground on our own intuitive experience of free will? Moreover, the only way free will can even hope to exist is if we give it free rein. Unguided by society, not subject to holistic piloting in the name of our group benefit, a similacrum of freedom can be found. To accept B. F. Skinner's insight (and Mark Twain's as well, surprisingly)[131] is to give up on the precious notion of individual freedom and dignity.

When they wrote in favor of the maximum protection for expression and sought to narrow the scope of the state's ability to control the self-expression of our citizenry, the Douglases, Blacks, Brennans, Holmeses, and Brandeises sought to preserve that narrow band of freedom in an age in which conformity has grown ever more present, an age in which the standards of rebellion have been appropriated by the forces of the market and recycled for profit. Wavy Gravy is not a musician today, but a flavor of ice cream. Standardization of popular culture, and the increasing irrelevance of all other culture feed the phenomenon as well. But the increased ability to communicate, to reach out for fellowship with others who share our views is a dazzling new prospect of our time.

That prospect is rejected by both the left and the right of the political spectrum. The right, who see the old simple monochromatic world of authority, obedience, and faith, continually—sometimes relentlessly—questioned, react to this erosion with fear, and seek to squelch the destroyers of

---

130. In addition to the sources cited in Chapter 6, *see*, for example, Robin D. Barnes, "The Reality and Ideology of First Amendment Jurisprudence: Giving Aid and Comfort to Racial Terrorists," in David Allen & Robert Jensen, *Freeing the First Amendment* (1995) at 253, 256–274.

131. Mark Twain, *What Is Man?* ed., A. B. Paine (1920).

surety. The left, who see their utopian visions of paradise postponed, wish to seize power to effect change, and in their frustration are forgetful or heedless of the coercive nature of power. Both act without thinking of the nature of humankind.

The human mind and spirit can be fragile; they need light and air to grow. The insistence on regulating views, the invocation of the crushing hand of the law into the realm of thought and idea may be appealing in the short term—even the Blues Brothers felt the need to silence Illinois Nazis—but the shelter the new critics of the First Amendment would provide is in fact stifling. Trusting the people to govern can be frightening, and may even in the last analysis fail. But it is worth the risk if it succeeds. There is always a new tyranny waiting to be born; freedom, on the other hand, has been growing throughout this American century.

As we enter the new century, the new millennium, we need to accept that the questioning of established verities, and the fighting of the newly emergent verities, will not cease. Injustice will never be fully routed, evil never wholly conquered. Those who seek control seem to believe the contrary, that with control some utopian moment can be reached. But moments are transient, and the structure of control will be left in place when corruption has set in—as witness the bureaucracies of the declining Roman and Chinese Empires. Humankind will never arrive at stasis, unless it is the stasis of death. Freedom is an embracing of the chaos—the pains and losses as well as the satisfactions and rewards—of life.

9

Epilogue
Free Speech In Wartime

AS THESE WORDS are written, in January 2004, the United States is again at war. Although this new conflict is being waged with congressional approval (but no actual declaration of war as yet), its parameters and nature are undefined. It is still too early to tell what effect the ongoing hostilities will have on free speech jurisprudence, although certainly what Holmes termed "the hydraulic pressure" to conform exerted by the times is appearing. Cases are now wending their way through the courts, and no doubt the Supreme Court will be required to address the issues presented by America's latest war, at this time an amorphous conflict against a changing cast of characters. Because the Court has yet to address these issues, only an impressionistic, more political analysis is possible here.

WAR AND PRESSURE TO CONFORM

Historically, war, whether hot or cold, has always led to heightened unity, and increased pressures to conform politically.[1] Traditionally, the freedom to dissent has suffered in times of hostility, even when dissent is limited to

---

1. This phenomenon is explored in many works; a good recent account from World War I through the Cold War is presented in William M. Wiecek, *The Legal Foundations of Domestic Anticommunism: The Background of Dennis v. United States*, 2001 Sup. Ct. Rev. 375 (2002). For general accounts encompassing adverse the effect of war sentiment on free speech doctrine, *see* Zechariah Chafee, *Free Speech in the United States* (revised edition, 1941); Thomas Emerson, *The System of Free Expression* (1970) and Harry Kalven, *A Worthy Tradition: Free Speech in America* (1988).

the means by which commonly held aims are to be furthered. Indeed, the need to protect speech criticizing "men and measures" in time of war was articulated by Justice Oliver Wendell Holmes in the very first dissent from a Supreme Court ruling on free speech, in *Abrams v. United States*, in which he vainly argued against the Court's broad reading of the Espionage Act permitting imposition of criminal liability for any intentional act, including speech urging curtailment of production that subsequently was deemed to have had a tendency to "cripple or hinder" the war effort:

> A PATRIOT might think that we are wasting money on aeroplanes, or making more cannons of a certain kind than are needed, and might advocate curtailment with success; yet, even if it turned out that the curtailment hindered and was thought by other minds to have been obviously likely to hinder the United States in the prosecution of the war, no one would hold such conduct a crime.[2]

That Holmes's concern that measured criticism of the government's conduct would be met with repressive action did not take long to eventuate. Indeed, in one instance, mere agreement with Holmes's *Abrams* dissent, and criticism of the lower court proceedings led to a striking instance of the private sector cooperating with government actors to silence criticism. One of the first scholars of the First Amendment, Zechariah Chafee, was a Harvard law professor of impeccable patrician antecedents who opposed socialism. Chafee nonetheless was deeply affronted by the trial and convictions in *Abrams* and the Supreme Court's affirmance of the convictions. The conviction under the Espionage Act of socialist protesters urging a general strike to dissuade the United States from seeking to overthrow the Russian Revolution struck Chafee as unfairly obtained and upheld on a legal rationale inimical to free speech.

Chafee published a law review article sharply critical of the trial judge's bias, the allegations that police brutality had been employed to obtain confessions, and, especially, the crabbed interpretation of the First Amendment used to affirm the convictions. Chafee strongly endorsed the rationale for free speech offered by Justice Oliver Wendell Holmes (himself a former Harvard law professor) in dissent.[3]

For his pains, Chafee found himself charged with misconduct by the university, based on the complaints of several alumni who acted in consultation with two of the prosecutors on the case. In May of 1920, Chafee described these alumni as "hot on my trail." In December of that year, he sig-

---

2. 250 U.S. 616, 626–627 (1919) (Holmes, J., dissenting).
3. Zechariah Chafee, *A Contemporary State Trial—The United States Versus Jacob Abrams, et al,* 33 Harv. L. Rev. 747 (1920).

nificantly revised the articles, pruning out factual errors, but also moderating his criticism of the judge as well as of the Assistant United States Attorneys who had prosecuted Abrams. Chafee also struck out his prior assertion that the whole proceeding had been "a disgrace to our law."[4] Despite this partial withdrawal, the offended alumni convinced the university to convene a disciplinary hearing at which Chafee was forced to defend himself against charges of improper behavior.

With the aid of the Assistant United States Attorneys (but, surprisingly, with only minimal help from J. Edgar Hoover who had falsely classed Chafee as an "Attorney for Radical Organizations"[5]), the disgruntled alumni compiled their evidence and presented their case that Chafee had been guilty of poor scholarship, inappropriate political behavior, and misconduct, and his termination was warranted. At the hearing, Chafee disclaimed sympathy with the defendants in *Abrams*, stating: "My sympathies and all my associations are with the men who save, who manage, who produce. But I want my side to fight fair."[6] Previously, Chafee had classed the defendants as men and women who "produced" books, furs, hats and shirtwaists, as opposed to Judge Clayton who "produced the Clayton Act," of which he disapproved.[7] Chafee's change of tone, concessions, and the unlikely support of Harvard University President Abbott Lawrence Lowell, an "arch-conservative" who nonetheless described himself as "an old fashioned believer in the constitutional protection of individual rights,"[8] turned the tide. The committee voted unanimously in Chafee's favor on the charge that he had made "consciously erroneous" statements, but found in his favor by a bare 6–5 majority on the question of whether the article "contained erroneous statements of fact which should not have been made" or should have been corrected in the Harvard Law Review.[9]

Chafee's experience, that of a thoughtful critic who sided with the so-called establishment but wanted "my side to fight fair" has an evocative power these days; the censorship imposed on Chafee was not governmental in

---

4. This discussion of Chafee's "trial" at the Harvard Club is drawn from Richard Polenberg, *Fighting Faiths: The Abrams Case, the Supreme Court, and Free Speech* (1987) 272–284; *see also* Peter H. Irons, *"Fighting Fair: Zechariah Chafee, Jr., The Department of Justice, and the Trial at the Harvard Club,"* 94 Harv. L. Rev. 218 (1981).

5. Hoover had Chafee subjected to background investigation, and the resultant report was filed as covering an "Attorney for Radical Organizations," but when Austen G. Fox, the lead prosecutor at Chafee's hearing, asked for a copy of the file, the FBI merely forwarded to Fox "a copy of Chafee's testimony before the Senate Subcommittee" investigating charges of illegal practices by the Department of Justice in arresting radical aliens during the "Palmer Raids." Polenberg, *Fighting Faiths*, at 274–275; 279.

6. Polenberg, *Fighting Faiths*, at 281.

7. *Id.* at 276.

8. *Id.* at 280.

9. *Id.* at 282.

nature but was rather the result of threats brought by his private employer, which acted to appease an angry alumni—and which also feared offending the government. During the so-called McCarthy era,[10] employees both public and private found themselves out of work and unable to find new jobs because of their alleged sympathies with the "enemy" in the undeclared war against communism.[11] During the Cold War, government employees' support for the opinions of Supreme Court justices unpopular with the FBI was probed as an indicator of disloyalty.[12] Justice William O. Douglas was understandably exercised when he found that among other questions concerning their reading and voting preferences, federal employees subjected to "loyalty-security" investigations were being asked, insinuatingly, "You rather like Justice Douglas?" in an effort to ascertain whether they had communist leanings. Douglas also quotes a transcript of such an investigation in which an FBI agent asks a government employee if that employee would vote for the Communist Party "if they came up with a candidate you liked. For instance, Justice Douglas, if he decided to run for President on the Communist Party?"[13]

Even more rampant than government terminations of employment based on political ideology and affiliation were dismissals by private employers, and the "blacklisting" of employees so terminated. The entertainment industry was especially feared and put under pressure to conform by purging its ranks of those who would not join in the anticommunist crusade.[14] This sort of unofficial censorship can be seen in the present time.

One such incident of private censorship resulting from criticism of the government took place soon after the September 11 terrorist attacks on the World Trade Center and the Pentagon. On September 17, 2001 "Politically Incorrect" comedian and provocateur Bill Maher took exception to President George W. Bush's labeling the suicide terrorists "cowardly," and stated on his late-night talk show that, "We [Americans] have been the cowards, lobbing cruise missiles from 2,000 miles away. That's cowardly. Staying in the

10. Professor Wiecek objects to the term "McCarthyism" on the cogent ground that the movement both pre-dated and survived the Senator from Wisconsin's opportunistic and grandstanding "surf[ing] its wave." 2001 Sup. Ct. Rev. at 375, n. 3.

11. *See, generally,* Corliss Lamont, *Freedom is as Freedom Does* (1956); Ellen Schrecker, *The Age of McCarthyism: A Brief History with Documents* (1994); Schrecker, *Many Are the Crimes: McCarthyism in America* (1999).

12. *See, for example,* William O. Douglas, *The Court Years: The Autobiography of William O. Douglas* (1980) at 61.

13. *Id.* Notably, Douglas had, only a few years before this questioning, turned down the opportunity to run for vice-president with first Franklin Roosevelt and then Harry Truman. James Simon, *Independent Journey: The Life of William O. Douglas* (1980); Bruce Allen Murphy, *Wild Bill: The Legend and Life of William O. Douglas* (2003).

14. *See,* Lillian Hellman, *Scoundrel Time* (1976); Dalton Trumbo, *The Time of the Toad* (1949); Louis Nizer, *The Jury Returns* (1966) at 225–438.

airplane when it hits the building—say what you want about it, it's not cowardly."[15] Response to Maher's comment was swift.

> ADVERTISERS such as Sears and Federal Express immediately pulled their ads. Some stations stopped airing the smart program. And White House spokesman Ari Fleischer got in on the action, stating during a press conference, "It's a terrible thing to say and it's unfortunate. There are reminders to all Americans that they need to watch what they say, watch what they do. This is not a time for remarks like that. There never is.[16]

Shortly after the controversial remarks, and Fleischer's rejoinder, ABC cancelled "Politically Incorrect."[17]

Some dismiss Maher's remarks as bad taste, and approve his dismissal, but it is disturbing to wonder what effect the White House's statements had on ABC's decision to fire Maher. ABC has claimed that the show was on the way out, and that may be the case. However, in a free society, a comedian's questioning the application of every conceivable epithet to terrorists, even epithets that do not really fit their conduct, hardly warrants a presidential rebuke, withdrawal of sponsor support, and cancellation. Fleischer's comment, however intended, that all Americans need to "watch what they say" was itself profoundly anti-American—if by pro-American we mean embracing freedom, questioning authority and opposing self-censorship.

Many other incidents have taken place since September 11. In the aftermath of the attacks, several newspaper columnists lost their jobs for criticizing the president's immediate reaction to the attacks,[18] cartoonists who did not side with the administration, such as Aaron McGruder, author of the popular cartoon strip The Boondocks, have seen their cartoons suspended or pulled from newspapers; less well-known cartoonists were simply fired.[19]

In opposing the war in Iraq, which toppled Saddam Hussein, the Texas country music group, the Dixie Chicks, have been boycotted and their CDs burned because Natalie Maines told a London audience that, "We're ashamed the president of the United States is from Texas."[20]

---

15. "Speaking With Bill Maher," *Chicago Sun-Times*, November 15, 2001, posted at <http://www.safesearching.com/billmaher/print/a_chicagosuntimes_111502.htm>.

16. *Id.*

17. *Id.*

18. *See* Matthew Rothschild, "The New McCarthyism," *The Progressive*, January 2002, describing the terminations of, among others, columnists Dan Guthrie and Tom Gutting, both of whose columns claiming that the president's not returning to Washington after the attacks on September 11 was "embarassing" to the Nation. According to Rothschild, both columns had been approved by the editors, who fired the columnists and published apologies in the wake of angry public response.

19. *Id.*

20. *See* Stephanie Zacharek, "Bush, Shame and the Dixie Chicks," March 18, 2003, posted at http://www.salon.com/ent/music/feature/2003/03/18/dixie_chicks/index.html.

Conservative columnist Ann Coulter disagreed with characteristic strenuousness to the president's effort to counterbalance vigorous response to the terrorist attacks with conciliation of Muslims worldwide,[21] and demonstrates one precept of this work: that censorship effects *all* those who challenge the orthodoxy of the day, conservative as well as liberal.

Coulter's words represented a particularly bellicose response. After eulogizing her friend Barbara Olson, who died in the terrorist attack on September 11, Coulter argued that the United States should not be overly nice (in the original sense of overly precise) in locating the actual terrorists, but should deem its enemies to include all those "cheering and dancing right now." With respect to such populaces, Coulter wrote, "We should invade their countries, kill their leaders and convert them to Christianity. We weren't punctilious about locating and punishing only Hitler and his top officers. We carpet-bombed German cities; we killed civilians. That's war. And this is war."[22]

As a result of her published opinion, Coulter was let go from her position as an associate editor at the *National Review* and her column was dropped. On October 3, 2001, Jonah Goldberg published a column, "L'Affaire Coulter: Goodbye to All That,"[23] explaining the *National Review*'s decision to terminate Coulter. Goldberg denied censorship on the part of the magazine, chided Coulter for her lack of professionalism, and noted that other columnists including himself at the *National Review* had expressed very pro-West, anti-Muslim viewpoints in the wake of the September 11 attacks without consequence. The publicity surrounding Coulter's termination, however, and the defensiveness of Goldberg's piece make clear that emotions were running high regarding what he terms "L'Affaire." Even the title of his column is itself defensive, coupling a reference to the Dreyfus Affair, in which Alfred Dreyfus, an *innocent* French Jewish officer was tried and convicted of treason in a classic distortion of justice caused by anti-Semitism, and a reference to Robert Graves' memoir *Goodbye to All That,* an *antiwar* classic.[24] These erudite allusions suggest that, at some level, Goldberg's lack of comfort with his own explanation almost amounted to what in criminal law is referred to as evidence of consciousness of guilt.

Public education has also been impacted by the wave of pro-war sentiment. An eighth-grader in Lakeport, California claims to have been singled out for punishment by his teacher for refusing to recite the Pledge of Alle-

---

21. Ann Coulter, "This Is War," September 12, 2001, posted at <http://www.nationalreview.com/coulter/091301.shtml>.
22. *Id.*
23. Jonah Goldberg, "L'Affair Coulter: Goodbye to All That," posted at <http://www.nationalreview.com/nr_comment/nr_comment100301.shtml>.
24. Robert Graves, *Goodbye to All That* (1929).

giance in his U.S. History and Constitution class. The teacher's alleged conduct—in a class on the Constitution, no less—if true, violated not only well-established constitutional principles acknowledged in theory, but flouted an explicit holding of the Supreme Court in *West Virginia Board of Education v. Barnette,*[25] in which the Supreme Court safeguarded the right of public school students to refuse to recite the Pledge. *Barnette* has been one of the leading cases in constitutional jurisprudence, and has led to a series of decisions protecting individuals and even corporations against not only "compelled speech" but against penalizing a "refusal to foster" speech with which the individual is not in agreement. In *Barnette,* the Court explained that "to sustain the compulsory flag salute, we are required to say that the Bill of Rights, which guards the individual's right to speak his own mind, left it open to public authorities to compel him to utter what is not in his mind."[26]

In another educational misfire, a high school "teach-in" in Madison, Wisconsin opposing war with Iraq had been approved by the school, but was cancelled by the school superintendent the day before it was scheduled, after

---

25. 319 U.S. 624 (1942).
26. *Barnette,* 319 U.S. at 633. *See also, Wooley v. Maynard,* 430 U.S. 705, 714 (1977) (striking as a violation of First Amendment the state requirement that automobiles display on their license plate the New Hampshire state motto, "Live Free or Die"). The "right to speak and the right to refrain from speaking are complementary components of the broader concept of the individual freedom of the mind" and thus "the right of freedom of thought protected against state action includes both the right to speak freely ands the right to refrain from speaking at all." Subsequent decisions have elaborated on these holdings as based on one of "the values lying at the heart of the First Amendment—the notion that an individual should be free to believe as he will, and that in a free society one's beliefs should be shaped by his mind and conscience rather than coerced by the State." *Glickman v. Wileman Brothers & Elliott,* 521 U.S. 457, 471–472 (1997) (*quoting Abood v. Detroit Board of Education,* 439 U.S. 209, 234–235 (1977). In *Abood* the prohibition against compelled speech was relied upon to recognize a First Amendment right against forcible financial support of an organization whose expressive activities conflict with one's own beliefs; in *Glickman,* the Court drew a narrow exception to this doctrine in upholding an enforced subsidy by fruit growers of generic advertisements for fruits, because: (1) the growers themselves were not required to communicate the message; (2) the message communicated—that fruits including their own wares were good—was not one they opposed; and (3) the First Amendment does not protect against the taking of funds on the ground that the funds would otherwise be used for expressive purposes. *Glickman* was itself distinguished (on the less than compelling ground that the fruit growers were extensively regulated, and the "assessment" of funds was an incidental part of such broad regulations) and a similar compelled subsidy struck down in *United States v. United Foods, Inc.,* 533 U.S. 405 (2001) (striking as "compelled speech" a levied sum of money required of fresh mushroom handlers under the Mushroom Promotion, Research, and Consumer Information Act, to fund generic advertisements promoting mushroom sales; The account of the current Pledge flap is drawn from Ucila Wang, "Boy's Parents Want Teacher Fired in Flag Flap," the *Press-Democrat,* January 8, 2003, posted at <http://www.pressdemocrat.com/local/news/08pledge.html>.

local conservative radio host Chris Kroc and local Young Republicans complained and organized opposition to it.[27]

To name one more instance, the University of California at Berkeley—an institution hardly noted for its conservatism—recently forbade the Emma Goldman Papers Project to mail out a fund-raising appeal which quoted Goldman on the subjects of suppression of free speech and on her opposition to war.[28] The quotations, which Berkeley officials stated could be "construed as political statement by the university in opposition to the United States policy toward Iraq," were written in 1915 and 1902, and contained strong denunciations of "war madness" as a "crime and outrage," while darkly prophesying that free-speech advocates "shall soon be obliged to meet in cellars, or in darkened rooms with closed doors and speak in whispers lest our next door neighbors should hear that free-born citizens dare not speak in the open."[29]

These instances, and others on a par with them, are disturbing reading, but do not sound the knell of repression of their own weight: the teacher was rebuked, Ann Coulter has gone on to publish a well-hyped (if not well reviewed) attack on the American Left, and Bill Maher has both published and resurfaced on HBO, whereas some victims of the McCarthy era were never able to rebuild their careers. The fates of the lesser-known columnists and cartoonists, however, is not clear.

More fundamentally, the First Amendment does not protect against non-governmental censorship, and thus the firing or censuring by private employers technically does not fit within the scope of a work on the First Amendment. Indeed, ABC, *National Review* and the other media employers could claim a First Amendment right to disassociate themselves from Maher, Coulter, McGruder and the other dissidents.[30] Thus, no abridgment of the legal rights of the provocateur, columnist, and cartoonist described here is made out. It is nonetheless hair-splitting to deny that they were subjected to censorship based upon their expressed views. The fact that the offending statements had all been previously approved and run suggests that the resultant termination or disassociation was as much motivated by fear as it was by political principle.

---

27. Matthew Rothschild, "Right Wing Radio Show Postpones Madison Teach In," December 6, 2002, posted at < http://www.progressive.org/webex/wxmc120602.html>.
28. Dean E. Murphy, "Old Words on War Stirring a New Dispute at Berkeley," *New York Times,* January 14, 2003, posted at <http://www.nytimes.com/2003/01/14/education/14BERK.html?8hpib>.
29. *Id.*
30. *See Boy Scouts of America v. Dale,* 530 U.S. 640, 655–661 (2000) (right of private organization to bar dissentient individuals from membership protected by First Amendment); *Hurley v. Irish-American Gay Lebian and Bisexual Group of Boston,* 515 U.S. 557, 573–574 (1995).

At one level, it could be claimed that this is free speech in action—hostile public response drove these speakers from the market. However, free speech is more than a legal principle; it is part of the American identity, part of how we define ourselves as a nation. Harry Kalven, Jr. called it a part of our "secular religion," and President Bush himself adverted to it as defining the "us" against the "them" of the terrorists in answering the question "why do they hate us" in his address to Congress after September 11:

> THEY hate what they see right here in this chamber: a democratically elected government. Their leaders are self-appointed. They hate our freedoms: our freedom of religion, our freedom of speech, our freedom to vote and assemble and disagree with each other.[31]

The centrality of free speech to our national identity urges us to deplore censorship, even when it does not come from the government. Even if there is no legal remedy for private censorship, the instances noted here do suggest that the reflex to censor has strengthened with the stress of the terrorist attacks and war. The right to disagree with each other so properly celebrated by President Bush cannot flourish if it is a mere legal doctrine, as opposed to a cherished and honored right. Indeed, the instances of Coulter and Maher can be read in an even more significant way: these individuals were hired to be provocative,[32] to be gadflies to the body politic, who spoke their perceptions without fear, to be, as Maher's program was titled, "Politically Incorrect." It says something about the state of free speech in the United States when dismissal results from well-known provocateurs provoking; if these individuals are not free to ask jarring questions, than who is? Such instances raise the question of where we stand today as a Nation, and whether the values of free speech are now in danger.

While the value of the some of the speech discussed here is open to question—Coulter's article strikes me as at best an effusion of spleen—the comments were plainly core First Amendment speech: thoughts and feelings questioning government reaction to a catastrophic attack on American soil. Both Maher and Coulter offered sincerely held viewpoints on that classic question of public concern in the immediate aftermath of the most appalling attack on this Nation since the bombing of Pearl Harbor. In particular, Maher was seeking to separate reality from propaganda in response to the attack, and his rebutting the government perspective so swiftly is exactly why

---

31. CNN.com/US, Transcript of President Bush's Address, September 21, 2001, posted at <http//www.cnn.com/us>.
32. Indeed, conservative columnist John Podhoretz has described Coulter as a "professional provocateur." John Podhoretz, "Blame the Voters," *New York Post*, January 28, 2003 at 23.

we have gadflies. Likewise, Coulter's rage is itself expressive of the pain and anger inflicted by the attack.

GOVERNMENT ACTION: LEADING BY EXAMPLE

Certainly, these instances raise concerns when joined with the administration's pronounced distaste with dissent; Ari Fleischer's comment concerning Maher was just the beginning. The administration's subsequent comments suggesting that dissenters from the post-September 11 expansion of powers in general—and with respect to Muslim immigrants in particular—are anti-American, stigmatizes dissent in a manner reminiscent of the "fellow traveler" slurs so favored during the Cold War. As Attorney General John Ashcroft so memorably stated shortly after the Maher incident:

> TO THOSE who pit Americans against immigrants and citizens against non-citizens, to those who scare peace-loving people with phantoms of lost liberty, my message is this: Your tactics only aid terrorists, for they erode our national unity and diminish our resolve. They give ammunition to America's enemies, and pause to America's friends.[33]

The lack of respect for differing points of view is troubling; the assumption that unity is of such paramount interest that the fundamental balance between the individual and the state should be changed without hesitation or public comment is at best unseemly coming from the Nation's top lawyer. Condemning the critics of new and untried policies for "aiding terrorists" is exactly the sort of heavy-handed "shaming" that was used to suppress dissent at the height of the Cold War.

Moreover, the federal government has been in a desultory way equating dissent with danger. Thus, in the months after the September 11 attacks, FBI and Secret Service agents investigated at least one avant-garde museum based on its political art, and the Secret Service interviewed at least one college student who had posters opposing the pro-capital punishment policies

---

33. *Senate Judiciary Committee Hearing on Anti-Terrorism Policy,* 106th Cong. (Dec. 6, 2001) (testimony of Attorney General John Ashcroft), quoted in David Cole, *Enemy Aliens,* 54 Stan. L Rev. 953, 954 (2002). Unfortunately, the passage of time has not blunted the administration's propensity to equate dissent with aiding America's foes; similar, although less strident comments were made by Donald H. Rumsfeld on September 8, 2003. See Douglas Jehl, "Rumsfeld Strikes Back at Critics on U.S. War on Terror," posted at <http://www.nytimes.com/2003/09/08/international/middleeast/08CND-RUMS.html?hp>

of then-Governor Bush, as well as a poster from a "Bush counter-inaugural," and a Pink Floyd poster asking, "Mother, should I trust the government?"[34] More recently, in October, 2002, university police officers, including one who served as a part time liaison with the FBI anti-terrorism task force, visited economics professor M. J. Alhabeeb at the University of Massachusetts at Amherst, "acting on a tip someone called in saying I am anti-American." when Professor Alhabeeb asked for clarification, the response was, "You are opposing the president's policy on Iraq."[35]

Other governmental actors have been employing the vehicle of anti-terrorism to earn headlines. One example took place as conflict escalated over how to handle Iraqi resistance to arms inspection. In late September, 2002, Representatives James McDermott (D., Washington) and David Bonior (D., Michigan), on a fact-finding trip to Baghdad, gave interviews to the American media, during which they "criticized U.S. efforts to pressure the U.N. Security Council to pass a new resolution designed to force Iraq either to accept unrestricted arms inspections or face military action."[36] McDermott was quoted as saying that "the president would mislead the American people" into war, and that he was trying to "provoke" war with Iraq.[37]

Shortly thereafter, New Jersey State Senator James Cafiero (R.) introduced a resolution calling for Attorney General Ashcroft to indict the two members of the United States Congress, on charges of treason, on the ground that the "public comments critical of the policies and the President of the United States made by United States Representatives Jim McDermott and David Bonior during a recent trip to Baghdad constitute an act of treason against the United States" asserting that their comments "gave aid and comfort to an enemy of the United States."[38]

One need not sympathize with the comments themselves to find Cafiero's response dangerous. Treason, as defined in the Constitution, takes place in the "Levying of War" against the United States, or of giving "aid and comfort to their Enemies," a term commonly understood to require a state of war, and to require a finding that an "overt act" has been committed by the alleged

34. Rothschild, "The New McCarthyism," *supra* note 18.
35. Matthew Rothschild, "FBI Goes on Campus," December 17, 2002 posted at <htp:// www.progressive.org/webex/wxymc121702.html>.
36. Joyce Howard Price, "Democrats Blast U.S. Line on Iraq," *Washington Times*, September 30, 2002.
37. *Id.*
38. Matthew Rothschild, "Some Call it Treason," October 23, 2002, posted at <http://www. progressive.org/webex/wxmc102302.html>; *see also* N. J. Sen. SCR 75 Cafiero, J./Connors, L. and <www.njleg.state.nj.us/legislativepub/ digest/20021017.pdf>.

traitor.[39] The jurisprudence of treason is sketchy, but to debase so grave a crime to fit a political statement by duly elected members of Congress speaking out on the subject of whether the United States should enter a war *before one exists* would criminalize any debate among the people as to any potential military action proposed by any incumbent administration. If such limits could apply to members of Congress addressing the press, then the law would leave no room for antiwar protest on the part of the citizenry. Moreover, in view of the fact that Cafiero as a state senator could only urge the Attorney General to action, and thus had no responsibility for any resultant prosecution, a resemblance to McCarthyist tactics and Cafiero's resolution appears.

Such incidents do not, of course, establish a conscious decision on the part of state or federal government to quash dissent. Indeed, in the various incidents of Secret Service and FBI investigation, the agents in question stated that they were responding to complaints concerning the subjects in question. However, these incidents do raise the question of whether our government stands as a guarantor of liberty, or whether it is subject to the same fears and paranoid impulses that beset individuals. Certainly the past record of the federal government, or the states, does not suggest that they will serve as a bulwark against repression. Past records and present intimations of a will to marginalize and disparage dissent become all the more concerning in light of the government's monopoly of much information and its desire to obtain more traditionally private information by expanding its ability to spy on its citizens and residents. It is fair to ask: How safe are our freedoms in such a climate?

GOVERNMENT ACTION REDUX: CONTROL OF INFORMATION

Access to governmental information, not surprisingly, has been tightened in the wake of the September 11, 2001 terrorist attacks. In terms of complying with the Freedom of Information Act (FOIA), Attorney General John Ashcroft has reversed a 1993 pro-disclosure policy propounded by then-Attorney General Janet Reno, who had instructed agencies not to use dis-

---

39. U.S. Const. Art. III, sec. 3 (1789). Notably, Ann Coulter's most recent book, *Treason: Liberal Treachery from the Cold War to the War on Terrorism* (2003), attempts to argue that American liberalism is itself an attempt to overthrow the government by invariably opposing American governmental decisions. Ms. Coulter's expansive definition of treason is without foundation in either law or logic, as is her defense of Senator Joseph McCarthy. Her continued equation of dissent with treason is ironic (and a little sad) in view of her own experience with censorship, as described above.

cretionary exemptions to the federal act unless they could point to a "foreseeable harm" that would occur from disclosure. In contrast, the Attorney General's October 12, 2001 memorandum informs all heads of federal agencies and departments that, "When you carefully consider FOIA requests and decide to withhold records, in whole or in part, you can be assured that the Department of Justice will defend your decisions unless they lack a sound legal basis or present an unwarranted risk of adverse impact on the ability of other agencies to protect other important records."[40]

Likewise, the new Department for Homeland Security, like the FBI, is exempted from whistle-blower protection. This is concerning, as only the extraction by members of Congress of an anti-retaliation pledge from FBI director Robert Mueller allowed Colleen Rowley to testify before Congress and reveal the extent and scope of bureaucratic risk aversion and avoidance of hard decisions that had handicapped intelligence gathering prior to the September 11 attacks.[41] By contrast, the Attorney General is looking for ways to further leakproof a notably reticent administration.[42]

Even more concerning to civil libertarians is the creation of an armory of legal surveillance techniques, and the passage of legislation that could lead to the tracking of ideas and thoughts as a means for finding the enemies of America.

On May 30, 2002, the Attorney General revised guidelines that had been put in place in the 1970s, in the wake of disclosures of abusive FBI surveillance of dissidents and activists, including the Reverend Martin Luther King. In so doing, the Attorney General jettisoned his predecessors' recognition that the FBI had in fact abused its authority to domestically spy on those who were guilty only of disagreeing with its long-time head, J. Edgar Hoover.[43] The guidelines had been crafted to assure Americans that their political gatherings would not be infiltrated by federal agents.

In announcing the abandonment of these guidelines, Attorney General Ashcroft stated ahistorically that in "its ninety-four-year history, the Federal

---

40. John Ashcroft, "Memorandum for Heads of All Federal Departments and Agencies," October 12, 2001, posted at <http://www.usdoj.gov/04foia/011012.htm>.

41. Michael McClintock, et al, Lawyers' Committee for Human Rights, *A Year of Loss: Reexamining Civil Liberties Since September 11* (September 1, 2002), <http://www.lchr.org/us_law/loss_report.pdf> at 12–13.

42. *Id.*

43. *See, for example, Final Report of the Select Committee to Study Governmental Operations with Respect to Intelligence Activities of the United States Senate,* 94th Cong. 2d Session (1976), the "Church Committee" Report; a legion of secondary works document Hoover's enthusiasm for surveillance over personal enemies, or even disciplines he deemed somehow untrustworthy; *see, for example,* Wiecek, *supra*; Lamont, *Freedom is as Freedom Does*; Douglas, *The Court Years* at 57–91; William O. Douglas, *Points of Rebellion* (1970) at 17–24; Mike Forrest Keen, *Stalking the Sociological Imagination: J. Edgar Hoover's FBI Surveillance of American Sociology* (1999).

Bureau of Investigation has been many things—the defender of the nation from organized crime, the guardian of our security from international espionage, and the tireless protector of civil rights and civil liberties for all Americans."[44] No doubt the numerous victims of harassive FBI surveillance might disagree with the Attorney General's laudatory assessment.

The new rule, as summarized by the Attorney General, is: "[T]hat, for the specific purpose of detecting or preventing terrorist activities, FBI field agents may enter public places and attend events open to other citizens, unless they are barred from attending by the Constitution or federal law."[45] A grace note concerning the historic grounds for these guidelines would perhaps have been too much to expect, but beyond the hymn to the FBI as a "defender of civil liberties," the Attorney General described the former guidelines in terms that suggested that they were mistaken when enacted: "[T]he guidelines mistakenly combined timeless objectives—the enforcement of the law and respect for civil rights and liberties—with outdated means."[46]

Other indicia that the expectation of privacy is steadily, stealthily shrinking can be seen in the administration's controversial surveillance initiatives. The Uniting and Strengthening America by Providing Appropriate Tools Required to Intercept and Obstruct Terrorism (USA PATRIOT) Act,[47] in addition to expanding the government's ability to communicate information among various agencies, allows for presumptively private information regarding Internet usage; telephone calls; and library, book store, financial, and educational records to be demanded by the government from providers, librarians, or shop owners.[48] The USA PATRIOT Act also contains a broad definition of what constitutes "domestic terrorism, " encompassing "acts dangerous to human life that are a violation of the criminal laws" if they "appear to be intended . . . to influence the policy of a government by intimidation or coercion" and if they "occur primarily within the territorial jurisdiction of the United States."[49] Concerns have been raised that the scope of this definition could extend to abortion activists, to environmental activ-

---

44. Prepared Remarks of Attorney General Ashcroft, May 3, 2002, posted at <http://www.usdoj.gov/ag/speeches/2002/53002agpreparedremarks.htm>.

45. *Id.*

46. *Id.*

47. Uniting and Strengthening America by Providing Appropriate Tools Required to Intercept and Obstruct Terrorism (USA PATRIOT ACT) Act of 2001, H.R. 3162 (2001). The scope of the legislation is quite broad; in view of this work's focus on freedom of speech, the sections dealing with the right to detain immigrants and others suspected of terrorist affiliations and even beliefs is not treated. For further details, *see* Cole, *supra* note 32. For a meticulously researched summary of the dangers to civil liberties and civil rights posed by the responses to the terrorist attacks, including the USA PATRIOT Act, *see A Year of Loss, supra* note 40.

48. H.R. 3162 at §§ 212, 215, 505, 507.

49. *Id.* at § 802.

ists, or indeed to many dissenters who seek to influence government behavior through what is called, sometimes euphemistically, "direct action."[50]

Another such initiative, not enacted at the present writing, Total Information Awareness, is the brainchild of the Iran-Contra veteran, Admiral John Poindexter, and has been summarized as "an experimental system being developed by the Pentagon that seeks to scan information on billions of electronic transactions performed by millions of people here and abroad each day, analyze them and flag suspicious activity for possible investigation."[51]

More ambitiously, as of late 2002, the Bush Administration was "planning to propose requiring Internet service providers to help build a centralized system to enable broad monitoring of the Internet and, potentially, surveillance of its users."[52] That so ambitious a plan may succeed is contended by privacy and free speech watchdogs; the growth of governmental and private employer or corporate surveillance, and the exponential increase of potential surveillance technologies have led the American Civil Liberties Union to conclude that "there are no longer any *technical* barriers to the Big Brother regime portrayed by George Orwell."[53] Indeed, as the ACLU report argues cogently, such surveillance can quite easily extend well beyond tracking Internet usage, to video surveillance of public spaces, data surveillance (e.g., recording the use of toll-booth speed passes and subway passes such as New York's MetroCards), and exchanging of library usage, financial, credit card and other transaction data that can provide a template to an enormous amount of associational activity the privacy of which have long been assumed—or, rather, taken for granted.[54]

As technology provides convenience, it also eliminates the difficulty of finding information about what Americans read, where they spend their free time, who they associate with. Convenience supplants privacy and forces us to examine the nature of the society in which we wish to live. Juxtapose such surveillance against the backdrop of the government's assertion of power to declare even American citizens "enemy combatants," whose indefinite

---

50. Nancy Chang, "The USA PATRIOT Act: What's So Patriotic About Trampling on the Bill of Rights," available at <http://www.ccr-ny.org/whatsnew/usa_patriot_act.asp>.
51. John Markoff, "Poindexter's Still A Technocrat, Still a Lightning Rod," *New York Times*, January 20, 2003, posted at <http://www.nytimes.com/2003/01/20/business/20POIN. html>.
52. John Markoff & John Schwartz, "Bush Administration to Propose System for Monitoring Internet," *New York Times*, December 20, 2002, posted at <http://www.nytimes,com/2002/12/20/technology/20MONI.html>.
53. Jay Stanley & Barry Steinhardt, "Bigger Monster, Weaker Chains: The Growth of an American Surveillance Society" (January 15, 2003) at 1; posted at <http//www//aclu. org/Files/OpenFile.cfm?id=11572>.
54. *Id.* at 1, 4–6 (private surveillance); 6–10 (government surveillance).

detention is subject to no limitation or meaningful judicial review,[55] and the solidity of the legal bedrock of our constitutional order begins to feel more like gravel.

The Value of Anonymity

One response to criticism of the increasing surveillance under which Americans are expected to live is the claim that the innocent have nothing to hide. This seemingly common-sense based retort is contrary to the political experience of this nation, dating back to the Framers of the Constitution. The most venerated and oft-cited treatise on the original meaning of the Constitution, *The Federalist Papers* (1789), was published under the pseudonym Publius by Alexander Hamilton, James Madison and John Jay. Indeed, the Supreme Court has long recognized that, "Anonymous pamphlets, leaflets, brochures and even books have played an important role in the progress of mankind."[56] The right to receive information, and to pursue one's own interest without fear of public scrutiny is likewise implicated in the right to discuss free from government scrutiny and monitoring.

Thus, as the Supreme Court held in the context of a challenge brought by the NAACP, then struggling against Jim Crow and pro-segregation governmental forces to change the social construct of racism:

> [C]ompelled openness to public scrutiny is likely to affect adversely the ability of [any group] and its members to pursue their collective effort to foster a belief which they admittedly have the right to advocate, in that it may induce members to withdraw from the Association and dissuade others from joining because of fear of exposure of their

---

55. Cole, *supra*, note 32; *see also Hamdi v. Rumsfeld*, 316 F. 3d 450, 476 (4th Cir. 2003) (holding that judicial review of detention is mandated, but that, "where, as here, a habeas petitioner has been designated an enemy combatant and it is undisputed that he was captured in a zone of active combat operations abroad, further judicial inquiry is unwarranted when the government has responded to the petition by setting forth facts that would establish a legally valid basis for the petitioner's detention." The Court bluntly concluded that "*Hamdi* is not entitled to challenge the facts presented" by the government. *Id.* As commentator Nat Hentoff notes, the ruling in *Hamdi* is especially troubling in view of the fact that the lawyer representing Hamdi's interests was unable to confer with him, and to question the veracity of the factual allegations contained in the two-page affidavit. Nat Hentoff, "Liberty's Court of Last Resort," *Village Voice*, January 24, 2003.
56. *Talley v. California*, 362 U.S.60, 64 (1960) (Black, J.); *See also McIntyre v. Ohio Elections Commission*, 514 U.S. 334, 131 L.Ed. 2d 426 (1995) (*following Talley*; striking as unconstitutional statute prohibiting the circulation of anonymous campaign literature).

own beliefs shown through their associations and of the consequences of this exposure.[57]

So critical is this interest in freedom from scrutiny of the individual's associations and beliefs, that a compelling state interest is required and disclosure must be limited to that which represents the narrowest possible intrusion on the protected right of association needed to serve that state interest.[58]

The right to privacy in associational activity has been upheld against weighty state and federal government interests—interests such as the importance of preventing voter confusion and fraudulent representations by partisans at the polls;[59] enabling voters to identify the bias of handbills directed at specific election issues;[60] and discouraging commission of hate crimes by imprisoned felons.[61]

The value of anonymity, as the N.A.A.C.P. example shows, is especially high in troubled political times, when quashing dissent is more likely. The question arises: Are we entering such a time? The first ingredient of a climate hostile to dissent, a government that does not see the need or even the legitimacy of dissent, appears to be in place, or at least growing, within the present administration. And in the increased arsenal of surveillance and diminishing expectation of privacy, the means for hobbling dissent may be emerging.

THE PRESENT COURT AND DISSENT

Any notion of the role the judiciary will play in addressing the inevitable challenges to these increased surveillance techniques, and to the various responses to September 11, is predominantly speculation at the present writ-

---

57. *N.A.A.C.P. v. Alabama ex rel Patterson*, 357 U.S. 449, 462–463 (1958).
58. *Id.; See Bates v. Little Rock*, 361 U.S. 516, 524 (1960); *Watchtower Bible and Tract Society of New York, Inc. v. Village of Stratton*, 536 U.S. 150, 151 L.Ed.2d 963 (2003) (striking as unconstitutional ordinance forbidding door-to-door canvassing to "promote" any "cause" absent obtaining a mayoral permit and signing a registration form).
59. *Buckley v. American Constitutional Law Foundation, Inc.*, 525 U.S. 182, 198–200 (1999) (striking state statute requiring petition circulators to wear a name badge identifying themselves and their party affiliation).
60. *McIntyre*, 131 L.Ed.2d 440–443.
61. *Dawson v. Delaware*, 503 U.S. 159, 169 (1992) (even in criminal sentencing procedure, where standard of permissible aggravating evidence is broader than evidence permitted to establish guilt of crime, state could not introduce evidence of defendant inmate's membership in racist prison gang; reaffirming and following *Bates*).

ing. Certainly, Justice Sandra Day O'Connor's statement that "we're likely to experience more restrictions on our personal freedom than has ever been the case in our country," was not particularly encouraging for civil libertarians, in view of O'Connor's position as a swing vote on the Supreme Court.[62] Justice O'Connor was speaking only two weeks after the horrific attacks on the World Trade Center and the Pentagon, and posed the question: "[A]t what point does the cost to civil liberties from legislation designed to prevent terrorism outweigh the added security that that legislation provides?"[63] Still, her comment captures the oddly flat, rather passive acceptance by the majority of the public to date of such abridgements of civil liberties as contained in the USA PATRIOT Act, and in the administration's other proposals for combating terrorism.

The present Court has not been particularly hostile toward free speech claimants, to the surprise of many commentators. While some decisions have allowed for greater regulation of content,[64] the strong decisions reaffirming First Amendment fundamentals in *Ashcroft v. Free Speech Coalition*[65] and *Watchtower*, as well as in *Reno v. American Civil Liberties Union*[66] make clear that the Court while nipping and tucking in some areas of First Amendment doctrine, has maintained the status quo on the whole, and is reaffirming some first principles in an encouraging style.

Even in the areas of so-called "lesser value speech," the Court has on occasion expanded protection beyond what the rulings of prior Courts required.[67] Notably, these decisions sometimes cut across presumed ideologi-

---

62. Linda Greenhouse, "O'Connor Foresees Limits on Freedom," *New York Times*, September 29, 2001, <http://www.nytimes.com/2001/09/29/national/29SCOT.html>.

63. *Id.*

64. For example, in *City of Erie v. Pap's A.M.*, 529 U.S. 277 (2000), the Court diluted the level of First Amendment protection extended to nude dancing in *Schad v. Mount Ephraim*, 452 U.S. 61, 66 (1981). To provide an older example, and correct an inference to be drawn from a previous statement, in *Turner Broadcasting System, Inc. v. FCC*, 512 U.S. 622 (1994), the Court, as I correctly noted in chapter 3, disavowed the application of deferential review of government regulation to cable television that it has allowed to broadcast media based on "scarcity" of government allotted airwaves; however, its application of supposedly traditional First Amendment principles to the cable medium allowed for more regulation than would be supported by such principles, as was pointed out by Bruce Johnson in response to the first edition of this work. *See*, Bruce E. H. Johnson, "Confessions of a First Amendment Hedgehog," JURIST: "Books on Law," September 2000, posted at <jurist.law.pitt.edu/lawbooks/revsepoo.htm>.

65. 535 U.S. 234, 152 L.Ed.2d 403 (2002) (discussed in Chapter 5, *supra*; employing verbal act logic to invalidate statute barring "indecent" representation of "virtual child").

66. 521 U.S. 844 (1997).

67. For example, in the context of commercial speech, the Court has in recent decisions afforded more substantial protection than it did just a few years previously. *Compare Greater New Orleans Broadcasting Assn. v. United States*, 527 U.S. 173, 182 (1999) with *Posadas de Puerto Rico Ass'n. v. Tourism Co.*, 478 U.S. 328 (1986). In the case of "fighting words," in

cal lines; Justice Thomas has led the way for arguing for an increase in the level of protection afforded commercial speech,[68] and it was Justice Scalia who authored the opinion in *R.A.V.* Justice Kennedy authored the opinions in *United States v. Playboy Enterprises*,[69] in which sexually oriented, non-obscene cable television programming was protected against a content-based regulation, applying strict scrutiny to the regulation. In *Legal Services Corp. v. Velasquez*,[70] the Court, again through Justice Kennedy, struck as unconstitutional the placing of restrictions on the arguments and tactics which could be employed by government-funded lawyers representing the indigent. In each of these cases, the Court recognized relatively recent precedent that could have been deployed in favor of the restriction on speech, but chose to limit or reject the prior decisions.

This is not to say that traditional ideological characterizations no longer pertain at all. In the recent case *Ashcroft v. American Civil Liberties Union*,[71] the justices sent back to the lower court the question of whether the Child Online Protection Act (COPA) was constitutional, fracturing on the rationale along more traditional ideological lines. Justices Thomas, Rehnquist, and Scalia thought that the effort to regulate "indecent" internet content by the local community standards they found in COPA was largely untroubling; Justices O'Connor, Kennedy (joined by Justices Ginsburg and Souter), and Justice Breyer, found that such an approach might impermissibly allow the most restrictive community in the Nation to dictate to the rest what would be tolerable online, but declined to find that COPA in fact imposed such a standard without further findings. Justice Stevens would strike the statute as violative of the First Amendment.

Beyond the simple placing of cases into the "won" or "lost" category, and the simplistic characterization of the current members of the Court as "for" or "against" free speech, there are undercurrents that could lead to a more subjective, or more value-laden, approach to free speech cases. In *Bartnicki v. Vopper*,[72] the Court struck down as unconstitutional the application of federal

---

R.A.V. v. City of St. Paul, 505 U.S. 377, 382–383 (1992), the Court extended protection even to "fighting words" when such words were being regulated not because of their inherent tendency to provoke violence, but because of their ideological content. *But see Virginia v. Black*, 536 U.S.—, 155 L.Ed.2d 535 (2003).

68. *44 Liquormart, Inc. v. Rhode Island*, 517 U.S. 484, 515 (1996) (Thomas, J., concurring); *New Orleans Broadcasting v. United States*, 527 U.S. 173, 197 (1999) (Thomas, J., concurring).

69. 529 U.S. 803 (2000) (striking as violative of First Amendment section 505 of the Telecommunications Act of 1996 requiring channels "primarily dedicated to sexually oriented programming" to "fully scramble or fully block" those channels or to limit broadcasting hours to those when children are less likely to be viewing to prevent children from viewing moments of programs which become clear through "signal bleed").

70. 531 U.S. 533 (2001).

71. 535 U.S. 564, 152 L.Ed.2d 771 (2002).

72. 532 U.S. 514, 149 L.Ed.2d 787 (2001).

and state statutes prohibiting interception of cellular telephone calls to the subsequent publication of the text of a cell phone conversation between a union president and the union's chief negotiator concerning the "need for a dramatic response to [the employer's] intransigence." The Court, in an opinion by Justice Stevens, found that the case presented a difficult balancing operation, between "important interests to be considered on *both* sides of the constitutional calculus" against the right to report and comment on public affairs, the Court found was ranged "privacy of communication," an interest which the Court also found rooted in the First Amendment.[73]

Justice Breyer, in an opinion joined by Justice O'Connor, stated that their joining of the majority opinion assumed that a deferential "reasonable balance" analysis would be employed as is proper when balancing competing constitutional values that cannot be reconciled, as opposed to a "strict scrutiny" test, "with its strong presumption against constitutionality."[74] In the case before the Court, they concluded, the statutes "do not reasonably reconcile the competing constitutional objectives" but were too onerous against the press, which had not acted unlawfully itself. Moreover, the lesser privacy interests of public figures (in this context, at any rate), and the low value of their speech, potentially threatening to "blow up porches" tipped the balance in favor of the media.[75]

This analysis, however, becomes more worrisome if one credits the assertion of Professor Paul Gewirtz that in *Bartnicki* the "competing values" to be weighed as co-equals are not, as Justice Stevens would have it, those of speech and privacy of communication—the right to choose when one's expression is to be public—but rather between the right to speak freely and the more generalized right of privacy which is not specifically enumerated.[76] Professor Gewirtz notes that in his opinion Justice Breyer distinguishes between "privacy and speech-related benefits" served by the statutes at issue, and suggests that "'privacy' benefits that are not 'speech-related' have some independent weight in the constitutional balance."[77] Gewirtz himself, who favors further privacy protection at the expense of the media's right to report, explicitly does not "rest my argument on a claim that media interference with 'privacy' violates a constitutional right of privacy."[78]

Gewirtz further claims that "Justice Breyer's separate opinions over the past few years take a more tolerant approach to laws limiting the speech of

---

73. 149 L.Ed.2d at 805 (emphasis in original), 804, and n. 20.
74. 149 L.Ed.2d at 806, 807 (Breyer, J., concurring).
75. 149 L.Ed.2d at 807–809 (Breyer, J., concurring).
76. Paul Gewirtz, *Privacy and Speech*, 2001 Sup. Ct. Rev. 139 (2002).
77. Gewirtz, 2001 Sup. Ct. Rev. at 158–159 & n. 66.
78. Gewirtz, 2001 Sup. Ct. Rev. at 172, n. 110.

some in order to enhance the overall system of free expression."[79] Taking from these separate opinions the notion that free speech may best be served by restraints on speech, and that when such is allegedly the case, strict scrutiny should not apply, Gewirtz argues that state actions that "strike a reasonable balance between their speech restricting and speech enhancing consequences" should be presumptively constitutional as enhancing speech as an "active liberty."[80]

From there, Gerwitz argues that under Justice Breyer's approach, "balancing" may be a more appropriate general approach to the conflict between speech and "several values other than speech," without being able to identify "how far Justice Breyer is prepared to go in this direction, what values are sufficiently important to justify speech restrictions, or how such balances will be made."[81] Despite the vagueness of this analysis, Gewirtz favors this approach, on the ground that "a more explicit and multifactored balancing of interests" is preferable to the convoluted system presently extant.[82] The underlying template of this approach, as summarized by Gerwitz, is "proportionality," a concept Gerwitz traces to cases from the European Court of Human Rights and the Supreme Court of Canada, and which Breyer has approvingly cited as avoiding "a simple test that effectively presumes unconstitutionality" in favor of "balanc[ing] interests," that is, "asking whether the statute burdens any one such interest in a manner out of proportion to the statute's salutary effects upon the others."[83]

Assuming that Professor Gewirtz is correct in glossing the intention and charting the developing jurisprudence of Justice Breyer, the Court may have its first advocate of holistic balancing since Felix Frankfurter. The instability of such an approach has already been discussed at length in Chapters 2 through 4, and even Gewirtz concedes that "for those who consider free speech to be highly vulnerable in our society, and who greatly distrust whether judges and legislatures will adequately protect it, allowing nonspeech values to trump speech values will always be a very risky business (and especially so in times of national stress)."[84] We are now in such a time of national stress: how will the Court, including Justice Breyer, fare?

---

79. Gewirtz, 2001 Sup. Ct. Rev. at 191, *citing United States v. United Foods*, 533 U.S. 405, 450–459 (2001) (Breyer, J. dissenting); *Nixon v. Shrink Missori PAC*, 528 U.S. at 337, 400 (2000) (Breyer, J., concurring); and *Turner Broadcasting System, Inc.*, 520 U.S. 180, 225 (1997) (Breyer, J., concurring in part).
80. Gewirtz, 2001 Sup. Ct. Review at 193, 191–193, *quoting* Breyer, *Our Democratic Constitution* (October 22, 2001) at 6–7.
81. Gerwitz, 2001 Sup. Ct. Rev. at 194.
82. Gewirtz, 2001 Sup. Ct. Rev. at 195, 195–196.
83. Gewirtz, 2001 Sup. Ct. rev. at 196, *quoting Nixon v. Shrink Missouri PAC*, 528 U.S. at 402, 403.
84. Gewirtz, 2001 Sup. Ct. Rev. at 194.

SURVEILLANCE AND THE COURT

In terms of Internet surveillance, the freedom of association may be vindicated as a source of protection—or not. What will the current Supreme Court think of the FBI's policy that it may attend and document "public" meetings of "suspicious" political dissidents? And will that policy apply to online use as well, with the constitutional imprimatur of the Supreme Court. The status of such monitoring is far from clear, but the Court's Cold War and Vietnam-era decisions are not encouraging.[85] And another source of potential protection of privacy, the Fourth Amendment, may not even apply.

That the Fourth Amendment's protection against unreasonable searches and seizures may not even be implicated may come as an unpleasant surprise. Because the hallmark for application of the Fourth Amendment is a "reasonable expectation of privacy," as society defines away the private, that which constitutes an objectively reasonable expectation diminishes.[86] Such a conclusion could be supported by the case law, and may be that which the Court reaches. As technology has increased the ability of aerial observers to peer into an individual's property, the individual's expectation that a fence guarding the perimeter of the property is sufficient to guarantee privacy has been deemed no longer objectively reasonable, such as to require the government to have probable cause prior to conducting an aerial visual surveillance of private property.[87]

However, the Court has not simply given technology a blank check; in *Kyllo v. United States*,[88] the Court, in an opinion by Justice Scalia, found that the use of a thermal-imaging device aimed at a private home from a public street to detect the use of special plant-growing lamps for raising marijuana

---

85. *See Laird v. Tatum*, 408 U.S. 1, 13 (1972) (holding that an Army Intelligence domestic surveillance program investigating dissidents did not by its mere existence sufficiently chill the right of free association to "entitle a private individual to invoke the judicial power to determine the validity" of the program. *Id.* at 11–15. The scope of the surveillance in question was described by Justice Douglas in dissent as "massive and comprehensive," (*id.* at 26), involving "virtually every activist group in the country," and employing "undercover agents to infiltrate these civilian groups . . . mov[ing] as a secret group among civilian audiences, using cameras and electronic ears for surveillance." *Id.* at 25 (Douglas, J., and Marshall, J., dissenting).

86. The application of Fourth Amendment scrutiny is triggered by the existence of an "objectively reasonable expectation of privacy" has been Fourth Amendment doctrine since *Katz v. United States*, 389 U.S. 347, 361 (1967) (Harlan, J., concurring); *see Smith v. Maryland*, 442 U.S. 735, 740 (1979) (*quoting Katz*).

87. *California v. Ciraolo*, 476 U.S. 207 (1989); *see Bond v. United States*, 529 U.S. 334, 337–338 (2000) (re-stating rule in *Ciraolo* but noting greater intrusiveness of physical seizures as opposed to visual surveillance).

88. 533 U.S. 27, 150 L.Ed.2d 94 (2001).

indoors constituted a search and was subject to Fourth Amendment's requirements. The Court rested its distinction on its conclusion that "preservation of that degree of privacy against government that existed when the Fourth Amendment was adopted" mandated a conclusion that "obtaining by sense-enhancing technology any information regarding the interior of the home that could not have been obtained without physical intrusion into a constitutionally protected area constitutes a search."[89]

The Court's decision will depend on which of several analogies is adopted. The Court will be offered the analogy of surveillance of an individual's Internet use to peering into a home and watching the resident select books from his or her shelves, or that of tapping the phone. Conversely, the Court could adopt the competing analogy of watching an individual enter a public space, whether to wander about the public square or to choose library books in a common, shared space. The kind of Internet browsing surveillance suggested by this is no less unreasonable than aerial photographic fly-overs, under the last comparison.

Yet such a chain of logic would lead to *no* expectation of privacy in terms of Internet browsing, and would open up for unlimited government review and analysis the web pages viewed by any individual at all, although e-mail might still retain significant privacy protection. This result would in turn lead to a chilling of speech on the Internet that would significantly undermine its potential to foster debate, and would place individuals on a par with corporate speakers. Security, of course, is a prime concern, but it could lead to an environment so stifling that our society would fundamentally be transformed. As eloquently explained by Justice Douglas in dissent in *Laird*:

> ARMY SURVEILLANCE, like Army regimentation, is at war with the principles of the First Amendment. Those who already walk submissively will say that there is no cause for alarm. But submissiveness is not our heritage. The First Amendment was designed to allow rebellion to remain our heritage. The Constitution was designed to keep government off the backs of the people. The Bill of Rights was added to keep the precincts of belief and expression, of the press, of political and social activities, free from surveillance. The Bill of Rights was designed to keep agents of government and official eavesdroppers away from assemblies of people. The aim was to allow men to be free and independent and to assert their rights against government. There can be no influence more paralyzing of that objective than Army surveillance.[90]

---

89. 150 L.Ed.2d at 102 (citation and internal quotation marks omitted) (*quoting Silverman v. United States*, 365 U.S. 505, 512 (1961)).

90. *Laird v. Tatum*, 408 U.S. 1, 28 (Douglas, J., dissenting).

Justice Douglas urged the Court in *Laird* to defend the very nature of American democracy from a government seeking to maximize the interest in security at the price of liberty. Without actually naming the military theory of replication in which opposing forces begin to mirror each other's behavior, Justice Douglas noted that, "When an intelligence officer looks over every nonconformist's shoulder in the library, or walks by his side in a picket line or infiltrates his club, the America once extolled as the voice of liberty heard around the world no longer is cast in the image which Jefferson and Madison designed," but more in the image of our Cold War foes.[91]

The hasty passage of the USA PATRIOT Act, the very name of which stigmatizes any disagreement, and the tepid response to proposed government regulation and monitoring of the Internet and other speech, do not bode well. And whether Supreme Court invokes Justice Douglas's call to first principles or follows the passions of the moment remains to be seen.

We stand at a crossroads, with wholly new issues of fitting our eighteenth century Constitution to the twenty-first century technology and its challenges. We have new resources—access to facts, fictions and representations on a scale that dwarfs the most magnificent library owned by any of the Framers. We also have new dangers—greater ease in killing masses of people due to technological advances; the use of our own transportation infrastructure to kill Americans, or to cripple our economy with the technologies that serve it so well. How our Congress, our president, our Court will propose to address these issues is still largely unknown. How We the People will grade their proposed solutions is even harder to predict. Will we passively accept whatever is offered? Or will We the People do our duty in defending freedom, and be heard, either supporting our leaders or opposing them, debating with a fervor that shows that the American Experiment is still alive?

At the present time, only three propositions are clear to me. First, positive engagement in the democratic process is more critical than ever. In the first edition of this book, I wrote—and it bears repeating here—that we now find ourselves in a situation where freedom of speech has become a "use it or lose it" proposition. Or, in the eloquent words attributed to Edmund Burke, "the only thing necessary for the triumph of evil is for good [people] to do nothing."[92]

Second, power needs guarding. Our government needs new powers, it has said, to deal with our new enemies. But as power grows, so does temptation. Abuse of power flourishes when it happens in secret, without criticism.

---

91. *Id.* at 28–29.
92. Justin Kaplan, ed., *Bartlett's Familiar Quotations* (16th ed. 1992) at 332, n. 3, reports that "vigorous searches" have failed to find the source for this statement traditionally attributed to Burke. *Id.*

As power becomes more familiar to even the most well-intentioned, it becomes easier to believe in the rightness of one's actions because of the righ-
teousness of one's intentions.[93] Who will guard the guardians, if We the
People nap in our electronically diverting playrooms? Burke's other great
maxim, that "among a people generally corrupt, liberty cannot long exist,"
comprehends, although it is not limited to, the specter of a populace so
besotted with pleasure as to abandon the exercise of political power to who-
soever will not join in the festivities.[94] Just this concern animates Aldous
Huxley's famous dystopic vision, and, according to at least two recent commentators, is closer to the American state of affairs than the more repressive, force-based regime depicted in George Orwell's *1984*.[95] As our voter
turnout continues to decline, and as only a minority in America now even
bother to vote, that specter cannot be disregarded.[96] Finally, that self-doubt—
self-questioning, at least—is a precious virtue in a democratic-republican
society. Holmes stated that "to have questioned one's first principles is the
mark of a civilized man."[97]C.P. Snow explained why, in depicting a fictional
debate between a British democrat (Lewis Eliot, Snow's alter ego) and
Reinhold Schader, a Nazi official:

> "No one is fit to be trusted with power, I said . . . No one. I should not
> like to see your party in charge of Europe, Dr. Schader. I should not
> like to see any group of men in charge at all—not me or my friends or
> anyone else. Any man who has lived at all knows the follies and wick-
> edness he's capable of. If he does not know it, he is not fit to govern
> others. And if he does know it, then he knows also that neither he nor
> any man ought to decide a single human fate. I am not speaking of
> you specially, you understand: I should say exactly the same of myself."

> Our eyes met. I was certain, as one can be certain in a duel across the
> table, that for the first time he took me seriously.

---

93. *See* Edmund Morris, *The Rise of Theodore Roosevelt* (1979) and *Theodore Rex* (2001) in which
    Theodore Roosevelt's increasing confidence as President is depicted as leading him to
    occasional over-certainty in his own action, as Morris phrases it, to believe that his ac-
    tions were right because he did them.
94. Edmund Burke, "Letter to the Sheriffs of Bristol" (1777).
95. Aldous Huxley, *Brave New World* (1946) and *Brave New World Revisited* (1956); George
    Orwell, *1984* (1948); Ronald K. L. Collins and David M. Skover, *The Death of Discourse*
    (1996) (critiquing free speech theory on the basis that it reinforces and fosters "the
    Huxleyan Nightmare," while protecting against the "Orwellian Nightmare.").
96. *See generally*, Richard G. Niemi & Herbert F. Weisberg, *Controversies in Voting Behavior*, 9th
    ed. (2001); William J. Keefe & Marc J. Hetherington, *Parties, Politics, and Public Policy in
    America*, 9th ed. (2003) at Chapter 6.
97. Oliver Wendell Holmes, *Collected Legal Papers* (1920) at 307.

"You do not think highly of men, Mr. Eliot."

"I am one," I said.[98]

We are all called, as a Nation and as individuals, to question the rightness of our own conduct and our own first principles. We are called to be civilized in Holmesian terms, in the sense that we are called to be people who recognize greater claims to truth and right than our own self-interest, and our own desires. Our receptivity to critics, even if in the last analysis they fail to persuade to a crucial distinction between a free and a subject people. A nation that silences its skeptics, its rebels, and its provocateurs is one which has ceased to look beyond the pronouncement of its onetime leaders, now its unquestionable rulers. In short, a little rebellion is good for the civic soul.

---

98. C. P. Snow, *The Light and the Dark* (1948) at 193–194.

Case Index

Subject Index

433